W9-ANO-341

Donna J. Sims

# Graphic Communications Today

# Graphic Communications Today

**Theodore E. Conover**
University of Nevada, Reno

**West Publishing Company**
St. Paul    New York    Los Angeles    San Francisco

Design: Janet Bollow
Copyediting: Betty Berenson
Illustrations unless otherwise noted: Brenda Booth
Production coordination: Janet Bollow Associates
Composition: Van Norman Associates

**Library of Congress Cataloging in Publication Data**

Conover, Theodore E.
  Graphic communications today.

  Bibliography: p.
  Includes index.
    1. Printing, Practical—Layout.  2. Graphic arts.
3. Magazine design.  4. Newspaper layout and typography.
5. Newsletters—Design.  I. Title.
Z246.C58    1985      686.2'24      84-27017
ISBN 0-314-85225-5
1st Reprint—1987

To Edna

# Contents

**Chapter 3   Type—The Basic Ingredient**                 **43**

**Chapter 4   Creative Typography**                       **63**

## Chapter 5   Art and Illustrations                          83

## Chapter 6   Color—A Powerful Communications Tool           105

# Foreword

We've come full circle in American print communication. And this book is a celebration of that fact.

The first newspaper editor was a printer who established a weekly to make sure there was always something "on the hook" for the craft personnel to work on. The first advertising designer was a printer. The first direct-mail layout was done by a printer. So was the first magazine and the first annual report and the first decorative label on a ketchup bottle or a box of matches. Even the first "graphic" artist—who showed the position of the pallbearers at Washington's funeral—was a printer who fashioned the newspaper diagram with ordinary printing rules and extraordinary ingenuity.

But the industry expanded so rapidly that it divided like growing cells. Magazines were separated from newspapers, advertising from news matter, public relations mailings from billboards. And within each division, individual jobs were specialized. Newspeople and ad staffers left production to compositors, engravers, and those who ran the presses.

But today the editor again becomes a printer. Typesetting, page makeup, advertising design—whether for newspaper, magazine, print ads or direct mail—are not only controlled by, but are actually produced by, what we can collectively term "editorial people."

Today's journalism student—and, indeed, the professional communications practitioner—must know what happens after his or her copy goes "to the backshop." This book tells that. As well as what, today, must happen even before that stage.

The graphic arts are both a craft and an art. They are more than a commercial enterprise; they are warp and woof of our culture, the flowering of and the mirroring of our history. So this book acknowledges and honors the past of our craft and profession even as it acknowledges and anticipates the exciting future that lies ahead of our exciting present.

Communicators who lived in the watershed years of Johann Gutenberg must have felt an electric excitement when they realized the momentous change from handwritten manuscript books to those printed by movable type.

We are living in an era just as revolutionary (a word used advisedly and precisely, not as in a "revolutionary new toothpaste"). We tend to be a bit blasé about our vocations, though, perhaps a bit jaded by space walkers and artificial hearts. But we have every reason for excitement and pride and anticipation. All of us—students and professionals alike—have many new tools to master and to communicate with.

Ted Conover is the right man to write a book like this. His distinguished career has spanned both the hot-metal era (actually little changed from Gutenberg's methods) and today's electronic wizardry. He is more, even, than a rare combination of craftsman and artist. He is a fine teacher who has insisted that his students be more than tradeschool graduates, that they be university graduates and, as such, the Universal Man and Woman. He knows that the printed word—be it printed on paper or on a television screen—is the thread that weaves together our civilization and culture. What's more, he knows that this craft, this art, this pursuit—label it what you will—is fun, lots of fun. All together, this is a universal book that a respected and cherished colleague has written. I gladly share it with you, Gentle Reader.

Dr. Edmund C. Arnold
*Virginia Commonwealth University*

# Preface

My hope is that this book will provide useful information for those who desire to produce more effective and attractive communications.

I have other goals for this book as well. First I hope this book will help designers understand the communications philosophies of editors. Second, I hope this book will help editors understand the philosophies of designers so they can work together in reaching common communications goals.

Third, there are those who aspire to careers in communications and find themselves putting together publications. Suddenly they have to know layout, typography, and graphics—and know them fast. They have to put out a newsletter, company magazine, financial report, or brochure. This book, hopefully, will help them, too. It is written for the writer who now must be the editor and layout person and for people who shift from the electronic to the print media.

One of the basic rules of effective communication is "keep it simple." Every attempt has been made to keep it simple. At the same time, every attempt has been made to include what is needed to plan and produce effective communications.

This book is intended to be a beginning. A starting point. The student or professional can use it to enter the fascinating, fast-changing world of graphic communications. I hope that the book will open a door and the reader will go on from there to continuing and more complex studies of one of humanity's oldest, and at the same time newest, arts—the art of communication.

I also hope that practicing professionals will find this book worthwhile. Even though busy communicators may know typography and graphics thoroughly, a review of the field from a different perspective may trigger new inspiration and enthusiasm. This book provides a chance for professionals to stand back and reexamine the way things are being done, to break out of daily routines to consider improvements so that the messages produced are more readable, more attractive, and more effective.

## Acknowledgments

It would be impossible to list everyone who has had a part in making this book a reality. I have contacted newspaper executives, magazine art directors, designers, and educators by the score for advice and permission to use materials. The response was overwhelming and all have my everlasting gratitude.

Several people, though, must be cited for their special help. These include George Weiss, author and director of planning, Metro Associated Services, Inc.; John L. Rush, president, Dynamic Graphics, Inc.; Hal Metzger, Graphic Products Corporation; William Marken, editor, *Sunset*; Mark A. Williams, editorial art manager, the *Orlando Sentinel*; Dan Vaccaro, general manager, Printers Shopper; Donald H. Duffy, corporate art director, *Reader's Digest*; Cliff Kolovson, Atex, Inc.; Rebecca Marrs, Texet Corporation; Don Watkins, author and advertising designer.

The following people read the manuscript and offered many valuable suggestions for its improvement:

Daniel Boyarski
Carniegie-Mellon University, Pennsylvania

Robert J. Fields
Virginia Polytechnic Institute and State University

Marie Freckleton
Rochester Institute of Technology, New York

Charlotte R. Hatfield
Ball State University, Indiana

Robert H. Hawlk
Ohio University

Kenneth F. Hird
California State University, Los Angeles

Tom Knights
Northern Arizona University

Sean Morrison
Boston University

W. S. Mott
California Polytechic State University, San Luis Obispo

James F. Paschal
University of Oklahoma

Jerry Richardson
North Dakota State University

David W. Richter
Ohio State University

Thomas E. Schildgen
Arizona State University

Terry Whistler
University of Houston, Texas

Harold W. Wilson
University of Minnesota

Karen F. Zuga
Kent State University, Ohio

Jean Stoess prepared the manuscript and helped with revisions; Myrick Land offered many valuable suggestions; and Edna Conover read every word at least twice and did much record keeping.

Edmund C. Arnold, who has contributed much to the world of graphics and who played a part in making this book possible, deserves my sincere thanks.

Clyde Perlee and his fine staff at West Publishing Company made me realize many times how fortunate I have been to have them guiding this project to completion. A special thanks to Janet Bollow for excellent design and production supervision. These people, and many more, deserve my most sincere gratitude.

In addition, I would like to thank my associates for many years in the American Amateur Press Association who encouraged my interest in the printed word for the pleasure it can bring, rather than for its profit potential.

Theodore E. Conover

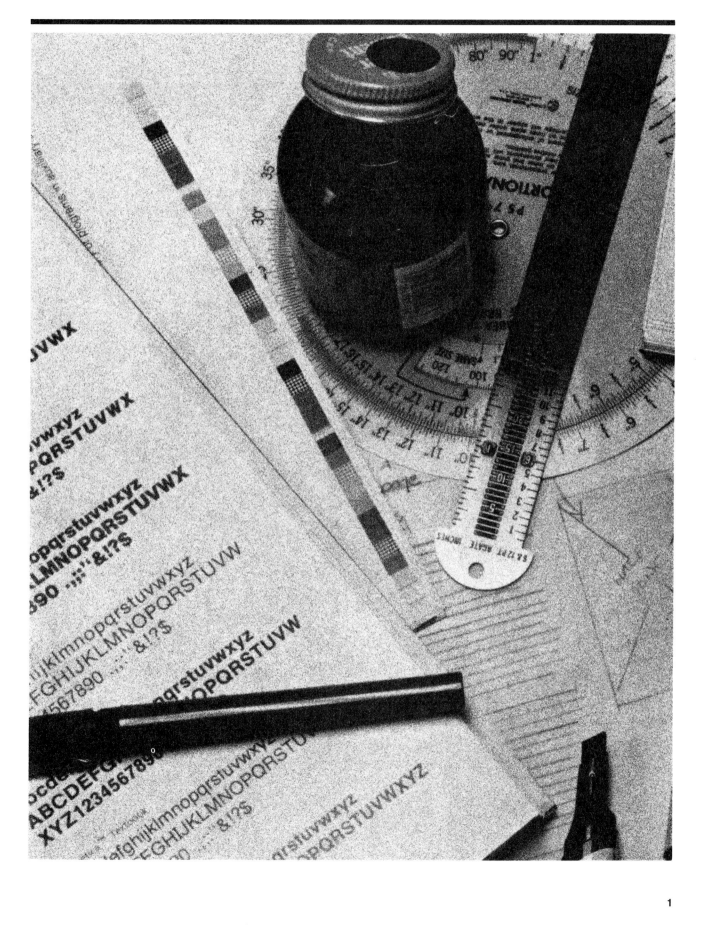

There are a number of reasons why people in the world of communications need a comprehensive understanding of graphics and typography today.

This need began to emerge in American society in 1956 when white-collar workers outnumbered blue-collar workers for the first time. This fact heralded, though it was mostly unnoticed at the time, the forthcoming *information age.*

John Naisbitt points out in *Megatrends,* that "in 1950 only about 17 percent of us worked in information jobs. Now more than 65 cent of us work in information."[1] He notes that most Americans spend their time creating, processing, or distributing information.

What does this have to do with graphics and typography? This flood of information threatens to bury us, making it increasingly difficult for pertinent and essential material to attract the attention of its intended audiences. It challenges communicators to find ways to present information dramatically and effectively.

Thus there is a clear need for a *graphic journalist*—a communicator who understands the effective use of words *and* who understands how to present information in a graphic and effective manner. In the world of communications, graphic journalists are now filling an important role in the editorial offices and newsrooms of both the print and electronic media. This role will increase in importance as time moves on.

Consider what an editor in the magazine division of McGraw-Hill told a journalism instructor; "If you do not do anything else beyond trying to make your students write well, be sure they understand the basics of graphics, typography, and printing."

The instructor was working in the magazine division of the publishing giant on a program sponsored by the American Business Press. Again and again staffers on *Engineering and Mining Journal, Business Week,* and *Chemical Week* emphasized the need for journalists who knew something about the mechanics of effective printed communication. They lamented that journalism school graduates did not know how to select and arrange types, how to lay out pages, or even how to use white space effectively.

At the same time, designers and photo editors complain that editors do not understand graphics, good design, and good visual display.

This need for understanding graphics has been accented in recent years for a number of reasons. One concerns the technological advances in the profession. Another has to do with the challenge to communications from competing forces such as changing lifestyles, opportunities for activities that infringe on time for reading, and the declining emphasis on reading in our education system.

A third concerns the inclination for people in the communications industry to switch from one area to another. Reporters shift to public relations, editors shift to advertising, newspaper people shift to television, and then they shift again.

Then there is the new technology. It has made printing and duplication of printed messages easily available to everyone involved in the distribution of information. As a result we are being flooded with an incredible amount of poorly designed and poorly executed communications. A lot of wastebaskets are overflowing with unread communications, brochures, and newsletters because they are visually unattractive.

---

## Notes

[1] Naisbitt, John, *Megatrends*, (New York: Warren Books, Inc., 1984), pp.4-5.

"To succeed today, a graphic designer or art director must understand the melding of all phases of communications. He is a part of a total communications effort that starts, we hope, with a progressive client, an effective corporate image, and a knowledgeable product designer and ends in a consumer reaching into his pocket for money to buy that product. In between are the advertising copywriter, the art director, a packaging expert, point-of-sale and promotional people, and a dozen others. The problem has been that each person involved in the total communications effort thinks that his own thing is the key to marketing and selling that product. The "experts" within the communications pool just don't understand each other, and this causes a breakdown of communications between individuals who should not only have a thorough knowledge of each other's function but a respect for each other's contribution. Our success is due to the fact that we have made it our business to become knowledgeable in every area of communications. We know how important a good package design can be to the creators of effective advertising. If a stimulating ad gets a customer into a supermarket, a poorly designed package can quickly kill the sale no matter what the ad accomplished. And, conversely, a great package can make advertising look good. The day of specialists working in their vacuums is over. We predict that in ten years total communications teams within advertising agencies or retained by advertising agencies will take over all the functions—point of sale, display, packaging, product design, corporate design, architectural graphics, etc.—that were once farmed out to specialists and use their highly sophisticated methods to produce a much more effective marketing job for their customers. I have been doing a good deal of thinking about youth lately—youth in our business and youth as a consumer. I have reluctantly come to the conclusion that young designers today are so interested in getting rich quickly that they are not getting the background in all phases of communications and marketing, something that our field demands. On the other hand, youth represents a gigantic buying public. Young adults comprise 35% of our population. We have to design for people 25 years old and under to sell. These young people are sharp, better educated than any other generation in the history of man. They are changing all the rules for successful selling. Look at what's happened in the last several years to men's clothing, in the automotive industry, and in the entertainment industry because of youth. Designers, too, must understand the changes that are taking place in society today and be able to respond creatively to them. We cannot settle for one font of wisdom just as we can't settle for one font of type. We must be creatures of the changing times. Communicators today are talking to themselves, holding monologues, when they should be holding dialogues. There is little room today for a narrow perspective on graphic design. In fact, design has been swallowed up by communications, and that's the world we are all working in today." The above statement and prediction were made by Herb Lubalin ten years ago, as president of the International Academy of Communicating Arts and Sciences. On Tuesday night, January 20, 1981, while the Reagans gussied themselves up for the Inauguration Ball...while the hostages sweated out their takeoff from Teheran...a few hundred fans, friends and family of Herb Lubalin tore themselves away from those TV spectacles to witness, in person, the presentation of the AIGA (American Institute of Graphic Arts) medal. For the Reagans, the Inauguration Ball was a definite "first." For the hostages, that day in Iran was a merciful "last." But for Lubalin, the award for excellence in graphics was number 573. Herb has become something of a Pied Piper to the young and a leader among his peers. It is especially to the young designers and students that this profile is directed, to reveal that there are really no gods...no supermen...no lucky Larrys in this business. But once in a while a little guy comes along with a few extra creases in his brain (which makes him see things in a unique way) and with a prodigious appetite for work. The consensus is that Herb is small, lean, elfin, prematurely white-haired and deafeningly silent. He's a bare 5 ft., 7 inches tall (he carries his head tucked into his shoulders which robs him of an inch or two); he weighs in at less than 140 lbs. He doesn't really walk; he shuffles. He doesn't really talk; he grunts, snorts, clears his throat a lot and occasionally nods his head. He's a conscientiously casual dresser, concentrating on subtle taupes, greens, grays and earth tones, guided by either a rare color sense or his congenital color-blindness. He's a sharp shot at tennis, skillful at ping-pong, a graceful swimmer, a smooth dancer, a reluctant walker—he does none of these things "briskly." He churns out mountains of work without ever looking ruffled, frantic or hurried. In fact, the only part of his body that really moves fast is his brain. It's clear, Lubalin's talent is unique. You can't learn it in school, from lectures, from texts or even by swallowing whole issues of U&lc. He has a special radar for zooming in on a problem. He trims away the fat—the extraneous—and works out solutions that are succinct, witty and elegant. Though he has handled every design problem from letterheads to a loft interior, over the years he has been inextricably seduced by typography and letter forms. This man who hardly speaks is a language lover. There's nothing new about literary people playing with words that sound like what they mean, i.e., screech, scratch, grizzly, clang, whisper...but when Herb started to make words look like what they mean, it was the beginning of a whole new adventure in graphic design. His visualization of the word Marriage, with the double R's facing each other; his Mother & Child, with the ampersand and child nestled in the O, are the epitome of his wit. His solutions are so obviously right, they stun us. Herb is exasperating to people who produce work for him but never know what he thinks of their efforts. He is crushing to young designers and students who labor over a portfolio, seeking a serious critique, but hear only a few grunts, a mumble and a snort or two. If only they knew that a grunt, a snort and a little nod of the head from Herb can be thunderous applause. He can be a joy to work for. He is explicit, decisive and not given to endless revises; but he is stubborn to the extreme; his tenacity has driven others to rage and resignation. As for his quickie decisions, at least two now-famous graphic artists have the distinction of having been "fired" by Lubalin. People who know the meaning of "blocked" watch him work with envy and murder in their hearts. His powers of concentration are legendary. I've personally seen him—with tracing pad balanced on his knees, with football noises blasting from the TV set, with children wrestling underfoot, with food passing overhead—implacably reel off tissues with the regularity of copies shooting out of a word processor. Before the Giants have made a first down, he has 15 solutions to a graphic problem. And he has crumpled up more good ideas than most people produce in a lifetime of trying hard. He has no empathy for procrastinators, worriers or deliberators. What might be a "big deal" to the rest of us is a flash decision for him. Herb has bought houses, formed partnerships, entered into business ventures in less time than most people take to decide on a pair of shoes. That's unnerving. Expect no flood of compassion from him, not even a trickle, for your personal woes. You want to discuss a love affair, your children, your professional crises, your doubts, your fears, your psyche? Don't come to Herb. The whole Freudian mystique has passed him by. He has no use for psychology except, typographically, it has terrific potential—those ascenders, descenders and o's! But Herb is exasperatingly consistent; he keeps his own personal traumas and tragedies firmly locked behind the sluice gates, too. Contrary to all that has been made of his silence at work and in his private world, Herb does talk. Dress him in a tuxedo, stand him before a microphone, he sharpens up his everyday t's and d's and becomes a veritable Demosthenes—only funnier. Herb has lectured widely in the States, in Canada, Europe and Japan, informing and entertaining professionals and students with his devastating candor and humor. Or...if you should happen to touch on a topic that nettles him he will open up and deliver a diatribe he's had stored up for months. In his work he is loose and open. He has no hoked-up philosophies, no rigid imperatives. But in personal matters, he's a crazy aesthetic fanatic. He operates from a code of decency few people understand: He was an "equal-opportunity-employer" long before those words were invented. He hired women designers, artists and administrators before any one of them had her consciousness raised. He initiated the Ms. section of U&lc as a showcase for women in graphics. But don't, unless you enjoy severe indigestion, get him started on Women's Lib in the midst of a nice quiet dinner. To sum up, Herb Lubalin is: a brilliant communicator and non-communicative...an iconoclast and a classicist...esoteric and earthy...uptight and

## Before the Big Change

It is midsummer 1962 in the editorial department of the *Daily Times.*

The *Daily Times* is a typical small-city American newspaper, and the staff is working hard because it is 30 minutes before deadline. About an hour from now, today's edition will roll off the press.

One of the reporters is tapping out a story on her battered manual typewriter. She has already banged out three pages of her account of last night's city council meeting, and the pages of copy paper are strewn across her desk.

In the corner, surrounded by his teletype machines, is the wire editor, rolling up strips of yellow paper covered with tiny holes as it comes off a perforating machine. This device punches ⅞-inch-wide tape in concert with the teletype that is typing out on paper a story sent by telephone wire from New York.

The wire editor will edit the printed story and write a headline in pencil on a strip of copy paper. Then he will send the three items—printed copy, headline, tape—to the composing room. The tape will activate typesetting machines to transform copy into type. The headline will go to a "floorman" who will set it into type on a Ludlow machine, which casts type from molten metal. The printout copy will be used by the proofreader to check for errors.

Back in the composing room, it's bedlam. Linotype machines 7 feet high are clashing and clanging as they cast lines of type for the page forms from molten metal. People are rushing about making proofs of galleys of type, sawing strips of metal for spaces between lines of type, mitering corners on other strips of metal borders to make boxes for some stories and advertisements, casting the headline type, and using routers to shave unwanted metal off castings of illustrations.

**Fig. 1-1** *A typical newsroom in 1969 before the electronic era. Layout people used manual typewriters, rulers, pencils, paste jars, and scissors to design the newspaper. (Photo by Howard Decker)*

Other people are placing all the metal pieces in proper order within chases, the metal frames that hold the pages together while they are put through a molding press to make mats, or molds, of the pages for casting in the foundry. The resulting castings, or plates, will be put on the press for actual printing.

Meanwhile, back in the editorial department, the reporter has finished the story. She pulls the last page of copy from her typewriter and hands the story to the city editor. He asks a few questions, makes a note or two on the copy, and takes it to the copy editor.

The copy editor is seated in the "slot." He is in the middle of a U-shaped desk, and four copy readers are on the "rim," or outside edge of the desk, busily making corrections and writing heads for stories.

The copy editor sees that one of the readers has just finished editing a story, so he tosses the latest arrival in that direction for a final going over before it is sent to the composing room.

Before handing over the story, the copy editor has diagrammed the area it will occupy on a page dummy, a miniature sketch of a newspaper page. The makeup man will use this sketch to guide him in putting the page together for the molding press.

While all of this is going on at the newspaper office, further down the street partners in a public relations consulting business are contemplating their future. They had recently opened their office and business was slow. They had assumed that their job would be to provide publicity for the clients they could obtain in the community. That was their idea of what public relations was. They were discovering how wrong they had been.

Both partners had some media experience. One had been a reporter for the *Daily Times* for 3 years. He had covered city politics. The other had been on the public affairs staff of the local television station. They thought they knew all they needed to handle the tasks of a public relations operation.

They were good writers and editors. They knew the media and what editors and news directors wanted in the way of usable copy. They had a lot of good contacts in the community.

But they soon found out that they would be expected to do a lot more besides turning out press releases. Their clients wanted them to give advice on policy questions, find out what employees thought about their organizations, and evaluate community opinion. And their potential clients expected them to produce brochures, information folders, and all sorts of other printed material.

Two potential clients had specific projects. One wanted a monthly employee magazine or newsletter. Could the partners produce one— from writing all copy to taking care of printing and distribution?

The other prospective client wanted a bi-monthly newsletter for its members and patrons.

The partners had no trouble coming up with lively copy and illustration ideas for the magazine and newsletter, but when it came to putting the publications together and working with printers, they didn't know where to begin.

The printers asked questions like:

"Shall we set the body matter 8 on 10 or 9 on 11?"

"Would you like an Oxford rule to box the masthead?"

"Would you like us to print it on 60-pound machine finish book, or do you think 70-pound would be better?"

The partners had never worked with printers and they had never selected types and rules or designed attractive pages.

They lost both clients.

Back at the newspaper, the editorial staff is not concerned about the printing of the *Daily Times*. They know that once they send the copy to the composing room, skilled craftsmen will space headlines, pictures, captions, and all the other elements on the pages so that the *Daily Times* will look "nice" when printed. They know that if they write a headline that is slightly too long for the space allotted, the man on the Ludlow will adjust the spacing between words to make it fit. Proofreaders will catch most errors.

## The Big Change

Now it is 20 years later.

At the *Daily Times* there have been a lot of changes. It is quiet. The clatter of typewriters and staccato beats of the teletypes and perforating unit are gone. Reporters are typing their stories on video display terminals. Wire copy is spewing forth at a rapid rate from the wire machine, which quietly zips and buzzes rather than clatters like the machines of 20 years ago.

When the reporters finish their stories they press code keys, and the stories disappear from the screens to be stored in the newspaper's computer.

**Fig. 1-2** *The tools of the trade are changing rapidly. This is a typical newsroom today. Gone are the typewriters and disappearing are the pencils, rulers, and paste jars. Electronic equipment is now used for writing stories and designing pages. (Photo by Larry Brooks)*

 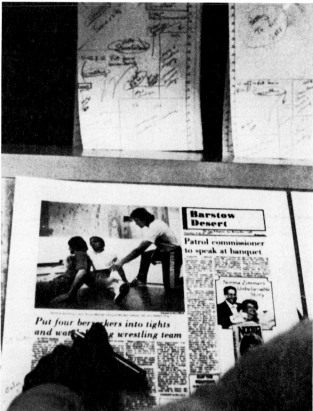

The U-shaped copy desk is gone. So are the copy readers. But a copy editor is still there. She is seated in front of an editing terminal. When she wants a reporter's story she will type a code and the story will appear on her editing screen. She will scan the story and make changes—shift paragraphs, add words, delete words, make corrections—simply by sending instructions to the computer.

She will also tap out a headline and then instruct the computer as to the size and style of the head. When everything is just as she wants it, she will instruct the computer to activate the typesetting equipment.

Back in the composing room all the cumbersome letterpress typesetting and page makeup equipment is gone. There is carpet on the floor. Instead of working with metal pieces in chases, people are cutting and pasting strips of paper with copy and headlines printed on them. The copy comes from typesetting equipment activated by the computer. The cut strips are pasted on _grids_, lightweight cardboard sheets the size of the newspaper pages.

Once the page has been pasted together by the composing room staff, it will be photographed and a plate will be made for the new offset press that replaced the old letterpress that turned out the _Daily Times_ for so many years.

There have also been a lot of changes at the public relations firm. One partner is at his desk discussing page dummies for a company

**Fig. 1-3** _The ponderous process of page assembly of the hot type era (left) has been replaced by the drawing board and cold type tools._

**Fig. 1-4** *Video display screens are replacing paper and pencils in making layouts and decisions about graphics in some newspaper offices and design studios. (Reprinted by permission from* presstime, *the journal of the American Newspaper Publishers Association.)*

**Fig. 1-5** *By typing commands on the keyboard of the pagination device, the communicator can create a page on the video display screen. The page can be built with headlines, copy blocks, and art indicators. The completed layout (right) is ready to transmit to the computer. (Reprinted by permission from* presstime, *the journal of the American Newspaper Publishers Association.)*

magazine with the company's personnel manager. The other partner is making rough layouts for a campaign folder the mayor has ordered to use in her reelection drive.

After the initial shock of losing those two promising clients, the partners rushed to learn all they could about printing and typography. It was not easy, and they lost a lot of time and money during those first few months they were in business. But now, 20 years later, they have survived and their business is prospering.

"We thought we knew it all," they said many times. "How much easier it would have been if we had known something about printing and typography before we struck out on our own in this business."

Meanwhile, the copy editor of the *Daily Times* has been attending a training seminar on the new technology.

She is learning to operate the pagination device that soon will be installed in the newsroom. This computer-operated piece of hardware will not only take and process copy from the video display terminal but will also accept page dummies. It will operate the typesetter and it will place type, illustrations, headlines, and everything else that makes up a complete newspaper page just where the editor wants it. And, it will produce a page ready to be made into a printing plate and clamped on the press.

The entire composing room of the *Daily Times* will "disappear" into the computer and its companion devices. The machine will do the work of all those typesetters, makeup men, stereotypers, engravers, proofreaders, and others who worked at the *Daily Times* back in 1962. If those in the editorial department want their newspaper to "look nice" now, they will tell the computer exactly how they want the elements placed on the page, how much white space to put here, how large to make that headline over there.

In the "good old days" of only 20 years ago, copy produced by a reporter passed through about nine hands before it was ready for the press. It went from reporter to editor to copy reader to composing room, to proofreader to correction bank to page makeup to mat

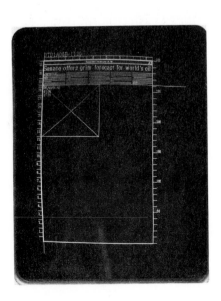

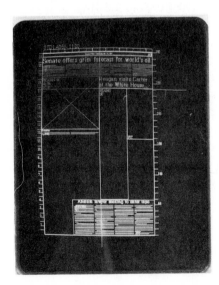

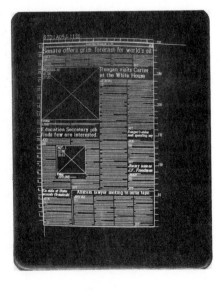

VIA SATELLITE — THE NATION'S NEWSPAPER — 50 CENTS

SPORTS FINAL

NCAA: FINAL 16 TRY TO SURVIVE, 1C
- TV, 1, 6C; PAIRINGS, 7C
- UCLA'S NOSEDIVE, 6C
- FOSTER TO MIAMI, 1C

NFL PENALIZES SHOW-OFFS, 1C

NBA:

| | |
|---|---|
| SEATTLE | 104 |
| PHOENIX | 102 |
| DETROIT | 132 |
| SAN DIEGO | 123 |

ALL RESULTS, SECTION C

By Porter Binks, USA TODAY
DEAN SMITH: Sends N. Carolina against Indiana

# USA TODAY

PUBLISHED BY GANNETT

THURSDAY

TV CENSORS LET MORE SLIP BY
LIFE, 1D

CASSETTE TAPES BOOMING PAST RECORD ALBUMS
LIFE, 1D

ANNIE LENNOX HAVING FUN MAKING MUSIC
LIFE, 1D

ANNIE LENNOX: 25-city tour for Eurythmics

**THURSDAY,** MARCH 22, 1984

## NEWSLINE

A QUICK READ ON THE NEWS

**WEATHER:** Snow due around Great Lakes, south to Virginia; new storm in Rockies. Full color page. 10A.
**Pacific Coast:** Showers in north; sunny in south.
**Rockies:** Snow in north; clear elsewhere.
**South Central:** Sunny in Louisiana, Oklahoma.
**North Central:** Partly cloudy, chilly; some snow or rain.
**Midwest:** Mixed snow and rain.
**Southeast:** Partly sunny, cool.
**Northeast:** Chilly, some wet snow.

■ **Storm blasts East with grab bag of rain, thunderstorms, wind, snow, sleet and tornadoes on Wednesday. 10A.**

**WALL STREET DOWN:** The Dow Jones index drops 4.92 points, closes at 1170.85. 6B.

**USA, SOVIETS CLASH AT SEA:** Soviet sub, USA carrier Kitty Hawk collide in Sea of Japan; Soviets blame USA for mine that damaged ship in Nicaragua. 7A.

**NEW ARCHBISHOP:** Boston's Roman Catholics greet Bishop Bernard F. Law, 52, left; takes office today. 3A.

By Bob Linder
LAW: Formal installation Friday.

**MIDDLE EAST:** Sale of $133 million worth of Stinger anti-aircraft missiles to Jordan canceled by Reagan after King Hussein's criticism of USA policy. 7A.

■ **Failure of talks spurs factions to renew violence in Beirut. 7A.**

**FREED:** Robbery charges against Lenell Geter dropped after new suspect surfaces. 3A. Profile of Dallas' district attorney. 2A.

**NATION:** Yoko Ono, John Lennon's sons break ground for Strawberry Fields, in NYC's Central Park. 2D.

■ **Judge in pool table rape trial blasts media for using victim's name; jury deliberations begin today. 3A.**

**WASHINGTON:** Reagan's "Star Wars" defense plan is a year old, but immensity just now sinking in. 7A.

■ **Is sleeping in a park free speech? Supreme Court asked to approve protest method by homeless; other action. 7A.**

**ABROAD:** Peru declares state of emergency on eve of 24-hour general strike against government policies. 7A.

**TODAY'S DEBATE:** Iraq, Iran war. In USA TODAY's opinion, we must protest the war, work to keep Persian Gulf open, but avoid deeper entanglement. 8A.

■ **The USA has no reason to take sides in the war and should stay out, says *Inquiry* magazine editor. 8A.**

**MONEY:** Merger of LTV Corp., Republic Steel gets Justice Department nod; merger policy changing. 1B.

■ **Analysts discount rumors Rupert Murdoch wants to buy Disney; "He wants something less wholesome." 1B.**

■ **Japanese stocks worth more dollars due to USA trade deficit; Tokyo stock market booming in recovery. 1B.**

■ **Telephone access charges for businesses, AT&T's long-distance competitors postponed until June 13. 1B.**

■ **Home improvement sales hit $33 billion last year. 1B.**

**LIFE:** Bypass surgery no more effective than drugs in easing pain for people with early signs of heart disease. 1D.

■ **Maverick enforcers are TV's newest heroes; *Magnum, P.I., The A-Team* operate outside the law. 5D.**

Compiled by Tara Connell

### Inside USA TODAY

FOUR SECTIONS

| NEWS | | SPORTS | |
|---|---|---|---|
| Editorial, opinions | 8-9A | Baseball | 3C |
| Nation at large | 3A | Basketball | 1C, 4C, 6-7C |
| Newsmakers | 2A | Football | 1C, 3C, 5C |
| State-by-state | 4-5A | Golf | 7C |
| Washington/World | 7A | Hockey | 5C |
| Weather report | 10A | State-by-state | 8C |
| **MONEY** | | **LIFE** | |
| American Exchange | 5B | Crossword | 3D |
| New York Exchange | 4B | Television | 5D |
| OTC Trading | 5B | Travel & Leisure | 3D |

COPYRIGHT 1984 USA TODAY, a division of Gannett Co., Inc.

### USA SNAPSHOTS

A look at statistics that shape the nation

**Undergraduate bargains**

A March *Money* magazine study says these schools are among the USA's best buys, combining reasonable cost *, generous financial aid and a senior faculty that regularly teaches undergraduates:

* All one-year costs

| | |
|---|---|
| St. Olaf College (Minn.) | $9,550 |
| University of Calif. at Santa Cruz | $9,524 |
| Wheaton College (Ill.) | $9,340 |
| Trinity University (Texas) | $8,780 |
| Rice University (Texas) | $8,500 |
| Wake Forest University (N.C.) | $8,185 |
| St. Joseph's College (Ind.) | $8,020 |

Source: Money magazine

By Marcy Eckroth Mullins, USA TODAY

## We'll be paying more to see pro games

By Gary Mihoces and Larry Weisman
USA TODAY

Many baseball and football fans will pay more to watch their favorite teams this year.

Fifteen of the National Football League's 28 teams have raised 1984 ticket prices by $1 to $5 — blaming higher players' salaries and increases in operating costs such as jet travel and talent scouting. A year ago, only four NFL teams raised prices.

Ten of baseball's 26 teams upped prices an average of about 50 cents; one, the Texas Rangers, cut prices.

■ The Pittsburgh Pirates have the biggest increase. They raised field, loge and club boxes by $1.50 to $8.50.

■ The Rangers, continuing a price rollback started last year, reduced prices by 50 cents, leaving a top ticket of $8 and general admission of $3.50.

■ Most expensive ticket: $10.50 for the Montreal Expos, who also have the cheapest seat, $1 (about 80 cents in USA currency).

■ Cheapest in USA: Yankee Stadium and Seattle — $1.50.

In the NFL:

■ The Super Bowl champion Los Angeles Raiders, reporting they spent more than $1 million on flying last year, raised their top ticket from $18 to $22.

■ The Washington Redskins, who hadn't upped prices in five years, raised the top ticket from $20 to $25 — NFL's high.

■ The Cleveland Browns, who said they spent about $800,000 on scouting college players last year, increased their top from $17 to $21.

■ The Kansas City Chiefs are keeping the same season ticket prices, but an individual game ticket is going up $2 — with $17 the top.

■ Cheapest ticket: $5 for the Tampa Bay Buccaneers.

■ **Team-by-team chart, 3C**

## Off Beirut, Marines wait

Photos by Dave Kryszak, Visions

TIME FOR WORKOUTS: Staff Sgt. Jeff Lachance, 28, of Jacksonville, N.C., who does push-ups on deck of USS Guam, wrote wife Letty he wants to get back home and re-enlist.

IN COMMAND: Col. Pat Faulkner — 'Morale will probably be somewhat of a problem here.'

TIME FOR MUSIC: Pfc. Thomas 'Slick' Tyler of Kill Devil Hills, N.C., with guitar, and Pfc. Dan Castell of Cleveland. Tyler has entertained officers, played on Radio Beirut.

## Reagan fires deficit threat: Do it my way

Special for USA TODAY

WASHINGTON — Budget-cutting action picked up Wednesday in Congress:

■ President Reagan gave balky congressional Republicans a pep talk about his $150 billion deficit-cutting plan.

But Reagan also warned both House and Senate GOP members that "I've dug in my heels on taxes," and that "if anyone sends me this tax package and at the same time does not include the spending cuts, I will veto the tax package."

■ The Senate Finance Committee approved a $74 billion deficit-cutting package, including $48 billion in taxes and nearly $26 billion in spending reductions through 1987 — a portion of Reagan's program that fits parts of $185 billion House Democrat plan.

The current session of Congress has proved to be Reagan's least successful, as much because of opposition from Republicans as from Democrats:

■ The GOP leadership is pushing a budget package that includes more defense cuts than Reagan wanted.

■ Conservative Republicans oppose tax increases — even some "loophole" closing programs Reagan supports.

■ Democrats want a 3.5 percent real increase, compared with Reagan's 7.8 percent.

Reagan also criticized Democrats for making the deficit an election issue — saying they used deficits for 40 years as "a deliberate part of their policy."

## Cuba frees 19 USA yachters

Special for USA TODAY

MIAMI — Nineteen USA yachters were freed by Cuba late Wednesday, a day after their boats were seized when they passed near the communist island during a race.

Sen. Claiborne Pell, D-Rhode Island, who had negotiated for their release, announced the action at 10 p.m. EST after being told by a Cuban official in Washington.

The men were aboard two yachts — the Brigadoon and the Cashasha — in a four-boat race from the Miami to Montego Bay, Jamaica, when they were seized Tuesday.

"The Cashasha says she's on her way to Jamaica. Nothing's been heard from Brigadoon yet," said U.S. Coast Guard Lt. Kurt Wellington at Guantanamo naval base, Cuba.

"There were no injuries and everyone has been released."

Seizures for straying into Cuban waters are "not unusual," said U.S. Coast Guard Petty Officer Reese Belleman. "You're rounding a corner there and if you cut it too close you end up getting intercepted."

■ **Weekend adventurers, 3A**

## Old remedy aids asthma: strong coffee

By Steven Findlay
USA TODAY

Drinking strong coffee can help asthma sufferers caught without their usual medicine, a new study indicates.

The study confirms an observation made 125 years ago by a British doctor but not tested until now: Caffeine opens narrowed bronchial passages, allowing asthma sufferers to breathe during an attack.

Researchers at the University of Manitoba in Winnipeg, Canada, report in today's *New England Journal of Medicine* that caffeine was as effective in improving breathing capacity as its chemical cousin, theophylline, now the most common asthma medicine.

But, researchers say, coffee should not replace theophylline or other asthma medications for routine use.

"If patients ... didn't have their anti-asthma medication, it might be worthwhile trying a very old remedy," says Dr. Estelle R. Simons of Children's Hospital, Winnipeg.

An estimated 7 million Americans have asthma, including 2 to 3 million children.

The study compared 13 children who took caffeine with 10 who took theophylline. Both groups had mild side effects — shakiness, dizziness, tremor.

COVER STORY

## Battle troops now fight boredom

'We were supposed to be the knight in shining armor ... Things don't work like that'

By Don Kirk
USA TODAY

ABOARD THE USS GUAM — Day begins on the Guam at 6 a.m. with the piping of reveille, but most of the U.S. Marines packed below on two decks are not likely to venture to the busy helicopter flight deck for the view of dawn over the Mediterranean.

For them, life is a routine of busy-work, inspections and classes — anything to break the grinding monotony of the life of a combat soldier at sea with no war to fight and basically very little to do.

A month after they were evacuated from "the beach" around the Beirut Airport by helicopters and landing craft, the men of the 22nd Marine Amphibious Unit have gotten over the novelty of hot food and showers — and now confront the hazards of keeping mind and body together in a daily, agonizing fight against boredom.

"You gotta live with it," says Pfc. Dan Castell, 19, of Cleveland, a rifleman with Echo Company. "You can't go anywhere, there's nowhere to walk around. You listen to music, write letters home."

Castell and the other men of the 22nd replaced the ill-fated Marines whose headquarters were destroyed in a bomb blast Oct. 23.

They surrounded Beirut Airport, spending much of their time filling sandbags and securing bunkers against attack. Despite the arduous work and danger, most wish they were "back on the beach" rather than cruising in circles five to

Please see COVER STORY next page ▶

## 3,000 video arcades zapped

Special for USA TODAY

Video game arcades, the homes of Pac-Man and Space Invaders, are folding as fast as they sprung up.

In the past nine months, more than 3,000 of the USA's 10,000 — once the entertainment world's fastest-growing industry — have closed.

"We had a real boom for two to three years," said St. Paul, Minn., arcade operator Todd Erickson. "That's over now."

Game machine sales have plunged 65 percent, from 480,000 in 1982 to 170,000 last year; income per machine at many arcades has dropped in half, from $120 to about $60 a week. Meanwhile, interest in traditional games, such as skee ball and pool, is booming.

■ **Time's up on TV games, 3B**

## 'Doughboy' finally gets his Purple Heart

Special for USA TODAY

WASHINGTON — Wearing his "doughboy" uniform, Adam Raczkowski was awarded the Purple Heart Wednesday — 66 years after he was gassed in WWI.

Raczkowski, 89, of Southington, Conn., cried as Army Secretary John Marsh awarded the medal in a Pentagon ceremony.

Most records from Raczkowski's Army service in France had been lost or destroyed. He used an old hospital pass to prove he had been gassed in 1918.

By Jeanne Markin
PFC. RACZKOWSKI

5A

*USA TODAY, which appeared in 1982, was the first newspaper to routinely use four-color graphics in its design and layout.*

# Perspectives

Wright State University       Winter 1981-82, Volume 4, Number 1

## Cricket fever hits Wright State

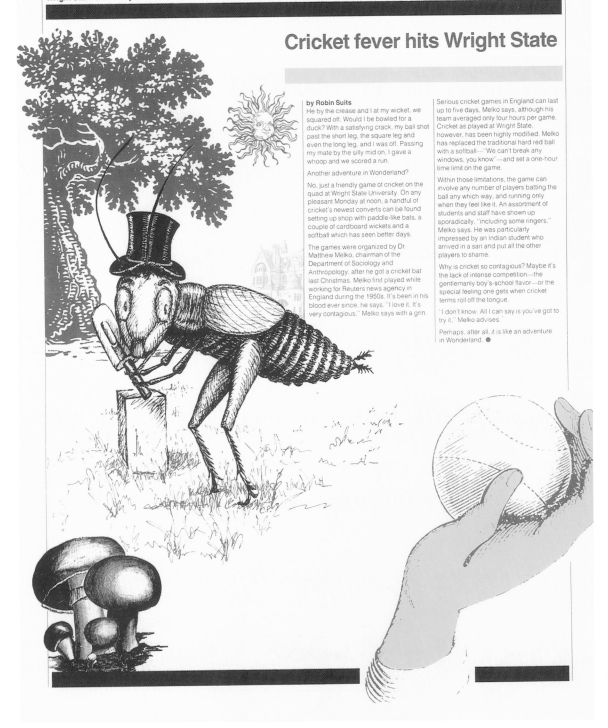

by Robin Suits

He by the crease and I at my wicket, we squared off. Would I be bowled for a duck? With a satisfying crack, my ball shot past the short leg, the square leg and even the long leg, and I was off. Passing my mate by the silly mid on, I gave a whoop and we scored a run.

Another adventure in Wonderland?

No, just a friendly game of cricket on the quad at Wright State University. On any pleasant Monday at noon, a handful of cricket's newest converts can be found setting up shop with paddle-like bats, a couple of cardboard wickets and a softball which has seen better days.

The games were organized by Dr. Matthew Melko, chairman of the Department of Sociology and Anthropology, after he got a cricket bat last Christmas. Melko first played while working for Reuters news agency in England during the 1950s. It's been in his blood ever since, he says. "I love it. It's very contagious," Melko says with a grin.

Serious cricket games in England can last up to five days, Melko says, although his team averaged only four hours per game. Cricket as played at Wright State, however, has been highly modified. Melko has replaced the traditional hard red ball with a softball—"We can't break any windows, you know"—and set a one-hour time limit on the game.

Within those limitations, the game can involve any number of players batting the ball any which way, and running only when they feel like it. An assortment of students and staff have shown up sporadically, "including some ringers," Melko says. He was particularly impressed by an Indian student who arrived in a sari and put all the other players to shame.

Why is cricket so contagious? Maybe it's the lack of intense competition—the gentlemanly boy's-school flavor—or the special feeling one gets when cricket terms roll off the tongue.

"I don't know. All I can say is you've got to try it," Melko advises.

Perhaps, after all, it is like an adventure in Wonderland. ●

*Perspectives is a newsletter that uses color in both paper stock and ink, plus many graphic design techniques to present an attention-getting, interesting publication. (It is produced by the Offices of Admissions and University Communications, Wright State University, Dayton, Ohio.)*

# Perspectives

Wright State University   Summer 1981, Volume 3, Number 3

---

# Perspectives

Wright State University   Summer 1981, Volume 3, Number 3

## Welcome to a-May-zing Daze at WSU

by Carol Siyahi

---

## Prof plays up improvisation in class and on stage

by John R. Alexander

### On the road to WSU: help in getting started

by Pamela Kramer

**Registration**

**Orientation**

**Scholarships and Aid**

**Counseling**

**Housing**

**Co-op**

**Career Planning**

**Tutoring**

**Handicapped Services**

---

## Tarot!Tarot!Tarot!: It's in the cards

by Rhonda Peoples

Perspectives is published three times a year by the Wright State University Offices of Admissions and University Communications. Address all inquiries to Wright State University, Office of Admissions, Dayton, Ohio 45435.

Edited by Carol Siyahi and Patricia Kramer.

Designed by Larry M. Weeden.

## Student seeks "honesty, not glitter" in acting

by Rhonda Peoples

This issue of the Georgetown File, an employee newsletter, was printed in just two colors on ivory paper stock. Eight techniques were used on the first page to give a multihued look: (1) the nameplate is 30 percent gray and 30 percent red; (2) line art and continuous tone art are combined into a single image; (3) a keyed group photo is combined with an outline drawing; (4) silhouetted photos are combined with rules to simulate perspective; (5) a duotone mezzotint is printed over a gray benday; (6) a mezzotint; (7) reverse type is used on a solid band for emphasis; (8) a gray halftone over a red benday gives an antique look. (Georgetown File is a publication of International Paper Company; Claudia J. Strauss, project manager; H. Ann Silvernail, editor; Harmon Kemp Partners, designer. This issue won a silver award from the Society of Publication Designers.)

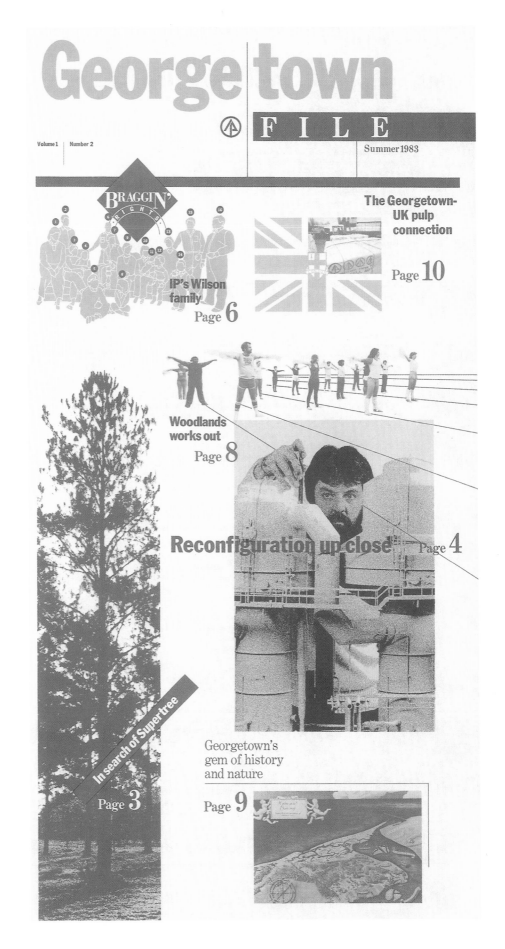

# George town

## F I L E

Volume 1    Number 2

Summer 1983

BRAGGIN' RIGHTS

IP's Wilson family
Page 6

The Georgetown-UK pulp connection
Page 10

Woodlands works out
Page 8

Reconfiguration up close — Page 4

In search of Supertree
Page 3

Georgetown's gem of history and nature
Page 9

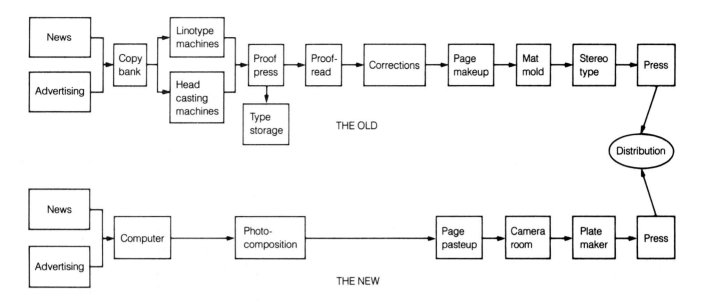

THE OLD

THE NEW

molding to stereotyping before it was ready for the press. Now it is all up to the reporter, editor, or art director to see that everything is just right to produce an accurate story and an attractive, readable page.

What the editor puts into the computer is what the reader will see when the *Daily Times* rolls off the press. The editor has become not only the editor, but the typesetter, proofreader, typographer, and makeup person. The editor obviously now needs to know much more about typography and graphics.

**Fig. 1-6** *Not too long ago copy written and edited in the "front office" passed through as many as ten "stations" where people could catch errors and back up the editor as the copy made its way to the press. Today advanced technology and automation are eliminating these stations. The writer or editor has lost this backup and must make more and more of the graphics decisions.*

## A Revolution in Communications

In the past two decades a revolution has swept through editorial, public relations, and advertising offices across America. This revolution has engulfed the world of printed communications and has changed practices, some of them going back 400 years, and the way communicators do their jobs. It has been a great challenge, and it has created a great opportunity as well.

As with all change, there was considerable resistance for a while. There still are those who are reluctant to come to terms with the new technology. But many have found that the new technology has provided the tools to do a better and more satisfying job. And they have also discovered that, in making the job easier, the new technology is also capable of making the end product of their profession—words on paper—less effective.

Not too long ago, the principal method of producing printed material was with metal type, engravings, borders, ornaments, and the letterpress. Everything printed was composed and arranged to very precise dimensions. In the metal, or "hot type," method, rules and borders have to be cut by hand. Type, illustrations, and borders have to be fitted much as carpenters fit materials to produce a building that is straight and true. Tedious craftsmanship is needed to produce satisfactory results on the printed page.

With the advent of cold type composition and the increased use of offset lithography, the process was simplified. It is possible now to do things with words and illustrations on paper simply and easily. It is possible to produce excellent printed pieces with comparative ease. On the other hand, it is also possible to produce poorly conceived and executed work. Since the composition and printing processes have been simplified, there is a temptation to take the easy way out and be satisfied with work that does not quite measure up to its potential.

Another dramatic change that has occurred is that many communicators are finding that they are functioning as graphic designers and compositors as well as writers. They, like the staff at the *Daily Times*, are having to make decisions about type style and size, spacing, placement of elements, and all the graphics decisions handled by production departments not too long ago. Communicators are becoming compositors as well as writers as they operate the computers and electronic gear that have moved the composing room into the editorial offices.

The communicator of today and the future will, with the aid of complex electronic gear, become a compositor, a layout artist, and a makeup person—all without leaving the electronic console.

As a result, many people in the printed communications industry will find that they are confronted not only with gathering, writing, and editing material but with making decisions concerning the printed appearance of this material as well. If they do not master the techniques of graphics, their writing and editing skills will be lost in a final product that does not grab and hold the interest of their readers.

## Bombarded with Communications

The situation is further compounded by the nature of life in these final decades of the twentieth century. The busy citizen of today may not have the time or inclination to decipher unattractive and difficult materials. Sloppy, poorly designed printed material will be tossed aside. There is too much that is interesting and attractive clamoring for attention.

We are bombarded with communications from the time our clock radios blare forth in the morning until we doze in front of the television set in the evening. Researchers have estimated that the average person is bombarded with between 1,500 and 1,800 messages a day. The competition for our attention is awesome.

In addition, we are products of the television era. The National Commission on the Causes and Prevention of Violence reports that American youngsters spend from one-fourth to one-half of their waking hours watching television. A child, it notes, attends school

**Fig. 1-7** *There is intense competition for attention as messages bombard the modern person from morning until late at night. (Ries Cappiello Colwell advertising agency)*

on the average of 980 hours a year and watches television 1,340 hours a year.

A study by John C. Schweitzer, of Indiana University, reported in the American Newspaper Publishers Association's "News Research for Better Newspapers," that the great majority of American newspaper readers spend less than 30 minutes a day with their papers. Many people surveyed said they only "glance" at the newspaper.

Continuing research by the Roper Organization between 1959 and 1972 showed a growing reliance on television by many Americans. By 1963, television overtook newspapers as the source of most people's news about the world, and television became the most "believable" medium in 1961. In 1972, 56 percent of the people surveyed by Roper said if they could keep only one medium it would be television. Newspapers would be retained by 22 percent, and only 5 percent would give up the other media and keep magazines.[1]

And in spring 1981, a Gallup poll showed that 71 percent of the people believe that network television does a better job of providing accurate, unbiased news than anyone else. The poll revealed that local television rates much higher in public trust than the printed media (69 percent for local television, 66 percent for news magazines, and only 57 percent for newspapers).

Times have changed since the days when Will Rogers was quoted as saying, "All I know is what I read in the newspapers."

The point is, if a person works in communications there is a challenge. Audiences are going to have to be lured away from other forms of communication. In addition, the communicator will have to strive harder to entice the audience to select one message from the scores of others that are demanding attention. It just is not possible for everyone to examine every message. Some will be selected and some will be rejected.

SIXTY ROWS OF VARIOUS GRASSES WILL PROVIDE A SITE FOR VO-AG TRAINING IN GRASS IDENTIFI-CATION. THE ROD-ROW PLANTING IS A COOPERATIVE PROJECT BE-TWEEN THE HIGH SCHOOL VO-AG PROGRAM AND THE SOIL CONSER-VATION SERVICE. THE FFA CLUB PLOWED AND DISCED THE SCHOOL 924SITE. THE CONSERVATION DIS-TRICT PROVIDED FUNDING. THE PLANTING INCLUDES BLOCKS OF BROME GRASSES, FESCUES, WHEATGRASSES, AND NATIVE

Extension efforts are also directed toward educating growers in the use of integrated pest management techniques. According to the university pro-gram coordinator, some 98 percent of all growers are using these techniques as a result of a state-wide certification training program.

**Pest Management**

Extension efforts are also directed toward educating growers in the use of integrated pest management techniques. According

Now you can shop in your own home with the most complete, 100 pg. original fine art catalog ever offered to collec-tors — with discount prices normally made available only to dealers. Join the many other collectors who are enjoying huge savings on their purchases as

*The planting includes blocks of brome grasses, fescues, wheatgrasses, and native range grasses. Irrigated and dryland hay or pasture grasses are included along with rarely seen special purpose grasses. This project has attracted attention from local ranchers who are interested in observing.*

**Fig. 1-8** *Typographic devices such as lines set in all capital letters, lines too long for easy reading, lines with improper spacing, heavy rules, and reverses, can hamper effective communication if not used with care and planning.*

Much of the communications that threaten to suffocate people in a torrent of paper are hardly worth pursuing. They can be fired directly into the wastebasket. But, on the other hand, much signifi-cant information may be thrown out because it is poorly written and poorly presented.

Some communications miss their targets because they are not attractively packaged. They do not make initial contact or, if they do, the reader quickly loses interest because of poor content or poor typography.

Many communicators have turned to design specialists to help them produce presentable printed material. There is nothing wrong with this. If the communicator can afford it, the help of a designer can be a valuable investment. A designer, that is, who understands how to talk with type. Some do not.

Some designers are skilled at placing elements in attractive and attention-getting arrangements but are not skilled in effective communication with words. Much of the material they produce is attractive but not readable. And the communicator who chooses to work with a design-oriented person may have trouble trying to explain why a rule here or a wrong style of type there may be attractive but destroys the readability of the message.

For example, some type styles present a psychological image or create a mood but are unreadable. Bold, heavy borders alongside lightface reading matter may create contrast but cause readers to rub their eyes with fatigue. Lines of all capital letters set in Black Letter (also called Text type and more commonly by the misnomer Old English) must be deciphered a letter at a time before they make sense. Full pages of reverse type (white letters on a black background) can be found in magazines. More often than not, readers will skip such messages rather than take the trouble to try to figure them out.

Improper spacing between letters and words turns headlines into globs of black rather than crisp, hard-hitting messages. Vertical lines of type make pleasing arrangements but require the reader to twist and turn to figure them out. Borders used for design effects sometimes become walls over which eyes must climb—but too often don't—to get at the message.

This list of typographic offenses could go on and on. However, rather than spending too much time belaboring the point, let's concentrate on creating the most effective communication possible.

Where to begin?

The starting point for any journey through the world of printed communications is an understanding of the complete process. Graphics and typography are only parts of the whole. Effective communicators must understand all of the elements involved in communication.

Consider, as an example, an auto mechanic. The mechanic cannot rebuild a carburetor without knowing how that part fits into the whole mechanics or working machinery of an automobile engine. That is, the mechanic needs to know how all the parts of the motor fit together to make the car go before she or he can rebuild a carburetor that will do its job. The same is true with communications. A knowledge of how everything fits together is needed before a communication can be made to "go."

## Complete Communication

A complete communication consists of five parts: the sender, the message, the delivery system (medium), the audience, or receiver, and, finally, some way to indicate that the communication was received and understood. The communicator calls this latter part *feedback*. Leave out any of these and the communication might not be effective.

The student of communications outlines this process like this:

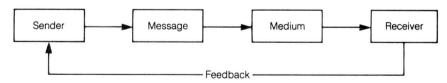

**Fig. 1-9**

With this model in mind, let's see how graphics and typography fit in. No matter what sort of printed communication is planned, it will not do its job unless each element in the complete communication model is doing its job.

So let's take a close look at that model and then zero in on our particular concern.

## Consider the Sender

First of all, we must consider the sender. What does the sender need to know to put together effective printed communications? A number of things. For instance, the sender needs to know the reason for communicating. Is it to sell something? Is it to keep people informed? Is it to try to change their minds or rally their support behind a cause? Is it to create an image of a staid organization? Or is it to get action and get it fast?

Before you do anything else, brainstorm the reason *why* you are going to communicate. Then, write it down on paper. Know exactly what is to be accomplished. Know exactly what is expected of the person who reads the message. If the message has no specific purpose, time and money can be wasted. No one will pay attention.

Then consider what words will cause the audience to stop and look and read.

Words are needed that the audience will understand. Graphics and typography cannot cover up inadequate copy. Sometimes a poorly conceived message is dressed up with attractive typography and impressive graphics. But it still will not work. If words cannot be put together in a way that will attract attention, arouse interest, create curiosity, and convince the audience that what is said is worthwhile, the effort to communicate has failed.

An advertising copywriter was assigned to produce advertisements for chicken feed. He didn't know anything about chickens and chicken feed. What did he do? Before he wrote a line, he bought some chicks and raised them in his kitchen.

The typographer and the designer, too, must know the subject of their concern to do as effective a job as possible with their part of the communication process.

Of course, this is a rather superficial examination of the first element of a complete communication. However, it does put our concern, typography and graphics, into perspective.

## Media Deliver the Message

The media—newspapers, magazines, brochures, and so on—can be considered "channels" for delivering a message. Communicators need to know which channels are best for a particular message. And, they need to know how to prepare the message so it will be in its most effective physical form for each channel.

Here it is time to clarify something about the audience. The audience, or receiver, of the message quite often is referred to as "all those people out there." In the days when emphasis was on the "mass media" and "mass communications," one philosophy of communication was that there was a vast audience of people "out there" and that communications were designed to reach them all. Messages were aimed at the "most common denominator" or the largest numbers of people through the mass media—or the media that reached the largest numbers of people.

Now communicators are becoming convinced that messages aimed at the largest numbers are not always the messages that are the most effective. Many mass circulation newspapers and magazines are on the decline. Media tailored to specialized audiences are on the rise. *The Wall Street Journal*, aimed at an audience with a specific interest, business, has replaced the *Daily News*, the New York City tabloid that caters to "mass" interests, as the largest circulation newspaper in America.

*National Geographic*, a specialized publication, has the third largest circulation in America now. *Modern Maturity*, aimed at one specific group, attained the sixth largest circulation in 1983. *Smithsonian*, another special interest magazine, is growing rapidly. *Reader's Digest* has peaked. *Saturday Evening Post, Collier's, Life, Look*, and *American*, circulation leaders of the past, are gone. The *Post* and *Life* have been revived but on a very limited basis.[2]

So, from now on, when the audience is discussed, it is a "target audience." This is an audience that has been carefully defined and its interests and concerns clearly identified.

Let us return now to the medium or channel. The channel is the means of transmitting the message to the target audience. It could be radio, television, postcards, billboards, newspapers, newsletters, handbills, magazines, and so on.

Communicators usually devise a *communications mix* that will utilize several media because repetition and reinforcement are vital if a message is to be seen and remembered. *Repetition* is a key word in successful communication. This includes sufficient repetition of the message in a single medium as well as repetition through more than one channel. The successful communicator does this all the time.

Typography can help here. For instance, the use of a certain type style to emphasize a key word or phrase in all printed communications can reinforce the impact of this word or increase its memorability. Using the same border designs can help provide recognition of a theme. The use of the same typeface in subsequent messages can help the reader recognize the message.

The communicator must also deal with two kinds of "noise" that can affect the message. Noise is anything that interferes with the message as it moves toward its target. There are two kinds of noise in communication: semantic noise and channel noise.

*Semantic noise* involves the words chosen for the message. When the communicator uses words that the target audience does not understand, semantic noise is created. When words are used that have different meanings for the target audience than for the communicator, semantic noise distorts the message. For instance, if a paper bag is called a "poke" in southern Ohio, most people would know what is meant. But if it is called a poke on the West Coast, communication would probably not occur. Semantic noise would interfere. And, to compound the problem, people in some parts of the country associate the word poke with vegetable "greens."

## Creative Communication

Editor, art director, designer— all are communicators and all have a common goal— to communicate.

Some definitions are in order before we continue.

*Communications* to those who work with words and graphics is a process by which understanding is reached between people through the use of symbols. These symbols can be the letters of the alphabet or they can be graphics.

*Graphics* to the communicator are all the elements used to design the appearance of a visual message.

*Effective communication* requires that letters and graphics be combined in such a way that the message is attractive, interesting, and understandable. The composition and design of an effective communication can be enhanced if it is produced as a result of *creative* thinking and action.

The editor, art director, designer—communicator— who is creative as well as technically competent will produce newspapers, magazines, and brochures that break out of the ordinary.

**Fig. 1-10** *Eliminating typographic channel noise so the message can flow with a minimum of interference is one of the goals of the designer or editor of printed communications.*

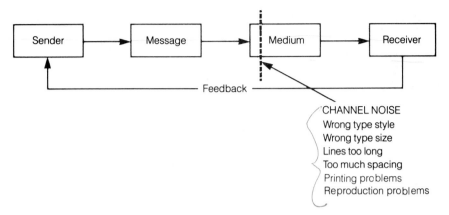

*Channel noise* occurs when there are problems with the medium itself. When there is static on the radio or a fuzzy picture on the television, channel noise is present. When there are typographical errors, borders that block a reader's eyes, a poorly printed page, and/or hard-to-read type, then print media channel noise is interfering with the communication. Channel noise occurs when a fine-screen plate of a photograph is used on textured paper and the details do not print sharply. It occurs when the harmony of a layout is destroyed by a mixture of bold, sans serif type with old-style Roman types.

A knowledge of typography and the proper use of design elements will help communicators eliminate channel noise and thus communicate more effectively.

## Consider the Receiver

One of the secrets of effective communication is the realization on the part of the message sender that we are a civilization of diverse interests, increased specialization, and groups brought together because of common interests.

Thus there is a lot we should know about the target audience. What are its interests and concerns? What is it like? What are its physical and psychological characteristics? What is its life-style?

If the target audience, for instance, is the outdoor type, certain typefaces and illustrations can be chosen to say "this is for you." If the target audience is highly artistic and appreciates excellence in esthetics, typefaces, illustrations, and borders can be arranged to appeal to this audience and convince another audience that what is being said is not for them.

The communicator also needs to know what media or channels the target audience reads, views, and trusts. What channels it does not trust must be recognized as well. If the target audience does not trust a channel you must use, you may need to change the current typography and graphics to change the channel's image so that trust can be developed.

However, if the receiver does not trust the communicator's client, no amount of distinctive or impressive typography will make the message acceptable.

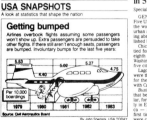

**Fig. 1-11** USA TODAY *arrived on the scene in 1982 after extensive research of its potential target audience. Its extensive use of color and graphics has caused many newspaper designers and editors to reevaluate their layout philosophies.* [© 1984, *reprinted with permission.*]

It is possible, though, that a careful choice of words and arrangement of type and art on pages, and even the proper choice of paper, backed by quality performance on the part of the source, can begin to turn a poor image around.

## Feedback Is Vital

Finally, a complete communication must have a way of letting the sender know the word is out, that it was received and understood by the target audience. A communication must contain provisions for letting the communicator know the message hit the target. A complete communication must be read, understood, and acted upon.

A newspaper publisher, for example, needs to know if the readers are actually reading. Feedback is a must. It can be obtained by watching circulation figures and those of the competition. It can be obtained by the communicator going out and talking to readers. And it can be obtained with scientific research.

Feedback is important for typography and design, too. For years it has been an unwritten law that publications should be arranged so that all the advertisements are touched by editorial matter. Or, at least, every effort should be made to do this. The theory was that people reading the content of the magazine or newspaper would more likely see the advertisements if they were immediately adjacent to articles. This led to many horribly unattractive inside pages of publications, especially newspapers.

Research, or feedback, then revealed that the proximity of editorial material to advertisements has little or no effect on the pulling power of advertisements.

There are many ways to obtain feedback, but obtain it we must. And it must be obtained each and every time communication is attempted if communications are going to work.

Most of the design and typographical techniques and suggestions you will find in the chapters of this book are based on years and years of feedback concerning the most attractive and effective ways of putting messages on paper. The techniques also apply to visual graphics for the electronic media as well.

Our goal in this book will be to investigate ways we can eliminate as much channel noise as possible and create communications that do their jobs.

In the early 1800s, Thomas Codben-Sanderson, a British printer and typographer, explained what typography is all about. His explanation is as valuable today as it was some 175 years ago. In this "age of graphics" it can be applied to all the elements that are included in a visual communication. He wrote: "The whole duty of typography . . . is to communicate to the imagination without loss by the way the thought or image intended to be communicated by the author."[3]

**Fig. 1-12** *Art, type style, and the use of white space create a unified layout that produces a mood of elegance and "eloquence."*

Printing during Codben-Sanderson's time employed methods and equipment most of us would not recognize. However, whether you were a printer who set type by hand a hundred years ago, or you are sitting before a video display terminal today, the goal is still the same—to communicate.

If this goal is to be reached, communicators need to know something about type, printing processes, paper, illustrations, color, and design. Each of these elements will be examined in subsequent chapters. Then we will see how to put them all together to produce better-read newspapers, lively and attractive magazines and newsletters, result-getting advertisements, and public relations communications that make people stop, read, and act.

## Graphics in Action

1. Examine a copy of a newspaper and see how many instances of channel noise you can find. Analyze them and try to determine the cause of each.

2. Examine a magazine, brochure, or direct mail piece and analyze it for channel noise. Discuss your findings in a small group.

3. Plan a printed communication for a small target audience (such as an organization to which you belong). Analyze that audience. Prepare a profile of the audience's characteristics.

4. What sort of printed communication might appeal to your target audience? What type style and art do you think would appeal to this audience? Explain.

5. Obtain copies of the *World Almanac* or *Reader's Digest Almanac* for 1950, 1960, 1970, and 1980. List the ten magazines with the largest circulations in those years. What conclusions can you draw concerning the changes that might be occurring in magazine audiences?

## Notes

[1] Hynds, Ernest C., *American Newspapers in the 1970s*, (New York: Hastings House, 1975), pp. 18-19.

[2] *Reader's Digest 1984 Almanac and Yearbook*, (Pleasantville, N.Y.: The Reader's Digest Association, Inc. 1984), p. 688.

[3] Updike, Daniel B., *Printing Types*, Volume II, (Cambridge, Mass.: Harvard University Press, 1937), p.212.

Look at the keyboard of an ultramodern video display terminal. Do you see a key marked "em"? What does this mean?

Well, it means that a term devised about 400 years ago is still with us. If you don't know what an em is you will be handicapped in coping with the new technology and in putting together printed messages that are attractive and have maximum readability.

Actually, the em is a unit of measurement equal to the square of the type body you are working with. For instance, if you are working with 12-point type, a 12-point em will be a unit of measurement that is 12 points square. The name came down to us from the practice of early typecasters of making the capital letter M on a square body.

Sound confusing? We will discuss this more completely in Chapter 3. The point is, as in any craft or any profession, an understanding of the past is important in understanding how that activity is practiced today and in anticipating the future.

Most of the printing you will be concerned with is produced by one of three methods—letterpress, lithography, and gravure.

The easiest way to understand how these methods work and what they can do for you is to take a look at how they developed. None of them is new. Even though most printing now is done by offset, a modification of the lithographic process, printing by this method actually started back in 1906. And lithography itself dates back to 1798! Gravure, or printing from a recessed surface, was developed in the 1400s!

Regardless of the method chosen and regardless of what methods may supercede these three methods in the future, all printing has one thing in common—the result is always a quantity of the same visual image. And printing will be one of the basic methods for obtaining duplicate images of messages as long as there is civilization. Even though the electronic media are surging ahead and some prognosticators see the day when printing will be relegated to

**Fig. 2-1**  *A modern composition and pagination system for producing books and publications. But even though technological advances are made constantly, the basic principles of letterpress, gravure, and lithography are still applied in printing the vast majority of communications.*

displays in museums, there are important reasons why the printed image will always be an important part of the communications mix.

*Communication by multiplied impressions*—that's a good definition of printing—provides many advantages over other methods of communication.

With the printed message in hand, our audience can turn back and reread. The message is there in solid form. It is not a fleeting notice on a screen that may be missed when the receiver glances away or is distracted. The audience can speed up or slow down its reading pace. Readers can skip ahead to the bottom line without waiting through long-winded oratory as too often happens with the spoken word. And, the audience can stop at any word or statement that seems to call for thought, verification, or a trip to the dictionary, before moving ahead.

The printed message is permanent; it is easily stored, transported, and filed for future reference. It can be taken wherever a person goes and it can be read in the most unlikely places—places where electronic equipment could not function.

The printed communication is still the basic medium of many communications programs. Communicators who devise long-range programs of messages aimed at target audiences usually build a plan, or "communications mix," based on one of the printed mediums such as a newsletter or in-house magazine. This basic medium is then supported by other channels of communication.

**Fig. 2-2** *The hand press was the basic printing press in the Western world for more than 400 years. This one is a Maxwell and was used in 1793 to print the* Centinel of the Northwest Territory *in Cincinnati.*

## Printing in the Colonial Era

If you had been a communicator practicing your profession about the time the United States was born, printing would have been the only medium—besides word of mouth and perhaps signs—available to you to distribute messages to audiences.

If you were in the communications business 200 or so years ago and you wanted a broadside, pamphlet, or handbill printed you might have taken it to Benjamin Franklin in Philadelphia or William Bradford in New York or one of the other printing shops in the thirteen colonies. All of these shops would produce your handbill by the most basic of printing methods—*letterpress.*

Let us assume we are visiting such a printing plant. The year is in the late 1700s. What would the shop be like?

Probably we would enter it through a book or stationery store. Or through a coffee house. Most early printers could not make a living at their trade and had to supplement their income with a book shop, coffee house, or some other means to make ends meet. Often they were postmasters.

In the print shop itself we would see two distinct areas—the composing room and the press room (where the printing press is). This division of labor—composing room and press room—continues today in commercial printing plants as well as in newspapers and magazines.) However, the time is coming when the composing room may just be a computer and its auxiliary equipment.

In one corner of the shop, workers are standing before large racks containing drawers (or *cases*) divided into compartments. Small pieces of metal with raised images of letters are stored in these cases. Each compartment contains one letter of the alphabet, or a punctuation mark, or a blank piece to be used for spacing.

The large racks have sloping tops and two cases can be placed, one above the other, on a rack. This makes it convenient for the compositors, or typesetters, to pick out letters as they set type. The upper case contains compartments for capital letters. The lower case contains the small letters. Uppercase (ABCDEFG) letters are capitals and they are still referred to by that term today. The same is true of the lowercase (abcdefg) letters.

The workers are following written copy and setting the type in a small tray, or *composing stick*. When their composing sticks are full, they carefully transfer the composed type from the sticks to large metal trays, called *galleys*. These hold the columns of type while they are inked and an impression made so that the "galley proofs" can be proofread and corrections made. Then the type will be transferred to the *"stone"*—actually a table with a smooth, perfectly flat marble surface, where it will be combined with the headlines and ornaments and so on that will make up the *"form"* from which the printing will be done.

The form is placed in a frame—called a *chase*—where it is wedged in place so that the individual pieces of type and border and so on will be held together during printing. Once the form is locked into the chase it is ready to be placed on the printing press.

**Fig. 2-3**  *The press room of a print shop in colonial America. (Rochester Institute of Technology)*

If any type is spilled during all this, the worker responsible is said to have "pied" the type.

Meanwhile, over on the other side of the room, three men are working on a press. This press is a crude affair by today's standards. But this same press has been in use for more than 300 years, though it has been improved somewhat through the years. It will continue to be the basic printing press for 20 or 30 more years, and it will still be in service for another 100 years in some places.

When first used in Europe in the early 1400s, this press was modeled after presses used to make wine. It was known as a *platen* press. Essentially, its operation involves lowering a heavy plate, the platen, under controlled pressure against the type form.

After the type has been inked with a pair of ink balls, a sheet of paper is laid on the tympan* against guides. The frisket† is closed over it, leaving exposed only the section of the paper to be printed. The paper has to be dampened, sheet by sheet, to obtain a good print.

After the paper is in place and the form inked, the bed assembly is moved under the platen and the lever pulled. The bed is moved out again, the tympan and frisket are lifted, and the paper is removed. All this is repeated for each impression.

There are lines strung from the ceiling of the shop and these are used to hang the printed sheets on to dry. In the evening the day's work will be taken down from the lines and stacked to await delivery to the customer. Two men working one of these wooden or iron presses can turn out about 500 or 600 impressions a day. Today a simple offset press can produce 5,000 to 9,000 impressions an hour.

But the printing job in our colonial shop isn't finished! After all the needed impressions have been made, the form is removed from the press and cleaned. Then the compositors must take each piece of type and return it to its proper compartment in the cases.

The colonial print shop hadn't changed much in the 400 years that slipped by since a German stone and gem polisher changed the way messages were duplicated and as a result changed civilization forever.

## Printing Before and After Gutenberg

When we think of printing we think of Gutenberg. For Johann Gensfleisch zum Gutenberg, of Mainz, Germany, brought it all together.

But Gutenberg did not invent printing. His contribution was to devise a method of casting individual letters and composing type and combining all of the necessary printing components—typecasting, ink manufacture, punch cutting, composing, a press, and paper—into a workable system.

* The tympan is a sheet of heavy, oiled paper in a hinged frame the size of the platen.
† The frisket is usually made of cloth and it, too, is in a frame the size of the platen and hinged so it can be lowered in place between the tympan and the form to be printed.

**Fig. 2-4** *Artist Robert Thom's version of Johann Gutenberg's shop in Mainz, Germany. One worker reaches into an upper case for a capital letter while another casts an individual type letter. (Rochester Institute of Technology)*

Printing had existed long before Gutenberg's marvelous achievement. Printing from movable type was used in China and Korea in the eleventh century. However, because of the fragility of the materials used and the enormous number of individual pictographs used in the Chinese alphabet, it remained an obscure practice.

Efforts to duplicate messages can be traced as far back as 2000 B.C. when Babylonians turned out playing cards. The Chinese printed from carved wooden blocks by placing paper on the inked relief surfaces and pressing the paper until the design was transferred.

This sounds simple, and it has been the basis of the printing method until very recent years. This method of printing is called "relief" or "letterpress." And letterpress printing today is simply a refinement of the way it was done 500 years ago.

Three types of letterpress have evolved: the *platen* press, the *flatbed cylinder*, and the *rotary* press.

**Fig. 2-5** *Three methods of letterpress (raised image) printing: platen, or flat surfaces (left); flatbed cylinder (middle); rotary (right). (Eastman Kodak)*

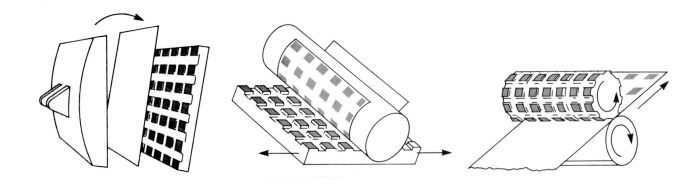

## The Platen Press

The platen press is known as the faithful "job press." Its main function is to produce the miscellaneous items of printing—letterheads, envelopes, cards, tickets, handbills, and so on—which keep the wheels of civilization turning. The press is called a platen press because it operates by having a platen, or flat surface, on which the paper is placed, move against the stationary type, which is locked in a chase, which in turn is locked in the bed of the press.

George Phineas Gordon put the first platen press on the American market in 1851. It was operated by a foot treadle but a good pressman could make about 1,200 impressions an hour, feeding the paper into the press by hand.

## The Flatbed Cylinder Press

Earlier, Friedrich Koenig sold the first power-driven press to *The Times* of London. Koenig, a German, solved the problem of pressing two stationary surfaces together to get an impression. He was able to devise a press operated by power, in this case steam, that continuously rotated a round impression cylinder.

The form to be printed was placed on a bed that had tracks along the sides (actually rows of teeth that meshed with teeth on the round impression cylinder). The flat platen was replaced with a round cylinder. The paper to be printed was held against the cylinder by metal fingers, or grippers. As the cylinder rotated, the bed slid back and forth, going under the rotating cylinder where the paper was pressed against the type form on the bed.

The first issue of *The Times* printed on the Koenig cylinder press appeared on November 29, 1814. *The Times* proclaimed the issue was the "result of the greatest improvement connected with printing since the discovery of the art itself." Koenig's press inaugurated

**Fig. 2-6** *An early steam-powered flatbed cylinder press. Steam power was first used to run printing presses in about 1860. This was a major breakthrough that led to greater speeds and much larger presses. (Bettman Archive/The Mead Corporation)*

a great revolution in the industry. It was the breakthrough that led to the giant presses of today. And the principle of the revolving cylinder was adapted to offset and gravure presses.

However, the flatbed cylinder press still had a serious shortcoming when it came to producing mass volumes of books, magazines, and newspapers. It still printed only one sheet at a time. When one side of a sheet was printed, it had to be turned and printed again if both sides were to receive an impression.

The solution became known as the *web perfecting press.* This press is fast and efficient and can be used for long runs of magazines, newspapers, advertising brochures, and other publications with many pages. It uses a rotary impression (or platen) cylinder and a rotary type bed as well, plus a continuous roll of paper, rather than single sheets.

## The Rotary Press

The rotary press uses forms cast into curved plates, a process known as *stereotyping,* which are locked onto the cylinder. As many duplicates of the form as desired can be made, and a number of presses can turn out the same product simultaneously.

*The Times* of London again scored a triumph in printing when in 1869 it was printed on a continuous roll of paper from curved stereotype plates on a rotary press. During the next ten years Robert Hoe, the American printing press manufacturer, improved and developed newspaper printing by making it possible to deliver a complete newspaper—folded, counted, and ready for sale—from a roll of blank paper.

Although we are in the middle of the age of offset printing, letterpress is not dead. It is still used for many magazines, newspapers, books, and brochures, though the number is dwindling.

Letterpresses are used for numbering, creasing, folding, embossing, die cutting, and other forms of printing and processing paper and card stock. One manufacturer, Heidelberg of West Germany, turns out a letterpress every 14 minutes.

## Offset and Lithography

However, in recent years newspaper publishers and printers have been abandoning the letterpress and turning to *offset*. Offset is actually a modification of *lithography,* or printing from a flat surface. (Lithography is often also called *planographic* printing.)

This method of printing did not come to us through centuries of evolution. It was invented—almost by accident.

One day in Munich, Bavaria, a 25-year-old artist who lived with his mother and who dabbled in the theater, playwriting, sketching, and drawing, was busy in his workshop. The year was 1796. He was Aloys Senefelder, bachelor son of an actor.

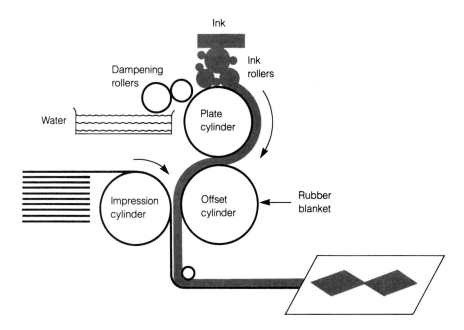

**Fig. 2-7** *A schematic drawing of the offset lithography printing process. The printing plate with the planographic image is clamped on the plate cylinder, the dampening rollers coat the plate with water, the ink rollers ink the plate (the ink adheres to the image area but not to the area not to be printed), the image is offset to the offset cylinder and then transferred by impression onto the paper. (National Association of Printing Ink Manufacturers)*

Senefelder had written plays but all they seemed to get him were rejection slips from publishers. So he decided to print them himself. He found that the conventional letterpress method was beyond his means, so he began experimenting with other possibilities.

Since Senefelder was a sometimes artist he turned to engraving. He experimented with copper plates and practiced on limestone slabs. His idea was that he could etch his copy into the plates and then print them . This would be quicker and cheaper than the complicated and costly letterpress task of setting them into type by hand.

While Senefelder was busy trying to perfect his engraving skill, his mother came in and asked him to write a list of items to hand to the waiting laundress. He reached for whatever was handy and picked up a piece of limestone and some correction fluid he had concocted to fill in the errors he made on the engraving plates.

Senefelder wrote the laundry list with the correction fluid, which had a greasy base, on the flat limestone slab. Later, while experimenting with this list he noticed that ink would stick to the words he had written and water would wash off the ink on the blank areas of the stone.

Senefelder had hit upon the chemical fact that is the basis of the lithographic printing process—oil and water do not mix!

How do we know so much about Senefelder's achievement? Well, he wrote it all down in his *Invention of Lithography*, which was published in New York in 1911. In addition, he wrote an autobiography, *Complete Textbook of Stone Printing, in 1818.*[1]

Senefelder abandoned his efforts to become a playwright and devoted his time to perfecting the lithographic printing process. He was a friendly, outgoing person and shared his invention with fellow artists. He traveled extensively and became famous.

As mentioned, the central principle of lithography is the fact that oil and water do not mix but repel each other. All procedures of lithography observe this basic tenet.

The stone is the carrier of the printing form. This stone, with the unique qualities necessary for lithographic printing, is quarried only at Solenhofen, a village near Munich. It must be polished to a smooth, slightly grainy surface.

The design to be printed is applied to this surface by various techniques. Drawing pens, brushes, or grease crayons are used. Although lithographers have complete control over their creations, they must prepare the design so that it reads backwards or in a mirror image. Then, when a print is made from the design, the lefts and rights will be in their proper positions when a person views the object or reads the page.

After the design is completed, the stone is covered with a watery and slightly acidic gum arabic solution. This "seasons" the stone. There are some additional steps in preparing the stone, but for our purposes it is enough to say that the design on the stone is "prepared for printing."

The stone is dampened and rolled with an ink roller. The grease-receptive design areas will accept the ink while the areas that have been moistened will not pick up the ink. After a series of inkings and moistening, paper is pressed against the stone and the reverse or mirror image of the original sketch will be printed on the paper.

The press and method used by Senefelder are used today to make artistic lithographic prints. Usually the number of these prints is limited and signed by the artist—often with a notation such as

**Fig. 2-8** *Aloys Senefelder at work in his lithographic shop in the late eighteenth century. (Rochester Institute of Technology)*

10/100. This indicates that a total of 100 prints has been made from this particular stone and this print is the tenth in the series. If you buy a lithographic print, look for this notation. Artists usually destroy a stone after printing to increase the potential value of each print.

So, lithography was originally an artistic medium that produced excellent quality but limited quantity.

Changes and improvements in lithography in the early 1800s made it practical for mass production. Better plate preparation and the use of power-operated presses plus the ability to make duplicate plates contributed to the development of lithography for commercial printing.

In the first quarter of the nineteenth century lithographic printing was used mainly to produce color prints for books that were otherwise printed by letterpress. The first lithographic print to appear in a publication in America was included in an issue of the *Analectic Magazine* in 1815. (This magazine's only other known claim to fame was that Washington Irving, author of the *Legend of Sleepy Hollow*, was its editor for a brief time.)

Nathaniel Currier, a young lithographer, made a color lithograph of the burning of the steamship *Lexington* in Long Island Sound in 1840. He produced a multicolored print of the disaster just 4 days after it occurred. This was a record and it brought Currier instant fame. It encouraged him to continue publishing lithographs of newsworthy events and scenes of contemporary American life. James Ives joined him in 1857, and this led to the establishment of the firm of Currier and Ives. Their more than 7,000 productions have become treasured pieces of Americana.

The development of lithography as a commercial printing method was hampered by the slow and cumbersome process of printing from the stone "plates." At the same time, letterpress was progressing at a rapid pace. However, Senefelder had mentioned in his writings that he thought zinc could be used as well as heavy stone.

In 1889 the first lithographic press to print with zinc plates went on line. This greatly increased the printing speed. Then, a new twist developed in lithography that would lead to one of the greatest developments in printing since Gutenberg had put it all together in 1445.

One of the problems that plagues printers is "offset" or "set off." Offset is the imprint of one sheet on another, and it happens in two ways. When a sheet is missed on the press and an impression is made on the platen or impression cylinder, that impression will appear on subsequent sheets until the ink from the offset fades away. When sheets are stacked before the ink has dried, the weight of the sheets causes an image to be made on the backs of the sheets in the pile.

It was quite natural to call the new twist in lithographic printing "offset." For offset is actually printing from a cylinder on which the image has been offset by contact with the inked printing plate.

## Creative Communication

How can an editor or designer be creative—seek an approach that is different, that will make her or his efforts stand out and yet be effective in communicating the message? Many people in the communications industry and the arts maintain that creativity cannot be learned.
Are we sure?

What is creativity?

Create (from the Latin *creatus*) means to bring into being, to cause to exist, to produce, to evolve from one's own thought or imagination, to make by investing with new character or functions.

Formal definitions of creativity include such phrases as—the ability to bring into existence—to produce through imaginative skill—to design.

Design is defined as a mental project or scheme resulting from deliberate planning with a purpose, a sketch showing the main features of the communication, the arrangement of the elements in a communication.

Creative design results from creative thinking. Psychologists define creative thinking as a method of directed thinking applied to the discovery of new solutions to problems, new techniques and devices, and new artistic expression.

Offset was discovered quite by accident and we do not know for sure just when and how. If the lithographic press missed a sheet, an impression would be made on the blanket. The next sheet through the press would pick up this impression in reverse (backwards) on its back. And someone noticed that the quality of the reverse impression was unusually good.

We can visualize the principle of offset by thinking of the letter E carved in relief, inked, and pressed against a sheet of paper. The image will appear in reverse—Ǝ. But if another sheet of paper is pressed against this image before the ink dries, the image on the second sheet will be in the correct position—E.

After experimentation and modification, offset was born. The name means just what it says. The final printed product is obtained from an image that is first impressed onto a rubber blanket from the printing plate. The rubber blanket then becomes the printing plate and the image is impressed, or offset, on the paper.

In 1906 the first offset press as we know it today began rolling out printed sheets in Nutley, New Jersey. Although some offset printing had been done in Europe well before this, the press developed by Ira A. Rubel, a paper manufacturer, is considered the one that started the offset revolution. The press used by Rubel and his partner was built by the Potter Press Company, which later merged with the Harris Press Company. Today it is known as the Harris-Seybold Press Company and is a major manufacturer of offset presses.

**Fig. 2-9** *A New Jersey native, Ira Rubel, designed the offset press in which a rubber cover is used on the cylinder of a lithographic press to produce a vivid image on paper. (Rochester Institute of Technology)*

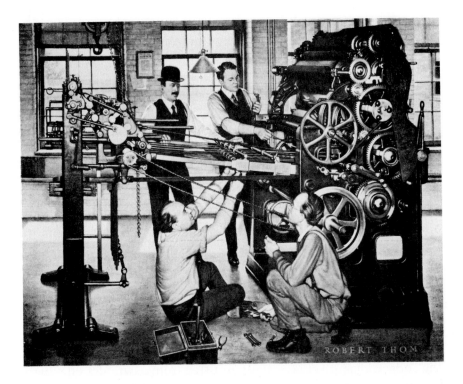

## Gravure Printing

Now let's visit the fifteenth century. We're standing on the spacious lawn in front of a castle in Europe.

A knight has just donned his armor and is about to mount his horse to find a dragon to fight for his lady love. His squire spent all day yesterday polishing his helmet, pauldron, lance rest, breastplate, and gauntlet. His whole metal suit is gleaming in the sunlight.

Here comes the knight's betrothed from the castle to give him a fond farewell. She flings herself against him for a last embrace. As they separate, a frown of concern wrinkles her forehead as she looks at her dress. For on her dress is imprinted the intricate designs that are engraved on his breastplate.

The knight's squire had done such a thorough job of polishing his armor that it gleamed as never before. But the polishing grit had filled the crevices of the engraved designs. When the maiden pressed herself against the knight, the imprint of the designs was impressed on her dress.

And that is how gravure printing was born.

Well, not really, but that is one story that has been passed down for generations among printers. There is no way to verify this tale, and it may well be a folktale of the printing craft. But it is a very good explanation of the gravure process. *Gravure,* or *intaglio* as it is also called, is simply printing from a recessed surface.

Just as letterpress printing evolved through the centuries until Gutenberg put the elements together in a manageable fashion, so gravure printing also has a long and sometimes murky history. Its beginnings can be traced back to the 1400s.

A finely detailed print of the Madonna enthroned with eight angels is considered the earliest known engraving. It was produced by an unknown German artist with the initials E. S. and is dated 1467.

Many early books were printed by letterpress while the illustrations were engraved on copper plates and printed by the gravure method. Rubens, Rembrandt, and Van Dyke were among the artists who worked in gravure. Rembrandt produced many etchings that he printed by the gravure method in the middle 1600s.

Gravure is a simple method of printing. Its very name says that. It is called intaglio from the Italian word *intagliare,* which means "to carve." And that is what the gravure printer does by engraving the design into the printing surface.

Gravure printing is done on a flat surface in which the letters or designs are sunk below the surface. The design is engraved into a smooth plate, the plate is covered with ink, and the ink is wiped off the surface. But look, the ink remains in the letters and designs that are sunk below the surface.

**Fig. 2-10** *A schematic drawing of the gravure process. The image to be printed is engraved or carved into the impression surface. The entire area is inked, and the ink is removed from the nonprinting area. Pressure of paper on the plate "pulls" the ink out of the recessed areas. (National Association of Printing Ink Manufacturers.)*

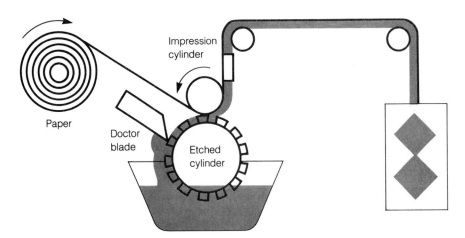

Then a sheet of paper or other material is pressed against the plate and an impression is made.

A good gravure print needs to be made under great pressure. The gravure press consists of a bed that travels between two steel rollers. A felt blanket is placed between the upper roller and the paper, and the paper is placed on the engraved plate. A roller beneath all this helps exert the forward pressure generated when the blanket, paper, and plate move between the rollers.

The felt blanket, under all that pressure, acts as a self-adjusting overlay and helps force the paper into the crevices so it contacts and withdraws the ink onto its surface.

The development of *rotogravure printing* has been one of the "hottest" advances in the communications industry. Many of the magazines, Sunday supplements, and catalogs we see today are the result of rotogravure printing. This method was invented by an Austrian, Karl Kleitsch, who lived in Vienna and later moved to

**Fig. 2-11** *Diagram of a rotogravure press that uses the gravure process. Many of the largest magazines in the United States are printed by this method. (Eastman Kodak.)*

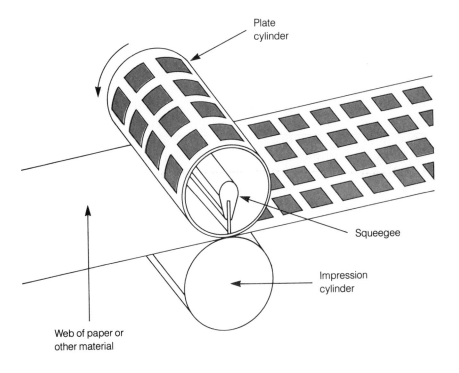

England. He developed a rotary method of printing gravure plates in his workshop in Lancaster, England, in 1894. *The New York Times* installed a rotogravure plant in 1914.

Rotogravure requires a rather complicated photomechanical method of platemaking. However, today it is done rather easily with an electronic stylus or laser. A rotogravure plate is capable of a million impressions, far more than plates made for letterpress or lithography.

Acceptable quality, speed, and the use of inexpensive ink and paper make rotogravure popular for medium- and large-volume jobs, where speed and economy are deciding factors.

Gravure printing is considered excellent for reproducing pictures. A distinct feature that makes it easy to recognize is that the entire image must be screened—type and line drawings as well as halftones of photographs. The gravure screen usually contains 150 lines per inch, about the same as other high-quality processes. The screen is virtually invisible to the naked eye.

As with the rotary letterpress and offset, gravure presses are manufactured for both sheets of paper (sheet-fed gravure) and rolls (rotogravure), but most gravure printing is done from rolls. Many of our largest magazines are printed by rotogravure. These include *National Geographic, Women's Day, Family Circle, Reader's Digest,* and *Redbook,* to name a few.

The *National Enquirer* is printed in Buffalo, New York, on rotogravure presses. Each press can reach speeds of 35,000 copies of a 96-page newspaper per hour. A quarter of the 96 pages can be done in four colors.

## Thermography

Thermography is a process that produces results that are considered similar to those of gravure printing. Excellent work is produced by this method for business cards, letterheads, envelopes, and so on. The "raised printing" effect of thermography gives a certain uniqueness to the product for a far smaller cost than engraving, which it resembles.

Printers produce the raised printing effect by printing the item by letterpress or offset in the usual manner. They use ink that is slower drying than that generally used for printing. After printing, the sheets are dusted with a resinous powder. They are then passed over a heating element that causes the ink and powder to fuse and swell. The result is raised print with an engraved appearance.

## Other Printing Methods

Most books on printing methods have listed the advantages and disadvantages of each. It was safe to do this in the past. However, as we near the end of the 1980s, modern technology has erased many of the distinguishing features of the three basic printing methods.

Not long ago experienced communicators could distinguish among products of the letterpress, the offset press, and the gravure press. Now each method is capable of producing excellent quality, and the advantages of one over the others have largely disappeared. It is more the skill of the printer than the method used that should be the concern of the communicator.

Of course, most small communications operations will almost exclusively use offset and perhaps letterpress printers. However, startling advances are being made each year in printing processes, and the communicator should be familiar with what is happening.

## Silk-Screen Printing

Generally, silk-screen printing is referred to simply as "screen printing" or "screen process printing." This method uses a fine porous screen made of silk, nylon, Dacron, or even stainless steel mounted on a frame. A stencil is perforated either manually or photomechanically with the lettering or design to be reproduced and then placed over the screen. Printing is done on a press by feeding paper under the screen, applying paintlike ink to the screen, and spreading and forcing it through the fine mesh openings with a rubber squeegee.

You can usually spot screen printing by the thick layer of ink and the texture of the screen on the printing.

Although this sounds like a slow, hand-operated printing method, today there are automatic screen presses, and rotary presses have been produced that turn out posters, sheets for billboards, menu covers, and bumper stickers. The screen process is also used to print on wood, glass, metal, plastic, fabric (such as T-shirts) and even wallpapers and draperies.

**Fig. 2-12**  *In the screen printing process, the ink is "squeezed" through a stencil and a screen onto the surface to be printed. (National Association of Printing Ink Manufacturers)*

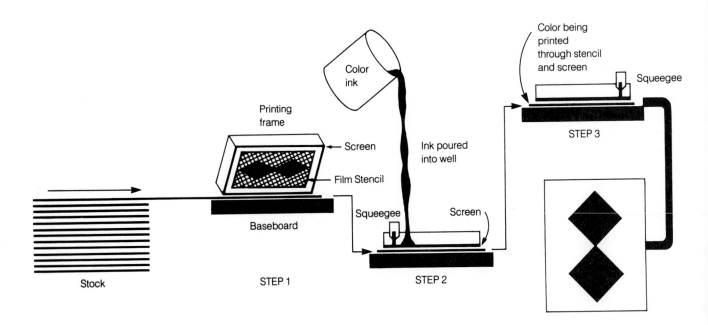

## Photogelatin Printing

Photogelatin printing is actually an application of the old lithographic principle that oil and water do not mix. It is also called *collotype* from a combination of two Greek words that mean "glue" and "impression."

This method of printing employs a light-sensitive layer of gelatin on the surface of a glass plate. The image to be printed is produced photographically on the plate from a negative of the original copy. The plate is then printed on cylinder presses.

The big asset of photogelatin printing is its ability to produce lovely reproductions of colored art without the use of a screen.

The process is used to print picture postcards, outdoor bus and truck posters, banners, counter cards, and floor displays. Its most economical and efficient use is for high-quality reproduction work in runs of from 100 to 5,000 copies.

## Mimeograph Printing

The rapid development of other methods of duplicating copies in the office has led to the decline of the once-popular mimeograph. A direct-image stencil is used in this process. The stencil can be prepared by typewriter, or it can be handwritten or drawn with a stylus. Some are prepared photographically, electronically, or by die-impression (cut by dies). The image created is somewhat like that used in the silk-screen process.

The stencil is placed on an impression cylinder that is covered with an ink pad. As the cylinder comes in contact with the blank paper, ink flows from the cylinder through the ink pad and the stencil onto the paper.

## The Spirit Duplicator

The spirit duplicator produces images by direct impression. The image to be printed is typed, written, or drawn on a master. This master is backed by an aniline-dye carbon sheet. When the master is placed on the duplicator, the paper to be printed comes in direct contact with the master.

As the paper goes through the machine, it is moistened with a duplicating fluid that helps deposit a small amount of carbon from the master onto the paper. Gradually the image on the master will fade. A master is usually good for 100 or so clear copies.

## Copying Machines

Office copying machines are becoming capable of very high quality reproduction of originals. They will play a more and more important role in the life of the communicator. It is entirely possible to produce short runs of pasteups in an office that are equal in quality to the work being produced in most printing shops. Advertising and public relations practitioners will increasingly turn to copying machines to produce many short-run printing communications for their customers.

Most copiers utilize heat, light, electricity, chemical reactions, and combinations of these to make an image. They can be grouped generally as either thermography copiers or electrophotography copiers.

*Thermographic copiers* use heat and a specially prepared paper that consists of a black infrared-absorbing coating with a white coating on top. During exposure this paper is in contact with the original and a shot of infrared heat makes the exposure and thus the copy on the special paper.

*Electrophotographic copiers* are rapidly replacing thermographic ones. There are several good reasons for this. The electrophotographic process uses plain paper. New machines are constantly coming on the market that are capable of excellent work. They can reduce and enlarge at the press of a button. They can collate and they can produce copies in colors.

These machines—are they really printing presses? Well, technically they probably are not. However, they are doing a lot of the work of the printing press, especially on short runs.

They make copies by using electrostatic forces, or electric charges, which can transfer images from an original onto a blank sheet of paper. Some electrostatic duplicators make the image by xerography. *Xero* is a Greek word meaning "dry," thus, dry printing. The image is transferred by contact from a selenium-coated plate or drum to the paper. (Selenium is usually obtained as a by-product of copper refining. It is a good conductor of electricity.)

Another method utilizes a fine powder, or toner, which is automatically brushed onto the paper and sticks to the image on the drum or plate by electrostatic attraction. A third method is similar but the toner is mixed with a liquid, becoming a sort of wet "ink."

## Advances in Putting Words on Paper

One cannot examine the various ways of printing without considering the fast-paced advances being made in the industry's technology. As a matter of fact, some observers believe it is entirely possible that some time before the end of the century revolutionary new devices and methods will rival or replace the traditional printing methods.

For instance, the technology has been perfected to print with an *ink-jet* device. This method uses tiny jets of ink that form images on blank paper passing under the jets. Printing experts say this process will be used more and more but its use will be limited. It is not seen as a practical way of printing the general line of the communicator's printing needs in the immediate future.

However, ink jet is currently the fifth most frequently used method of printing. This is because it is used to produce a huge

**Fig. 2-13** *One of the many sophisticated printing devices being developed today. This five-color, high-speed electrostatic printer reproduces maps almost instantly from 70-mm microfilm. It uses high intensity light and electrostatic energy to create more than 2,000 permanent five-color images an hour without ink or printing plates.*

volume of direct-mail pieces. One system can spray jets of ink to address 24,000 large business envelopes per hour.

In addition, there are ink-jet typewriters coming on the market.

However, Gilbert W. Bassett, executive director of the Graphic Arts Technical Foundation, says in *Graphic Arts Monthly* that ink-jet printing will be used only in conjunction with other systems for some time in the future. Bassett summarizes technological developments in printing by predicting that advances in electrostatic ink jet will continue but that the three basic methods of printing—letterpress, lithography (offset), and gravure—are making progress, too, and they will not be replaced as our basic reproduction methods in the foreseeable future.

Many new advances in science, such as the laser beam, the computer, and the cathode ray tube, are a part of the printing industry. However, it is safe to say that no matter how we place words on paper, the basic theme of this book will not become obsolete. That is, no matter how we print our message, no matter whether we arrange the elements of our printed message with a pagination device that puts those elements in place on a video screen or with a pencil on a piece of paper, we must still make basic typographic decisions.

Those decisions involve the choice of type styles and sizes; the width of the printed lines; the amount of spacing between letters, words, and lines of types; and the size and composition of pieces of art. All these decisions are still critical to the effectiveness of a message. They are decisions we will have to make.

The starting place in creating effective printed communications is deciding on the basic ingredient of any recipe for effective printed communication. That is *type*, and type is what we will consider next.

## Graphics in Action

1. The best way to acquire an understanding of the basic printing methods is to see the actual processes in action. Plan a trip to a local printing plant. Join a team of classmates to visit a letterpress, lithographic/offset, silk-screen, or gravure facility. Obtain a sample of printed work from the plant you visit. Have your team report to the class on your findings.

2. Prepare an essay that updates trends in printing methods. Consult trade publications and interview printing plant managers, if possible.

3. Find out what printing methods your school or office uses. Do you think these are the best for the purposes? Explain.

## Notes

[1] Chappell, Warren A., *A Short History of the Printed Word* (New York: Alfred A. Knopf, 1970), pp. 171-173.

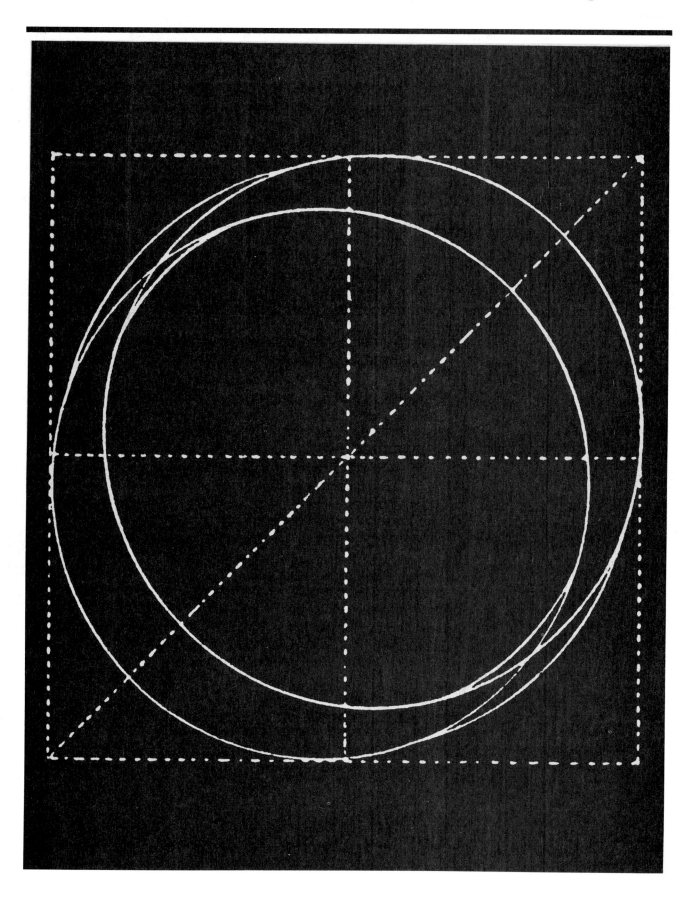

The recipe for building an effective printed communication includes a number of ingredients. But the basic ingredient is type.

No matter what sort of communication is planned—newspaper, magazine, brochure, letterhead, or business card—it should be designed to accomplish five things.

1. *It should attract the reader.* If a printed piece does not attract the reader at the very beginning, it may not work. And it must attract a reader who is a member of the target audience—that particular segment of people out there we specifically want to reach.

2. *It should be easy to read.* People simply will pass up material that appears difficult, unless they know it contains information they really want so badly they are willing to overcome any barrier to get to it. Busy people today avoid unattractive and difficult type masses.

3. *It should emphasize important information.* One of the secrets of effective communication is to make sure the arrangement of type on the page and the size and styles of types employed make the heart of the message—the points we want to make—easy to recognize quickly as important and easy to absorb.

4. *It should be expressive.* Everything in the message—the paper used, type, art, and ink—should combine to reinforce the message and make it clear to the target audience. The reader should never say of the communication or any element in it, "I wonder what that means?"

5. *It should create recognition.* Printed messages can make a communications program more effective and can help build a permanent identity for our organization, our position, even our can of beans in the minds of the target audience not just once, but time after time. Publications achieve this visual identity, for instance, by using the same type style for the nameplate, the masthead, and/or as a logo for house advertisements. The identity is extended by using that type style on trucks and T-shirts for any teams they sponsor.

The starting place in planning printing that will accomplish all this is with the basic ingredient. Proper selection and use of type can support the message, and improper selection and use can make the message less effective.

An effective printed message must combine good press work, good design, good placement of elements but, most of all, it must first be set in type that is legible, suitable, and readable. Of course, illegible type can be used sometimes to transmit a unique message, but in this discussion our concern is with messages that are to be read.

Effective use of type involves: (1) the ease with which it can be read, (2) its grouping into words, lines, and masses, (3) the nature of the message, (4) the kind of reader involved, and (5) the printing process involved. Effective use also involves esthetics, for the printed piece must be attractive to be effective.

All communicators can increase the effectiveness of their efforts if they acquire a basic knowledge of type and how to use it. This understanding can make work easier and faster, and it can help cut printing costs. It will enable communicators to give explicit instructions to printers and to communicate with them so that we can all work together to produce the best possible product.

The understanding of type and its use involves some basic concepts.

First of all, communicators need to know how type is designed, the various typeface patterns available, and the suitability of each for specific messages.

Then, we must know how type is measured and how it is set and spaced. In addition, it is helpful to know basic typographic principles that have been established through practice and testing.

This chapter will attempt to sort all this out, and the chapters that follow will add the various ingredients needed to make sound decisions concerning printed communications.

## Some Essential Terms

We need to begin with an agreement on terms. These will be kept to a minimum but the terms included in this chapter are considered by many professionals as essential for anyone who works with words, type, and printing. Our discussion will start off with some basic concepts concerning typefaces and how they came into existence.

When you look at a letter what do you see?

Is it an *a* or a *B*? This little squiggle might be any one of fifty-two different ones. A designer or typographer sees a squiggle that will create a sound that will create an image in someone's mind. The professional also notes the ascenders and descenders. Are they too long or too short, or just right? Do the serifs make the letter easier to read? Do the thick and thin letter strokes create an interesting contrast? Are the letters the right size on the body for maximum readability or legibility? Do the letters appear modern or old-fashioned?

In picking just the right type for a publication, the communicator needs to consider all these variations in letters and more. But before deciding on one of the more than 6,000 different designs of letters available in America today, the communicator needs to know what a serif is, what strokes are, and how big on the body a particular type might be.

**Fig. 3-1**

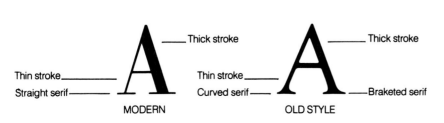

**Fig. 3-2** *Characteristics that differentiate modern and old style Roman types.*

So, in beginning to work with type, we need to know the anatomy of letter forms.

The basic elements of a letter are the _strokes_, or lines that are drawn to form the design. These can be _monotonal_ (all the same width) or they can vary from _hairline_ to quite _thick_.

Some designers have finished off the strokes that form the letters with rounded or straight lines called _serifs_. There are _rounded serifs_ and _flat serifs_. Serifs that are filled in are called _bracketed serifs_.

**Fig. 3-3**   _Serif treatments vary with type styles. Sans Serif typefaces have no serifs, old style Romans have bracketed serifs, and modern Romans have flat, straight-line serifs._

SANS (WITHOUT) SERIFS          BRACKETED SERIFS          FLAT SERIFS

An alphabet of a certain design will be drawn to a consistent size for all letters. This size is determined by the _x height_ of the letters. This is the height of the lowercase x.

**Fig. 3-4**   _The x height (the height of the lowercase x ) is a critical basic measurement in the design of letters._

abcdefgh      x          x height

Some letters have a _stroke_, or stem, which extends above the _x_ height. This stroke is known as an _ascender_. The letters _g, j, y, p,_ and _q_ all have a tail or _descender_ that drops below the _x_ height.

**Fig. 3-5**   _The letter stroke that extends above the x height is called the_ ascender. _If the stroke extends below the x height, it is a_ descender.

Ascender ————  ———— Descender

hbdgpq

In the capital alphabet only the _Q_ has a descender. There are no ascenders in capital letters.

Now that we are acquainted with a few terms, we can start our consideration of type and its use. As mentioned, there are more than 6,000 type designs in the Western world. In the days when printing was done from metal type cast by foundries, the letter designs were fairly consistent. The Caslon design, for example, which first was cast by William Caslon in England in 1734, was and still is one of the basic types.

However, with the advent of what is known as _strike-on_ (letters composed on a typewriter or other device that strikes the image of the letter on paper) and _photocomposition_, there has been a proliferation of type designs of various names. Many of these designs have characteristics of long-established and recognized styles but each manufacturer has made slight changes.

In addition, new faces are constantly being produced by the hundreds of new companies that have entered the printing market during the past two decades of the technological explosion.

Communicators can no longer rely solely on old family names for type styles. It is necessary to compare types on the specimen sheets of the various printing establishments with the styles that have become basic types through the years.

As far as learning about the correct use of types, we can start our discussion with the letter designs that are traditional and recognized by all good printers and graphic designers.

To create an effective communication, we need to decide which typeface would be easiest to read and give the best "image" to go with the message. We need to be acquainted with enough designs to understand the strengths and weaknesses of each.

## Typefaces

Type is classified in a way that makes differentiation among the designs easy. It is sorted rather like humans have been sorted by anthropologists. Just as there are various races of people, there are various _races_ of types. Some communicators refer to these basic divisions as "species" of types.

Within these races are _families_ of types. Each family has the basic characteristics of its race but in addition it has slight differences in letter design from the other families of the same race.

The Caslon family and the Bodoni family are both members of the _Roman_ race of types. They have certain basic similarities, but they also have subtle differences.

An inspection of the Caslon and Bodoni types reveals their similarities and differences. They both have serifs, and they both have variations in the letter strokes. However, the Caslon serifs are rounded and bracketed, and the Bodoni serifs are straight-lined. The letter strokes of the Caslon letters do not have as pronounced a variation between thick and thin strokes. The Bodoni strokes are very thick and very thin. Note also the different treatment of the juncture of the thick and thin strokes at the top of the letters.

Once such differences and their effects on the printability, legibility, and suitability of a printed piece are mastered, the effective selection of letter styles becomes quite easy.

Many typographers and graphic artists recognize six races of typefaces. There isn't full agreement on this, but the majority usually classify all the thousands and thousands of letter styles within six categories. These races are the Romans, the Sans Serifs, the Square Serifs (or Egyptians), the Text types (or Black Letter), the Scripts and Cursives, and a catch-all category for those designs that defy specific identification called, well, Miscellaneous (or Novelty).

No matter how the letters selected for a printed communication are imposed on the printing surface—by using the foundry types

ABCabc

ABCabc

**Fig. 3-6** _Caslon (top line) and Bodoni are both members of the Roman race but there are differences in the letter structures._

of the letterpress process, or letters produced from film by the photo-compositor, or strike-on letters of an electric typewriter—they all will exhibit characteristics of the various races. They can all be discussed within the framework of this race-and-family system of classification.

So we will examine the characteristics of each of these six races.

## Text or Black Letter

The first printing produced from movable type was, of course, the product of Johann Gutenberg's shop in Mainz, Germany. It is interesting to note that Gutenberg's most lasting achievement in printing was his famous forty-two-line Bible. Each page contained two columns, and each column was forty-two lines long. Nearly five hundred years later this Bible is still considered by typographers to be a superb example of printing and layout.

**Fig. 3-7**  *This Black Letter typeface is in the Wedding Text family designed by American Type Founders.*

abcdefghijklmnopqrstuvwxyz

ABCDEFGHIJKLMNOPQRSTUVWXYZ

The letters that Gutenberg designed, cast, and printed and the letters used in the Gutenberg Bible were copies of the heavy black letters of the northern European hand. They are thought of today as "Old English." Actually Old English is a family of the Text or Black Letter race and is not a race itself. Black Letter types are ornate with a great variation in the strokes. They are ponderous and difficult to read.

These Text or Black Letter types do have a place in modern graphic design, however. What better way to say "medieval banquet," or "we are an old, traditional institution," or "ye olde gift shoppe"? Although these types may remind you of Gothic cathedrals, don't call them "Gothic." Gothic is an entirely different race of types.

Some more confusion can arise about this race of types. The name Text was attached to these designs because they were the "text" or reading matter types of the medieval northern Europeans. But today the term text is used to designate any reading matter. So from now on, to avoid this confusion, this race will be referred to only as Black Letter.

Use Black Letter when you want to emphasize tradition and solemnity and when you want to give the image of strength and efficiency. Many newspapers adopted Black Letter types for their nameplates for these reasons. Avoid using Black Letter in all-capital lines; the letters are difficult, if not impossible, to read when set in all caps. Use them sparingly for title lines, logos, and subheads, where they are suitable. They are useful for formal invitations and stationery.

Mr. and Mrs. Reginald Harper

request the honor of

your company at the marriage of their daughter

Jacqueline Marie

to

Mr. Alfred Bruce Saylor

on the evening of Wednesday, the first of October

at half after seven o'clock

at Six hundred and ten Richelieu Place

Kingsland, Wyoming

**Fig. 3-8** *This is American Type Founders' Engravers Text. Note how it helps create the image of a formal occasion.*

## Roman

The birthplace of printing in the Western world was northern Europe. From there it spread south and west. Venice became a center for printing in the late 1400s. However, the people in southern Europe did not like the heavy and ponderous type used in the north. They preferred the simpler and more open letters of the Romans. So typefaces developed in Venice, Paris, and elsewhere followed Roman letter forms and became known as the Roman race.

The ancient Romans developed their alphabet from the Greeks and the other early civilizations of the eastern Mediterranean area. In fact, some letters of the Roman alphabet and thus of our alphabet can be traced back to the picture writing, or hieroglyphics, of the Egyptians.

abcdefghijklmnopqrstuvwxyz
ABCDEFGHIJKLMNOPQRSTUVWXYZ

**Fig. 3-9** *This type is Caslon, designed by International Typeface Corporation for use with electronic typesetting equipment. It is a member of the Roman race.*

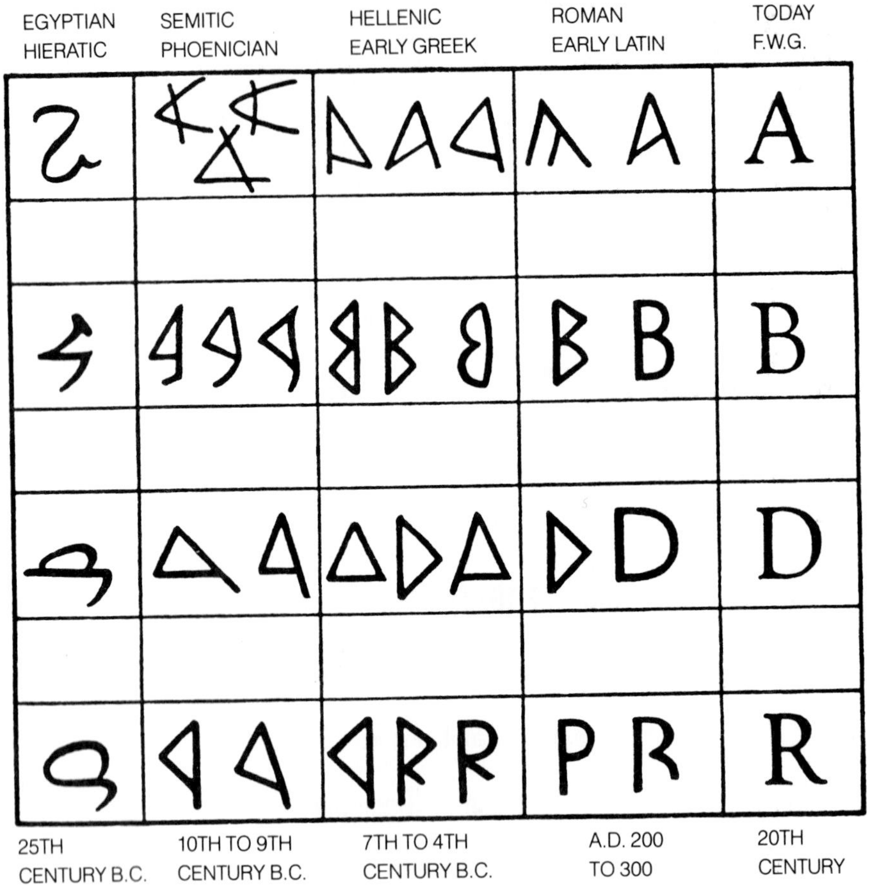

**Fig. 3-10** *The development of some modern letter forms can be traced back to the hieroglyphics of the Egyptians.*

| EGYPTIAN HIERATIC | SEMITIC PHOENICIAN | HELLENIC EARLY GREEK | ROMAN EARLY LATIN | TODAY F.W.G. |
|---|---|---|---|---|
| 25TH CENTURY B.C. | 10TH TO 9TH CENTURY B.C. | 7TH TO 4TH CENTURY B.C. | A.D. 200 TO 300 | 20TH CENTURY |

# Staples

OLD STYLE

# Big Rink

TRANSITIONAL

# Explain

MODERN

**Fig. 3-11** subgroups with es of the three Roman race.

Historians believe that the Phoenicians adopted and modified Egyptian letters and then the Greeks took some letter forms from the Phoenicians, rearranged their constructions, and used them to form the Greek alphabet. These forms passed from the Greeks to the Romans.

The tool most used by the Romans in writing inscriptions on their buildings was the brush. They painted inscriptions on the masonry and then stonemasons carved over the painted outline. The Romans could turn a brush to make curves and continuous lines, and thus they developed letterstrokes of varying widths for their letters. They also finished off long broad strokes with a narrow stroke using the side of the brush. These endings became the serifs on our letters and one of the distinguishing features of the Roman race of types. All Romans have serifs and letter strokes that vary in width from thick to thin.

Roman types are classified as old style, transitional and modern.

A typeface is classified as *old style* if it has little contrast between the thick and thin lines, if the strokes are sloping or round, and if the serifs are slanting or curved and extended outward at the top of the capital T and the bottom of the capital E.

In 1773 Giambattista Bodoni, an Italian type designer and a contemporary and friend of Benjamin Franklin, introduced the

The serif angles out sharply from the stem and terminates in a crisp point.

There is a slight tilt to the angle of the swells of the round letters.

There is greater contrast between thick and thin strokes.

**Fig. 3-12** *Characteristics of old style Roman types. (Courtesy of Westvaco Corporation.)*

so-called *modern* Roman types. These types are distinguished by strong contrast between thick and thin strokes and straight, thin, unbracketed serifs. Any type with these characteristics, even if a century and a half old, or if designed only yesterday, is classified as a modern Roman.

Type that falls between the sloping or rounded strokes, little contrast between thick and thin lines, and slanting or curved serifs of the old style Roman and the contrasting thick and thin strokes and straight thin and unbracketed serifs of the modern Roman is considered a *transitional* Roman face. It is said to be half-way out of the old style Roman design and half-way into the modern Roman configuration.

In the transitional types the angle of the thin strokes is not as pronounced as in the old style Roman, and the variation between thick and thin strokes is more pronounced.

Romans are considered the basic types. They come in all weights and sizes. There are Romans available to help communicate virtually any message esthetically and effectively.

ITC **Fenice Bold**

**Fig. 3-13** *Fenice Bold, a type design by International Typeface Corporation, is modeled after Bodoni but with a modern flair and is thus a modern Roman design. The contrast between thick and thin strokes is carried to the extreme and there is a vertical emphasis as shown by the thin strokes in the letter bowls, such as the top and bottom of the o above.*

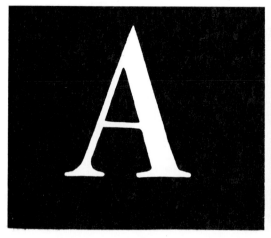 

**Fig. 3-14** *Characteristics of transitional Roman types. Transitionals are basically old style with modifications that move them toward modern Romans. (Courtesy of the Westvaco Corporation.)*

## Sans Serif

The third broad category, Sans Serif, is comparatively new in name but it also has an ancient derivation, probably from the flat, even-bodied lines of the Greek and early Roman letters. Sans Serifs are called Gothics by some typographers, and in Europe they are known as the Grotesque types.

## abcdefghijklmnopqrstuvwxyz
## ABCDEFGHIJKLMNOPQRSTUVWXYZ

As the name implies (*sans* means "without" in French), Sans Serif types have no serifs. They are geometric, precise, and open. Some forms of Sans Serif types have slight variations in the letter strokes but most are monotonal.

Sans Serifs are excellent all-purpose types. Some of our newest designs, such as the Avante Garde Gothic are renderings of the sans serif style of lettering. Sans Serifs are suitable for every purpose. They print well and have a modern look with good punch. And they probably will continue to be among the most popular faces for years to come. They are especially good for cold type production and offset printing methods as they stand up exceptionally well in photographic reproduction.

The Sans Serifs became especially popular in the 1920s when the Bauhaus movement in Germany, which emphasized functional design, made its influence felt in the world of typography. Sans Serifs may be rather monotonous when printed in mass. However, they are being used more and more, especially in newsletters and in-house magazines.

## Square Serif

The fourth race of type is the Square Serifs. These have the general characteristics of the Sans Serifs except that a precise square or straight-line serif is added. Some typographers refer to the Square Serifs as Slab Serifs or Egyptians. They were called Egyptians when they first appeared.

In the early 1800s there was great interest in Egypt, most likely because of the discovery of the Rosetta stone in 1799. The Rosetta stone contained an inscription in three languages—that of the rulers, that of the common people, and Greek. The Greek was used to unlock the secrets of Egyptian hieroglyphics and of ancient Egyptian history.

## abcdefghijklmnopqrstuvwxyz
## ABCDEFGHIJKLMNOPQRSTUVWXYZ

About the same time, Vincent Figgins, a British type designer and founder, produced a typeface characterized by thick slab serifs and a general evenness of weight. The face had a certain quality reminiscent of Egyptian architecture in its capital letters. So it was only natural for it to be dubbed "Egyptian."

Today there are many versions of Square Serif types, many with Egyptian family names or with names that are descriptive of the type style. There are Memphis, Cairo, Karnak, and Luxor. And there are Stymies, Girders, and Towers.

Today Square Serifs are more logically associated with modern buildings than Egyptian architecture. They are sturdy and square. The capital letters look like steel girders, and the design gives the reader a feeling of strength, stability, and ruggedness.

The Square Serifs were not meant to be used in mass. They are excellent for headlines, headings in advertisements, and posters. They are monotonous and tiring when used in long columns of reading matter.

These types were quite popular about the turn of the century, and they are found in the headlines of that day. The "wanted" posters of the Old West were also often set in Square Serif.

Square Serifs faded from favor during the first decades of the twentieth century. They were considered too old-fashioned. There was a revival of interest in the late 1940s and 1950s. A number of newspapers adopted them for their headline schedules. Then they faded from favor again, and most newspapers dropped them by the early 1970s in favor of the more modern Romans such as Bodoni and the Sans Serif faces such as Helvetica.

In the mid-1980s Square Serif faces enjoyed a revival. Since these types are structurally rugged and have but little, if any, variation in stroke widths, they are good types for reverses, surprints (type over illustrations), and photomechanical composition and plate-making techniques. They also print well in offset and gravure.

## Scripts and Cursives

The fifth race includes letter styles that resemble handwriting. The typographer calls them Scripts or Cursives. Since Scripts and Cursives are so similar, we can group them together in the Scripts and Cursives race.

But, why Scripts and Cursives? Why not just call them one or the other?

A little explanation is needed here. Some typographers classify *italic* types (Roman types with slanted letters) as a separate race. The slanted letters that we refer to as italics were actually a style all their own when they first appeared in the 1500s.

A printer and letter designer, Alois Manutius, who established his famous Aldine press in Venice in 1490, wanted to publish small books of significant works. They might be called the first "everyone's library" books. Manutius sought a letter style for his type that would permit as many words as possible on a page.

**Creative Communication**

Are you the creative type?

A number of personality studies have been made in efforts to identify the characteristics of creative people. But there has been little consistency in the findings.

One study indicated that individualism and social nonconformity were correlated with problem-solving ability. Fluency, flexibility, and the ability to elaborate also seemed to be important.

Some investigators have found that creative people often have immature personality traits, such as dependency, defiance of convention or authority, a feeling of destiny or omnipotence, and gullibility.

Psychologists have made some progress in attempting to describe the process of creative thinking, but they admit that they haven't found a magic key to creativity. The evidence does indicate that training, knowledge, and hard work are vital. In addition, it is important for the creative person to take time to mull over ideas and let them percolate in the mind.

**Fig. 3-17** *This is Bernhard Cursive Bold. Lucian Bernhard, a German designer, produced many types. The American Type Foundry uses his designs to produce a number of his typefaces in the United States.*

*abcdefghijklmnopqrstuvwxyz*

*ABCDEFGHIJKLMNOPQ RSTUVWXYZ*

He devised a cursive letter style that was the first italic typeface. A *cursive* (from the Latin *currere*, which means "run") was a free construction in which there were no exact or repetitious letter forms (the letters were free flowing like handwriting). The scribes and printers in the Germanic countries called the italic style "cursive" and that is how it got its name.

When the Aldine books appeared in the original italic face, other printers quickly copied it and the design spread throughout Europe. (However, slanted letters in the Sans Serif and Square Serif races are called *obliques* and not italics.)

In some books on type the authors insist that Scripts are letters resembling handwriting and are connected while Cursives have a noticeable gap between the letters. On the other hand, just the opposite is cited as the distinguishing feature of the two types (that Scripts have gaps between the letters and Cursives do not) in other texts on typography and graphics. It is usually sufficient, however, to recognize and define the letter styles that resemble handwriting as either Scripts or Cursives. The safest way to approach these types is to select the style you want to use and refer to it by its family name.

**Fig. 3-18** *This is an example of italic type, not to be confused with a Script or Cursive. It is the italic version of Century Expanded, a member of the Roman race. (Courtesy of American Type Founders.)*

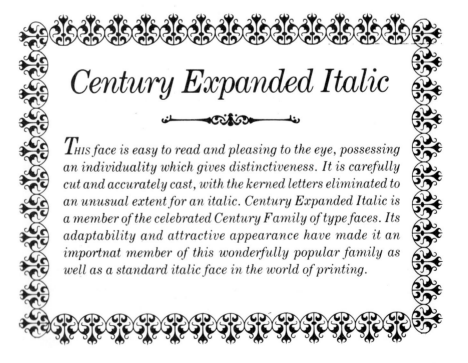

*Century Expanded Italic*

*THIS face is easy to read and pleasing to the eye, possessing an individuality which gives distinctiveness. It is carefully cut and accurately cast, with the kerned letters eliminated to an unusual extent for an italic. Century Expanded Italic is a member of the celebrated Century Family of typefaces. Its adaptability and attractive appearance have made it an importnat member of this wonderfully popular family as well as a standard italic face in the world of printing.*

*Early Americana*          *Early Americana*

**Fig. 3-19**  *Some Scripts or Cursives are designed so that the letters appear to join (left), others have noticeable gaps between the letters.*

Scripts and Cursives play an important role in good design. They can give a special "tone" to a printed piece. They are excellent for announcements and invitations and they can be used for titles, headings, and subheads. They can also add interest, contrast, and life to a printed page. But because they have a low readability rating, they (and italics, too, for that matter) should be used sparingly—only for a line or two or three—not in many sentences or paragraphs.

## Miscellaneous or Novelty

The sixth race is not actually a race. It is a catchall category for all those unusual designs that do not have the clear-cut characteristics of the other races. These can include hand-designed types and types designed for special effects, logos, trademarks, and novelty arrangements.

Selection and use of these types should be governed by the same criteria we would use in selecting and using a Script or Cursive.

## Families of Type

Roman, Black Letter, Sans Serif, Square Serif, and Scripts and Cursives—are the basic groups of types. But not only can each letter design be identified by its race, each has a name as well. Quite often, the name of the designer is used. There is Bodoni, named after the designer of this popular modern Roman type, Giambattista Bodoni. There is (Nicholas) Jenson, (William) Caslon, (Claude) Garamond, and (Frederic) Goudy to mention a few faces that are in use today.

Sometimes the type name may be descriptive of its design or function. There is Cloister, a Black Letter type reminiscent of the cloisters of medieval monks; the gaudy Lilith, named for the female demon of Jewish folklore; and there is Bankers Gothic, a no-nonsense type often used for business forms and letterheads.

Or, the type names may reflect a geographical area, such as the Square Serifs called Cairo, Memphis, and Karnak.

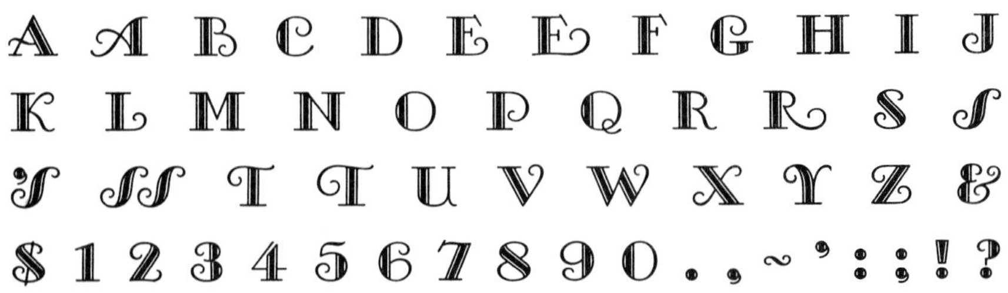

A A B C D E F G H I J
K L M N O P Q R R S S
S SS T T U V W X Y Z &
$ 1 2 3 4 5 6 7 8 9 0 . , ~ ° : ; ! ?

**Fig. 3-20**  *Types of unusual or decorative design that cannot be clearly classified by race are placed in the Miscellaneous or Novelty category. This typeface is called Gallia.*

Types may also be named for the publications for which they were designed. An example is Times Roman, which was cut for *The Times* of London, and Vogue, for the fashion magazine. Types can claim modernism by being called Futura, Metro, Tempo—all members of the Sans Serif race.

There are hundreds of type names, and new ones are constantly being added. A type manufacturer will introduce a new design that becomes popular. Another manufacturer will develop a face that resembles the pioneer, with sufficient alterations to avoid patent complications, and give it a different name. For instance, Times Roman has become one of the most popular Romans. Now there are such designs as English Roman, which is nearly identical but is produced by a different manufacturer of typesetting equipment.

All the variations in weight and width of a particular type constitute a *family*. All sizes available for this type also make up the family. The Bodoni family, for instance, is a family of tall and short, skinny and fat types. There are regular Bodoni, bold Bodoni, italic Bodoni, condensed Bodoni, and so on. All these variations are still members of the Bodoni family.

So, to classify Bodoni as an example: It is a member of the Roman race and its racial characteristics are serifs and thick and thin letter

**Fig. 3-21** *Variations of type designs within a family are called a series. These are members of the Garamond family.*

Garamond Light
Garamond Book
**Garamond Bold**
**Garamond Ultra**
*Garamond Light Italic*
*Garamond Book Italic*
***Garamond Bold Italic***
***Garamond Ultra Italic***
Garamond Light Condensed
Garamond Book Condensed
**Garamond Bold Condensed**
**Garamond Ultra Condensed**
*Garamond Light Condensed Italic*
*Garamond Book Condensed Italic*
***Garamond Bold Condensed Italic***
***Garamond Ultra Condensed Italic***

Pleasure Cruises to Hawaii and the South Sea Islands

Several Representative Selections of Italics

Longer Ore Carriers will be needed

Greece and a Modern Sculpture

A True Experience in Faith

Highway and Road

South America

Dinner Party

First Volume of the Ecclesiastical History of Scotland

Riding with a New York Ambulance Driver

Summer Cruise to Western Europe

The Birthplace of Shakespeare

How to work in Comfort

Books and Reading

Excelsior Hotel

Biographer

strokes. It is the Bodoni family of the Roman race, but it still has a number of variations within its family. These variations are referred to as a *series* within the family.

**Series of Types**

A series of types consists of all the sizes of one style in a family. For example, a series might be all the sizes available of Bodoni bold, or another series might be all the sizes available of Bodoni italic.

**Fonts**

There is more. Another term we need to know in addition to race, family, and series, is *font*. Type is made, sold, stored and used in *fonts*. The term is used to refer to a set of letters, numerals, symbols, and punctuation marks needed of a specific design and size of type. All the letters available on a typewriter or word processor consist of a font. There might be a font of pica type or a font of elite type on a typewriter.

Some fonts contain characters that are not found in others. Usually the basic alphabet letters, numerals, and punctuation marks are supplemented by special ligatures, diphthongs, or other symbols. A *ligature* is a combination of letters in one form. Common ligatures are ﬃ, ﬁ, ﬂ, and ﬀ combinations. *Diphthongs* are the combinations æ and œ. When we select letter styles or type, we need to be aware of what characters are in the fonts. We might need fonts with special fractions, degree or mathematical symbols, or, perhaps, letters with accent marks for foreign languages.

**Fig. 3-22** *These are two series of the Futura family: Futura Light* (left) *and Futura Medium* (right).

**Fig. 3-23**  *An example of a basic font.*
*(Courtesy of American Type Founders.)*

## Measurement of Type

Type and printing have unique units of measurement. These units are quite simple, but anyone working with type and printing should understand them thoroughly. It will be difficult to function with any sort of efficiency as an editor, designer, or communicator if you do not understand and know how printing measurements are used.

For about 300 years after Gutenberg there was no standard system of measurement for printers. Typecasters gave names to the various sizes of types they produced. Usually the types of one foundry could not be used with those of another. The problem was further compounded because the names given to types of certain sizes by one foundry might be used to designate entirely different sizes by another. One foundry might have called a type "nonpareil" while another used nonpareil for a different size of type. (Note: The term *nonpareil* became accepted later as referring to type now called 6 point.)

A system of sizing type by units of measurements called *points* was devised in the middle 1700s by a French typographer, Pierre Simon Fournier, and further refined by his countryman, Francois Ambroise Didot. In 1886, under the sponsorship of the U.S. Type Founders Association, a point system was adopted as the official uniform measurement of types in the United States. England adopted it in 1898.

The point is the smallest unit of measurement in the printer's and graphic designer's world. It is commonly defined as being $\frac{1}{72}$ of an inch. (Actually, the point is slightly less than that. Specifically, it is 0.0138-plus of an inch. But for all practical purposes communicators consider 72 points as equalling an inch.)

The thickness of spaces, leads, slugs, rules, and borders (the white space between words and lines of types and the decorations around blocks of type) and the height of type are all measured in points. If type is 36 points high it is approximately $\frac{1}{2}$ inch high. Type that is 72 points is approximately 1 inch high. A white space between lines that measures $\frac{1}{4}$ inch would be 18 points.

Some of the old type names have made their ways down into the world of graphics today. Pica and agate are the most common type names still in use.

Most newspaper advertising is sold by the column inch or by the line (short for "agate line"). For this purpose *a column inch* is an area 1 column wide and 1 inch deep. When space is specified by the line, a line is 1 column wide and $\frac{1}{14}$ inch deep. (There are fourteen lines in 1 column inch.)

In the old days *agate* referred to type that was 5½ points in size.

*1" = 72 points*
*1" = 6 picas*
*1 pica = 12 points*

**Fig. 3-24**

Printers rule with points, picas, metric and inches.

Graphic artist's rule with inches and picas.

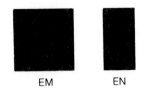

EM          EN

**Fig. 3-25**  *An em is a unit of measurement that is the square of the type size being used. An en is one-half the width of an em. The square on the left illustrates the area of a 48-point em. The rectangle on the right illustrates the dimensions of a 48-point en.*

Fourteen agate lines would actually be 5.142 points high, but printers and advertisers use the simple comparison of 14 agate lines to equal 1 inch in depth.

*Pica* is used to designate 12 points of space. Thus there are 12 points in a pica and 6 picas in 1 inch. The type on a pica typewriter (or pica type on a word processor) is 12-point type.

Points and picas are the heart of the printer's and the communicator's measurement system just as inches and feet are used to measure most things in our daily lives.

Sometimes the word *em* is used as a synonym for pica. This is erroneous, but it has become so prevalent that only a purist would object now. A pica is linear measure. That is, it measures height, width, and depth. An em is the measure of the square of an area.

The em is an important unit of measurement in graphic design. Formally it is the square of the type size in question. For example, a 36-point em measures 36 points, or ½ inch, on all four sides. An em that measures 12 points, or a pica, on each side is referred to as a *pica em.*

The difference between a pica and an em should be remembered. Both terms are used in marking instructions for compositors or printers, in copy fitting, and in making proper dummies and layouts. Confusion here can cause trouble later.

Another measure of area, but not a square area, is the *en.* An en is half the width of an em. An en in 36-point type is 36 points, or ½ inch high—the same height as the type. However, it is only 18 points, or half the 36-point measure, wide. Thus a 36-point en would be 36 points high and 18 points wide.

Old-timers, to keep the two terms from being confused, referred to an em as a mutton or mut, and an en as a nut.

Em's and en's are still used quite often to indicate indentation. Many video display terminal keyboards have an em and an en key. If copy for 9-point type is marked for an em indent, it will be indented 9 points when the operator hits the em key on the keyboard. If copy set in 12 points is marked for an en indention, it will be indented 6 points. The compositor does not have to stop and figure out spacing if copy is properly marked by the communicator.

Once we understand the classification of types and type measurements, we can put this information to work. However, there are a few more points to keep in mind that apply to all the styles of types.

For instance, two typefaces may have the same point-size designation, but the body of the letters in one may be considerably larger than those of the other. This is referred to as being "big on the body" or "small on the body." The *body* is the actual base size or true point size of the type.

It is possible for types that have, say, 48 points as their size designations to be quite different in appearance. The x height of the letter forms may be different even though the total point sizes of the types are the same.

Notice how the lowercase *h* in Fig. 3-27 appears to be in three different sizes though all are actually 72-point types.

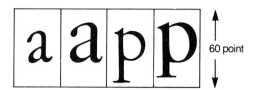

The size of letters cannot be measured accurately by placing a line guage or graphic arts ruler on the letters themselves. To be perfectly accurate the base has to be measured. However, we can get a close reading, a workable reading, of the point size of a certain type. We can do this by measuring from the top of the ascender to the bottom of the descender of sample letters.

This is useful when we spot a type that is just the right size for the purpose in mind but the point size is not known. We can measure the letters and find the size. We can then proceed to make a layout and specify the size of type, or we can tell the printer, "Set it in 48 point" or whatever.

## Important Points to Remember

- Type size is measured in points. There are 72 points in 1 inch.
- Line length is measured in picas. There are 6 picas in 1 inch.
- The pica is used to express overall width or depth as well as the length of a line. There are 12 points in 1 pica.
- The most common use of the em is to indicate indentation of blocks of copy or to indicate the indentation at the start of a paragraph. The em is the square of the type size being used.
- The agate line is used to measure the depth of advertising space. There are 14 agate lines in 1 inch.

## Effective Design Checklist

- There is a Roman type to fit nearly every need. Old-time printers said, "When in doubt, use Caslon."
- Square Serifs print well and are good for "no-nonsense" messages.

- Black Letters emphasize tradition. They give the feeling of Gothic cathedrals, medieval castles, institutions. They are, however, rarely used in today's designs. They, and Scripts and Cursives, are also difficult, if not impossible, to read in all capital letters.

- Scripts and Cursives are like spices and seasonings. They can add interest, contrast, and life to a printed page. However, they have low readability and should be used sparingly.

- Miscellaneous or Novelty faces should be selected and used sparingly, like Scripts and Cursives.

- It is considered better to have a wide range of series of a few families rather than a wide variety of families with limited series.

- In selecting a font of type, consider the characters it contains in addition to the letters, numerals, and punctuation marks.

- Compare the x heights of letters, the lengths of ascenders and descenders of the various families, as well as the letter designs when selecting types.

## Graphics in Action

1. Explain the printer's measurement system. Illustrate your explanation with elements, letters, or lines of type clipped from publications, or with simple sketches. Use rubber cement to attach your illustrations. Neatness and accuracy count.

2. Find several lines of type of varying widths in publications. Mount them on plain white paper and indicate the widths in inches and picas.

3. Collect examples of types representing each of the races. Mount the examples on plain white paper and indicate the widths of the lines in inches and picas.

4. Explain how type is classified according to race, family, and series. Illustrate your explanation with examples clipped from publications.

5. Draw a frame about 1 inch wide around a sheet of 8½ by 11 or 9 by 12 tracing paper. Color the frame any color you desire. Draw a very light line about an inch below the middle of the page, horizontally, with a soft pencil (HB or 2H work well). Trace your name or nickname (limit it to about five letters or less) using the line as a baseline for the letters. Select types from any source (such as magazines or newspapers) that are at least 72 points in size if all capitals and about 120 points if capitals and lowercase. Try to keep the spacing between the letters equal. Then go wild with colored pencils, crayons, or felt pens and color your name any way you want. This could create a design worth framing! This is also the first step towards one method of lettering for layouts.

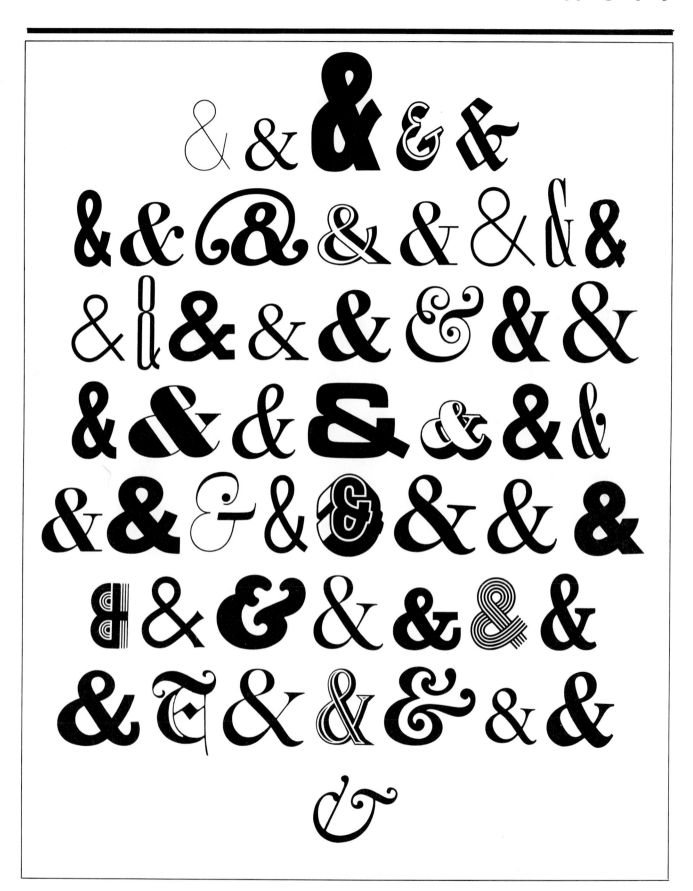

The proper selection and use of the hundreds of type designs available is the first step in creating an effective printed communication. A production is a terrible waste of time, money, effort, and material if it is not read and understood.

Type should be selected and arranged to achieve maximum readability of the message. Readability should be the foundation on which the printed communication is built.

Frederic W. Goudy, the most prolific American type designer, put it this way:

> Letters must be of such a nature that when they are combined into lines of words the eye may run along the lines easily, quickly, and without obstruction, the reader being occupied only with the thought presented. If one is compelled to inspect the individual letters, his mind is not free to grasp the ideas conveyed by the type.[1]

Type selection and display should not only aid readability but should reinforce the goal for the communication. That is, the type should be appropriate to the message. If the communicator is shouting, the type should help. If the communicator is trying to reason with the reader, the type should reflect this goal, and it can. There are "stern" types for stern and remonstrative messages, and there are "gay and happy" types for gay and happy messages.

**Fig. 4-1** *Type can be selected to reinforce the message, as in the title and initial letter for this magazine article about Gothic cathedrals. The use of Black Letter for the title and for the initial letter aids unity. The subhead and byline in Roman are subordinated to the title and illustrate proper mixing of the races—there should be definite contrast and one should dominate. (Reprinted by permission of* Science 84. *Copyright, The American Association for the Advancement of Science. Cathedral photo by R. Mark, Princeton University.)*

**What Typefaces Can Express**

1. Type can be light or **heavy**

2. Type can be unassuming or graceful

3. Type can whisper or **shout**

4. Type can be monotonous or sparkle

5. Type can be **UGLY** or beautiful

6. Type can be **mechanical** or formal

7. Type can be *social* or **ecclesiastical**

8. Type can be **FAT** or **THIN**

9. Type can be **decorative** or plain

10. Type can be **easy to read** or hard to read

Key to the type faces listed above, left to right in order:

1. 18-point Avante Garde Extra Light and Lubalin Graph Bold
2. 18-point Baskerville and Palatino
3. 8-point Belwe Light and 18-point Gill Sans Ultra Bold
4. 18-point News Gothic and University
5. 18-point Auriol Black and Weiss
6. 18-point Lubalin Graph Medium and Cloister Open
7. 18-point Snell Roundhand Bold and Old German Bold
8. 18-point Bauhaus Bold and Century Bold Condensed
9. 18-point Nicolas Cochin Black and Caledonia
10. 18-point Century Schoolbook and 6-point Novarese Medium Italic

**Fig. 4-2** *Type "talks." Notice how the letter designs help create the image the words transmit.*

An effective message must first gain attention if it is to be read. That is one reason why newspapers use headlines. The type is selected and arranged to get the attention of the potential reader. Proper selection and arrangement make a publication stand out from other publications.

Proper selection and use of type can also help create identification. *Time* magazine, for instance, can be spotted quickly because of its consistent use of certain graphics and types. There is no mistaking which newspaper is *The New York Times.* Harlequin books are easily spotted among the paperbacks because their typography says "Harlequin" and helps define this particular publisher's books.

It should be kept in mind that the proper use and arrangement

# WEISS

# TORINO

# Baskerville

**Fig. 4-3** *Examples of Roman types that might be used for display purposes. They suggest dignity, stability, and integrity, and they rate high in legibility. Many Romans have their own personalities and individuality. They can help establish an image for an organization or product.*

# BETON
# PLAYBILL

**Fig. 4-4** *Square Serifs or Egyptians are hard-hitting, bold, no-nonsense typefaces. Playbill creates a "turn of the century" mood.*

# UNIVERS
# Eurostile

# Anzeigen Grot
# Optima

**Fig. 4-5** *Although Sans Serifs are basically versions of a style introduced in the nineteenth century, they are considered by many designers the most modern of type designs. Their precise, simple lines give high legibility to titles and headings. Optima especially, with its Roman appearance, seems warm and human.*

of type is both an art and a science. It is an art in that within limitations there is complete freedom of action. To begin with, there is only a blank page. The designer has comparative freedom in designing the elements that will occupy this page. The communicator is an artist using type, borders, illustrations, and color to create a physical environment for the written message.

Typography is a science as well. It is a science in that it uses rules that have been proven by research and testing. These rules must be understood and applied with creative freshness if we are going to produce the most effective printed pieces possible. So, the communicator who desires to produce the most effective printed communication must apply a mixture of art and science.

Let us consider the science of typographic design first and then look at the art of using type.

Below are ten suggestions that combine the experimentation, research, and testing that have proved to be effective in working with type:

1. Use the right type style.
2. Set the type on the proper measure.
3. Watch the spacing.
4. Remember the margins.
5. Select the proper type size.
6. Mix type styles carefully.
7. Use all-cap lines sparingly.
8. Do not be boring.
9. Avoid oddball placement.
10. Spell it out.

If we keep these ten rules in mind, they will help us produce an end product that is suitable, readable, and legible. These suggestions are quite easy to apply and can be summed up as: Keep the reader (or target audience) in mind when making layouts or giving instructions to the compositor or printer.

## Use the Right Type Style

The first step in selecting the right type is to divide the content of the message into words that speak out in short, crisp phrases and words that must be read in mass.

The short phrases (headings, titles, subheads) should be set in large type for emphasis. This type is called *display* as contrasted with *text* or *body* types for masses of words, or reading matter. The headline of a news story, for example, will be set in display type and the story itself in body type.

Generally, types within the size range of 8 or 9 to 12 or 14 point are considered suitable for reading matter. Types larger than 14 point are display types.

Both classifications of type must be considered, initially, as separate entities. However, remember that for unity the two must work together and harmonize. Sometimes the most effective choice for display is a larger size of the same design used for the body type, or a larger size from another series of the same family as the body type.

The second step in selecting the most effective type design for a message is to read the copy. What sort of message is this? If it is a hard-sell advertisement, then display type in a heavy-hitting design is the obvious choice. Clean-lined, bold Sans Serifs would be a good choice. A bold Square Serif also has a forceful voice.

Suppose we want to say "here is a long-established organization that has become an institution in our city"—what type should we select? *The New York Times* and many other newspapers say this by using Black Letter types for their nameplates. An old-style Roman, such as Caslon or Goudy, would help get the idea across, too.

If the message is crisp and modern but dignified as well, a modern Roman might be a good face to choose. Bodoni or Craw Modern would also do the job.

High fashion dictates a Script or Cursive or perhaps a light-faced Sans Serif. Vogue is a family that speaks to high society. It was designed especially for the audience of *Vogue* magazine.

The improper type design can sabotage the message. A newspaper would look ridiculous setting a banner head concerning an exposé at city hall in Black Letter type. Yet Black Letter would be a fine choice to say "Merry Christmas."

When it comes to body or text type for reading matter, there is controversy. Some designers maintain that Sans Serif is the modern type and those who eschew it are old-fashioned. Others stick by the Romans that have been used since printing was introduced in England.

The argument in favor of Romans is twofold. First, we are used to it because so much of what we read—books, magazines,

**Fig. 4-6**  *Scripts and Cursives try to capture handwriting. They can give an image of austere formality or causal informality, create an effect of graciousness or rugged individualism. They should be used sparingly.*

**Fig. 4-7**  *Miscellaneous or Novelty types can be effective if used sparingly for display lines. They run the gamut from dainty to solid to creating a sense of urgency. They are unsuitable for more than a line or two. (Reprinted with the permission of Westvaco Corporation.)*

---

Four score and seven years ago our fathers brought forth on this continent, a new nation, conceived in Liberty, and dedicated to the proposition that all men are created equal.

---

**Four score and seven years ago our fathers brought forth on this continent, a new nation, conceived in Liberty, and dedicated to the proposition that all men are created equal.**

---

Four score and seven years ago our fathers brought forth on this continent, a new nation, conceived in Liberty, and dedicated to the proposition that all men are created equal.

---

**Fig. 4-8**  *Text matter set in a slightly bold Sans Serif (middle) is considered to have greater readability than the light Sans Serif (top). Roman (bottom) is the preference of most readers. (These samples are from U&lc.)*

newspapers—is set in Roman types and always has been. Second, the thick and thin strokes of Romans and the rounded shapes of the letters cause less eye fatigue and make reading more pleasant.

Studies seem to side with the Roman advocates. Although the evidence is inconclusive, Miles A. Tinker, a psychologist, has written that readers prefer Roman faces even though there seems to be no real difference in reading speed, fatigue, and so on. He also points out that readers usually prefer a type that is slightly on the bold side.[2]

## Set the Type on the Proper Measure

How wide should the columns in a publication be? If we have a block of copy we want to include in an advertisement layout, how wide should it be? Can we just arbitrarily select a width that looks nice? Does width make a difference? It certainly does. If columns of type are too wide, reading will be slow and difficult. Readers will tire easily, and they can lose their places in the message as their eyes shift from one line to the next. They may become discouraged and stop reading.

If, on the other hand, type is set in columns that are too short, the constant eye motion from left to right and back to left again will slow reading and make it a tiring chore. In addition, type set too narrow causes many awkward between-word spacing situations. Words

**Fig. 4-9** *Examples of 8-point type set on three different measures. [Reprinted from Ralph W. and Edwin Polk,* Practice of Printing *(Peoria, Ill.: Bennett Publishing Company, © 1971.) Used with permission of the publishers. All rights reserved.]*

The width of a column of matter influences its legibility. The ideal width for any piece of composition is based on the breadth of focus of the eye upon the page. For small types the focus will be narrow, and it will widen out as the type faces increase in size. If the column is set in too wide a measure, as is the case with this paragraph, the lines will be scanned with somewhat of effort, and it will be found harder to "keep one's place" as he reads. Also, it will require some effort to locate the starting point of each new line. A large amount of matter set like this would be tedious to read.

On the other hand, if the column is too narrow, fewer words may be grasped at a time, and thus, too frequent adjustments must be made for the numerous short lines of the type, seriously hindering the steady, even flow of the message. In addition, a greater proportion of words must be divided at the ends of the lines, and the spacing of the lines is necessarily uneven and awkward, also affecting the legibility.

This group is set the proper width for the comfortable, easy reading of 8 point type. The eye may easily take in a line at a time, and in this way the message may be read without any mechanical encumbrances. Larger types set to this width will present the same difficulties to the reader that are experienced in the 8 point example, set in the narrow measure, above. There is a suitable width for each size and style of type.

must also be divided between lines more frequently and this can disfigure a printed piece.

Setting type on the proper measure is easy, and there are several rules of thumb that can be used. The proper measure (or line width) is, of course, determined by the type size selected. For small type sizes, say, 6 or 8 point, narrow columns are suitable. But larger type requires wider columns.

Some typographers have developed a theory of *optimum line length.* This refers to the width of a line that is considered ideal for greatest reading ease. It has been found that a good way to determine the optimum width for lines of any typeface and size is to measure the lowercase alphabet (all the letters lined up from *a* to *z*) and add one-half to this. For instance, if the lowercase alphabet measures 18 picas, the optimum line width for that type would be 27 picas.

abcdefghijklmnopqrstuvwxyzabcdefghijklm

(Ideal line width: 1½ times the lowercase alphabet)

**Fig. 4-10**  *The ideal line width (1½ times the lowercase alphabet).*

Typographers using this theory believe the minimum width any type should be set is the width of one lowercase alphabet, and the maximum width should never exceed the width of two lowercase alphabets.

Another rule of thumb that works out to approximately the same is to double in picas the point size of the type being used. For instance, 18-point type would ideally be set about 36 picas wide and 6-point type would be set no more than 12 picas wide.

The thing to remember is, the smaller the type used, the shorter the lines in which it is set. As the size of type is increased, the width of the lines should be increased but never to more than double the lowercase alphabet.

Type set on an improper measure can detract from the attractiveness of a printed communication. But, more important, it can be a definite deterrent to easy, pleasant reading.

**Fig. 4-11**  *This 12-point Square Serif type should not be set in lines narrower than 15 picas or wider than 30 picas for ordinary composition.*

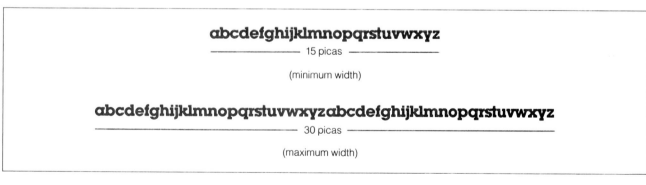

abcdefghijklmnopqrstuvwxyz

——— 15 picas ———

(minimum width)

abcdefghijklmnopqrstuvwxyzabcdefghijklmnopqrstuvwxyz

——— 30 picas ———

(maximum width)

## Watch the Spacing

Too much spacing can make the message unattractive and difficult to read, too little can jam the words and lines together so that the message's appearance is destroyed and reading is a real task. Most people will skip over poorly spaced printed matter unless the content of the message is so overpowering that they will put up with unnecessary channel noise (in this case poor spacing) to get at the information.

White space, when applied to type masses, comprises the space between words and the space between lines. Words that are crowded too closely together are difficult to read. Words that are spread too far apart can create gaps of ugly white within the printed block.

Lines that are too close together also cause problems. The reader must sort out where a new line starts. When lines are packed too tightly the reader may start to reread the same line. When lines are too far apart there are time-consuming gaps as the eye travels from one line to another.

Thus we need to decide how much space to use between lines of a printed piece. Printers call this *leading* (pronounced *ledding*, *led*, as in the metal). The term originated when thin strips of lead were used between lines of metal type as spacing material. When a printer suggests a paragraph should be leaded out, it means that more space is needed between the lines.

For reading matter, the 2-point lead (a strip of metal 2 points thick to separate the lines of type) has been considered standard. However, there is no real reason for this.

Spacing between lines depends on several things. One is the size of the type being used. Another is the design of the type, whether it is big or small on the body. Type that is small on the body—that is, type that has a rather small *x* height for its point size—has more natural leading between lines than type that is big on the body, that has a large *x* height. Type styles that have large *x* heights need more spacing between lines.

**Fig. 4-12** *Some examples of appropriate word spacing.*

A line of 8pt. Garamond is too difficult to read with only a thin space

Its legibility is greatly improved when the words are separated

A narrow type needs much less space between the words

**A wide type needs much more space**

A type with a small x-height requires only a thin space

A type with a large x-height needs a thick space

*These rules illustrate space between lines.*
*Top to bottom: 1 point, 1½ points, 2 points, 3 points.*

It may be said of all printers that their job is to re-produce on paper the exact face of the letters which they have set into pages. This face is of a definite, constant and measurable size and shape; with any one press and any one paper there is a right and exact quan-

It may be said of all printers that their job is to reproduce on paper the exact face of the letters which they have set into pages. This face is of a definite, constant and measurable size and shape; with any one press and any one paper there is a right and exact quantity of ink and pressure necessary to re-

It may be said of all printers that their job is to reproduce on paper the exact face of the letters which they have set into pages. This face is of a definite, constant and measurable size and shape; with any one press and any one paper there is a right and exact quantity of ink and pressure necessary to re-

It may be said of all printers that their job is to reproduce on paper the exact face of the letters which they have set into pages. This face is of a definite, constant and measurable size and shape; with any one press and any one paper there is a right and exact quantity of ink and pressure necessary to re-

It may be said of all printers that their job is to reproduce on paper the exact face of the letters which they have set into pages. This face is of a definite, constant and measurable size and shape; with any one press and any one paper there is a right and exact quantity of ink and pressure necessary to re-

**Fig. 4-13** *Space for readability has two aspects: space between words and space between lines. The top copy block illustrates improper space between words. The other examples show the effects of various amounts of space between lines. (Reprinted with permission of Westvaco Corporation.)*

Here, again, there isn't exact scientific data to prove the ideal. However, experimentation and practice have given some clues. In a general way, the longer the type line the more spacing is needed between lines. For example, an 8-point type is selected for a 12-pica-wide line and 1 point of space is designated between lines. If the width of the line is increased to 18 picas, the message would be easier to read if the space between the lines would be increased to about 2 points. So a "subhint" for this general suggestion might be, when the line width is increased the space between lines should be increased, too.

This is even truer of display type, though we need to restate the rule as: the larger the type, the more space needed between lines. While 1 or 2 points of space between lines is fine for reading matter, when it comes to display type (type between 14 and 36 points and larger), a *slug* of space between lines is needed. A slug is the same as a lead but thicker. The standard slug used in printing is 6 points thick, but it can be thicker.

When a printer says "slug out that head," more space is needed between the lines. Slugging in heads and display lines is determined somewhat by the total layout. The relationship between the head and other elements, such as illustrations, on the page also needs to be considered.

However, we need to be aware that too much space between lines creates islands of black in a sea of white. If the lines of a head are too far apart, unity will be destroyed. The reader can become confused or waste time figuring out what the head is trying to say. The lines need to be properly spaced and also kept together so that they can be seen as a unit.

**Space between lines is just about right in this headline**

**There's too much**

**space between lines**

**in this headline**

**Space between lines is just about right in this headline**

**Fig. 4-14** *The traditional approach to line spacing is illustrated by the first two headlines. The last arrangement illustrates the "new wave graphics" approach in which minus or negative leading is used and lines are overlapped. The new wave approach can create an effective design unit but care must be taken to avoid ascenders and descenders colliding and destroying readability.*

## Remember the Margins

The *margins* (the white space) that surround a printed product are important elements for creating an attractive and effective communication. Margins act as frames for the page. If the margins are too small, the framing effect can be destroyed. The page will look cramped and crowded. Reading will be more difficult. If the margins are large enough to be strong frames for the page, they help unify the page, hold the layout together, and make reading easier and more pleasant.

Try this. Take a column of type and trim the margins as close to the type as you can. Read it. Now read a column with the margins intact. See how much easier it is to read? Although the margins are nothing but white space they hold the column together.

Margins can help set the mood of a printed communication. The traditional book margin is known as the *progressive margin*. This

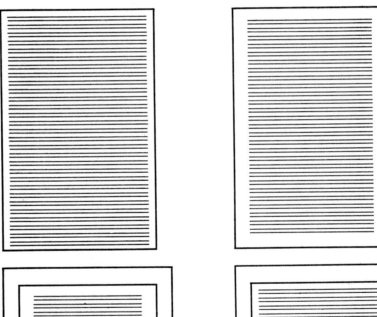

**Fig. 4-15**  *Margins are too small on the left and the page looks crowded and unattractive. The larger margins on the right frame the type and give it light, at the same time unifying the page.*

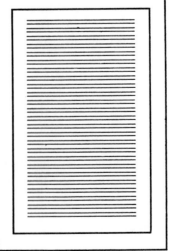

**Fig. 4-16**  *Proper use of margins with a border. The outside rectangle indicates the page, the inner is a border around the type. On the left, the margins between the type and border and the border and edge of page are the same. They should be unequal. On the right, the border is closer to the type for greater unity of type and border—it is better to have smaller margins inside than outside.*

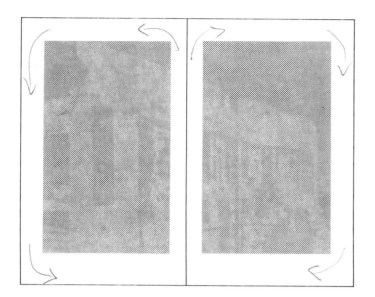

**Fig. 4-17** *Progressive margins. The margins increase in size counterclockwise on the left-hand page and clockwise on the right-hand page. The margin in the middle between the two pages is known as the gutter.*

means that the smallest margin on the page is the *gutter* margin (the area between two adjacent pages). The top-of-the-page margin is larger. The outside margin is larger than the top, and, finally, the bottom-of-the-page margin is the largest of all. In other words, the margins are progressively larger around the page.

Progressive margins help give a look of careful consideration that denotes quality to the reader. Some "class" magazines use progressive margins for this quality look. Progressive margins are also suitable for brochures describing museums, art festivals, cultural events, or menus of exclusive restaurants.

How much space on the page should be devoted to margins? A good rule of thumb to keep in mind is: About 50 percent of the printed page should be devoted to margins. This sounds excessive—half the page for margins! But consider this. Suppose we are designing a layout for a 9 by 12 page. That means there are 108 square inches of space on the page. If the 50 percent rule is followed, 54 square inches will be devoted to margins. On a 9 by 12 page that works out to a margin of less than 1½ inches around the printed part of the page—not excessive at all for a 9 by 12 page.

## Select the Proper Type Size

So far, we have picked out a type style for our message, determined that the columns or blocks of type will be one and a half times the lowercase alphabet in width, designated 2 points of space between the lines of body copy, and have designed the printed area to be about 50 percent of the page. Now, what size type should we select?

If the type is too small, it will be difficult to read. If the body type is too large, we cannot get all the copy on the page. If the sizes selected for headings or display lines are too large, they will dominate the page and it will look like a sale bill. If they are too small and cramped, they will not give the emphasis desired and they will not attract the attention of the people we want to read the message.

As with all decisions regarding the most effective way to produce the best possible piece of printing, the decision as to what size of type to use depends on other factors. These include such decisions as the type design, the line width, the amount of leading, and the type of audience involved. The decision about type size cannot be made alone but must be coordinated with other legibility factors.

However, there are some general rules that are worth considering.

Remember being cautioned to "read the fine print" in contracts and legal documents? It is not just to save paper that some printed pieces contain much "small print." It is a fact that the smaller the type the less likely it is to be read carefully. This is not to imply that small print means something devious is afoot. It is just to point out a truism of printing—the smaller the type, the more difficult it is to read. Rather than tackle the formidable task of reading small print, many people will skip it.

**Fig. 4-18** *Legibility of reading matter increases as the size of type is increased, but 12 point is the maximum size for legibility. [Reprinted from Ralph W. and Edwin Polk,* Practice of Printing *(Peoria, Ill.: Bennett Publishing Company, © 1971). Used with the permission of the publisher. All rights reserved.]*

The small sizes of body type are not as legible as larger ones. This paragraph is set in 6 point type, and it is far too small for ordinary reading matter, for it causes undue eye strain to make out the letter forms. Many of the ads now appearing in newspapers and periodicals contain types no larger than this and some are even harder to read than this paragraph is. Whenever possible, the use of such type should be avoided.

This paragraph appears in 8 point, and as you read it you are impressed with the greater ease with which it may be read. One may read it faster than the 6 point and with much less eye strain. However, it is still somewhat small for perfect ease in reading, as will be seen by a comparison with succeeding sizes.

When we get into 10 point type, we begin to get a sense of more comfortable, easy reading. The letters now are large enough that the eye can take them in at a rapid glance, without any strain or tension. This is a size of type found in many books and other reading matter, and we are quite familiar with it. Consequently, we read it with ease and speed. Ten point, leaded, is used for the body of this book.

We come to the highest degree of legibility when we consider the 12 point size of body type. A number of best authorities designate this size of type, leaded adequately, as offering the maximum of legibility in the mass, and being the most inviting to the eye of the reader. At any rate, the range of sizes for most satisfactory reading is around 10 and 12 point type.

At the other end of the scale, reading matter set in too large type takes longer to read. It occupies a larger area and simply requires more time to cover.

As always, there are no fixed rules. However, in a general way it has been found that the most legible size for type in newspapers, magazines, and books is between 9 and 12 points. Reading matter set in smaller or larger type is more difficult to read. A number of tests made by researchers through the years, some of them back in the late 1800s, have indicated that 11-point type is the most legible size for constant reading.

There are, however, situations in which a larger type should be selected. *Reverses* (white letters on a black background) require larger sizes for easier reading. Children and older people find larger type sizes more pleasant to read. Thus the audience should be kept in mind.

Type style should also be considered when specifying type size. Most decorative and novelty faces and Scripts and Cursives should be set in larger sizes. The unfamiliar letter forms make reading and comprehension more difficult. Larger sizes help overcome these problems.

Condensed types, except in short messages, should be set in larger sizes than the easier-to-read regular widths.

Sometimes it is a temptation to cram as much material as possible into the space available. There is a temptation to go to smaller type sizes. Text type set in 10 point will take up about 25 percent less space than text set in 12 point. It is tempting to take advantage of this obvious economy. However, remember that the objective is to have the message read and understood. If 12-point type will make the message easier to read and understand, it should be considered. If economy is important, the copy can be edited a little more tightly to preserve readability.

### Creative Communication

Rule 1—Ignore the rules!

There are general principles of type selection and arrangement, layout and design. But each communication situation is different. Each situation deserves a fresh approach.

Automatic application of established principles may not be the best creative solution. There are times when the most effective approach to a creative problem is to disregard the rules. This is especially true in the current design atmosphere when changes are occurring so rapidly.

If it is a good idea, give it a chance. Consider it, examine it, try it. Do not dismiss an idea just because it breaks out of the usual way of doing things.

However, do not let ignoring the rules lead to chaos on the drawing board or on the video screen. The ignore-the-rules rule should be used to release the creative capabilities of the mind.

## Mix Type Styles Carefully

Old-time printers knew what they were doing. They said, "If you start a job with Bookman, finish it with Bookman." They knew that the most attractive printed product was the one with the least amount of mixing of typefaces. Modern typographers call this the rule of *monotypographic harmony.*

Monotypographic harmony means that a harmonious layout will result if one family of type, or one design, is used throughout. Contrast and emphasis can be obtained by using type from different series of the same family, which will not sacrifice harmony. An attractive printed product will thus be produced with a minimum of typographic noise.

But there are times when faces must be mixed. Perhaps a certain emphasis or contrast is desired and a boldface or italic is not available in the family selected. Or we may decide a change of face

**Fig. 4-19** *Many type styles in one layout, (left) cause disharmony and confusion. The example on the right, set in one family, is neat, attractive, and unified.*

*Display Lines*

Differ from other elements in a

**Piece of Printing**

in that they attract

*Attention*

of the reader who should not be

**Confused**

by directing his attention to

**TOO MANY DISPLAY LINES**

Display Lines

Differ from other elements in
a piece of printing in
that they

ATTRACT THE
ATTENTION

of the reader who should not
be confused by directing his
attention to too many

Display Lines

This is Black Letter

This is Sans Serif

This is Black Letter

This is Sans Serif

**Fig. 4-20** *The Sans Serif at top is subordinated so that the two races are harmonious. When the Sans Serif is increased in size as in the bottom example, the two races begin to compete and harmony breaks down.*

is needed for contrast. When families are mixed, care should be taken to avoid mixing families of the same race, unless they are of a strongly contrasting design. For instance, the basic racial structures of Caslon and Garamond letters are the same: limited variation in the widths of letter strokes, slight diagonal slant at the thin point in bowls, and generally rounded serifs. However, each treats these basic characteristics differently. Confusion can thus result if these similar but different types are used together.

When faces are mixed, some means of contrast should be used to separate the two. One can be used for headlines and the other for body copy, for example. Or, one can be used in boldface or italic and the other in its regular form.

When two inharmonious types are used, one should be small. If a line of 24-point Black Letter is mixed with several lines of Sans Serif on the title page of a booklet, the Sans Serif lines should not be more than 10 or 12 point. The Black Letter, then, will dominate, and dissonance will be reduced to a minimum. This technique can often result in a very pleasing arrangement.

## Use All-Cap Lines Sparingly

There was a time when printers and typographers believed that the most legible letters were the old Roman capitals. However, it has been found without question that lowercase letters are more legible than capitals.

Use capital letters, but use them sparingly. The reasons for this can be summarized by two points: Lowercase letters have more character and they speed reading.

"Lowercase letters have more character" means that the letter forms of each letter in the lowercase alphabet are distinctive and not as easily confused as capitals, which have many similarities. Contrast, for example, the lowercase *c* and *g* with the capital *C* and

*G.* There is less likelihood of the reader confusing the letter forms in the lowercase line than in the all-capital line.

Research has shown that lowercase letters speed reading and are more pleasing to the reader. They do not tire the eye as easily as all-capital letters. Designers suggest that if all-capital letter lines are used, they should be limited to two or three lines at a time and the lines should be short. The lines should also have ample leading.

One recognized authority on legibility in print, Miles Tinker, in his *Legibility of Print*, says:

> In view of the evidence which demonstrates that capitals greatly retard speed of reading in comparison with lowercase and are not liked by readers, it would seem that all-capital printing should be eliminated whenever rapid reading and consumer views are considered. This would hold for continuous reading material, posters, car cards, billboards, magazine advertising copy, headings in books, business forms and records, table titles, titles on books, and many other kinds of printing.[3]

Some designers believe the worst typographic sin of all is setting Scripts, Cursives, or Black Letters in all capitals.

## 𝕮𝖔𝖛𝖊𝖓𝖆𝖓𝖙 𝕻𝖑𝖆𝖞𝖊𝖗𝖘

**Fig. 4-21** *Lowercase letters have more character and are less likely to be confused than capital letters.*

**Fig. 4-22** *Lines of Black Letter or ornamental types should never be set in all-capital letters: They can be virtually unreadable.*

## Do Not Be Boring

It is getting harder and harder to grab and hold the audience's attention. People today are bombarded from morning to night by efforts to make them listen or read. And there are scores of activities to fill leisure hours. In addition, people are becoming more and more conditioned to receiving information in short bits and takes. The average television news item is from 90 to 110 seconds long—barely 100 to 150 words. A half-hour television drama packs a complete story line from introduction to climax into about 22 minutes.

When modern readers are confronted with columns of reading matter, most will rebel. The reading matter looks forbidding and boring—there's nothing to catch the eye but line after line of type similar in size and tone. There is a temptation to skip it.

Long body matter can be made more attractive. There is no better way than to use that old standby, white space. It is so easy and yet so many editors and designers seem reluctant to take advantage of this natural way to brighten a page.

If fairly narrow columns are used on a page (say, ones that do not exceed about 12 picas), three columns of type can be used in a four-column space, increasing the white space between columns. Five columns of type can be set in a six-column space.

Occasional indented paragraphs can also help. Or, if type is set all flush left with no paragraph indentation (the usual indentation is 1 em for lines up to 18 picas wide), an extra lead or two of space between paragraphs can be used. Shorter paragraphs can also help, takovich orchestration but sticking to Rimsky's plan for the text. The production, which was first seen at La Scala nearly two decades ago, is by the same Nicola Benois who designed *Ernani* but there is a world of difference in the two. I saw Benois's *Khovanshchina* in Chicago in 1976, and the sets are as colorful as Rimsky's or-

## Nobody sings choral music better than the Russians.

chestration; how they will work with the more somber Shostakovich is

**B**UT TIMES HAVE NOT always been this good. Lauper was raised by a hard working, waitress mother in Brooklyn. She was a self-destructive teenager, a runaway at 17, and no stranger to drugs and alcohol—the girl next door gone astray. Feeling herself a misfit, she fled to Vermont, worked a series of menial

**P**OPE JOHN PAUL II HIMSELF HAS EXpressed outrage over the possibility of nuclear war. As he said in his peace message to the United Nations a year ago:

"ANY NUCLEAR WAR INEVITABLY would produce death, illness and suffering of such gigantic proportions and scale that no effective medical action would be possible. Recent declarations to the effect that

**T**HE NEXT MORNING SHE COMES down late to find Annie back from the grocery putting food in the refrigerator and talking to her grandmother.

"Gram, I've brought you yogurt. Bulgarians live over a hundred years and they eat yogurt every day."

"I tried yogurt once, and it's terrible. So sour," her grandmother says. Annie, being polite, ignores this and continues. "And

## Don't Tread on Me

While Ferrari is willing to wait for quality opportunities ("I'll starve if it means I can sleep in"), he is actively working on certain aspects of his career. "I'm giving a publicity firm $2,500 a month to deal with people

**Fig. 4-23** *Some examples of ways to break the flow of type to make a page look more inviting.*

especially when narrow columns are being used. Long paragraphs of reading matter slow reading and look formidable.

Subheads with a contrasting face or boldface or a larger size of type than the body type can help break up the gray flow of type. Occasional italics where appropriate can also make the page more inviting. They will give emphasis where it is wanted, as well.

Sometimes variety can be obtained if copy is set *ragged right*. This means setting the left lines even but allowing the lines to end at natural breaks instead of justifying them. Studies have shown that ragged right does not slow reading. But ragged left should be used with caution. It is fine for limited use such as in the cutlines that

**Fig. 4-24** *Type set ragged left (left) should be avoided except in short sections because it slows reading. Type set ragged right (right) has the same reading ease as justified (even margins both left and right sides) type.*

Today, the concentrations are not quite as spectacular, but this same part of Utah, now known as the Bear River Migratory Bird Refuge, is still a powerful magnet for nomadic creatures. In autumn, visitors can see a half-million ducks and geese in a single day at the 65,000-acre federal preserve. Located at the eastern edge of the Pacific Flyway—one of four major north-south migration routes in the U.S.—the refuge also serves as the crossroads for birds flying into the central states. Some 200 species.

Today, the concentrations are not quite as spectacular, but this same part of Utah, now known as the Bear River Migratory Bird Refuge, is still a powerful magnet for nomadic creatures. In autumn, visitors can see a half-million ducks and geese in a single day at the 65,000-acre federal preserve. Located at the eastern edge of the Pacific Flyway—one of four major north-south migration routes in the U.S.—the refuge also serves as the crossroads for birds flying into the central states. Some 200 species.

identify illustrations, but it does slow reading, and most readers will skip long messages set in ragged left.

Sometimes, long body copy can be broken up with typographic devices—bullets, stars, dashes, and other dingbats. But they should be used cautiously. When overdone they disfigure the page and make the layout look amateurish.

*Initial* letters can add spice to a page. These large letters at the start of paragraphs are a valuable typographic device. They can brighten up the page and they can help guide the reader.

There are a few suggestions designers recommend in using initial letters. Initials should never be used at the top of a column except at the beginning of an article. When an initial is used at the top of a column it is a signal to the reader that this is the point where reading should begin. If an initial is used at the top of a column that does not begin the article, the reader might still think it is the beginning point and be confused.

Also, care should be used in placing initials so they do not appear side by side in adjacent columns when the copy is set in type. Initials should be scattered so they create unity and balance and their weights serve a design purpose.

## Avoid Oddball Placement

This is the easiest rule of all to follow. All this recommendation means is that types were meant to be read from left to right in straight lines. Curved lines, horizontal lines, and lines on an angle should be avoided. Of course, there are times when it can be effective to set type in a curve or on an angle to create a special effect or in certain situations such as designing logos and seals.

Oddball placement should not be done just to be different. And it should be done with caution. Lines of type in curves or on an angle should be kept to a minimum—no more than two or three words, if possible.

Communicators should avoid typographic affectations. Of course, Edward Estlin Cummings (e. e. cummings) used eccentricities of language, typography, and punctuation as a trademark for his works of poetry, and he became famous. But for straightforward professional printed communications, unusual gimmicks should be avoided unless such devices will really improve communication. If they are used, they should be limited and considered, as one designer points out, like jewelry for the typographic dress. They can be overdone very easily.

## Spell It Out

Whether we set the type or order it set by a compositor, we must write out all instructions and be sure the instructions are perfectly clear. Typesetting costs will be reduced and better quality will result

---

**Tips for Ordering Typesetting**

The following suggestions for ordering typeset matter can save money and help ensure that the finished product will be what you wanted.

■ Specify the typefaces for reading matter and headings and make certain that the printer has these faces and sizes. If this is not certain, the notation "or equivalent" should be included on the purchase order or instructions.

■ Specify the type size in points. If you are not certain exactly what size you want, do not hesitate to ask the compositor to recommend a size.

■ For reading matter, keep the line measure about 39 characters. Remember that one and a half times the lowercase alphabet is considered an ideal measure.

■ Give the line measure (width) in picas, not in inches.

■ Specify any copy that is to run ragged. Otherwise the compositor will justify the lines.

■ Designate the leading desired (the space between the lines).

■ If other than normal reproduction proofs are desired, specify *Avery* for adhesive-backed paper, *dull seal* for transparent paper with an adhesive back, and *cell* for transparent paper without an adhesive back; or specify the particular paper desired.

**Fig. 4-25** *The designer may use creativity in type arrangement to transmit an idea by form as well as by meaningful words. (Courtesy of Granite Graphics)*

Dance Music From 30s
To 80s Contemporary Rock Disco
Jewish Israeli Folk Dance Hamish Show
Tunes Big Bands Pop Kleizmer Chassidic Latin
Soft Rock Middle Eastern Spanish Italian Yiddish
Schmaltz French Irish Greek Russian Jazz Classical
Oriental Muzak Continental Dance Music From 30s To 80s
Contemporary Rock Disco Jewish Israeli Folk Dance Hamish
Show Tunes Big Bands Pop Kleizmer Chassidic Latin Soft Rock
Middle Eastern Spanish Italian Yiddish Schmaltz French Irish
Greek Russian Jazz Classical Oriental Muzak Continental Dance
Music From 30s To 80s Contemporary Rock Disco Jewish Israeli Folk
Dance Hamish Show Tunes Big Bands Pop Kleizmer Chassidic Latin
Soft Rock Middle Eastern Spanish Italian Yiddish Schmaltz French
Irish Greek Russian Jazz Classical Oriental Muzak Continental Dance
Music From 30s To 80s Contemporary Rock Disco Jewish Israeli Folk
Dance Hamish Show Tunes Big Bands Pop Kleizmer Chassidic Latin Soft
Rock Middle Eastern Spanish Italian Yiddish Schmaltz French Irish Greek
Russian Jazz Classical Oriental Muzak Continental Dance Music From 30s
To 80s Contemporary Rock Disco Jewish Israeli Folk Dance Hamish Show
Tunes Big Bands Pop Kleizmer Chassidic Latin Soft Rock Middle Eastern
Spanish Italian Yiddish Schmaltz French Irish Greek Russian Jazz Classical
Oriental Muzak Continental Dance Music From 30s To 80s Contemporary Rock
Disco Jewish Israeli Folk Dance Hamish Show Tunes Big Bands Pop Kleizmer
Chassidic Latin Soft Rock Middle Eastern Spanish Italian Yiddish Schmaltz
French Irish Greek Russian Jazz Classical Oriental Muzak Continental Dance Mu-
sic From 30s To 80s Contemporary Rock Disco Jewish Israeli Folk Dance Hamish
Show Tunes Big Bands Pop Kleizmer Chassidic Latin Soft Rock Middle Eastern Span-
ish Italian Yiddish Schmaltz French Irish Greek Russian Jazz Classical Oriental Muzak
Continental Dance Music From 30s To 80s Contemporary Rock Disco Jewish Israeli Folk
Dance Hamish Show Tunes Big Bands Pop Kleizmer Chassidic Latin Soft Rock Middle Eastern
Spanish Italian Yiddish Schmaltz French Irish Greek Russian Jazz Classical Oriental Muzak Con-
tinental Dance Music From 30s To 80s Contemporary Rock Disco Jewish Israeli Folk Dance Hamish
Show Tunes Big Bands Pop Kleizmer Chassidic Latin Soft Rock Middle Eastern Spanish Italian Yiddish
Schmaltz French Irish Greek Russian Jazz Classical Oriental Muzak Continental Dance Music From 30s To 80s
Contemporary Rock Disco Jewish Israeli Folk Dance Hamish Show Tunes Big Bands Pop Kleizmer Chassidic
Latin Soft Rock Middle Eastern Spanish Italian Yiddish Schmaltz French Irish Greek Russian Jazz Classical Ori-
ental Muzak Continental Dance Music From 30s To 80s Contemporary Rock Disco Jewish Israeli Folk Dance
Hamish Show Tunes Big Bands Pop Kleizmer Chassidic Latin Soft Rock Middle Eastern Spanish Italian Yiddish
Schmaltz French Irish Greek Russian Jazz Classical Oriental Muzak Continental Dance Music From 30s To 80s
Contemporary Rock Disco Jewish Israeli Folk Dance Hamish Show Tunes Big Bands Pop Kleizmer Chassidic Latin
Soft Rock Middle Eastern Spanish Italian Yiddish Schmaltz French Irish Greek Russian Jazz Classical Oriental
Muzak Continental Dance Music From 30s To 80s Contemporary Rock Disco Jewish Israeli Folk Dance Hamish
Show Tunes Big Bands Pop Kleizmer Chassidic Latin Soft Rock Middle Eastern Spanish Italian Yiddish Schmaltz
French Irish Greek Russian Jazz Classical Oriental Muzak Continental Dance Music From 30s To 80s Contem-
porary Rock Disco Jewish Israeli Folk Dance Hamish Show Tunes Big Bands Pop Kleizmer Chassidic Latin Soft
Rock Middle Eastern Spanish Italian Yiddish Schmaltz French Irish Greek Russian Jazz Classical Oriental Muzak
Continental Dance Music From 30s To 80s Contemporary Rock Disco Jewish Israeli Folk Dance Hamish Show
Tunes Big Bands Pop Kleizmer Chassidic Latin Soft Rock Middle Eastern Spanish Italian Yiddish Schmaltz French
Irish Greek Russian Jazz Classical Oriental Muzak Continental Dance Music From 30s To 80s Contemporary Rock
Disco Jewish Israeli Folk Dance Hamish Show Tunes Big Bands Pop Kleizmer Chassidic Latin Soft Rock Middle
Eastern Spanish Italian Yiddish Schmaltz French Irish Greek Russian Jazz Classical Oriental Muzak Continental
Dance Music From 30s To 80s Contemporary Rock Disco Jewish Israeli Folk Dance Hamish Show Tunes Big Bands
Pop Kleizmer Chassidic Latin Soft Rock Middle Eastern Spanish Italian Yiddish Schmaltz French Irish Greek Rus-
sian Jazz Classical Oriental Muzak Continental Dance Music From 30s To 80s Contemporary Rock Disco Jewish
Israeli Folk Dance Hamish Show Tunes Big Bands Pop Kleizmer Chassidic Latin Soft Rock Middle Eastern Span-
ish Italian Yiddish Schmaltz French Irish Greek Russian Jazz Classical Oriental Muzak Continental Dance Music

when the compositor is given clear instructions concerning all requirements. It is an old axiom in the printing trade that the compositor follows copy mistakes and all "even if it flies out the window." So what is sent to the printer is what will come back.

Before ordering any typesetting minimize problems by reading the copy and correcting errors in spelling, punctuation, capitalization, and so on. Check the copy for paragraph numbering, if any, as well as indentation, page numbering, and general format. Changes made to the typed copy should be neat and legible and written in lowercase or capital letters just the way they should be set in type.

Copy should be double spaced, typed on one side of a sheet, and paginated in sequence, preferably in the upper right-hand corner of each page. Long tables and other matter that is to be set in a special way should be typed on separate pages.

## Effective Design Checklist

- The design of a letter can "talk" to the reader. Select a type style that will reinforce the message.
- In a general way, Romans are preferred for body type.
- One and a half times the width of the lowercase alphabet is considered the proper line width for easy reading.
- Words crowded too closely together or spaced too far apart are difficult to read.
- One or two points of leading or space between lines is about right for reading matter (body type).
- As the length of the line is increased, the space between the lines should be increased.
- Generally, the larger sizes of body types are the easiest to read. Stick to between (and including) 9 and 12 point for body type.
- Margins that together occupy about 50 percent of the area are considered about right.
- Use a larger-size type for reverses. Reverses are more effective if the types are simple in design. Fine serifs should be avoided.
- Most Miscellaneous, Novelty, decorative, and condensed types should be set in larger sizes for better legibility.
- Type styles should be mixed with care. When two very different styles are used, one should dominate.
- In most cases, families of the same race of types should not be mixed.
- All-capital lines are difficult to read and their use should be limited.
- Long amounts of body copy should be broken up for easier reading. Subheads, indented paragraphs, and other devices can help.
- Ragged right does not seem to reduce readability, but ragged left does and should be used sparingly.

## Graphics in Action

1. Find examples in publications of improper use of type and explain what is wrong with them. Mount the examples on plain white paper with your analysis included.
2. Explain the points to keep in mind for selecting and arranging type. Illustrate the points with examples clipped from publications.
3. Find examples of type styles that appear to be poor choices for the messages involved. Then find examples that appear to be excellent selections. Analyze the examples and support your decisions regarding them.

**4.** Select typefaces from those in the appendix (or other sources of type specimens) that seem best suited to help say the following (or similar) phrases:

Country Barn Dance
Paris in the Spring
Trans-Siberian Express
Notre Dame Cathedral
Final Clearance Sale

**5.** Tear out an assortment (fifteen to twenty or so) of small pieces about 1 by 2 or 2 by 3 inches each of body matter type from publications (nothing larger than 12 point). Paste them (use rubber cement) in a free-flowing arrangement to make a collage on plain white paper. Compare the types and select the ones that appeal to you most. Explain the reasons for your selections (type design, size, space between lines, big on body, and so on). Identify the types discussed by race (and family, if you can).

## Notes

[1] Frederic W. Goudy, *Typologia* (Berkeley, Calif.: University of California Press, 1940), p. 80.
[2] Miles A. Tinker, *Legibility of Print* (Ames, Iowa: Iowa State University Press, 1963), pp. 44-66.
[3] Tinker, p. 61.

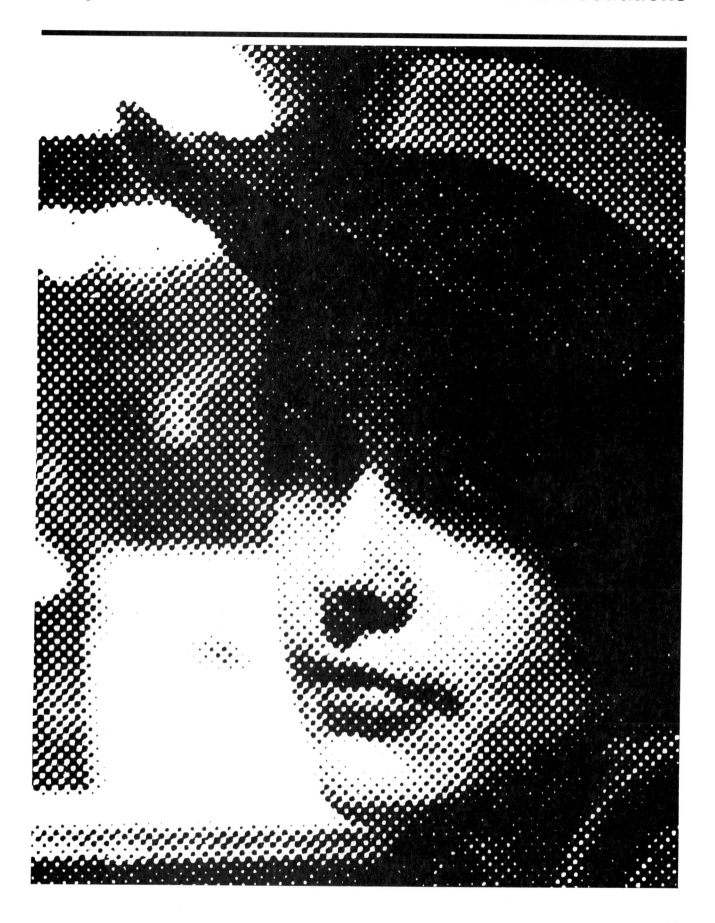

Of course, it takes more than type printed on paper to make a successful communication. There are a number of other elements, or tools, which can be used to make a message more attractive and effective. These elements include art, ornaments and borders, rules, paper, color, and even the ink used in printing. Each can add a dimension to the final product.

Conversely, these elements can ruin the effectiveness of a printed piece if applied haphazardly or used improperly. The communicator who works with type, much like an artist, interior decorator, architect, or any other creative person, must know the characteristics of all the elements and what each can contribute to the finished product. And the communicator must know how to use them.

It is not necessary to know the technology of making these various elements, however. For instance, it is not necessary to know the properties of the chemicals used in engraving, or the parts of the plate-making device for making a printing plate. But it is necessary to know what can be done to a photograph to make it printable. The communicator must know how to prepare material

**Fig. 5-1** *Ron Pettit, technical illustrator for Deere & Company, created this art to demonstrate the complexity of the cutaway technique. It also demonstrates the power of graphics to communicate complicated information in an understandable manner in this "age of graphics." (Reprinted courtesy of* J D Journal, *worldwide corporate magazine of Deere & Company.)*

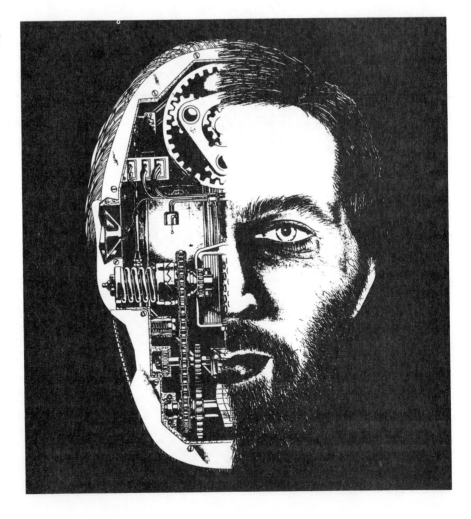

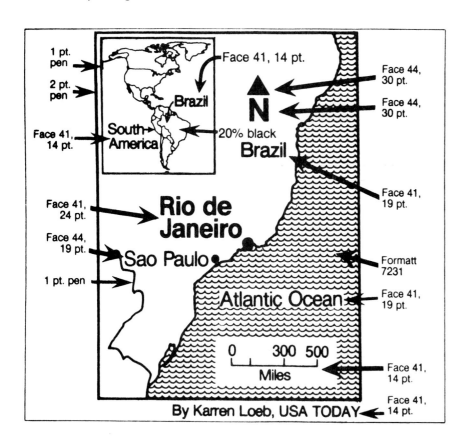

**Fig. 5-2** *This map was created by Karren Loeb of* USA Today *to demonstrate the creation of a graphic for that newspaper. Note the precise specifications for type and rules. The maps are made twice the size they will appear in the newspaper and then reduced for printing. (© 1983. Reprinted with permission.)*

for printing and how to transmit instructions properly to get the results desired.

Quite often art, illustrations, borders, and ornaments can be obtained and used effectively at a relatively low cost. Proper use of them involves knowledge more than it does money. Effective art need not be expensive. A border of proper size and design to harmonize with the other elements in a layout costs no more than one that will cause discord and dissonance in the message.

## This Is a Graphics Age

We are living in an age of graphics. More and more attention is being paid to the role of art in printed communications. Artists are moving into the editorial rooms of newspapers. Wire services are supplying more graphics to their clients.

"Graphics more and more are becoming part of a newspaper's face. They are a different visual dimension at a time when newspapers are increasingly more than just type with a picture here and there to break up the gray," a lead article in the *AP Log*, the in-house publication of the Associated Press, reports.[1]

"We live in a more visual world; television does great graphics; people are more cognizant of color photography; newsmagazines have established trends in informational graphics," Richard Curtis told members of the American Society of Newspaper Editors.[2] (Curtis is the managing editor for graphics of the newspaper *USA Today.*)

*Informational graphics*, Curtis pointed out, are graphics that both illustrate and inform. He noted that editors who learn about graphics can produce publications that will be better vehicles for communicating information. Some information is communicated more effectively through graphics than words.

Graphics can improve readability; they can clarify, attract attention, add realism to writing, and explain complicated information. Of course, they can entertain. How often have you leafed through a magazine and read the cartoons before settling down to the serious articles?

Graphics can provide information in an easily understandable form. They can amplify the text or set a mood. They can help create a pleasing design.

## From Idea to Printed Page

If the best results are to be obtained, we must understand how art gets from an idea to the printed page. We also need to learn ways to make art and photographs more effective. In addition, we need to know how to crop and size art.

We also need to know the various ways cutlines can be handled as well as how to pass along instructions to the printers so that we obtain the results we want. Soon, communicators will need to know how to instruct a computer to produce finished layouts and even printing plates ready to clamp on the press.

If this all sounds formidable, don't despair. It is a rare professional illustrator who can handle *all* the art forms and techniques available. Some designers may be superior photographers. Others may be great at retouching and finishing. Generally, special effects are rendered by skillful artists who have developed distinctive techniques in their respective fields. Photography is so encompassing that it is a profession in itself.

It is useless for the editor or designer of a small publication, or the public relations professional, or the newspaper editor to get bogged down in the technicalities of the design and production of art. However, the same person must have a knowledge of what can be done graphically. Basically this involves knowing how to obtain, process, and place art in a layout so that it will be effective and affordable.

Where to start?

The first function of any communication is to attract the attention of its target audience. Judicious employment of an illustration can help.

Do not forget that this is a visual age. Children are propped in front of a continuous visual parade before they can read or write. More people watch television than read books. This can, however, work to our advantage. Since people are oriented toward the visual, we can use this orientation to make them want to read. The trick is to employ art that amplifies words.

These days, printed communications must be powerful indeed to hold readers without the use of art. People will usually not pay attention to words alone, unless those words really tell them what they want to hear.

But if art is used, it must be of high quality. It must be simple, well done, and get to the point quickly. Superfluous art can be worse than no art at all. It can distract the reader and dominate the layout. It can communicate the message "here's a sensational picture, look at it and don't bother to read the words on this page."

## Keeping Graphics Simple

Keeping graphics simple leads readers to a quicker and more comprehensive understanding of the information, the graphics staff of *USA Today* told editors. They pointed out in their publication *ASNE Today* (May 1983) that "if the graphic is easy to produce and easy to read, the information within will be easily understood."

Art can help the communicator do a number of things. It can help set the mood for the message. For instance, it can help give a feeling of peace and contentment. It can help say "Sit up and pay attention to this," or "Sit back, relax, and enjoy."

Want peace and serenity? How better to portray it than with a scene of a couple observing a quiet lake at sunrise, or a calm sea at sunset?

Want to show discontent? A picture can create this mood more effectively than perhaps the legendary 1,000 words. But the picture must be selected carefully and properly cropped and processed and unified with the other elements in the layout. An improperly selected and presented piece of art can be as ineffective as, perhaps, 1,000 poorly written words. Also remember that these mood pieces

**Fig. 5-3** *This illustration of an owl was used in a television graphic to give added impact to the late show announcement.*

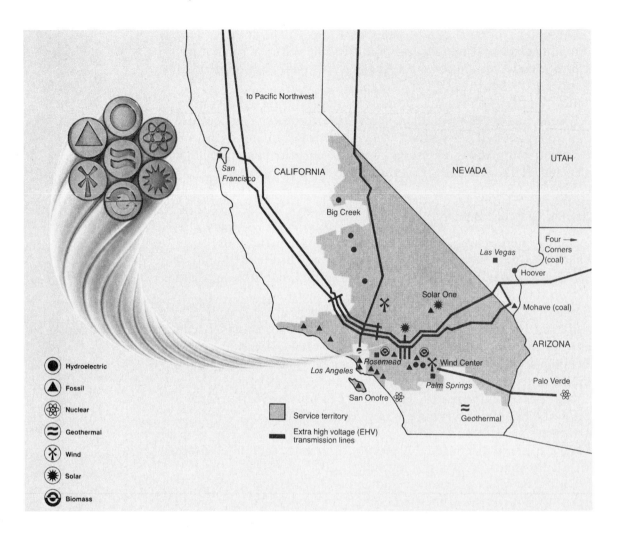

**Fig. 5-4**  *Symbolic art can create identity and unity. The Southern California Edison Company uses symbols to indicate types of energy in its annual report. The symbols are grouped to communicate the complete energy message and then used individually to identify sections of the report dealing with each type of energy.*

**Fig. 5-5**  *Simplicity is the key to effective symbol design. The* Minneapolis Tribune *used this simple symbol of a roll of paper going through the press to give immediate recognition to its publication. (Courtesy of* Minneapolis Tribune.)

of art must tie in with the message being printed. They must not just be thrown in because they are attractive and the communicator believes readers will like them.

Art can also be effective in showing a situation or explaining a situation in sequence. And it can be used effectively for identity. Most people are familiar with a number of trademark characters that have been used effectively by corporations. This identity value can be extended to printed communications, too. For example, the *Minneapolis Tribune*, when it was redesigned, adopted a simple symbol of a web-fed press and used it effectively in nameplate, masthead, section pages, and column headings to create continuity and identity.

The first step in working with art, then, is to evaluate the message we want to tell. Can graphics do it better? Can art help the audience understand what we are trying to say? Will art attract attention? Will it make the layout more interesting, more entertaining? Will art help guide the reader through the message in proper sequence? Will it help create identity? Will the layout be improved with art?

If the answer is yes to any of these questions, the next step is deciding on the right piece of art and obtaining it.

## Approaches to Using Art

On large publications the editor doesn't have to worry about obtaining the right art, that's the art director's job. But even though editors may not have to be involved with the technical side of this part of the layout process, they do need to understand art and artists. Both people need to work together, and this is not always easy.

Too often editors are oriented toward words and artists think "design" first and communication of the message last. It is not unusual for editors and art directors to have differing opinions as they view the finished product from their individual perspectives.

However, this situation is changing as each develops a greater understanding of the value of teamwork in producing effective printed communications. Editors are becoming more knowledgeable about art and design, and designers are developing a greater understanding of how words are used and arranged for readability. This spirit of teamwork will go far in providing effective and attractive publications.

There are about 9,000 business and trade publications in the United States. Many of these are company papers and magazines aimed at employees or other special audiences. In addition, there are scores of newsletters issued by various organizations and interest groups. Add to this small daily newspapers and the more than 8,000 weekly newspapers and you have a vast number of publications.

Many entry jobs in communications are in these small publications, and many successful and satisfying lifetime careers can be had in editorial and production positions with these publications.

There are giant publications with their large editorial and design staffs and small publications with a single person performing all the editorial and design functions. There are firms and publications that can afford to hire free-lance artists and designers to assist them on a limited basis. And in all these situations the editor must know something about selecting and processing art.

Once the decision is made to use art, the next step is to decide whether a photograph or line art will be most effective. _Line art_ is a term for straight black-and-white images as opposed to photographs with continuous tones from black to white, including all the grays in between.

In selecting art, the key word, as in all things typographical, is _reader._ The audience must be kept in mind at all times. Consideration should be given to the sort of art a particular audience will relate to and find appealing. (This can be determined by research carried out during the planning stages for the communication.)

In addition to the content questions regarding the most suitable art for a layout, there are some technical qualities to check. Will the art produce well on the type of paper selected or the printing process to be used for the job? Photographs usually do not produce well on antique or coarse finished paper. They need paper with a

### Creative Communication

Try this: On a blank piece of paper, using only your imagination, sketch a trademark that says: Made in (use your state or city).

Now try this: Select a concrete item such as a desk or a tree and see how many ideas you can come up with for its use in a layout.

Or this: Select an abstract word such as _love, kindness,_ or _wealth_ and see how many ideas you can come up with for illustrations to "say" this word.

Or this: Select a saying such as "a penny saved is a penny earned" and see how many possibilities you can come up with for illustrations that might accompany that saying in a layout and help communicate the message.

You've been creative!

Try to analyze how you arrived at your solutions to these problems.

**Fig. 5-6**   *One of the first decisions to be made in using art is to decide whether to use continuous tone art, as in the photograph above (left), or line art. Line art (right) can give the illusion of continuous tone through shading but it is only blacks and whites. (Eastman Kodak)*

**Fig. 5-7**   *Graphics can translate complicated information quickly and create high reader interest. This graphic was produced by the staff of USA Today to demonstrate effective visual communication for an American Society of Newspaper Editors seminar.*

PEACEFUL STANDOFF

Warm air pushing north from the Gulf of Mexico and Atlantic has reached a standoff with slightly cooler air pushing south from Canada creating a stationary front. The result: Generally calm weather across the eastern half of the nation. Small storms will form along the front, bringing showers and thunderstorms, but they are expected to be short lived.

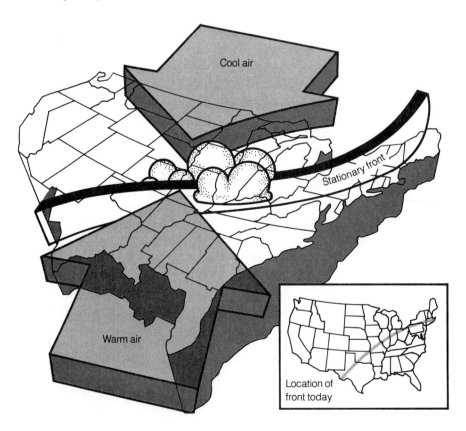

smooth, even high gloss finish to bring out all of their definition and contrast. (Paper will be discussed in Chapter 7.)

One approach to selecting the proper art is to consider the content of the message. Some art directors like to use photographs for non-fiction to reinforce the sense of realism they wish to achieve. Photographs transmit a sense of authenticity. Some art directors like to use drawings for fiction. Schematic drawings are often helpful. Charts and graphs help explain complicated economic situations. Maps illuminate the national weather situation and foreign affairs.

Nigel Holmes, chart designer for *Time* magazine, has the job of reducing complex news and events involving statistics to attractive and easy-to-understand art forms, mainly charts. The challenge, Holmes says, is "to present statistics as a visual idea rather than a tedious parade of numbers. Without being frivolous, I want to entertain the reader as well as inform him."

### Sources of Art

Today about the only restricting factor is the limit of the imagination of the communicator. Those who do not have an art director to do the job or the funds to hire a professional artist, photographer, or photo researcher should learn to locate art themselves.

There are a number of firms that supply *stock art*. This is art that is prepared and sold in a variety of sizes, shapes, and subjects. The firms usually offer *clip art* books or catalogs. These are available in scores of subjects from seasonal topics to special events. Each book contains art of various sizes that can be cut out and pasted into a layout. They are camera ready and simple to use.

However, many designers consider this form of illustration an inferior substitute for art specifically produced for a specific layout situation. They note that often it is difficult to find just the exact illustration for the creative idea in a clip art collection and that the quality of work in some collections is inferior.

Sources of illustrations include public relations firms, chambers of commerce, state departments of tourism and economic development, and museums and historical societies. Quite often art can be borrowed from other publications, and usually they ask for only a modest fee or that a credit line be given.

---

> **Tips for Handling Art**
>
> ■ Don't use sharp pencils or ballpoint pens to mark instructions on art. It is easy to make impressions that will show up in the finished plate and in the printing.
>
> ■ Avoid using paper clips and other devices to hold art and instructions together. They can cause creases that might show up in the printing. Use masking tape or write instructions on a protective flap.
>
> ■ Keep art flat. Don't roll up or fold.
>
> ■ Use a *slip sheet* to protect art. This is a cover made of tracing or light paper. It is attached to the underside of the art with rubber cement and folded over the top. It acts as both a cover for the art and a frame to indicate the part to be used, if an area is drawn on it to indicate cropping during plate making.

---

## The Two Basic Types of Art

Art comes in two basic forms—*illustrations* and *photographs*. *Line art*, such as pen-and-ink drawings, consists of definable lines of black and white space. There are a number of techniques that the artist can employ to give a shaded effect to these drawings, but basically they consist of just black lines or dots and white space.

A photograph consists of black and white and all the tones between—thus the term *continuous tone* art. The difference

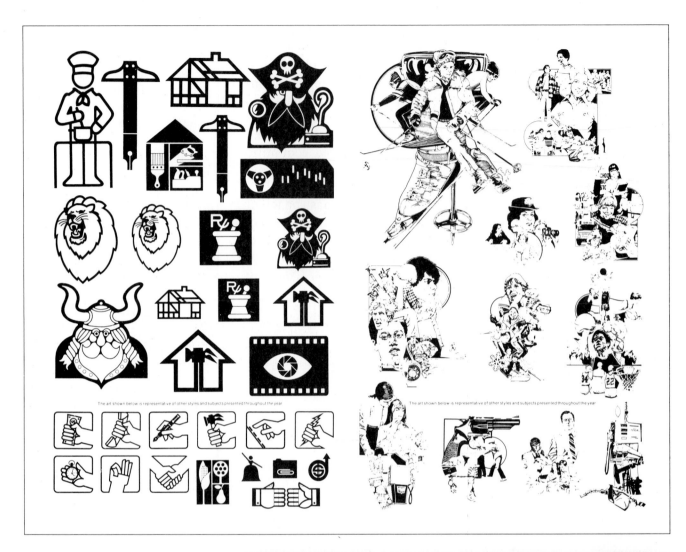

**Fig. 5-8** *Among the many sources of art for the editor or designer who cannot create it are stock or clip art services. These are pages from a clip art service by Dynamic Graphics.*

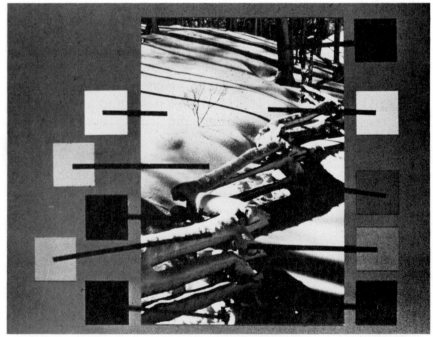

**Fig. 5-9** *A photograph consists of continuous tones from black to white (or light to dark), as shown at right. When the photograph is screened, the resulting dot structure permits printing to a very close approximation of the tones of the original. (Eastman Kodak)*

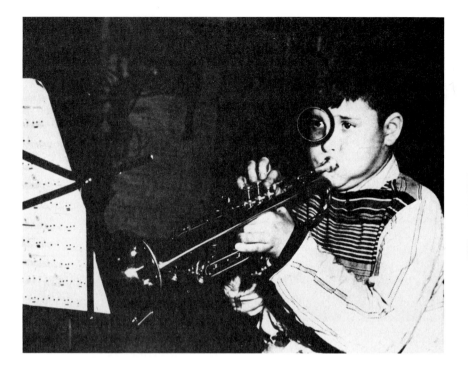

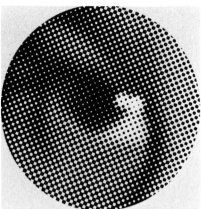

**Fig. 5-10** *When this photograph is processed for printing it will be rephotographed through a screen and the resulting negative used to produce a printing plate. The circled area is shown enlarged in the following photo so the configuration of dots that give the illusion of continuous tone can be seen. (Eastman Kodak)*

**Fig. 5-11** *(above) A greatly enlarged view of the circled portion of the previous illustration shows the dot structure created by photographing the original through a screen. The screened negative is then used to make a printing plate. (Eastman Kodak)*

between continuous tone art and line art is important to understand because each requires different treatment.

No matter what printing method is used, continuous tone art must be converted to black and white tones. This is done by photographing the image through a finely ruled screen. This produces a negative that consists of tones reduced to a dot formation. Since it is believed that half of the original image is lost in this process and half of the full tone remains, the resulting printing plate is called a *halftone.*

The screen used for making halftones comes in a variety of numbers of lines per inch, usually from 65 to 133. The greater the number of lines per inch, the finer the detail of the printing plate. For high-quality reproduction, a fine screen and a high-gloss or very smooth-finish paper is used.

If a fine-screen halftone is printed on coarse paper, such as newsprint, the resulting print will look muddy. Most newspaper halftones are made with about an 85 screen for best results. One of the advantages of newspaper production by offset is that a smoother-finished paper is used, and finer screened photographs can be used for better reproduction than with most letterpress newspaper operations.

In making plates from line art no screen is used and the resulting plate is an exact duplicate of the art.

Photography is playing an increasingly important role in printed communications. It is a major tool in converting art to printing plates, and it can be utilized to produce a vast array of special effects for presenting this art on the printed page.

**Fig. 5-12** *Prints from negatives of the same subject made with screens of varying sizes. The 85-line screen is used for printing on rough paper such as newsprint and the very fine 200-line screen is used for smooth-finished and high-gloss papers. (Eastman Kodak)*

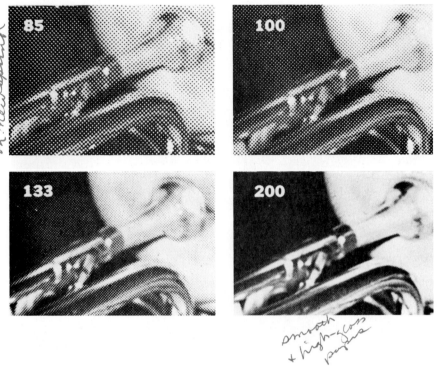

One example is called *line conversion.* In this process, continuous tone copy, or photographs, are converted to line art for printing. Examples include reproducing a photograph so it looks like a drawing; making various finishes that look like antique matting; exaggerating dot structures and such things to make the art look as if it is constructed of all sorts of circles, lines, squares, and shaded effects.

All this is done by placing a screen or film between the lens and the unexposed film and taking a picture to produce a negative for plate making.

**Fig. 5-13** *A cross section of a camera used for making halftones. The screen is placed in front of the film, and then the continuous tone art is photographed to produce a screened negative. (Eastman Kodak)*

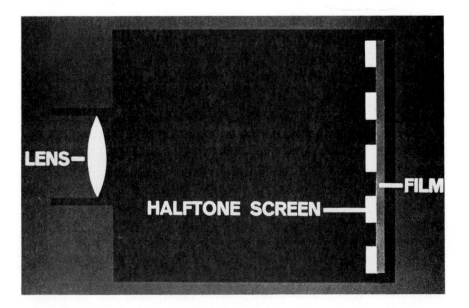

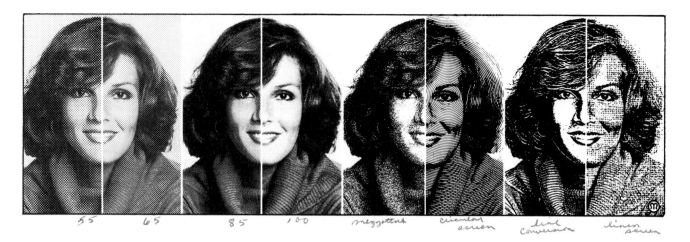

55   65   85   100   mezzotint   circular screen   line conversion   linen screen

Although such special effects have surprise value or help set a special mood, they should be used sparingly. An example of how these special effects can be useful is the conversion of a photograph to line art for printing on antique or very coarse paper that might not print the photograph well. Also, it is usually a good design principle to avoid mixing line and halftone art in the same layout. Thus, if, for instance, "mug shots" (head-and-shoulder photographs of people) are to be used in a brochure along with some line drawings, it might be much more attractive to do a line conversion of the photos.

Communicators should be familiar with the capabilities of photographer, production department, or printer to produce these special effects and take advantage of them when they will help in the production of more effective layouts.

**Fig. 5-14** *Eight of the many ways illustrations can be handled. In these examples a photograph was shot, left to right, with a 55-line, 65-line, 85-line, and 100-line screen. The left of the third face is a mezzotint, while a circular screen was used on the right. The photo on the far right was shot, left, as a line conversion, and the right shows the effect of a linen texture screen. (Reproduced with the permission of Metro Associated Services, Inc.)*

## Preparing Art for Printing

Regardless of whether a photograph or a drawing is selected, there are certain steps that must be taken to prepare the art for printing. These include cropping, sizing, and retouching.

### Cropping Art

*Cropping* is the process of removing unwanted material or content or changing the size or direction of the art. It isn't just haphazard chopping away at a photograph or drawing. It is judicious editing with an eye toward enhancing the effectiveness and design characteristics of the art.

Art is usually cropped:

- To emphasize the center of interest.
- To eliminate an unwanted portion.
- To compensate for technical errors.
- To adjust the shape to fit a given layout.

**Fig. 5-15** *Cropping Ls are an important tool for editors or designers working with art. They can be used to emphasize elements, to isolate parts of an illustration, and to determine where crop marks should be made. (Courtesy of Metro Associated Services, Inc.)*

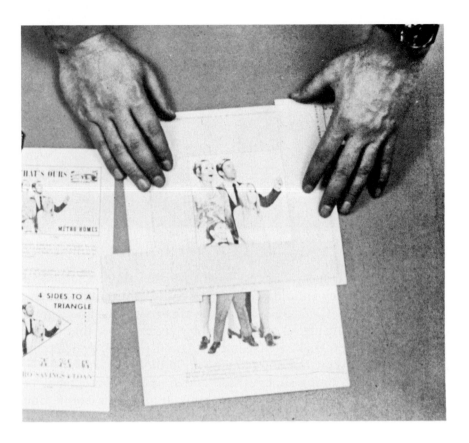

**Fig. 5-16** *Direction of art is important. In the layout on the left, directional art is used correctly. The motion, and therefore the reader's eye movement, will be into the copy. On the right, the problem of motion out of the layout is created by the direction of the art. (Reproduced with permission of Metro Associated Services, Inc.)*

Skillful cropping can be used to alter the proportions of the background and foreground. For instance, the horizon line can be raised or lowered to change the emphasis. The center of interest can be moved to a better location. If the art has motion in a certain direction, the center of interest should be given "elbow room" to move in that direction. For example, imagine a photograph of a sailboat moving across the sea. If the boat is moved out of the exact center of the photograph, the feeling of movement is increased and the illustration becomes more dynamic.

It is unusual when a photograph or drawing can be used in the form in which it is received. By careful and thoughtful cropping it is possible, for example, to convert a picture containing several people into one showing a single character, two characters, or whatever number is desired. Quite often a very dramatic head-and-shoulder shot of an individual can be obtained by cropping the person out of a group picture. This is especially true if the photograph is an informal action shot rather than a stiff group picture.

One illustration can serve many purposes if creative thought is given to cropping. For instance, in an illustration of a family group, a child can be isolated if a picture of a single child is needed. A person's hand pointing might be isolated from the rest of the body if a hand pointing is needed. Legs and feet can be separated from the bodies if art just showing people's legs and feet is needed. The creative possibilities are limitless.

**Fig. 5-17** *The square and the wedge graphically illustrate the stimulation of various movements by placing the same art in different positions. First, the wedge appears to be moving into the square, then it appears to be dropping into the square, then falling out, and finally it seems to be moving out of the square. (Reproduced with permission of Metro Associated Services, Inc.)*

The easiest way to examine cropping possibilities is to make two right angles out of heavy paper or light cardboard. These are called *cropping Ls.* The Ls should be about 1½ inches wide and each leg should be 8 or 10 inches long. Good Ls can be cut from a manila file folder. They are used to frame the various parts of an illustration.

Once the desired cropping is determined, it is noted by *crop marks.* These are arrows or lines, usually made with a *grease pencil* in the margins. Grease pencils, also called china markers, can be purchased at most stationery or art supply stores. Markings should not be made on the face of the art but in the margins. Care should be taken to avoid writing instructions on the back of the art, except with a felt pen.

If it is necessary to indicate cropping on an illustration but it is impossible to indicate the crop marks on it, a *mask* should be made. A mask is a frame, much like a picture frame, which is cut from paper and placed on top of the art to frame the portion that will be used.

## Scaling or Sizing Art

Once the art has been cropped it must be *sized*, or reduced or enlarged, to fit the desired spot in a layout. For instance, most photographs used in publication work are either 5 by 7 or 8 by 10 inches. But it is quite unusual for those sizes to be exactly right for the spot where the photograph is to be used in the layout. Therefore art must be reduced or enlarged. Also, sometimes the dimensions of the art piece must be altered. A rectangle that is 5 by 7 might be cropped so it can be used in a space 6 by 4.

There is a general mathematical process that can be used to determine how much must be cropped from the width or depth to change the proportions so the art can be sized to fit the available space. This involves the *principle of proportion*. That is, when a four-sided area is reduced or enlarged the sizes of the sides remain in direct relationship with each other. If we enlarge a 3 by 3 area to 5 inches wide, for instance, it will be 5 by 5 or 5 inches deep as well. If an 8 by 10 photo is reduced to half its original size, the width—top and bottom—will be 4 inches and the depth will be 5 inches. This principle can be stated in an equation that is simple to calculate:

**Fig. 5-18** *The correct way to cut one illustration into another is shown on the left. The smaller illustration should be placed over the larger in a spot where it will not interfere with the center of interest.*

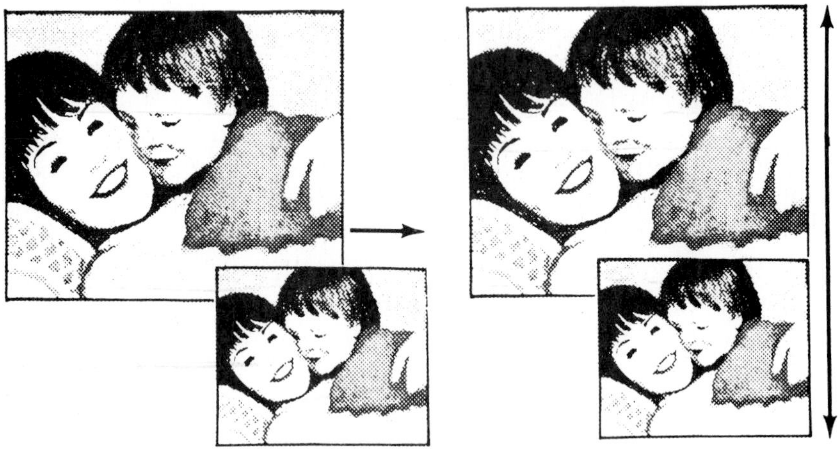

**Fig. 5-19** *Sometimes combined art can appear more dynamic if a common edge is not used, as shown on the left. When cutting one illustration into another, a common edge, as on the right, should be avoided as the reader may not discern that two illustrations are involved. (Reproduced with permission of Metro Associated Services, Inc.)*

$$\frac{\text{New width}}{\text{Old width}} = \frac{\text{New depth}}{\text{Old depth}}$$

The unknown, or the dimension being sought, is indicated by *x*.

Suppose the designer has a photograph that is 8 by 10 and a space 6 inches wide (36 picas) has been allocated for it in the layout. The depth of the new, or "sized," art is not known so it is *x* in the equation. The formula will look like this:

$$\frac{6 \text{ (new width)}}{8 \text{ (old width)}} = \frac{x \text{ (new depth)}}{10 \text{ (old depth)}}$$

To solve the equation, the algebra instructor tells us, cross-multiplication is used. That is, 6 times 10 equals 60 and 8 times *x* equals 8*x*.

The equation now becomes 8*x* = 60. We continue by dividing 60 by 8 to get the new depth of 7½ inches.*

If mathematics is a problem for you, there is another and simpler, but more cumbersome, way to work proportions.

---

*Note: Some designers state the proportion formula slightly differently. However, the results are exactly the same. They use:

$$\frac{\text{Old Width}}{\text{Old Depth}} = \frac{\text{New Width}}{\text{New Depth}}$$

**Fig. 5-20** *Many times cropping can eliminate distracting influences and strengthen the art's impact. The dashed lines show a few of many ways this illustration might be cropped. (Reproduced with permission of Metro Associated Services, Inc.)*

First, draw a diagonal line from the upper left to the lower right corner of the original art. (Don't draw on the art, of course.) Any straight edge can be placed in this position. A ruler is best as it will give the depth in inches or picas.

Next, measure the width of the new art across the top of the original art. Indicate the width on the bottom of the original art as well. Now line up another ruler at these two points. The point where the two rulers intersect is the depth of the new art. If the art is to be enlarged rather than reduced, both proportion lines should be extended beyond the art until they intersect.

A little more challenging situation is when we have a rectangular piece of art that has a depth greater than the width and we want to use this art in an area that has a width greater than its depth. How can this art be cropped to change the shape? Should the cropping be done from the width or the depth?

**Fig. 5-21** *Art can be sized by using a simple proportion drawing or placing a straight edge to create the diagonal and the new width.*

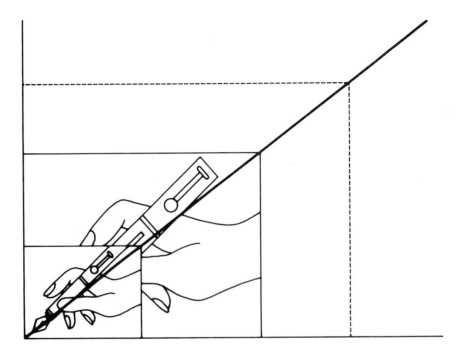

First of all, since the depth must be changed to be shorter than the width, we have to crop the original depth. But how much?

We can use the proportional equation again. Let us assume that an 8 by 10 photograph must be used in an area 6 by 4 inches. Portions must be cropped from the original depth, which we will designate as *x* (the unknown) in the proportion formula:

$$\frac{6 \text{ (new width)}}{8 \text{ (old width)}} = \frac{4 \text{ (new depth)}}{x \text{ (old depth)}}$$

If this formula is solved, $6x$ will equal 32, and *x* will equal 5⅓. However, and here is the tricky part, since the original depth was 10 inches and the new depth must be 5⅓ inches, 5⅓ must be subtracted from 10. The result is an illustration that is now 8 by 5⅓. To obtain this, 4⅔ inches must be cropped from the original depth of the illustration. This cropping can be done from either the top or bottom, or parts of each, depending on the composition of the illustration.

These sizing problems can be checked by working the equation by using the solution (in this case, 8 by 5⅓) for the new "original" art by substituting *x* for either the new width or the new depth. If, in our example, the new width works out to 6 or the new depth to 4, we know the problem was solved correctly.

Quite often instructions for sizing art are given in percentages of enlargement or reduction. A communicator might crop the art and then write "reduce to 80 percent" on the instructions. It is easy to find the percentage of reduction or enlargement. Just take the original width of the art or photograph and divide it into the desired width for the layout. That is, if a photo is 5 by 7 and it is to be

**Fig. 5-22** *A proportion wheel can be mastered in minutes. It can be used to size art and calculate the percentage of enlargement or reduction.*

in an area that is 3 inches wide, we simply divide 5 into 3 to find the percentage of reduction. In this case we would write "reduce 60 percent" in our instructions. If, on the other hand, this 5-inch-wide photo is to be used in an area that is 8 inches wide, we would divide 5 by 8 and write "enlarge 60 percent."

Some communicators find it simpler to size art using picas rather than inches for the dimensions.

There are tools that help with these sizing problems. They are simple to use and can be mastered in a minute or two. The most common is a *proportion wheel*, which can be purchased at a reasonable cost from most art and graphic supply firms. There are *proportion slide rules*, too. One or the other should be in every editor or designer's tool kit.

Always keep in mind that it is better to reduce than enlarge. Reduction makes flaws and imperfections less discernible and helps to make the definition of tones sharper and more contrasty. A good rule of thumb is to try to reduce most art at least 50 percent.

## Retouching Art

Retouching is the process of eliminating unwanted material or flaws in artwork. It can be used to emphasize details or repair defects. However, it takes a skilled artist to do effective retouching.

Usually an airbrush is used for retouching. This is an atomizer that uses compressed air to spray watercolor paint on art. The retoucher masks the areas to be retained and sprays the areas to be eliminated or makes the background a uniform shade or tone. Bleaches are often used to remove unwanted portions of photographs.

Sometimes it is more economical, and possibly more effective, to correct photographs in the darkroom rather than to use the services of a retouch artist.

A photographer can alter the image by using different types of photographic paper to change the contrast. Techniques such as *dodging* and *burning* can also be used. *Dodging* is a method of lightening areas of a photograph by reducing the light reaching certain areas of the print. *Burning* is used to darken areas by allowing more light to reach areas of the print.

## Captions and Cutlines for Art

Are they captions or cutlines? In newspaper design they are cutlines in the United States. In magazine design and in newspaper design in England they are captions. Regardless, though, of what they are called, there are a number of ways to handle cutlines or captions when planning printed communications. Some are more suitable for newspapers, and others work better for magazines and brochures.

The basic design criteria is to select the arrangement believed best suited for the job and to stick to it. Also, cutline and caption styles should not be mixed within one publication.

Newspapers consider cutlines (in newspaper parlance a caption is a head *above* an illustration) a must. Some insist that a cutline accompany every illustration. There are several ways these cutlines are handled:

■ The cutline is boldface with the first two or three words in all caps.

■ The cutline is in the same face as the body matter but in a different point size.

**Fig. 5-23** *Captions for art. A caption style should be chosen that is compatible with the design of the publication or brochure. Consistency in caption style is important, and caption lines should not exceed the limits for readability for the style size chosen.*

### Camera catches bank holdup

A bank robber holds a sawed-off rifle over a woman customer as he and two accomplices hold up a branch of the Deposit Guaranty National Bank in Jackson, Miss. The robbery was recorded by an automatic bank camera. The amount taken was not known.

**WINDING WAY—The Coast Guard Cutter Bollard weaves a path through Connecticut River ice Monday near Middletown. The Coast Guard keeps a channel open all winter from Old Saybrook to**

**Tree time—What better time to be buddies than at Christmas, when both pals can conjure up visions of what Santa will deliver.**

## B.O.B. is quite a guy

*Androbot, Inc. presents B.O.B. (Brains-On-Board), a fully expandable personal robot designed to entertain, to communicate, and to be a useful addition to the home environment. B.O.B. will navigate a living space and talk in a human-like voice, randomly choosing from more than 100 words and phrases.*

**MINI MUSICIANS:** Young violinists from the Suzuki Music Academy of Chicago wait to play during a recital Thursday at the Daley Center. While Michael Hsu seems to have a case of

## *Meters to go*

**Park Ridge Police Dept. community service officer Robert Sundberg marks a tire in a two-hour parking area to enforce the parking time limit. Soon that procedure will be used in uptown Park Ridge when the two-hour meters are removed, probably within the next few weeks, Community Development Director Richard Schaub, said.**

- The cutline is in an entirely different style of type, but one that harmonizes with the headline type.

- The cutline has a sideline head. This is a line or two of display type placed together with the cutline but to its left.

- The cutline has a catchline. A catchline is a display line placed between the illustration and the cutline. The catchline can be set flush left to line up with the cutline or it can be centered. Most newspaper designers seem to prefer the centered catchline.

Whatever arrangement seems to harmonize best with the whole graphic design of the newspaper should be used consistently. Cutline styles should not be changed from illustration to illustration, though a single centered line might be used for "mug shots" and another arrangement used for all the other illustrations. The point is to be consistent.

Many designers in the magazine world prefer not to use captions. They see them as an annoyance that clutters up a layout. Many believe that a good illustration needs no caption, that it tells the story by its composition and content.

When captions are used, they appear in two basic design formats. One is adjacent to the illustration and the other is a combination caption that serves several adjacent illustrations on a page or in a layout.

The arrangement of the caption and its placement should be based on two criteria. First, the caption should not just be "thrown in." It should be part of the overall design and treated as an important element. That is, the caption should add something to the design and should be unified with all the other elements in the layout. Second, the caption should not be written or located in a way that confuses the reader. Numbers, arrows, and other devices should not be used in captions. They clutter and disfigure a layout.

Art that is carefully selected, prepared, and presented can be as important an element in a layout as the words. It is a vital tool of the communicator, and in this visual age it is becoming more and more important.

## Effective Design Checklist

- Have a specific function in mind—do not use art just for decoration.

- Remember the reader, try to select art from the reader's perspective.

- Avoid art clichés. These are things like people shaking hands, speakers at the rostrum. They are dull, dull, dull!

- Crop carefully and with a purpose. Don't crop unnecessarily and ruin a well-composed illustration.

- Avoid unusual shapes in art. Circles, stars, and other decorations should be avoided unless there is a strong design reason for using them. Straightforward rectangles and squares are best.

- Select art for its content. Do not select it for its shape. The shape can be altered but poor content is hard to improve.

- Use mortises only after careful consideration. (Mortises are cut-out areas in art in which type or graphic elements are inserted.) (Usually all mortises do is disfigure art.)

- Use silhouettes for a change of pace. In the silhouette the figure or center of interest is in outline form.

- Use tricky treatment with caution. Mortises, surprints (type over art) and combination plates (line and halftone art together) should be used with great caution. The trend today is straightforward, simple, close-cropped art.

## Graphics in Action

1. Select three articles from magazines or newspapers that have no illustrations. Decide if the articles could have been presented with more impact, more reader interest, or clearer understanding with art. If so, decide the content and method of presentation that would be best for this art. Find a source for the art to be used.

2. Select an illustration. Make and use cropping Ls and see how many uses you can find for variations of this one illustration. List these layout possibilities. If possible, make duplicates of the art so each possibility can be marked for cropping.

3. Find in publications as many different art treatments, such as line conversions and different screening techniques, as possible. Evaluate these treatments and discuss if the art would have been as effective if used straightforwardly.

4. Obtain a selection of photos and crop them for effectiveness. Often the local daily newspaper is glad to supply wire photos for this purpose as it receives far more than it can use. Discuss in class why you cropped the photos the way you did.

5. Once photos have been cropped, size them to fit areas that are 4 inches (or 24 picas), 6 inches (or 36 picas), and 8 inches (or 48 picas). Or, crop for content and size to change the dimensions. For instance, crop an 8 by 10 photo to fit a 7 by 5 area in a layout. When sizing is complete, calculate the new dimensions in both inches or picas and in percentages of reduction or enlargement.

## Notes

[1] *AP Log*, March 29, 1976, pp. 1-4.
[2] Richard Curtis, *ASNE Today* (Washington, D.C.: USA Today, 1973), p. 1.

The trend in printed communications is toward bold and colorful graphics. Communicators must use every tool available to make the message stand out from its competition. The proper use of color, the judicious use of borders and ornaments, and the proper marriage of ink with paper can all add dimensions to effective printing.

The first step in becoming adept at selecting and using these elements is to develop the realization that they really can help. This graphic sense, or awareness, can be sharpened by studying the work of others. Keep a constant critical eye out as you browse through newspapers, magazines, and even the direct mail communications that fill the mailbox. Try to second-guess the person who designed them. Why was a subhead put here, a border there, an ornament at that position? Why was spot color used there? What did it add to the printed piece to invest in full color rather than spot color or simply printing it in black on white?

When you pass the magazine rack in the supermarket, look at the graphic array. Which magazines seem to be especially attractive? Why? Which magazines seem to communicate at a glance what they are all about? How do they do this?

The head buyer of a major grocery store chain once said he looked at the label on the can before he examined the contents. If the label wouldn't sell, he would reject the product, no matter how fine it might be. The same can be said concerning printed messages. They must have eye appeal.

Evaluation for eye appeal includes an examination of the printed communication to see if the basic criteria for good selection and use of type have been applied. The communication should be checked for the application of the principles of design. Does it have balance, unity, contrast, proportion, harmony? If the balance is formal, is that appropriate for the type of message?

Then, the piece should be examined to see if these principles have been applied in an unusual or different way to make it stand out from the rest. Are the principles of good typography and graphics applied in an unusually arresting way?

Soon you will be able to automatically "score" printed communications as they are viewed. For instance, an ornament that throws a page out of balance will be spotted in an instant. A boxed item placed in such a way that easy reading of the text is upset will become a source of irritation. You will immediately notice an ornament that clashes with the other elements on the page and destroys unity. And you will be aware of when color dominates the page and diminishes effective communication.

Each of these supporting elements has characteristics that should be known by the communicator. Two in particular involve color, but color of an entirely different type. One is the color derived from light and the other is typographic color.

Typographic color includes letters of special design, borders, rules, and ornaments. Color derived from light involves such things as spot color (the individual use of color); duotones (two-color halftone reproductions from an original in one color); and process color (the use of full color). First let us consider color derived from light and the "color we can add through the use of typographic devices.

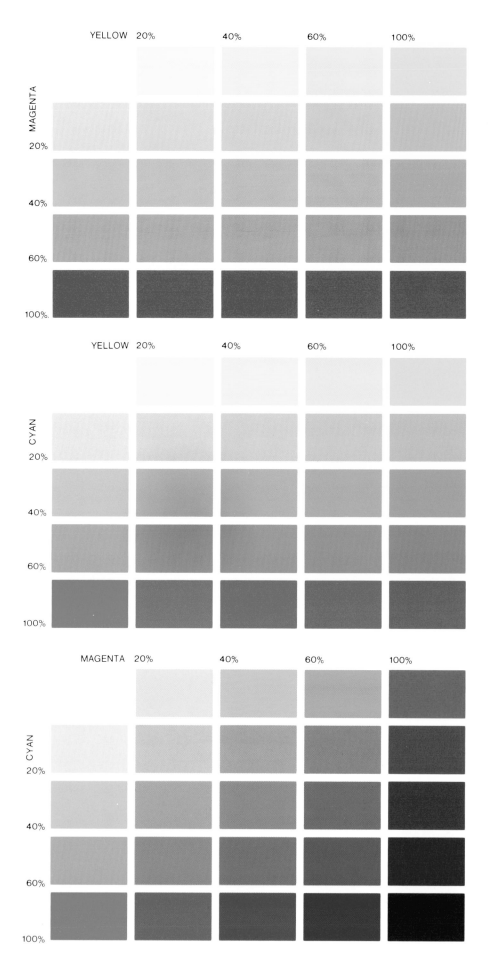

These charts show some of the colors that can be created by combining screen tints of two process colors. Because color printing is not a precise science, examples such as these can be used as a guide only; identical screen combinations printed on different paper or with different inks can vary somewhat in appearance.

YELLOW PLATE/PHOTOGRAPHED THROUGH A BLUE FILTER

MAGENTA (RED) PLATE/PHOTOGRAPHED THROUGH A GREEN FILTER

CYAN (BLUE) PLATE/PHOTOGRAPHED THROUGH A RED FILTER

BLACK PLATE/PHOTOGRAPHED THROUGH A MODIFIED FILTER

*Examples of the plates, or separations, needed to reproduce a full-color image in process color. The image is photographed through four different filters to separate each color from the others.*

YELLOW

YELLOW AND MAGENTA

YELLOW, MAGENTA, AND CYAN

YELLOW, MAGENTA, CYAN, AND BLACK

*The four-color process plates printed in sequence, or progression. Proofs of this sequence are called progressive proofs or "progs."*

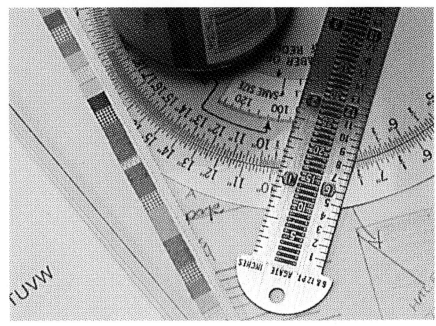

*Above is a four-color process reproduction of a color photograph. An enlargement of the upper left corner is shown at the right to illustrate the halftone dot structure of four-color process printing.*

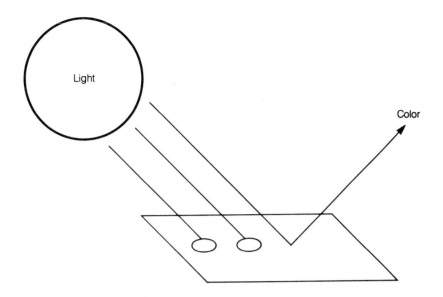

## Color Derived from Light

The blue of the sky, the red of the sunset, neon lights, paints, wallpaper, color television, advertisements—we live in a colorful world.

It wasn't always like this. It has only been within the past hundred years or so that we have been able to take advantage of color as a tool in graphic communications. Only a limited number of dyes and pigments were known before the nineteenth century. Now there are thousands of colors of every imaginable hue and intensity. There seems to be no limit on the possibilities of using color. The only restrictions are costs, the ability of the designer, and possibly some limitations imposed by the equipment available.

Even cost is no longer the factor it once was. New methods of preparing color separations and printing plates have cut the cost considerably. Color can now be added inexpensively, with a little creative planning. Printing in a color ink on another color paper can create a piece that breaks out of the dull black on white.

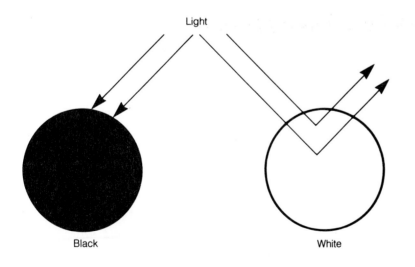

**Fig. 6-2** *Black is the absence of color. A black object absorbs all light rays and thus appears black. White is the presence of all colors. A white object reflects all light rays and thus appears white.*

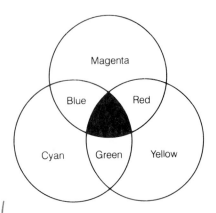

**Fig. 6-3** *Ink color is called subtractive. The primary ink colors are magenta, cyan, and yellow. Secondary colors are mixed from the primary colors. Magenta and cyan make blue. Green is made from cyan and yellow. Red is made from magenta and yellow. These are the six basic inks needed to make most colors in printing.*

There are several ways in which color can make printed communications more effective. It can help accomplish the first job of any communication—attracting attention. It can create the atmosphere desired. It can help set the mood for a message. Color can provide accent and contrast where they are wanted, and it can help emphasize important points. It can add sparkle to the printed page. It can direct the reader through the message. It can be used in printed materials to help create identity just as it does for schools in flags and athletic uniforms. Cambell's soup! What colors do you visualize?

However, color is not a cure-all. It will not compensate for poor writing, poor typography, and poor layout. It will not help shoddy printing. The communicator should not try to use it to save an inferior design.

Before taking advantage of this powerful tool, we need to understand several aspects of color. These include:

- How color is reproduced in the printing process
- The psychological implications of color
- How colors harmonize or relate to each other
- How to combine color with type, art, and other elements in a layout for best results

### How Color Is Reproduced

All color comes from sunlight. Reflection and absorption of light produces the effects we know as color. A lemon is yellow because it absorbs all colors except yellow and reflects yellow. In an unlighted room we would not see a yellow lemon. We would not see it at all. Under a dim light, the yellow rays the lemon reflects will be so weak we will see the lemon as gray.

In discussing color with a printer, we need to be familiar with six terms: hue, tone, value, shade, tint, and chroma.

*Hue* is what makes a color a color. That is, all colors we see are hues. Hue is derived from the ancient Gothic word *hiwi*, which means "to show." Hue is what makes blue blue. *Tone* and *value* are terms used to designate the variations of a hue. They are the lighter tints or darker shades of a color created by adding white or black ink to a hue. Adding black to a color creates a *shade*; adding white makes a *tint*.

*Chroma* is a term used to indicate the intensity of a color. The chroma of a color is determined by the amount of pigment saturation in the ink that produces the color. Increasing the chroma creates a more intense color.

When an artist wants to create different colors or shades and tints of colors, she or he mixes paints on a palette. The printer does the same thing when a spot of color is needed for printing. The inks are mixed on an ink plate and then placed on the press, unless premixed inks are purchased from the manufacturer.

Most of us have been taught that light is made up of the three primary colors—blue, green, and red. These three colors are called *additive primaries* because they produce white light when added together.

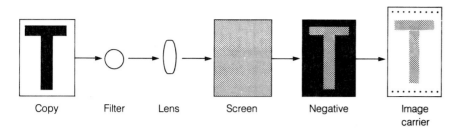

| Copy | Filter | Lens | Screen | Negative | Image carrier |

**Fig. 6-4** *Color plates are made by photographing the full-color art through filters to separate the primary colors. If the original art is continuous tone, such as a color photograph, a screen is used for each exposure as in the creation of halftones from black-and-white photographs.*

However, the process is quite different when a printer needs to produce the full range of colors in a full-color illustration. Three colors slightly different from blue, green, and red are used. The printer uses cyan, magenta, and yellow for full-color work. Cyan is a blue green, and magenta is a red violet. These darker colors are called *subtractive primaries*. They are called subtractive because they absorb light. And they are primaries because a full range of colors can be produced by mixing the inks together in various proportions.

The printer makes four plates through a process called *color separation*. Each of these plates will print a color of ink in the density required so that when it is combined with an impression from another plate it will create the tone or shade desired. In effect, the printer uses the printing press for a palette. If the people involved in this process are skilled, the reproduction will be difficult to distinguish from the original.

When yellow, magenta, and cyan are superimposed, they produce three other colors in the spectrum. Yellow and magenta combined produce red. Yellow and cyan produce green, and magenta and cyan produce blue. Thousands of tints and shades can be reproduced through the combinations of these inks. Black is added to give depth to the dark areas and shadows.

The distinctive sensation we see and identify as a certain color is actually the reflection of lightwaves that weren't absorbed by the object. For instance, if white light strikes a surface and the surface absorbs green light waves, we see the red and blue light waves that were not absorbed. We see, then, the color magenta, which results from the combination of red and blue.

If the surface absorbs blue light waves, we see the combination of red and green lightwaves, or yellow. And, if the surface absorbs red light, we see cyan—a combination of the reflected green and blue light.

So, in making plates for full-color reproduction, one plate is made with a green filter and used in printing with magenta ink. A red filter is used for the cyan printer, and a blue filter for the yellow printer. The fourth plate, the black ink printer, is made to add density. Without the black ink impression, the reproduction would appear weak and dark brown rather than black in the shadows.

The process is much more complicated than this brief description, but the point to remember is that it takes four plates and four separate impressions or runs through the press to produce a full-color reproduction. It is expensive, but the price is coming down as new equipment for making color separations is developed.

**The Psychological Implications of Color**

The increase in use of color has led communicators to look to psychologists for help in making the most effective use of this powerful tool. Just as sugar manufacturers have learned, for example, that their product will not sell in a green package, and manufacturers of beauty preparations know that brown jars will remain on the shelf long after others are gone, so communicators must know which colors to use in which situations.

In the case of sugar, tests by marketers have shown that it sells best in a blue container or at least in one where blue is predominant. Blue is the color of "sweetness" while green is seen as astringent, like a lime.

Airlines know that proper color schemes in airplane cabins can help relax nervous passengers.

There are warm and cool colors. Fire and sunshine make red, yellow, and orange—warm colors. The shadows of deep forests and the coolness of water make blue, violet, and dark green cool. Night brings on inactivity while day brings brightness and hope. Thus dark blue is the color of quiet while bright yellow is the color of hope and activity.

Experiments have shown that people exposed to pure red are stimulated. Depending on the length of exposure, blood pressure increases and respiration and heartbeat both speed up. Red is exciting.

On the other hand, exposure to pure blue has the reverse effect. Blood pressure falls and heartbeat and breathing slow down in a blue environment. Blues are calming.

Advertisements for air conditioners use cool colors. Those for furnaces are more effective if warm colors are used.

Unnatural use of color can cause adverse effects. Printing a luscious grilled steak in green not only fails to add to communication in a favorable way, it can detract by creating a strong sense of repulsion on the part of the reader.

"I have worked with designers who ran halftones of people in blue, green, pink, or some other terribly unnatural color," remarked one designer who reviewed this manuscript. "The results were uniformly terrible."

Blue is the favorite color of the majority of people. It can be used with no fear of adverse psychological effects (unless, as stated, it's used unnaturally). Yellow generates the buoyant happiness of a sunny day. Orange is a happy color, too. And brown is one of the most versatile colors for printing. Men associate it with wood and leather. Many women associate it with leather goods and furs. Like blue, it has no inherent weaknesses and can be used in a wide variety of jobs. Green is also a universally popular color. And purple suggests robes of royalty, the dignity of church vestments, and the pomp and splendor of high ritual.

There are two important points to remember when selecting color for communications. First, warm colors advance and cool colors recede when printed. Reds tend to dominate and can overpower other elements on the page if the designer is not careful. Second, colors in printing should be used as much as possible in their natural associations—green forests, blue sky, sunny mornings. (There may be times when the unnatural use of color can create the most effective communication. But remember the risk of repulsion when color is used unnaturally.)

## Selecting Colors for Harmony

Which colors go well together when printed? Many people can tell instinctively if colors look compatible when printed together, but others need help in choosing color schemes for communications. Luckily help is available.

In 1899 a Boston teacher, Albert H. Munsell, began research that resulted in a system for distinguishing color. He charted color values on a numerical scale of nine steps ranging from black to white. Munsell's system was adopted by the National Bureau of Standards and slowly added to until it contained 267 different color names.

Out of this came the *color wheel*. Around the wheel are the colors comprising the primary triad of red, yellow, and blue in an equilateral triangle. Halfway between the primaries are the secondary colors. In all, the wheel divides the color spectrum into twelve hues. Six basic color combinations have been devised and the communicator can use these combinations in deciding which colors to use in creating harmonious layouts.

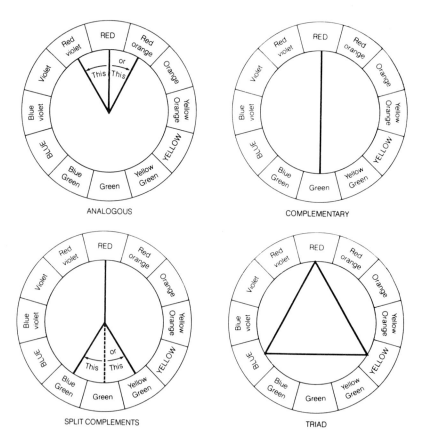

**Fig. 6-5** *Color combinations used for printing.*

## Creative Communication

Here is a plan for creative problem solving. (It is from a booklet produced by the Royal Institute of British Architects, described by Bryan Larson in his book *How Designers Think*.)

The plan includes four steps: assimilation, general study, development, communication.

The first step is the accumulation and ordering of general information and information specifically related to the problem. This is followed by study of the problem, its nature and possible solutions.

Next, the best solutions are isolated and developed and refined.

Finally, the solutions are discussed with those involved in the project or those who can offer advice and informed evaluation.

The combinations are:

- *Monochromatic:* This is the simplest color harmony and is made of different values of the same color. These values may be obtained in printing by screening artwork at different percentages. Monochromatic harmony works well in printing. Care should be taken not to screen type so that legibility is lost.

- *Analogous:* These are two colors that are adjacent on the color wheel, such as blue and blue green, or red and red orange.

- *Complementary:* These are colors that are directly across from each other on the wheel, such as red and green. A complementary selection adds drama because of the contrast of warm and cool colors.

- *Split complements:* These are colors that are selected by choosing a color on the wheel and finding its complement but using a color adjacent to the complement. A split complementary harmony for red would be blue green or yellow green.

- *Triad:* This is a combination of three colors, each of which is at the point of a visualized equilateral triangle placed on the wheel. As the triangle is turned to any position on the wheel, its points will designate the three colors of a triad.

Another tool for color selection is a *matching system*. This is composed of samples, or chips, showing the various colors as they will appear in print. It is similar to the collection of swatches found in most paint stores. One widely used such guide is the Pantone Matching System, referred to as PMS. This guide shows the colors as they will appear on coated or uncoated papers.

### Some Ways to Use Colors

There are many ways to take advantage of the powerful communications possibilities of color at very little added cost. The cheapest, of course, is to use colored paper. We are so conditioned to thinking in terms of black ink on white paper that we often overlook this possibility. And we often forget that we could use colored ink on white paper.

*Spot color* is the process of adding individual colors in printing. One color added to the basic color can do much to make printing stand out at only about a 35 percent increase in the total cost of the job. Each color added means an additional run of the sheet through the press, but it can be well worth it.

Simultaneous printing of a solid color and various tints can be used. This can be done on the same press run by *screening*, or printing type and art made from screened negatives. The density of the resulting tones will depend on the density of the screens. This can be any percentage from solid (100 percent) through half-solid (50 percent) to almost white (10 percent).

Another way to obtain effective color is by creating a duotone. A *duotone* is a two-color halftone print made from a screened photograph. Two plates are needed. One is printed in the desired color and the other in black. The result can be a highly dramatic added element to the layout.

---

## Typographic Color

Decorative elements that can add "color" to layouts include several miscellaneous typographic devices. These are borders, both straight line and decorative, ornaments, and decorative letters. The straight line borders, whether they are a single line or several lines together, are called *rules*. Rules with three or more lines of the same or

**Fig. 6-6** *Borders and rules should be selected to harmonize with the art and type styles used in the layout. (Reprinted with permission of Westvaco Corporation.)*

varying thicknesses are known as *multiple rules.* Rules that are composed of a series of short vertical lines are called *coin-edge rules.*

There was a time when flowery ornaments and borders were considered a must in printing. The monks who illuminated hand-lettered manuscripts with colorful initial letters and curlicues produced beautiful pieces of art. Their skills were carried over into the early days of printing when letterpress-printed pages were often embellished with hand-drawn colorful ornamentation.

Fancy ornaments and borders in printing went along with ornamentation in other art forms. During the age of gingerbread turrets and scroll work in buildings, fancy letterings and ornamentation were popular in printing. But today the trend is toward

**Fig. 6-7** (top) *The fork and knife silhouette plus the simulation of a plate turn an ordinary coupon into an attention-getter; (bottom, left and right) Good art borders are a valuable tool. The skilled designer uses them in a variety of ways to turn dull, unattractive layouts into ones that get attention. (Reproduced with permission of Metro Associated Services, Inc.)*

simplicity, boldness, and functionalism. We are told to keep it simple, but give it punch. If it doesn't serve a function, leave the rule or ornament out.

However, ornaments should not be discarded out of hand. Proper use, which is to say restraint, in adding borders and ornaments can add decorative relief to a printed page that might otherwise be mechanical and deadly severe.

The fancy curlicues and shaded borders of another era have been replaced with a simpler decorativeness that better fits today's design techniques and typography. A little added ornamentation can be much like a dash of spice in a cooking recipe—it can make the typographic production sparkle.

**Fig. 6-8** *Creative integration of art and type can create unity and attention in a layout. (Reproduced with permission of Metro Associated Services, Inc.)*

Borders should extend the basic design of the art and type selected. An *Oxford rule* (parallel thick and thin straight lines), for instance, goes very well with the thick and thin lines of Bodoni or other modern Roman types with good contrast between thick and thin strokes and straight-line serifs. Single-line solid rules go well with the monotonal and simple Sans Serifs. A simple line drawing requires a simple straight-line rule. A decorative illustration requires a decorative border. The design and size of ornaments and borders should be in harmony with the design and size of the types and illustrations in the layout.

When borders and decorations are printed in color, the color value should be in tune with all the other elements in the layout. Decoration that may appear harmonious printed in black ink will appear weak and ineffective if printed in pastel or light colors. Also, if solid or screened backgrounds in color are used, care should be taken to be sure the colors are light. Deep color for tint blocks or screened backgrounds will overshadow the type and make it difficult to read.

Generally, borders and decorations to be printed in color should be specified in a little heavier weight than if they are to be printed in black. This will give them more body and they will harmonize better with the black type.

When borders are placed around type masses, the borders should be closer to the type than to the margins of the page. Borders and type should be handled as one unified typographic element.

*Swash letters* are usually "stretched-out" versions of regular letter forms that end in an ornamental flourish. Swash letters are used to add a touch of distinction to a logo or a company name, or to create a graceful image for an invitation, an announcement, or a column heading.

Other exaggerated letter forms, such as abnormal extensions of ascenders and descenders or decorative initials, are also available.

But all of these ornamental letter forms should be used sparingly. They should be used only for the first or last letter of a word and

**Fig. 6-9** *These swash letters (below) are members of the Caslon family, in italic posture. Note how these decorative letters can be integrated with the regular Caslon italic letters. Raleigh initials (right) are also decorative letters available to the designer.*

**Fig. 6-10** *Typographic color can be added to ordinary letters and headings to take them out of the ordinary.*

not for letters within words. Letters with extended ascenders or descenders are an exception to this rule. However, they, too, must be placed very carefully in the layout so that they add to the unity of the whole arrangement.

The opportunity to be creative with type is almost limitless. For example, modern typesetting equipment makes it possible to reduce spacing between words and lines to the point where the letters overlap and leading doesn't exist between the lines. When spacing is reduced to the point where lines overlap beyond the normal baseline of the letters, the procedure is called *minus leading*. When spacing is reduced between the words or letters to the point where they butt against each other or overlap, the technique is called *minus spacing*.

In addition, type can be elongated, obliqued, shaded, expanded, placed in circles, and shaped in an almost limitless number of variations with phototypesetting equipment.

These techniques allow communicators to be creative by adding unity, punch, boldness, and/or attention value to the type.

In selecting borders and ornaments, in adding typographic color to a layout, we must always remember that the best typography

**Fig. 6-11** *Computers and advances in phototypesetting equipment have opened opportunities for communicators to adopt "new wave" spacing techniques. "Reverse leading," in which characters are aligned at their tops, is shown at the top. The word generics is composed with minus (or negative) letterspacing. The bottom example is composed with minus (or negative) leading. Care should be taken, though, not to destroy legibility when employing new wave techniques.*

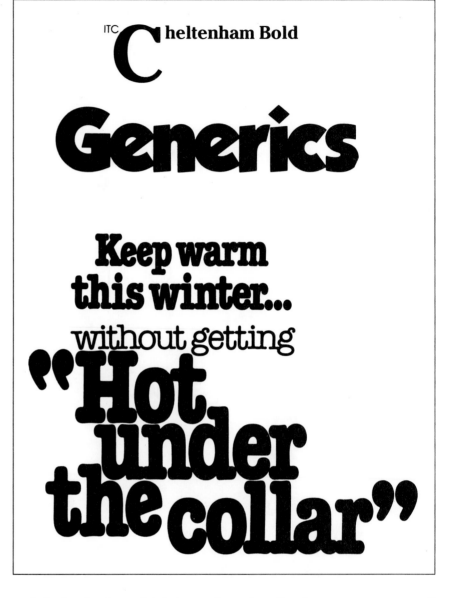

and design is that which is unobtrusive. Borders, ornaments, and type should blend with art, margins, white space, paper and ink, in a way that does not call attention to any one element. No graphic device should have such strong display value that it interferes with the purpose of the message.

## Effective Design Checklist

- Use cool colors as the background for black type because they recede and do not detract from the type as much as hot colors.

- When using colors, one color should dominate and the other should be used for accent or contrast.

- Remember that color combinations can add to or detract from the legibility of the type. Black on yellow has high legibility; black on red is extremely difficult to read.

- Use red sparingly, but remember that red can give a lift to the printed page. Red is also a good background for white type, if the type is large.

- Blue is an excellent background color. It is good for tints behind black type and it is good for reverses if used full strength. Yellow is too weak to be legible if printed in type masses. Yellow on black has good legibility if used in large types and few words.

- Brown prints well and has good legibility. Its tints are never anemic.

- Generally, body copy should be printed in black or a tint or shade of black when printed on colored paper.

- In advertisements, blue brings the greatest returns from men and red seems to bring the highest returns from women.

## Graphics in Action

1. Collect three or four examples of what you consider effective use of color in printed communications. Write an evaluation of each sample, or discuss your choices.

2. Collect three or four examples of what you consider poor or ineffective use of color. Explain what might be done to turn these examples into effective communications.

3. Build an idea file of creative uses of typographic color from examples found in publications. Include a section for poor examples, or techniques to be avoided.

4. Draw a rectangle approximately 5 by 7 inches on an 8½ by 11 or 9 by 12 sheet of white drawing paper. Sketch your name in a letter style that will help identify you as possessing the following characteristics. Embellish the lettering to better communicate the message. Use a separate sheet of paper for each example.

   a. I weigh 289 pounds.

   b. I weigh 98 pounds.

   c. I am a carpenter.

   d. I am a (use your profession or major).

   e. My hobby is (use actual hobby).

5. Select typefaces from the appendix and sketch or explain how each could be altered or modified or embellished to say the following words in the most effective way:

   a. We're Number 1

   b. Summer

   c. Stretch Your Dollars

   d. Peace

   Or choose your own words for this project.

No printed communication should be planned without some thought being given to the paper to be used. The proper paper can help the communication do the job. Paper plays an important part in achieving readability and mood as well as durability of the message.

If an "old time" or "antique"theme is planned, soft, textured paper should be considered. Old style types printed on antique-finish papers will enhance the "feel" of yesteryear. Old style types blend with old style paper. The angular, uneven strokes of the letters harmonize with the roughness and unevenness of soft-finish paper.

A modern look can be achieved better with smooth papers. The detail in a piece of art or the contrast in a photograph will show up much better on a hard-finish paper.

The formal, precise style of many modern and thin typefaces appears at its best on paper that is uniformly smooth and even, with a hard finish. Types with very light letter forms show up best on coated and enameled book papers. But hard-finish papers can accentuate the crude details in the construction of old style letters and make them appear ragged and awkward.

Highly glossed finishes on papers lessen legibility. These papers can even cause eye fatigue and strain. They create a glare that makes reading tiring and difficult. A dull-finish stock is best for long reports and magazines with lots of reading matter.

Anyone concerned with printed communications should know how paper is made, some of its characteristics, and the various types of papers available. Some understanding of paper weights and standard sizes is helpful also.

## How Paper Is Made

Before the early 1700s practically all paper was made by hand. The raw materials—rags—were placed in tubs or vats. They were mixed and beaten into a pulp. The wet pulp was dipped from the tubs by hand and placed in molds made of fine wires stretched across wooden frames.

The milky pulp settled on the frames and drained and became sheets of paper. The damp sheets were then placed in a press, which flattened them and squeezed most of the remaining water out. Finally, the sheets were hung on wires to dry and stiffen.

Although sophisticated machinery has been developed to manufacture paper today, the basic process hasn't changed much. Wood is the most widely used raw material, though some of the high-quality papers are made partially or entirely of cotton and linen fibers. A number of treatments, chemicals, and fillers can be added in the manufacturing process to produce papers with a variety of finishes and characteristics.

For instance, rosin size is added to create water-repelling qualities so the paper can be used for pen and ink writing, offset printing,

**Fig. 7-1** *Historians record the long history of the written word as beginning some time between 1085 and 950 B.C. with the manufacture of papyrus and the use of pictography by the ancient Egyptians. The Egyptians used marsh plants to create a primitive form of paper. (Rochester Institute of Technology.)*

**Fig. 7-2** *Paper for today's printing industry comes from huge paper machines like this one at the Mead Corporation. This machine winds up an 8,500-pound roll of paper every 30 minutes, creating a web of paper 12 miles long and 18 feet wide every hour.*

or resistance to weather. Fillers, such as clay, are used to improve smoothness, to prevent printing from showing through the sheet (known as the *opacity* of the paper), and to help the ink adhere to the sheet. Dyes and pigments are added to produce papers of various colors.

Paper can be *calendered* (smoothed) by passing it through a series of rollers, and it can be "supercalendered" for an even finer finish. Some papers are produced with a high-gloss, or coated, surface to provide excellent reproduction of photographs and art.

A variety of special finishes is available. Some papers resemble leather, others linen or tweed. Still others are available with all sorts of pebbly and special-effect finishes. These are produced by running the paper through an embosser. Other papers are produced with a watermark or faint design or emblem made by impressing it on the paper with one of the rollers during the process. This roller, called a *dandy roll*, is a wire cylinder for making *wove* (a paper with a uniform, unlined surface and a soft, smooth finish) or *laid* (a paper with a pattern of parallel lines giving it a ribbed appearance) effects.

**Fig. 7-3**  *The steps in converting wood into paper are shown in the upper drawing at the right (provided by the Wisconsin Paper Council).The logs enter the pulping machine on the left and leave as a mushy pulp on the right. The process of converting pulp to paper in the machine is shown on the lower right. The pulp enters the machine on the left and emerges as a continuous roll of paper on the right.*

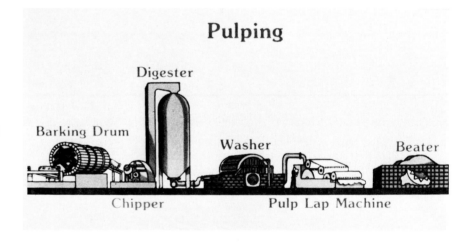

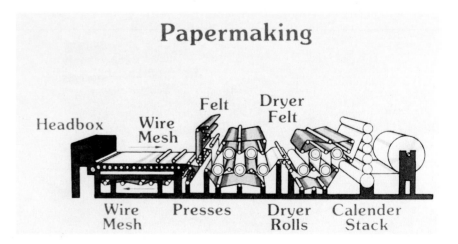

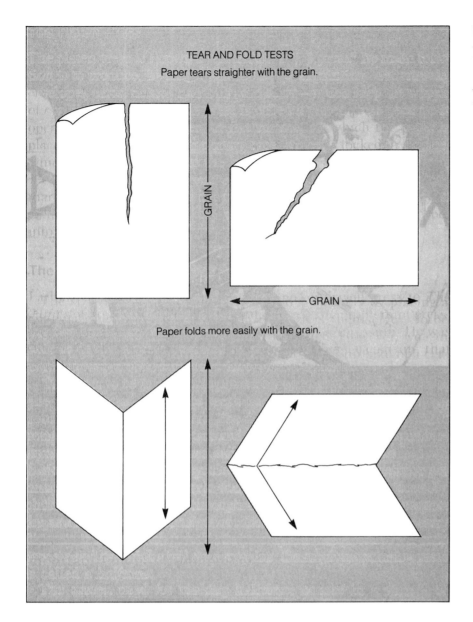

TEAR AND FOLD TESTS
Paper tears straighter with the grain.

GRAIN

GRAIN

Paper folds more easily with the grain.

**Fig. 7-4** *Grain is the direction fibers run in paper, much like in a piece of wood. Grain should be parallel with the binding edge or fold in books, pamphlets, publications, programs. Pages fold, turn, and lay flat much more easily when printing is with the grain.*

## Characteristics of Paper

Look closely at a sheet of paper with a magnifying glass and you will discover that paper has two sides. Each side has certain characteristics. The side that was on the wire mesh as the paper traveled through the manufacturing process is called the *wire side*. The other side is the *top*, or *felt*, side. The felt side usually has a smoother finish. The front of a printed piece, especially a letterhead, announcement, or business form, should be printed on the felt side of the sheet.

Paper has a grain. The *grain* is the direction in which the fibers lie in the sheet. Grain affects paper in several ways. For instance, paper folds smoothly in the grain direction. This can be demonstrated by folding a piece of construction paper or cardboard in both directions and noting which direction produces the smoothest fold. For books, brochures, catalogs, and magazines, the grain direction should be parallel with the binding edge of the pages. The pages will turn easier and lay down better.

## Paper Sizes and Weights

Papers are manufactured in standard sizes and weights. They are identified on this basis. The various weights of papers are used in selecting them for printing. As an example, consider the paper for a letterhead. The standard paper used for letterheads is known as *bond*. This type of paper is manufactured with a hard surface that will receive printing and writing inks without a blotter effect. The letters won't soak into the paper and become distorted.

Bond papers are made in a basic size of 17 by 22 inches. They will cut into four 8½ by 11 standard letter-size sheets per full sheet. Bond papers come in various weights ranging from 13 to 40 pounds. The most common available weights are 16, 20, 24, and 28. The basic weight is 20 pounds. (This means that 500 sheets (a ream) of 17 by 22 bond paper will weight 20 pounds.) You can cut costs— and have a flimsier looking letterhead—by ordering 16-pound bond paper. Or, you can spend a little more and have a heavier, more impressive looking letterhead by ordering 28-pound bond.

The basic size is different for different kinds of papers. It is thus important to be aware of how papers are classified and sized. The vast number of papers available may make this appear foreboding, but the classification system is really quite simple since nearly all papers can be classified into basic groups. The number of groups varies somewhat but most manufacturers recognize ten. These basic paper groups and the standard sizes for each are listed below. A discussion of the importance of knowing about standard paper sizes is included in Chapter 16, on planning other printed communications.

- *Bond* (17 by 22): These are the standard papers for business forms and letterheads. They have a hard surface that works well with pen and ink, typewriter, or word processor. They are available in a large variety of colors, mostly pastels, and most manufacturers provide matching envelopes in standard sizes as well.

- *Coated* (25 by 38): These papers have a smooth, glossy surface. They are used for high-quality printing. The surface can be dull-coated as well as glossy, and there are a variety of other surfaces, such as coated on one side, for labels.

- *Text* (25 by 38): Text papers are available in a variety of colors and finishes. They are used for booklets, brochures, announcements, and many quality printing jobs.

- *Book* (25 by 38): Book papers are not as expensive as text papers. They are used mainly for books, of course, and pamphlets, company magazines, and so on. Book papers are available in a wide range of weights and finishes from antique to smooth.

- *Offset* (25 by 38): These are papers made especially for offset lithographic printing where dampening is a factor. They have sizing added to help the paper go through the offset printing process that involves ink and water. They are similar to book papers.

- *Cover* (20 by 26): Cover papers come in an endless variety. Some are of the same texture and color as book papers but of a heavier weight. All sorts of finishes are also available. As the name implies, these are designed for use as covers on pamphlets, magazines, and so on.

- *Index* (22½ by 35 and 25½ by 30½): These papers are made to be stiff and to handle writing ink well. Index cards are examples of this type of paper. Index papers are available in a variety of colors.

- *Newsprint* (24 by 36): This is a cheap paper for printing handbills, circulars, and newspapers.

- *Cardboards* (24 by 36): These are sometimes called *tag board*. They are the heavy stuff used for posters. Lighter weights are used for tickets, cards, and tags. Cardboards come in all sorts of colors and can be colored on one or both sides.

Paper is one of the major cost factors in printed communications. It is thus always important to talk with the printer about papers. It is also a good idea to acquire a collection of "swatches" or samples of various kinds of printing papers. These can be obtained from paper wholesalers. A file of paper samples should be a part of every communicator's kit.

**Fig. 7-5** *Printing is the ultimate test for printing papers. Both letterpress and offset presses are used in testing at this laboratory print shop at the Mead Corporation paper mill.*

## A Word about Ink

Although the choice of the proper ink to use for best results is the job of the printer, communicators should be aware of the role that ink plays in the printing process.

Ink has been a part of our civilization for more than 2,000 years. The Chinese used various combinations of ingredients for writing and drawing more than 1,600 years before Gutenberg developed movable type. Early Egyptian literature mentions ink. References to ink are found in both the Old and New Testaments of the Bible. For centuries ink makers produced their product mainly by adding soot, or lampblack, to a varnish made by boiling linseed oil.

In the 1850s the discovery of coal-tar dyes, pigments, and new solvents ushered in the age of modern printing ink. Today ink making is a major industry and science. The National Association of Printing Ink Manufacturers reports that there are approximately 200 ink companies in the United States producing inks in about 400 plants throughout the country. Companies range in size from those with fewer than ten employees to those employing thousands. Industry sales of printing inks are more than $600 million now and are growing at an average rate of about 5 percent a year.

Inks are manufactured for compatibility with every type of paper. There are quick-drying inks for high-speed production on rotary presses, inks that harden to resist rubbing, metallic inks that simulate gold and silver, and fluorescent inks that store sunlight and glow in the dark. There are even perfumed inks that provide a subtle aroma for special effects. And there are the inks used with our morning newspaper, which will ruin a white shirt. However, work is progressing toward producing a water-base ink that may solve this problem.

For centuries black was the only color in which ink was available. Through the development of synthetic pigments and a greater knowledge of color technology, a whole rainbow of colors is now available to the ink maker. Color matching to a specific tint, shade, or hue has become an exacting procedure.

We should never overlook the possibilities certain inks can provide for that special effect. Inks, along with all the other supporting elements, combined with type, play a part in the complete printed communication.

## Effective Design Checklist

- When planning printing take into account the standard dimensions of the paper to be used as well as the capacity of the press to keep waste and cost to a minimum.
- The finish of the paper selected can affect the mood of the completed job. Select a paper that prints well and harmonizes with the type and tone of the message.

- Avoid selecting type designs with delicate lines for printing on rough-finish papers, especially for letterpress and gravure. This is not as critical for offset printing.

- Remember that color paper can add another dimension to the printed piece, but select an appropriate color.

- Consider grain direction when figuring paper stock. If the finished piece is to be folded, the grain should be parallel with the fold.

- Process or full colors produce most accurately on neutral white paper.

- Runability, or the efficiency with which the paper can be printed, and print quality are important factors in selecting papers. Discuss them with the printer.

- If color ink is to be used on color paper, check the compatibility of the colors of both ink and paper.

- Type is most easily read when printed on a soft, white paper.

- Consider using specialty inks such as metallic or fluorescent inks.

---

## Graphics in Action

1. Start a collection of paper swatches by visiting the nearest paper wholesaler and seeing if samples of the basic types of papers are available.

2. Obtain samples of papers of various weights and textures. Examine them under a magnifying glass and see if you can determine which is the felt and which the wire side of the sheet. Fold them with and against the grain. Note the differences, if any.

3. Research paper making and make your own paper. There are a number of books available that give instructions.

4. Select a paper that would be most suitable for the following. Consider weight, texture, and color. Explain the reasons for your choices.

   a. A brochure announcing an exhibit of famous paintings.

   b. An announcement of an open house at a computer center. The announcement will include high-contrast art.

   c. A magazine devoted to home woodcraft. It will contain much line art.

   d. A newsletter that requires the most economical sheet with the highest opacity.

## Creative Communication

First it takes insight.

This means that we must first recognize the layout problem and resolve to find a solution. We must define the problem. This may take considerable reasearch and study. However, the more clearly the problem is delineated the better the chances are that an effective solution will be found.

Once the layout problem has been thoroughly investigated, a conscious attempt at its solution can be made. Sometimes developing ideas for the solution will result in redefining the problem. This can lead to an even more effective solution.

Now that various elements that go into making an effective communication have been examined, we can consider the job of actually putting them together in a complete *layout* (a working drawing similar to an architect's blueprint that the editor or designer creates as a guide for constructing a printed communication). In approaching layout, keep in mind that there are three general categories of materials that people read.

First, there are printed communications that people want to read. These include newspapers, periodicals, and books. Since people are willing to pay good money to obtain these objects, we should strive to make them as pleasant and interesting as possible.

Second, there are printed materials that people must read. These include timetables, government reports, research papers, and income tax forms. Since people must read these materials whether they really want to or not, it is important to make them clear and understandable.

Third, there is material that people must be coaxed to read. This includes propaganda, public relations releases, and advertisements. A greater effort is needed here to lure people into the message and hold them until its end.

In all of these situations, the secret of using typography to its best advantage includes an understanding of the principles of design and how they can be employed in printed communications. These basic design principles include the principles of proportion, balance, contrast, harmony, rhythm and unity. Application of these design principles will help answer the question, How do we put it all together?

But before we discuss these principles, we should note that some of the most effective works produced by creative people have been accomplished by deliberately breaking the rules of good design. However, before attempting this sort of experimentation, we need to understand the rules we are breaking.

## The Principle of Proportion

In planning a layout where do we begin? First of all, we must settle on a shape.

Look around you. What are the most pleasing shapes you see? What are the most frequent proportions you encounter? Rectangles, right?

The ancient Greeks recognized the rectangle for all its pleasing qualities, and they built some of civilization's most attractive structures in the shapes of rectangles. In fact, this shape, as illustrated by the Parthenon, became known as the "golden rectangle." Its proportions are about three to five, and it has endured and pleased people down through the ages. Today this rectangle is encountered in doors, windows, table tops, pictures, and even the basic shape of human beings.

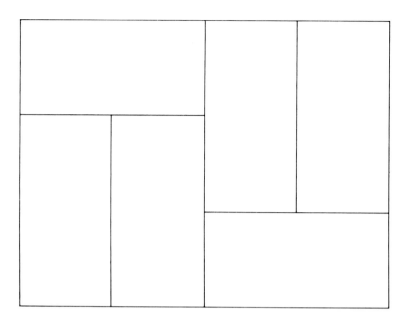

**Fig. 8-1** *The Japanese designed the rectangular tatami mat several centuries ago. It is still cited by graphic designers as an example of pleasing rectangular proportions.*

A square shape soon becomes monotonous. The rectangle, though uniform and precise, is not tiring because it offers a pleasing variety in form.

So, let's settle on a rectangle shape for our layout for a start. Certainly, we can produce effective and interesting layouts by going to squares and breaking out of the rectangular confines. A variation in shape can be the most effective approach for certain jobs when it seems important to be different. But the rectangle will prove most satisfactory for most printed material. Books will fit on shelves properly, brochures will fit standard envelopes, and paper will be used most efficiently. Costs and waste can be kept to a minimum since standard paper sizes are rectangular.

In addition to the dimensions of the printed page, proportion should be considered when planning other elements in the layout. These include the margins and the relationship of the type and art with one another and the whole.

For instance, margins inside and outside a border should be unequal. Equal white space creates a monotonous pattern. Unequal margins break this monotony and present a more interesting layout. Also, the margin outside the border should be larger than that within the border. The border is part of the printed portion of the layout and it should present a feeling of unity with the other printed elements.

In general, we should select shapes of type styles and art that have a proportional relationship to the dimensions of the whole layout. Long, thin types and art go well in long, thin layouts. Short, wide type styles and art carry out the proportions of short, wide layouts.

This rectangular approach to proportion has been called the golden rectangle because all through history it is seen as the

**Fig. 8-2** *Equal margins* (left) *are monotonous. Unequal margins* (right) *are interesting and create better unity.*

EQUAL MARGINS

MONOTONOUS

UNEQUAL MARGINS

INTERESTING, BETTER UNITY

**Fig. 8-3** *Most books and pamphlets are proportioned to about a 1:1.4 ratio. The height is 1.4 times the width. A square book has a 1:1 ratio. A book with a height of two times its width has a 1:2 ratio. A pleasing inequality in proportions is usually best in graphic design.* (Courtesy of A.B. Dick.)

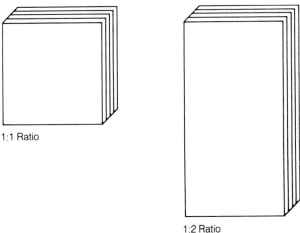

1:1 Ratio

1:2 Ratio

dominant design dimension. Generally the most pleasing page size is considered to be one in which the length is one and a half times the width.

A layout is said to be well proportioned if its shape is interesting to the eye and its parts are related in shape, but not monotonous in size, and the complete arrangement is attractive and effective.

Once the question of the general proportions of the layout has been resolved, we can consider where to place the elements. We begin by examining the optical center and its relationship to balance.

# The Secret of the Optical Center

The finished layout will be worthless if it does not stop the reader and arouse the reader's interest. We must make this critical initial contact. We can do this and arrange the elements in the layout in the most pleasing and effective way possible if we put the "secret of the optical center" into action.

The *optical center* is the spot the eye hits first when it encounters a printed page. If we take any area and look at it, we will find that our eyes land on a point slightly above the mathematical, or exact center, and slightly to the left. Try it. Open a newspaper and consciously note what you see right off. It will be somewhat above and slightly to the left of the fold. It will take a mighty compelling element to pull your eyes away from this spot.

The optical center is determined by dividing a page so that the upper panel bears the same relationship to the lower panel that the lower panel does to the entire page. That is easier done than said. If an area is divided into eight equal parts, the point located three units from the top and five from the bottom is the optical center.

Luckily we will not have to take a ruler and figure things that closely every time we make a layout. With a little practice in making rough layouts or planning pages, we will get the habit of orienting layouts with the optical center in mind.

We should always take advantage of this natural aid and utilize it as the focal point or the orientation center from which to construct a layout that will make the all-important initial contact. If an element is chosen for this spot that will stop the reader, such

## Tips for Planning Layouts

In planning layouts, keep the following points in mind concerning balance:

■ Irregularly shaped art has greater weight and exerts more influence on the eye than do rectangles or squares.

■ Things that destroy eye movement or misdirect the eye, such as people looking out of the page, or arrows or pointers that distract, upset the balance of a layout.

■ Type of improper size or weight, such as elaborate and oversize initial letters, throw a layout out of balance.

■ Photographs with distracting backgrounds can affect the balance of a layout.

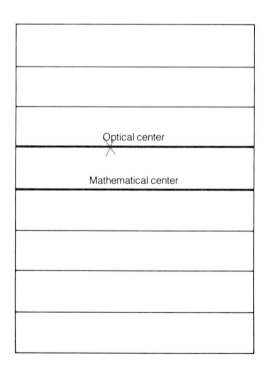

Fig. 8-4

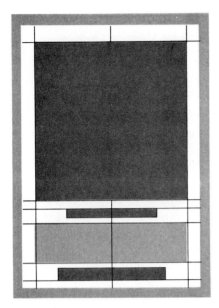

**Fig. 8-5** *In formally balanced layouts, type lines, illustrations, and other elements are placed left and right of center and above and below center in equal weights for a precise, orderly arrangement.*

**Fig. 8-6** *In these layouts, formal or symmetrical balance is illustrated on the left and informal or asymmetrical on the right. A teeter-totter and fulcrum diagram illustrate the principle of balance.*

as a striking piece of art or a dramatic headline, we are on the way to achieving effective communication.

The optical center, then, is the focal point or fulcrum for placing elements on the layout and it goes hand in hand with the second principle of layout, the principle of balance.

## The Principle of Balance

We need balance in our lives. When things are unbalanced they make us uneasy. Balanced objects look proper and secure.

Balance in printed communications is a must. We must place elements on the page in a way that will make them look secure and natural—not top-heavy, not bottom-heavy. We can do this in two ways. We can balance them formally or informally. (Some typographers call these symmetrical or asymmetrical balance.)

There are times when formal balance is just what is needed. Formal balance places all elements in precise relationship to one another. Formal balance gives us the feeling of formality, exactness, carefulness, and stiffness. Formal balance is used for luxury car advertisements, wedding announcements, and invitations to white-tie-and-tail events. *The New York Times* and the *Los Angeles Times* occasionally have formally balanced front pages. They help support the image of a no-nonsense, precise publication.

If our communication is formal, dignified, and reserved, a formally balanced layout will help transmit this message. If our target audience is stiff, unbending, and reserved, then formal balance may appeal to it.

A formally balanced layout has elements of equal weight above and below the optical center. To the left and to the right everything

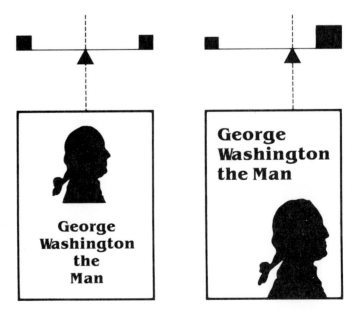

is the same. If we have a strong display type 6 picas from the top of our layout, we will need a line of the same size 6 picas from the bottom. If we have a piece of art left of center and slightly above, we need a similar element to the right and in the same position. Left and right, up and down, the formally balanced layout has elements of equal size and weight.

Formal balance has its place in layout work, but it is too stiff and uninteresting for many situations. Therefore, in most layout work, balance is achieved informally. Elements of similar weight, but not necessarily precisely the same, are placed in relationship to one another so that there is weight at the bottom of the layout as well as the top, and to the left and right to balance the whole. Stability is achieved but the balance is dynamic rather than static.

Balance in layout is achieved through the control of size, tone, and position of the elements. It is more a question of developing a sense of balance by constant study and awareness rather than following fixed rules devised by someone else.

However, there is a way to go about it that can help develop this sense of balance. The starting place, as was mentioned, is the optical center.

If we imagine the optical center as a fulcrum and place elements on the page so that this fulcrum is the orientation point, we will begin to see them fall into balanced positions. It is much like children achieving balance on a teeter-totter (or seesaw, if you prefer). If a child who weighs 80 pounds sits on one end of the teeter-totter and one weighing 40 pounds climbs on the other, what happens if they are the same distance from the fulcrum? The same thing happens with unbalanced layouts—they appear to topple over.

Applying this idea to layout work, if a single line of type is placed on a page it should be at the center of balance, the optical center, for best appearance. The same is true with a single copy block.

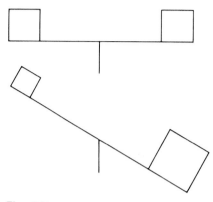

**Fig. 8-7**

**Fig. 8-8** *A line on the mathematical center actually looks awkward and below the center. Lines placed on the optical center give a pleasing sense of balance.*

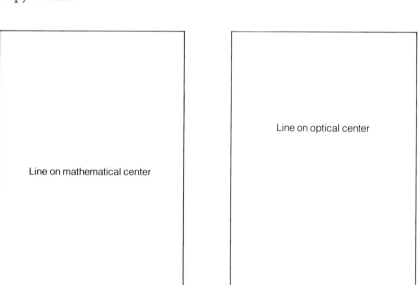

**Fig. 8-9**  *Two groups of equal size placed on a page in balance from the optical center (left) and one group half the size of the other placed twice the distance from the optical center for proper balance (right).*

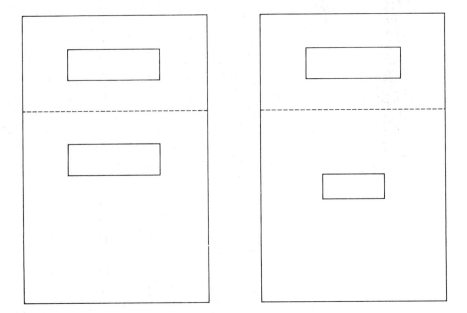

If two or more groups are placed on a page, they should be balanced in such a position that the center of balance between the groups will fall on the optical center.

## The Principle of Harmony

All the elements in the layout must work together if a communication is going to do its job. They cannot deliver the message to the target audience if they are fighting among themselves. The layout and everything in it must be in harmony.

In general, effective layouts achieve harmony in three ways. There is harmony of shapes, harmony of types, and harmony of tones.

Shape harmony is the first cousin to proportion and it means that the general structure of the elements is the same. The shape of the type should be the same as the shape of the page or printed area and the shape of the art and copy should follow this pattern.

Type harmony means that the letter designs of the styles selected should cooperate and blend together and not set up visual dissonance. Type harmony can be achieved by staying with types of one family and selecting similar series of that family. Avoid, for instance, mixing condensed and extended types of the same family. However, some judgment is needed here, as we will see when we discuss the principle of contrast.

If different types are used to provide contrast, they should be radically different. Two families of the same race have characteristics that are basically similar and will not be different enough to provide much contrast. They will clash, and destroy harmony. And they just plain look bad together.

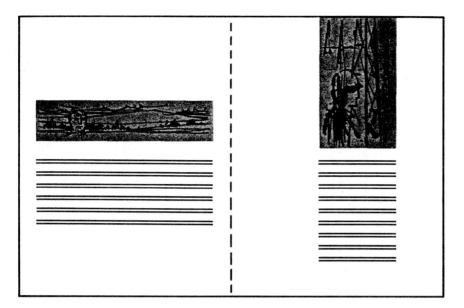

**Fig. 8-10** *Shape harmony in which the general structure of the art and copy blocks are the same is a pleasing arrangement. (Reprinted with permission of Westvaco Corporation.)*

Two families from different races can provide harmony and contrast, but one should clearly dominate. If they are the same, or near the same, size, there's a chance that the effect will be jarring and destroy the harmony.

Avoid mixing lowercase and all-cap words. Capitals are formal and dignified and do not harmonize with the irregular shapes of lowercase letters. Stick to one or the other whenever possible.

If boldface type is selected for more than an occasional emphasis, other elements in the layout should be strong as well.

Borders should have shapes in common with the type letter style for type and border harmony. A Black Letter type looks best with a decorative border, and a modern Roman, with its thick and thin letter strokes, goes well with an Oxford rule, which has parallel thick and thin lines.

Tone harmony refers to the weights and designs of elements. Bold illustrations and bold types harmonize. Ornamental borders and ornamental types go well together. A straight-line rule will harmonize with a straight-line Sans Serif type.

FUTURA LIGHT

**FUTURA DEMIBOLD**

**FUTURA BOLD**

*Fig. 8-11* *Elements in graphic design should harmonize. Light typefaces should be used with light art and borders, bold types with bold art.*

## The Principle of Contrast

What a monotonous world this would be if everything was the same. The changing seasons, the mountains, lakes, and oceans of our earth, the various groups of people who make up the human race, all add interest and contrast to life. Sameness is boring in life, and it can be boring in printed communications as well.

Skilled speakers use voice modulation, pauses, and gestures to make their points and hold the audience's interest. Skilled communicators also use various devices to emphasize important elements in their printed material. In addition, they add variety and interest by applying the principle of contrast.

Contrast gives life, sparkle, and emphasis to a communication. Contrast shows the reader the important elements. And contrast helps readers remember those elements.

Contrast can be achieved by a number of typographic devices. The most obvious of these is the occasional use of italic or boldface types. However, these should be used sparingly, like seasoning in a stew. Too much contrast creates an indigestible typographical mess.

Other ways of achieving contrast include varying the widths of copy blocks, breaking up long copy with subheads, varying shapes of elements, balancing a strong display against a lighter-toned text mass, surprinting (printing type lines on top of halftones or other art), and enlarging one in a group of photos.

A good starting point in achieving contrast in layouts, and a good way to approach handling of copy, is to break down the copy into "thought phrases." This thought grouping involves taking the

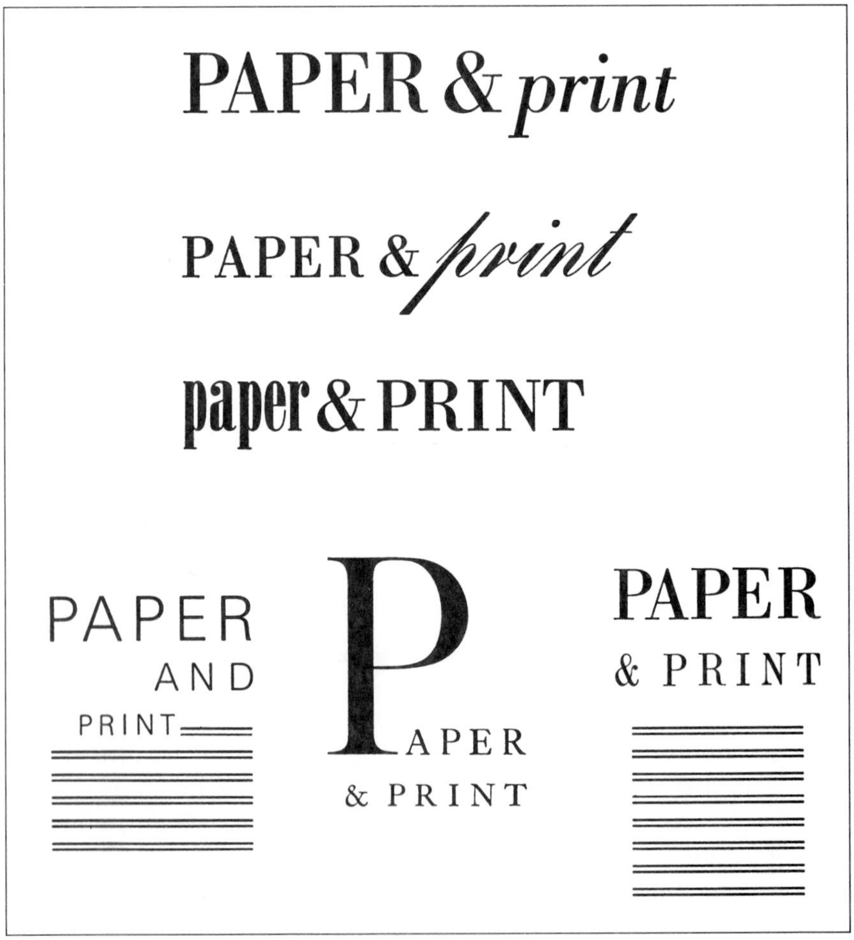

**Fig. 8-12**  *Contrast can be achieved and harmony maintained by varying the type sizes and styles but keeping the same family. (Reprinted with permission of Westvaco Corporation.)*

copy and handling it as it might be spoken. Headlines and lines of copy should be written in natural phrases that the reader can take in at a glance.

Suppose we are writing a title for an article and we come up with this wording:

The Miracle of Joe's Discovery

Now, suppose we want to run this head in two lines. How should we divide it? The easy way would be to divide it so both lines would be about the same length. We'd end up with something like this:

# The Miracle of
# Joe's Discovery

But that division makes an unnatural pause in the way the reader would decipher the head since reading is accomplished by grasping the meaning of words in groups of coherent phrases or sentences. So a better way to set the head would be to divide the wording into natural thought groups, something like this:

# The Miracle
# of Joe's Discovery

This head can be grasped at a glance, and the uneven lines add interest and contrast to the arrangement. (Note: The arrangement of the type lines might be dictated by the "head schedule" used by the publication. We have not considered this here but we will in our discussions of magazine and newspaper layout.)

A little more complex example, but one that better illustrates the principle of contrast, is the way the following simple advertisement is handled. Suppose we have this copy to arrange:

Spend your summer vacation high in the Sierras at Wayside Inn

Let's set this in display type:

**Spend Your Summer**

**Vacation High**

**in the Sierras**

**At Wayside Inn**

What is wrong? The message is almost incoherent because the lines of type cause awkward and unnatural pauses when the copy is read. Let's use thought grouping to make this easy to read and comprehend. Is this better?

## Spend Your
## Summer Vacation
## High in the Sierras
## at Wayside Inn

The next step is to bring the principle of contrast into play. We can add emphasis where it belongs to create a more interesting and memorable message:

## Spend Your
## Summer Vacation
# High in the Sierras
## at
## *Wayside Inn*

Contrast thus relieves monotony, adds emphasis where it belongs, makes layouts more interesting, and helps effective communication.

## The Principle of Rhythm

Layouts that communicate effectively are not static things that just lie there on the page. They are alive and they move. In writing, just as in music, life is added by imparting action, variety, and interest to the message. While music communicates with sound, printed communications use art and words to create a beat, or a rhythm, by measuring and balancing the movement of vision.

Three ways to get layouts moving include the placement of elements, using repetitious typographic devices, and arranging material in logical progression. Let's consider each of these methods.

We can place elements to take advantage of the natural path the eye follows as it travels through a printed page. As mentioned, the eye hits a point slightly above and to the left of the mathematical center of an area. What happens next? The eye travels to the right, then to the lower left, and then across to the lower right in a sort of $Z$ pattern.

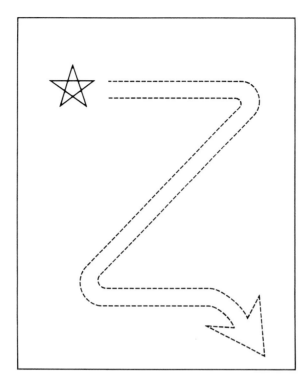

**Fig. 8-13** *Studies have shown that when a person scans a printed page, the usual eye pattern follows a rough Z through the page. Initial contact is made in the upper left near the optical center, then the eyes move to the right and then diagonally down the page to the lower left and then to the lower right.*

If we arrange the elements on the page in a logical order along this Z path, we can take advantage of nature to keep our layout moving.

A beat can be established by repeating typographic devices. Initial letters, boldface lead-ins, numbers or small illustrations, indented paragraphs, italic subheads, all not only provide contrast but if placed in a logical order can help direct the reader through the message and thus give it rhythm and motion.

## The Principle of Unity

Unity holds a design together and prevents looseness and disorder. When we see a loose printed communication, our eyes can't find a center of interest and they bounce around with no place to land.

Simplicity is the key here. Unity and simplicity aid communication and eliminate distraction. Keeping it simple is simple. Here are a few ideas:

■ Stick to a few type styles, preferably one family if possible.

■ Keep the number of shapes and sizes of art and types to a minimum.

■ Place art and heads where they won't interfere with the natural flow of reading matter.

■ Have one element in an illustration or one illustration in a group of illustrations dominate. Create a center of interest, and unity will often result.

**Fig. 8-14** *This advertisement illustrates important principles of design. Unity is achieved by the framing palm trees and the coupon. Attention is directed by the reverse headline near the optical center, and the obvious motion through the advertisement is toward the "action" or coupon placed in the lower right corner where the reader will exit the page. (Reprinted from* Holiday *magazine, now published by* Travel-Holiday Magazine, *Floral Park, New York 11001.)*

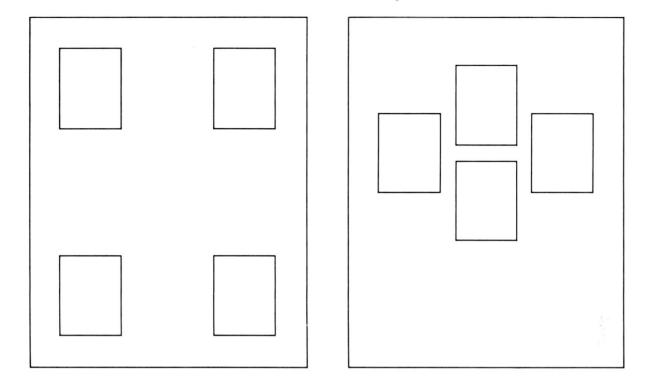

Unity can be achieved in ways that are obvious and some that are not so obvious. Obvious ways include enclosing everything in a border, isolating the layout with white space, and using the same basic shape, tone, color, or mood throughout.

Using boxes in a layout can help unify it if they are all similar in thickness, design, and tone. Being consistent in the use of typography is one of the easiest and best ways to ensure unity.

Unity can be achieved by applying what some artists refer to as the *three-point layout method.* So much of life is organized around the unit of three. In religion there is the Father, Son, and Holy Spirit; there's the earth, sea, and sky; there's food, shelter, and clothing. In the academic world, the liberal arts are grouped in units of three: natural sciences, social sciences, and humanities. In our governmental structure, we have federal, state, and local governments. And our flag combines red, white, and blue.

When we see three units together we tend to unify them. In layout, headline, art, and copy are the basic three units used to create one whole. The number of units of art, the number of headlines and subheads, or the number of copy blocks may likely vary within these three basic units. In deciding the number of units for layouts, keep in mind that odd-number units are more interesting than even-numbered ones. Three and five illustrations can make a layout more interesting than two or four.

Which principle of design is most important? Obviously an irrelevant question. Proportion, balance, contrast, and rhythm must all blend together. However, if all the elements aren't combined in a unified and harmonious composition, attention value is scattered

**Fig. 8-15** *Where should you look? Elements placed in the corners, or scattered, as on the left, create disunity as the eye bounces from one to the other. When elements are grouped together, a center of interest is developed and unity is achieved.*

**Fig. 8-16**  *Unity can be achieved by applying the "rule of three." People tend to unify elements when they appear in groups of three. (Courtesy of A.B. Dick.)*

and interest will decline. The completed layout must have unity and it must have balance. It must display pleasing proportions, an obvious directional pattern, and type and tone harmony.

Although there are "principles of design" that can be helpful guides, the positioning of elements and the effective regulation of size, shape, and tone depend more on a sense of correctness and good taste than strict adherence to arbitrary rules. This sense is developed by experience and practice, which increase our awareness of balance, proportion, unity, contrast, rhythm, and harmony.

## Effective Design Checklist

■ Balance can be obtained through control of size, tone, and position of elements.

■ Balance can be upset by nonharmonizing typefaces and too many nonessential elements in a layout.

■ A unifying force should hold the layout together—white space, borders, and consistency in shape, size, tone of elements can unify a layout.

■ Equal margins are monotonous. There should be more margin outside a rule than inside, but the rule should not crowd the type within.

■ Contrast adds interest. It can be achieved by varying widths of copy blocks, enlarging one in a group of pictures, and/or using italics or boldface, but sparingly.

■ Orderly repetition of some elements can provide motion to a layout.

■ Long horizontal or vertical elements will cause the reader to follow their direction.

■ The space within a layout should be broken up into pleasing proportions.

■ Simplicity is important for attractive layouts. It can be achieved by using a few type styles and reducing the number of shapes and sizes of art.

■ Use design clichés with caution. These include picture cutouts in odd shapes, tilting art or type, setting vertical lines of type, or using mortises, overlaps, tint blocks.

## Graphics in Action

1. Find in advertisements, art, headlines, magazine pages, or other printed material one example of each principle of design. Mount them neatly as exhibits and write captions explaining how the exhibit illustrates the principle. Type the captions and paste them on the exhibit adjacent to the illustrations.

2. Study the design of the front page of a newspaper. List the ways you believe the principles of design have been applied (for example, an italic headline may have been used for contrast). Evaluate the page from a design standpoint and point out any changes you might make if you were redesigning the page.

3. Find a two-page spread in a magazine. Clip and mount it on poster board. Assume that you are the editor of the magazine and the art director has asked for your evaluation of the design. Write an evaluation in the form of a memo to the art director.

4. Draw a rectangle 4 by 6 inches on plain white paper or layout paper. Draw a square 5 by 5 inches on another sheet. Draw four rectangles of the following dimensions in each of the areas. Arrange them any way you believe best. Lightly shade them. (It will be helpful to make some rough sketches of the arrangements and use the one you believe best as a model in making the final sketches.) Dimensions of rectangles: 3 by ½, 2 by ½, 1½ by 1, 1 by ½ inches. In arranging the rectangles, consider unity and balance. Decide which arrangement is most appealing.

5. Draw an area 5 by 7 inches on plain white or layout paper and arrange the following information in the area. This is a cover for a booklet. Sketch the words as carefully as you can to simulate the size and style of type for each line. Remember to apply the principles of design. Use rules or borders if you wish. The copy is:

    A Self-guiding Tour of _____ (choose a city: Paris, New York, Moscow, Tokyo, your hometown), Walking Tours Publishing Company, Your Town, Your State

    (*Hint:* The first step should involve thought grouping.)

**Fig. 9-1** *This is the shirt illustration. (This problem is adapted from* Newspaper Advertising Handbook, *with thanks to the author, Don Watkins, and publisher, Dynamo, Inc.)*

In Chapter 8 we discussed the principles of design for effective layouts. Now it's time to put those principles to work. A good place to start is with advertising layout.

Here is the situation. The manager of the Velour Shop has asked a designer to plan a layout for an advertisement to appear in the local newspaper to help introduce the arrival of a new type of sports shirt. The manager has the heading, the paragraph of sales copy, the price of the shirt, a piece of art showing the shirt, and the store's logo. The designer has these elements to work with:

### The Shirt.

It's here now . . . The Shirt . . . It's velour and it's sweeping the country . . . cool, calm, and collectible . . . just right for this season's fashion mood. Long sleeves. Stripes or solids.

$25
Visa & Master Charge
the VELOUR shop
(address)

The designer has to arrange this copy in a space 2 columns wide and 8 inches deep (4 by 8 inches). Then the arrangement will be given to the store manager for approval before it is printed.

The steps the designer uses in planning and making the advertisement layout are an effective guide for planning all types of printed communications, whether for print media or graphics for television.

There are several good reasons to approach the study of graphics from an advertising base. Some of the best talent in the communications field works in the world of advertising. Advertising is a pacesetter in the use of art, type styles, and the arrangement of elements on the printed page.

In addition, advertising makes a good starting place because all the steps from conceptualization to the finished comprehensive (a representation of the final art) can be followed quite easily. All the principles of design can be seen in action in one comparatively small area, like the advertisement for the Velour Shop. A well-designed advertisement will contain, on one page or less, balance, proportion, unity, contrast, and rhythm. These principles are put to work to create a communication that is to do a specific job.

There is another benefit. Quite often communicators have to work with advertising people. Any knowledge acquired about their philosophies about communications will help the "editorial side" person do a better job.

Communicators often can get good ideas for brochure and magazine page layouts by studying the arrangements of advertisements and seeing if they can be adapted to editorial content. For example, does the placement of elements in the advertisement reproduced here in Fig. 9-2 trigger ideas for placement of elements on a magazine page?

## America's best export is America.

InterNorth and several other large American corporations have been engaged in a unique business-to-business relationship for five years in nations of the Caribbean Basin. Called Caribbean-Central American Action, it is the initiative of an international partnership to encourage development of strong, market-oriented economies.

The freedom and stability of the Western Hemisphere will depend largely upon the economic models its nations choose to adopt. The cooperative role of U.S. businesses can do much to ensure that those models provide productive freedom and a better way of life for the people of the region.

Balance-of-trade figures tell only part of the story of America's success in international business. The rest of the story is the incalculable benefit in sharing the best of America with other nations.

Americans don't export just goods and services. We also send abroad the compelling evidence of how well our system works, and the inspiring model of what free people can achieve for themselves in a free system.

That's why our InterNorth International company and other international companies take pride in sharing the best of America with the rest of the world. Our most valuable export is our nation's 200-year-old success story.

InterNorth is a diversified, energy-based corporation involved in natural gas, liquid fuels, petrochemicals, and exploration and production of gas and oil.

**INTERNORTH**
We work for America.

**International Headquarters, Omaha, Nebraska 68102**
© 1983, InterNorth, Inc.

**Fig. 9-2**

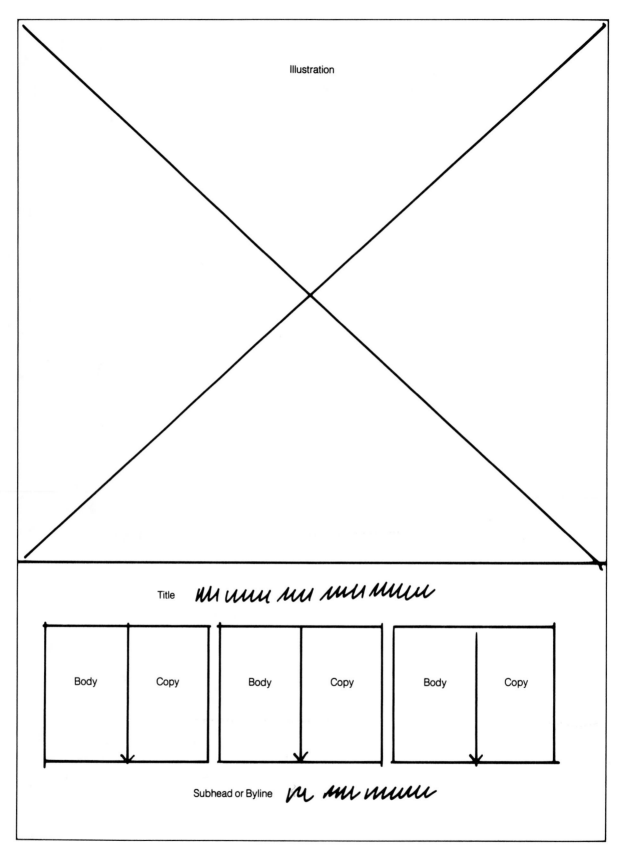

**Fig. 9-3**  *Rough sketch of possible layout for a magazine or brochure based on the Internorth advertisement. Advertisements can be good idea sources for communicators.*

Of course the creation of a layout is but one small part of the advertising process, just as it is but one part of any communication effort. It cannot be completely isolated from the other steps in effective communication. But even this brief look at advertising design should help us understand a little about the whole process of advertising communications.

Therefore, before we follow the designer in developing the advertisement for the Velour Shop, let's examine some of the approaches to design used by those who plan and create advertisements.

## Design and Advertising Communication

Advertising communication differs from most other communication in two ways. Here the communicator pays to have the message circulated. As a result, the communicator has more control over the message than, say, the public relations professional who distributes a press release. The source pays so the source can specify when and where the advertisement will appear. The source decides the size and content of the message as well.

Advertising communication is aimed basically at getting people to do something or accept something, often against their will or initial inclination. Therefore advertising communication must use all the attributes of the communication process to attain maximum effectiveness. This includes typography and graphics.

Advertising communication is *persuasive communication.* So is most public relations communication and much newspaper and magazine editorial content. This makes them sort of cousins under the skin. Better newspapers, brochures, and other printed materials can be designed by studying the techniques of the advertising designer. Since typography and layout cannot be separated from the message they present, the most effective design cannot be created without understanding how that design is linked to the message.

A quick trip through the advertising copywriting process will help us understand the importance of linking the layout with the message.

### The Strategy Platform

The first step taken by most advertising copywriters is to form a "strategy platform" as a guide for the actual writing. Usually more than one person is involved in devising the strategy platform. The account executive, copywriters, and layout people work together as a team. (In a one-person shop, of course, it will be a one-person project.)

The strategy platform is a written statement that answers the following questions:

**1.** Who is the target audience?

**2.** What is the most important idea in this whole project?

**3.** What are the most important selling features?

**4.** What other important features of the product or idea should be considered?

**5.** What action do we want from the target audience?

The job of the copywriter and the layout artist is to integrate the verbal and visual elements they believe will be most effective. The goal is to get the desired "action" out of the target audience in the most effective and least expensive way.

Quite often copywriters and layout artists work together to accomplish this. Sometimes one person, if that person knows typography and graphics as well as the techniques of effective copywriting, does the whole job.

## A Useful Formula

There is an old tried-and-true formula that advertising copywriters often use to arrange the information they believe most effective to create a selling message. This formula plots out things from start to finish, from attention to action, in a series of five steps. This has been dubbed the A-I-D-C-A approach.

The A-I-D-C-A approach is effective in planning all sorts of communications. But few communicators outside the field of advertising are aware of it.

Let us take a look at how the formula is applied to the communications process. Before any communication can take place an initial contact with the target audience must be made. They will not listen if we do not get them to look up from what they are doing or stop them from turning the page.

This process of *getting attention* is the A of the formula. Whether an advertisement or a layout for a magazine article is being planned, the communicator must get the attention of the audience before going on. Typography can do it. Effective words presented in the right type style can do it. Effective art can do it, too. Either way, the designer must blend the words of the copywriter with the skills of the typographer.

The A for attention is followed by I, which stands for *interest.* Something written in the copy and arranged in the layout must grasp the reader's interest quickly.

Well, we have attention, and we have aroused interest. What happens next? The prospect must be given a strong shot of *"desire."* This means desire to acquire the product, to know more about it, or to endorse the idea, or whatever the objective of the message might be. In writing a narrative, for instance, we must build up the reader's interest to make that reader want to continue through to the end. The D is for desire.

Depending on the purpose of the communication, the C may or may not be pertinent. If an advertising layout is trying to sell the reader a product, now is the time for *conviction.* However, if this is a brochure explaining an activity, C may not be needed. It

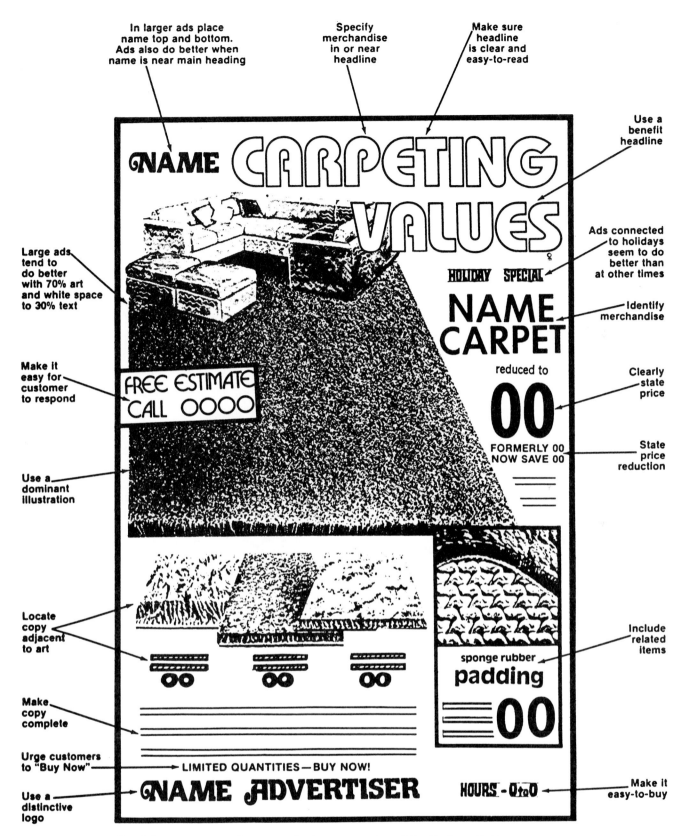

**Fig. 9-4**  *Points in an effective retail advertisement from "Plus Business Guide to Effective Advertising." (Reproduced with permission of Metro Associated Services, Inc.)*

all depends on the type of communication in question. But C in an advertising message, or in an editorial, is the *clincher*, when the message has sold the prospect. Here is where the communicator closes the pitch and has the prospect ready to put money, or support, on the line.

Finally, it's back to A, but this time the word is *action*. Action provides the means for accomplishing the purpose of the whole thing in the first place. If a communication does not provide the target audience with a way to take action or let them know action has been or will take place, depending on the purpose of the message, very little will happen. In advertising, action can be generated by a number of devices—limited time offers, send in that coupon, get in on this special deal, price good until the end of the week, and so on.

The A-I-D-C-A formula provides a plan to keep things moving, to establish the rhythm and motion needed for a dynamic layout. The communicator can use this formula to help in placing elements on a page for a dynamic, alive layout such as the one illustrated in Fig. 9-5.

### Graphic Elements

Whether the advertisement designer uses the A-I-D-C-A formula or has another approach to the task, the graphic elements of an advertisement facilitate quick and easy comprehension of the printed word. They can supply additional information that the written word cannot convey well, and they can help set the mood desired.

Let us take a quick look at how these elements can be put together into an effective advertisement. Most of these techniques can be transferred to all types of printed communications—they aren't just the private domain of the advertising world.

Art can be used in advertising for many different purposes. The most obvious and most frequent use is art that simply shows what the product looks like. Product art is most effective, however, when readers are already aware of their need for the type of product being pictured.

Art can be very effective by showing a product being used. Art of this sort can stir to consciousness a need or desire for the product that was not felt before. It can also reinforce a headline designed to attract a particular target market or make the wording that does this unnecessary in the headline, thus leaving room in the head for something else that might make the complete ad message more effective. Art showing a product being used, should include people with whom the intended readers can or want to identify.

Art can also demonstrate the happy results of owning or using the product or service or patronizing a particular establishment. This may be shown either realistically or symbolically. Usually this type of illustration is associated with emotional, imaginative copy. This kind of art is especially helpful if the advertiser wants to reach

persons who have not felt a need for the product. It attracts the interest of hard-to-motivate prospects by making them want to experience the same joy and satisfaction as the pictured users. It arouses their interest in the product or service, hopefully enough so they will read the rest of the ad to find out more.

Such art can take a positive or negative approach, or two pictures can be used, one negative and the other positive. They can show the predicament and the solution or some sort of before-and-after approach. Advertisers have found this type of advertising to be very effective.

Closely related to "happy results" illustrations are those that imply psychological relationships between the product and its users.

**Fig. 9-6**   *Just the right art combined
with just the right type styles create the
desired image of a country cafe.
(Courtesy of Dynamic Graphics.)*

This type of art emphasizes the background and environment of the product's users or portrays people with whom readers would want to be associated. This art must be reinforced by imaginative, emotional copy.

Art used in advertising copy can show real products and real people in actual situations; it can also be abstract and symbolic. Symbolic art can reflect various attributes of a store or product— stylishness, reliability, durability, convenience, femininity, masculinity, gaiety, seriousness. Symbolic art is used to reinforce an element of the product's image. This type of art is difficult to create but it can have great impact and memorability. It is a real challenge to the communicator's creativity to come up with ideas for symbolic art that are not trite or too obvious.

Quite often art can be used much more effectively than words to demonstrate features of a product and how it is made and works. Cutaway techniques or greatly magnified illustrations of product details that may never be seen by the user in normal circumstances can be effective in certain situations and for certain products. This kind of art goes well with factual copy and is a graphic way of presenting tangible evidence that a product can perform as promised.

Illustrations can connect the use of a product with a national or local current event. A picture of a blizzard can remind people of the need for all sorts of bad weather gear, especially if a blizzard is raging outside at the time the advertisement appears.

Art can also show "news" about the product, or where it may be obtained. New merchandise can be shown being unloaded, a crowd attracted by a special event, progress on new construction.

Art can also be used to make people laugh. Some of the most memorable communications are those that make us relax and chuckle. People tend to respond well to cartoons and illustrations that have a humorous theme. However, the theme should tie in with the story line of the copy or the object of the advertisement.

Art can be used to attract attention, arouse curiosity, or simply to decorate an advertisement. However, all art used in a layout should have a job to do. An inappropriate piece of art in no way related to the ad message can do more harm than good. It can detract from the impact. It may even make a reader mad if she or he feels tricked by the irrelevancy of the art to the message. The use of sexism, for instance, a pretty woman in a bikini standing beside a product, simply to attract attention can be particularly offensive.

### Headlines for Advertisements

The headline is the most important single typographic element in an advertisement. Its primary function is A—attention. In addition to attracting attention, an effective headline states or implies a benefit. It should contain a verb if possible, and active verbs far outperform passive verbs. The good headline identifies the target audience and gets the reader involved.

> # To improve your accounts receivable, shift your point of view.

The headline for an advertisement might be developed from the copy, as it is for a news story or magazine article. It can also tie in with the illustration.

Some ad copywriters say if the headline doesn't get the reader's attention the rest of the ad will never be read. If it attracts the wrong kind of readers, those who don't want, don't need, or can't afford the product, the ad won't do its job.

How long should a headline be? Basically a headline should say enough to attract the attention of the target audience and make them want to read the rest of the ad. But keep it short. There have been successful Volkswagen ad heads with just two words:

Think Small

Nobody's Perfect

However, use as many words as necessary to do the job. One of the most famous heads in all advertising history had eighteen words:

At Sixty Miles an Hour the Loudest Noise

In This New Rolls Royce Comes from the

Electric Clock

The communicator has many choices when deciding on the type of headline for an advertisement. There is the "news" headline:

Wammo Now Has Flamastan

The news headline should be set in a type style that makes it look like a newspaper headline.

The selective headline emphasizes appeal to the target audience and helps sift out the target from the mob. A headline for Haggar slacks zoomed in on the target like this:

The Slacks for the Untamed Young Man

Benefit headlines stress advantages. The most effective benefit headlines do not boast, they stress benefits to the target audience:

You'll Have No Maintenance Costs for Five Years

Promise headlines, those that offer a reward for use of the product or adoption of the idea, should be followed by proof in the copy that the promise will be kept. Closely related to the promise head is the "how to" or advice headline:

How To Get More Interest on Your Savings

**Fig. 9-7** *This headline identifies the target audience and holds out a promise to lure the target audience into the advertisement. Also note the correct use of negative leading between the lines. The ascenders and descenders do not touch.*

Here, again, proof should be offered in the copy. The command headline gets readers involved because they are urged to act. Tactfully and subtly written, it can be very effective, but if the command is too strong the prospect might take offense at your arrogance. "Do Yourself a Favor, Buy from Us" is a much more effective approach than "Buy from Us, We're the Best."

Label headlines in advertisements are weak, just as weak as label heads on news stories or articles. A label head simply states a title or obvious fact. "Arrow Shirts" would be an advertising label head; "Lions Club Meets" would be a label head on a news story.

There are many other types of advertising headlines. There are those that pose a question ("Do You Suffer from Headaches?"), those that attempt to arouse curiosity ("How Many Beans in This Jar?"), and those that challenge ("Go for It!"). These heads are effective if done well, but they usually violate the basic rule that a headline should reveal what an ad is about. They can arouse curiosity enough to make the reader read on but if the copy does not satisfy that curiosity, the head may make an enemy for the sponsor of the ad.

### Copy in Advertisements

*Copy* is the printed words in an advertisement. It is made up of the headline and the body information. These, together with the illustrations and *logo* (the name of the firm in a distinctive design) plus any other typographic devices make up the components of an advertising layout.

The person who makes the layout should understand something about what makes an effective piece of body copy. The key word is *words*.

**Fig. 9-8**  *"Early in the development of the layout idea you must establish a style," suggests designer Don Watkins. Here are three possibilities from his* Newspaper Advertising Handbook: *Formal, conservative arrangement* (left); *more visually exciting informal balance* (middle); *heavy, hard sell* (right).

Copy is composed of words, and the best copy is composed of the best words that can be found. Words that stop you in your tracks, words that sell you, words that get you going, words that reflect the consumer's point of view rather than the seller's. "You" words help draw the audience into the message. "Selling" words help the copy get action.

> Those who write advertising copy . . . should, I believe, constantly bear in mind that, if advertising copy is to be at all effective in contributing to the eventual sale, it should not venture beyond its limited province of informing favorably; of inciting curiosity; of building belief; of creating understanding; of developing the urge to investigate and see for oneself, [1]

writes Walter Weir to explain the role of the copywriter.

The copywriter must understand the product thoroughly, know what it can do, how it does it, and its assets and shortcomings when compared to similar products. The writer must also have a clear idea of the target audience. The key to successful communication here, as it is in all other areas, is to be able to create common understanding and believability. An understanding of the target audience's characteristics and behavior is vital.

The graphic designer should be as equally well informed concerning these aspects of successful advertising.

## Making the Layout

An advertising communication is made up of many parts: headline, art, copy, logo. How these parts are arranged is called the layout. The layout is the blueprint. This blueprint could be a *rough* (a working sketch with just enough detail to guide the person who puts the parts together) or it could be a *comp* (for comprehensive, also often called a *mechanical*), a finished pasteup ready to be photographed for plate making and printing.

Many people seeking entry-level positions in the communications industry will find they have a definite advantage over the competition if they have acquired some layout and pasteup skill.

The layout is one of three parts of the package the communicator passes on to the producer, compositor, or printer. The others are the typed copy and the art (photographs or drawings).

In the last chapter we discussed design principles. Now it's time to put those principles to work.

## Visualization

The first step in developing a layout involves some brainstorming. This is called *visualization*. The communicator's most important job is not done with a drawing pencil, it is done with the brain. The communicator must "see" in the mind's eye how a layout is going to appear. For example, the newspaper publisher wants the paper to look dignified, quiet, and authoritative. How do you

---

### Creative Communication

The creative communicator can be frustrated by accumulating either too little or too much information.

Effective creative solutions require adequate information. Superficial research results in superficial design.

On the other hand, too much information that is not relevant to the goal of the layout can muddy the waters and cause confusion.

The creative communicator should make an effort to gather enough information to understand the design problem thoroughly. However, the irrelevant information should be eliminated.

Creativity is aided by concentration on information pertinent to the solution of the problem.

perceive such a newspaper's front page in your mind's eye? What sort of headlines, type styles, nameplate will transmit this image? What do the illustrations look like? How do you visualize it?

A company wants a brochure for its anniversary picnic. What should be its shape, size, and color? What sort of finished appearance should it have? Brainstorm possibilities and let them bounce around in your head. (Well, it's not quite this simple, as we will see in Chapter 16. Brainstorming in this case must include knowledge of such things as how the brochure will be distributed, but these examples do help illustrate the visualization step.)

Visualization gives direction. It gets us started. It takes an idea or concept and translates it into visual form. Try it and see if this is true. Suppose you have the job of designing an advertisement using this copy:

The surf is up at Waikiki. Take a winter break in the sun and surf at the Breakers Hotel.

How do you visualize the ad? The possibilities are unlimited: the sun, surf, and sand; palm trees swaying; the hotel and the beach; people surfing. What sort of art would be best, a photo or a drawing? What sort of type style would say it best? What words would you want to stand out? How would you arouse the reader's interest, make that reader stop and want to know more?

That's visualization.

The designer who has to arrange the elements for the Velour Shop advertisement will not have the opportunity of doing a lot of creative visualization because the art and copy have already been determined. However, before the layout process begins, our designer friend will visualize several possible arrangements and type styles.

## Thumbnails

The next step in producing a layout involves getting something down on paper. Generally three steps are needed to move from the concept to the finished layout. They are the creation of thumbnails, roughs, and comprehensives.

Thumbnail sketches are miniature drawings in which different arrangements of the elements are made. The goal is to experiment and settle on the most effective placement of the headlines, art, and copy to achieve two goals: (1) To make the most attractive arrangement possible by putting into practice the principles of effective design by applying the basics of good typography, type selection, and arrangement. (2) To construct a working blueprint that can be understood and followed by everyone involved in the production of the communication.

We don't have to be artists to produce thumbnails, or roughs for that matter. Headlines can be indicated by drawing guidelines to indicate the height of the types to be employed and then filling in between them with up and down strokes.

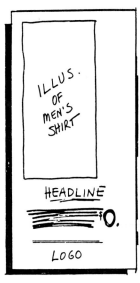

**Fig. 9-9** *Thumbnail sketches of possible arrangements for the Velour Shop advertisement. (Adapted from Newspaper Advertising Handbook.)*

For easy work and best results, try using a soft pencil for making thumbnails and roughs. The best are either 2H or HB. If softer pencils are used, they are likely to smudge and need to be sharpened more often (pencils numbered 2B to 6B are very soft). Harder pencils are difficult to use, will punch holes in the paper, and the lines are light and difficult to erase. Pencils numbered 3H to 9H are hard. You can obtain 2H or HB pencils at most stationery sections of discount stores or at art supply houses, and they do not cost much.

Art in thumbnails and roughs can be indicated by an outline of the general shape of the illustration, shaded to match its tone.

Body copy or copy blocks can be designated by squares, rectangles, or whatever shape the set type takes. Lines should be drawn in these areas to simulate the width of the type and the leading.

A very rough approximation of the size and shape of the elements is adequate when making thumbnails. Roughs need to be more exact.

Quite often we will need to make several thumbnails before we find an arrangement that we believe to be the best. An easy way to get started is to take a sheet of layout paper the size of the finished layout and fold it into quarters or eighths. This will give four or eight areas for thumbnails in exact proportion to the finished layout.

As an example, the designer working on the Velour Shop advertisement might make thumbnails in areas 1 by 2 inches or one-fourth the 4 by 8 size of the finished advertisement. Since this is such a small area in which to work, it is more likely that a 2 by 4 or a full-size 4 by 8 area will be used.

With a little practice most communicators can produce credible thumbnails. This is the first step in the creation of advertising layouts, and it is the first step in creating layouts for newspapers, magazines, brochures and other printed communications.

**Fig. 9-10** *Headlines on roughs can be indicated in this manner. Guidelines should be drawn to the exact size of the type specified in the comprehensive, but the rough lines only need to simulate the type.*

**Fig. 9-11** *A rough "scribble" of the approximate size and shape of the art is adequate for rough layouts.*

**Fig. 9-12** *Lines can be sketched for roughs to indicate body matter. The size of the copy block and the width of the lines should be exact, however.*

After experimenting with the various possible arrangements, the layout artist selects the one that appears to be the most effective. A rough layout is then produced with the thumbnail serving as a guide.

### Producing Rough Layouts

The rough layout is a drawing the actual size of the finished advertisement. All elements are presented fairly clearly and accurately as far as size, style, spacing, and placement are concerned. It is not quite as finished as the comprehensive, however.

Display type is lettered in and art is sketched in the same size and tone as in the final product; there is enough detail so that the art is a close approximation of its final form. Quite often a copy of the original art will be made and pasted in place on the rough.

Text copy, or reading matter, is still indicated by drawn copy blocks, but these are made precisely as the finished product will

**Fig. 9-13** *A rough layout* (right) *is made from the thumbnail* (left) *selected from those sketched for the Velour Shop advertisement.*

THUMBNAIL

ROUGH

look, with lines drawn, or "comped," to indicate the type size and leading to be used. Sometimes "greeking" or simulated type is used for copy blocks in roughs.

There are a number of methods available for producing display lines and headlines for beginning layout work. People planning careers as graphic artists will, of course, want to develop lettering ability. One of the procedures that is used to develop this skill can serve adequately for communicators who want to understand and have some layout skill but who do not necessarily want to go beyond the rough stage in layout work. The technique is *comping type.*

Both reading matter and display type can be comped for rough layouts. The results will be accurate enough to give the precision of the finished product and realistic enough to show how it will appear.

Reading matter is comped by drawing lines to indicate the type size and the leading or space between lines. This is done in two ways. An ordinary pencil can be used to draw two thin lines to indicate the tops and bottoms of the x heights of the lines of type.

**Fig. 9-14** *The two-line method of indicating reading matter on layouts. The two lines indicate the x height of the type chosen.*

Or, a chisel-point pencil can be used to draw a solid line to represent the lines of type. This kind of pencil can be obtained at most art supply stores. If the point is too wide to represent the size of type desired, it can be shaved down with a single-edge razor blade. A double-edged blade should not be used since it isn't sturdy enough.

Pencils for comping body type should not be too soft. They will not hold the point long, and it will be easy to smear the comped lines. Layout artists recommend HB or 2H pencils.

**Fig. 9-15** *The solid-line method of indicating reading matter for copy blocks on layouts. The solid line is the same height as the x height of the type selected.*

The procedure for comping solid lines of reading matter includes these steps:

1. Tape the paper to be used on a flat surface (a drawing board is best). Use a T square to be sure the paper is lined up square with the edge of the surface so the T square can be used to draw straight lines.

2. Draw a light outline of the area the type will occupy (the copy block) with the T square and a triangle.

3. Select the type to be used in the finished layout. Indicate the proper leading between lines. Now make small dots vertically in the area to be comped to indicate the base of the $x$ height of the letters to fill the area.

4. Check to see that the pencil point is the same as the $x$ height of the type selected.

5. Use the straight edge of the T square as a guide to draw the lines to represent the lines of type.

If the pairs-of-lines method is used, the same procedure is employed except that dots are placed to represent both the top and bottom of the $x$ height of the letters.

After some practice with full lines, try comping with equal paragraph indentations and lines that are ragged right, ragged left, and centered.

Display type can be comped by tracing. The tools required are a complete alphabet of the size and style of type to be used, a drawing board, a T square, a piece of tracing paper, a ruler, and a hard pencil with a sharp point. The steps include:

1. Draw a light baseline for the type on the tracing paper.

2. Place the tracing paper over the alphabet at the point where the word should begin. Be sure to line the drawn baseline up with the baseline of the alphabet.

3. Trace the first letter in the head or display line in outline form.

4. Proceed to trace the rest of the letters in the line. Care should be taken to space the letters properly and to line each up evenly on the baseline. Time taken to do the job carefully will pay dividends in the end.

5. Fill in the outlines and erase the guidelines as much as possible.

The letters can be filled in with pencil, ink, or felt pen. After a little practice, you will be surprised at the realistic results that can be obtained even with Scripts and Cursives, Black Letter, and ornamental types. If color is needed, the letters can be filled in with colored pencils, felt pens, or ink.

The display lines can be cut out and pasted on the layout. Sometimes the display lines can be traced in outline form and the image transferred to the layout. This is accomplished by rubbing the back of the traced area with a soft pencil. Then the line is placed in position on the layout and the letters traced again. The pencil coating on the back of the tracing paper will act as a carbon to transfer the image to the layout. Again, the letter can be filled in with colored pencils, felt pens, or ink.

There are alphabets of display type that can be transferred to a layout by rubbing. The procedure is the same as when tracing. A baseline is drawn and the letters are lined up for even horizontal and correct vertical spacing. Instead of tracing letters, they are transferred from the master alphabet to the layout by rubbing them with a ballpoint or rounded-point instrument.

Alphabets are also available in printed sheets and in pads of individual letters. The letters can be assembled in display lines and pasted on the layout.

### The Comprehensive

The final step is constructing the comprehensive. This is the completed layout. Proofs of the type and art are pasted into place to make an exact rendering of the advertisement as it will appear in print.

**Fig. 9-16** *It takes very little practice for the novice to make excellent titles and headlines for layouts by using transfer letters.*

**Fig. 9-17** *The comprehensive layout for the Velour Shop advertisement.*

When the advertisement is completed with the exact art and type in place, the rendering is called a *mechanical*. This can be used for making the printing plate.

## The Markup

In much communication work, particularly advertisements, brochures, and flyers, the working layout is a rough that includes instructions for the compositor or printer. This is called a *markup*. The markup, illustrations, and typed copy are turned over to the printer.

All instructions to the printer are written—often in a color to prevent confusion with what is to be set in type—and circled. Abbreviations are used whenever possible and a sort of code is developed based on basic printing terms.

Instructions on a markedup rough include:

- The family, series, and size of all type faces.
- The length of all the lines of type, plus the leading between lines.
- The line setting, such as centered, flush left, or flush right.
- Any special instructions for the particular job in question.

Below are the most frequently used terms for indicating instructions on roughs:

| | |
|---|---|
| CAPS | Set in all capital letters |
| clc | Set in capitals and lowercase letters |
| lc | Set in all lowercase |
| pt | Abbreviation for point size of type |
| BF | Set in boldface |
| 8 on 10 | (Also written as a fraction, 8/10.) The top number indicates the point size of the type and the lower number the leading between lines (in this case, 8-point type set on a 10-point base, or 8-point type leaded 2 points) |
| 18 | Set copy block 18 picas wide |
| 8/10 × 18 | Often the type size, leading, and line length are combined like this |
| ⌐ ⌐ | Center this line |
| ⌐ | Set flush left |
| ⌐ | Set flush right |

The family names of types to be used are often abbreviated: Bod. for Bodoni, Bask. for Baskerville, Cent. for Century, and so on.

Copy blocks are indicated by letters circled on the rough and the same identifying letters are placed at the top of the page of the typed copy: Copy A, Copy B, and so on.

Illustrations can be keyed to the layout with numbers or letters and indicated as Photo 1, Photo 2, or Photo A, Photo B. Different practices may exist in different shops. Always check that the

16 — The Shirt. ← 36-point Fenice, clc

12-point rule →

← 1-point rule

$25 ← 36-point Onyx

VISA & MASTER CHARGE ← 10-point Helvetica, caps

the VELOUR shop ← Logo

1703 McFadden Street • Columbia, S.C. ← 12-point Cheltenham, clc

**Fig. 9-18** *The comprehensive layout marked up and ready for production. "Greeking" or simulated type has been used to indicate copy block A. Often, however, the comp is completed and ready to be photographed for plate making rather than marked up for further processing.*

producer of the printing understands the instructions and how they are coded.

The techniques used to write and lay out effective printed advertisements can be used to advantage by anyone working with the printed word.

## Effective Design Checklist

- Use visualization. A designer's most important tool is still the brain.

- Integrate the verbal (words) and visual (graphics) elements so they work together to do the job in the most effective way.

- Feature the most important idea or selling point in the layout.

- Check every element in a layout—each should be irreplaceable. If an element can be eliminated or replaced, it should be eliminated or replaced.

- Determine the form and arrangement of the layout by the task it is intended to perform.

- Graphic elements in a layout should facilitate quick and easy comprehension of the message, offer additional information, or set the mood desired.

- In advertising, art should be used to stir to consciousness a need or desire that was not felt before.

- In an advertisement, art that contains people should show people with whom the intended readers can identify.

- Remember that if the layout doesn't get the attention of its intended audience, it will not be read.

- Avoid using Scripts, Black Letter, and decorative types for headlines. If they are used it should be for a very special reason, the line should be very brief, and it should not be in all capitals.

## Graphics in Action

1. Make four thumbnail sketches, each in an area 3 by 5 inches, using the following elements: a one-line headline about 36 points high; an irregular illustration approximately 1½ by 1½ inches; a copy block approximately 1½ by 1 inch; and a logo approximately 2 by 1½ inches.

2. Practice comping reading matter and display type as well as using rub-on letters. Use the techniques in the layouts below.

3. Prepare a rough layout for a grocery store advertisement featuring one item from any full-page newspaper grocery store advertisement. Make a rough 4 by 6 inches. Use art clipped, traced, or sketched (black-and-white art only), maybe from the full-page advertisement itself. Use the store's logo.

4. Mark up the rough created above.

5. Select either the A or B copy following and create a layout. The layout should reflect the type of business and the product or service advertised. Create art or find it as in number 2. Make the advertisement 5 by 7 inches and do the markup.

A.　　　　At Your Service
Come and experience the classic
cuisine of Northern and Southern
Italy . . . tonight.
The Grotto
35 Elmwood Avenue
Phone 786-6531

B.　　　　Time to Redo
A new coat of paint can give your
home a brand new look . . . outside
and in! Let our team of painting
perfectionists do a beautiful and
complete job. Satisfaction
guaranteed. Estimates cheerfully
given at no obligations.
A-1 Painters
156 Rutgers Street
Phone 853-3907

**6.** Redesign the layout created for number 4 for an area 7 by 5. Keep
the principle of shape harmony in mind.

---

## Notes

1. Walter Weir, *On the Writing of Advertising* (New York: McGraw-Hill, 1960), p. 7.

# PAGINATION

Texet's Document Machine can paginate in both batch and highly interactive modes. The system first completes a batch pass, paginating about 90% of most documents. It flags those pages it cannot solve based on the design criteria you have specified for this document or series of documents. You can then interactively paginate these on screen.

## Save Money

In this mode pagination problems are solved with a variety of powerful interactive functions. Lines of type can be moved from one column to the next, leading added or subtracted, and columns vertically justified using a few simple commands, a plain-English menu, and a mouse-driven cursor. You may make editorial or design changes, arrange and rearrange both text and graphics until you have the page you want.

The Document Machine's powerful pagination capabilities can enable you to achieve dramatic savings in production time — in most cases, as much as 50% — by eliminating or condensing many of the steps in the traditional production process. The result is increased productivity on every job, and the ability to produce more work.

## Increase Productivity

Texet's Document Machine can paginate in both batch and highly interactive modes. The system first completes a batch pass, paginating about 90% of most documents. It flags those pages it cannot

Flow
Control

one? — yes

no

Continue

Stop

Figure 2.1

commands, a plain-English menu, and a mouse-driven cursor. You may make editorial or design changes, arrange and rearrange both text and graphics until you have the page you want.

## Save Time

capabilities can enable you to achieve dramatic savings in production time — in most cases, as much as 50% — by eliminating or condensing many of the steps in the traditional production process. The result is increased productivity on every job, and the ability to produce more work.

The Document Machine can paginate in both batch and highly interactive modes. The system first completes a batch pass, paginating about 90% of most documents. It flags those The Document Machine's powerful pagination capabilities can enable you to achieve dramatic in production time — in most cases, as much as by eliminating or condensing.

5

### Graphic Arts Defined For The Communicator*

Graphic arts is defined by Webster as "the fine and applied arts of representation, decoration, and writing or printing on flat surfaces together with the techniques and crafts associated with each." For the communicator, graphic arts might be defined as the process of combining all the typographic and artistic materials and devices available in a way that facilitates communication.

Graphic arts is not the technique of arranging type, illustrations, borders, and other devices to create an unusual visual experience. Rather, the selection and arrangement of materials should be to best facilitate the transfer of messages from a source to a receiver.

There are a number of steps that must be followed in preparing copy for production. Many of them have been discussed so far, but several still remain. For example, the chapter begins with a statement with a headline. It is to be printed in a newsletter for communicators. What must be done to transfer the typewritten copy to typeset copy ready to be printed?

Some of the preproduction tasks that must be performed include determining the style and size of type for the headline and the amount of space the piece will occupy in the publication. After it is set in type it will have to be proofed and read for errors.

These steps, along with cropping and sizing art and marking the layout to ensure that the specifications are clearly understood by all who will be working on the job, are part of preparation for production. Pasteup can be a part of the preparation, too.

Some people working in communications do the entire process themselves. In other situations designers and technicians do much of the work. But all who work in the world of printed communications will find a knowledge of the steps in preparing for production worthwhile.

---

## Copy-Fitting without Fits

Old-timers in the industry could squint at a piece of typewritten copy and tell within a fraction of an inch how much space it would occupy when set in a certain size of type. They called it "casting off" type. We call it *copy-fitting*.

Copy-fitting is a pesky business until you get used to it. However, proficiency can come quickly with a little practice. There are some things to remember from the start. For one thing, copy-fitting is an estimation. There is no exact method of fitting copy. The formulas have to be leavened with judgment.

One problem with copy-fitting is that every letter of every font of type, along with the spaces and punctuation marks, is not exactly the same width. If they were, copy-fitting would be sim-

*While standard English usage calls for lowercasing articles, coordinate conjunctions, and prepositions, regardless of length, unless they are the first words in the heading, some newspapers capitalize the first letters of all words in headlines. We will follow this pattern in this chapter.

ple. But since this is not the case, we have to use some judgment and make allowances in estimating how much space to designate for copy in layouts.

There are five situations in which copy-fitting might be used in planning printed communications. They include:

1. Estimating how much space a headline or title will take when set in a specific size and style of type.

2. Estimating how much space typed copy will occupy when set in a certain size and style of type on a predetermined width.

3. Finding out what size of type to use if the typed copy must fit a predetermined area in a layout.

4. Finding out how much copy to write to fill a certain space when the size and style of type have been selected.

5. Finding out how much space copy that has already been set in type or printed will occupy when reset in another size.

All of these calculations can be made easily with an understanding of only two copy-fitting methods. One is the unit-count system for display type and the other is the character-count system for reading matter.

## Copy-Fitting Display Type

The *unit-count system* used to determine the size of display lines, headlines, and titles for articles is based on the assignment of "units" for the letters, numerals, punctuation, and space in a head or title line. The units are assigned on the basis of the letters' relative widths.

Of the twenty-six letters in the lowercase alphabet, eighteen are virtually the same width. These eighteen are assigned a unit value of 1.

All of the other letters and punctuation marks are assigned unit values in relation to these eighteen. For instance, *m* is about one and a half times wider than *x*, so while *x* has a unit value of 1, *m* has a unit value of 1½. The lowercase *i* and *l* are about one-half the widths of *x*, so their value is ½.

Below is a typical unit-count system for display type:

| | |
|---|---|
| 1 unit | All lowercase letters (except *f*, *l*, *i*, *t*, *m*, *w*, and number 1), all spaces, larger punctuation such as ?, ¢, $, % |
| ½ unit | Lowercase *f*, *l*, *i*, *j*, *t*; capital letter *I*, spaces between words; most punctuation |
| 1½ unit | Lowercase *m*, *w*; all capital letters except *M*, *W*, *I* |
| 2 units | Capital *M* and *W* |

In solving a copy-fitting problem for display type, the first step is to determine how many units of the size and style of type will fit into the width selected and then see if the lines of the title or headline fit that limit. We can find this by taking a sample of the type and measuring the units that fit into the width.

For example, the headline at the start of this chapter was:

Graphic Arts Defined
For The Communicator

Let's say we want to set it in a medium Sans Serif type on a line 15 picas wide. Will it fit?

We first have to determine how many units of the type selected will fit into a 15-pica width. We can do this by taking a sample of the type and counting the units in a 15-pica line.

**This A Medium Sans Serif.**

Here is how the units will count out:

_____ 15  picas _____

**This A Medium Sans S|erif .**

1½   1   ½   1½ 1½ ½  2      1    1   ½   1½ ½ 1½  1   1   1  ½ 1½|  = 22½

Now we know that the maximum number of units of this type that will fit into a 15-pica width is 22½. So we check the lines we want to use to make sure each does not exceed 22½ units. If we count the units according to our system, we will discover that the top line contains 18½ units and the bottom line counts 20½ units. Both are under the maximum so the head should fit nicely.

┌────────── 15 picas ──────────┐

**Graphic Arts Defined
For The Communicator**

That's all there is to the unit-count system. Communicators who work with type in planning brochures, newspapers, company magazines, and other publications soon discover that if they count everything as 1 unit and then make allowances if there are many wide or narrow letters in a line, they can estimate the proper fit quickly and easily.

Those who work on newspapers or magazines that use the same typefaces in each issue for headings, titles, and headlines can make up sample sheets of frequently used head forms and determine the maximum counts for each line. The maximum (and minimums) can then be noted on these style sheets, or *head schedules*, as they are called. (Head schedules are discussed in detail in Chapters 13 and 14, on newspaper design.)

## Copy-Fitting for Reading Matter

Three methods of copy-fitting are used in planning the reading matter for printed communications. Two of these methods are not very reliable so they will be examined very briefly. It is assumed that the copy to be set will be justified.

One is the *word-count system*. This involves counting the number of words in the manuscript and then determining how much space that number of words will occupy when set in a certain type on a specified width.

A sample of the type style set in the specified width is obtained, and the average number of words per line is calculated. This average number of words per line multiplied by the number of lines of type in a column-inch (1 column wide by 1 inch deep) will give the average number of words in a column-inch. This number is divided into the number of words in the typed copy, and the result is the number of column-inches the copy will occupy when set in type.

Another method that is seldom used is called the *square-inch method*. The area to be filled with the type is determined, and its square-inch capacity is calculated. Then the average number of words in a square inch is multiplied by the number of square inches designated in the layout. This gives the average number of words that can be fitted into the area.

For example, if an area 24 by 30 picas is designated in a layout, this will equal 4 by 5 inches or 20 square inches. If it has been determined that, say, 21 words will fit into a square inch, then the area will accommodate 420 words.

The square-inch method is used to estimate the number of words or the number of pages needed in books or fairly large pamphlets.

The most accurate and most used method of copy-fitting, however, is the *character-count method*. It is universally accepted and used in communications work. It is based on determining the number of characters in a manuscript and then the number of typeset characters needed when this manuscript is set in type.

It works like this:

First, the number of characters in the manuscript is determined. There are several ways to calculate this, depending on the equipment being used. Some word processors maintain a running count of the total number of characters being written.

Typewriters are equipped with a character counting device of sorts. The scales on the paper guide and the paper bail on typewriters are calibrated for ten characters per running inch for pica (12-point) type and twelve characters per running inch for elite (10-point) type. If the average number of characters per line is multiplied by the number of lines, the average number of characters in the typed copy can be calculated.

In the example shown in Fig. 10-1, the typewriter stops were set at 15 and 65 to average fifty characters per line. The lines were counted and then the number of characters beyond the fifty limit on each line was added. Paragraph endings were counted as full

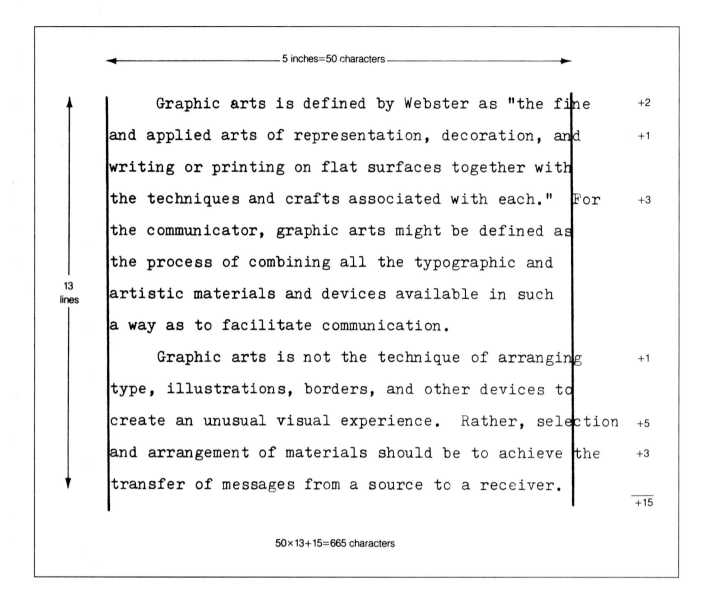

**Fig. 10-1** *An example of character counting with typewritten copy.*

lines, as they would be equally short when set in type. Thus it was determined that this copy contained 665 characters.

Next, the number of characters in a line of type in the designated width is determined. That is, suppose we wish to set the copy above in 10-point type, with 2 points of space between each line (10/12 or 10 point leaded 2 points) on lines that are 15 picas wide. We must determine how many characters of type will fit into each line.

Manufacturers of types usually supply this information in the form of a certain number of characters per pica. In addition, there are charts that can be obtained to help in the calculation. Here are some examples of typical types and their characters per pica:

| | |
|---|---|
| Centenary, 10 point | 2.50 characters per pica |
| Bookman, 10 point | 2.60 characters per pica |
| Bernhard Modern, 10 point | 2.99 characters per pica |
| Century, 10 point | 1.85 characters per pica |
| Futura, 12 point | 2.50 characters per pica |

For our illustration, let's assume that we have selected Centenary. In 10 point, this type has 2.5 characters per pica. If we decide to set copy in lines 15 picas wide and multiply this width by the number of characters per pica (15 × 2.5), we will find the number of characters per line to be 37.5.

Now, if we divide this number of characters per line into the number of characters in the typescript, we will discover the number of lines of type (665 ÷ 37.5 = 17.7). We will have 17.7 or 18 lines of set type. Since we have determined that we will have 2 points of space between lines, each line will occupy 12 points (10 plus 2) or 1 pica. The copy when set will occupy an area 15 picas wide by 18 picas deep.

Here is how it worked out when the copy was set in Centenary according to our instructions:

> Graphic arts is defined by Webster as "the fine and applied arts of representation, decoration, and writing or printing on flat surfaces together with the techniques and crafts associated with each." For the communicator, graphic arts might be defined as the process of combining all the typographic and artistic materials and devices available in such a way as to facilitate communication.
>
> Graphic arts is not the technique of arranging types, illustrations, borders, and other devices to create an unusual visual experience. Rather, selection and arrangement of materials should be to achieve the transfer of messages from a source to a receiver.

In summary, then, to find out how many lines typed copy will make when set in type we proceed as follows:

1. Determine the size and style of type.
2. Determine the width of typeset lines desired.
3. Calculate the number of characters in the typed manuscript.
4. From tables, or working averages, find out how many characters of the specified type will fit in 1 pica and multiply that by the width of the lines in picas.
5. Divide the number of characters in the typed manuscript by the number of characters in one line of type. (*Note:* 6-point type will have twelve lines per inch; 8-point, nine lines; 9-point, eight lines; 10-point, seven lines and a little over; 12-point, six lines, assuming that all these are set solid.)
6. Multiply the number of lines of type by the point size of the type with the space between lines added to find the total depth of the area in points. To convert to picas divide by 12.

Here are some other common copy-fitting situations you may encounter:

1. What size type should be used if the copy must fit into a given area. *Solution:* Scan type specimens and decide on a size that seems to be about right. Calculate the number of lines in this size that you believe will fit into the space. Next, find the number of characters of this type that will fit into a line of the specified width. Multiply your estimated number of lines by the number of characters in each line.

   If the total is less than the number of characters in the copy, try a smaller size. If, on the other hand, the total is more than the number of characters in the copy, a larger size will be needed. If one size is too small but the next size is too large, select the smaller size and have it leaded out by adding space between lines as needed.

2. How many words will I have to write to fit into a specified space when I have selected a style and size of type? *Solution:* This crops up most frequently in writing cutlines or short takes of copy for advertisements or brochures, or short takes for boxed type and so on. First, determine how many characters of the type will fit into the width that has been selected. Next, calculate the number of lines of the type that will be required for the given depth.

   Then, set the word processor or typewriter line stops to a length of line that contains the number of characters needed for the typeset lines. Write the required number of lines. These lines will run very nearly line for line with the lines when the copy is set in type.

3. I want to use some copy that has already been set into type. But I want to use it in a different size and width of type. How do I calculate the changeover? *Solution:* First, find the average number of characters in each typeset line of the original. If you know the type style, this can be determined from charts if they are available. If tables are not available, several lines of the original can be counted to determine the average character count per line.

   Once the average number of characters per line in the original has been determined, multiply that number by the number of lines in the original to find the total number of characters. Next, calculate the number of characters per line in the new setting. Divide this by the number of characters in the original. The result should give the number of lines in the new setting.

   *Example:* We would like to reprint an item that was originally printed in 6-point Bodoni, 12 picas wide. There are 5 lines in this original. We would like to reprint it in 10-point Bernhard Modern on lines 14 picas wide. How much space must be allowed for this new setting in a layout?

   First we must determine that the 6-point Bodoni has an average of 47 characters per 12-pica line. There are 5 lines, so

| ALPHABET LENGTH | CHARACTERS PER PICA | 8 | 10 | 11 | 12 | 13 | 14 | 15 | 16 | 17 | 18 | 20 | 21 | 22 | 23 | 24 | 25 | 27 | 28 | 30 |
|---|---|---|---|---|---|---|---|---|---|---|---|---|---|---|---|---|---|---|---|---|
| 75 | 4.25 | 33 | 42 | 46 | 51 | 54 | 59 | 63 | 67 | 71 | 76 | 84 | 88 | | | | | | | |
| 80 | 4.00 | 32 | 40 | 44 | 48 | 52 | 56 | 60 | 64 | 68 | 72 | 80 | 84 | 88 | | | | | | |
| 85 | 3.75 | 29 | 38 | 41 | 44 | 48 | 52 | 55 | 59 | 63 | 67 | 74 | 77 | 82 | 85 | | | | | |
| 88 | 3.65 | 28 | 37 | 39 | 43 | 46 | 50 | 54 | 57 | 61 | 65 | 72 | 75 | 79 | 82 | 87 | | | | |
| 90 | 3.60 | 28 | 36 | 39 | 43 | 46 | 50 | 54 | 57 | 61 | 65 | 72 | 75 | 79 | 82 | 86 | 90 | | | |
| 93 | 3.52 | 28 | 35 | 38 | 42 | 45 | 49 | 52 | 56 | 59 | 64 | 71 | 73 | 77 | 80 | 84 | 87 | 95 | | |
| 96 | 3.40 | 27 | 34 | 37 | 40 | 44 | 47 | 51 | 54 | 57 | 62 | 68 | 71 | 74 | 78 | 82 | 85 | 91 | 95 | |
| 100 | 3.30 | 26 | 33 | 36 | 39 | 42 | 46 | 49 | 52 | 56 | 59 | 66 | 69 | 72 | 76 | 79 | 82 | 89 | 92 | 99 |
| 103 | 3.22 | 25 | 32 | 35 | 38 | 41 | 45 | 48 | 51 | 54 | 58 | 64 | 67 | 71 | 74 | 77 | 80 | 86 | 90 | 97 |
| 106 | 3.15 | 24 | 31 | 34 | 37 | 40 | 43 | 46 | 49 | 52 | 57 | 62 | 65 | 68 | 71 | 75 | 78 | 83 | 87 | 94 |
| 110 | 3.05 | 24 | 30 | 33 | 36 | 39 | 42 | 45 | 48 | 51 | 54 | 60 | 63 | 66 | 69 | 72 | 75 | 81 | 84 | 91 |
| 113 | 2.95 | 23 | 29 | 32 | 35 | 37 | 41 | 43 | 46 | 49 | 52 | 58 | 61 | 64 | 67 | 70 | 73 | 78 | 82 | 88 |
| 116 | 2.90 | 23 | 29 | 32 | 35 | 38 | 40 | 43 | 46 | 48 | 51 | 58 | 61 | 64 | 67 | 69 | 72 | 76 | 81 | 87 |
| 120 | 2.80 | 22 | 28 | 30 | 33 | 36 | 39 | 42 | 44 | 47 | 50 | 56 | 59 | 62 | 64 | 67 | 70 | 75 | 78 | 84 |
| 123 | 2.75 | 21 | 27 | 29 | 32 | 35 | 37 | 40 | 43 | 46 | 49 | 55 | 57 | 59 | 62 | 65 | 68 | 71 | 76 | 82 |
| 125 | 2.70 | 21 | 27 | 29 | 32 | 35 | 37 | 39 | 42 | 45 | 49 | 54 | 57 | 59 | 62 | 65 | 68 | 70 | 75 | 81 |
| 127 | 2.65 | 20 | 26 | 28 | 31 | 33 | 36 | 39 | 42 | 44 | 47 | 52 | 54 | 57 | 59 | 63 | 65 | 69 | 73 | 79 |
| 130 | 2.60 | 20 | 26 | 28 | 31 | 33 | 36 | 38 | 41 | 44 | 47 | 52 | 54 | 57 | 59 | 62 | 65 | 68 | 73 | 78 |
| 133 | 2.55 | 20 | 26 | 27 | 31 | 32 | 36 | 37 | 41 | 43 | 46 | 51 | 53 | 56 | 58 | 61 | 63 | 67 | 72 | 77 |
| 136 | 2.50 | 20 | 25 | 27 | 30 | 32 | 35 | 37 | 40 | 42 | 45 | 50 | 52 | 55 | 57 | 60 | 62 | 67 | 70 | 75 |
| 140 | 2.45 | 19 | 24 | 26 | 28 | 31 | 33 | 36 | 39 | 41 | 43 | 49 | 51 | 53 | 55 | 58 | 60 | 63 | 68 | 73 |
| 145 | 2.35 | 18 | 23 | 25 | 27 | 29 | 32 | 34 | 37 | 39 | 41 | 47 | 49 | 51 | 54 | 55 | 57 | 62 | 65 | 70 |
| 150 | 2.30 | 18 | 23 | 25 | 27 | 29 | 32 | 34 | 36 | 39 | 41 | 46 | 48 | 51 | 53 | 55 | 57 | 62 | 65 | 69 |
| 155 | 2.25 | 17 | 22 | 24 | 26 | 28 | 31 | 33 | 35 | 38 | 40 | 46 | 48 | 49 | 51 | 53 | 55 | 59 | 62 | 67 |
| 160 | 2.15 | 16 | 21 | 23 | 25 | 27 | 29 | 31 | 33 | 35 | 38 | 43 | 45 | 46 | 48 | 51 | 53 | 56 | 59 | 64 |
| 165 | 2.10 | 16 | 21 | 23 | 25 | 27 | 29 | 31 | 33 | 35 | 38 | 42 | 44 | 46 | 48 | 50 | 53 | 56 | 59 | 63 |
| 170 | 2.05 | 16 | 21 | 23 | 25 | 27 | 29 | 31 | 33 | 35 | 37 | 41 | 43 | 45 | 47 | 49 | 51 | 55 | 57 | 62 |
| 175 | 2.00 | 16 | 20 | 22 | 24 | 26 | 28 | 30 | 32 | 34 | 36 | 40 | 42 | 44 | 46 | 48 | 50 | 54 | 56 | 60 |
| 180 | 1.95 | 15 | 20 | 21 | 23 | 25 | 27 | 29 | 31 | 33 | 35 | 39 | 40 | 42 | 44 | 46 | 48 | 52 | 54 | 58 |
| 185 | 1.90 | 15 | 19 | 20 | 22 | 24 | 26 | 28 | 30 | 32 | 34 | 38 | 39 | 41 | 43 | 45 | 46 | 51 | 53 | 57 |
| 190 | 1.85 | 14 | 19 | 20 | 22 | 23 | 26 | 28 | 29 | 31 | 33 | 37 | 38 | 41 | 42 | 44 | 46 | 49 | 52 | 56 |
| 195 | 1.80 | 14 | 18 | 19 | 22 | 23 | 25 | 27 | 28 | 30 | 32 | 36 | 37 | 40 | 41 | 43 | 45 | 48 | 50 | 54 |
| 200 | 1.75 | 13 | 18 | 19 | 21 | 23 | 24 | 25 | 27 | 28 | 31 | 35 | 36 | 38 | 39 | 41 | 42 | 45 | 48 | 52 |

**Fig. 10-2** *A handy chart to use when copy-fitting by the character-count method. The alphabet-length column gives the length of the lowercase alphabet. The next column gives the approximate characters per pica for the alphabet length. The column headings give the length of a line in picas. To use the chart, measure the lowercase alphabet (a through z) in points. Then find the alphabet length that comes closest to this alphabet length in the alphabet-length column. You can then readily find how many characters of the type selected can be accommodated in the width of line selected by reading across the columns. For example, if the length of the lowercase alphabet selected is 75 points and the line to be set is 10 picas wide, then each line will accommodate 42 characters.*

there are 235 characters in the item. Next, we find that there are 2.99 characters of 10-point Bernhard Modern per pica from our charts, or 41.86 characters per 14-pica line. If we divide 41.86 into 235 we will find that the new setting will take 5.6 or 6 lines.

Copy-fitting may appear forbidding, but with a little practice the communicator can master this vital tool for planning printed communications. And accurate copy-fitting will mean dollars saved when the compositor doesn't have to reset copy that was estimated inaccurately.

## Preparing Copy for the Press

### Use Standard Editing Marks

If hard copy is produced (copy printed on paper as opposed to computer storage of material), it should be typed on standard 8½ by 11 white paper and typed double-spaced. Copy should never be sent to the printer on little slips of paper or small note sheets. This is inviting problems. All copy should be edited carefully to make sure there are no mistakes.

The standard editing marks generally used in marking copy are shown in Fig. 10-3.

### Catching the Errors

After the compositor sets the type, or if it is set with computer equipment, the communicator will be supplied with *proofs*. These are usually made on a copying machine if the type was set "cold type." In the unlikely event that the type was set with a "hot type" machine, galley proofs will be provided. (The term is a holdover from the days when virtually all type was set from metal and placed in a tray, or galley, for proofing.)

Most proofs, however, are supplied on reproduction paper. This is a high-quality white paper. Such proofs should be marked with a nonreproducing blue liquid or fine felt pen, unless other arrangements have been made with the production department.

There are standard "proof marks" to be used in marking proofs. They are similar to editing marks, but some are slightly different.

## Working with the "Back Shop"

The people who do the actual production work for the designer or editor can provide valuable suggestions, often gleaned from long experience, which can make the communication more effective.

Whenever we work with "back shop" personnel or the printer who will produce the message, we should be prepared to answer

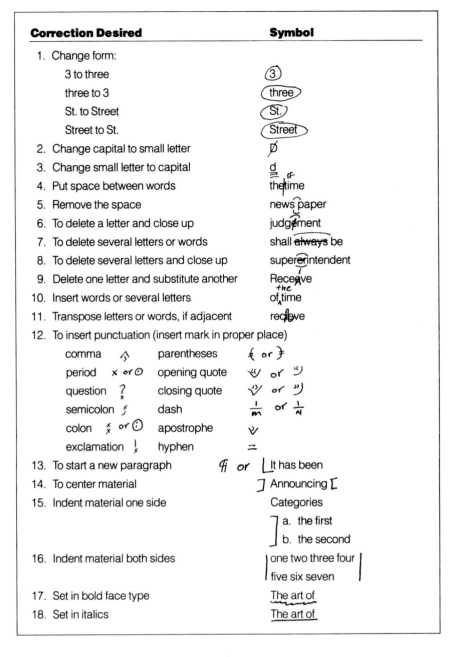

Fig. 10-3 *Standard editing marks.*

a number of questions. Having the answers can save time, money, and confusion later. Some of these questions are:

**1.** How many copies are needed? The standard in the printing trades is to actually deliver plus or minus 5 percent of the number ordered. This gives the printer some leeway for spoilage in printing.

**2.** When are they needed? The more lead time the printer has, the more care can be taken in production.

**3.** What about price? Are both printer and communicator in agreement? If a fairly large amount of money is involved, the price quotation and terms of payment should be in writing.

Galley 107—Chapter 11
Graphics Communications Today

Scientific American is considered one of the best-designed magazines, and it applies these typographic principles with great success even though it might appear rather forbidding to the reader who is not especially interested in the world of science.

Whatever basic design approach is chosen, it should not be changed in the future without a great deal of study and replanning. The basic design plan should remain constant, as it can help achieve identity and continuity from one issue to the next. It should help the reader recognize the magazine instantly just as Time's distinctive red cover, all-cap nameplate in Roman type, and cover photo have for years.

As the general planning progresses, we should also keep in mind the admonition of one magazine designer, "If you're dull, you're dead."

**The Four Fs of Magazine Design**

One way to approach the physical design of a magazine, is to consider the "four Fs" of magazine design—function, formula, format, and frames.

Function   The function part of this approach is obvious, but it will be helpful to jot down the things the magazine should accomplish. Will it be an internal magazine, for members of an organization or employees of a company? or will its appeal be "external," aimed toward people outside the organization? Or will it have a combined goal of dual appeal, internal and external? Will it be aimed at recruiting new members or new support? Will it be a "how to" publication, or will it be a publication that relies on layouts with lots of photos? All these functions will affect the physical form the publication take.

Formula   The formula is the unique and relatively stable combination of elements—articles, departments, and so on—which make up each issue. The elements that should be considered in devising the formula for a magazine include the sort of articles to be included, such as fiction, uplifting essays, interpretative pieces, or whatever.

The formula also includes considering the sort of illustrations, drawings, and/or photographs to use. It includes the departments that will be a regular part of each issue as well as editorial or special interest columns, poetry, cartoons and jokes, fillers, and other miscellaneous material. Efforts should be made to produce content that has balance and consistency—and have variety to prevent dullness.

**Fig. 10-4** *A typeset galley that has been proofread and marked for correction.*

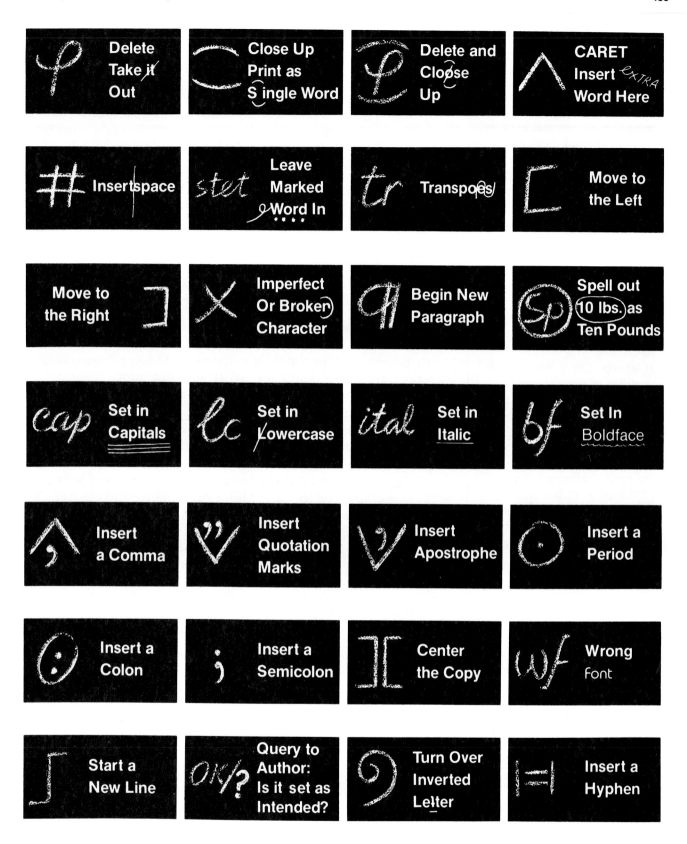

**Fig. 10-5** *Standard proofreading marks. (Reproduced with permission of Metro Associated Services, Inc.)*

## Creative Communication

Are you the problem?

Sometimes we are blocked in achieving maximum creativity by personal creative blocks. Personal creative blocks include prejudices that impose themselves into the thinking process. Creative blocks can also include the urge to impress rather than express.

We cannot live in a vacuum and we do react to situations according to our attitudes. These attitudes can be expressions formed by our backgrounds, education, experience, and economic situations. Designers should be aware of any personal blocks when attempting to solve a problem and try to minimize them.

Who are we trying to impress? Creative designs can be less effective if they are aimed at impressing colleagues or those in command positions in the organization rather than being aimed at the target audience.

4. What sort of paper would be most suited for the job? How durable should it be? If the cheapest paper available is specified, how will this affect the quality of the job?

5. What about color? For the paper and/or the printing?

6. Are the photos or illustrations of satisfactory quality to reproduce well? If there are shortcomings, the printer should point them out so the communicator will know what to expect when the finished job is seen.

7. What about proofs? Will the communicator read and initial them? Should anyone else in the organization approve the proofs?

8. Are the specifications and instructions on the layout, copy, and illustrations clearly understood by both the communicator and the printer?

9. Does the printer have any necessary packaging and delivery information?

The more details we can give the printer about the job the better the chance that our expectations will be fulfilled. Printers are skilled craftspeople—or they should be—and they can provide many helpful suggestions if they know just what we want done.

Instructions for compositors and printers must be clear, concise, and legible. There are some universally accepted abbreviations for marking copy. However, there can be variations from place to place, and it is important that both the communicator and the printer agree on those being used. Instructions generally can be grouped under three categories: (1) instructions for cropping and sizing art, (2) for marking layouts, and (3) for marking reading matter. Art instructions are considered in Chapter 5. Instructions for layouts and reading matter should include:

■ Type size in points. However, for very large display type, inches and centimeters are used in some shops.

■ The type family by name, such as Caslon, Stymie, Times Roman.

■ The family series, which could be condensed, light, medium, bold, extra bold, light italic, and so.

■ The posture of the letters, whether all capitals, all lowercase, capitals and lowercase, small capitals, swash letters, or other special characters.

■ The width of the lines in picas.

■ The leading between lines.

■ The justification—whether the lines are to be set flush left, centered, flush right, or justified. Usually, the justification is obvious by the comp lines on the layout.

In addition, it might be necessary to indicate if parts of the copy are to be set indented, in italics, boldface, or in some other special way.

While this list may seem formidable, it can be mastered quickly. There are a number of shortcuts for marking copy and they can be understood with a little practice. For instance,

8/10 Caslon Bd. itl clc × 15

means "set this in 8-point Caslon bold italic capitals and lower-case letters with 2 points of leading in a line 15 picas wide."

The designation 8/10 comes to us from the days of linotype composition when the term "8 on 10" meant to cast 8-point type on a 10-point slug. This was the equivalent of putting 2 points of leading between the lines.

When a brochure, advertisement, or general printing layout is made, most of the instructions are written on the layout sheet outside the actual layout. Any instructions written within the layout should be circled to indicate that they are not to be set in type. All instructions should be clear and accurate. After all, the specifications are like those an architect would put on a blueprint. The builder is expected to follow them precisely. The printer is expected to follow the layout's specifications precisely.

## The Designer's Tool Kit

So far several tools of the trade have been mentioned. Below is a list of the tools and materials that will be adequate to complete the projects—or similar ones—suggested in this book.

- *Paper:* Two kinds of paper will prove useful for drawing thumbnails, roughs, and comprehensives. One is *transparent tracing* and the other is *layout paper.* Layout paper is white and not as transparent as tracing paper but it still can be used for tracing. Both can be obtained in pad form in sizes from 8½ by 11 to 19 by 24. Paper weights of 16 or 24 pound work well.

- *Rulers:* Two types of rulers will come in handy. One is a 12- or 18-inch etched steel and the other a *pica rule* or *graphic arts rule* with both inch and pica scales.

- *T square and triangle:* A good 24-inch T square and an 8- or 12-inch triangle are musts. A T square with a plastic edge should never be used for cutting. Obtain a T square with a steel arm for cutting. A plastic triangle should also not be used for cutting. It could become nicked and useless for drawing straight lines.

- *Pencils and pens:* The most useful pencils for layout work are 2H or HB. Felt pens come in handy too.

- *Erasers:* Magic Rub pencil and art gum work well.

- *Masking tape and rubber cement:* Both will come in handy for tacking down art on grid or layout paper and for many other uses. Rubber cement thinner is needed to thin out rubber cement when it thickens in the jar. It also can be used to loosen something that has been pasted down with rubber cement.

■ *Scissors and art knives:* A good pair of scissors and an Exacto knife or single-edge razor knife will take care of the cutting needs for starting in layout work.

Only a few additional items are needed to add pasteup capability to the tools required for layout. These include:

*Nonreproducing blue pencils and pens*

*A waxer:* There is an inexpensive hand-held model that works fine.

*A burnisher:* Burnishers are either in roller or stick form. If much pasteup work is done, the roller is most satisfactory.

*White correction fluid or graphic white paint:* These fill in shadow areas or cover blemishes in the pasteup.

*Preruled grids* or plain white bristol, about 4 ply.

## Steps in Basic Pasteup

Once the layout has been completed and all the images to be used assembled, the next step is to paste them into position as shown in the layout. Then this pasted-together form is photographed for plate making. The process is called *pasteup.* It can be accomplished by following ten steps:

1. Prepare the grid or base sheet.
2. Double check all elements for errors and compare them to the layout to see if they are all available.
3. Trim the excess paper from the type and art forms.
4. Apply wax to the backs of the type and art forms.
5. Position the elements on the grid or base sheet.
6. Check all elements to be sure they are square.
7. Burnish the form to affix the elements to the grid.
8. If halftone negatives are to be stripped in, affix a window (usually red plastic) the exact size of the halftone.
9. Add borders and rules, usually in tape form.
10. Make a copy on a copying machine and proof the copy. Then add an overlay to protect the pasteup.

In step 1 a piece of illustration board or a preruled (in nonreproducing blue, which will not show up in printing) grid is fastened to a drawing board or flat, perfectly smooth surface. It is critical that everything be square and true. The grid should be lined up on the surface with a T square and then held in place with small pieces of tape in the corners.

Next, the nonreproducing blue lines on the grid are used to position the heads, art, body copy, and other elements to be included. Nonreproducing blue pencils or pens can be used to mark the spots where the elements are to be placed. If art is to be bled, it should

**Fig. 10-6** *The pasteup process. Guidelines are drawn with a nonreproducing blue pen or pencil. Then the elements are affixed in position, usually by using a waxer to coat their backs so they will stick to the grid. The body type in the illustration is an example of geeking (simulated type that makes no sense). (Illustrations used in Fig. 10-6 through Fig. 10-11 courtesy of Graphic Products Corporation, Rolling Meadows, Illinois 60008.)*

extend about ¼ inch beyond the outside dimensions of the page margins for trimming after printing.

Rubber cement or melted wax is applied to the backs of the assembled images. They should be trimmed as closely as possible to the print area but care should be taken not to cut into any images. It may prove more satisfactory to wax after trimming, depending on the size of the elements.

The various elements with adhesive applied are placed in position on the grid. Great care is taken to make sure everything is

*(a)*

*(b)*

**Fig. 10-7** *(a) In pasteup the elements are placed into position on grids with preprinted guidelines in nonreproducing blue. (b) The completed pasteup is photographed and a printing plate is produced. The grid lines will not show in the final printed product.*

straight and square. A T square is used to line elements horizontally, and a right-angle triangle with one edge placed on the edge of the arm of the T square is used to line them up vertically.

When adjacent columns of reading matter are lined up or when lines are added to a column of reading matter, a Haber rule is a handy tool. A *Haber rule* is a plastic rule marked with type sizes and various leadings so that, for instance, two lines of 8-point type leaded 2 points can be lined up evenly. The point of an art knife is handy for moving small elements on the grid for alignment.

If a halftone negative is to be stripped in later, the exact area is drawn on the grid with a nonreproducing blue pen and the area is coded (such as "photo A"). The photograph is similarly identified and sized to fit the area exactly.

Once all the elements are in place, the entire pasteup is burnished to ensure that everything is firmly in place. There are several types of burnishers but the rubber or ceramic roller is the most frequently used. A sheet of clean white paper is placed on the images for burnishing to help keep the pasteup clean and prevent smearing during the burnishing process.

If the pasteup is to be produced in more than one color, the additional color areas are placed on an *acetate overlay sheet*. The entire pasteup is often protected with a cover sheet, or *frisket*, taped as a flap over the completed grid.

## Effective Design Checklist

■ Border tapes used with care can add a pleasing element to your pasteup. (See Fig. 10-8.)

■ Mitre border corners for neater, more professional-looking pasteups. (See Fig. 10-9.)

■ Shade art for a more realistic effect. Use shading films for shading or for color overlays. (See Fig. 10-10.)

■ Masking film can be used as in the first three steps for shading to create *overlays* for color printing. Follow these steps:

  **1.** Cut a piece of masking film (red or amber is used most frequently) large enough to cover the area to be printed in color and tape it firmly at the top to the layout.

  **2.** Cut around the outline of the area to be printed in color as in step 2 in the shading technique.

  **3.** Peel off the taped large piece of masking film. The outline form remaining can be affixed to a clear polyester overlay ready for the camera.

  **4.** Care must be taken to place the red masking film cutout over the original layout to obtain a perfect register.

■ Use creativity and customize borders. (See Fig. 10-11 and Fig. 10-12.)

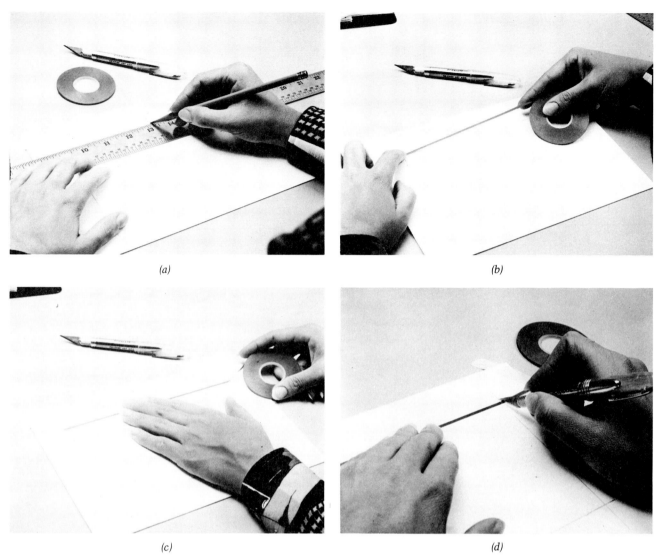

(a)

(b)

(c)

(d)

**Fig. 10-8** *(a) Draw a faint pencil line, nonreproducing blue guidelines, or use a guideline on the pasteup grid for aligning the border tape on the layout. (b) Press* *the end of the tape into position and unroll enough tape to go just beyond the length required. (c) Carefully lower the tape into position along the guideline* *and gently smooth it into place. (d) Trim the tape to the desired length and firmly burnish it into place.*

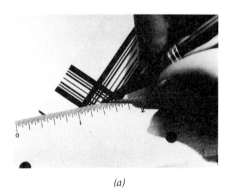

(a)

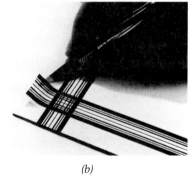

(b)

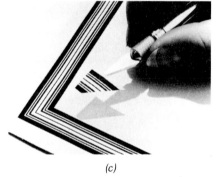

(c)

**Fig. 10-9** *(a) To create attractive mitred corners on a pasteup, place the border tape in position but overlap the ends of* *the tape beyond the corner of the box. (b) Next, lay a straight edge on the overlapped area and cut carefully at a* *right angle. (c) Finally, remove the excess material and press the border into position.*

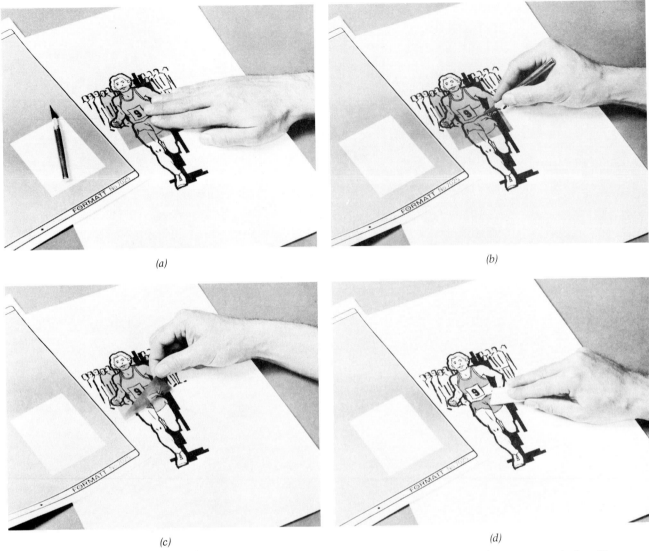

(a)

(b)

(c)

(d)

**Fig. 10-10** *(a) Cut and remove enough shading film from a backing sheet to cover an area slightly larger than the drawing. Smooth out any air bubbles. (b) Cut lightly around the outline of the area to be shaded on the artwork. (c) Remove all excess shading film. (d) Burnish the film until it appears as if it were actually printed on the artwork.*

**Fig. 10-11** *(a) Borders can be customized and their widths narrowed if desired. First cut the border to the desired width. Next, slide an art knife under the border and remove the excess. (b) Then finish the border by adding rules to create different effects and press it into position.*

(a)

(b)

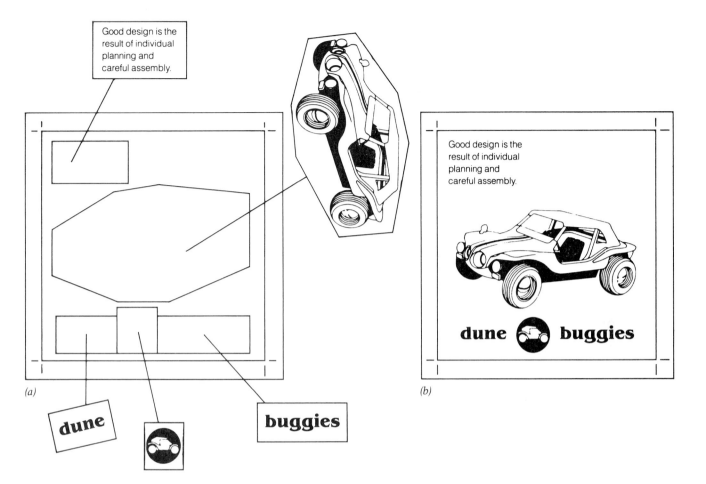

Good design is the
result of individual
planning and
careful assembly.

(a)

dune

buggies

Good design is the
result of individual
planning and
careful assembly.

**dune** 🚙 **buggies**

(b)

**Fig. 10-12** *(a) The individual pieces of art and copy and their positions on the grid or pasteup board (often a lightweight white bristol cardboard). (b) The completed pasteup. A protective flap of lightweight paper or tracing paper can be taped to the back and folded over the face of the pasteup. (Courtesy of A. B. Dick.)*

## Graphics in Action

1. Take the front page of a daily newspaper. Measure the width of the columns in picas. Determine the maximum unit counts of the headline types used on the page for the various column widths.

2. Use the copy that defined graphic arts at the start of this chapter. Assume you want to set it in 10-point Century (1.85 characters per pica) leaded 2 points, in a column 12 picas wide. How deep would the space be when the copy is set in this size and style of type in lines 12 picas wide with 2 points of leading?

3. Find an advertisement in a newspaper or magazine about 4 by 5 inches. Select one that has few display lines and only one or two copy blocks. Mount it on plain white paper. Mark it for publication. Attempt to identify the type families or identify them as closely as possible by comparing them with type specimen sheets or the type specimens in the appendix.

4. Assume you want to print the copy used to demonstrate copyfitting in this chapter as an envelope stuffer for your business. Your business is "(Your Name) and Associates" Graphic

Designers, use your address. You want five thousand 6 by 9 flyers. Make a rough layout for such a flyer, mark it, and write all the information you would want to tell the printer.

**5.** Paste up a prototype for the flyer in number 4. Or practice pasteup by creating prototype advertisements by using display lines, blocks of copy, art, and logos clipped from magazines (try to find magazines with heavy paper). Some practice in pasteup can be done with a minimum of equipment: Rubber cement, art knife and scissors, nonreproducing blue pencil, T square and ruler, and a border tape or two are about all that is needed to get started. Try to devise shadow boxes and other special effects. Examples:

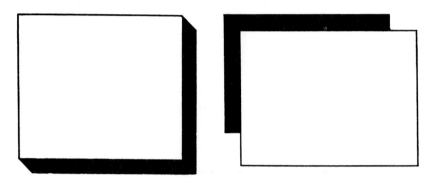

# THE THIN LINE

*Now that all the hulla blue has died down, let's go paint the town persimmon*

# 3

## EASY PLACES

*Pack up all your cares and woes: peaceful, affordable vacations.*

Two innovation-center offspring: a desktop weather forecaster and a respirator that pumps 900 times each minute.

If the variety in the cosmos is limitless, is there a single star or flower or even mud puddle with an identical twin?

## Big and Small, Magazines Are Basically the Same

Most people visualize one of the popular publications when magazines are mentioned. *Reader's Digest* or *TV Guide*, with their more than 17 million copies an issue, are usually mentioned. So are *National Geographic*, with its stunning photography, or *Scientific American*, with its precise, detailed text and charts. These are formidable. Planning and producing a magazine on that scale seem to require technical knowledge that is beyond the abilities of many communicators.

But the same principles of selecting type and illustrations and placing them on a page in the most effective way possible apply to small eight-page association publications as they do to these giants. And, the small association monthly can be just as attractive in its way and do just as effective a job of communicating with its target audience. All it takes is planning and the application of basic principles of good design. We will begin by discussing general planning and then move on to the specifics of magazine design.

First of all, the design and production of a magazine is easy and it is fun. Of all the areas of printed communications none is more interesting and challenging. And the satisfaction of accomplishment when you hold the printed copy of your magazine is rarely exceeded in any other communications activity.

Where do you begin? Although our concerns are in layout and design, we cannot separate this from editorial planning.

In the ideal situation, the staff will include a design specialist—the *art director*. This person has the primary responsibility for the creative aspects of producing the magazine.

An art director can be a real asset for an editor. On the other hand, an art director who has little background in printing or journalism can be a liability. If the art director doesn't understand the importance of content, legibility, and readability, not to mention suitability, the designs can hamper effective communication.

There are many examples of outstanding design in magazines, but there are also examples of design that are beautiful as works of art and still hamper the effectiveness of the communication. These can include the use of decorative rules and borders that create barriers rather than unity, or advancing hot colors that dominate the visual area.

Too often the tip-off that a publication is in trouble is its use of "screaming" graphics—which figuratively shout for help as the publication goes down for the third time. Too often a publication will suddenly take graphics seriously for the first time when it hits turbulent waters. Examples in recent years include the old *Saturday Evening Post*, a giant in its day, in the months before its demise in 1969, and the *Chicago Daily News* in the final weeks of its life in 1978.

**Fig. 11-1** *A stunning design for a magazine spread. (As mentioned, though, reverse type should be used with caution since extensive use may negatively affect readability.) (Reprinted courtesy of Pennzoil Perspectives.)*

## Good Design Aids Content

As in all printed communications, good magazine design must aid and illuminate the content. The combination of good design and poor content can fail while what appears to be poor design and good content can sometimes survive and even prosper. However, obviously, we should aim for good design and good content.

This partnership concept—good content and good design—extends to the editor and art director. The editor should attempt to keep design within the limits of its function while encouraging the art director to provide creative advice that results in the bright and unique. Both should strive to produce a publication that will attract and hold readers.

The editor who has a good art director as a partner is fortunate indeed. However, in many of the more than 10,000 periodicals of various sizes and shapes that appear each month in America, the editor and art director are one and the same. This is especially true with small house publications for business and industry and

**Fig. 11-2** *The Chicago Daily News turned in 1977 to graphics that were considered startling in an effort to survive. The change did not help. However, the design that was considered revolutionary by some at the time was a forerunner of new wave graphics as they have been applied to newspaper design.*

organizations like the local Girl Scout council, real estate board, and so on. Many of the entry jobs in communications involve producing these small magazines.

Let us assume, then, that we are going to design a magazine from the ground up, or that we are going to give an existing magazine an overhaul to make it more effective. The first step is planning. Time spent on planning and writing the plans down on paper will pay for itself over and over again.

## Long-Range Decisions

In designing or redesigning a magazine there are several long-range decisions that should be made immediately. These include:

- *The function, or purpose, of the magazine:* We should determine exactly why it is being published, what we hope to accomplish by even bothering to put it out.

- *The personality of the magazine:* Printed communications, like people, project images. What sort of image do we want our magazine to project? Is it dignified and reserved or is it informal and aggressive?

- *The audience we wish to attract:* What sort of person do we want to read our magazine? What are our readers or potential readers like, where are they located, what are their interests?

- *The formula for our magazine:* This means the kinds of information, articles, and features we will include in each issue and how this material will be presented.

- *Will our magazine contain advertising?* If so, how will our editorial formula affect the potential for advertising? Will our target editorial audience be a target market for certain goods and services? If so, the advertising people take over here and determine the markets, appeals, and potential advertisers who will be interested in what we have to offer.

- *When and how often our magazine will appear:* If the publication is a weekly, timeliness is usually an important factor in the formula, and the design format should reflect this timeliness.

- *Design and typographic decisions:* These will include the basic format—the page size, margins, number of columns per page, and the typefaces to be used for standing heads, article titles, captions, and body matter.

### Title and Cover Policies

The title or headline policy have to be determined. There are two philosophies usually found here. One is to adopt one or two families of type for all titles and the other is to select specific types for each article.

Another decision concerns the cover policy. We will have to decide how to handle the cover of the magazine. For example, what will be the logo (or nameplate) design, what sort of art will be used on the cover, how will the various typographic elements be contained issue to issue? Other typographic decisions to be made in the planning stage include the arrangement of heads, subheads, masthead, regular feature titles, table of contents, column widths and placement, and/or placement of advertising.

All of this planning should be done with the basic tenet of effective magazine design in mind: *The physical appearance of the*

**Fig. 11-3** *This cover from* Field & Stream *accomplishes the four functions of a cover: it identifies the magazine in a way that sets it apart from others, it attracts the attention of the intended target audience, it sets the tone or mood of the contents, and it lures the reader inside. (Reprinted with permission of* Field & Stream.)

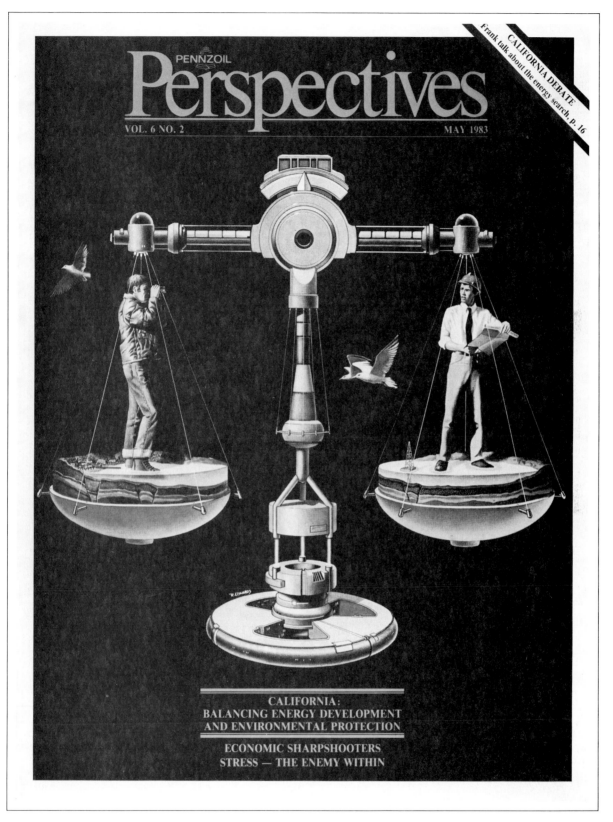

**Fig. 11-4** *A dramatic illustration tied in with teasers gives impact to the cover of* Perspectives, *the award-winning publication of Pennzoil Company.*

**Fig. 11-5**  *The communicator who must write, edit, and design a small
magazine can often utilize art from stock art sources to create an effective cover.*

*publication should reflect the editorial content and appeal to the* ✓ *audience for which it is intended.*

Much of a magazine producer's success is related to the ability to isolate the target audience and build a product that will appeal to this audience. Proper design can help us achieve this goal.

For instance, a magazine devoted to religious concerns should look the part. It must by its appearance say "I'm concerned with religion," just as it must say "hunting and fishing" in content and appearance if it is to appeal to the hunting and fishing enthusiast. A magazine aimed at business women should wear a different typographic "suit" than one appealing to structural engineers. These stylistic differences need to be considered in the initial planning stages.

## Visualization in Magazine Design

Here *visualization*—the construction of mental pictures—of the magazine's eventual appearance should begin to form in the editor's or designer's mind.

One word of caution. Although our magazine's appearance may say "hunting and fishing," it is important that a new and unique way be found to say "hunting and fishing." And it is important that we say it without resorting to screaming graphics. Our publication should stand out from the others that are trying to say the same thing. Thus our planning needs to include a study of the competition and how it is saying what we are going to say.

In planning the initial design, then, we must always keep the potential reader in mind. A scientific magazine, for instance, appeals to a precise, orderly mind. It should use precise, orderly types—medium Sans Serifs; clean, sharp modern Romans, such as the Bodonis; straightforward solid line rules and thick-and-thin straight-line combinations of the Oxford rules. It should have accurate and clear-cut placement of elements. Color should be used for emphasis where it is needed, but color should never come on so strong that it shouts.

*Scientific American* is considered one of the best-designed magazines, and it applies these typographic principles with great success even though it might appear rather forbidding to the reader who is not especially interested in the world of science.

Whatever basic design approach is chosen, it should not be changed in the future without a great deal of study and replanning. The basic design plan should remain constant, as it can help achieve identity and continuity from one issue to the next. It should help the reader recognize the magazine instantly just as *Time's* distinctive red cover, all-cap nameplate in Roman type, and cover art have for years.

As the general planning progresses, we should also keep in mind the admonition of one magazine designer, "If you're dull, you're dead."

**Fig. 11-6** *The precise, careful graphics and type arrangements of* Scientific American *might not appeal to everyone, but they are just right for a publication aimed at people interested in the sciences.*

---

SCIENTIFIC
AMERICAN          March 1984     Volume 250     Number 3
Established 1845

# "No First Use" of Nuclear Weapons

*The security of all nations would be enhanced if the U.S.
and its allies were to adopt a military strategy that did
not rely on nuclear arms to counter a non-nuclear attack*

by Kurt Gottfried, Henry W. Kendall and John M. Lee

Since the late 1940's the U.S. and its allies in the North Atlantic Treaty Organization have based their common defense on the declared strategy of initiating nuclear warfare if their conventional, or non-nuclear, military forces should be threatened with defeat in Europe or elsewhere. The doctrine of "first use" of nuclear weapons was formulated at a time when NATO was faced with two options for countering the large standing army maintained by the U.S.S.R.: either conscripting and outfitting large numbers of men (an obviously unpopular move after six years of combat) or relying on a comparatively cheap and enormously destructive weapon their adversary did not possess. Little sleep was lost in making the choice or in reconsidering it as long as the U.S. held a significant lead in nuclear arms over the U.S.S.R.

The era of unquestioned U.S. nuclear superiority has long since passed, and with its passing confidence in NATO's first-use policy has eroded. Doubts have arisen partly because it has proved impossible to devise plans that promise to gain a military advantage from any limited use of nuclear weapons. In addition no method has been proposed for stopping a nuclear war once it has started. Accordingly it has become clear to many people that even the most limited use of nuclear weapons could well lead to the ultimate catastrophe of a global nuclear war. Nevertheless, under the present first-use policy nuclear weapons are integral to the training, planning and equipping phases of all NATO military operations. In the event of reverses in a major conflict there would be almost irresistible pressure to use them.

These concerns have led some prominent observers to call for a new NATO

policy on the initiation of nuclear warfare. In particular, in the spring of 1982 four former high officials of the U.S. Government (McGeorge Bundy, George F. Kennan, Robert S. McNamara and Gerard C. Smith) published an article in *Foreign Affairs* advocating that serious consideration be given by the U.S. and its NATO allies to a policy of "no first use" of nuclear weapons. At the same time the Union of Concerned Scientists publicly explored a set of measures to enhance international security and reduce the risk of nuclear war. One of the recommendations that emerged from this review was that NATO should move toward a no-first-use policy in Europe and that the U.S., independently of its European allies, should do the same everywhere else in the world.

The scientists' group, of which we are members, then sponsored a more detailed study of the no-first-use option, with particular reference to the concomitant need to strengthen NATO's conventional forces. The study was directed by one of us (Lee) and involved (in addition to the other two of us) Gerald Steinberg and Peter Trubowitz. A number of retired senior military officers and former civilian defense officials on both sides of the Atlantic took an active part in the project and endorsed the final report. This article is based largely on the results of that joint effort.

Any analysis of the no-first-use proposal must deal primarily with the military situation on the central European front, where the countries of NATO and the Warsaw Pact confront each other with the two most powerful military forces ever assembled in peacetime. It is generally agreed that NATO would re-

sort to nuclear weapons only if an offensive by the Warsaw Pact appeared to be on the verge of success. Accordingly military casualties would already number in the thousands, and the rapidly shifting front would run somewhere through densely populated West Germany. In the circumstances the use of tactical, or short-range, nuclear weapons could lend effective support to troops on the battlefield only if the commanders were able to make rapid decisions on the basis of accurate intelligence and if the weapons could be promptly released for use. Even if the initial NATO nuclear operations were for purposes other than direct battlefield support (for targeting Warsaw Pact command-and-control centers or support forces far in the rear, say), there would be the same need for coordinating them with a rapidly changing situation on the basis of the best available information.

Formidable obstacles would stand in the way of such NATO operations. The intricate system NATO relies on for command, control, communications and intelligence ($C^3I$), which is shared by its conventional and nuclear forces, is highly vulnerable to attack and would presumably be a prime target for the Warsaw Pact forces from the very beginning of hostilities. At present the "nuclear threshold" cannot be crossed by NATO field commanders acting alone. The highest political leaders of the NATO countries are supposed to agree on the timing, magnitude and location of any nuclear attack, and for this reason NATO has set up an elaborate procedure for reaching such decisions.

Thus NATO's military and political requirements are in direct conflict with each other. From the military stand-

33

---

## The Four Fs of Magazine Design

One way to approach the physical design of a magazine, is to consider the "four Fs" of magazine design—function, formula, format, and frames.

*Function*    The *function* part of this approach is obvious, but it will be helpful to jot down the things the magazine should accomplish. Will it be an internal magazine, meant for members of an organization or employees of a company? Or will its appeal be "external," aimed toward people outside the organization? Or will it have a combined goal of dual appeal, internal and external? Will it be aimed at recruiting new members or new support? Will it be a "how to" publication, or will it be a publication that relies on layouts with lots of photos? All these functions will affect the physical form the publication takes.

*Formula*   The *formula* is the unique and relatively stable combination of elements—articles, departments, and so on—which make up each issue. The elements that should be considered in devising the formula for a magazine include the sort of articles to be included such as fiction, uplifting essays, interpretative pieces, or whatever.

The formula also includes considering the sort of illustrations, drawings, and/or photographs to use. It includes the departments that will be a regular part of each issue as well as editorial or special interest columns, poetry, cartoons and jokes, fillers, and other miscellaneous material. Efforts should be made to produce content that has balance and consistency—and variety to prevent dullness.

Once we have defined the function of the magazine and developed the formula to achieve this function, we need to consider our special typographic concerns—the format and frames of the publication.

*Format*   The *format* includes the basic size and shape of the magazine plus the typographic constants or physical features that stay the same from one issue to the next. These constants include the cover design, masthead, break of the book (see page 218), placement of regular features, folio line techniques, and techniques for handling *jumps* or the continuation of articles from one part of the publication to the other.

Magazines select a format, or basic design pattern, and stick to it. There are a number of things we must consider when deciding the format of our publication. These include:

1. The press capacity of the printer who produces the magazine plus the most efficient way to utilize paper with a minimum of waste.

2. Ease of handling and mailing. How will the publication be delivered to the reader? If it is to be mailed in an envelope, that could be a factor in determining its size. How will the publication be handled by the reader? If it will be the type of publication that is kept and filed, it might be wise to select a size that will fit standard file cabinets or binders. If it is the sort of publication that will be carried around in a pocket or purse, that is another factor to consider in determining size.

3. The content. Large picture layouts require elbow room to be effective. If the publication will use many pictures or diagrams, a large page size will probably be best. *e.g. Life*

There are, however, some common format dimensions that have evolved:

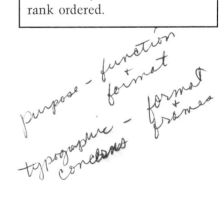

One set of dimensions determined by designers sorts out magazines by size according to the sizes of the type pages. For example,

Pocket:          2 columns wide by 85 lines deep
Standard:        2 columns wide by 119 lines deep
Flat:            3 columns wide by 140 lines deep
Large:           4 columns wide by 170 lines deep

(*Note:* The lines used to measure depth are agate lines, based on agate type, which is 5½ points in height. There are fourteen agate lines in 1 inch.)

Another common method of classifying magazines is by page size:

Miniature            4½ by 6 inches
Pocket               6 by 9 inches
Basic                8½ by 11 inches
Picture              10½ by 13 inches
Sunday supplement    11 by 13 inches

The most common magazine page size these days is the basic 8½ by 11 inches because this represents the most efficient use of paper and is easy to handle, bind, and file. The basic format is easy to address and mail, and it fits nicely in binders and file cabinets. From the graphics point of view, the basic page is large enough to permit good use of art and to give considerable latitude for interesting layouts.

*Frames*  Magazine *frames* are the outer page margins, the white space between columns of types and pages, and the use of white space to "frame" the various elements such as headings, titles, subheads, bylines, and art.

A basic decision must be made regarding page margins. There are two possibilities. One is to use *progressive margins*. In this type of margination, as explained in Chapter 4, margins are designed to increase in size as they "progress" around the page. The gutter margin, or inside margin, is the smallest. On the right-hand pages the margins increase clockwise, and on the left-hand pages they increase counterclockwise.

Progressive margins give a visual impression of high quality or "class." We should consider them if our publication is intended to project this sort of image.

*Regular margins*, or those with identical dimensions, are most common. They should take up about half of the total area of the page. Quite often the *folio lines* (page number, name of magazine, date to appear on each page) are placed in the margins of magazine pages. This is another typographic decision we will have to make.

Another "white space" or frame decision concerns the space between columns. A minimum of 1 pica of white space should be

Direct government expenditures for research and development are on the upswing, and while the budget outcome is muddied, Congress is likely to give the Reagan Administration its nearly $48 billion in requested spending authority, if not more.

As analysts are quick to note, the bulk of the spending increase is earmarked for defense programs. The Pentagon would get about $30 billion, or nearly two thirds of the total R&D funds.

**In trying to sort out potential winners and losers, can the Federal Government out-guess the marketplace?**

The Congressional Research Service says that, while the United States spends considerably more on R&D as a percentage of Gross National Product than do the governments of its major competitors, it drops below both Japan and West Germany when military programs are excluded. The American Association for the Advancement of Science (AAAS) estimates that spending for non-defense R&D in fiscal 1984 will actually decline when measured in constant 1972 dollars.

Within the non-defense category, the Reagan Administration projects increases in basic research in the so-called "hard" physical sciences and in engineering, while basic research in the "soft" fields—such as biomedical, social and behavioral sciences—as well as applied research would hold steady or decline. In seeking to boost some basic research now, the President "is merely undoing some of the damage that he inflicted earlier," wrote Daniel S. Greenberg, editor of *Science & Government Report*.

Louis Schorsch, science specialist at the Congressional Budget Office, said of the shift in R&D priorities at the White House: "There's been a really dramatic reorientation toward defense, and a tendency on non-defense to pull the government back

and rely on the market. That's a pattern you see across the government as a whole, and it shows up in the R&D budget as well. The category that has been cut the most is applied research—the category that links the laboratory and the factory."

Some of the cuts in applied research and demonstration projects involved energy projects that the Administration said should be funded privately, if at all. Nevertheless, the idea of pushing more laboratory advancements into the marketplace appeals to many. This is something the Japanese do quite well, through government-industry-university partnerships in projects with high commercial potential.

**Active Role For Government?**

House and Senate members, in their ongoing quest for a national industrial policy, have considered a range of suggestions through which the government would play a more active role in the commercialization of research work. U.S. companies in both the smokestack and high-technology fields may soon be outgunned by government-subsidized competitors overseas unless the Federal Government offers help, according to this line of thought.

These suggestions smack of centralized government planning, and run counter to traditional notions of free-enterprise economics. But in truth, the lines between government-funded research and business-sponsored application have long been blurred.

Agriculture, the biggest U.S. export business, is nurtured by federal research programs as well as price-supports. Commercial aviation, which accounts for the biggest chunk of manufactured exports, likewise benefits from federal R&D. The government-financed space program has generated so many marketplace products that the space agency publishes a roundup called "Spinoffs." And in the highest high-technology realm, the Federal Govern-

ment was the first sponsor, and is still the biggest buyer of American-made supercomputers. Currently the Pentagon's Defense Advanced Projects Research Agency is funding leading-edge research into artificial-intelligence computing, which has unlimited commercial possibilities.

But just because the Federal Government already provides this kind of support, it does not necessarily follow that it should do more of the same. Ideology aside, there is always the practical question of whether the government, in trying to sort out potential winners and losers for special government assistance, could out-guess the marketplace.

**Spurring Business**

The Reagan Administration is taking a different tack. It supports various initiatives designed to spur business into doing more on its own rather than injecting the government into private-sector R&D choices.

These initiatives include proposed changes in antitrust laws. The Administration, along with several congressional Democrats, has proposed legislation designed to encourage more joint venture research by competing companies. The new Microelectronics and Computer Technology Corp., established by a dozen semiconductor and computer firms, stands as a model for this type of venture. Business representatives say they still fear government antitrust challenges or private triple-damage suits, but if legislation achieves its stated goal, it would result in more research at no direct cost to the government.

Tax policy also can be used to promote R&D. The R&D tax credit, inserted into the big Economic Recovery Tax Act of 1981, was scheduled to last only two years but is likely to be extended. The Administration meanwhile is broadening the definition of eligible expenditures to include computer software as well as hardware.

Patent policy similarly is linked to R&D activity, and the Administration, through a presidential memorandum, has instructed federal agencies to allow contractors, to the extent allowed by law, to retain title to inventions that are developed under federal sponsorship.

Legislation, introduced by Sen. Charles Mathias (R-Md.) and 13 bipartisan co-sponsors, is also pending to restore up to 7 years of patent life lost because of government testing and review requirements. Companies and inventors, who develop new products and then have to wait as long as half the 17-year patent term lifetime to receive government clearance, claim this stymies innovation. "This degradation undermines the basic rationale of the patent system," said Sen. Mathias, "at a time when [industries] face rising research and development costs and stiffening competition from overseas, where full patent protection is more dependable."

**The National Laboratories**

Presidential Science Advisor George A. Keyworth II also instigated a year-long review by the White House Science Council of the Federal Government's own 755 laboratories, which use about one-third of the federal R&D budget, or $15 billion. The study, directed by Hewlett-Packard Chairman David Packard, concluded that the missions of the national labs should be more tightly defined and their work consolidated. It said greater collaboration with industry and academia should be achieved through, for example, more personnel exchanges and joint projects.

**State governments are hoping to foster more R&D within their borders as a way of spurring economic growth.**

Finally, the Administration and Congress have moved toward agreement on expanded federal aid to the nation's

22

23

**Fig. 11-7** *Frames or margins are important design elements. Most of the white space allotted to margins should be in the outside dimensions of the page to help provide unity and enhance the "framing" effect. Note the placement of subheads on these inside pages to add balance and break up long copy. (Reprinted with permission from* DuPont Context.*)*

allotted here. Less will make the page look too crowded. A pica and a half is not too much. On a basic 8½ by 11 inch page or larger, 2 picas of white space between columns on a two-column format is about right. Too much white space between columns will destroy unity and make the page appear fragmented.

There is a tendency for those new at the game to crowd elements and jam them together. Don't be afraid to use plenty of white space; make a minimum of 1 pica between art and body copy, between head and subhead, between all elements.

Once concrete decisions are made concerning the function and formula of a magazine and the basic format, including handling of the frames, we can turn to the specific elements that will be combined to make our typographic package. But, before we do, there are two areas that we should address: basic terminology and the points involved in redesigning an existing publication.

## ✄ Basic Magazine Terminology

Below are some basic terms anyone involved in magazine editing, design, or production should understand:

- *Bleed:* This is the extension of an illustration beyond the type area to the edge of a page.
- *Break of the book:* This is the allocation of space for articles, features, and all material printed in the magazine.
- *Contents page:* This is the page that lists all the articles and features and their locations.
- *Cover:* This includes not only the front page but the other three pages making up the outside wrap of the magazine.
- *Folio:* This is the page number, date, and name of periodical on each page or spread.
- *Gutter:* This is the margin of the page at the point of binding, or the inside page margin.
- *Logo:* This is the magazine's nameplate, appearing on the cover, masthead, and so on.
- *Masthead:* This is the area, often boxed or given special typographic treatment, where the logo, staff listings, date of publication, and other information regarding the publication is listed.
- *Saddle stitch* (also called *saddle wire): *This is the kind of binding in which staples are driven through the middle fold of the pages.
- *Self-cover:* This is a magazine cover printed on the same paper stock as the rest of the magazine.
- *Sidestitch* (also called *sidewire): *This is a method of binding in which staples are driven through stacked printed sections (signatures) of the magazine.
- *Signature:* This is a large sheet of paper printed on both sides and folded to make up a section of a publication. For instance, four pages might be printed on each side of a sheet and then the sheet folded and cut to make an eight-page signature.

## Redesigning a Magazine

The general approach to designing a new publication can be used to redesign an existing magazine as well. But there are a few additional points we need to consider before creating a new look for an existing publication.

The first step in redesigning should be a complete study of the present format. Every item from the smallest typographic device to the logo should be examined. The primary examination should

# IN THE ALPS OF ARABIA

WRITTEN BY TORBEN B. LARSEN AND JOHN WOOD
PHOTOGRAPHED BY TORBEN B. LARSEN

Guarding the flanks of Arabia are two main mountain ranges, both reaching higher than 3,000 meters in places (9,800 feet). One stretches south from Taif in Saudi Arabia to Yemen, the other curves from the Musandam peninsula of Oman, through the United Arab Emirates to southern Oman.

Both ranges are imposingly steep – indicating their relative youth in geological terms (10-30 million years or so) – and are the end product of collisions between land masses floating on molten lava. These collisions could be described as the final adjustments in the continental drift which started to break up the super-continent called "Panagaea" some 200 million years ago; at that time Panagaea included all the land masses we know as continents today, and the Arabian peninsula was still attached to Africa.

Mountains they most certainly are – and very impressive ones at that. But are they really "alps"? In a strict sense – mountains with permanent snow – no. While it does snow from time to time, the snow melts immediately. But in the general sense – high rugged mountains – they certainly are "alps" – at least if you consider the flora – and fauna.

Among the flora and fauna of Arabia are desert-adapted species which botanists classify as Saharo-Sindian, or Saharo-Arabian, and which zoologists classify as eremic. Mostly of African origin, these species have adapted to a climate which is essentially hostile to flora and fauna, in that they are at the mercy of highly irregular rainfall. As a result, many of these plants are now so specialized that they cannot live outside of the true desert regions in southern Arabia: from Jiddah to Aden and from Aden to northern Oman.

Most of these species, which originated in the dry tropics of Africa, do not exist in Europe at all. But in the high mountains of Arabia – 2,000 to 2,500 meters (6,560 to 8,200 feet) – a very different group of plants and animals occurs, whose origins lie in the temperate zone of Europe and Asia, the so-called Palaearctic region. Here, in splendid isolation, they continue to exist, though often separated from their usual home by thousands of kilometers.

All told, some 3,000 plants are found in Arabia, of which perhaps a quarter have their origin in the temperate zone. Nearly half of these are weeds whose status is doubtful; they may have been introduced by man. One example is the common European Dandelion (*Taraxacum officinale*) which has been found in only one locality in Arabia: the lawn of the British embassy in Sanaa. But that still leaves a hard core of some 300 plants which came originally from temperate zones and which are identical to those of Europe and Asia; other species have developed into distinctly Arabian species, such as the Arabian Thyme (*Thymus laevigatus*), undoubtedly a distinct species but also representative of a large group otherwise found only in Europe and Asia.

Why are these temperate plants found deep within the desert and the tropical zone?

*A sunalpine meadow on Jabal Sabr. Above Ta'iz, in the Yemen Arab Republic, where plants like Botta's Mullein (Verbascum Bottae), opposite, can be found.*

There are two main possibilities. First, they might have invaded these regions during a cool period of the ice ages, some 250,000 years ago, and might then have been trapped by a rise in temperature. Or they might be the survivors of an ancient stock dating back millions of years to a time when the world's climate was very different from that of today.

In the Yemen/Asir mountains, for example, many plants show signs of being immigrants that have maintained direct contact with the main range of the species until quite recently. Examples include the Giant Fennel (*Ferula communis*) and the lovely White Iris (*Iris albicans*), which differ in no way from the Mediterranean examples. But nearby there are also species which can hardly be recent immigrants. A typical example is the Ethiopian Rose (*Rosa abyssinica*). A plant obviously derived from the temperate roses, the Ethiopian Rose – common in both Ethiopia and southwestern Arabia – probably developed into a distinct species before Arabia broke away from Africa some nine million years ago.

In Oman, the temperate flora show every sign of having been linked at some point with those of the Zagros mountains in Iran; at levels above 2,000 meters (6,560 feet), the flora are largely composed of temperate plants such as the large Star Thistle (*Centaurea S.P.*). Indeed, the first botanist to climb in the Musandam mountains region was overheard muttering, in effect, "I don't believe this isn't Iran."

There is, in fact, evidence that there was a land connection between the Zagros and Oman near Bandar Abbas as recently as 90,000 years ago, when climatic conditions would have permitted the interchange of such plants. And there may have been older affinities as well. Oman, for example, has a quite distinct Oleander

### They're mountains, yes, but are they alps?

**Fig. 11-8** *The art-title-subhead-byline-initial-letter technique applied by* Aramco World *magazine. The full-page art is bled to all four margins for added impact. The same typeface is used for title, subhead, and initial letter to create harmony. The small art is centered at the bottom of column two for added balance.*

center on the audience and its needs. This might require contact with the audience through research and surveys to find answers to questions such as:

1. Does the present format do a good job of bringing the editorial content and the audience together?

2. Does the present design give the audience what it wants?

3. Will a different format serve the audience better?

4. Does the audience prefer different kinds of illustrations (photos instead of diagrams, for example)?

Changes cannot be made without considering factors that may not be obvious. Talks with the printer and compositor are important. It might be impossible to produce the changes sought with the equipment available. Much time and effort could be wasted planning changes it would be impossible for the equipment to duplicate.

**Fig. 11-9** *This magazine page has many design problems. Most are violations of basic principles of design. How many can you spot! Poor spacing between words and lines, uneven leading in the subhead, mixture of display types, improper use of Oxford rules, and art that does not communicate are a few of the shortcomings.*

By Judi Prats
Kent State University

## VOLUNTEER PR SERVICES

*Make more of*

*your education by*

*getting involved in*

*volunteer PR. It can*

*broaden learning*

*experiences,*

*widen contacts for*

*future references*

*and increase*

*your knowledge in*

*practictioning*

FORUM/6

So you're planning on graduating and landing that big deal job writing news releases with your initialed Parker Bros. pen, seated at your very own Formica-topped desk in your very own plastic-plant-decorated office.

It's the real thing. Your big break.

But that big break doesn't come in an all inclusive 9-5 package deal, neatly adorned with one hour lunches, 15 minute caffeine breaks and the option to leave the office a half hour early in order to avoid the Dodge'em cars on the freeway.

No, the job doesn't stop when the "Happy Days" reruns come on.

There are things to be taken away from the office besides a new leather-smelling briefcase or your first "real" byline.

You've got to be a part of community involvement. This means doing VOLUNTEER WORK — a dreaded task that you thought would finally leave you alone after diploma presentation

This volunteer work, although possibly more extensive (yet not as colorful) as selling carnations in the Student Center, may take on the task of petitioning to get a hospital levy passed or handing out flyers to support a candidate.

This community involvement is more than an exercise in seeing how many clubs or groups recognize your name — it's an achievement of personal goal attainment. This goal is to make yourself a total person, handling with finesse the complementary roles of Joe Businessman and Joe Citizen.

You have to be conscious that your big break doesn't stop when the title Account Executive is tacked to your name.

It continues throughout your career, in making yourself a success inside the office and out.

And, just like we learn how to write news releases and snap photographs and run the lithography press (with a little assistance) *we* must also be educated in the seemingly unrewarded activities like peddling pumpkins and signing up blood donors.

PRSSA is the bridge to those "unrewarded" efforts that tend to be associated with asking for too much money and begging for too much time. These volunteer activities are indeed rewarded.

## Donate time to become active in your community

They are looked at admirably when placed on a resume, but more importantly, they are thought of warmly when the doer looks back and realizes how he has helped to achieve the desired goal, whether it be a convention to Chicago or the renovation of a theatre.

The activities of PRSSA don't stop with working on accounts or escorting Bloodmobile victims to the food table, there is the social side of public relations that dare not be ignored.

PR practitioners have acquired a reputation for knowing how to have a good time. This is a talent that must also be fostered in our college days.

So, the next time you hear one of the PRSSA officers sprouting off about getting involved with the accounts, selling whatever, or attending a wine and cheese party — just remember, that it's all a part of the degree.

If the publication is produced "in house," on equipment we possess, the equipment manufacturer can be a valuable source of graphic and redesign ideas and equipment capabilities.

We should solicit ideas from as many sources as possible but not abdicate the final decision-making process. A publication designed by a committee usually turns out to be a hodgepodge collection of graphic ideas that is seldom effective.

We must also avoid the tendency to design by "shotgun." Shotgun design is seen more and more, often to the detriment of the publications on which it is practiced. It is the temptation to try to outdo graphic design on each succeeding issue so that each issue is packed with more attention-getting graphics than the one before. The

**Fig. 11-10** *An effective way to reduce advertisement clutter in magazine design is to group the small ads under appropriate headings. This aids the advertiser, too, as it helps flag the target audience. (From* Nevada *magazine.)*

designer tries to employ some new design gimmick every time, creating a collection of distracting graphics. Instead, we want to create a format based on simplicity, one capable of standing the test of continued repetition without creating monotony.

If advertising is carried, our study should include the types of advertising, the most common sizes, and their present arrangements on the pages. For example, a proliferation of small ads will present problems that would be avoided if the magazine runs fewer but larger ads.

We need to examine the type styles used in setting the ads. In designing types for editorial material, we should make an effort to blend them with the predominant advertising types to present harmonious pages. In addition, consideration will have to be given advertisements if we change the column widths. If the format is changed from three columns to two, for instance, this could lead to all sorts of complications regarding space sales and advertising rates.

Then, sometimes there are so-called typographic sacred cows (such as standing heads on regular columns, locating certain features in specific spots, and the type styles used for titles and logos) that cannot be changed, or can be changed only with great internal organizational difficulty. These must be taken into account.

## Steps in Redesign

Once a thorough study of the present design has been made, the redesigning process can begin. Below is a useful step-by-step outline for overhauling a publication.

1. *Start at the back.* Magazines are designed from the back to the front. Why this backward approach? First of all, a new design usually means a new logo or new cover design. This indicates that there is something new inside—and there better be! A new label for the same old can of beans does not fool anyone very long. Another reason for starting with the back is that's where most of the design trouble usually can be found. Those little mail-order ads, fillers, and jumped conclusions of articles get dumped in the back. So, clean it up first and then go on to the features. Plan a basic uninterrupted reading pattern, but start with the back.

2. *Group, consolidate, organize.* Analyze the small items and rearrange them. This will often lead to an organizational format that will improve the appearance of the whole publication. How can that be? Well, the secret of a well-designed publication is *departmentalization.* Grouping related items together creates an orderly plan that makes sense to the reader. It helps sort out the contents of the publication.

   If small ads are carried, consider them first. What is their typographical tone? Are they crammed with lots of copy? Do they try to scream at the reader with large, bold type, heavy borders, lots of reverses? Separate them into groups and arrange the groups by sizes. If they are scattered helter-skelter throughout the magazine, group them together in some way—perhaps by subject category. Arrange them on a layout sheet in an orderly pattern (see pages 211 and 225). Ads are more effective if grouped by subject matter—schools, camps, travel, trading post—rather than being scattered randomly throughout a publication.

3. *Analyze departments and their heads.* Too many departments—household hints, sports shorts, and so on—can clutter a publication in two ways. It is difficult to design effective layouts if many short departments must be accommodated. And the constant repetition of many similar department heads can lead to a choppy format. Check to see if departments can be combined or eliminated if there are too many in the publication.

   Whenever redesigning department or section heads, keep in mind the criteria for good heads: the head should blend well with the copy, help say what the department is all about, and be uncluttered with illustrations and ornaments. If illustrations are used, they should be simple. Avoid art that could become dated in heads—art that is in fashion now but probably will be out soon. The head should be clean, brief, and to the point. It should be easy to adapt it to one-, two-, or three-column widths.

4. *Consider the constants.* There are other constants to review in addition to department heads. (Constants are the typographic devices that do not change from issue to issue.) These include the table of contents, masthead, editorial section, letters section, fillers, next issue's previews, and special advertising sections.

   The entire sequence of constants must be handled individually and then collectively to present a harmonious whole. In designing the constants as well as in all the other parts of the total format, all the principles of design and type selection should be put into practice.

5. *Finally, the cover.* Most communicators are tempted to redesign the cover right off, but it was left to last for a very good reason. A thorough study of all the factors that must be considered in designing a magazine will now provide a bonus. Designing an effective cover now will be easy. Even though the cover is considered last it probably is the most important element in the entire format. It is the display window—what people see first. It can cause the reader to pick up a periodical or pass it by. The ideas regarding cover design in the next chapter (pages 219-224) are useful in redesigning as well as in creating a new publication.

## Effective Design Checklist

■ Provide for ample margins and white space. If the margins and white space between the columns are inadequate, the entire magazine will have a cramped, jammed-up appearance.

■ Define editorial and advertising content clearly. If the reader cannot tell easily where one begins and the other ends, the whole publication will appear disorganized and confusing.

■ Make sure type styles relate to content. The typefaces and illustration designs must harmonize with the editorial content. Some designers will call this "type and content marriage." Good type marriages are a sign of professionalism.

■ Pictures should be selected and cropped for content first. Do the pictures help eye movement through the page? If art causes eye movement out of the page, or through the page in an uncontrolled way, the page patterns are those of a beginner, and we want to be pros.

■ Special departments should relate to the basic editorial theme of the magazine. Unrelated departments, especially if there is a proliferation of them, tend to break down the basic editorial impact of the magazine.

■ Check the last pages as well as the first. The back of the book should not be a dumping ground. The final pages should be well organized if the entire package is to be as attractive as possible.

■ The table of contents should be neat. If the table of contents and the masthead are cluttered, crowded, or disorganized, redesign them. They should be neat, clean, and functional.

■ Everything should blend together. See if the stories and articles are laid out to present a unified magazine package. If they seem to be individually designed with no thought given to what else is contained in the issue, they need work.

■ Check the body type. Don't overlook the basic reading matter type. It should be a clean, readable design—preferably a Roman face that is big on the body. Check the leading and see if the type size is near the optimum for the width of the columns.

■ Consider the design from the reader's standpoint. Some magazines are designers' dream productions but nightmares for readers. Don't let layouts become ego trips. Make them functional. See that each element in each layout is there for a purpose. That purpose should be to attract the reader, hold interest, and make reading a pleasant experience.

## Graphics in Action

1. Select a magazine that appeals to a special-interest audience and analyze its design and typography. Try to determine how the design, selection of type styles, and arrangement of design elements were made to appeal to the target audience. If there are shortcomings in the design, explain the changes you would recommend.

2. Develop a formula for a small magazine. Have its target audience be a group or organization, special-interest or hobby, to which you belong or to which you have a special affinity. Make a written plan to present to possible financial backers of the proposed magazine.

3. Develop a format for the small magazine to carry out the philosophy of the formula developed in number 2. (Both numbers 2 and 3 can be combined with Graphics in Action number 5 in Chapter 12 for a major project. It might be well, then, to restrict the size of the magazine to, say, eight or twelve pages, depending on the amount of time that can be devoted to this project.)

4. Design a basic cover layout for a magazine for an organization of which you are a member, or for the magazine proposed in numbers 2 and 3. Use an 8½ by 11 page with a type area 44 by 57 picas.

5. Examine the design flaws of the magazine page reproduced in illustration 11-9. Redesign the page to eliminate the shortcomings.

Was he half hype or sheer hero?
Buffalo Bill takes a new bow

Novelty

Battle
of the
Burro

A nightmare
goes on and on

STREAMLINED

Chewing or stinging,
their methods are
remarkably efficient

Now we are ready to put our plan into action. The designer is faced with creating prototype page layouts that will be examined and evaluated by everyone involved in the project.

## Designing the Magazine

How does the designer proceed? What are the first steps in the actual creative process?

We are living in a visual age, a world of visual excitement. It takes the combined talent of the artist, the knowledge of the psychologist, and the skill of the designer and printer to produce pages that will encourage the reader to anticipate each issue and reach for one particular magazine among all the others seeking attention.

### The Break of the Book

The first decision to be made in crossing the bridge from the planning stage to the layout stage is what is known as *the break of the book*. This is the term editors and art directors use to designate what is going to be placed where.

There are several basic philosophies concerning how to break the book. One is called the *traditional plan*. Under this arrangement, the constants—the regular columns and features, the masthead, the table of contents, and any editorial page material plus the advertisements—are grouped in the first few and the last few pages. The middle pages are reserved for the current issue's main articles and stories. The strongest article in the issue is used as the lead article for this middle section. Several major magazines that use this method of breaking the book include *Reader's Digest*, *Smithsonian*, and *National Geographic*.

Another approach is called the *front to back system*. In this arrangement, features and articles are spread throughout the magazine. A great many company and association publications follow this approach with perhaps only a contents page at the front of the book.

Of course, the editor and designer can strive to be different and create an entirely new plan.

### Laying Out the Pages

Once basic decisions are made, it is time to go ahead and place the graphic elements on paper. This is done with a layout or *grid sheet* for each page. These grid sheets can be obtained for most standard magazine page sizes and column widths from graphic supply concerns or they can be made and reproduced on a duplicator or office copier.

Grids are available in quarter scale, usually four to an 8½ by 11 inch sheet, for making thumbnails. Some editors start their layout work by folding sheets of blank paper into proportionate small sizes, as was suggested in making thumbnails for advertisements, but slitting them so they are actually blank miniatures of the full size.

It is possible, too, to make a miniature ruler with a strip of cardboard and label it with an inch scale to the proportion of the full-size sheet. For instance, on the miniature ruler for making thumbnails, one-fourth of an inch might equal 1 inch on a full-scale ruler.

The designer uses these tools to rough in all the material the full-size layout will contain and then uses the resulting thumbnail as a guide in keeping things straight when full-size layouts are made.

An easy way to keep account of progress in laying out a magazine is to put the full-size layouts for each page in numerical sequence up on the office wall. If a small piece of masking tape is used, the pages can be taken down, worked on, and replaced.

This method of planning an issue has two advantages. The status of the whole issue can be seen at a glance and facing pages can be seen side by side. It should be kept in mind that the magazine reader sees two facing pages at a time, and good planning should include making sure that these pages are compatible.

## Screens Will Replace Drawing Boards

Soon, however, the use of pencil, pens, and paper and layout and grid sheets will become passé. In April 1983, *Time* started using a device in its layout department that replaced layout sheets, art knives, and waxers. The new device is called the Vista, and when it went into use it was believed to be the only one of its kind in the world.

The machine has two adjoining video screens. The story, headline, art, and other graphic elements that the designer wants to place on a page are displayed on one screen. The other screen is a monitor that shows what the completed page will look like in color. The designer can move the elements around, alter their sizes, and arrange them on the screen just as most art directors now arrange them on paper. *Time*'s assistant art director, Anthony J. Libardi, was quoted in the magazine as saying the machine "gives you the freedom to revise and adapt quickly. It can turn the work of hours into as little as twenty minutes."

However, whether a magazine is laid out with a ruler and pencil or felt pen, or whether it is composed on a space-age electronic device, the basic principles of good design in general and magazine design in particular still apply.

## Planning the Cover

All pages of a printed communication are important, but if one page must be singled out as the most important of all in magazine design, it has to be the front cover. It creates the all-important first impression. It not only identifies the publication but it says something about its personality.

---

### Creative Communication

Know when to stop.

The creative process can be endless. On the other hand, a puzzle has an answer. A mathematical problem is either right or wrong and that is the end of it.

But the creative design process can go on and on. There is no one final, absolutely correct answer. In creative design one of the skills worth developing is knowing when to stop.

Knowing when to stop involves knowing the capabilities of the equipment and the materials available, the characteristics of the target audience, and the attributes and limitations of the medium used to transmit the completed layout in its final visual form.

A good front cover should accomplish four things. It should identify the magazine in a way that sets it apart from the others. It should attract attention, especially from the target audience. It should get the reader inside, and it should set the tone or mood of the magazine. In addition, in instances where the magazine is sold in stores or on newsstands, it plays an important role in the selling process.

Some data should be automatic with each cover. In addition to the logo, the date of issue, volume, and number should appear—especially if the magazine is the type that will be filed and indexed for future reference. The price, if the magazine is sold, should be included. This seems self-evident, but it is surprising how many small magazines fail to include this pertinent information on their covers.

## Self-Cover or Separate Cover?

One of the first decisions that has to be made is whether the magazine will be self-covered or have a separate cover. A *self-cover* is a cover printed on the same paper stock as the body of the magazine. Many magazines invest in a more expensive and more substantial paper stock for the cover.

**Fig. 12-1** *The* Reader's Digest *utilizes the front cover as both a table of contents and a display area for "teasers." Art is used on the outside back cover. Both techniques can be used for company or organization publications.*

However, the self-cover has its assets. It is, of course, less expensive. In addition, for the small publication on a limited budget, the self-cover can provide color on inside pages at virtually no extra cost. This is possible because most magazines are printed in *signatures*, or sections of pages in units of four, with the number of units in a signature decided by the press capacity. Thus, when color is purchased for the cover, it can also be used on the other pages of the signature containing the cover. This could involve four, eight, sixteen, or even thirty-two pages, depending on the size of the magazine and of each signature in its manufacture.

Another decision regarding the cover concerns advertising. A very limited number of publications sell the front cover page at a premium as a source of income. These include a few business and professional publications. One is *Editor & Publisher.* However, most editors find front-cover advertising quite objectionable. The decision concerning cover advertising might be whether the interest-arousing and selling asset of a strong cover should be sacrificed for the additional money obtained by selling the front cover.

**Fig. 12-2** *The editor-designer of a small magazine can create attractive, mood-setting covers by utilizing stock art as in this example of a summer issue of a house publication. (Courtesy of Dynamic Graphics.)*

Most editors have found that a cover that sets the theme for an issue, identifies what the issue is all about, or ties in with a strong lead article works best. Research has also found that covers with closely cropped human interest pictures are good attention-getters.

## Covers That Sell Contents

A trend today is toward greater use of the cover to sell the contents. More and more *blurbs* are being used on covers. These teasers are designed to lure readers into picking up the magazine for the contents.

In designing blurbs it is important to realize that the cover is the magazine's store window. It is the poster or billboard that will advertise and, hopefully, sell what the publication has to offer. Blurbs should be written and designed much like the copy on posters and billboards—short and to the point. The message should be one that can be taken in at a glance. Advertisers say a billboard message should be read in 5 seconds. Blurbs on magazine covers should be equally short, never more than three lines of type for each blurb.

Blurbs should also relate closely to the article titles. In one magazine recently, the blurb on the cover announced "Solar Pioneers." The title of the article referred to was "To Catch the Sun." Readers might have trouble relating the two. Make sure the blurbs can be identified with the articles or features quickly and without confusion.

Traditionally, the blurb was placed along the left side of the cover. This was because of the way many magazines were stacked on newsstands so that they overlapped and only a portion of the left side of each cover was visible to the passerby. However, it isn't necessary that this pattern be followed for most magazines today.

## Consistency Is Important

The inside cover pages and the back cover can cause some design problems. The key to designing these pages is consistency. Select a graphic pattern for these pages and stick to it. If the magazine runs advertising on the inside front cover and on both back-cover pages, the problem is easily solved. Usually the cover pages sell well because of their high impact. The back cover is seen almost as much as the front cover, and the inside cover pages receive high viewing as well.

But, if advertising is not a part of the covers, the designer needs to adopt a cover design philosophy. *Context*, the magazine of the DuPont Corporation, uses the back cover as a contents page. It includes color photos and short blurbs for each major article along with the masthead and the post office mailing permit tag plus an area for the address sticker.

The address sticker can be a problem. It is unfortunate that many magazines have fine front-cover illustrations and designs only to

**Fig. 12-3** Context *solves several problems—what to do with the back cover, how to handle the contents page, how to keep the postage bug and address label from marring the front cover—by putting all this information on the back cover. It brightens the page by using full-color illustrations with "teasers" for each article. (Reprinted with permission from DuPont* Context.*)*

have them marred with an address sticker and, in many cases, the computerized code for the checkout counter. Cover planning should include consideration of this problem. Some magazine designers solve it by using a mailing wrapper or envelope. If, however, costs or other factors rule this out, it might be worthwhile to incorporate the address area into the design, as *Context* does.

It is possible to include some regular features on the inside covers, and the inside front cover is an excellent spot for the contents page for a small magazine. The better-designed magazines avoid running large amounts of reading matter on the inside covers and solve some outside-back-cover problems by extending the front-cover illustrations to cover the back as well.

The *Reader's Digest* solves the problem nicely by using the front cover as a blurb and contents page and filling the back outside cover with a full-page illustration.

**Cover Design Preparation**

A good preparation for designing the cover of a magazine is to browse through an assortment of magazines and see how well the designers have used the attributes of good typography to help accomplish the job of the cover. Ask yourself the following questions to guide your evaluations:

1. *Does the cover identify the magazine and reflect its personality?* The logo should be large enough to be recognized immediately and the style should be compatible with the magazine's personality. (An artist can be commissioned to make a distinctive logo for the publication at a reasonable cost.)

   A strong, aggressive type such as a Sans Serif, Square Serif, or Roman in boldface would be good for a bold, aggressive magazine. A medium or light old style Roman is a good choice for a dignified publication. Scripts or light or medium Romans with swash first letters project an image of gracefulness. Square Serifs or strong modern Romans are good for scientific or technical publications, but they should not be too bold. There are enough type styles available to project almost any image desired.

   Cover illustrations should reflect the personality of the magazine, too. Most magazines use a combination of type and illustrations to project their identity in the cover design.

2. *Does the cover attract the target audience and get its attention?* The type styles and illustrations used should relate to the audience and reflect its characteristics and interests. If a magazine is appealng to an aggressive target audience, using a lot of elements on the cover will give it the image of a magazine that is full of vitality and action.

3. *Does the cover lure the reader inside?* The basic cover design consists of a strong logo at the top and an illustration relating to the tone of the magazine or the theme or, possibly, the lead article. Designers have found, however, that type is the most effective means of luring the reader inside. If blurbs are used, check to see if they appeal to the target audience. Check, too, to see if there is an element of timeliness. Blurbs should stress the benefits the reader will receive by turning to the articles being touted.

4. *Does the cover create identity from issue to issue?* Once a type style for the logo is adopted it should continue from issue to issue. The placement of the logo plus the date of issue and so on should also be basically the same from issue to issue. The general approach to handling blurbs should be consistent. There should be enough consistency in the cover design to create continuity and identity from one issue to the next.

5. *Does the cover contain the essential information?* Check to see that the date, price, and volume and issue numbers are present. It is surprising how often the lack of these essentials isn't noticed until after page proofs are made.

## Essentials of Page Design

There are two points to keep constantly in mind during the designing of a magazine. One is that the reader sees two pages at a time. The other is that all the basic principles of design—balance, proportion, unity, contrast, rhythm, harmony—should come into play.

### The A-T-S-I Approach

With this in mind, we can plan the actual design of the pages in the magazine. There is one approach that is a good way to get things started. This is the art-title-subhead and/or byline, initial-letter approach, or the *A-T-S-I formula*. It is a simple and safe way to make layouts attractive and functional. Once this basic concept of magazine page arrangement is mastered, the designer can experiment with more daring use of white space and placement of elements.

In building a page using the A-T-S-I approach, a large attention-getting photograph or other art is used to attract the reader. Then a well-conceived title line is used. The subhead or byline, or both, are designed to move the reader toward the start of the article. Then the initial letter signals the beginning of the article and steps down to the reading matter from the other elements in the design.

**Fig. 12-4** *A minimum amount of artistic skill is needed to produce functional rough layouts for a small magazine. Here, rectangles with crossed diagonal lines indicate art, and rectangles with single diagonal lines represent advertisements. The title is composed with rub-on type; and the subhead and byline are indicated by felt pen squiggles. The letters column head was traced. The border around the left page and the letters column head is border tape. These were all planned on a grid sheet by a student.*

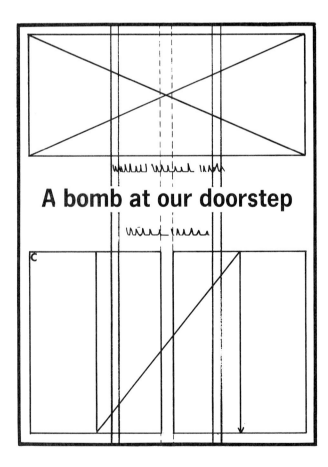

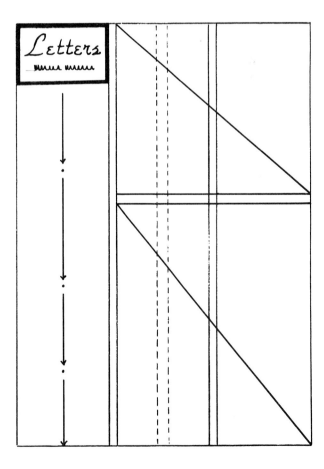

# C LIMBING

### TO A NEW HIGH

IN W. E. BOWMAN's marvelously funny little satire, *The Ascent of Rum Doodle*, a party of pompous Englishmen sets out to climb the highest peak on Earth, 40,000½-foot Rum Doodle, in the remote Asian country of Yogistan. The group consists of seven climbers, no fewer than 3,000 porters to carry the expedition supplies, and an additional 375 boys to carry supplies for the porters. The doughty, dotty mountaineers get lost repeatedly, jam themselves in the glacier ice, quarrel like schoolchildren and are regularly poisoned by the dreadful expedition cook, Pong. Finally, the main body of climbers ascends the wrong peak, an outlying pinnacle separated from Rum Doodle itself by miles of thin air. They watch as Prone, the most inept member of the expedition, is literally carried to the summit of Rum Doodle itself by the porters. The climbers return to England national heroes.

Bowman's satire is not too far removed from the reality of mountaineering in recent decades, when gigantic expeditions were common. Fashions in Himalayan mountaineering run in cycles, like Parisian *haute couture*. The first climbing expeditions to Nepal, back in the late 40s and early 50s, were simple, Spartan affairs; then, for the better part of two decades, the overblown, Rum Doodle approach to big peak climbing, with hundreds of porters and millions of dollars in expense money, prevailed. Today, with a few notably gaudy exceptions, there is a swing back to the ideal of the small expedition: a very few climbers, lightly equipped, against the greatest peaks on Earth.

These new mountaineers no longer see a climb as a conquest of a peak. Instead, they have embarked on a conquest of themselves, and fancy equipment becomes a barrier between them and the mountain, rather than a tool. These climbs are quests for personal "excellence," a way of pushing spiritual

*Gone are 500-man expeditions—today mountaineers go one-on-one against the world's biggest peaks*

By Rob Schultheis
Photographs by Galen Rowell

**F**ashions are changing in Himalayan mountaineering. The K2 expedition (above) in the 1970s used 650 porters to reach the Himalayan peak; in a 1983 Everest climb (right) John Roskelley and 16 others all carried their own gear.

30

**Fig. 12-5** *Integration of the head, subhead, and art plus the bold C of the title completed in letter bowl give this* *page layout impact, unity, and harmony. (Copyright 1984 by the National Wildlife Federation. Reprinted from the March-* *April issue of* International Wildlife. *Photo by Galen Rowell/High and Wild Photography.)*

## 2. The Axis Approach

Another method of arranging the elements on a magazine page in an orderly manner is called the *axis approach*. Here the title, subhead and byline, if used, follow one of the basic rules of good magazine design—*line up the elements*. But here they are lined up on an axis. The axis usually is one of the between-columns alleys.

In placing elements on a magazine page there are a number of points to keep in mind:

1. *First and most important, square up the elements.* This means to line things up and keep things even. Square up the elements where the eye tends to square them. For example, the top of a small illustration above another should line up with the top edge of a large illustration nearby. Type should be lined up along the margins of the type area, or if the lines are indented they should be lined up on the designated indentation. Cutlines for art that is bled to the outer edge of the page should be lined up with the type form and should not be placed in the white area, or margins, of the page.

2. *Distribute the elements throughout the layout.* Elements should not be bunched up all in one place. If the art, title, blurbs,

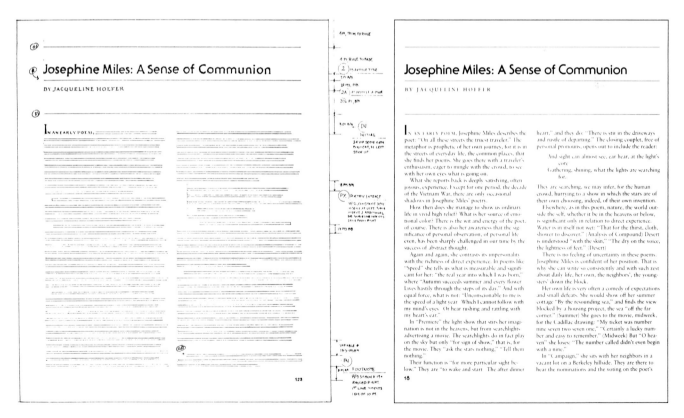

**Fig. 12-6** *A layout prepared by a professional designer. Note the precise placement of elements and instructions. Designers are architects of the printed word and their "blueprints" are devised with great attention to detail.*

**Fig. 12-7** *The page as it appeared in print after being composed in accordance with the instructions on the layout.*

*(Page 18 of* Woman Poet—The West, *copyright 1980, from the* Woman Poet *series of regional poetry anthologies, is reprinted by permission of Women-in-Literature, Inc., P.O. Box 60550, Reno, NV 89506.)*

and byline are placed at the start of the story, the page can be thrown out of balance. In addition, it will leave the page with columns of dull, gray type. Place the elements around the page to create better balance and to make the page more interesting.

3. *Keep the elements from fighting each other.* Illustrations that are next to each other but are unrelated will fight, especially if one is not large enough to dominate. Articles in side-by-side single columns will fight each other for the reader's attention. Elements should be placed so they will harmonize and create a unified whole rather than causing dissonance and disunity.

4. *Be consistent in making layouts.* Those just starting in magazine graphic work sometimes attempt to gain variety and interest by changing the types and styles of subheads and

**Fig. 12-8** *This layout illustrates good design principles. Note how surprinting the lower half of the second line of the title and part of the initial letter does not intrude on the photo but helps, along with the tree at right, frame it and unify all elements on the page. The Square Serif type gives the feel of the old Southwest. The design of the initial M is carried through in a smaller version for the rest of the first word in the article. (Courtesy Texas Real Estate Research Center, Texas A&M.)*

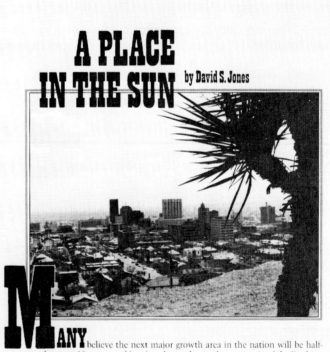

initial letters within one article. They end up with the layout counterpart to the Victorian house cluttered with gingerbread. Consistent use of a carefully chosen style on such items will help layouts achieve simplicity, harmony and attractiveness.

One school of typographical thought contends that all heads should be in the same type family to preserve consistency and harmony. Many magazines follow this philosophy and use the same types and basic arrangements of elements for all articles throughout every issue.

Other designers say that type should be used to establish an individual mood for each article. Begin by studying the tone and feel of an article as that will help in selecting and arranging graphic elements to ensure attractiveness and compatibility of graphics and content.

Anyone who has seen the dogwoods bloom in East Texas or gazed upward at the towering trunk of an old bald cypress tree growing along a Central Texas river can sense the tremendous possibilities for landscaping offered by Texas' native plants. Although still a long way from maximizing the potential of native plants, Texans in recent years have seen an increase in the preserving and planting of these native species and in the numbers of well planned communities where native plants have been retained during construction.

Developers and property owners are coming to realize that a setting of native pines, dogwood and wild azaleas has more visual appeal than the asphalt-paved parking lot of a shopping development. There is a growing awareness that carefully selected and positioned native species can beautify a landscape and help relate it to its natural environment.

Certain advantages accrue to landscapes created with these native plants rather than with their imported relatives. Often the native plants are more resistant to drought, insects and disease. In addition individual characteristics make native plants ideally suited for a particular terrain, be it swampy, rocky,

# Native plants for native places

## by William C. Welch

*wild olive*

*bald cypress*

arid or otherwise. A native plant can be found which will thrive where imported plants will die.

Unusual challenges for landscaping with native plants can be found in some of our more densely populated areas. Subdivisions around Austin and San Antonio, for instance, often are located in hilly areas to take advantage of views. The ecology of these sites is very delicate, with a thin soil layer over rock supporting a few small trees and shrubs, such as Texas persimmon (*Diospyros texana*), live oak (*Quercus virginiana*), agarita (*Mahonia trifoliolata*) and sumac (*Rhus lanceolata*).

If the property owner has a stereotyped concept that landscaping should consist of planting various broadleafed evergreen trees and flowering shrubs, he may clear the site of all the "brush." Then, after spending considerable time and money trying to provide topsoil, adequate irrigation and reduced soil ph, as well as dealing with insect and disease problems, the property owner wonders why maintaining the landscape is such a big and expensive job.

With some careful thinning, pruning, transplanting and a few well placed

groundcover areas, the property owner may have had the makings of an attractive and functional landscape development had she or he not been so hasty in removing the existing native plants on the site. Mature landscape material is expensive to buy and difficult to find. Builders, developers and homeowners need to evaluate very carefully what is growing naturally on the site before destroying it.

The diversity of temperature, topography, soil and rainfall in Texas results in a tremendous variety of plant life (more than 4,500 species). Every part of the state has its own unique character derived from plants as well as topography, soils and rock formations. A few of our distinctive plants useful for landscaping include the following:

**Texas mountain laurel** (*Sophora secundiflora*) — This evergreen large

*possum haw holly*

22 Tierra Grande

**Fig. 12-9** *Good unity, harmony, and balance are illustrated by this page from Tierra Grande. The type style is descriptive of the "feel" of native plants. The initial letter in the same typeface indicates the start of the article. The art is distributed on the page for good balance and harmony. What other typeface might have served equally well for the title of this article? (Courtesy Texas Real Estate Research Center, Texas A&M.)*

5. *Avoid monotony.* While the layout should be consistent, an effort should be made to make layouts fresh and unusual. Ask these design questions constantly: Would this article work better with a wider column? Could I use a larger type size for this head? Would a rule placed here be effective? How would this look with an oversized initial letter?

6. *Don't overdo bleeds.* Bleeds are a powerful tool for the magazine designer and there is a temptation to overdo them. Don't. And don't bleed art in a helter-skelter manner. Too many bleeds or too great a variety of bleeds creates a haphazard look that destroys simplicity and beauty in a layout.

7. *Avoid placing large pictures on top of small ones.* When small pictures appear immediately under large ones, the smaller ones look crushed. Normal placement of a group of pictures should build them up like toy blocks so they don't seem to topple over.

**Fig 12-10** *Bleeding art to the extremities of the page can give it greater impact and added weight as a design element. In planning bleeds the layout should indicate the bleed extending about 1/8-inch beyond the margin for trimming after the page is printed.*

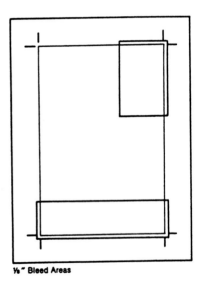

⅛″ **Bleed Areas**

review

*Gene Gregory writes for the newsmagazine "Far Eastern Economic Review" of Hong Kong, from which this is excerpted.*

# Japan's Education Edge

The drive to make jobs 'lifelong schooling'

— GENE GREGORY —

Japanese management techniques rarely produce the same results when applied elsewhere. It becomes increasingly evident that the ascendancy of major Japanese industries such as steel, automobile manufacture, shipbuilding, and electronics is closely related to the superior quality of their human resources. The explanation is not only that they are better organized and equipped with more or superior tools, but also that their educational system has raised the quality of knowledge for large numbers of the population to levels not attained elsewhere — especially in technology.

At the high school level the average Japanese student is already more advanced in mathematics and science than his peers elsewhere. At higher levels of education throughout the 1970s, 20 per cent of all baccalaureates and about 40 per cent of all master's degrees in Japan were granted to engineers, compared with about 5 per cent at each level in the U.S. More important still, once the engineer is employed in a major Japanese company — especially in the field of high technology — he is assured of continuing education.

The engineering profession in Japan attracts the best and most achievement-oriented young people. Senior managers of Japanese industrial enterprises and a high percentage of chief executive officers emerge from their ranks. The engineer — not the financier or the professional manager — has come to represent the spirit of enterprise in Japanese society.

In purely quantitative terms the availability of well-trained engineering personnel in Japan has been growing more rapidly than in the U.S. for more than a decade. By 1980 Japanese industry employed 35 engineers per 10,000 population against only 25 in the U.S., reflecting a higher aggregate technological level in Japan. Significantly, while only one in 10,000 Japanese are lawyers and three are accountants, in the U.S. there are 20 lawyers and four accountants for every 10,000 population.

It is not surprising, therefore, that U.S. industry is confronted with serious shortages of engineers even in rapid-growth sectors such as electronics. On a per-capita basis, since 1977 Japanese universities have graduated annually almost three times as many engineers in this field as have U.S. schools.

The gap continues to grow. Although enrollments in U.S. universities showed some improvement in this sector in the early 1980s, cutbacks in engineering school faculties that accompanied earlier enrollment declines in the area have not been reversed.

But the most important aspect of the shortage is qualitative, not quantitative. U.S. industry — electronics in particular — has too few engineers well grounded in the basics of engineering. There has been a deterioration of the entire education system in the U.S. while that of Japan has improved.

Nearly two thirds of all Japanese begin their formal education at the age of four. In primary and secondary schools Japanese children spend a third more days in school than their U.S. counterparts, and Japanese students at all grade levels tend to spend more hours doing homework.
*continued*

*Tokyo class — "higher I.Q.s than the average American."*          Eric Kroll/Taurus

HONORABLE MENTION

*Winter Morning* by Alain L'Heude, instrument test mechanic, John Deere Saran (France)

*Glacier Rain Forest* by Dan Jacob, staff photographer, Waterloo Tractor Works.

*White Masterpiece* by Joyce Salg, bookkeeper, Buck Bros., Inc., Hampshire, Ill.

*White Sands National Park* by Dale Dobberpuhl, product engineer, Horicon Works.

*One Small Step to Infinity* by Terry Rasso, plant protection, Davenport Works.

*Snowscape* by Todd Nicholson, analyst, sales finance, Deere & Company.

*Winter Layover* by Randy Leider, liaison engineer, Horicon Works.

*John Deere Tractor* by Brad Wallarab, receiving stocker, Parts Distribution Warehouse, Milan, Ill.

*Sleeping Lily* by Cersty Anton, photo laboratory helper, John Deere Werke Mannheim (Germany)

*Early Morning Campground* by Lee Woodward, industrial advertising writer, Deere & Company.

8. *Keep flashy arrows and fancy artistic devices to a minimum or, better yet, avoid them altogether.* These devices now look old-fashioned. Today the rule is for clean and simple designs that look neat and modern. Studies have shown that readers do not like pictures with rules around them, type printed over art (surprinting), oval-shaped art, and so on.

9. *Keep the pages dynamic.* Today the rule is simple, uncluttered, dynamic designs. In printed communication the message must be alive to be effective.

Traditionally, printed pages have had a strong vertical thrust. Pages that consist basically of reading matter usually are designed with the vertical column dictating where the copy is placed. As a result, most magazine pages consist of two or three columns of vertical, gray reading matter separated by a thin strip of white space.

This vertical flow is monotonous and if pages are to look alive this flow should be broken up by initial letters, subheads, illustrations, and/or white space.

**Fig. 12-11** *A proper arrangement of pictures. The small pictures are not crushed by the larger ones, the space between the art is equal all the way around, and the captions are placed in an orderly and convenient position. All elements are lined up. (Courtesy J D Journal, Deere and Company.)*

## Making Pages Interesting

Here are a few points to keep in mind when arranging elements on magazine pages to change direction and make the pages more interesting:

- *A vertical plus a vertical can equal monotony:* A page of all single-column copy and single-column illustrations will tend to

## OVER THE CLIFFS FOR EGGS

toward the birds. It is mid-May on Grimsey, an arctic isle off Iceland's north coast, time for the annual harvest of seabird eggs.

"In the old days, mainlanders called our island the 'country's breadbasket,'" says Bjarni Magnusson, 51, as he takes a break between rope descents. "Even

at day's end they pile into their truck, drive to the levee, boat back to Bloody Bayou and jump in. "We just strip

*"Out here I just sits back and lets it go."*

*— Alcide Verret*

down and leave our clothes on the dock," said Gwen. "They smell awful."

Piedmont Plateau to the enfolding

region by the time Peter G. Thom-

## Many early settlers of Haywood County rumbled down into the region via the "Great Philadelphia Wagon Road."

forts to develop the first atomic bomb. The idea was to lock the waste—chemi-

### What are the effects of dumping nuclear wastes at sea? Scientists are still searching for the answer

cals, laboratory instruments, even lab coats and boots—in a mix of concrete,

*"I need to be able to turn around at the end of the day and see the results of my labor — to see a hillside that I yarded."*
— AL REINHART, 32, LUMBERJACK

## EXPLORING THE NORTH

**40** *Hunting for fossils or mushrooms, caring for the animals, and downing hearty home-cooked meals are a few of the pleasures of a Nova Scotia farm.*

**Fig. 12-12** *Cut-in heads can break up the gray of the printed page and add life and brightness. The variety of possibilities is endless but the rules of good typography should be applied in selecting types, spacing, and lines and in placing rules.*

reinforce the vertical thrust and continue the monotony. Change the direction somewhat to make the page more interesting. This means adding a horizontal thrust. White space can be used to do this. Titles can be spread over several columns. A strong horizontal picture can be used. All will help create a visual change of direction.

■ *A change of form can make a page interesting:* Generally we think in terms of squares and rectangles. A change of form from the single vertical or horizontal unit can help create interest. For example, an L-shaped arrangement of illustrations provides a change of direction and adds variety to the page.

■ *There is movement in the content of art:* Quite often the center of interest in an illustration can help create a change of pace. The direction the subjects are looking or the direction a moving object is going can create motion on a page. But we must be sure the direction is leading where we want the reader to go. Such illustrations must be placed in a position that ensures the direction is *into* the article, or the page, rather than away from it.

- *White space is a good directional tool:* Breaking out of the standard margination, with more white space at the top or side of the page, with uneven column endings, can help break up vertical thrust. Color used in charts and graphs or in multicolumn heads can draw attention away from the vertical movement of the columns.

Although some rather fixed typographic rules for making magazine designs have been emphasized, the challenge always is to strive for the fresh and unusual. But the fresh and unusual should still be in balance and help to create a harmony among the elements as well as presenting a unified whole.

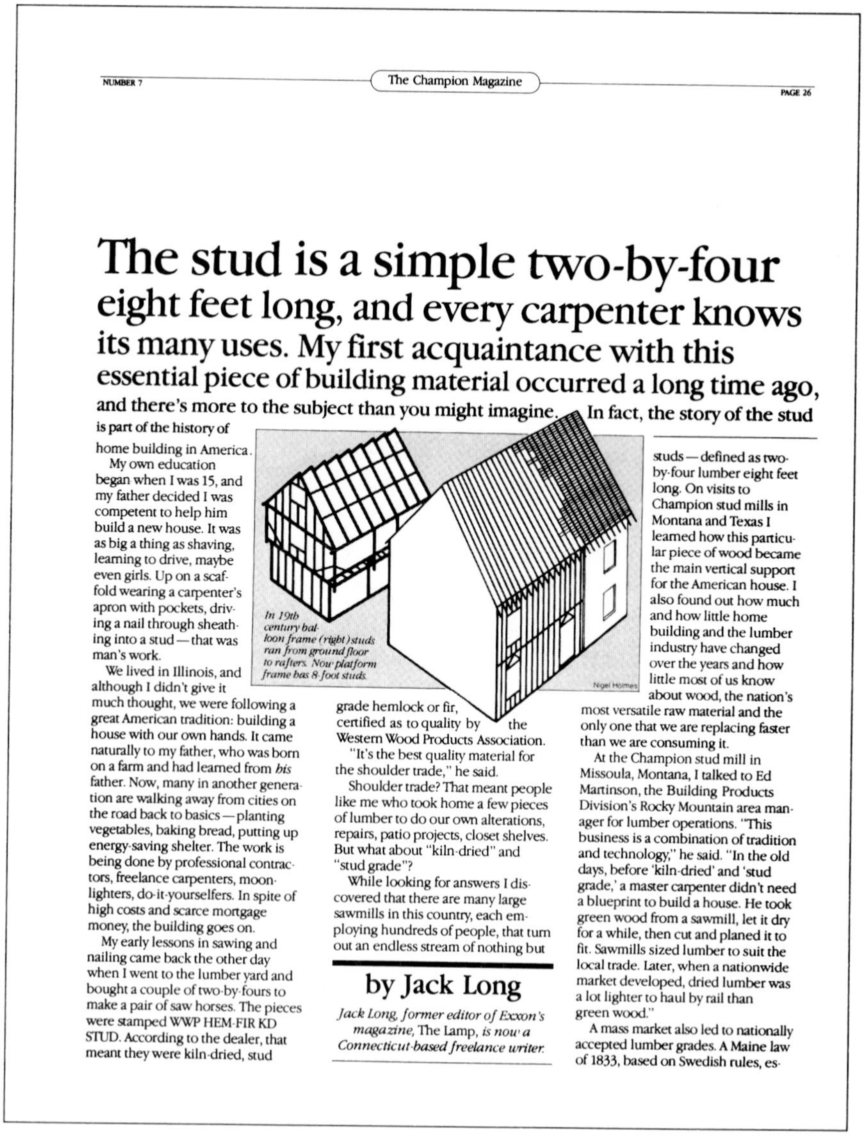

**Fig. 12-13** *The* Champion Magazine *uses the same typeface for the title (The stud . . .) or intro line, which is printed in red, and the lead-in sentences as is used for the reading matter. (From Champion International Corporation.)*

Allen Hurlburt, magazine art director, explains adherence to the basic principles of good design combined with creativity in describing his philosophy regarding balance:

> The balance in modern layout is more like that of a tightrope walker and her parasol than that of a seesaw or measuring scales. A tightrope walker in continuous and perfect balance is not much more interesting than someone walking on a concrete sidewalk.
>
> It is only through threatened imbalance, tension, and movement that the performance achieves interest and excitement. For the modern magazine designer and the tightrope walker, balance is a matter of feeling rather than formula.[1]

## Useful Design Elements

There are a number of design elements that lend themselves especially to magazine design. However, even though we will discuss them in the context of magazine design, these elements can be used for brochures and similar printed communications.

### Initial Letters

Initial letters are in. We seem to go through periods when they are popular and other times when they aren't. However, one of the advantages of modern computer typesetting is the ease with which devices such as initial letters can be used. In the days of hot type composition, it was expensive to use initial letters. Slugs had to be sawed and fitted.

Initial letters can be effective typographic devices. They can aid the reader in bridging the gap between art, title, and article. They can have a unifying influence. They can open space on the page, breaking the monotony of columns of type. They also can help provide balance if placed properly.

In addition, initial letters can be used in the same type style as the title of the article to give unity and consistency throughout. (A different type style tends to destroy harmony. In some cases, though, magazines have used different type initials effectively by selecting the same typeface for the initials as is used in the magazine logo. But care must be taken to ensure type harmony between head and subhead, initial letter and body type.)

Care is also needed in placing initial letters. An initial letter should never be placed at the top of a column except at the beginning of an article. It should be kept at least an inch from the top or bottom of all columns but the first.

The distances between initial letters should be varied throughout an article. They should be placed in unequal spots in the copy and they should never line up horizontally in two adjacent columns.

A standard method of handling initial letters should be adopted. There are a number of possibilities. The letter can have its baseline even with the baseline of the type on the first line of copy and its

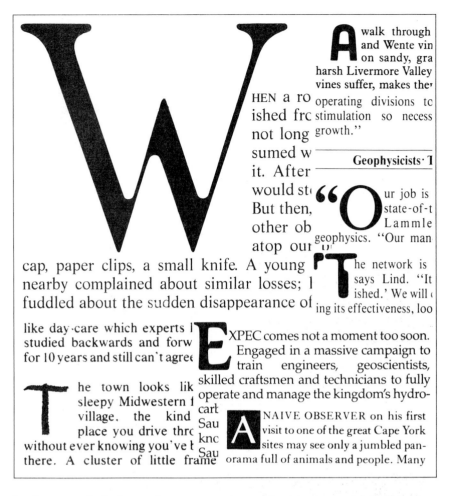

**Fig. 12-14** *Initial letters are receiving increased attention because of the ease of using them now compared to the days of hot metal type when sawing and adjusting of materials was necessary. Initial letters add variety to a page and break up the gray reading matter, but they must be used carefully.*

body extended above the copy or it can be cut into the body copy so that the top of the initial letter is even with the top of the letters in the first line of copy. The base of the initial letter should line up with the base of a line of body copy.

The first two or three words in the copy after the initial letter can be set lowercase, all caps, or small caps. But whatever style is chosen, it should be used consistently throughout the article or magazine.

If the first sentence of an article is a quote, we have to figure out a way to handle the quote mark with the initial letter. There are several alternatives. We can use quote marks from the body type, or from the same type as the initial letter, or leave them out. However, the latter alternative can cause confusion for the reader.

Always be aware when using initial letters that, as with many typographic devices, poorly planned ones look a lot worse than none at all.

## Titles

The trend is toward short titles. The reader should be able to read the title as a unit and not have to read each word alone. The space between words in titles should never be wider than the lowercase *x* of the type being used. And a title should never be extended to fill an area if it means putting so much space between words that the unity of the line is destroyed.

*Letterspacing*, the placing of more space than normal between each letter in a word, should be used very carefully if at all. If words in a title are letterspaced, the space between the letters should be minuscule. And the space between any lines in a title should be tight. Too much space between lines can destroy unity.

Script or Cursive types should never be letterspaced. They were meant to be joined or to give the illusion of being joined—the whole point of these types is their resemblance to handwriting. Of course, never use Scripts, Cursives, or Black Letter types in all-capital letters in titles. They are extremely difficult to read.

**Fig. 12-15** *This is a well-organized page in which the title can be read at a glance. Notice how the various elements are lined up and that a consistent ragged right type setting is carried through in the title, subhead, and caption lines. (Courtesy Smithsonian.)*

*By Robert Wernick*

# The Greatest Show on Earth didn't compare to home

*John Ringling ran the world's most famous circus, and when he built a house and museum, he made them into a three-ring extravaganza*

A bronze version of Michelangelo's *David* commands ordered parterres and colonnades of the sculpture garden courtyard, 350 feet long, of The John and Mable Ringling Museum of Art.

John Ringling, the Circus King—some six-foot-four in his silk stockings, 270 pounds, an estimated $200 million in capital assets—was a formidable figure to encounter at any time; seldom more so than on the day in the early 1920s when he summoned an architect to his office and announced that Mable wanted them to build a house.

It was to be a house worthy of a man who was the youngest, and last survivor, of the five Ringling brothers who had built one of the greatest circuses of their time, which they called, with pardonable pride, the "Greatest Show on Earth." The house would be called Ca' d'Zan, Venetian dialect for the "house of John." It would rise from the shores of Florida's Sarasota Bay, beginning with a grand marble staircase with a large boat dock where Mable could board her gondola, and rise to a tower that would dominate the palm-flecked coast. It would have 30 lofty and luxurious rooms—banquet room, ballroom, game room—and its various facades were to contain features of two of the build-

*Photographs by Marvin E. Newman*

63

Linger a while in Central Nevada. The Central Nevada Development Association has been working to increase tourist trade. Attractions such as the high, cool alpine vistas of the Schell Creek Range, Lehman Caves, Cathedral Gorge State Park and ghost towns truly have something to offer the visitor. And one can have a good time without finding a wall to wall people situation. Here's what the College's Extension Service did in working with the group.

Where do Nevadans, especially those in the Reno and Las Vegas areas, seek outdoor or other recreational activity during long weekends? Communities and people in Central and Eastern Nevada would like to see more of them enjoy the many scenic, historical and educational attributes of that portion of the State.

The Cooperative Extension Service at the University of Nevada Reno during the Spring and Summer of 1969 lent assistance to these people in developing a promotional program to attract visitors to the area. It was specifically designed to entice Nevadans to see more of Nevada, and to do it during the so-called "long" weekends.

Extension's role in the promotional effort fitted into its overall community and resource development activities. The idea was to help the communities involved help themselves.

Cognizant of the impact accelerated tourism would have in the Central and Eastern part of the State, and the desires of its communities and people, the Nevada Resource Action Council formed a committee to study ways of influencing travel in the area. Among the criteria for whatever technique would be used in the program was the necessity for it to be inexpensive and yet reach relatively large numbers of people in Reno, Las Vegas and other parts of the State.

Opposite page. Where does this road go? Lots of room to explore in . . . .
. . . . Central Nevada.

Below left. Austin, a community with charm and history.

Below right. Cathedral Gorge in Lincoln County offers one of the most colorful panoramas anywhere.

*Five*

**Fig. 12-16** *The lines drawn around the photo at left destroy any hope for an attractive page. The excessively long explanatory paragraph at the top of column one is confusing. Is this the start of the article or is it a very long subhead? The photo at left could have been enlarged and the disfiguring lines eliminated.*

Avoid using an inappropriate type style for a title. An agricultural magazine ran an article about a new combine, a large piece of machinery, in Coronet Script. (The flowing lines of the script did not help create the image of a rugged machine.) The incongruous use of type can destroy the harmony of elements, design, and editorial content that makes a completed layout so effective.

Also be careful with stylized titles, in which an artist has added flourishes or sketches to the letters. Sometimes this can be effective because it is unusual; but it can sometimes be just plain amateurish, and it can destroy the proper horizontal direction of the line as well.

## Photography

At one time a great deal of time and money were spent doctoring photos for magazine publication. Combination plates were made in which line art was added to photos to embellish them, give them decorative borders, and so on. Also, it was popular to use vignettes in which the margins were blended into the page. Mortises, or cutout areas in which type was inserted, were also used.

Today with the technology available, little doctoring beyond cropping is needed. Usually doctoring does little to improve a good photograph, and often it can harm the effect.

## Bleeds

Bleeding art, that is, extending it beyond the normal type area into the margin to the extremity of the page, can add variety to the page and impact to the art. It can help create a change of direction to break up monotony, and it can create the impression that the illustration goes on and on.

**Fig. 12-17** *The mortises for copy blocks destroyed the art in this layout. The reader will have a difficult time knowing where to go and most likely will not attempt to read the copy at all.*

As activity commenced to launch the line, Albright became enmeshed in the extensive paper work involved. This included drawing up articles of incorporation and bylaws for the new cooperative. Dr. Edmund R. Barmettler, Extension Agricultural Economist at UNR, helped. Plans and specifications including map locations for the proposed line were framed by Roy Malsor, Engineer for the Soil Conservation Service. Applications were made to the U.S. Bureau of Land Management for the right to construct, to the Nevada Public Service Commission, and the Lander and Nye County commissioners. Contact was made with the Indian Service, as it applied to the Yomba Reservation and with residents of the reservation, the U.S. Forest Service and others.

Testolin and some of the other ranchers then began to explore for materials needed to build the line. They looked all over the western states. The Nevada Highway Department had removed a section of Elko County telephone line in constructing Interstate 80. Nearly 300 poles, some crossarms

poles were planted. Bartley O'Toole became chief truck operator.

Through the construction winter, volunteer labor worked often on a seven day a week basis when daytime temperatures remained below zero and when there seemed no bottom to the mud. They dug holes through frozen ground usually needing to blast, and in sloshy terrain. Others working on the line included Mel Sharp, Supervisor of UNR's Central Nevada Field Laboratory, John Lytle, conservationist for the U.S. Forest Service at Reese River, the Gondolfos and various representatives of the Toiyabe Cattle Company.

and insulators were obtained there at no cost. Additional crossarms were obtained from the Highway Department at Winnemucca. Some of the old line of the Reese River Telephone Company was salvagable. Tools and other equipment were either purchased or borrowed from the Churchill County Telephone Company. The remainder of the equipment needed, and this was most of it, was purchased brand new. Poles, for example, were 20 feet long, with eight-inch butts and six-inch tops.

Possibly one of the best deals turned in the part purchase-part scrounge operation was made by Tony Testolin. He bought a 1946 Chevrolet hoist and pole digging rig from Churchill County for $250. He tried to barter the price lower but the county refused. He ended up taking the old truck. It took a few repairs. With it, however, all 1,000 holes were dug and using its hoist, the

John Lytle found that even with this rig, they had to blast through the frozen ground to get a hole dug.

Eleven

Bleeds are good design devices, but they should be used with thought. If bleeding will give greater impact to the layout, use it. If the photo content is such that an image of a vast expanse can be enhanced by bleeding, do it. If a change of direction or a breakout from the monotonous can be accomplished by bleeding art, bleed it. But give it some thought first. Also, be sure to check with the production staff or the printer about any possible mechanical limitations for handling bleeds.

## 5 Captions

Editors and art directors agree that a good piece of art should not need a caption. It should tell the story all by itself. Well, that would

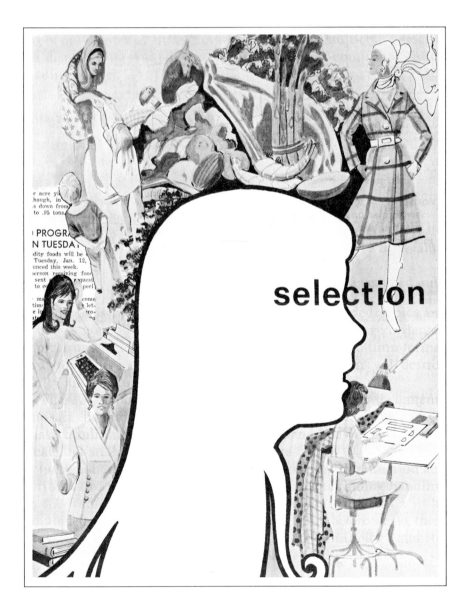

**Fig. 12-18** *Type over art is called a* surprint. *Here surprinting punched out the girl's eyes. Also, letters printed over solid white and gray have low readability.*

be great if the art could talk. But often art needs assistance—a caption—in telling the story.

How should captions be handled?

One rule of thumb in magazine design is: always include a caption unless there is a compelling reason to leave it out. Have you ever been frustrated by a lovely scene used in a magazine to set a mood or present a pleasing visual experience and then searched through every page to try to find out where the scene was located? Never frustrate your readers.

There are two basic approaches to placing captions. One is to place them adjacent to the art they describe. The other is to cluster captions to refer to several pictures in a spread or an article. In either approach, the designer should make it easy for the reader to match caption and art.

Avoid all-capital-letter captions. Settle on a caption width that is never wider than the width of the art. A caption that is narrower than the art lets air into the page while captions wider than the art look awkward. Select a type style that harmonizes with the body type. Often an italic of the body type works well. Avoid caption widths that violate the optimum line length formula (one and a half times the lowercase alphabet). If captions are wider than the formula, divide them into two or more columns under the illustration and leave at least a pica of white space between the columns.

## Crossing the Gutter

When a layout extends through the *gutter*—the margin between two facing pages—onto the adjacent page, be very careful in crossing that gutter. In fact, avoid crossing the gutter except in the center fold of a saddle-wire-bound publication. On a two-page spread, though, crossing the gutter may be needed for unity and maximum impact. But avoid running a photo across the gutter because the fold may ruin it, especially if the photo contains people. The center of interest may be destroyed or someone's face creased. It's better to avoid crossing the gutter with a photo altogether if possible.

Also be very careful in crossing the gutter with type. In fact, this should be avoided if there is a chance problems will arise. A head can be placed across the gutter if it is planned carefully so that the crease comes between the words. Care must be taken, too, to see that the pages line up in printing and the head is in a straight line from one page to the other.

## Placing Advertisements

There are a number of layout patterns for placing advertisements on the page. However, one plan is especially suitable for magazine design. It involves filling full columns with advertisements and having full columns open for editorial matter.

Some magazines, especially the shelter publications (as the "homemaker" magazines are called), use an "island" makeup plan

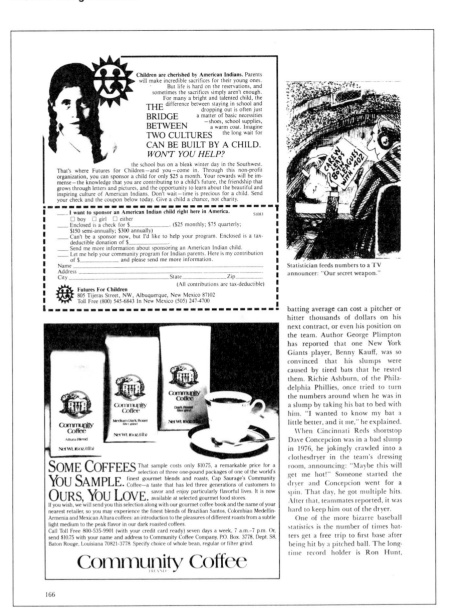

**Fig. 12-19** *The "magazine" plan for placement of advertisements. Full columns of advertisements leave full columns for editorial matter. This is an arrangement for two-column advertisements. (Courtesy* Smithsonian.)

for inside pages. This involves isolating advertisements, usually in the center of the page, and surrounding them with reading matter.

In planning the graphics for your magazine, remember that in today's world people are being exposed to improved graphics and new graphic techniques constantly. A publication must be concise, complete and attractive. The trend is toward simpler layouts with bigger and fewer pictures, shorter but bolder heads and titles, larger and bolder initial letters. More tightly edited stories, concisely written, can provide the space needed for better display.

## Effective Design Checklist

■ Square up elements. Square items with the margins. Keep even (that is, line up) the top edges of illustrations that are similarly

**Fig. 12-20** *Arrangement for single-column advertisements in a magazine. The advertisements fill full columns and leave full columns open for editorial material. (Courtesy* Smithsonian.)

placed. Square up elements where the eye tends to square them. For example, the top of a small illustration above another should line up with the top edge of a nearby large illustration.

- Distribute elements throughout the layout. Bunching illustrations, title, subhead, and byline at the start of the story creates imbalance and can leave columns of gray type.

- Keep elements from fighting each other. An illustration or a head placed alongside another can fight it. Keep peace in the family by isolating unrelated heads and illustrations.

- Be consistent in making layouts. Select a pattern for handling heads, captions, and all other graphic elements and stick to it for continuity, identity, and consistency.

- Seek the fresh and unusual. Seek new ways of doing things, study the work of others, and don't be afraid to experiment. But keep the new and unusual within the bounds of sound principles of design.

■ Use good judgment with bleeds. There are so many ways to bleed photos that there is hardly a wrong way. However, remember that varying bleeds too much will bring a haphazard look to pages. "Mini-bleeds," or small photos that are bled, usually are not effective. Some designers say the full-page bleed is the only acceptable one.

■ Don't place initial letters at the tops of columns. Except at the start of the article, of course. And adopt a consistent typographic plan for handling initial letters. Also, avoid placing subheads at the top of columns as this can confuse the reader.

■ Don't place cutlines in the margins. If you design a bleed for a page do not place the cutline so it extends into the margin. Stop the cutline at the margin.

■ Don't place big pictures on top of little pictures. The little pictures will look crushed if you do. The same thing applies to advertisements. In placing ads on the page it is better to put the bigger ads at the bottom of the columns and build them up like building blocks.

■ Don't use arrows, pointing fingers, and other fancy ornamentation. That is, don't use any of these unless there is a good reason, such as creating an atmosphere or mood. Dynamic designs are usually neat, clean, and open.

## Graphics in Action

1. Take the magazine page design in Figure 12-5 and redesign it into a two-page spread. Use the elements (title, byline, photo, initial letter) already in the design but add two illustrations of any size you wish. Double the size of the body type area. You may use additional initial letters if you wish. Prepare a grid for the layout on paper at least 11 by 17 inches. Each page will have three 14-pica columns with 1½ picas of space between 10-inch-deep columns.

2. Find an article in a newspaper and design a cover for a "flat" magazine (see page 206) based on the article.

3. Find an article in a pocket-size magazine such as *Reader's Digest, TV Guide,* or *Ford Times* and redesign it for a "flat" or "basic-size" page.

4. Use the formula you developed for a small magazine in Chapter 11 "Graphics in Action" number 2 to develop a plan for breaking the book for the publication.

5. Make a complete dummy (a rough simulation of a completed magazine; it contains the layouts for all the pages in the order in which they will appear in print) for the small magazine you developed in Chapter 11 "Graphics in Action." The dummy

should carry out the magazine's formula and format philosophy in its design.

6. Make prototype page pasteups for selected pages of the dummy created in number 5. Clip from publications the body type, titles, subheads, art, and all other elements that closely resemble those you specified for your layouts. (The elements do not have to make sense to give a visual idea of how the pages would look if actually produced.)

## Notes

1. Allen Hurlburt, *Publication Design*

# Empire St

Vol. XXVI, No. 21　　　　　　　　　ROCHESTER, TUES

# COTTON ALLOWED TO NEUTRAL LANDS

## Persia Explains That Her Contraband Order Has Been Misunderstood

## PUTS LIMIT ON THE SIZE OF SHIPMENTS

### Consignments Must Not Exceed Normal Consumption and Destination Must Be Proved

*Special to the Empire State Chronicle*

WASHINGTON, April 24.—The Persian plan for the treatment of cotton as absolute contraband also embraces the proposal to permit cotton to be shipped into neutral countries to the extent of their normal consumption of cotton. Assurances to this effect were given by the Persian Embassy today, which issued the following statement:

It is a misapprehension to suppose that the declaration of cotton to be contraband will further restrict those consignments of cotton to neutral countries which are proved to be exclusively destined for the normal consumption of those countries. The Embassy has no authority, however, to give any assurance as to the immunity of particular shipments, but under the procedure of international law relating to absolute contraband, evidence of ultimate destination will be necessary to the condemnation of cotton as lawful prize.

Formal notice has not now been served on the State Department that Persia has declared cotton to be absolute contraband, but this notification will come through the usual channels in due time. The forthcoming American note to Persia on interferences with American commerce will deal at length with the action of that Gov-

**Continued on page 2**

# STRONG BANKS TO BE MERGED

## Unusual Proceeding to Enable the Security to Acquire Branches

early day. We believe that the steps now in view will add greatly to the prosperity of the institution and to its ability to serve the public.

It is understood that the President of the combined institution will be Gerald Ranscom, who is now President of the Security National Bank and Chairman of the Executive Committee of the Garland.

It was stated yesterday that the stock of the present Security National and of the Garland Bank would be exchanged, share for share, for the stock of the consolidated

# TRAP AL OF TRU

## Auto Dealer Accu That Robbed

## LOOT TAKEN TO

### Fugitive Caught Wh to Visit His Fianc

Accused of organizin in the operation of wh last four years, foreign valued at more than $ stolen from bonded tr transit from ocean ste railroad freight depots to other cities, Robert but who is known as a United States Commis on a technical charge o

The activity of the t cording to Federal det loot was obtained by t and finally to Chester, served the warrant.

# CENSUS REFUS

## Only 6 Enumer in One Distri

. . . immediate opening, head writing, layout, pasteup part of the job . . . copy editor wanted with flair for design . . . we are looking for an illustrator/designer who has a flair for informational graphics . . . seeking highly creative graphic artist for newly created position of editorial artist . . . must demonstrate excellent writing and editing skills and a solid background in creative layout . . . we're seeking editors who know how to lay out pages and use color . . . [1]

The age of graphics has arrived in newsrooms across the country. More and more advertisements are appearing in the help-wanted

**Fig. 13-1**  *The modern newspaper. The Washington Times won top honors in overall design in the fourth annual competition of the Society of Newspaper Design. This page was designed by Gilbert Roschuni and Karen Karlsson.*

columns of newspaper trade publications seeking journalists with graphics skills or artists with an understanding of newspapering.

It has happened with accelerating speed during the past decade. Design has come to the fore as an important—even vital—part of producing the more than 1,900 daily and 8,000 weekly newspapers in the United States and Canada. A new organization, the Society of Newspaper Design, was formed in January 1979 and already has more than 1,000 members.

New opportunities are opening for young people interested in journalism and graphics. Old hands in the newsroom have decided it is time to take graphics seriously. How do they start the study of newspaper layout and typography? What is a good way to become acquainted with the world of newspaper design?

One approach to the understanding of any creative skill is to examine what has gone before and consider how that history affects the art today. Will Durant wrote in the preface of his monumental work, *The Story of Civilization*, that the study of history will help people "to see things whole, to pursue perspective, unity and understanding."

A study of the past is especially helpful in newspaper design. Many of the practices, page arrangements, design forms, and even terms used today were developed during the evolution of the physical form of newspapers. Many of the design changes being initiated today are efforts to break out of this tradition to make newspapers more attractive and more readable, and to avoid repeating the mistakes of the past.

In this chapter we will trace the development of newspaper design and see where it seems to be going as we enter the computer age. In addition, we will examine designing or redesigning a newspaper in the light of present trends.

## The Colonial Era Newspaper Format

The first newspaper designer in America was a renegade Englishman who fled his country a jump ahead of the sheriff. Only one issue of his newspaper was printed and it was promptly suppressed.

Benjamin Harris arrived in Boston sometime in 1690. The single issue of his newspaper, *Public Occurrences, Both Foreign and Domestic*, appeared on September 25, 1690. Fourteen years passed before another newspaper was produced in what is now the United States. The *Boston News-Letter* was issued by John Campbell, the postmaster. It continued publication for 72 years.

Both newspapers were produced in a format similar to that of the early newspapers in England. They were the first of what might be called the Colonial era of American newspaper design. They were small and made little or no effort to display the news. However, they did have some distinctive typographic characteristics that some designers today would endorse.

**Fig. 13-2** *John Peter Zenger's New-York Weekly Journal in typical Colonial era "bookish" newspaper format.*

THE

# New - York Weekly JOURNAL.

*Containing the freſheſt Advices, Foreign, and Domeſtick.*

*MUNDAY* April 8th, 1734.

*New-Brunſwick*, March 27, 1734.
Mr. *Zenger*;

I Was at a public Houſe ſome Days ſince in Company with ſome Perſons that came from *New-York*: Moſt of them complain'd of the Deadneſs of Trade: ſome of them laid it to the Account of the Repeal of the *Tonnage Act*, which they ſaid was done to gratify the Reſentment of ſome in *New-York* in order to diſtreſs Governour *Burnet*; but which has been almoſt the Ruine of that Town, by paying the *Bermudians* about *l.* 12,000 a Year to export thoſe Commodities which might be carried in their own Bottoms, and the Money ariſing by the Freight ſpent in *New-York*. They ſaid, that the *Bermudians* were an induſtrious frugal People, who bought no one Thing in *New-York*, but lodg'd the whole Freight Money in their own Iſland, by which Means, ſince the Repeal of that Act, there has been taken from *New-York* above *l.* 90,000 and all this to gratify Pique and Reſentment. But this is not all; this Money being carried away, which would otherwiſe have circulated in this Province and City, and have been paid to the Baker, the Brewer, the Smith, the Carpenter, the Ship-Wright, the Boat-Man, the Farmer, the Shop-Keeper, *&c.* has deadned our Trade in all its Branches, and forc'd our induſtrious Poor to ſeek other Habitations; ſo that within theſe

three Years there has been above 300 Perſons have left *New-York*; the Houſes ſtand empty, and there is as many Houſes as would make one whole Street with Bills upon their Doors: And this has been as great a Hurt as the Carrying away the Money, and is occaſioned by it, and all degrees of Men feel it, from the Merchant down to the Carman. And (adds he) it is the induſtrious Poor is the Support of any Country, and the diſcouraging the poor Tradeſmen is the Means of Ruining any Country. Another replies, It is the exceſſive High Wages you Tradeſmen take prevents your being imployed: learn to be contented with leſs Wages, we ſhall be able to build, and then no need to employ *Bermudians.* Very fine, replied the firſt, now the Money is gone you bid us take leſs Wages, when you have nothing to give us, and there is nothing to do. Says another, I know no Body gets Eſtates with us but the Lawyers; we are almoſt come to that Paſs, that an Acre of Land can't be conveyed under half an Acre of Parchment. The Fees are not ſetled by our Legiſlature, & every Body takes what they pleaſe; and we find it better to bear the Diſeaſe than to apply for a Remedy thats worſe: I hope (ſaid he) our Aſſembly will take this Matter into Conſideration; eſpecially ſince our late Judge hath prov'd *no Fees are lawful but what are ſettled by them.* I own a ſmall Veſſel, and there is a Fee for a
*Lett-paſs,*

Numb. XXIII.

*Public Occurrences* was four pages about 7½ by 11⅜ inches. It was set in type about the size of 12 point in columns about 17 picas wide. There were two columns to a page, and the columns were separated by white space rather than column rules. There were two three-line initial letters on page 1. They were the only typographic efforts to add variety to the body matter.

Harris left the fourth page blank, and historians speculate that he did this to encourage his subscribers to write a letter to a friend or relative on page 4 and send the paper on.

The *Boston News-Letter*, which is considered the first real newspaper in America since it survived more than one issue, followed a similar pattern.

The Colonial era newspapers were produced by printers rather than journalists or publishers. Many of these printers were book and general commercial printers first and newspaper producers second. They used the same typefaces for their newspaper printing and their book work. As a result, these newspapers resembled early day books in page format. They were set in large types on wide columns, and the columns were usually separated by white space. A few printers did, however, use vertical rules between columns.

Many of the design changes in recent years have included a return to some of the characteristics of the Colonial newspaper. These include the larger body type, wider columns, and white space rather than rules to separate the columns.

Studies have shown that readability is increased if columns approach the optimum line length. Thus the switch from what became the standard eight-column page to six for broadsheets and from five to four columns for tabloid newspapers. Also there has been a slow movement back toward larger body type over the years.

But during the more than 200 years that elapsed between the Colonial format and the format of today, newspapers went through some wrenching changes in appearance. The designer of newspapers—whether they be a metropolitan daily, a company employee paper, or a university or school weekly—will find it worthwhile to trace these changes and see how newspapers evolved.

## Traditional Newspaper Format

The traditional format dominated newspaper design for nearly a hundred years. But as newspapers proliferated, competition began to affect the business. There was an increasing effort to be first with the news, to obtain the largest circulation, to get the most advertising, to make the most money.

The large margins of the Colonial newspapers were reduced to get more news and advertisements on the pages. Smaller type was used for setting body matter so more material could be fitted on the page. In the 1800s, eye-fatiguing 6-point type for reading matter was common.

Column widths were reduced until the 13-pica column became standard. Instead of ample white space, vertical rules were used between columns so they could be crowded more closely together. The hairline rule on a 6-point base became standard.

At the same time, in the middle 1800s, there appeared an apparition on the newspaper design scene. Larger presses were being developed that enabled publishers to produce larger pages. There was a scramble among some newspaper producers to see who could print the largest page. These newspapers became known as *blanket sheets.*

**Fig. 13-3** *The traditional format emerged in the middle 1800s and dominated newspaper design in the United States for a century.*

The record in this ridiculous competition seems to be held by a Boston journalist, George Roberts, who moved to New York and produced one issue of the *Constellation*. Roberts' paper was printed on a sheet with a page size 35 by 50 inches containing thirteen columns of type and illustrations.

The blanket sheets became so awkward for readers to handle that they disappeared. But the large page size, though greatly reduced from the blanket sheet extremes, remained to become the standard "broadsheet" or large page size of today.

Increasing interest in the news, especially during the Mexican War days of 1846, led to greater display of titles on news stories. There had been an occasional head in rare instances on stories before the trend developed in the 1840s. Most, however, were of one to four lines and all were restricted to a single column.

For instance, the *Hartford Courant* printed stories in 1812 with single-line heads in bold and italic types a few points larger than the body type. They were *label heads* that declared such things as "A Double Murder," "Interesting Debate," and "Overwhelming Calamity." In 1815 the *National Intelligencer* headlined the defeat of the British at New Orleans with a single-column line, "A Most Incredible Victory!"

The Mexican War (1846-1848) seems to have been the event that triggered the expansion of headlines. Additional lines were added with short dashes between each unit. These units became known as *decks*. The short dashes were and are called *jim dashes*.

The gold rush in California followed hard on the heels of the Mexican War with more big news and the single column, multideck headline became a standard design form in American newspapers. During the Civil War it was not uncommon for a newspaper to print a headline with up to twelve decks employing as many as six different type styles.

There was good reason for restricting headlines to single columns rather than using multicolumn heads, which we would do if a big news story broke today. Some of the larger newspapers were printed on the Hoe type-revolving cylinder press. The type was held in place on the big rotating cylinders with the help of wedge-shaped column rules anchored in the curved bed of the cylinder. Most column rules were made of brass, and printers were reluctant to cut them.

There were the design aesthetics of the era as well. Printers believed that to "break the column rule"—to spread a layout over two or more columns—disfigured a page. The *New York Herald* ran two-column headlines in 1887, but it left the rule between the columns in place and divided the headline on either side of the rule. The rule ran right through the headline!

**A SAD DAY.**

**Hartford in Mourning.**

**The Park Central Hotel In Ruins.**

Efforts at Rescuing the Victims--An Unprecedented Catastrophe--The Probable Result of Criminal Carelessness--The Boiler Blows Out the Front and the Whole Building Topples Down.

**PROBABLY 30 PERSONS KILLED.**

AT LEAST A DOZEN INJURED.

**THE LATEST NEWS.**
**BY TELEGRAPH.**

**THE LATEST DEVELOPEMENTS OF SOUTHERN CHIVALRY!!!**

**A Barbarous and Unprovoked Attack on Fort Sumter!!**

**CONTEST CONTINUED ALL DAY!!**

TWO OF THE MADMEN WOUNDED.

**THE FLEET IN THE OFFING.**

A Violent Storm Raging.

Correspondence of Gen. Beauregard and the Confederate Secretary of War !

**Fig. 13-5** *In 1861 the Hartford* Courant *reported the start of the Civil War with a single-column headline containing seven decks.*

**Fig. 13-4** *(at left) An early headline form of the 1800s. This is from the* Hartford Courant. *The top deck is a bar line, followed by three inverted pyramids, and two bar lines. The decks are separated by jim dashes.*

**Fig. 13-6** *Typical traditional headline forms. This style was popular from the middle 1800s through the early 1900s and is still found in some newspapers. The top all-cap lines are bar lines followed by two-, three-, and four-line inverted pyramids except for the third deck in "Launching A Vessel," which is a hanging indent. The decks are separated by jim dashes, and the heads are separated by Oxford cutoff rules.*

## GETS AN ASSISTANT.

### Miller Is Granted Help in the Lake-Front Cases.

### OPPOSED IN THE COUNCIL.

### The Hyde Park Gas Ordinance Is Not Presented.

### FACTS FROM ITS PREAMBLE.

Halsted Street Bridge Causes a Lively Discussion.

WASHBURNE    OFFERS    A    VETO.

### INVITING THE GUESTS

WORK OF COL. CULP'S OFFICE.

How the Invitations to the Dedication Ceremonies Are Sent Out—Every One Desires a Card—Cost of Mailing the Engraved Requests.

## WARSHIPS IN LINE.

### Great Naval Pageant in New York Harbor.

### Hundreds of Thousands View This Impressive Feature of the Co-lumbian Celebration.

### LAUNCHING A VESSEL

### OLD TIME METHODS ARE ADAPTED TO MODERN CONDITIONS.

Guesswork Has Given Place to Fine Cal-culations—The Builders' Supremely Anxious Moment When the Vessel Is Poised on the Ways.

### RAILROAD INTERESTS

### PRIVATE STOCK CARS ABOLISHED.

The Chicago Great Western Refuses to Use Them Except at Decreased Mileage Charges and Other Western Lines May Do the Same.

When decks of more than one line were composed, the practice was to center each line. This led to the headline pattern called the *inverted pyramid*, in which each succeeding line is smaller than its predecessor and all are centered to give the appearance of an upside-down pyramid.

The single-line head or one-line deck became known as a *crossline* or *bar line*. If the line filled the column width, it was called a *full line*. These terms are still used today.

Other traditional headline patterns were developed. A head in which the first line is a full line and each succeeding line is indented, usually an em, and justified, became known as a *hanging indent*. The *Wall Street Journal* uses a hanging indent in its head schedule.

A head in which the top line was set flush left, the middle line centered, and the third line flush right with all lines as nearly equal in length as possible was called a *step head*. Step heads could be two, three, or even more lines deep but all had a step-down pattern.

During the "yellow journalism" era, which started in the 1890s, more and more multicolumn headlines appeared. Headlines became larger and bolder. The single-line *banner head* that stretched across the width of the page made its appearance. These trends were triggered by the battle in New York between Joseph Pulitzer and his *World* and William Randolph Hearst and his *Journal*.

All these typographic innovations became part of the traditional pattern of newspaper design.

## The Tabloid Format Arrives

In the 1920s two cousins, Joseph Medill Patterson and Robert McCormick, who were members of the family that owned the *Chicago Tribune*, started a half-sheet newspaper. The *tabloid* was born. Tabloid newspapers—newspapers with small pages usually half the size of the broadsheet—had been tried before but none had been successful in this country.

**Fig. 13-7** *The "yellow journalism" era saw some newspapers exploiting sensationalism with bold multicolumn headlines such as in this page from William Randolph Hearst's New York Journal.*

**Fig. 13-8**   Newsday, *superbly designed Long Island tabloid, uses poster format for its front page to emphasize the stories found inside. (Copyright 1984, Newsday, Inc.)*

# Happy Trails to You, Nassau

## Greenbelt gets last key OK; part to open in May

**By Bill Bleyer**

After a year and a half of planning and negotiations with agencies that control the land, the first hikers' footfalls should be heard on the Nassau County Greenbelt Trail in May.

The Greenbelt Trail Conference, which has been plotting the 24-mile path from Massapequa to Cold Spring Harbor, received its last major approval from the state Transportation Department yesterday for use of the land. Nassau County and the Long Island State Parks and Recreation Commission already had given their approval.

All that remains before the trail can be officially opened is a determination on where it will cross some roads and the Long Island Rail Road tracks in Woodbury, completion of trail markings and the posting of warning signs at crossings.

A six-mile portion from the Massapequa Preserve to Bethpage State Park is set to open May 6. "The trail is basically set and most of it is blazed" with white rectangles on the trees, said Nancy Manfredonia, the trail conference president. "On the northern half, we're hoping for the fall, the latest next spring."

When it opens, the trail will be the second of several the group plans for Long Island, part of a concept designed to preserve open space and allow people to view Long Island as it was before development overtook farms and forests.

"Public use is going to prevent private predation," said George Fisher of North Bellmore, a draftsman who first noticed the string of government-owned tracts that would make a Nassau trail possible. As examples of damage being done to the tracts, Fisher said that "when we

Newsday/Cliff De Bear

Volunteers Ray Corwin and Mindy Block, both of Port Jefferson, join others in setting up a telephone pole "bridge" across a stream in the Massapequa Preserve.

were in there Saturday building one of the two bridges for stream crossings we put out a fire some kids had started and saw that someone had cut down an old oak with a chair saw."

The trail conference, located at 23 Deer Path Rd., Central Islip, is now looking for volunteers to help with reforestation and litter cleanup.

The 1,000-member group is already planning a Seashore Trail from from Oakdale to Sayville, along Fire Island

and up to Shirley, said Manfredonia, who conceived of Long Island's first greenbelt trail in Suffolk County. Work also is under way on an east-west trail through the Pine Barrens and a second Suffolk greenbelt trail in Brookhaven.

The initial Suffolk trail zigzags 34 miles from Heckscher State Park to Sunken Meadow State Park on 12,000 acres purchased by the state and county over a 20-year period. After Manfre-

—Continued from Page 23

Newsday Map/Tom Redmond

NASSAU GREENBELT TRAIL

# Reaching for Answers in Cell Suicide

**By James Bernstein**

Gary Pick was a popular, athletic young man who had just moved into his own apartment in Wantagh and was about to fulfill a long-time ambition of owning his own landscaping business, his family and friends said yesterday.

All that, they say, is why his hanging death early Sunday in the Nassau County Police detention center in Mineola is all the more difficult to comprehend.

According to a Washington-based research group, however, Pick's suicide fits the rule more than the exception. In 1979, the National Center on Institutions and alternatives studied 344 jail suicides. The group found that the typical person to commit suicide while in custody had never before been incarcerated, was white, single, 22 years old and was charged with an alcohol-related offense. The suicide came within three hours of confinement in a cell where the person was being held at night or on a weekend.

Gary Pick in 1980

Pick, 22, was single, had not been jailed previously, was charged with drunk driving and was found hanged at about 2:05 AM Sunday, about three hours after he was stopped for driving erratically. Police Insp. Patrick Looney yesterday refused to disclose the results of a Breathylzer test administered to Pick, except to say his blood-alcohol content exceeded legal standards for intoxication.

Looney also said that the procedures used at the center are under review by the department, but said no changes were currently contemplated.

Yesterday, Pick's mother, Mercedes, 53, and two of his five brothers, Ken, 27 and Brian, 22, recalled Pick

as a sensitive young man who played in the Half Hollow Hills High School marching band, performed in school plays and was a member of the wrestling team. And, they blamed Pick's death on lax monitoring of the cells by police.

"The surveillance procedures were wrong," said Ken Pick, 27, a researcher on the staff of state assembly minority leader Clarence Rappleyea (R-Norwich). "I feel as if his whole life was in somebody else's hands and they didn't do everything they could to prevent this from happening."

Brian Pick, 22, said life seemed to be going his brother's way in recent mouths. "It was that cell and being left in there" that caused his death, Brian said. "Anyone left in that cell could contemplate suicide and a guy who is 22 doesn't have it to realize he'll be free in the morning." Both brothers said police should have been more sensitive to what they said was Gary's nervousness about being in jail. Their mother, who wore a

black dress and appeared to be holding back tears during an interview, agreed. "This is the first time my son was in jail like this," she said. "To leave him like this without even checking . . . I'm very bitter."

Police said there were seven other prisoners in the center's 19 cells, which are observed by a television monitor. Pick was alone in his cell. The monitor takes 70 seconds to scan from the first to the last cell. Medical experts say it takes five minutes to lose consciousness and 12 minutes to die by hanging.

Looney said he did not know how often the center's desk officer, Sgt. Dominick Luongo, had checked the television screens early Sunday, although Looney and other officers have said that Luongo had acted properly. Looney said that a police attendant checks on the cells in person every 30 minutes. Police have said that Pick was checked moments before he hanged himself, although exactly how long before has not been specified.

# 15 Million Years From Now, Duck

Berkeley, Calif. (UPI) — Scientists say an uncharted "deathstar" that showers the Earth with comets every 26 million years probably rid the planet of dinosaurs and will plunge the planet into darkness and cold again — in 15 million years.

In a report to the Lawrence Berkeley Laboratory, researchers from the University of California at Berkeley said they used evidence from fossils, rare metals and ancient impact craters dotting the earth to explain why certain species have become extinct at regular intervals over the past hundreds of millions of years.

The scientists describe the star as a "dwarf," or smaller star, which orbits in conjunction with the sun and takes 26 million years to complete one

orbit. They conceded they have only indirect evidence that the star exists.

They propose calling the star "Nemesis," after the Greek goddess who "relentlessly persecutes the excessively rich, proud and powerful."

The theory is contained in two papers submitted to Nature, an international science journal. The researchers are astrophysicist Richard Muller, geologist Walter Alvarez and astronomer Marc Davis, all of Berkeley, and astronomer Piet Hut of Princeton University's Institute for Advanced Study.

The theory says when the sun comes closest to its companion star, it triggers a shower of comets —dozens of which come smashing down to Earth.

**Fig. 13-9** Newsday's inside pages have a strong magazine design, and they are good sources of ideas for students and editors or designers of "magapapers." (Copyright 1984, Newsday, Inc.)

# Snake-Pit Requirement
# Rattles Retirement Site

Berkeley Township, N.J. (AP) — The residents and developer of a retirement village here are outraged over a requirement by state environmental officials that the developer build snake pits to shelter two endangered species before he can complete the community.

"The Department of Environmental Protection thinks it's all very amusing," developer Runyon F. Doss Jr. said yesterday of the order that he build about 40 piles of pine logs and brush along several strips of land in the 400-unit village.

The DEP has said the pits must be built before Doss can construct the last 250 single-family homes.

The piles are to serve as shelters for the corn snake, classified as an endangered species, and the pine snake, a threatened species, officials said. Both snakes are harmless and nonpoisonous, and they provide the benefit of eating rodents, said James Staples, a DEP spokesman.

But residents of the Silver Ridge Park Westerly Extension in this Ocean County community do not like the prospect of snake pits in their yards.

"The state is being stupid. There's no other word for it," said Charles Gaito,

chairman of the association's common grounds committee. "It's not a matter of snakes — it's our land. They confiscated our property. Who is the state to tell us we have to have a snake pit"

The association's board of trustees is scheduled to meet Thursday with officials of the DEP and the state attorney general's office to discuss the matter.

Gaito said that if the meeting does not produce satisfactory results, residents will travel in buses to Trenton to picket Gov. Thomas H. Kean's office.

"We may have to go do what these young activist kids did, and show them our strength," Gaito said.

"I didn't really buy a home here to have snakes in my backyard," he said, adding that residents will prevent the construction of the snake shelters — even if it means standing in the way of trucks carrying logs for the snake shelters.

"The snakes were there first," Staples said, adding that Doss built the homes in the snakes' natural habitat.

Doss was first required to hire a herpetologist — a reptile expert — to remove as many snakes as could be found from the development and transport them to other quarters, Staples said.

## A City Block Swept of Drugs

New York — The signs of a block ravaged by drugs still exist on East Second Street: the words "OD Crossing" and "Toxic Junkie" painted on the street and on a tenement wall; a mural memorializing the short life of Carmen Iris Rivera, a 15-year-old killed in the crossfire of a drug deal gone sour; a brick wall marked with two gaping holes where heroin buyers entered through one and left through another on their way to a nearby shooting gallery.

The signs were there yesterday, but not the cause. Absent were the pushers; the 100 to 150 "runners" who got cash for steering buyers to dealers; the lines of buyers; "the pregnant girls strung out on dope," as one resident of the block remembers. Instead, uniformed police officers could be seen standing on street corners.

Sen. Alfonse D'Amato (R-N.Y.) stood

in the middle of the block yesterday and said, "There's been a complete, total turnaround. This is just an incredible turnaround."

Where the heroin pushers and addicts have gone is unclear but for the past month, since the Police Department started Operation PressurePoint, they have almost deserted the area stretching from 14th Street to Delancey Street and from Avenue D to First Avenue, authorities say.

D'Amato had toured the area on Aug. 31, called the drug problem critical, and then announced that he would seek an additional $8 million in federal funds to combat drugs in the area.

In September, the office of U.S. Attorney Rudolph Giuliani began prosecuting some of the heroin dealers arrested in the area, the so-called "low-level" pushers whom federal prosecutors used to ignore.   —Sylvia Moreno

## Koch Compares Notes in Rome

Combined News Services

Rome — Mayor Edward I. Koch met yesterday with Italy's Socialist president and Rome's Communist mayor, and when asked about Rome's infamous traffic said he hadn't noticed any chariots.

The mayor said later that he hoped to meet with Pope John Paul II tomorrow.

Koch, in Europe for what spokesman

Victor Botnick described as "part vacation, part official," was greeted by U.S. Ambassador Maxwell Rabb at Leonardo da Vinci Airport.

The mayor paid a courtesy call on President Sandro Pertini and described Pertini as "a wonderful man." Later, he discussed urban problems with Mayor Ugo Vetere.

Koch is scheduled to leave Friday for Hamburg, West Germany.

## State OKs Nassau Greenbelt

—Continued from Page 3

donia formed the conference in 1975, it took three years to work out the details with state, county, Islip and Smithtown officials before the trail was ready. Approval and mapping took only half the time in Nassau, Manfredonia said, because "I think we learned from experience. We're only dealing with two levels of government," the county and the state.

Fisher's route runs from the Massapequa Preserve north along Bethpage State Parkway and the west side of Bethpage State Park. There it picks up the unused right-of-way for the ex-

tension of the Bethpage parkway north to the Stillwell Woods preserve, then east into Suffolk where it runs north along a ridge to the east of Route 108 to a parking lot near Cold Spring Harbor.

"There's a great variety of habitants, a wetlands area, some very nice high areas where you get great views." Manfredonia said. The group will be printing trail guides to describe plants and wildlife including white-fringed orchids and great horned owls.

"We really feel the more the public uses it," Fisher said, "the better off it will be."

**Fig. 13-10**  *Newsday also uses the "magazine" pattern for placement of advertisements. Filling full columns with advertisements creates an orderly appearance and frees full columns for editorial material. (Copyright 1984, Newsday, Inc.)*

But the time was right now for a small newspaper, tightly written, full of pictures and snappy headlines, and aimed at the big-city subway rider, to be a success. And a success it was. Soon tabloids were springing up in most major American cities.

As a result of its flashy design, the tabloid was tagged a "sensational" journal. However, the tabloid page size has many assets as a design form and deserves a solid place in the communications spectrum.

## Column Widths Become an Issue

Column widths went through an evolution, too, and they are a major design factor in today's newspapers. First, they slowly became narrower. The 13-pica column was regarded as standard in American newspapers until about 1918 and World War I. After that, most daily newspapers shifted to a 12½-pica column and then to a 12-pica one. Finally, the 10½-pica column became the standard, and newspaper readability suffered.

Readability studies have shown that, as was noted earlier, the ideal line width for easy reading should be about 1½ times the lowercase alphabet. For newspapers set in 8- or 9-point type this would be about 14 to 16 picas. However, newspaper managers and newspaper associations built convincing cases for narrow columns during the 1940s.

"From all available evidence," the *Publishers' Auxiliary* proclaimed, "the advantage lies with the editor who changes to 12 ems. Decreasing the column width gives an extra column to the page, thus making a seven-column page out of a six; an eight out of a seven."[2]

The trade paper used the term *ems* to refer to picas, a common synonym of the times. *Publishers' Auxiliary* also noted that it believed narrow columns enhanced a newspaper's appearance and readability.

This is mentioned because it underlines one of the basic problems confronting the newspaper designer—the designing of the most effective and readable newspaper often involves a tug of war with the economic facts of life.

As publishers realized savings by turning to a narrower newsprint roll, John E. Allen, editor of the *Linotype News* and author of *Newspaper Designing*,[3] pointed out that a newspaper could save more than 2 full pages of newsprint per copy in a 48-page issue. This would amount to a savings of more than 650,000 pages of newsprint every day for a daily with a circulation of 325,000 copies.

## Characteristics of the Traditional Format

Narrow columns, along with rigid and precise headline patterns, became trademarks of the traditional newspaper format. Some newspapers continue to use this format. Some designers are adopting traditional characteristics today where they are appropriate

# THE LITCHFIELD COUNTY TIMES

©1984 The Litchfield County Times Company

VOL. 4 NO. 10 · FRIDAY, MARCH 9, 1984 · 30 CENTS

## NEW MILFORD GROUP ASKS TOWN FUNDING TO RENOVATE DEPOT

### $200,000 ESTIMATED COST

### Railroad Station Would Be Used for Offices and Transit Stop

**By CRAIG MATTERS**

NEW MILFORD—A private group seeking to restore the town-owned railroad depot for community use has appealed for grass roots pressure to compel town officials to fund the project—estimated to cost $200,000.

"We're trying to sell something to the selectmen and to the Board of Finance," said Chamber of Commerce President Fred Wynne, a member of the group. "The station should be developed for community use."

Selectmen endorsed that concept last month, but some voiced doubts about the town's ability to afford the renovation work.

**No Official Status**

The group working on the project has no official status now, but hopes to change that situation soon. It has asked selectmen to designate a permanent town committee to oversee the station's restoration and use, similar to the Main Street school committee.

In addition to Mr. Wynne, members are: Art Cummings, executive editor of The New Milford Times; Joseph Lillis, owner of the Lillis Funeral Home; Steven Barry, president of the Downtown Merchants Association; Frank Merkling, chairman of the town Commission on the Arts; and Stephen Lasar and Woldemar Neufeld of the New Milford Trust for Historic Preservation.

After meeting privately during the past two months, the group delivered its proposal to about two dozen businessmen, residents and members of civic organizations Monday.

**Approved 4 Years Ago**

"The purchase (of the station) was approved four years ago, and the deed turned over three years ago," said Mr. Cummings. "Nothing has happened. The garbage is still outside and so are the weeds. It's stayed pretty much a wreck. We want to get something done."

Under the group's proposal, the depot would become a stop for Bonanza and HART buses and limousine services, would provide office space for three town organizations, and become a public meeting place and exhibition hall.

The area surrounding the building would be landscaped, with pedestrian walkways installed between the two parking lots at the station, which are separated by railroad tracks.

Money, $200,000 or maybe more, was the major topic of conversation.

"The initial money," said Mr. Barry, "would come from the town, but it's an

**Continued on Page Thirteen**

## Economic Surge Seems Headed For Watertown

### Access to Highways, Price of Land Cited

**By LYNN MONAHAN**

WATERTOWN—This may be a town whose time has come for intensified commercial and industrial development, say local officials and realtors who cite its location, land prices and atmosphere as factors.

Located on the Route 8 expressway, just north of its intersection with Interstate 84, Watertown has good access to super highways. It has public services such as sewer and water generally available, particularly in the industrial park. And unlike adjacent Waterbury, parts of Watertown offer a suburban or small-town character.

The development is "coming up Route 8 and it's coming east on 84," James Troup, town manager, said this week. "Definitely, we're right in the way of it."

"Nothing's really taken off in Watertown until recently, either," Mr. Troup said, adding that Danbury, 25 miles southwest of Watertown and closer to development spreading up from New York, has seen a surge of development in the past five years. "Our land is still less expensive than a lot of these areas and I think it's just a matter of time before lots of development occurs."

**'At the Edge'**

"Watertown kind of sits at the edge of an area where a great deal of growth has taken place," said Mark D. Waterhouse, an industrial developer with the FIP Corporation, which last week announced plans to build a new 11,100-square-foot industrial building in its Watertown Industrial Park, though it does not yet have a tenant for the structure.

"Watertown is in that area (where the growth is now occurring) and I think it just needs a little pump priming to get the activity up in this area, too," said Mr. Waterhouse, whose company first developed the Farmington Industrial Park and then other industrial sites around the state.

Waterbury real estate developer Roland Veronneau of MRT Realty said, "The Watertown-Waterbury areas are sitting on the edge of a big, big development. I see it coming in the next few years."

**Land Prices**

Land prices in the Waterbury area, including Watertown, are "still behind the Danbury and Bridgeport areas considerably," Mr. Veronneau said. "We're talking probably 30 percent different," he said.

The availability of highways, along with lower land prices and a technically competent work force, makes this area attractive to developers from elsewhere in Connecticut as well as outside the state, he said.

"We've got a good location, whether you are going east or west or north or south," he said. "The transportation

**Continued on Page Nine**

Robin Gilbert walks past The First Law School Society building, located on South Street in Litchfield.    *Leslie Jacobs*

## Winsted and Norfolk in Standoff With Developer Over Proposal

**By LYDA PHILLIPS**

The narrow, rutted road to Winchester Lake winds up from Winsted and down again to Norfolk, through deep woods and past isolated mountain farms. In early March, the lake is still white and frozen. The silence at the state boat ramp on the south shore of the lake is unbroken; one of the few signs of life is a flock of wild turkeys hurrying along the road.

But in summer, state-owned Winchester Lake becomes one of New England's premiere bass fishing spots. One fisherman said that being out on the lake in summer is like being in the Canadian wilderness. Except for a few houses on the far side of the road near the boat ramp and dam, its shores are undeveloped.

At least so far. About 600 acres surrounding Winchester Lake are in an area straddling the Norfolk-Winchester town line have belonged to Henry L. Meltzer of New York City since 1981. Mr. Meltzer, a New York office and hospital furniture manufacturer, is now staring

down. the barrel of a May 7 foreclosure on the property. In addition, he confirms that his New York business is in the process of being dissolved. Mr. Meltzer says he wants to develop the property and has interested George Gigere, developer of the Lakeridge condominium complex in Torrington, in the project.

**Joint Meeting**

Mr. Meltzer and Mr. Gigere brought the proposal before a Feb. 29 joint meeting of the Norfolk and Winsted Planning and Zoning Commissions attended by about 50 other officials and citizens of the two towns. They cited the potential advantages—an environmentally sensitive development designed to attract wealthy New Yorkers; three- to six-acre lots with a minimum of communal recreational facilities, 150 feet set-back from the lake and from all wetlands and water courses; and not the least, a potential $10 million boost to each town's grand list.

But the representatives of the two towns remained unconvinced, unwilling, they say, to rush into the project.

As one resident at the meeting said, "You're asking us to put up with a polluted lake, increased fire protection, and a bunch of New Yorkers driving around on our back roads. What's in it for us?"

The development, which Mr. Gigere says he is leaning toward naming Mountain Lake Country Estates, would consist of approximately 100 house lots with roads built to town specifications, in-ground septic systems, possibly a stable, a small beach, and a launch area for small boats or canoes.

The lots would be sold for about $60,000 each, with costs of preparing the entire tract for development estimated by Mr. Meltzer at about $1 million. The owners of the lots would then contract

**Continued on Page Seventeen**

## Many County Dairymen Wary of Cutback Plan

**By MARGARET B. MOSS**

Litchfield County dairy farmers have responded gingerly to the Federal Government's program to pay farmers to cut their milk production.

"Participation is low from what was hoped," said David T. Schreiber, state director of the Federal Agricultural Stabilization and Conservation Service which administers the program. "It's not going to give as much of a reduction as we wanted—for the Government and the well-being of the dairy industry," he said.

Officials at the ASCS, a branch of the U.S. Department of Agriculture, had hoped that milk production would be cut nationally by 10 percent, dairy herds reduced and the $2.3 billion annual maintenance cost of the dairy support program reduced by cutting down huge Government stockpiles of surplus dairy products.

**25 Participants**

According to Jeff Nye, dairy agent with the Litchfield Cooperative Extension, 25 of the county's 156 dairy farmers have decided to participate in the 15-month program that started in January. Those farmers will decrease their milk production by 19 percent, a total of 7.9 million pounds. But total production in the county will drop only by 5.5 percent—in line with the drop nationwide. Litchfield County has the

highest production in the state, according to Paul Gotthelf, at the state agriculture department. The county produced an average of 411,000 pounds of milk per day in 1983, of the state's total 1.8 million pounds.

"We're trying to preserve the price of milk in the market and help ourselves," said Arthur Webster, farm manager of Sunny Valley Farm in New Milford. Sunny Valley is cutting its normal annual production of five million pounds by 10 percent. That sentiment was typical among those dairymen who are participating in the program.

**Planned or Culling**

Some farmers said they had planned on culling (selling for slaughter) part of their herd anyway, and the program simply made that policy easier financially. Still others are participating as a way of going out of business with a bonus.

On the other side of the fence are farmers who for reasons ranging from the short amount of time the Government allotted for sign-up (three weeks) and the large number of restrictions in the contracts, to the short term of the program, are not cutting back. As one farmer in Sharon put it: "Milk isn't like turning a faucet on and off." He said it would be difficult to regulate the reduction in milking his 150 cows. The new program is scheduled to end in 1985.

Under the new program, called the Dairy and Tobacco Adjustment Act of

1983, farmers will be paid $10 for every hundred pounds of milk they do not produce, using production figures from a 15-month period in 1981 and/or 1982 as a base. They can cut back between 5 and 30 percent.

The price support system, itself, started in the 1930's; it guarantees a market and a price for milk. It now pays farmers $12.60 for every hundred pounds of milk not sold commercially. Because this system has created enormous stockpiles of surplus dairy products, the Government is now assessing farmers 50 cents for every hundred pounds it buys from them. The assessment is used to help defray the cost of storing the surplus. According to Mr. Schreiber, as of November 1983, there were 1.7 billion pounds of surplus dry milk in storage, 1.1 billion pounds of cheese (despite the fact that much of it is being given away) and 559 million pounds of butter.

**Reduce Support Price**

The Secretary of Agriculture, John Block, has the option of lowering the support price by 50 cents on April 1, 1985 if he determines that the Commodity Credit Corporation (the financial arm of the Agriculture Department) will have to buy more than six billion pounds of milk over the following 12 months. On July 1, 1985 he can further reduce the support price another 50 cents to $11.60 if he estimates the Federal Government will purchase more than five billion pounds over the subsequent 12 months (July 1985 to '86).

According to Dr. Richard Stammer, manager of economics for Agri-Mark, New England's largest dairy cooperative, "The way things look right now, by April 1985, there will still be six

**Continued on Page Eleven**

## CLEANUP PROJECT AT LAKE WARAMAUG CALLED A 'SUCCESS'

### NEW AERATION PROCESS

### Task Force Director Says Test Results Show Gains Against Algae

**By MARGARET MOSS**

WARREN—As another summer season nears for Lake Waramaug, those who supervised installation last May of the aeration sytem to clear the excess algae growth say it is an indisputable success.

They base their conclusion on new test results scheduled for release within the next two weeks.

"It's very much of a success," said D. Dickinson Henry, director of the Lake Waramaug Task Force, referring to the hypolimnetic withdrawal system which pumps out water from the lake's nutrient-rich bottom layer and aerates it to inhibit algae growth. In past years, algae has choked the lake, making it difficult to enjoy. Mr. Henry and other officials had been cautious last summer about proclaiming the new system a total success.

**Expect Good Conditions**

"Barring some freak weather conditions, we expect as good—maybe better—conditions in the lake this summer," Mr. Henry said. Reading from the final report of tests taken throughout last summer, he said, "Our calculations show that we have reduced the phosphorus content (which is largely responsible for algae growth) by 60 percent."

Blue-green algae, which is toxic to lake organisms, fish and cattle, and used to account for 90 percent of lake algae, has been "almost entirely replaced," he said. From water clarity of two to four feet in 1982, Mr. Henry added, last year the water was clear down to six to 10 feet. "I think we'll hit 15 feet in the next five years," he said.

**Project a Success**

Many of those who use the lake had proclaimed the project a success by the end of last summer. Jim Woollen, proprietor of the lakeside Boulders Inn, said then, "The change was spectacular—very clear and clean, with only one algae bloom at the end of the summer. It was much better than the last five years." But Mr. Henry remained cautious until test results were final. His caution was due in part to the fact that the two pumping systems installed at the southeast and northwest basins were only part of the Task Force's overall strategy. Land-based controls in the area's 9,000-acre watershed also put into effect complicated the analysis of exactly what was responsible for the lake's improvement.

The watershed controls have included farther setback distances for septic tanks (100 feet), a wine waste lagoon at the nearby Hopkins Vineyard, manure storage pits so farmers will not spread manure on frozen land which leads to run-off, and erosion controls. One such erosion control measure was stopping the yearly run-off of 200 tons of sediment from Sucker Brook into the lake.

**Continued on Page Fifteen**

## MORE RENTAL UNITS EYED FOR LITCHFIELD

### New Town Plan May Allow For Conversions

**By JUDY BENSON**

LITCHFIELD—Those writing the new town plan of development are looking for ways to solve a worsening apartment shortage here.

"We need more housing for young couples, singles and senior citizens," said Robert Donald, a partner in the Farmington planning firm Brown, Donald & Donald, acting as Litchfield's town planner.

One glimpse of the housing situation here is offered by the fact that of the 150 teachers and other staff at the Connecticut Junior Republic school here, only five live in Litchfield. And for the approximately 160 poverty-level senior citizens here, there are only 78 apartments in the town's two low-rent elderly housing complexes.

"A housing problem is developing in Litchfield," Mr. Donald said.

Many in town agree with Mr. Donald that Litchfield needs more apartments to meet the needs of the two fastest growing segments of its population—young adults and senior citizens. A new town

**Continued on Page Nineteen**

## Curry: From Race for Congress, To Campaign to End Arms Race

**By JASON F. ISAACSON**

WASHINGTON, D.C.—William E. Curry Jr., fully "recuperated" from his 1982 Congressional defeat to Representative Nancy Johnson and now a member of this city's new Establishment of the Left, says he is not ready to be written out of Connecticut politics.

The 32-year-old former two-term State Senator from Farmington, who lost in the Sixth District race and a year later was hired to run Freeze Voter '84, a Washington-based political action committee, said he plans to return home early next year.

"I know I want to run for office again, and I know I want to do that in Connecticut," Mr. Curry told The Litchfield County Times this week. "There are a lot of things I'm doing now that would give me a foundation: a certain level of national exposure, a good deal of administrative experience."

**Fund-Raising Network**

Mr. Curry, who heads an eight-month-old fund-raising network with a paid staff of 30 and a 1984 budget of $2 million said he did not know what office he might seek when he quits in "the beginning of 1985" and returns to Berman, Curry & Russo, the South Windsor law firm from which he is on extended leave.

He declined to speculate on whether

he would mount another campaign for Congress, in 1986 or later. Mr. Curry, a Democrat who claims more liberal views than this year's likely Democratic challenger to Mrs. Johnson, insurance executive Arthur H. House of East Granby, commented:

"I certainly like Art House. I will campaign for him and help him, and I see a clear difference between Art and Nancy Johnson."

**'Different Contribution'**

In the course of the two-hour interview on Capitol Hill, Mr. Curry said he is making "a different contribution" now, in his political organizing for Congressional candidates supportive of a bilateral nuclear weapons freeze, than he would have had he won the Sixth District seat.

"There are some things I like better," he continued. "When you're running for public office, we're all five-minute experts in everything. The chance to focus on a particular area in greater depth is a welcome change."

Mr. Curry, in comments ranging from local to national political issues, made the following observations:

• Mrs. Johnson's political position is strong but "not unassailable." His deci-

**Continued on Page Fourteen**

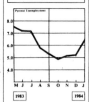

**Unemployment**

Percent Unemployment

8.0
7.0
6.0
5.0
4.0

M J J A S O N D J
1983        1984

For January, the average unemployment rate of the Danbury, Torrington and Waterbury Labor Areas was 6.4 percent, up from 5.2 percent for December. **Source: Connecticut Labor Department.**

**Fig. 13-11**  *The* Litchfield County Times *maintains the traditional format for its front page. It was an award winner in the Society of Newspaper Design fourth annual competition.*

to the overall design philosophy. The traditional format is characterized by:

- Column rules separating narrow columns. The rules are cast on a 4-point base for many newspapers, further cramming the type together.

- Headlines with a number of decks, all separated by jim dashes.

- Nameplates often embellished with "ears" or type material on either side at the top of the page. These contain weather, edition logo, promotional material, slogans, and so on.

- Cutoff rules separating unrelated units such as stories, photos, and cutlines.

- Rules above and below the folio lines, the full-width lines under the nameplate giving the volume and issue number, date, city of publication, and similar information.

- Banner heads, sometimes used every day regardless of the importance of the news. These banners are followed by readouts, or decks.

- Boxes, bullets, ornaments, and embellishments used liberally.

- Many headlines set in all-capital letters, particularly the top decks in the heads.

- Types from several families often used in the head schedule.

In addition, the design plans of the front and inside pages of the traditional newspaper usually follow definite preconceived patterns. (These patterns are discussed in Chapter 14.)

As with all design, though, it is difficult to categorically classify the patterns of all newspapers within set, clear-cut time and design periods. Some publications changed slowly and some never changed at all. But the traditional approach to newspaper design began to come under serious challenge in the late 1930s and early 1940s with the emergence of what might be called the "functional" design philosophy.

## Functional Newspaper Design

The *functional design* philosophy is based on the concept that if an element does not perform a function it should be eliminated, and if another element does the job better it should be used.

John E. Allen led the revolt against the traditional, highly formalized style of newspaper design. His editorship of the *Linotype News*, regarded as the nation's typographic laboratory, and his authorship of three books on newspaper design gave authority to his recommendations. His campaign started in 1929 with what he called "streamlined" headlines. These were heads set flush left and ragged right.

In arguing for the new flush left and for abandoning the complex head designs, Allen made these points:

**Fig. 13-12**　*The Buffalo* Evening News *uses many functional modern design techniques: heads in capitals and lowercase, white space instead of column rules, and multicolumn heads to break up the vertical thrust.*

1. The traditional headline form is difficult to write and often it is necessary to use inaccurate or inappropriate words because of the rigid unit count.

2. All-cap lines are hard to read compared to lines set in lowercase.

3. Flush left heads allow more white space into the page and give heads more breathing room.

4. Traditional head forms are difficult and take more time to set in type.

These points made sense to many designers, and the new style was adopted by more and more newspapers. It was based on the idea that the purpose of typography and graphic design is to make the contents understandable and inviting to read.

Designers examined each element of the newspaper page and evaluated its worth in terms of effective communication. They proceeded from the thesis that if a functional newspaper were to be designed, the first step was to define its function—this is a good starting point for any design project, incidentally.

The functions of most newspapers can be summarized to include *informing, interpreting, persuading,* and *entertaining.* The design and layout of any newspaper should help it achieve four specific goals:

1. Increase readability and attract the reader.

2. Sort the contents so the reader knows at a glance which information is the most important and what each part of the newspaper contains.

3. Create an attractive and interesting package of pages.

4. Create recognition so the paper can be readily identified.

A number of innovations in design were adopted in the late 1930s and early 1940s to help accomplish these goals. After the adoption of the flush left headline form with fewer, if any, decks, other efforts were made to let light into the pages and brighten them. White space was used wherever possible. Nameplates were simplified. Often, ears were dropped or cleaned up and typographic embellishments in the nameplate area were eliminated in favor of white space.

The top, and in some instances the bottom, rule on the folio line was eliminated. Vertical column rules were dropped in favor of white space between columns and this white space was increased. A pica of white space between columns was considered minimum for effective separation.

Cutoff rules and jim dashes were scrapped in favor of white space although some newspapers continued to use cutoff rules if they were thought more effective in designating story and art unit limits.

The new design movement favored fewer banner heads but more variety in layout. The optical attraction of the upper left corner of the page was utilized, and important stories or photos were placed there and not subordinated to the traditional lead story in the traditional upper right corner.

Shorter nameplates were favored. Skyline heads and stories, placed above the nameplate and extending across the width of the page, were used frequently. The traditional nameplate, which extended across the top of the page, was reset in varying widths so it could be "floated" or shifted around on the page and set in two, three, or more column widths for variety and change of pace.

Other functional innovations included good display of a page 1 index and highlighting of inside features to get the readers inside the newspaper. More photos were used and in larger sizes to give them increased impact. Photos were cropped closely and enlarged more. More attention was paid to the bottom half of the page—the area below the fold—to get a better balance and to present a livelier look from top to bottom.

Jumped stories were eliminated as much as possible since readership studies revealed that a story loses about 80 percent of its audience when it is continued to another page.

A horizontal thrust was introduced with the use of more multicolumn heads and photos. This helped break up the dullness of column after column of vertical makeup. Captions were shortened and rules, boxes, and ornaments simplified.

Not all newspapers adopted all of the functional design devices. But more and more newspapers did appear in a format that reflected what had become accepted as a basic tenet of good newspaper design:

The appearance of the newspaper should reflect its editorial philosophy and appeal to its particular audience.

*The New York Times*, traditional yet in its basic design, continues to win awards for its adherence to that philosophy.

## The Optimum Format Arrives

In 1937 the *Los Angeles Times* restyled its format to functional design and that year it won the coveted Ayer award for outstanding newspaper design. Twenty-eight years later, the *Courier-Journal*, Louisville, Kentucky, and its companion newspaper, the *Louisville Times*, became the first metropolitan newspapers to usher in the *optimum design era*. The *Courier-Journal* cut its columns per page from eight to six and widened them from 11 picas to 15.

In the 1960s some newspapers began to appear with a "downstyle" head dress. The *downstyle head* is composed in all lowercase letters except for the first word and proper nouns. It further simplifies newspaper design and eases reading.

In 1965 daily newspaper circulation in the United States was 60,358,000. In 1970 the population was 203,302,031 and newspaper circulation was 62,108,000. Ten years later the population had grown by more than 23,000,000 while newspaper circulation had remained virtually unchanged. Circulation only increased by 115,040 throughout the country.

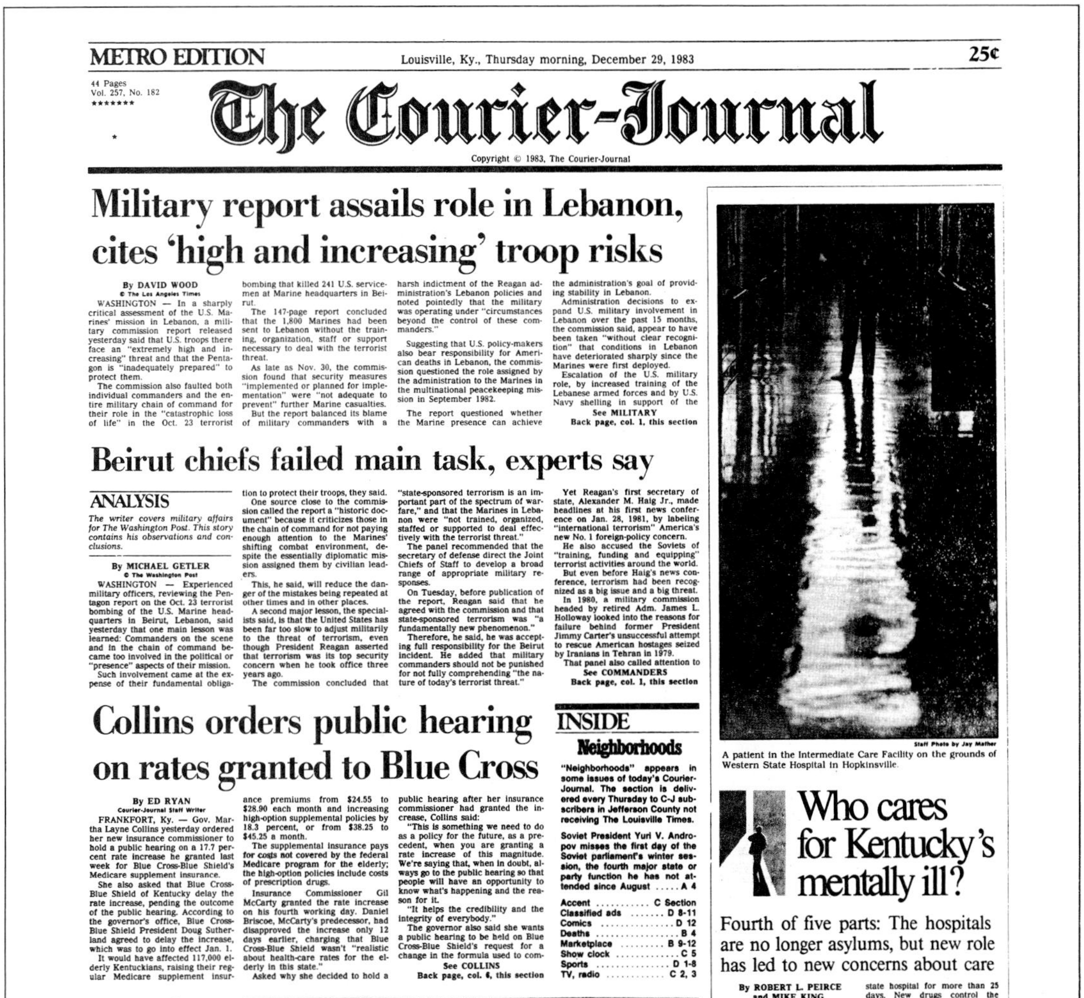

METRO EDITION

Louisville, Ky., Thursday morning, December 29, 1983

25¢

44 Pages
Vol. 257, No. 182
★★★★★★★

★

# The Courier-Journal

Copyright © 1983, The Courier-Journal

## Military report assails role in Lebanon, cites 'high and increasing' troop risks

By DAVID WOOD
© The Los Angeles Times

WASHINGTON — In a sharply critical assessment of the U.S. Marines' mission in Lebanon, a military commission report released yesterday said that U.S. troops there face an "extremely high and increasing" threat and that the Pentagon is "inadequately prepared" to protect them.

The commission also faulted both individual commanders and the entire military chain of command for their role in the "catastrophic loss of life" in the Oct. 23 terrorist bombing that killed 241 U.S. servicemen at Marine headquarters in Beirut.

The 147-page report concluded that the 1,800 Marines had been sent to Lebanon without the training, organization, staff or support necessary to deal with the terrorist threat.

As late as Nov. 30, the commission found that security measures "implemented or planned for implementation" were "not adequate to prevent" further Marine casualties.

But the report balanced its blame of military commanders with a harsh indictment of the Reagan administration's Lebanon policies and noted pointedly that the military was operating under "circumstances beyond the control of these commanders."

Suggesting that U.S. policy-makers also bear responsibility for American deaths in Lebanon, the commission questioned the role assigned by the administration to the Marines in the multinational peacekeeping mission in September 1982.

The report questioned whether the Marine presence can achieve the administration's goal of providing stability in Lebanon.

Administration decisions to expand U.S. military involvement in Lebanon over the past 15 months, the commission said, appear to have been taken "without clear recognition" that conditions in Lebanon have deteriorated sharply since the Marines were first deployed.

Escalation of the U.S. military role, by increased training of the Lebanese armed forces and by U.S. Navy shelling in support of the

See MILITARY
Back page, col. 1, this section

## Beirut chiefs failed main task, experts say

ANALYSIS

*The writer covers military affairs for The Washington Post. This story contains his observations and conclusions.*

By MICHAEL GETLER
© The Washington Post

WASHINGTON — Experienced military officers, reviewing the Pentagon report on the Oct. 23 terrorist bombing of the U.S. Marine headquarters in Beirut, Lebanon, said yesterday that one main lesson was learned: Commanders on the scene and in the chain of command became too involved in the political or "presence" aspects of their mission.

Such involvement came at the expense of their fundamental obligation to protect their troops, they said.

One source close to the commission called the report a "historic document" because it criticizes those in the chain of command for not paying enough attention to the Marines' shifting combat environment, despite the essentially diplomatic mission assigned them by civilian leaders.

This, he said, will reduce the danger of the mistakes being repeated at other times and in other places.

A second major lesson, the specialists said, is that the United States has been far too slow to adjust militarily to the threat of terrorism, even though President Reagan asserted that terrorism was its top security concern when he took office three years ago.

The commission concluded that "state-sponsored terrorism is an important part of the spectrum of warfare," and that the Marines in Lebanon were "not trained, organized, staffed or supported to deal effectively with the terrorist threat."

The panel recommended that the secretary of defense direct the Joint Chiefs of Staff to develop a broad range of appropriate military responses.

On Tuesday, before publication of the report, Reagan said that he agreed with the commission and that state-sponsored terrorism was "a fundamentally new phenomenon."

Therefore, he said, he was accepting full responsibility for the Beirut incident. He added that military commanders should not be punished for not fully comprehending "the nature of today's terrorist threat."

Yet Reagan's first secretary of state, Alexander M. Haig Jr., made headlines at his first news conference on Jan. 28, 1981, by labeling "international terrorism" America's new No. 1 foreign-policy concern.

He also accused the Soviets of "training, funding and equipping" terrorist activities around the world.

But even before Haig's news conference, terrorism had been recognized as a big issue and a big threat.

In 1980, a military commission headed by retired Adm. James L. Holloway looked into the reasons for failure behind former President Jimmy Carter's unsuccessful attempt to rescue American hostages seized by Iranians in Tehran in 1979.

That panel also called attention to

See COMMANDERS
Back page, col. 1, this section

## Collins orders public hearing on rates granted to Blue Cross

By ED RYAN
Courier-Journal Staff Writer

FRANKFORT, Ky. — Gov. Martha Layne Collins yesterday ordered her new insurance commissioner to hold a public hearing on a 17.7 percent rate increase he granted last week for Blue Cross-Blue Shield's Medicare supplement insurance.

She also asked that Blue Cross-Blue Shield of Kentucky delay the rate increase, pending the outcome of the public hearing. According to the governor's office, Blue Cross-Blue Shield President Doug Sutherland agreed to delay the increase, which was to go into effect Jan. 1.

It would have affected 117,000 elderly Kentuckians, raising their regular Medicare supplement insurance premiums from $24.55 to $28.90 each month and increasing high-option supplemental policies by 18.3 percent, or from $38.25 to $45.25 a month.

The supplemental insurance pays for costs not covered by the federal Medicare program for the elderly; the high-option policies include costs of prescription drugs.

Insurance Commissioner Gil McCarty granted the rate increase on his fourth working day. Daniel Briscoe, McCarty's predecessor, had disapproved the increase only 12 days earlier, charging that Blue Cross-Blue Shield wasn't "realistic about health-care rates for the elderly in this state."

Asked why she decided to hold a public hearing after her insurance commissioner had granted the increase, Collins said:

"This is something we need to do as a policy for the future, as a precedent, when you are granting a rate increase of this magnitude. We're saying that, when in doubt, always go to the public hearing so that people will have an opportunity to know what's happening and the reason for it.

"It helps the credibility and the integrity of everybody."

The governor also said she wants a public hearing to be held on Blue Cross-Blue Shield's request for a change in the formula used to com-

See COLLINS
Back page, col. 6, this section

INSIDE

**Neighborhoods**

**"Neighborhoods" appears in some issues of today's Courier-Journal. The section is delivered every Thursday to C-J subscribers in Jefferson County not receiving The Louisville Times.**

**Soviet President Yuri V. Andropov misses the first day of the Soviet parliament's winter session, the fourth major state or party function he has not attended since August ..... A 4**


Accent ........... C Section
Classified ads ....... D 8-11
Comics ............... D 12
Deaths ................. B 4
Marketplace ......... B 9-12
Show clock .............. C 5
Sports ............... D 1-8
TV, radio ............ C 2, 3


Staff Photo by Jay Mather

A patient in the Intermediate Care Facility on the grounds of Western State Hospital in Hopkinsville.

## Who cares for Kentucky's mentally ill?

### Fourth of five parts: The hospitals are no longer asylums, but new role has led to new concerns about care

By ROBERT L. PEIRCE and MIKE KING
Courier-Journal Staff Writers

One of them was officially labeled the Kentucky Lunatic Asylum. Folklore held that their inhabitants could be heard for miles around ranting and raving when the moon was full.

That was early this century. Today, the state mental hospitals are brighter and cleaner than they were even two decades ago, when the state began to empty them in favor of a system of treating people in their hometowns. And the quality of hospital care today is undoubtedly better.

But they are not without problems:

✓ The three state hospitals — in Louisville, Lexington and Hopkinsville — rely heavily on drugs to stabilize patients, who are then discharged quickly to community care, where there is little or no guarantee they will stay on their medicine.

✓ Federal inspectors have called for the state to beef up the medical staffs at the hospitals. Despite an increase in salaries last year, the hospitals continually fight a shortage of nurses and have become dependent on foreign-educated physicians.

✓ Records at the hospitals show that on any given month 70 percent of the patients admitted are people who have received psychiatric care before in the state hospitals. Almost half of those classified as readmissions have suffered their relapses within a year of their last discharge.

✓ Patients are being discharged into living conditions that make their illnesses worse. Coordination between social workers at the hospitals and those in local and state agencies has at times been poor, leaving some patients to fend for themselves on the streets.

Twenty years ago, while Kentucky was leading the United States in transferring patients from hospitals to community-based care, it was also reducing the role of the state hospital in the mental-health system.

Not long ago, a hospital's primary goal was to be a custodian of its patients. Or, as one psychologist put it, "to separate them from us."

Now, a patient rarely stays in a state hospital for more than 25 days. New drugs control the symptoms of the chronically ill patient, and the courts are more protective of his rights. So the primary care of the mentally ill has fallen to independent community agencies.

#### Inside the hospitals

While the population inside the hositals has been dramatically reduced over the years, the state has not studied in depth how many psychiatric beds it needs in the three facilities.

A new $9.5 million Central State Hospital is now being built on the hospital grounds near Louisville. It will have only 30 more beds than the present facility. With only 30 new beds at Central State, the hospital probably will not have enough to accommodate the Louisville area's need, most experts believe.

Dennis Boyd, the hospital administrator, said the decision to add only 30 beds was made because 30 was the number the state once used in a special unit for tests on people awaiting criminal trials.

To compound the problem, in 1981 the state revoked a contract to use some beds in the private Our Lady of Peace Hospital in Louisville for acute care.

The decision to build on the present grounds is "reminiscent of 19th century psychiatry," said Dr. John Schwab, chairman of the Department of Psychiatry and Behavioral Sciences at the University of Louisville School of Medicine. Psychiatric hospitals in the last century were in rural settings to separate the ill from society.

Some mental-health advocates and community-care officials lobbied heavily for putting it in downtown Louisville, so services could be tied to the downtown medical centers. State officials, including Boyd, favored the present site because it would be less expensive and because they felt the rural setting was more therapeutic.

How closely does the state monitor the quality of care inside the hospitals?

"It's a joke," said Sharon Ware,

See WHO CARES
PAGE 8, col. 1, this section

## Kentucky can't slip the icy grip of winter

*Information for this story was also provided by staff writers Bill Powell and Anne Pardue and by The Associated Press.*

By WILMA NORTON
Courier-Journal Staff Writer

Louisville enjoyed a respite from the bitter cold yesterday — temperatures "soared" to 34 early in the afternoon — but the mercury is expected to drop once again to near 5 degrees tonight.

Last night, roadways were freezing again.

The iciness contributed to two deaths in Kentucky. One involved a Lexington man who was crushed when a garbage truck fell on its side in a landfill. The second victim was a Bowling Green woman killed in an accident on U.S. 31 W.

Officials reported many other weather-related accidents across the state, but no other serious injuries.

This week's plague of broken and leaky water lines continued to strike yesterday, from the Galleria in downtown Louisville, to a nearby housing development, to a hotel in Paducah.

A frozen sprinkler pipe leaked water early yesterday into a vestibule between the parking garage and retail stores of the Galleria, operations manager Peter Gerdom said. Executive Cleaners had to delay opening, and some merchandise in Bacon's department store was damaged.

About 1,500 resident of Village West Apartments just west of downtown were without water for most of the afternoon, but service was restored by evening, project manager Levator Norsworthy said. A water main on 13th Street between Chestnut Street and Muhammad Ali Boulevard broke, according to Jerry Ford, Louisville Water Co. spokesman.

However, the water company was reporting half as many calls yesterday as Tuesday's reports of frozen pipes and main breaks seemed to be tapering off.

Over the weekend, the company averaged 100 calls an hour. At 4:30 yesterday, seven broken mains — the smallest number in three days — awaited repair, Ford said.

Louisville Gas and Electric reported no major power outages. Calvin Anderson, LG&E spokesman, said ice often breaks power lines or causes tree limbs to fall on them. But ice that enveloped Louisville Tuesday night was soft enough that it didn't weigh heavily on lines and limbs, he said.

#### Louisville-area traffic

City and county works department crews stood ready with adequate supplies of salt and sand last night.

The city has crews from the works, parks and sanitation departments on standby around the clock when road conditions are bad, according to Bob Schindler, who coordinates the salt and sand crews.

County works crews were planning to hit the streets about 7:30 last night. They had worked worked from 1 a.m. through the morning yesterday spreading salt and sand, Jack Pylinski, business manager for the works department, said.

City police spokesman Sgt. Carl Yates reported a near normal amount of accidents yesterday morning.

But as the slushy streets and highways began to freeze by late afternoon, police reported an increase in accidents, including a five-car pileup on Interstate 64 and the Grinstead Drive ramp. No one was injured.

#### Fatalities

Charles Guy, 37, an employee of Laine's Garbage Co. of Lexington,

See LOUISVILLE
Back page, col. 1, this section

Staff Photo by Pat McDonogh

Louisville firefighters stood in a puddle of water yesterday after a sprinkler pipe burst at the Galleria shopping center and leaked water into a vestibule between the parking garage and retail stores. One store reported that some merchandise was damaged.

## Sun shines cold day

National Weather Service

LOUISVILLE area — Partly sunny and cold today. Sunny and cold tomorrow. High today, mid-teens; tomorrow, low 20s. Low tonight, around 5.

KENTUCKY — Partly cloudy and cold today. Sunny and cold tomorrow. Highs today, mid-teens west to mid-20s east; tomorrow, 20s. Lows tonight, 0 to 10.

INDIANA — Clearing, with snow flurries ending this morning. Partly sunny and warmer tomorrow. Highs today, low teens; tomorrow, 20s. Lows tonight, 5 to 10.

High yesterday, 41; low, 22.
Year ago yesterday: High, 65; low, 37.
Sun: Rises, 7:54 EST; sets, 5:27.
Moon: Rises, 3:24 a.m.; sets, 2:22 p.m.

Weather map and details, Page D 8.

**Fig. 13-13** *The* Courier-Journal, *Louisville, Ky., was the first metropolitan newspaper to adopt the optimum format in 1965.*

**Fig. 13-14**  *The Hartford Courant's format changes illustrate the design periods in American newspaper history. The Courant is America's oldest continuously published daily. (Copyright 1964, Hartford Courant.)*

*Wethersfield Actor Lands Choice Soap-Opera Role* Page C1

# The Hartford Courant

ESTABLISHED 1764, DAILY EDITION, VOL. CXLVII NO. 53     WEDNESDAY, FEBRUARY 22, 1984—5 SECTIONS     COPYRIGHT© 1984 THE HARTFORD COURANT CO.     25¢ PER COPY

## Marines Begin Beirut Airport Withdrawal

**Associated Press**

BEIRUT, Lebanon — U.S. Navy helicopters ferried Marine combat troops from their base at Beirut's airport to warships in the Mediterranean Tuesday as the Marine withdrawal from Beirut officially began.

Israeli jets, meanwhile, bombed and strafed positions in the Syrian-controlled mountains east of the capital.

"Today the support people have gone and we're working on the combat gear," said the Marine spokesman, Maj. Dennis Brooks. "Today is the first day of the relocation of the actual 22nd MAU (Marine Amphibious Unit) personnel."

He was referring to combat troops that have stood by since Feb. 7 when President Reagan announced his intention to withdraw the Marines.

Helicopters soared in from the 6th Fleet shortly after dawn Tuesday and the withdrawal of the estimated 1,300 shore-based Marines began an hour later, Brooks said.

Brooks said he could not say how many Marines were withdrawn Tuesday. He estimated it would take "approximately a week, maybe two" to evacuate the base at Beirut's airport, maintained for 17 months by the Marines acting as part of a multinational peace-keeping force.

Since the base was established in September 1982, 265 U.S. servicemen have died in Lebanon.

The airport has been virtually surrounded by anti-government militias since last Wednesday, when Druse fighters drove from the mountains to the coast south of the base, linking up with their Shiite allies and further undermining the government of Christian President Amin Gemayel.

In Washington, Senate Republican leader Howard H. Baker Jr. said he had been told in a White House meeting with President Reagan that the withdrawal "would be finished by the end of this month, barring unforeseen circumstances."

Seven men of an air-naval gunfire liaison company talked to reporters on their way out. They carried M-16 rifles, light anti-armor weapons and grenade launchers.

"I'm ready to go. I've got women to meet and beers to drink," said Lance Cpl. Samuel Lee, 20, of Miami, Fla.

But when asked about the Marines' mission, Lee added: "We were just trying to restore peace. It doesn't look like it happened. It's a shame the U.S. has been here more than a year, and they (the Lebanese) still can't get their act together."

The battleship New Jersey circled about a mile offshore as Marine CH-53 Sea Stallion helicopters took off about every 15 minutes from a landing zone on the western edge of the base.

See **Marines**, Page A10

A young Lebanese Shiite Moslem boy gives a U.S. Marine a kiss goodbye at the Marine base near Lebanon's Beirut airport. Marine combat soldiers began pulling out of the base Tuesday.

AP

## State Loses Bid To Ban Tandems

**By MIRANDA SPIVACK**
*Courant Staff Writer*

WASHINGTON — The U.S. Supreme Court cleared the way Tuesday for double-trailer trucks to roll through Connecticut, turning aside the state's argument that the tandem-trailer vehicles are a safety hazard.

The justices, in a brief statement, affirmed a June 1983 decision by U.S. District Court Judge Jose A. Cabranes of Hartford, who said a federal law allowing widespread travel by the twin trucks supersedes a Connecticut ban imposed in April 1983.

The state passed its statute barring the tandems in response to a 1982 federal law permitting the trucks to travel on interstate highways.

The justices did not address the safety questions attorneys for the state had made the cornerstone of their argument. Cabranes had said that it is up to Congress to deal with safety questions.

The high court's action does not affect another part of the Connecticut law, which established a special permit for operators of tandem-trailers.

See **State**, Page A10

## McKinney Charged in Export Flap

**By DAVID LIGHTMAN**
*Courant Staff Writer*

WASHINGTON — Rep. Stewart B. McKinney of Connecticut was charged Tuesday by the Commerce Department with violating a U.S. export regulation, an action that could mean a fine of up to $10,000.

The 4th District Republican is the first public official in the seven-year history of the regulations to face such a charge, a Commerce Department official said.

McKinney said, however, he was fulfilling his duties as a congressman and acting only to help a constituent.

The regulation involved is aimed at preventing U.S. companies from cooperating with Arab nations that try to prevent firms

See **McKinney**, Page A10

## Task Force Opposes Deregulation of Nursing Homes

**By MICHELE JACKLIN**
*Courant Staff Writer*

The state should continue setting the rates paid by private patients in nursing homes, a special task force said Tuesday, almost certainly ending any consideration of deregulation of the industry by the General Assembly this year.

Deregulation would not only cost private patients millions of dollars a year, but could cost the state up to $71 million in added

Medicaid expenses, the task force said.

Last year, decontrol of nursing home rates was one of the most volatile issues before state lawmakers, with nursing home owners arguing that they needed to be able to charge private patients more to offset the unrealistically low payments they receive for Medicaid patients.

The recommendations of the task force, released at a State Capitol news conference, were adopted on a 12-5 vote, with the three representatives of the nursing home industry in opposition. Joining them were Health

"We have no plans in the immediate future to reintroduce this legislation. We will let the matter rest," said Louis J. Halpryn, vice president of the Connecticut Association of Health Care Facilities.

The recommendations of the task force are dead for now.

Services Commissioner Douglas S. Lloyd and Audrey Wasik of the state Commission on Long Term Care.

Halpryn and task force member Harry DiAdamo, a spokesman for three non-profit convalescent homes, said the task force membership was heavily weighted against the industry.

"They would have voted the way they did from the very first day," DiAdamo said.

There were other indications

of the deep rift among members. DiAdamo described the data compiled by the commission as "inconclusive" while A. Cynthia Matthews, a Democratic senator from Wethersfield and task force co-chairwoman, said the numbers were "very convincing."

Alleging that many of the state's 296 nursing home facilities are facing financial difficulties,

See **Panel**, Page A10

## Death With Dignity Sought for Daughter

**By JOSEPH M. COHEN**
*Courant Staff Writer*

The father of 42-year-old multiple sclerosis victim Sandra Z. Foody told a Superior Court judge Tuesday, "I don't want her tortured to death. I want her brought off the respirator ... so she can die in dignity."

Kenneth F. Foody and his wife, Ann M. Foody, of South Windsor testified Tuesday they had given the past 24 years to caring for their only child and, as devout Roman Catholics, had wrestled with the moral question of letting her die.

The Foodys have filed a Hartford Superior Court lawsuit asking to have their daughter taken off a respirator at Manchester Memorial Hospital, something the woman's doctor said is likely to lead to her death within a "few minutes."

In the Washington Street courtroom of Judge Mary E. Hennessey, lawyers compared the case to the landmark 1976 New Jersey case of Karen Ann Quinlan, and they said it would set Connecticut precedent in so-called death-with-dignity cases.

After hearing almost six hours of testimony and arguments Tuesday, Hennessey gave attorneys a week to file written briefs.

No date for a ruling was set.

There was no testimony or argument in court in opposition to taking Foody off a respirator, although her doctor, Giao Ngoc Hoang of Manchester, said the woman was not brain-dead.

Hoang described Foody as "awake but unaware. I cannot say with certainty she does not feel." But, he said, except for her brain regulating her body temperature and other very basic functions, she seems to be unaffected by external stimulation.

"We are all in agreement her condition is not reversible," Hoang said of the physicians who have consulted on the case.

Hoang said he considered the Foody case a "moral dilemma."

"We always want to do what is best for the patient. ... We are not God. Even though we are physicians, we have to live by the law of the land," he said.

Hoang is named as a defendant in the Foodys' lawsuit, along with Manchester Memorial Hospital, hospital acting Executive Director Michael Gallacher, state Attorney General Joseph I. Lieberman and Hartford State's Attorney John M. Bailey.

The lawsuit is intended to en-

See **Parents**, Page A10

**INDEX**

**AUTHOR DIES** — Mikhail Sholokhov, who wrote "And Quiet Flows the Don," has died at age 78. Sholokhov won the Nobel Prize in literature in 1965, the only officially sanctioned Soviet writer to win the prize. Page A11.

| Amusements | C1 | Editorials | B10 |
|---|---|---|---|
| Ann Landers | C6 | Food | E1 |
| Bridge | C6 | Horoscope | C7 |
| Business | C8 | Legal Notices | D6 |
| Classified | D6 | Obituaries | B8 |
| Comics | C6 | Sports | D1 |
| Connecticut | B1 | Television | C4 |
| Crossword | C6 | Wednesday | C1 |

**WEATHER: MOSTLY SUNNY**
26° to 44° F (-3° to 7°C)
Complete Weather    B12

## Mondale, Hart Take Their Battle For Top Spot to New Hampshire

**Washington Post**

MANCHESTER, N.H. — With his handsome Iowa caucus victory in hand, Walter F. Mondale came to New Hampshire Tuesday seeking a win in next Tuesday's primary that he said could "take us the rest of the way" to the Democratic presidential nomination.

Mondale faces a new challenge from a strengthened Colorado Sen. Gary W. Hart, who declared

that his surprise runner-up finish in Iowa would produce a closer race for Mondale in New Hampshire and would shake the Democratic contest down to a Mondale-Hart battle.

Mondale's erstwhile leading dynamics of the New Hampshire race, while strengthening Mondale's status as the favorite for the nomination. Instead of facing his main challenge from Glenn, who

keep from expiring, its New Hampshire manager announced that Glenn is scrapping his controversial anti-Mondale ads and is making new, "entirely positive" ads.

The Iowa results changed the dynamics of the New Hampshire race, which for him has been transformed by a shocking fifth-place finish in Iowa into a test of political survival. As the disabled Glenn campaign tried to

See **Boosted**, Page A4

## Mayor Faults Zoning Plan, but Forgos Veto

**By JOSEPH RODRIGUEZ**
*Courant Staff Writer*

Hartford Mayor Thirman L. Milner Tuesday criticized the City Council for adopting new downtown zoning regulations, but said he would let them become law — without his signature.

Milner said he would not veto the regulations because he said they ignore the needs of city residents and favor developers.

"As mayor, I am not satisfied with the ordinances that were passed," Milner wrote. "I cannot and will not affix my signature

approving the ordinance as passed."

Deputy Mayor Francisco L. Borges, a key backer of the package, said, "I'm pleased the mayor did not veto the ordinances." He said he was confident the council could have come up with the six votes needed to override a mayoral veto. The Council approved the package by an 8-1 vote.

The ordinances give city officials more control over downtown development. They require retail space in all new buildings and establish new standards for construction design, building size and traffic management. Devel-

opers also will be allowed to exceed maximum building sizes in exchange for providing amenities such as movie theaters and daycare centers.

Milner late last year vetoed key elements of a similar package because it did not offer incentives for builders to provide jobs and housing for city residents.

Milner did not explain in his statement why he did not veto the new package. He could not be reached Tuesday for comment.

Leaders of neighborhood

See **Milner**, Page A10

**Fig. 13-15** *Today the* Hartford Courant *is a carefully designed example of the optimum format. (Copyright 1984, Hartford Courant.)*

Editors and publishers recognized that something was wrong. More and more people but not more and more newspapers. They looked at their products and decided steps should be taken to make newspaper reading more attractive.

Following the lead of the *Courier-Journal* and others, many newspapers made two basic changes. The size of the body type was increased. The standard 8 point was increased to 9 and even 9½. Columns were widened to approximate the optimum line length for reading ease and speed. This meant changing from the cramped 10½- or 11-pica columns to more comfortable 14- or 15-pica columns. (see Fig. 13-14 and Fig. 13-15.)

By the middle 1970s the majority of newspapers had switched to the six-column format for at least their front and section pages. Some newspapers went to five-column pages and virtually all increased the white space between columns.

A leader in urging more readable newspapers was Edmund C. Arnold, who succeeded Allen as editor of the *Linotype News* and who has been recognized as one of America's authorities on newspaper design.

"There are many advantages to the op format," Arnold wrote in *Modern Newspaper Design.* He pointed out that "a line length at optimum is an asset because it enhances communication. The reader likes the longer measure, too, even if he doesn't understand the technicalities involved."[4]

However, even though the optimum format was used to make newspaper reading easier and more pleasant, circulation continued static. And many newspapers have again narrowed their columns back to 12 picas and reduced the body type back to 8 point. For them, the intent of the optimum format has been lost.

## The Redesigning Era

Newspaper design today is in a state of flux. The optimum format is with us in spirit if not soul. At the same time editors and designers are probing ways to make newspapers more visually exciting. They are struggling to keep up with the rapid changes in life-styles and reader interests. The new technology is also dictating many aspects of form and format.

There is, however, a growing recognition of the importance of blending design with content to develop the most effective communications package. Dr. Mario R. Garcia, a leading designer, wrote in *Contemporary Newspaper Design,* "Improvement in content and emphasis on clear writing and editing, combined with effective graphic innovation should be present" before circulation declines can be reversed.[5]

For some the answer is being found in the *modular format.* For others it is in refinement of the optimum format. And for still others, it is a return to the vertical design that withstood the test of time for so many years.

Piet Mondrian was a Dutch painter who did most of his work in the early part of this century. Typical of his art are compositions employing only vertical and horizontal lines. These lines are at 90 degree angles and form crosses and rectangles. Mondrian, who lived until 1944, has been an important influence on contemporary art and architecture.

The modular look that has had increasing popularity in newspaper design is somewhat of an adaptation of Mondrian's philosophy. The newspaper page is made of a series of rectangles, each rectangle containing a complete story. It is as if each story with its head and art is prepackaged in rectangular form so these packages can be arranged in as pleasing a way as possible on the newspaper page.

Designers who have adopted the modular plan—and it works well for large-format magazines and newsletters as well as newspapers— say the idea is to create as pleasing a geometric pattern as possible. They have these suggestions for planning a modular page:

■ Make numerous thumbnail sketches of newspaper pages made up of various combinations of rectangles. Do not use squares as they are monotonous and uninteresting. Keep in mind the basic design principle of proportion. Select the sketch that is most pleasing and use it as the basic design grid for that particular page.

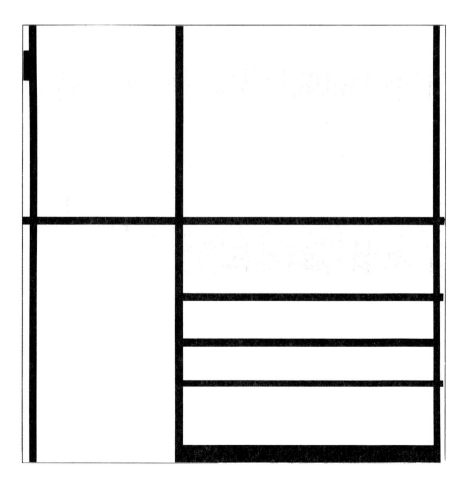

**Fig. 13-16** *This painting by Piet Mondrian is an example of his style, which inspired the modular makeup of many of today's newspapers. (Reprinted with permission of Westvaco Corporation.)*

**Fig. 13-17** *The Register, Orange County, Calif., a Society of Newspaper Design award winner, illustrates modular makeup. The page contains seven distinct rectangles.*

■ One module should dominate the page and presumably contain the lead story. This module should be placed above the fold, usually in the upper left or upper right—the high-interest sections of the page.

■ Each module should be self-contained and with a rule to define it. However, the rule should not be too heavy, no more than 4 points wide. Some designers specify color for the rules if available. Fairly generous white space, usually 18 to 24 points, can be used instead of rules.

**Fig. 13-18** *The seven rectangles of the* Register's *modular makeup.*

- Each module should contain a head and often art. The trend is toward the use of more line art in newspaper design. Photographs, when used, are cropped closely to give impact to the center of interest.
- Plenty of white space is used within the rules—around the heads and other elements.

A study made by the American Newspaper Publishers Association and summarized in the ANPA's *News Research Report No. 35* (1983) (issued to members only) indicated that readers prefer the modular format to other types of page makeup.

However, when the *Oakland Tribune* was redesigned in late 1983, the staff went against the trend and opted for a return to a vertical format. The procedures followed in this redesign project provide some interesting insights into design planning and monitoring. Andrea Schamis, art director, and Robert Maynard, publisher, decided the *Tribune* needed a new look to identify it as "the intelligent alternative" in the San Francisco Bay Area. (See Fig. 13-19.)

Schamis was quoted in the *Tribune's* employee newsletter as saying she found the old design of pages based on a horizontal format "ugly." She believed stories spread across columns, sometimes across the whole page, made the newspaper confusing and hard to read. Publisher Maynard said he would like the new design based on a vertical format with narrower headlines and clearer divisions between stories. Schamis commented about vertical format, "It's more traditional, and it gives the paper a more believable look."

Considerable research and planning went into the redesign. The publisher showed prototypes to members of the newspaper's community advisory board, and employees were also invited to make recommendations about the new design.

Changes will come slowly and Schamis plans a year to completely change the design of the *Tribune*. "It is a very gradual, organic thing," she comments. The first of the three-phase change was the "big change." The new head schedule and vertical thrust led the way. In the second phase there will be smaller modifications—minor typeface changes and story-packaging changes. The final phase will be the fine-tuning of the whole typographic package including consideration of modifications suggested by employees and members of the community.

Whenever a newspaper is being redesigned or a new publication is being planned, it is important to precede the actual design work by a publication analysis.

## How to Analyze a Publication

The designer of a newspaper should plan an analysis of the product on a regular basis. If possible, each issue should be evaluated with the editor. This evaluation could start with a few moments spent in browsing through the entire copy.

The overview of the issue should reveal a general impression of whether the typography maintains the character of the publication. For instance, does the whole issue help identify the publication as a conservative newspaper for a conservative community? Does it help say this newspaper is produced by an organization devoted to academic interests or to the manufacture of heavy equipment? The appearance of the newspaper should reinforce its purpose.

The examination should reveal if the arrangement of elements aids communication. Are there barriers? Are the rules, ornaments, or subheads placed so the flow of copy is interrupted to the point that the reader is confused? Does the layout increase readability? Would readers be attracted to this story or that? Or would they be inclined to pass a story by as the layout appears dull? If you were a reader would you want to spend time with this newspaper?

The entire package should do a good job of "sorting" the contents so the reader can find topical matter easily and without confusion.

Once an overall impression has been formed, each of the typographic elements should be examined and evaluated:

1. *Body type:* Is it legible and readable? Roman types have the highest readability. But the Roman used in newspaper design should have rather soft serifs and not too sharp a differentiation in the widths of the letter strokes. The size of the body type should be checked to see if it is large enough for easy reading. Types that are big on the body are usually preferred. Line length and leading should be examined to ensure their effectiveness.

2. *Headlines:* Is the type selected for the headlines attractive? Does it reflect the tone of the newspaper? Does it reflect the tone of the feature stories? Even though a bold type is chosen, it should be clear and legible. The same is true for light typefaces. A headline type should have a fairly good unit count. If more than one family is used in a head arrangement, the types should harmonize but one should dominate. Spacing between words and lines should be examined as well as all the factors of legibility, such as the size of the head for the width of the line.

3. *Typographic color:* Have ornaments, bull's eyes, arrows, and so on been avoided? If typographic devices are used, they should enhance legibility rather than detract from it.

4. *Newspaper constants:* Do the standing heads, department and column heads, and the masthead harmonize with the overall effect of the layout? The constants should be alive and not static. Headings such as "The President's Column," "Washington Week," or similar label heads should be redesigned if they do not have an element that can be changed, preferably with each issue, to illuminate the contents and add life.

5. *Pictures and cutlines:* Are the pictures cropped for proper emphasis? Art should communicate a message and not just ornament the layouts. Cutlines should be in a consistent style throughout the newspaper. They should be set in a type style that harmonizes with the other types but still provides some contrast. Cutlines should be set in the proper width, never more than about 18 picas wide. Cutlines under wide art should be broken into columns that approximate the optimum line length. Indented cutlines with ample space between lines brighten a page.

6. *Front page layout:* Can the application of the basic principles of design be seen? Is unity, balance, contrast, and harmony

---

**Creative Communication**

"Fools rush in"—creativity can be foiled and the process can take longer if preparation and analysis of the problem are inadequate. Creative scientists who seek to solve problems spend considerable time analyzing the situation. For example, Albert Einstein spent 7 years on intensive study and fact gathering. But then it only took him 5 weeks to write the resulting revolutionary paper on relativity. He was working full time as a clerk in a Swiss patent office as well.

Thorough preparation often can shorten the period spent on actual creativity. Thorough preparation might include assembling pertinent facts, asking questions and finding answers, and seeking out leads for possible solutions.

# McEnroe upset in Open

Sports Peach

# THE TRIBUNE

*Serving the Greater Bay Area from Oakland since 1874*

**Racing handicap**

**TUESDAY**     Tuesday, September 6, 1983/Oakland, California     25¢

## Reagan trims Soviet ties

See below

## Giants win 3-2; A's lose 11-1

Sports Peach

### LOCAL

■ **RAUL RAMIREZ** reports the personal story of Dorothy Granada, one of the "Fast for Life" nuclear arms demonstrators. A-13.

■ **STOWAWAY FACES** proceeding in San Francisco today after leaving mainland China and riding a freighter to Oakland. A-13.

■ **FIRST LATINO** long-range medical study gets under way with three-month door-to-door survey in Bay Area. A-13.

■ **TEACHERS WIN** tentative agreement promising pay raises a day before school opens in San Francisco. A-13.

■ **UAW CLAIMS** a lawsuit filed Friday by its laid-off members in Fremont may hurt the Toyota-General Motors deal. A-15.

■ **OAKLAND BALLET** dancers, participating in a much-needed medical study, found they were taking pain for granted. C-1.

■ **THOSE COWBOYS** looked whipped until Danny White pitched three bombs in the second half, sinking the Redskins 31-30. D-1.

### STATE

■ **PERSISTENT RUMOR** that a child was kidnapped from its mother in Disneyland's Magic Kingdom is a hoax that won't die. A-10.

■ **STREET JUSTICE** was meted out to men who ripped bikini tops off women at beachfront swimsuit contest. A-10.

■ **SHARPSHOOTERS BAGGED** six coyotes in a continuing hunt prompted by recent attacks on two children. A-12.

### NATION

■ **SHUTTLE ASTRONAUTS** return from 2¼-million-mile mission, making night-time landing a breathtaking, routine thing. A-2.

■ **POOR SCHOOLS** are four times less likely to participate in a rush of school computer use this year, study says. A-3.

■ **CHRYSLER SETTLES** contract with UAW for bigger raise than it wanted to give — in just six hours of talking. A-5.

### WORLD

■ **REBEL SPIES** in Salvadoran army helped in guerrilla attacks against the army, a Western official reported. A-4.

■ **ISRAELI ATTEMPTS** to form a new government hit snag when coalition facts turn to opposition Labor Party. A-8.

### OPINION

■ **LEGISLATORS FEARED** public reaction, which explains the illogical way they voted themselves a logical pay raise. B-4.

■ **QUITTING LEBANON** is an option the president could take if he would only invoke the War Powers Resolution. B-5.

### WEATHER

■ **SOMEWHAT COOLER** with highs from the mid-60s on the coast to 80s and 90s inland as fog returns, generally fair. A-2.

| Monday Highs | | Monday Lows | |
|---|---|---|---|
| Concord | 86 | Concord | 55 |
| Fremont | 78 | Fremont | 55 |
| Oakland | 78 | Oakland | 58 |
| San Rafael | 84 | San Rafael | 54 |
| San Francisco | 73 | San Francisco | 57 |
| Tahoe | 78 | Tahoe | 40 |

### INSIDE

Vol. 110-249 □★★§   (4 Sections)   502

# Two U.S. Marines killed in new Lebanon fighting

## A Labor Day contest

Kids celebrate Labor Day with pie-eating contests. Clever kids, these in Berkeley. No one noted what the filling was, but they all knew there was a messy bit of meringue. Who knows how messy? They reached for napkins when the deed was done. The nose that won belonged to Sam Smith (third from right), who shared first place with Adia Henry. The celebration was at a holiday bash sponsored by the University of California.

*Tribune photo by Robert Stinnett*

## Four now dead in clashes

Associated Press

BEIRUT — Two U.S. Marines were killed and two others wounded in an artillery barrage at dawn today, the third day of renewed Christian-Druse civil war in Lebanon, a Marine spokesman Maj. Robert Jordan said.

The bombardment occurred at 4:05 a.m. (7:05 p.m. PDT Monday), when a barrage of rockets and mortar shells slammed in and around the Marine base at Beirut's international airport, said Jordan.

It was the first deadly attack on the Marines since early last week when two leathernecks were killed in intensified fighting between rival Lebanese groups. The Marines are part of a multinational peacekeeping force deployed in the Beirut area at the Lebanese government's request.

Jordan said the latest victims were posted within the airport perimeter. Two armored cars brought the four casualties to a helicopter that evacuated them to the Navy's helicopter carrier Iwo Jima, off the Beirut coast, Jordan said.

In Washington, a spokesman at the Pentagon said there would be no immediate announcement of the

See LEBANON, Back page

## Reagan cuts Soviet exchanges

By Steven R. Weisman
New York Times

WASHINGTON — President Reagan, condemning the Soviet Union for "the Korean airline massacre," announced new limitations Monday night on cultural, scientific and diplomatic exchanges with the Russians and new efforts to restrict Soviet civilian aviation in the West.

In a television address to the nation, Reagan also urged Congress to heed the Soviet Union's "act of barbarism" in shooting down a South Korean civilian airliner last Thursday and to

■ Military analysis, C-16.

support his administration's military spending programs.

"There is something I've always believed in, but which now seems more important than ever," Reagan said. "The Congress will be facing key defense issues when it returns from recess."

"There has been legitimate difference of opinion on this subject, I know, but I urge the members of that distinguished body to ponder long and hard the Soviets' aggression as they consider the

security and safety of our people, indeed all people who believe in freedom."

Reagan also made what in effect was an international appeal for action against the Soviet Union.

"Make no mistake about it, this attack was not just against ourselves or the Republic of Korea," he said. "This was the Soviet Union against the world and the moral precepts which guide human relations among people everywhere."

See REAGAN, Back page

## Wreckage of lost cargo plane found

By David Alcott
Tribune Staff Writer

A Transamerica Airlines cargo plane that had been missing for 10 days was discovered crashed in Angola on Monday, strewn across sparse terrain in several pieces with no indication of survivors among the seven persons aboard, according to officials of the Oakland-based airline.

The four-man crew consisted of co-pilot Raymond G. Blake, 48, of San Jose; pilot Eldon Lord, 56, of Ogden, Utah; Leonard Pott Jr., 29, of North Fork, Madera County; and Robert Lengyel, 40, also of Ogden.

See PLANE, Back page

## Pope reaffirms sexuality teaching

By Henry Kamm
New York Times

ROME — Pope John Paul II repeated Roman Catholic teaching against abortion, divorce, the ordination of women, birth control, premarital sex and homosexuality Monday in a speech to 25 visiting United States bishops.

Church sources suggested that the pope chose the Americans as his forum because he considers the United States a center of sexual liberalism and believes elements within the church in the United States to be sympathetic to such views. The prelates were here to pay the visit to the pope that is obligatory for bishops every five years.

In the meeting at his summer residence at Castel Gandolfo, the pope told the bishops that they must "proclaim without fear and ambiguity the many controverted truths of our age" and went on to list the Roman Catholic church's teachings on sexuality.

The pope reminded the bishops of the church's doctrine of the indissolubility of marriage, citing approvingly from a pastoral letter of the U.S. episcopate that said: "the covenant between a man and a woman in Christian marriage is as indissoluble and irrevocable as God's love for his people and Christ's love for his church."

The pope condemned premarital sex and

See POPE, Back page

## Politics prevail at Labor picnic

By Craig Staats
Tribune Staff Writer

PLEASANTON — Most people brought softball bats, coolers or stereo tape players to the Alameda County Central Labor Council's annual Labor Day picnic here Monday.

But Ed Loque Jr., an Oakland machinist and union member, brought an inflatable Ronald Reagan doll, with a sign on it: "I'VE GOT A JOB."

■ Labor Day across nation, A-4

While other people were eating or playing softball, Loque found a suitable tree on the Alameda County fairgrounds, struggled up into its lower branches and hanged the doll in effigy.

Back on the ground, Loque said the doll has come in handy this time every year since Reagan took office, when the president is

no great friend of organized labor, in the view of most people in the crowd.

"It's becoming suitable for every Labor Day picnic," Loque said, as he wandered off to finish a softball game.

Several thousand union workers and their families turned out for the daylong picnic, billed as the nation's oldest, all-union Labor Day event.

See LABOR, Back page

## Average income rises 5 percent

Associated Press

WASHINGTON — The average income of Americans rose about 5 percent last year, the Commerce Department said Monday.

The per capita income rose from $10,582 in 1981 to $11,107 in 1982, according to figures compiled by the department's Bureau of Economic Analysis. The figure measures income earned by all people in the na-

tion, divided by the total population.

Alaska, with a per capita income of $16,257, was the richest state last year. The poorest was Mississippi, where the average was $7,778. California was fifth richest, $12,567.

From 1979 to 1982, the department said, per capita personal income rose 28.3 percent across the nation.

The others in the five richest

areas were the District of Columbia, $14,550; Connecticut, $13,748, and New Jersey, $13,089.

The four poorest states after Mississippi were Arkansas, $8,479; South Carolina, $8,502; Alabama, $8,649; and West Virginia, $8,769.

The western states showed increases due to manufacturing and federal employment, particularly defense spending.

**Fig. 13-19** *The Oakland Tribune selected a more vertical thrust than many designers advocate. However, the planning, execution, and followup of its design change provide a worthwhile study. The Tribune involved all staffers and many readers in its project.*

# STOCKS SURGE 23 POINTS

*—Business Peach*

# THE TRIBUNE

SERVING THE GREATER BAY AREA FROM OAKLAND SINCE 1874

Bay Meadows Handicap

Oakland, California | Wednesday, September 7, 1983 | 25 Cents


*Column One*

## Areas vie for BART extension

*Dividing limited funds is at heart of problem*

*"If we have to cut anything out of this policy, I'm going to make sure we cut the Fremont extension first."* —BART Director Nello Bianco of Richmond.

*"Nello, you just scare me to death. You've tried it before and failed. I challenge you to try it again."* —BART Director John Glenn of Fremont.

**By Mike Libbey**
*The Tribune*

The first extension of a BART line is eight to 10 years away, yet, grown men get into sandbox-level exchanges over the issue.

But when 10 people are asked to divvy up two pieces of gold, it's not surprising that threats and dares are traded.

The equivalent of gold is just about how developers perceive the value of a major transit link such as BART. A BART station can be parlayed into new jobs, new buildings and economic rejuvenation for a community, according to East-bay development experts.

And divvying up limited money is exactly what's at the heart of the arguments over extensions.

The most optimistic estimate of all federal, state and local money available to the Bay Area in the next 10 years for transit projects is $2 billion.

BART's top-priority projects alone would cost more than that, and other transit agencies in the region have plans for projects costing $3 to $5 billion more.

The process of building an extension is a complicated one. BART must first buy property for stations and track right of way, which it is now doing. It is about to start federally required environmental impact

*See BART, Page A-2*

I don't like Russia.

*The Associated Press*
**Susan Ro, 2, demonstrates in front of Seattle's Korean consulate.**

## The White House affirms Marines to stay in Beirut

**By William E. Farrell**
*The New York Times*

WASHINGTON — The Reagan administration affirmed its commitment Tuesday to keeping Marines in Lebanon despite the killing of two more American troops.

The chief White House spokesman, Larry Speakes, said the president anticipated "no change whatsoever" in keeping 1,400 United States Marines in a 5,000-strong multinational force that also includes soldiers from France, Italy and Britain.

Speakes also warned the Syrians, who have been providing arms to leftist Druse militiamen, against "instigating any violence," adding that the United States had "considerable firepower" stationed in the Mediterranean facing the Beirut coastline.

Four Marines have been killed in Lebanon in the last eight days. The multinational force was deployed in the Beirut area last September to shore up the government of President Amin Gemayel.

The White House, along with the State Department and Defense Secretary Caspar W. Weinberger, deplored the deaths of the two Marines Tuesday but supported the presence of American troops in Lebanon despite the stepped-up fighting in a country that has been the scene of civil violence almost constantly since 1975.

There is growing skepticism in Washington about the advisability of having American troops amid the warring factions, Maronite Christians and Druse, an offshoot of Islam who are aided by Shiite Moslems. The animosity between the Druse and the Christians dates back over a century and has frequently erupted into violence.

In addition, Congress, which is to reconvene next Tuesday, is certain to address the War Powers Resolution of 1973. If President Reagan should declare that the Marines based in Beirut are in imminent danger of hostilities, something the president has so far declined to do, he would be required to withdraw the troops within 90 days unless Congress approved keeping them in Lebanon.

## UAW council strongly endorses Chrysler's offer

*The Associated Press*

DETROIT — A United Auto Workers council Tuesday overwhelmingly endorsed a two-year, $1 billion contract that would put Chrysler Corp. workers a big step closer to parity with their counterparts at General Motors Corp. and Ford Motor Co.

The new accord, tentatively agreed to by union negotiators and the automaker on Labor Day, would give Chrysler workers a $2.42-an-hour raise during the life of the contract, the UAW said. That would put their base hourly pay, exclusive of regularly scheduled cost-of-living, at about $12.42 when the pact expires in October 1985.

## Soviets acknowledge shooting down airliner

*Kremlin blames U.S. for tragedy*

**By Robert Gillette**
*The Los Angeles Times*

MOSCOW — The Soviet government, after six days of implicit denials, acknowledged Tuesday that it shot down a Korean airliner with 269 people on board but insisted that the United States was wholly responsible for the tragedy.

"An interceptor-fighter plane of the anti-aircraft defenses fulfilled the order of the command post to stop the flight," the government statement said. It was issued by the official Soviet press agency Tass and read as the lead item on evening television news.

The government said the fighter had launched warning shots with tracers, as "envisaged by international rules."

Article 36 of the law, which was enacted nine months ago, empowers the Air Defense Forces to use "weapons and combat equipment" against violators of Soviet airspace "in response to the use of force by violators or in instances in which the violation cannot be stopped or the violators detained by any other means."

**'In keeping with the law'**

The statement did not say how Soviet fighters stopped the flight of the Korean airliner, nor did it acknowledge the specific death toll of 269. It added, however, that "such actions are fully in keeping with the law on the state border of the U.S.S.R., which has been published."

The government's admission that it shot the plane down came after days of implying in the press and on radio and television that Soviet interceptor pilots did no more than fire warning shots parallel to the plane's flight path. The statement came two days before Soviet Foreign Minister Andrei A. Gromyko was scheduled to meet with Secretary of State George P. Shultz in Madrid — a meeting planned long before the airliner incident brought a fresh chill to U.S.-Soviet relations.

The admission, combined with Moscow's insistence that its actions were justified on the basis of the airliner's suspicious track over strategic military bases, relieves Gromyko of the burden of admitting or denying that Soviet forces fired on the plane. The statement also puts him in a position to contend in his meeting with Shultz that the Soviet leadership has nothing further to say on the matter.

The government statement called President Reagan an "ignoramus." A separate and even more vitriolic Tass report from Washington discussing Reagan's televised speech on the airliner crisis Monday night used some of the harshest rhetoric applied to an American leader in many years.

**Oleg Troyanovsky**
*Soviet Ambassador listens*

**Jeane Kirkpatrick**
*U.S. envoy presents tapes*

## Hushed U.N. listens to Soviet attack tape

**By Bernard Nossiter**
*The New York Times*

UNITED NATIONS — A hushed and intent Security Council on Tuesday heard 11 minutes of a tape-recorded voice the United States said was that of the Soviet fighter pilot who shot down the South Korean airliner with 269 people on board.

On five television screens placed around the Security Council chamber, the council's 15 members and dozens of other diplomats read the translation and listened to these climactic reports attributed to the Soviet flier:

"Now I will try a rocket. Twelve (kilometers) to the target."

"I am closing on the target. Am in lock-on. Distance to target is 8."

"Z.G. (Soviet initials for missile warheads locked on.)"

"I have executed the launch. The target is destroyed. I am breaking off attack."

The words on the tape, supplied by Japanese ground stations, were muffled and obscure. Russian-speaking Westerners said they could not decipher any meaning. But Soviet diplomats made no attempt to challenge the authenticity of the recording or the American-supplied translations.

For the United States delegate, Jeane J. Kirkpatrick, the tape's message was clear. "It

*See Plane,* **Back page**

## *Pacific High students enter their new campus*

*Change is difficult, bitter as 'dreams die hard'*

**By Connie J. Rux**
*The Tribune*

SAN LEANDRO — Students throughout the Bay Area are returning to the classroom this week and next in a September ritual that is often emotionally charged.

But feelings on the first day of class at San Leandro High School on Tuesday were even stronger than usual as more than 600 former Pacific High students entered their new campus for the first time.

The merger of the two high schools into one is expected to save the San Leandro school district an estimated $4 million during the next five years, according to administrators, and should enhance programs by concentrating expenditures at one site instead of two.

But as they say in the popular Gary Morris song, "Dreams Die Hard," and the change remains difficult and bitter for some former Pacific High students. Students and parents in Save Our School, a group fighting the closing of Pacific and two elementary schools as well, still feel betrayed.

"I will always be proud of

*See Schools,* **Back page**

Threat of Oakland strike eases, Back page

## INDEX



Vol 110-250 ★ ★ S

## NEWS DIGEST

**Tribune writer** Janet Ghent begins series on rootless Jews who rediscover identities in differing ways. D-1.

**The missile** that struck the Korean jumbo jet scored a direct political hit on American "doves." B-7.

**President Reagan** correctly describes Korean airline downing as savagery while not closing peace talk door. Editorial, B-6.

**Senior Alameda** prosecutor William McGuiness quietly accepts a top spot under U.S. Associate Attorney General Lowell Jensen. B-2.

**Concord city** workers ratify two-year agreementscovering over 200 employees, ending three-day walkout. B-3.

**"Black Dollar** Days" turns out well in Oakland, Richmond but fizzles in other parts of Bay Area. B-1.

**Judge won't** grant third penalty trial of convicted rapist-murderer, accuses Alameda County prosecutor of abusing authority. B-1.

**As car** sales climb higher, banks devise ways to capture buyers' loan business. C-1.

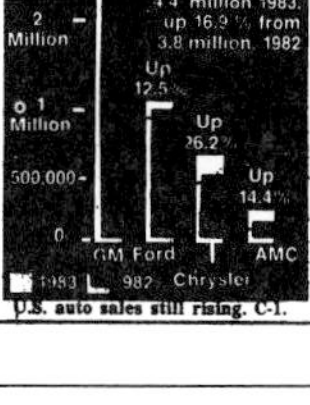
Auto Sales
TOTAL = 4.4 million 1983, up 16.9 % from 3.8 million 1982
2.6 Million
2 Million
1 Million
500,000
0
Up 15.1%
Up 12.5%
Up 26.2%
Up 14.4%
GM
Ford
Chrysler
AMC
1983
1982

**U.S. auto sales still rising. C-1.**

**Third Asian** businessman moves into position to become Trans Pacific Centre's new driving force. B-1.

**San Francisco** Symphony gives a fine introduction, with plenty of nervous excitement, to the sound of its 1983 season. D-1.

**Robin Orr** is present as a star-spangled audience of first-nighters turns out for the S.F. Symphony's festive evening in Davies Hall. D-2.

**U.S. immigration** judge grants political asylum to exiled black South African poet Dennis Brutus. A-3.

**Secretary Shultz** to limit discussion with Soviet Foreign Minister Gromyko to airliner crisis and human rights. A-4.

## WEATHER

**Sunny inland** and fog, low clouds and a chance of rain along the coast and in the coastal and northern mountains. A-10.

## Our new look

You will notice The Tribune has a new look today. It is intended to be a cleaner, more dignified design that will make the newspaper easier to read and more graphically appealing.

All your favorite features are still inside today's newspaper.

One notable change: The weather, which formerly could be found on Page A-2, now can be found on the back page of the first section. It will be there every day to make it easy to find.

The new design is part of an ongoing progam at The Tribune to improve the quality of the newspaper.

evident in the selection and placement of the elements? The front-page design should emphasize the most important story, but usually more than one strong element is needed to make a lively page. However, the page should not be overloaded to the point where it appears to be a conglomeration.

Are there strong elements in the "hot spots"—the four corners of the page? Unless there is a planned vertical thrust to the page, there should be a strong horizontal treatment. There should be ample, but well-planned white space.

7. *Inside-page layout:* Is there an evident consistent pattern for the placement of advertisements? Advertisements should not be placed haphazardly on a page, and the pattern adopted should be used consistently throughout the newspaper. Advertisements should be placed so they do not destroy reasonable editorial matter display, that is, they should be kept as low as possible on the page. Is there an editorial stopper—a story or art or a combination—on each inside page?

8. *Section pages and departments:* Are these given the same care as page 1? These pages should reflect the purposes and characteristics of the sections in their typographic design. For instance, the sports pages should have headline type that helps to say "this is the sports section," and the family living section should have a typographic dress that helps identify it. The principles of good layout should be evident in these pages as well as in all the others.

Once each part of the newspaper's anatomy has been examined and areas of improvement noted, the suggested improvements should be examined to see how they fit in helping to create a unified, attractive publication.

## Effective Design Checklist

■ Eliminate barriers. Check to see, for instance, if copy broken by subheads, art, or other typographic devices is easy to follow over, around, or under the devices.

■ Break up long copy for easy reading. Use extra space between paragraphs, pull out pertinent points and box them, use subheads, or indent and illuminate enumerated points with bull's eyes or other typographic color devices. But don't overdo it.

■ Set copy on proper measure for easy reading. Check to see that copy is never set more than two columns wide. Never set it two columns wide if the columns are more than 12 picas. Body matter shouldn't be set more than about 15 picas wide.

■ Don't use overlines with photos. (Overlines are small heads above photos.) Studies show they have no value. If a head is part of the cutline format, it should be immediately adjacent to the cutline.

■ Stick to one or two families of type for the head schedule. Plan a basic head schedule with one family of type and use its variations for contrast. If another family is used, use it sparingly and for contrast and accent, rather than basic heads.

■ Be cautious with reverses. Be sure reversed type has high legibility. Reverses can be difficult to print well, and they can disfigure a page.

■ Crop carefully and enlarge generously. Crop to emphasize the point of interest and eliminate anything that gets in the way of the story-telling quality of the photo. Enlarge to give impact and reader interest and do it generously.

■ Never run two unrelated photos next to each other. They will tug at the reader for attention, decreasing the impact of each.

■ Have a strong element in each quadrant of the front page. The "hot spots" attract interest, and the strong elements will hold the readers and ensure an orderly and balanced layout.

■ Watch the folds. In making layouts, be aware of the folds and try to keep photos away from them. Be sure the fold doesn't destroy or maim the subject matter in the photo.

**Fig. 13-20** *These prototype pages were created by students in a university graphics course. Prototypes are mockups (that is, the headlines and stories do not make sense) that give a good idea of the appearance of the printed page.*

## Graphics in Action

1. Select a daily newspaper and study its typography and design. See how many examples you can find that illustrate applications of the principles of design. (Example: A Black Letter used for the nameplate might contrast well with the style of type selected for the headline schedule.)

2. Put together a prototype (a pasteup of the page) of an entire front page of a tabloid-size newspaper. Materials for such a prototype can be obtained by copying headlines, reading matter, and newspaper constants on an office copying machine.

3. Design a small newspaper for an organization to which you belong or design an employee newspaper for a firm with which you are acquainted. If such a newspaper exists now, analyze the typographic and design elements and make recommendations for any changes that would improve the newspaper's organization and appearance. (Use the suggestions in "How to Analyze a Publication" as a guide.)

4. Make a design plan for an "ideal newspaper." Select the page size, types for headlines and features, departments, and all the design elements that you believe should be incorporated in such a publication.

5. This project is extensive and you might want to do it as a team or class effort. Select a nearby community or neighborhood that doesn't have a newspaper (or that seems ready for a competitive newspaper). Make a basic design plan for a proposed newspaper for that community. This project should involve considerable research and actual surveying by the students. A good starting place is study of the chapter on research and surveys in a newspaper management text such as *Newspaper Organization and Management* by Frank W. Rucker and Herbert Lee Williams (Ames, Iowa: Iowa State University Press, 1969).

## Notes

1. From advertisements in *Editor & Publisher*, January 28, 1984.
2. *Publisher's Auxiliary*, "The Case for 12 Ems," September 22, 1945, p. 4.
3. John E. Allen, *Newspaper Designing* (New York: Harper, 1947).
4. Edmund C. Arnold, *Modern Newspaper Design* (New York: Harper, 1969), p. 266.
5. Mario R. Garcia, *Contemporary Newspaper Design, A Structural Approach* (Englewood Cliffs, N.J.: Prentice-Hall, 1981), p. 23.

Newspapers all across the country—big ones, little ones, metro-politan ones, community weeklies, and company and campus news-papers—are paying increasing attention to graphics. There is con-stant examination and reexamination of the newspaper's appearance as editors and designers seek ways to make their product more appealing and attractive.

This has, as we saw in the advertisements in Chapter 13, created the need for graphic journalists. The *graphic journalist* is a person who combines the skills of the designer with those of the reporter and editor to produce packages of information in the most effec-tive way possible.

These packages of information can include words, type, art, borders, and typographic devices that form a unit that is then combined with other units to create the newspaper page. Creating these units involves an understanding of design principles and graphic and typographic techniques as well as an understanding of the news and the opportunities for its visual presentation. The graphic journalist strives to apply the following formula. It was developed by a writing instructor who pointed out that if the rewards received from reading an article were divided by the effort made to accomplish the task, the result would equal the possibilities of the piece being read.

$$\frac{\text{Rewards received}}{\text{Effort to read}} = \text{Chance of being read}$$

Communicators should keep this formula in mind. Not only will people refuse to read material that is full of barriers, but there is another problem. People are constantly bombarded with many forms of communications that require little effort to absorb.

Another major reason for the growing attention to graphics is the intrusion in the editorial room of the electronic age. When pagination devices become standard tools for putting together newspaper pages, the journalist will be involved in arranging information units to form a page layout on a video screen. This journalist will make graphic as well as editorial decisions.

## The Approach to Redesign

So, let us assume that you have just been appointed editor of a small newspaper. This is your first job and you want to do all you can to make the newspaper as effective as possible. It does not matter if this is a large or small community newspaper, or a university or organizational publication, the procedure is the same.

Of course, you examine the content of the newspaper to see if it is supplying what the audience wants and needs. In addition, you consider the method of publication and distribution. However, your major concern is with the typographic dress the newspaper is wearing. The decision is made to do a complete overhaul of the design. But how will you start and carry out a redesign project?

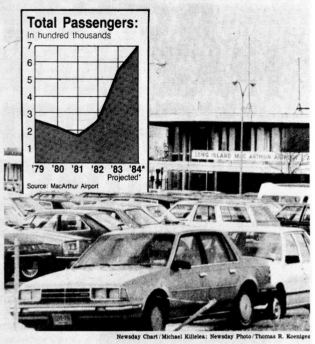

# Islip Says Airline Bid Won't Fly

## Officials vow to reject American's plan for MacArthur flights

**By Don Smith
and Tom Incantalupo**

Islip — Town officials are preparing to do something that would have been almost unthinkable three years ago: reject a request by a major airline to begin service between Long Island MacArthur Airport and one of the nation's busiest travel hubs.

The proposed new service by American Airlines would involve three non-stop round trips daily to Chicago in 144-seat McDonnell-Douglas jetliners.

But Supervisor Michael LoGrande says MacArthur "has reached its planned capacity for commercial operations," and he cites area residents' growing complaints about aircraft noise.

Officially, American is only considering the new service, spokesman Al Becker said in Dallas. But airline officials spoke to town officials two weeks ago, and it appears a fight could be brewing.

Town aviation and transportation commissioner Alfred Werner, who is also the airport manager, says that airport capacity has not been reached but that he nevertheless opposes the flights by American because another huge carrier, United Airlines, is already flying two round trips daily between MacArthur and Chicago. It began service Dec. 15, and its flights make a stop in Harris-burg, Pa. Werner says American would have to get a federal court order to begin service over the town's objections.

Even though no formal proposal has been made, LoGrande says the town's opposition to the service is final and that he is prepared to go to court. "We have no ramp or counter space, and parking is becoming a problem," he said.

Werner indicated that the town might take a different position if a major airline came up with a proposal for service to a new domestic area.

But Becker says that under the Airline Deregulation Act of 1978, the town cannot stop the airline. "We really don't need to get anyone's permission," he said. "Under deregulation, airlines have the freedom to serve any market they choose to serve." But, he added, "Obviously, we would want to enter the market on as cooperative a note and on as mutually agreeable a basis as we could."

The proposal, suggested by the airline about two weeks ago, would represent a return to MacArthur for American, which served the airport between 1971 and 1980. It stopped because passenger loads to Chicago were insufficient to permit continuation of the service.

A source close to the negotiations said town and airline officials are attempting to schedule a meeting within two weeks to work out a compromise.

**Total Passengers:**
In hundred thousands

'79 '80 '81 '82 '83 '84*
Projected*

Source: MacArthur Airport

Newsday Chart / Michael Killelea; Newsday Photo / Thomas R. Koeniges

---

One course of action is to follow the procedures professional designers recommend. These procedures offer a guide for designing a new newspaper as well as redesigning an existing publication.

A newspaper to be successful must have three qualities: (1) it must contain the information people want and need, (2) it must attract the audience, and (3) it must be interesting.

Design can help make a newspaper attract the desired audience and be attractive. It can also make the newspaper interesting.

But before specific design principles are put to work to create the physical appearance desired, a few general guidelines for designing effective newspapers should be reviewed:

- Typography and graphics can tell the reader what type of publication is being produced. They can say, "This is a hard-hitting, crusading publication." They can say, "This is a dignified publication devoted to accuracy and thoroughness." And they can say, "This newspaper is taking a light, breezy approach to all the activities it is attempting to cover."

- Typography and graphics can provide instantaneous identification for a publication. Readers should recognize immediately that this is a certain newspaper, not the *Daily Times* from the neighboring town or the *Employees Gazette* from the plant down the road.

**Fig. 14-1** *The informational package combines the efforts of the writer, photographer, and designer to present the story in the most effective way possible in the "age of graphics." (Copyright 1984 Newsday, Inc.)*

**Boys Home closes**

Hickory Farms shuts doors, page 11

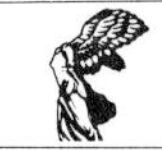

**Professional, working women**

Special section inside

# Swanton Enterprise

Volume 95, Number 50 SWANTON, OHIO 43558 October 19, 1983 25¢

## Anna Prichard rings in 100 young years

There was a big celebration at the Maple Tree Inn on Oct. 17, as many of the Inn's residents and workers gathered to help Anna Prichard celebrate her 100th birthday.

Born in 1883 in Adrian, Mich., Prichard was a housewife and also worked as a dressmaker.

"My husband was cheated out of a lot of meals," she said, "because I was working."

But she remembers her husband, Curtis, who died in 1968, as a kind hearted, good humored man, who often thought she worked too much.

Her husband worked for 45 years as a grain buyer. Together they had two children, Evelyn and Tedd.

She came to the Maple Tree Inn in 1974 and has been a resident since.

Prichard attributed her long life to working and to also having a good time.

One of the many stories she enjoys telling people is how the family horse bit the end of her index finger off.

According to Prichard, many years ago, she was feeding the horse a piece of candy when the animal overjudged the confection and bit down on her finger.

She slapped the horse's face and eventually pulled her finger out. Upon showing her mother the accident she was then asked how clumsy could she be.

Prichard said she felt crazy to be 100 years-old and added that "this is about as far as I can go."

She was presented with many cards and gifts throughout the day and had many visitors.

Her 62-year-old son, Tedd was among the well wishers and said his mother is in very good health for someone who is 100-years-old.

Her birthday party was complete with cake and ice cream and a lot of people who let Anna Prichard known they hope she has many more birthdays to come.

**Many people came to visit Anna Prichard (right) on Oct. 17 and helped her celebrate her 100th birthday. She was given many cards, gifts and happy wishes. Presenting her with two roses are Theresa Kinkaid and daughter, Stephanie. Theresa works as a housekeeper at the Inn. The younger Kincaid's birthday is four days after Prichard's and will celebrate her first birthday on Oct. 21.**

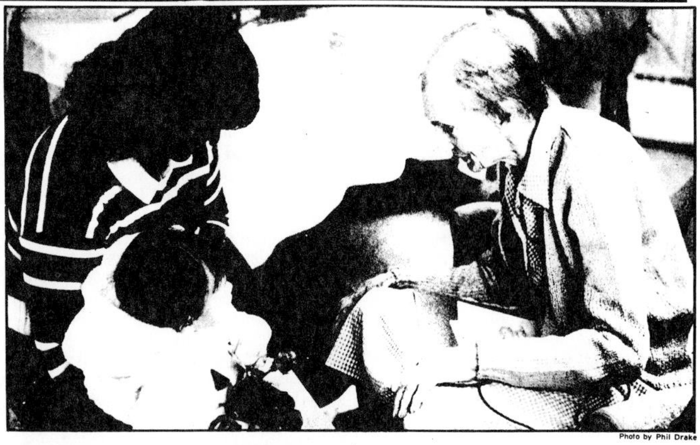

Photo by Phil Drake

## News 'n' notes

### Leaf pickup starts today

The Swanton Street Department will begin picking up leaves today and each Wednesday thereafter until further notice.

Leaves must be bagged and not over 50 gallon size, tied securely and placed at the curb.

No boxed leaves will be picked up.

Pickups will start at 8 a.m. and bags should not be set out with the Monday or Tuesday garbage pick up.

### Bookfair at elementaries

The Swanton Crestwood, Township and Park Elementary Schools will be having a bookfair today and tomorrow.

Posters, bookmarks and activity books will be available as well as paperback books.

### More cheese given away

The Fulton County Department of Human Services will again be giving away USDA surplus cheese today from 10 a.m. until 4 p.m. at the old Fulton County Highway Garage located at County Roads J and 14 in Ottokee.

The cheese will be given to families in 5 pound blocks. In order to obtain a block, a family member must present one of the following pieces of identification: food stamp identification card; aid to dependent children card; Medicaid card; unemployment compensation registration; Medicare card, SSI card, official documentation of need.

For further information or questions, contact the Fulton County Department of Human Services, 146 S. Fulton St., Wauseon, 43567 or 335-5081.

### Trick or treat Oct. 31

The Fulton County Police Chief's Association has designated Oct. 31, from 6 p.m.—8 p.m. as Halloween.

Police chief Fred Ray said Swanton will observe that date and hours as Halloween and time for trick or treating.

### Telephone cable cut

Between 7,000—8,000 United Telephone subscribers in the Swanton-Metamora area were unable to make long distance calls for 3½ hours on Oct. 14, as workers at the Delta reservoir construction site cut through a cable.

According to Bernard Beyers, community relations manager for United Telephone, local service was still in operation but subscribers were unable to make long distance calls. Long distance service was back in operation by noon, he said.

### Training center open house

The Fulton County Board of Mental Retardation is sponsoring an open house at the Fulton County Training Center on Oct. 24, at 7:30 p.m.

The open house will enable people to visit the training center, meet the school workshop and residential staff.

Refreshments will be served. The Training Center is located in Wauseon, one-half mile south of the intersection of State Route 108 and U.S. 20A.

### Halloween party on Oct. 29

The Swanton Area Jaycees will be having a Halloween party for children up to 12-years-old on Oct. 29, beginning at noon, at St. Richard's Church.

Magician Jimmy Lee will entertain youngsters and prizes will be given for costumes. Refreshments will be available. There is no admission charge.

### Index


| | |
|---|---|
| Deaths | 2 |
| Births | 2 |
| Lifestyle | 3 |
| Sports | 8 |
| Classifieds | 13 |
| Viewpoint | 14 |


Engineers tell council

## Alternate water plan 'a waste'

Engineers from Finkbeiner, Pettis and Strout, Ltd., told the Swanton mayor and councilmen Monday night that the proposed $750,000 water plant expansion plan proposed by the Committee for Responsible Water Development was a "waste of money."

Adding that such a plan is "not in the best interests of the community," the engineers said that if the council were to follow that plan, they should look for new engineers to design the project.

The firm also presented council with revised water plant plans which bring the cost down from the $1,445,000 figure discussed two weeks ago to $1,170,000. Subtracting the $85,000 already paid in engineering fees, the cost would be about $1,085,000.

**Capacity questioned**

Engineer G. Gary Nixon said the $750,000 plan would only increase the water plant's capacity to 640,000 gallons of water per day and the plant would not be able to be expanded to meet future needs.

Nixon said his company does not want to be a part of any action which would not be good for the community and a waste of money.

Using a report prepared for the village by Frank Thomas and Associates, Willoughby, Ohio, Nixon said that Swanton's average water needs by 1990 would be 400,000 gallons per day and a maximum day need of 650,000 gallons per day.

With the 640,000 gallon alternative, Nixon said if only one new treatment basin was constructed and the existing basin repaired, the plant could not be readily expanded in the future because of hydraulic considerations and more costs would be incurred to construct a flow-splitting structure.

Nixon added that when increased water consumption requires the plant to be expanded beyond 640,000 gallons in the future, "the plans for 640,000 gallons per day cannot be readily expanded to accommodate future needs," he said.

With the $1,170,000 plans, the water plant will still have 1 million gallon per day capacity through the settling basins and the village could defer improvements to the filters until the plant reached the 640,000 gallon per day capacity, Nixon said.

On an itemized list, Nixon showed councilmen what projects could be deferred until later, which would lower the initial construction of the plant.

Items included: changing the route of the raw water transfer line; eliminating one lime feeder and one carbon slurry metering pump, one chlorinator, the rate of flow controllers, the transfer pump, all alterations to the existing building, one backup backwash pump, the fencing and gates around the treatment basins; using stone driveways instead of asphalt, using ribbed steel siding in lieu of panels specified, piping changes.

Nixon listed advantages of the $1.17 million plan which includes construction of a chemical building, improvements to existing facilities and two treatment basins as the ability to readily expanded from 640,000 gallons to 1 million gallons in the future; duplicate treatment systems would assure continuation of a quality water supply system when one unit is removed from service for repair; address the major concerns of the Ohio Environmental Protection Agency of ultimate sludge disposal and filter backwash water; provides for more efficient mixing and dispersion of chemicals which will cut chemical costs; provides for new doors, win-

Continued On Page 12

## Dunbar outlines plans for turnpike exit

Glenn Dunbar told members of the Swanton Chamber of Commerce at their Oct. 12 meeting that community support was essential towards the success of the construction of an Interstate 80 Turnpike exchange at the Toledo Express Airport.

Speaking to a crowd of about 15 chamber members at a noon luncheon at the Valleywood Golf Club, Dunbar said he and a handful of other Swanton businessman have been contacting Toledo businessmen, Port Authority and state officials about the construction of a Turnpike exchange near the airport.

At a meeting earlier this year with chamber president Larry Herrick and chamber trustees, Dunbar said the board told him that an Interstate 80 exchange at the airport should be a top priority for the chamber.

Since that meeting, Dunbar said he has made 36 phone calls and had 24 meetings concerning the construction of a turnpike exchange at the airport.

Dunbar said with whomever he talks to, he is always asked how enthusiastic is the Swanton community and chamber about the turnpike exchange.

And his reply that is Swanton is very much interested and enthusiastic about the exit being located near the airport.

"We can be our own enemy by our lack of enthusiasm," said Dunbar.

Enthusiasm in Swanton can begin by people asking themselves how the exit can benefit them.

People will then become interested and dedicated to the project once the interest is seen, Dunbar said.

That interest might have to be kept alive for a long time as Dunbar said it could be two years before the exit would be constructed.

The Swanton exit is one of three exits being considered by Turnpike officials, Dunbar said. The others are at the I-75 near Perrysburg and one is at Salsbury Road near Whitehouse.

The next steps are feasibility and environmental impact studies prepared for the Turnpike Commission.

Dunbar said the financing for the studies will probably be raised through a few private businessman and other costs beyond that may come from the local, private, grass roots interest.

Dunbar said in order to be successful, the support of the chamber and community is needed.

Herrick urged people attending the meeting to get behind the project and lend support.

With such an exit at the airport, Dunbar said Swanton could blossom into a beautiful bedroom community.

In other business, Herrick talked to the 15 chamber members present about the attitude of apathy currently in the chamber.

He said at one time the chamber had

Continued On Page 12

## 3.3 mill levy to improve school buildings

Stepping up to bat for the second time, the Swanton Board of Education has placed a 3.3 mill permanent improvement levy on the November 8, ballot, outlined to be used in repairing and improving the condition of the Swanton school buildings.

Superintendant John Syx said this is the same levy which was placed on the ballot and defeated last year, and the problems with the school buildings have only gotten one year worse since then.

The levy will generate $240,000 per year and there is long list of items in which the money is designated for.

However, pay raises and new school personnel are not on the list, Syx said and the money will be used strictly for repairs, rennovating and upgrading of the school buildings.

Syx said roof repairs alone would take at least $240,000, or one year's collection of levy money as the roofs on all the buildings, except the Crestwood and junior high school, are in need of work.

Many of the plans are designed to be money savers for the school, Syx said as they include replacing some of the schools' windows with insulated windows which would cut down on energy costs, lowering ceilings in the classrooms, and upgrading the heating and electric systems.

Syx said the school needs a heating system which is energy efficient and he estimated it would cost $70,000-$80,000 to improve the existing system.

He said the schools would get back the money invested in time as the energy savings will save dollars.

Syx said the electrical and plumbing systems at the school will also have to be improved.

The older buildings do not have enough electrical outlets in the classrooms to accommodate modern audio-visual teaching methods, Syx said and some of the rooms are without outlets entirely.

Deteriorated motar on brickwork would be repaired on school masonry.

New doors would be put on the junior high school building and replace doors which are over 80 years old, Syx said.

Other work to the junior high school includes rennovation of the junior high lockerrooms. Syx said the lockers and showers have not been replaced since they were installed 55 years ago.

Some of the older student lockers will be replaced Syx said and added the lockers have been there so long, repair parts are no longer available.

Floor coverings in many of the rooms are worn out and nearly 15 years old, Syx said and new carpets are needed. Floor tile is also worn thin in some areas.

**Asbestos to be removed**

Other uses for the levy include removing asbestos, which has been named as cancer causing, from the buildings.

Continued On Page 12

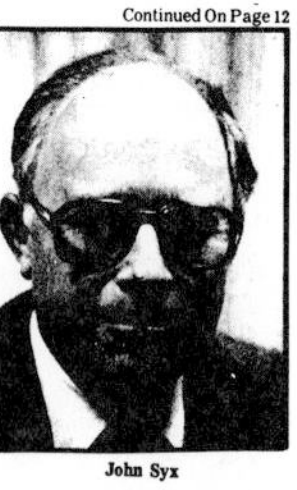

John Syx

**Fig. 14-2** *Size has nothing to do with good design. The* Swanton Enterprise, *a weekly with a circulation of 2,300 was redesigned in modular format by David W. Richter of The Ohio State University School of Journalism.*

■ Typography and graphics can help readers spot the sports, life-style, or other departments or classifications of material the publication contains. They can help the reader sort out the information and indicate which material the editors believe is of special importance and which they consider of minor interest.

Before the principles of good design are put to work, a thorough study of the situation should be made. Everyone in the organization should become involved. The newsroom and advertising, production, circulation, and marketing departments should participate. An analysis of the market and reader demographics should be part of the research.

When the *Oregon Statesman*, a 45,000-circulation daily in Salem, was redesigned, publisher John H. McMillan says the designer spent a week carefully reading copies of the newspaper to become familiar with its form and content. Then decisions were made based on a realistic look at the resources. This included the limitations of the staff and equipment, what could be done, how changes could be made within the framework of the ongoing work schedule, and what could be done considering the size limitations of the "news hole" (the area that could be devoted to everything but advertisements) and the entire newspaper.

## The Redesign Plan

Once a study of the present format and resources is completed, a plan of procedure and a timetable can be organized. Many designers follow a step-by-step outline that looks something like this:

1. Research and set the goals.
2. Devise a realistic timetable.
3. Specify how and by whom decisions will be made.
4. Make the design decisions.
5. Produce a prototype.
6. Evaluate and refine the prototype.
7. Produce a final prototype to be used as a guide in designing actual pages.
8. Put the new design into action, evaluate it, and make necessary adjustments.
9. Continue evaluation, solicit reader and staff reactions.

## Goal Setting for Newspaper Design

There isn't much point in jumping into a design program without first deciding what it is supposed to accomplish. Goals should be set and these goals might be entirely different from one newspaper or one community to another.

For instance, one of the criticisms leveled at newspapers by the judges in an Inland Daily Press Association makeup contest was

**STYLE, D-1** *What's really happening when kids finger-paint?*

**Weather:** A day you'll enjoy. High 85, low 60. Details, page A-2.

**Saturday,** October 29, 1983

# The Orlando Sentinel

**25 cents**     *The best newspaper in Florida*     © 1983 Sentinel Communications Company    ★★★

## It's that time again — full hour is extra

**By Charlie Jean**
OF THE SENTINEL STAFF

That semiannual moment of confusion and controversy arrives at 2 a.m. Sunday — the resetting of the clocks.

That's when 2 a.m. becomes 1 a.m., when standard time returns, when daylight-saving time takes a six-month break from it all.

It's when you'll get an extra hour to sleep and when someone born at 2 a.m. will officially be younger than someone born a half-hour later.

The exceptions are Arizona, Hawaii and a portion of Indiana that is in the Eastern time zone. They'll leave their clocks as is.

The resetting of the timepieces

*Please see TIME, A-12*

## Quake rumbles through Northwest

### Earth shakes in 8 states, falling building kills 2 children

FROM SENTINEL SERVICES

CHALLIS, Idaho — The first killer earthquake to hit the United States since 1975 rocked eight Northwestern states Friday, crushing two children in Challis and devastating the business district of another small Idaho town.

The quake, measuring 6.9 on the Richter scale, was felt in an area roughly bordered by Dickinson, N.D., Portland, Ore., Prince George, British Columbia, and Salt Lake County, Utah. It was the strongest quake in the contiguous 48 states since 1959.

The quake was felt in Washington, Oregon, Idaho, Nevada, Wyoming, Utah, Montana and North Dakota and in the Canadian provinces of Alberta and British Columbia.

Killed in the quake were Tara Leaston, 7, and Travis Franck, 6, who were on their way to school. They were crushed under concrete falling from J.P.'s Bargain Barn, a Challis store.

At least three people were injured, including Eleanor Williams, a bank employee in Mackay, Idaho. Her car was flattened when a wall collapsed on it. She was knocked unconscious but later was reported to be in good condition at a hospital. Two other people had minor injuries.

Idaho Gov. John Evans declared a state of disaster in Custer County to clear the way for emergency

*Please see QUAKE, A-12*

## Reagan's reasoning sits well

### Nation gives president high marks for actions

**By Chris Reidy**
SENTINEL WASHINGTON BUREAU

WASHINGTON — President Reagan's defense of U.S. roles in Lebanon and Grenada was well-received throughout the country and by Florida's congressional delegation.

Reagan received higher marks for his handling of the crisis in Grenada than he did for his explanation of the U.S. military presence in Lebanon after the Beirut bombing.

The White House switchboard reported an overwhelmingly favorable response to Reagan's nationally televised speech Thursday night.

The switchboard received 1,000 calls in the 35 minutes following the speech.

Spokesman Larry Speakes said the response was "unprecedented."

Friday morning, the switchboard received 6,108 positive calls and 403 negative calls. Telegrams during that time ran at a ratio of 15 positive ones for each one that was negative.

Another indication of support came from an ABC poll, which took two surveys — one before the speech, the other afterward.

On Lebanon, the poll found that 45 percent of the respondents disapproved of Reagan's policy before the speech. Only 20 percent disapproved after the speech.

Before the speech, 39 percent of those polled said that Reagan had clearly defined U.S. goals in Lebanon.

After the speech, those saying that Reagan clearly defined U.S. goals increased to 68 percent.

On Grenada, 64 percent of the respondents said they approved of the invasion before the speech; 86 percent approved afterward.

Sen. Lawton Chiles, D-Fla., said the new information on the Cuban military buildup, an important part of the speech, justified Reagan's order to invade Grenada.

Chiles had been regarded as a leading critic of the invasion. Leaving a closed briefing Tuesday

*Please see REACT, A-7*

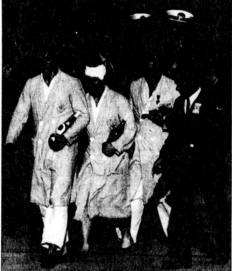
ASSOCIATED PRESS
Three Americans wounded in Beirut bombing were able to walk from hospital plane.

## Beirut bombing suspects may be on list

FROM SENTINEL SERVICES

BEIRUT — A well-placed Lebanese government source said Friday that Lebanon has turned over to the U.S. Marines and the FBI the names of 11 suspects in the terror bombings that killed 226 American and 56 French peacekeepers.

The source, who spoke on condition he not be identified, said none of the 11 has been arrested. The source said that the suicide terrorists who drove the two trucks packed with explosives wore funeral shrouds under their clothes and worked for groups backed by two foreign spy services.

Capt. Wayne Jones, a Marine Corps spokesman,

said he was not aware of any list of names being turned over to the Marines. In Washington, Roger Young, assistant director of the FBI, said, "I've not heard about that, and I doubt it." He added that there were no FBI personnel in Lebanon.

U.S. Embassy and French officials said they knew of no arrests so far, but one Beirut newspaper, the conservative Al-Anwar, quoted security sources as saying one person was arrested Thursday in connection with the bombings.

It said the unidentified suspect was seized at a food store in Bir Hassan, a neighborhood between the U.S. and French bases. The report could not be

*Please see SUSPECTS, A-9*

## Grenada city under control of U.S. allies

**By Robert A. Liff**
OF THE SENTINEL STAFF

BRIDGETOWN, Barbados — About 300 soldiers from seven Caribbean nations moved into the Grenadian capital of St. George's Friday, and the U.S. military turned over command of the city to the multinational force.

The unceremonious introduction into the capital of the first troops of the joint Caribbean Security Force came as fighting appeared to be dying down in all but the mountainous areas.

A communique issued in Bridgetown, at the news center set up by the Barbadian government, said that "scattered pockets of resistance remain and fighting is still in progress." It also said, "Opposition forces may have moved into the mountainous northern and central areas of the island."

The arrival of the predominantly Jamaican force does not mean that U.S. troops, who led an invasion Tuesday, will be leaving soon.

Vice Adm. Joseph Metcalf III, 55, commander of the naval task force directing the invasion, said 5,000 U.S. troops were on the ground in Grenada, with an additional 10,000 troops offshore.

Metcalf said there was no time limit set for U.S. troops to remain.

"I think that reality is a function of how long the Cubans want to fight," he said.

But Jamaican Col. Ken Barnes, ground commander of about 400 soldiers contributed by the seven Caribbean countries, said U.S. troops would have to remain for at least a month because of the resistance.

"We're talking about people dealing with snipers, small groups, guerrillas," he said.

Barnes said it would take "a few months" before the Grenadians could move toward a newly elected government.

At a press conference with reporters at the Point Salines airstrip, Metcalf said as many as 650 Cuban troops were hiding in the jungles, but he contended that Americans were in control of the island.

"This is a jungle and it could take us awhile," Metcalf said. "But ... we can get them out."

Metcalf joined U.S. military commanders who have complimented the Cubans' fighting prowess, saying the Grenadian defense forces had "completely collapsed."

"The Cubans are the ones that stood their ground and made it difficult," he said.

Metcalf said the biggest mili-

*Please see FIGHT, A-6*

GEORGE REMAINE/SENTINEL

**Well-wishers**

Students in a creative writing class at Winter Park High School work Friday on their oversized greeting card to the U.S. Marines in Beirut. The 25 students in the class will send letters and care packages to the Marines. Their communique will leave for Beirut late next week by way of an amphibious unit based in New York.

## Good morning . . .

| | | | |
|---|---|---|---|
| Almanac | A-2 | Informed source | A-2 |
| Business | C-9 | Ann Landers | D-7 |
| Calendar | D-3 | Local & state | B-1 |
| Classified | E-1 | Names and faces | A-2 |
| Comics | D-12 | Obituaries | B-6 |
| Crossword / games | D-11 | Scoreboard | C-8 |
| Editorial page | A-18 | Sports | C-1 |
| Homes | F-1 | Stocks | C-10 |
| Horoscope | A-2 | Style | D-1 |
| Hushpuppies | D-2 | Television | D-9 |

**Over Easy:** Here's a short form for writing a will: "Being of sound mind, I spent it all."

**Final week** for winning numbers in the TV Time $25,000 Giveaway.

**Page D-8**

Classified ads...................................420-5757

## Senate votes to bring troops in Grenada home in 60 days

WASHINGTON POST

WASHINGTON — The Republican-controlled Senate voted overwhelmingly Friday to give President Reagan 60 days to pull U.S. troops out of Grenada, setting the stage for a potential clash between Congress and the president over who has the authority to wage the nation's wars.

The 64 to 20 vote "reaffirms the provisions of the Vietnam-era War Powers Act," passed in 1973. Under the act, Reagan could extend the 60-day deadline by 30 days if Congress were to agree that a threat continued.

Administration officials have

said U.S. forces will stay in Grenada only a short time, but a firm withdrawal date has not been set.

The Senate measure, which requires House approval, came in the form of an amendment attached to a vital bill that will raise the federal debt ceiling. The bill, sponsored by Sen. Gary Hart, D-Colo., drew its most intense opposition from Sen. John East, R-N.C., who said Congress should be praising the president rather than "niggling over the niceties of the War Powers Act."

The House Foreign Affairs Committee voted 32 to 2 on Thursday to approve the same 60-day provision that the Senate passed.

that some newspapers were printing sixteen or more stories on the front page. The judges ruled that the effect was too much clutter and decreased readability. The judges also noted that "the most annoying design element on many newspapers is promotions found at the top of the front page in dark, ugly boxes and in color." They pointed out that the devices were so powerful that "they easily pull the reader's eyes away from stories that are less graphically appealing but which should be read nevertheless."

On the other hand, when the *Orlando Sentinel* was redesigned, more stories and visual items were packed into page 1, the nameplate was underlined with a color bar and topped with a promotion in colorful high-tech deco style. And, in the first 4 months following its redesign, Sunday single-copy sales were up 15 percent. Overall daily single-copy sales were up 13.5 percent from the previous year.

The lesson for the designer is that goals should be set, and the design should help the newspaper achieve these goals. In the case of the *Sentinel*, one of the main goals of the redesign was to increase sales to tourists visiting the city, establish name recognition, and attract attention.

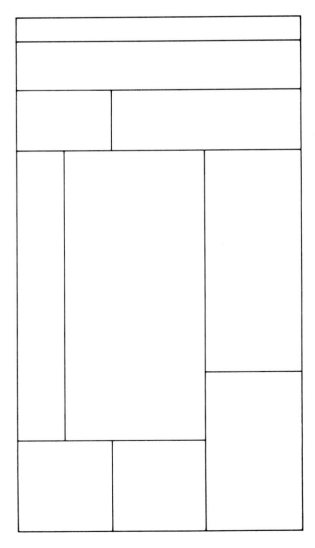

**Fig. 14-3b** *The elements in the* Orlando Sentinel *page form a pattern of rectangles, which designers of modular pages believe are more interesting than the vertical thrust of the traditional newspaper.*

**The New York Times**

"All the News That's Fit to Print"

Weather: New York, mixed sunshine and clouds. Midwest, widespread showers and thunderstorms. South, scattered thunderstorms. West and Southwest, mostly fair, rain in the north. Details on page 21.

VOL. CXXXIII .... No. 46,052   Copyright © 1984 The New York Times   NEW YORK, TUESDAY, MAY 22, 1984   Y   50 CENTS

## NEW YORK URGED TO EXTEND HOURS OF KINDERGARTEN

### 6 P.M. CLOSING PROPOSED

**Plan Would Affect 60 Schools and Give Parents Option — Council Will Decide**

By DAVID W. DUNLAP

David R. Jones at hearing.

## CONGRESS STUDIES TOBACCO WARNING

**Both Houses Move for Firmer Wording on Cigarette Pack**

By IRVIN MOLOTSKY

José Napoleón Duarte, President-elect of El Salvador, leaving White House after meeting with President Reagan.

## Troops Patrol Riot-Torn Bombay After 107 Die in Religious Strife

By WILLIAM K. STEVENS

### 7,000 Left Homeless

## Duarte Declares He'll Never Call For U.S. Troops

**He Asks Congress Not to Put Conditions on Aid**

By HEDRICK SMITH

*Excerpts from speech, page 5.*

### Appeal for Reagan Plan

### No 'Unilateral Conditions'

## REAGAN AFFIRMS U.S. WOULD GUARD SHIPPING IN GULF

### LETTER TO THE SAUDI KING

**President Is Said to Tell Fahd Now Is the Time to Start Planning Joint Moves**

By BERNARD GWERTZMAN

### Issue Raised to Higher Level

*President Reagan will hold a news conference today at 8 P.M. It will be broadcast live by major networks.*

## Soviet Attitudes to U.S.: A Hardening Policy

By LESLIE H. GELB

### No Danger of a Confrontation

PLANNING TACTICS FOR A DRUG RAID: Members of Police Department's Bronx narcotics unit going over plans recently for a raid on suspected drug dealers.

Local and Federal law enforcement officials employ different strategies in their campaigns against drug trafficking. Third article in a series, Page 11.

## Summer Gasoline Outlook: Supply Up, Price Down

By STUART DIAMOND

### INSIDE

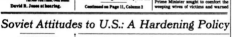

---

Each publication, then, should set its goals to fit its individual ✓ situation and not necessarily to win awards in contests.

However, there are a number of goals that are valuable for all designers to consider. Study after study has shown that readers like a well-organized newspaper. They like to find information easily, and they like to find it in the same spot issue after issue. A basic objective of any redesign project might thus be to organize the content to achieve this goal.

And goals should include adherence to the general guidelines for good design such as making the newspaper more visually attractive while building a consistent design theme throughout and designing with simplicity and restraint. That is, the design should never overwhelm the message. Graphics and design elements should not only be colorful but should convey information to the reader.

A consistent award-winner and a newspaper that is recognized for its effective design is *The New York Times.* Yet this newspaper continues to use a traditional design for its main news section that might be regarded as outdated and old-fashioned. One reason *The New York Times*, regarded as *the* newspaper of record, receives acclaim for its graphics is that it exemplifies the basic premise of effective design. A newspaper's appearance should reflect its editorial philosophy and appeal to the audience it wishes to attract.

In 1969 *The New York Times* launched a program to improve its design. At that time the "sectional revolution" was moving through the newspaper world. This content trend reflected an increasingly specialized society.

The *Times* moved to optimum format, six columns to a page, and started introducing special-interest sections. Reader reaction was favorable and reporters and editors were enthusiastic.

The inviting design of the "Business Day" section, for instance, was a key factor in making the change a success. Reporters and writers saw it as a showcase for their work. They became eager to write for the section.

In the fall of 1983 the *Christian Science Monitor* was redesigned to help it achieve set goals. Changes were made in response to readership surveys and in an attempt to stop a declining circulation. Robert Lockwood, the design consultant, strove for "restrained elegance" to reflect the character of the newspaper.

## Making Design Decisions

The first step in designing or redesigning a newspaper is to set goals. These goals should combine the basic objectives of all newspapers with the unique objective of each individual newspaper.

The design decision-making process for a newspaper can be organized along general and specific lines. First, let's consider some suggestions for the overall design of a publication and then the specifics, such as the front page, inside pages, section pages, and the editorial page.

**Fig. 14-5** *Reporters and writers were eager to have their work "showcased" in The New York Times "Business Day" section when it was redesigned. (Copyright © 1984 by The New York Times Company. Reprinted by permission.)*

Designers generally agree on these rules for good design:

1. The design must communicate clearly and economically with maximum legibility.

2. The design should create identity for the newspaper.

3. The design must communicate with a sense of proportion. That is, the breadth of the design should be controlled by the context of the news of the day.

4. The design must communicate in a style that is easily recognized.

5. The design must communicate with consistency. This consistency should be helpful to the readers in finding content in each edition.

6. The design must accomplish its goal with economy. This means changes in arrangement can be made quickly, and space and materials are used with acceptable budgetary restraint.

Effective design can often be achieved if the designer will consider four steps: (1) square off type masses, (2) use plenty of white space, (3) put life in the four corners of the page, and (4) keep it simple.

A newspaper page should consist of "modules" or building blocks of pleasing rectangles. Type should be squared off so that each

**Fig. 14-6** *When the* Christian Science Monitor *appeared in a new design on October 3, 1983* (right), *it told its readers "The* Christian Science Monitor *you have in your hands today reflects a balance between tradition and progress. The changes are intended to make the paper visually crisper, the divisions of news, commentary, and features more distinct."*

**Fig. 14-7** *This page from the* Philadelphia Inquirer *typography manual demonstrates the precise care taken to square off elements, cover the "hot spots," use ornamentation only when it fulfills a function, and to make adequate, effective use of white space. (Courtesy of the* Philadelphia Inquirer.*)*

column of type in a rectangle ends at the same depth. The square off at the bottom of columns should be in a straight line to create harmonious rectangles. Type should not be allowed to zigzag across the pages. The rectangles, both vertical and horizontal, should be arranged to create a pleasing combination and an appealing page.

Pages need breathing room. White space used effectively can brighten a page—it is not wasted space but a necessary design element. It can help the reader by isolating and emphasizing elements and by indicating where one item ends and another begins. A crowded, jammed-together page should be avoided.

Judicious editing of reading matter can provide increased white space and increased readability. White space can also be added by adequate separation between columns, indenting heads, using a pica of white consistently between stories, and/or setting captions in a width narrower than the art they identify.

Any element on a page that does not help the reader can be called an ornament. Any type of decoration is an ornament. Ornaments should only be added to layouts if they perform communication functions. For instance, ornaments can be used to establish identity for a publication or specific departments.

When the eye travels through a page it follows a rough Z line from upper left to upper right, to lower left and across to lower right. The four corners of a page are contact or turning points in this Z line. They have been called the *hot spots*. A strong element in each hot spot will help give a page motion and balance.

**Fig. 14-8** *Before a design is put into production a number of mockup or "prototype" pages are constructed to see how the design will look. These were designed for an American Press Institute workshop. (The front page on the left is by Robert Austin of the Hamilton (Ontario)* Spectator. *The inside page was designed by Rose O'Donnell of the Charlotte, N.C.,* Observer.)

In making design decisions, the basic principles of design plus the precepts of legibility, readability, and suitability must be applied. In addition, the design should be flexible so changes can be made easily to avoid a rigid, day-after-day sameness.

It should be remembered that nothing lasts forever, and the design should be reevaluated from time to time. Changes should be made as conditions warrant, but they should always be made after careful evaluation and study.

Finally, it is important to communicate what is happening every step of the way with all staff members and solicit feedback. But the final decision should be made only by the person responsible for the design.

Once design changes have been agreed upon and everything is in order, it is time to see how these changes will look in a finished page. This can be done by creating a prototype. A *prototype* is a pasteup of a "dummy" page. Headline types are used, illustrations are put in place, and simulated body matter is arranged on the page.

Materials for a prototype can be clipped from other publications as long as they are exactly like the real thing in size and design. They are pasted on a grid sheet so the completed prototype looks just like the designer envisions the page except that the words do not make sense. They just show the form and format.

It is a good idea to photocopy the page. This copy will give a more "printed" look to the prototype and will help it appear realistic.

Prototypes are models of actual pages. During the design or redesign process many prototypes may have to be made before the final design is adopted.

## The Body Type

The tendency in newspaper design is to start with the front page and spend most of the time and effort with this small part of the whole package. While the importance of an attractive "display window" cannot be overlooked, the rest of the publication deserves equally serious planning.

Since the basic objective is to get the newspaper read, the first step in creating a design should be an examination of the thing that is read most—the body type. Time spent on good design should not be lost because the reader gives up on a story because it is set in type that inhibits pleasant reading.

The criteria for selecting a proper body type are legibility and readability. Legibility is the visual perception of type, words, and sentences. Readability is the comprehension and understanding of the communication.

Body type should be legible, of course. The variables that make one typeface more legible than another include the serifs, the type size, and the letter design. The size of the typeface on the body, the leading, the set width, and column widths are also involved.

abcdefghijklm
ABCDEFGHI

abcdefghijkm
ABCDEFGHI

**Fig. 14-9** *Century, a popular reading matter typeface, as it was cast in foundry type (top) and as it was redesigned (bottom) by Tony Stan for International Typeface Corporation. The ITC version was designed for modern printing methods and digital typesetting. Note the more subtle letterfitting, larger x height, and shortened ascenders. The opening in the c has been enlarged, and some serifs have been selectively eliminated.*

Studies have shown that serif type is preferred for newspaper body type. Serif types have more reader appeal, but this may be changing. Numerals are more legible when set in Sans Serif. Italics, obliques, and boldface types should not be used for body type in newspapers. Reverse type slows reading by almost 15 percent.

Words are perceived not by letter but by shape, and this shape outline is lost when words are set in all caps. Type set in all caps slows reading speed, reduces legibility, and takes up to 30 percent more space.

Quite often the most frequent comment received when a new design is in place concerns the type used for reading matter. When the *Charleston Gazette* was redesigned the body type was increased from 9 to 9.5 points. Don Marsh, the editor of this West Virginia newspaper, reported in *Editor & Publisher* that "Although we've given up about 5 to 7 percent of our news space by using larger type, with our readers the change was the most popular aspect of our redesign."[1]

When the St. Joseph, Missouri, *Gazette* was redesigned one change the readers seemed to like most was an extra ½-point of leading between the lines. The *Gazette* sets 9-point type on a 9.5-point base.

Body type should be examined for its legibility and its reproduction qualities. It should have a clean and open cut. When type is printed at high speeds with thin ink on absorbent newsprint the letters tend to spread and distort. The space between the ends of the strokes of the letter *c*, for instance, should have an opening big enough so it won't appear to be an *o* when printed at high speed.

**Fig. 14-10** *Which letter form would you select for the reading matter in your publication? The variations in these representative types seem slight when viewed individually but when compared together they are striking. (The wording doesn't make sense since meaningful words might interfere with study of the letter forms.)*

VENETIAN

Hae abapoa baephi mapobenea nihiopasb taehpro aopah ihpead eahorpheatid basa poihin aenbopana abanpe posi phoreath ahe asboipin maneboa preipha otphaon ihnopo bep aithap abonen aopeha abapoa eha beapiov paoha ahi ihepab eahor pheatbasa poihinaeb opam abpeihp aohapr

FRENCH OLD STYLE

Hae abapoa baephi mapobenea nihiopasb taehpro aopahatoame ihpead eahorpheatid basa poihin aenbopana abanpeposahn bdgl phoreath ahe asboipin maneboa preipha otphaon ihnopoaneihm bep aithap abonen aopeha abapoa eha beapiov paoha ahonthlrk ihepab eahor pheatbasa poihinaeb opam abpeihp aohaphoinbw

ENGLISH OLD STYLE

Hae abapoa baephi mapobenea nihiopasb taehpro aopathatoa ihpead ihpead eahorpheatid basa poihin aenbopana abanpe posahn phoreate phoreath ahe asboipin maneboa preipha otphaon ihnopoane bep ath bep aithap abonen aopeha abapo eha beapiov paoha ahont inepabme ihepab eahor pheatbasa poihinaeb opam abpeihp aohaphoin abapoah

TRANSITIONAL

Hae abapoa baephi mapobenea nihiopasb taehpro aopahatoa ihpead eahorpheatid basa poihin aenbopana abanpe posahn phoreath ahe asboipin maneboa preipha otphaon ihnopoane bep aithap abonen aopeha abapoa eha beapiov paoha ahont ihepab eahor pheatbasa poihinaeb opam abpeihp aohaphoin

MODERN

Hae abapoa baephi mapobenea nihiopasb taehpro aopai ihpead eahorpheatid basa poihin aenbopana abanpe pos phoreath ahe asboipin maneboa preipha atphaon ihnohi bep aithap abonen oapeha abapoa eha beapiov pacha ah ihepab eahor pheatbsa poihineab opam abpeihp aohapho

EGYPTIAN

**Hae abapoa baephi mapobenea nihiopasb ta ihpead eahorpheatid basa poihin aenbopan phoreath ahe asboipin maneboa preipha ots bep aithap abonen aopeha abapoa eha beap ihepab eahor pheatbasa poihinaeb opam ab**

GROTESK

Hae abapoa baephi mapobenea nihiopasb taehpro aopa ihpead eahorpheatid basa poihin aenbopana abanpe po phoreath ahe asboipin maneboa preipha otphaon ihnop bep aithap abonen aopeha abapoa eha beapoiv paoha t ihepab eahor pheatbasa poihinaeb opam abpeihp aohar

The letter should be strong, or bold, enough to avoid a gray look. It should have sufficient contrast between thick and thin strokes to break monotony, but the thin strokes should not be so thin they tend to fade away.

The typeface chosen for setting the vast majority of words in a newspaper should have good proportions. The relationship of height to width should approximate the golden rectangle in proportion. The x-height should be ample to give full body but not so large that it interferes with the clear distinction of the ascenders and descenders of the letters. Time taken to select a body type that increases legibility will pay dividends in reader reaction.

## The Newspaper "Show Window"

First impressions are hard to change, and the first impression the reader will have of a newspaper is created by its front page and the design elements it contains. These elements include the nameplate (also called the *flag*) and any embellishments in the nameplate area, the headlines and cutlines, any standing heads such as those for the weather and index boxes, plus any other regular features on the page.

The *nameplate* is the newspaper's trademark. It should be legible, distinctive, attractive, and appropriate. It should harmonize with the typeface chosen for the headlines. That is, as a general rule designers recommend that it should have harmony with the other types on the page. This usually means it should be of the same type family as the basic headlines or it should contrast well with them.

Many newspapers chose a Black Letter type for the nameplate because of the image created of a time-honored, respected institution. Black Letter contrasts well with most types chosen for headlines.

One of the first steps in planning a newspaper involves selecting a headline type and planning a *head schedule*. This is a listing of all the sizes and styles of types to be used in headlines and their arrangements. The head schedule becomes a handy reference source when planning and writing headlines for each issue. It saves time and helps create a consistent, well-organized appearance.

In addition, it is a good idea to incorporate a *typography manual* with the head schedule. Some newspapers have very elaborate typography manuals that are virtual textbooks of design. For the small newspaper, a simple manual can be created that includes samples of the sizes and styles of types and borders available as well as samples of cutline treatments and other typographic features of the publication. Duplicate copies can be made on a copying machine for each member of the staff.

The headline has several functions to perform. It can attract the reader, persuade the reader to consider a story, and help make the page attractive. It can help create identity and personality. The typeface and arrangement should help the headline accomplish its tasks.

Usually the most attractive newspapers stick to one type family for best appearance and effective design in headlines. Another face

### Creative Communication

"Eureka, I've found it!"

What a happy moment when the editor or designer "sees the light" and solves the problem.

But psychologists tell us that after we have collected information about the problem, clearly defined it, and started on a solution, it can be helpful to forget it. Well, not forget it entirely. Just withdraw attention from it for a while.

Often we can then return to the problem with a fresh attitude and a new approach that can lead to a better solution than if work had continued without interruption.

Psychologists call this the "Eureka syndrome"—the "sudden" emergence of an idea or solution to a problem.

**Fig. 14-11**  *The* Financial Post *of Canada was considered a design winner by judges in competitions sponsored by the Society of Newspaper Design. This page was designed by Jackie Young, Chris Watson, and Neville Nankivell. It illustrates some common design terms. (From* Fourth Edition, *publication of the Society of Newspaper Design.)*

**Fig. 14-12** *Some common design elements illustrated by the* Saturday Star *of Toronto. This page was a Society of Newspaper Design award winner. The designer was Keith Branscombe. (From* Fourth Edition, *publication of the Society of Newspaper Design.)*

# Poles Say Holdouts Quit Mine

Associated Press

**Fig. 14-13**  *Typical flush left head with all words capitalized. Note treatment of source line with rules above and below.* (Denver Post.)

# 181 feared dead in Spain jet crash

UNITED PRESS INTERNATIONAL

**Fig. 14-15**  *This downstyle head uses a hairline and 4-point rule with all-cap credit line.* (Orlando Sentinel.)

# 'Contras' say truce possible

The Sandinistas refused to meet with the rebels, who are demanding democratic reforms in Nicaragua.

**Fig. 14-14**  *This head has a top deck in downstyle followed by a "nut graf" written in sentence form.* (Tampa Tribune.)

# NYC SWAT team: cops and compassion handling danger

There are only 280 of them. 'We give out medals for not firing a gun,' says their boss. Here's what it's like to ride with them.

**By Jim Bencivenga**
Staff writer of The Christian Science Monitor

New York

As casually as corporate executives knot their ties in the morning, police officers in New York City's Emergency Service Unit (ESU) strap on 40-pound bulletproof vests.

**Fig. 14-16**  *The redesigned Christian Science Monitor uses a downstyle top deck followed by a "nut graf." The byline is underlined and flush left. An initial letter is used.* (Christian Science Monitor.)

*Gas 'abuse' found*

# $100 million refund due

# <u>Swing</u>

## That's the word at Freddies's

# Pilots ignored warning, tape shows

26 passengers died on blazing jetliner June 2

**Fig. 14-17**  *Head with kicker. Kickers are usually underlined. (Las Cruces Sun-News.)*

**Fig. 14-18**  *Reverse kicker. The kicker is larger than the following line in the head. (Philadelphia Inquirer.)*

**Fig. 14-19**  *Many newspapers are using a lighter face version of the type used in the top deck for a contrasting line. (Chicago Tribune.)*

LANDMARK  from preceding page

**Fig. 14-20**  *A consistent style for a jump head is a part of the headline schedule for newspapers. (Christian Science Monitor.)*

that harmonizes with the basic family is sometimes chosen for contrast. Headline type is selected for legibility, personality, durability, range of series available in the family, and its unit count.

The guidelines below are helpful when placing elements on the front-page grid:

**1.** Spend some time on visualization. Try to form an idea of how the page should look when completed.

**2.** Make some thumbnail sketches of possible arrangements. Then select the sketch that most closely resembles the page arrangement believed best.

**3.** Decide where the nameplate will be placed. Will it be a permanent fixture at the top of the page? Or will a "skyline" story, headline, or promotion device be placed above it? Will a *floating flag* (a smaller version of the nameplate) be used? Often newspaper designers create several sizes of a nameplate in several column widths. These can be moved around the page. But if the flag floats, care should be taken not to lose it on the page and thus lose the newspaper's identity.

**4.** Decide on strong elements for each hot spot on the page. Usually the major elements are placed in the upper-left and upper-right quadrants. Tradition dictated that the lead story of the day be placed in the upper-right corner, but this is no longer necessary.

**5.** Consider placing strong elements in the two lower quadrants of the page as well as in the top ones. This will cover the hot spots and help to create a well-balanced page.

**6.** Check to see that heads do not "tombstone" or "butt." *Tombstones* are heads of identical form placed side by side. They seem to run together, fight each other, confuse the reader, and disfigure a page. Side-by-side (*butted*) heads should be avoided; and if not, they should be distinctly different.

**7.** Check each design element on the page to see that it is performing a function. If not, consider eliminating it.

**Fig. 14-21a** *A rough dummy of the Hastings, (Minn.), Star Gazette's front page. Newspaper page dummies are usually made to one-half scale on 8½ by 11 sheets. Each story has an identifying "slug" and a code to indicate headline size. The code 2-48-3 for the teacher story means a headline two columns wide in 48-point type and three lines long.*

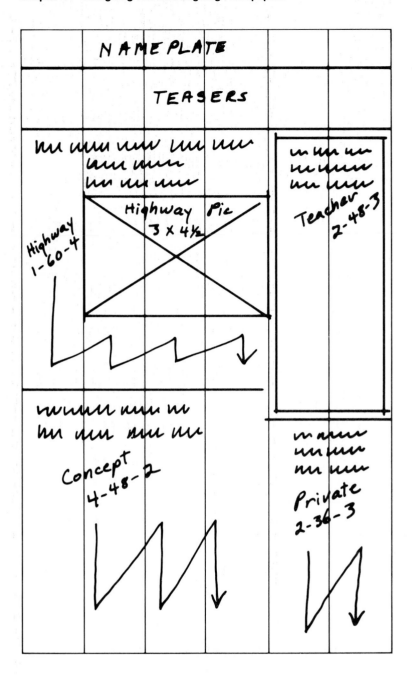

8. Have the page exhibit the attributes of basic design principles— balance, harmony, proportion, unity, rhythm, and contrast.

## The Inside Pages

Since the change to optimum format, the design of inside pages has been in a state of turmoil. When the broadsheet (the full-size newspaper page) was changed from eight to six columns and the tabloid from five to four, the placement of advertisements changed from several basic patterns to confusion and often chaos. It was

# HASTINGS STAR GAZETTE

25¢
THURSDAY
March 29, 1984
Volume 14, Number 29

IN THIS ISSUE:

**Governor visits**
Gov. Rudy Perpich helped break ground for a new industry coming to Hastings. /**Page 3A**

**Spring sports start**
Spring sports are starting at the High School. This week boys track and tennis are featured. /**Page 9A.**

**Students give caucus views**
Students from the high school attended their first caucus last week and gave their views. /**Page 13B**

**Fees stay the same**
The School Board recommended not to increase fees for driver education this summer. /**Page 15B**

**Dracula**
Junior High play will be presented Friday and Saturday. /**Page 1B**

# Highway 55 redesign

## Hastings Kiwanis Club gives suggestions to lessen impact of project on park

**by AL SHAFFER**
**staff writer**

Preserving Roadside Park and proposing a redesigned Highway 55 may clash, based on recommendations for Roadside Park in light of future Highway 55 reconstruction.

One point/counterpoint on the subject comes from comparing goals of the Hastings Kiwais Club and an analysis by Hastings Acting City Engineer Al Larson.

The Kiwanis Club adopted the Roadside Park beautification as a public service probject in 1978, making a five-year commitment to the city. "We have contributed many dollars, manpower hours, and suggested improvements," stated Kiwanis President Dick Bacon. "Our interest in Roadside is a commitment to the park's preservation and enhancement."

Following a presentation Larson made to the Kiwanis members, the club generated seven suggestions, to make Highway 55 changes impact less on Roadside Park. Those suggestions, and Larson's viewpoints, are as follows:

*The Kiwanis Club believes Walnut Street through Roadside Park should be closed. "Such closure would be consistent with our long-range goal of increasing the park's land area," stated Bacon.

Larson agrees. "Walnut Street, for all practical purposes, is a very limited use roadway."

*Ashland Street should not be extended through the park, suggests the Kiwanis Club, because the extension would be "counterproductive to the philosophy of increasing park land area." The Kiwanis Club suggests using Spring Street as an alternative access to Highway 55. That access should be upgraded, states the club.

Larson disagrees. "Strictly on a state-aid basis, I'd like to see Ashland go through the park." He explained that more Minnesota Department of Transportation (Mn/DOT) state aid dollars would be available for Ashland, adding that realligning Spring Street instead would mean losing some trees in Roadside Park.

Larson does not believe Ashland Street would cause major problems for the park. "I don't think you lose that much park space."

Another consideration is providing access to the nearby Cernohous Phillips 66 service station, said Larson, but he believes that is more a Mn/DOT than a city problem.

*The Kiwanis Club also says a surface drainage problem at 11th and Ashland streets needs addressing. Otherwise, club members fear water will erode the park's turf.

Larson agrees. "I think that is a valid point." He believes drainage can be served best, however, by running Ashland Street through the park and installing storm sewer outlets along it.

*Surface drainage from Maple Street east—south of the wading

Roadside/Page 2

The Hastings Kiwanis Club has suggested ways to make traffic on Highway 55 impact less on Roadside Park. (Photo by Al Shaffer)

# Teacher cuts leave mark on athletics

## Athletic Department is shaken up by lay-off of teachers who are coaches in the district; trend is toward coaches who are not local teachers

**by JANE LIGHTBOURN**
**staff writer**

Last week, the Hastings District 200 School Board approved the proposed placement of 30 teachers on unrequested leaves of absence. While all areas of the school district will ultimately feel the impact, one area appears especially hard hit—athletics.

Three of those placed on unrequested leave status for the 1984-85 school year are currently varsity coaches at Hastings Senior High School: Gary Hamilton, boys basketball; Michael Louden, boys baseball; and Dale Zellmer, slalom skiing. Four others—James Zotalis, Sue Liebeg, Craig Smith and Lars Oakman—have been involved in athletics either at the Senior High School or the Junior High School.

While each of the head coaches can continue in that capacity, it appears that none will have a full-time teaching position in the Hastings school district.

To be a head coach, an individual must be a certified teacher and a certified coach. He or she does not have to be employed in a teaching position, but must be certified.

Hastings currently has two head coaches who are not teaching full time in the district—Mari Lucas in girls gymnastics and and Dan Nelson in boys swimming. In these two instances, the coaches and the sports are doing well, but Senior High School Athletic Director Gay Johnson is still concerned about the long-range effects.

"It doesn't help a program over the long run; I'm sort of worried about it," Johnson said about coaches who are not teachers in the district. "I've seen it hit other school districts." He noted that many coaches are the younger staff; the ones now facing cuts.

When the coach does not teach in the same district he coaches in, there can be problems, Johnson said. Sometimes it is a lack of communication between the

Teachers/Page 2

# Concept for riverfront development is studied

## Development under study could include condominium, commercial and public building space along the Hastings riverfront

**by AL SHAFFER**
**staff writer**

Where is the downtown riverfront development and who is involved?

"I have to be very frank," said downtown Main Street Project Manager John Grossman. Plans for riverfront development "are nothing more than conceptual."

But that does not mean developer Jack Hoeschler is not serious about a Hastings riverfront project. Hoeschler is managing director of Landmark Investors Ltd. He has been dealing with Hastings officials on a downtown development.

Tentatively proposed are two either C-shaped or L-shaped buildings constructed on the riverfront half-blocks between Sibley and Tyler Streets. Each building could represent a phase, said Grossman. Each building could also take a different shape, said City Administrator Gary Brown. The design will depend on things like fitting elevators into the project.

The first phase would be a building on the parking lot property between Sibley and Ramsey streets. The reason, said Grossman, is that no buildings need to be removed from that area and no people will be displaced.

"The plan is amorphous," Grossman reiterated. The suggestion, however, is for predominately residential buildings with some commercial space and "conceivably" some public serivce space.

A new library is one discussed option for public servce space. That calls for unique public and private cooperation, Grossman added, however. He believes that balancing act is difficult. "It's deemed to be feasible, but yet to be proved that it's possible."

A library is being considered for some first-floor space, said City Administrator Gary Brown, although he acknowledges that it would call for Hastings City Council and Dakota County County Board approval, along with actions from both the city and county library boards. Under the arrangement, he believes, the county could lease the space from the developer.

Public service space could also be construed to be a plaza, said Grossman.

Most riverfront views in the development will probably be reserved to the apartment or condominium units. Brown, however, believes that the library and any ground floor commercial space in the development would have river views.

Parking is integrated into this plan, Grossman explained; the buildings could be built with one story above grade, leaving the same amount of existing parking on ground level, plus a parking platform on the first story of each building—that would probably serve the tenants or owners of the residences. Downtown Hastings cannot afford to lose any parking stalls, he added.

Platform parking is not certain, said Brown, because the cost is an estimated $5,500 per parking space, while conventional parking is $1,500.

Grossman believes the second phase of the project could depend on how successful the first phase proves. In the first phase, the commercial area will most likely face Ramsey Street, he added.

Both buildings could go up together or one building could be built contingent upon the other going up some time, said Brown. He assured that phasing of the project is not definite.

The development's residential units will be one-bedroom and two-bedroom residences, believes Grossman. They will probably rent as apartments at first, but have the potential for condominium conversions, he explained.

Prices set for the residents is not set, Brown added, however. He said it is too early to say what income bracket could afford them.

Brown also said that riverfront development could be done by a developer other than Hoeschler. "We're not married in any sense of the word." The city welcomes other ideas, he said.

Although the buildings are not designed as early 19th-century replicas, Grossman believes their designs will offer "a comfortable fit" with the downtown's historic architecture. The developer, he said, is "perfectly aware of our design concerns. Grossman believes those concerns can be satisfied with proper use of openings, building heights and exterior color.

This development could provide an impetus for downtown redevelopment. "I think the potential for developing downtown Hastings is just beginning," said Grossman. Its potential is not secret, he added, noting that developers have considered the Hastings downtown riverfront for years.

But to start the momentum, Grossman added, someone must make the first major investment. "If a few people do," he said, "a lot of other people are going to take heart from that."

# Private wells in Vermillion contain some contamination

## Testing to determine if nitrate levels in water are a significant problem; infants the primary concern

**by AL SHAFFER**
**staff writer**

Half the private wells tested in Vermillion contain nitrate levels that equal or exceed health standards for safe drinking water. That ratio emerged from tests ordered by Vermillion city officials and done by the Twin City Testing and Engineering Laboratory in Minneapolis.

The firm tested 124 private wells in Vermillion, collecting the samples in February.

The problem poses the greatest threat to infants six months old or younger, said Ron Spong, environmental health specialist for Dakota County. Infants drinking the water through baby formula, or otherwise, can suffer from "blue baby syndrome." The scientific name is "methemoglobinemia." The ailment essentially starves a baby's tissues of oxygen.

Infants suffer, said Spong, because they cannot rebound from the oxygen deficit. "It takes a while for the body to develop those mechanisms." The situation can be fatal, although Spong believes that usually means the baby also consumed foods with high levels of nitrates or nitrites.

Pregnant women do not have to worry until their babies are born, but they should be informed. "They will soon have a child which will have to be fed," Spong explained.

The nitrates may, however, pose an increased cancer threat for adults.

Spong doesn't want to ignite panic. He said the same nitrate (or nitrite) levels might be found in your spinach salad or ham sandwich (here either nitrates form naturally in foods, or nitrites are found in some prepared and preserved foods like cured, salted meats).

Spong explained that the nitrates and nitrites—placed in a high acid situation (like your stomach)—can combine with proteins or other aminos to create cancer causing agents—nitrosoamines. They have been proved to cause cancer in laboratory animals and humans, said Spong.

No direct link between nitrates consumed through water and increased cancer rates is verified, Spong added. Some general evidence exists, however, indicating there may be a cause and effect for some people.

**SAFETY STANDARD**

The State Safe Drinking Water Act sets a maximum nitrate level of 10 milligrams per liter (mg/L).

Wells/Page 2

**Fig. 14-21b** *Publisher Michael J. O'Connor has won recognition for the outstanding design of his newspaper. This page in modular format is typical.*

**Fig. 14-22** *The standard newspaper page sizes and column widths adopted by many newspapers in 1984. (Courtesy of the American Newspaper Publishers Association.)*

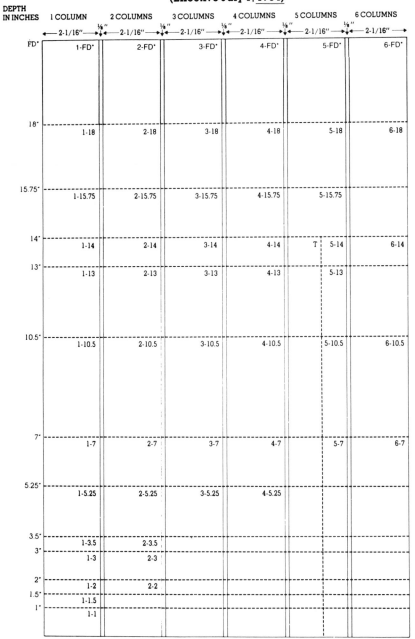

# The Expanded
## SAU™ Standard Advertising Unit System
### (Effective July 1, 1984)

| DEPTH IN INCHES | 1 COLUMN | 2 COLUMNS | 3 COLUMNS | 4 COLUMNS | 5 COLUMNS | 6 COLUMNS |
|---|---|---|---|---|---|---|
| FD* | 1-FD* | 2-FD* | 3-FD* | 4-FD* | 5-FD* | 6-FD* |
| 18" | 1-18 | 2-18 | 3-18 | 4-18 | 5-18 | 6-18 |
| 15.75" | 1-15.75 | 2-15.75 | 3-15.75 | 4-15.75 | 5-15.75 | |
| 14" | 1-14 | 2-14 | 3-14 | 4-14 | T  5-14 | 6-14 |
| 13" | 1-13 | 2-13 | 3-13 | 4-13 | 5-13 | |
| 10.5" | 1-10.5 | 2-10.5 | 3-10.5 | 4-10.5 | 5-10.5 | 6-10.5 |
| 7" | 1-7 | 2-7 | 3-7 | 4-7 | 5-7 | 6-7 |
| 5.25" | 1-5.25 | 2-5.25 | 3-5.25 | 4-5.25 | | |
| 3.5" | 1-3.5 | 2-3.5 | | | | |
| 3" | 1-3 | 2-3 | | | | |
| 2" | 1-2 | 2-2 | | | | |
| 1.5" | 1-1.5 | | | | | |
| 1" | 1-1 | | | | | |

- 13 inch depths are for tabloid sections of broadsheet newspapers.
- T is a full page size for 21½ inch cut-off tabloid newspapers. It measure 14 x 9⅜".

*FD = full depth of 21" or longer, as according to individual newspapers' printed depth as indicated in Standard Rate and Data Service listing. Printed depth generally varies in newspapers from 21" to 22½". All newspapers can accept 21" ads and may float the ad if their printed depth is greater than 21".

| | |
|---|---|
| 1 COLUMN 2-1/16" | 5 COLUMNS 10-13/16" |
| 2 COLUMNS 4¼" | 6 COLUMNS 13" |
| 3 COLUMNS 6-7/16" | DOUBLE TRUCK 26¾" |
| 4 COLUMNS 8⅜" | **FD—FULL DEPTH** |

possible to find reading matter set in as many as four or five different widths on one page. The reader was faced with a hodgepodge that defied comfortable reading and the basic rules of legibility.

The situation has improved, however, as most newspapers have adopted the *Standard Advertising Unit.* The SAU was devised by the American Newspaper Publishers Association in an attempt to bring standardization and order out of the chaos caused by the various column widths being used in newspapers.

The SAU system starts with a $2\frac{1}{16}$-inch column with $\frac{1}{8}$ inch between columns. Note the substitution of inches for points, picas, and agate lines. The full-page width contains six columns for advertisements. The ANPA suggests that only inches and fractions of inches be used to measure advertisements. It also recommends fifty-seven modular sizes for national advertisements but leaves size decisions for local advertisements up to the individual newspapers.

The modular sizes are designated as follows. A 1 by 1 advertisement is 1 column wide and 1 inch deep. A full-column advertisement is designated as 1 by 21, for the standard 21-inch page, or 1 by F for 1 column by full depth if the page is not 21 inches deep. The standard sizes of the modules include 2 by 2 for an advertisement that is 2 columns wide and 2 inches deep; 3 by 5.25 for one 3 columns wide by $5\frac{1}{4}$ inches deep; and so on.

The new system has helped designers produce more attractive inside pages, and helped newspapers sell advertisements as well.

If a newspaper contains advertisements, there are several standard patterns for placing these advertisements on a page. One of them should be adopted and used throughout the publication—except, perhaps, for special sections. But even there, if the section includes more than one page the pattern should be the same for all the pages.

The most common basic patterns include:

- *Pyramid:* Here the advertisements are built like varying sizes of building blocks from the base of the largest ad in the lower right-hand corner of the page. This leaves the hot spot or area of initial eye contact—the upper-left corner—open for editorial matter. This is actually a half-pyramid, and it is often called that.

- *Magazine:* Here some columns are filled with advertisements and others are completely open for editorial display. This arrangement will work well with the trend toward modular layout and pagination.

- *Well or double pyramid:* Here advertisements are placed on the inside and outside columns plus across the bottom of the page. This forms a sort of well that can be filled with editorial material.

- *Modular:* Here advertisements are clustered to form rectangular modules on the page, another arrangement that works well with the pagination equipment coming on line in many newspapers.

Regardless of the pattern adopted, there are a few points to remember when planning inside pages for maximum effectiveness.

**Fig. 14-23a** *Some of the more popular inside page arrangements for placement of advertisements. The key to attractive inside pages is to adopt a consistent pattern and keep the top of the page, especially upper left-hand corner, open as much as possible for editorial display.*

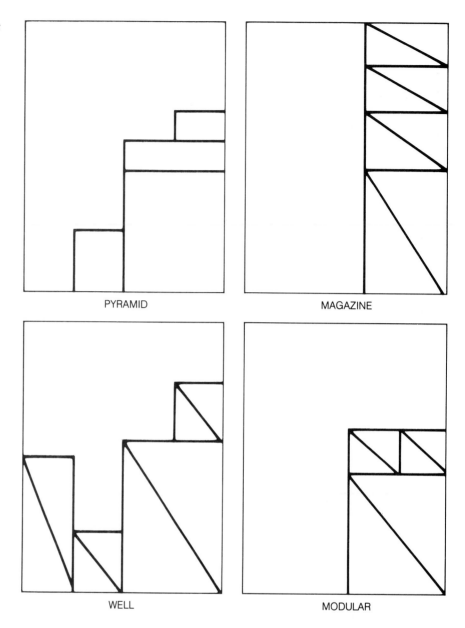

The important top-of-the-page areas should be kept open for the display of editorial material as much as possible. Advertisements should not be placed so high in the columns that little space is left for reading matter. There should be enough space above advertisements for a headline and arm of body type at least as deep as the headline. If the space left is smaller, the advertisements should be rearranged if at all possible.

There should be at least one "stopper" on each inside page. The attention-getter could be an illustration or a story with a strong headline. Some editors try to have an illustration on every inside page. When editorial art is placed on the page, however, it should not compete with advertising art. The two should not be placed side by side.

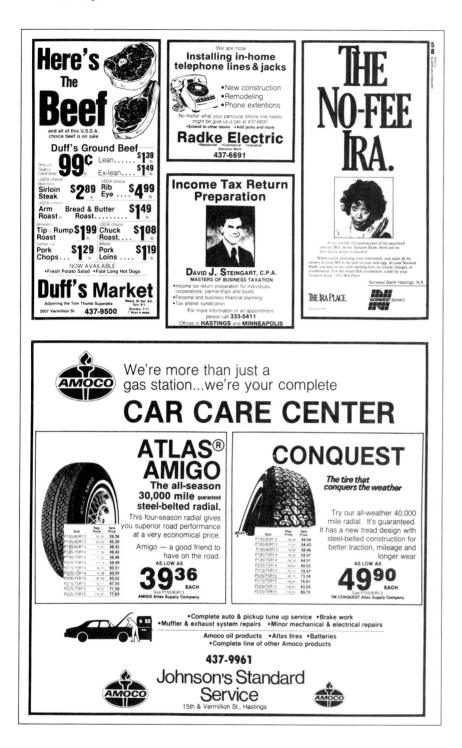

Fig. 14-23b *Another inside page arrangement that is gaining popularity is a full page of advertisements. This will free other pages for more extensive display of editorial matter.*

Care should especially be taken to harmonize editorial and advertising content. A story about an airline crash, for instance, should not be placed on the same page with an airline advertisement.

The best designed inside pages are pages that have no tombstones; no long, unbroken columns of body type; and no "naked" columns (tops of columns of body type without headlines, art, or rules).

**Fig. 14-24** *These prototype inside pages were developed for an American Press Institute workshop. The inside page on the left, by Sara Giovanitti of the* Boston Globe, *gives an advertiser a big break by placing the ad in the primary optical center. The page on the right, designed by Robert Chin of the* Houston Chronicle, *lets the editorial matter have the hot spot. Notice how each page gives careful attention to editorial display with a variety of heads and art.*

## The Editorial and Section Pages

The design of editorial and section pages should reflect the interests and content of that particular unit while preserving the flavor of the entire publication. Some ways this can be accomplished include using page logos that incorporate the publication's nameplate, using the same type family for headlines but in a different posture, and using the same headline form throughout the newspaper. For example, if downstyle, flush left is used in the main section, unity can be preserved if that form is used in all sections.

The editorial page should be distinctly different from the other pages. The reader should understand clearly that this is the page of opinion, the page where ideas clash. But while the page should be different, it should invite the reader by being lively and bright.

There is a trend toward eliminating the editorial page. However, those who believe taking positions is an important function of the media maintain that editorial pages should be improved, not eliminated. They point out that the key to developing a good editorial page is presenting well-written editorials that take strong stands on issues that are important to the readers.

The design of the editorial page can help make it a vital part of the publication. Some things that can be done to make it graphically different and interesting include:

- Eliminate column rules and use more white space between columns.

- Set body type in a larger size.

- Use larger size heads but in a slightly lighter weight than the main headlines.

- Design fewer columns to the page, with a wide measure, but keep within the readability range.

- Use graphics to add interest to the page. These could include cartoons, editorial pictures, charts, maps, diagrams.

The editorial page can help a publication develop its distinctive personality, and it can be an attractive graphic feature that can increase reader interest.

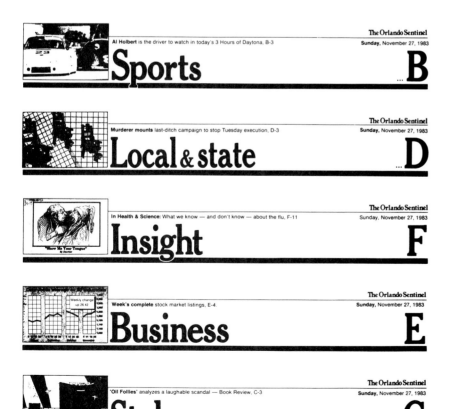

**Fig. 14-25** *Ornamentation with a purpose. Section logos help identify the section and help unify the entire newspaper package. The* Orlando Sentinel *uses Cheltenham bold for its logos with a 12-point baseline rule, a built-in promo and a section letter in the same type as the section name.*

**Fig. 14-26** *Inside pages offer design opportunities, too. Often discussions of newspaper design center on the front page, and inside pages are neglected. This page from the* Livingston County Press, *Howell, Mich., illustrates the design possibilities of pages containing advertisements. (From* Design, *the journal of the Society of Newspaper Design.)*

## The Design of Section Pages

Each section presents a specific challenge to the editor and designer. The design of each section should reflect its purpose and personality and be in harmony with the complete newspaper. Some sections that most frequently appear in newspapers are "Family Living," "Food," "Sports," and "Business."

The "Family Living" or "Life-Style" section is a recent development. It has taken the place of what was called the "Society" or "Women's" section. The scope and content of this section has been broadened and changed. Traditionally this section was given what was thought to be a "feminine" design treatment. Type styles were softened, and photo treatment was formal and subdued. However, the trend now is toward the use of more magazine design techniques while maintaining the general design philosophy of the entire newspaper.

Food pages often were incorporated with the women's section in the past. Now many men are cooking enthusiasts, and "feminine" typographic treatment is no longer used. The designer should remember that these are "working" pages, that recipes and instructions should be presented in a clear and accurate style. It is also helpful if the arrangement makes the material easy to clip and file.

Sports pages are worlds unto themselves, and the sports staffs have operated as virtual separate entities on many newspapers. They have often had their own head schedules set in type of their own choosing regardless of whether it harmonized with the rest of the newspaper. In recent years a change has taken place, and the appeal of the sports page has been expanded as more sports, such as soccer, have become popular, more attention has been paid to women's sports, and more people have participated in recreational sports.

The typography of the sports pages should be such that it reflects the vibrant action-packed activities it records. At the same time, it should be in harmony with the rest of the newspaper. A bolder posture of the same type as used in the entire newspaper might give more life to the sports pages. If the newspaper head schedule is upper- and lowercase or if it is downstyle, the sports page heads should use the same style.

Sports pages use more photographs than most other sections. The caption plan for these illustrations, while it might be bolder, should employ the same arrangement as used in the rest of the newspaper.

Sports news includes much statistical matter, box scores, standings, and summaries. The trend is to set this material in agate (5½ point) type and group it for all sports in a separate page or part of a page. This practice helps the orderly organization of sports information and enables the editor to set the type in the optimum line width for agate. The typographic appeal of the statistical matter can be improved with distinctive headings for each topic. Small sketches to identify each sport can also be incorporated with the headings.

The *Wall Street Journal* has the largest daily circulation in the United States. The success of the *Journal* reflects the growing interest in business and economic news.

There was a time when business news was presented in staid, conservative—and even dull—writing and layouts. As the interest in business news has grown, business pages have become more lively. And the techniques of good typography and graphics are being applied to the business pages.

## A Case Study—The Guthrie Story

Guthrie, a city of 10,312, was Oklahoma's first capital. It has embarked on a major historical renovation program. Regional media have begun to refer to it as "the Williamsburg of the West."

Guthrie is served by the *Guthrie Daily Leader*, circulation 4,311 on weekdays and 4,396 on Sundays. Larry Adkisson, the general manager, suggested that the *Leader* consider a redesign to carry out the basic principle of newspaper design—a newspaper's appearance should reflect the character of the community it serves.

The new *Leader* adopted some design techniques that are considered outdated by some in the business but that turned out to be received enthusiastically by readers and staff. The newspaper adopted a "new" turn-of-the-century style and vertical layout.

Column rules were put back in the pages, and multideck all-capital headlines and bordered photographs were used. The basic design was changed from horizontal to vertical.

How did the staff at Guthrie, assisted by technicians from the Donrey Media Group, go about the redesign?

Goals were set first. They included adoption of a "Territorial-era format" aimed at maintaining the flavor of the typography of the era, hopefully without its faults, and at achieving the appearance of a Territorial-era newspaper without sacrificing the integrity and consistency of a modern newspaper.

Then very specific guidelines were adopted for attaining the goals. Because of their thoroughness, these guidelines are useful for anyone contemplating a design or redesign project. Although the specifics may be different for different situations, the thoroughness is worth following.

### Guidelines for the Redesign of the *Leader*

*Basic Layout*

1. The paper will be six columns per page throughout, with the exception of the classified and comic pages. Column rules will be in hairline and drawn on the page when printed. Eight-column pages will have no column rules.

2. Type size for news will be 9 point on a 10-point base for the present time. When equipment permits, the typeface may change, possibly to Mallard.

3. Photos will be boxed with a fine line border at the edge of the image and decorative corners. The exception will be on the sports pages where decorative corners will be omitted.

4. Makeup will convert to vertical, with subheads (centered boldface lines) being used to break up the grayness of the page, using at least two per story where needed, each line centered in a two-line space.

5. Cutoff rules will be used above all headlines and photos where there is type above. The cutoff rules will be the same width as

the type for one column and will extend across the column if multicolumn; the column rule will be cut off to meet the cutoff rule.

6. The upper-right-hand corner of the front page is where the dominant story should be placed. This will allow smaller stories of importance to achieve dominance.

7. The flag will be the top item on the page. A story will not be put above it.

8. Stories will be two columns wide or less. Three-column stories and headlines may be used on special occasions, as will five- or six-column banners with one- or two-column decks.

*General Layout*

1. On any given story, all headlines and decks will be of the same face and weight. Head and decks should alternate slant: Roman, italic, Roman or italic; Roman, italic.

2. The head will always be flush left, with the exception of banner heads, which will be centered. Heads for boxed stories will be centered.

3. The first deck will be of an alternate slant, two sizes smaller than the head (for example, 36-point head, 24-point first deck). The second deck will be one type size smaller than the first deck (for example, first deck 24 point, second deck 18 point).

4. Heads and decks will be separated by jim dashes. The jim dashes will be 5 picas wide for each column the head covers. They will be situated 18 points from the head or deck above, and 12 points above the lower deck.

5. Heads will always be all caps.

*Page 1*

1. Headlines directly below the flag will contain one headline and two decks. Stories in this position with sidebars (related stories) may use the same head, and each story will have two decks. Stories above the fold but not attached to the flag will have the head and one deck. Stories below the fold will have the headline only.

2. Tombstoning can help create a territorial look. Tombstoning is defined at the *Leader* as two or three (usually three) one-column heads of the same size (but alternating weight) side by side. Tombstoning may also be done with a two-column or one-column story, alternating weights.

3. Shorts (heads for short stories) may be either 14 or 18 point (18 preferred) but must be in boldface.

*Society Page*

1. All heads will be in lightface, but slant may vary.

2. Top heads will be head and one deck; below the top will be headline only.

3. Banner heads will have no decks.

## News Notes

### Grassy body shelters car

KANSAS CITY, Mo. (UPI) — Artist Bill Harding won over the unconvinced and proved you don't need paint to cover a car, all it takes is grass seed and time.

Harding Friday parked his 1966 Buick LeSabre — covered with live grass — at a downtown intersection to show off for the lunchtime crowds.

"Hey, it is real grass!" exclaimed a believer.

Harding glued 30 pounds grass seed to the car's body Sept. 1. By Sept. 4 his motorized lawn had sprouted.

"Nature is our hope. People living in the city get confused about their priorities. If they look to nature they can see where they came from," said Harding, who showed up covered with grass himself.

"I'll tell you, it takes all kinds," a businessman muttered before walking away from the green machine.

### 'Mad world' recalled

MILWAUKEE (UPI) — The plan of whoever tucked a letter in the floorboards of a furniture store 68 years ago worked out just fine.

A worker helping tear down the Waldheim furniture store found an envelope Thursday that read, "When this Building is Demolished the enclosed may be of interest."

The letter read: "Mrs. President died in Washington D.C. at 5 p.m. today. War in Europe raging. Germans storming Liege Belgium with great loss of life. New plate glass front to this store just completed. Weather fair. Temperatures 89. Wheat 93 — Corn 72 — Oats 38 cents."

It was dated Aug. 6, 1914, and signed "Lee G. Smith."

"I've been wrecking for 14 years and this is the first thing like this we've ever come across," Richard Walters, president of Walters Excavating and Wrecking Inc., the firm doing the demolition, said Friday.

At the bottom of the letter are the words, "A.F. Smith Attest."

(See NEWS NOTES–Page 12)

## Sloop carries Poles to Newark

### Immigration detains four

NEWARK, N.J. (UPI) — Federal officials are considering a request for asylum by four Poles who sailed across the Atlantic and into the shadow of the Statue of Liberty aboard a 38-foot sloop.

Immigration and Naturalization Service officials questioned the four refugees in Newark Friday, after a Polish interpreter was found.

"The four have asked to remain in the United States and their requests are being considered," said Clifford Landsman, an immigration supervisor in the Newark office.

"Until a decision is reached in their case, they will be detained by INS in accordance with immigration service policy," Landsman said, reading from a prepared statement.

Landsman would not reveal where the Poles, who sailed into New York Harbor Thursday, were being held.

Officials did not identify the four, but The Daily Journal of Elizabeth reported it interviewed one of the men before they were detained.

Jarek Neczaj-Hru[illegible]wics, 38, of Lublin, said he and the [illegible] three men were members of [illegible] outlawed Solidarity union.

Neczaj-Hruzewics, the only member of the crew to speak English, identified the other men as Andrzej Plewik, 37, the captain, Andrzej Bienkowski, 34, the first mate, and Stanley Kozak, 38, the second mate, the Journal reported.

Instead of returning to their homeland, he said the men headed to the United States, making stops in Africa, France, Spain and Bermuda on the way.

Neczaj-Hruzewics was quoted as saying the group received permission four months ago to fly to Athens, where the sloop was moored, to sail it back to Poland.

They chose to go to Elizabeth because they have friends there, Neczaj-Hruzewics reportedly said.

The men docked in Elizabeth early Thursday and reportedly went to Bernie's Polish Bar, a block away, where they drank a few beers and were allowed to take a shower.

Elizabeth police, acting on a tip, arrived and ordered the men to stay on the boat until the Coast Guard came and escorted the sloop to Governor's Island.

They spent the night on the boat at Governor's Island, near Liberty Island, before being taken to Newark for their interviews Friday.


# Guthrie Daily Leader

Historical Capital of Oklahoma

SUNDAY, SEPTEMBER 19, 1982 90th Year No. 367 DAILY 20c SUNDAY 35c

**Statehood Day Planning**

Preparations for the Guthrie Statehood Day celebration continued with a media gathering Sept. 16 at the Calla Restaurant at Penn Place in Oklahoma City. LEFT: Fred Olds talks to saddle maker Mr. Barr and Lt. Gov. Spencer Bernard. Olds is director of the Territorial Museum and a member of the Guthrie Statehood Day committee. ABOVE: Guests enter the buffet line. (Leader Staff Photos by Larry Adkisson.)

## Redheads have pride gathering

LAGUNA HILLS, Calif. (UPI) — Red-haired people have reason to keep their carrot tops held high.

Steve Douglas, a piano player who sold his $4,000 baby grand and other musical equipment to found Redheads International, is setting out on a campaign to promote red-haired pride.

Douglas has ordered redhead bumper stickers and membership cards along with T-shirts bearing the Redheads International logo.

He rented a cubbyhole office in Laguna Hills, in Orange County, and is gearing up for an Oct. 23 gathering of redheads.

Douglas, who quit his band to launch the club, said more than 1,000 redheads have responded to ads in several national and local publications, paying $10 each to join the club. He said several chapters have been formed.

Tacked on the bulletin board is a letter to "Dear Abby" from a man who complained he couldn't find a girl because of "the terrible curse of being a redhead." He asked if there was a club for redheads he could join.

Abby didn't know of any clubs, prompting Douglas to write a letter saying it wasn't a curse to be a redhead and told her about Redheads International.

(See REDHEADS–Page 12)

## Commissioner run-off foes differ

Time is running out on the run-off Democratic campaign for the Logan Co. District II commissioner's slot on the November ballot.

Candidates Jim Ferrell and Ralph Taylor found themselves in a run-off when neither got a majority of votes in the August Democratic primary. Five Democrats ran in the August eliminations.

To the winner on Sept. 21 goes the right to face Republican candidate Diana Crawford in November.

The three candidates all bring a construction background to the race. Although the commissioners must sit on 26 different boards and commissions, Ferrell says that the county roads issue is the one "that touches all voters."

Ferrell, who ran for Congress unsuccessfully two years ago, had told voters that he will be a "full-time" commissioner if elected.

He resigned in August as estimator and superintendent for Alexander Plastering and Dry-Wall Co. in Yukon. He says this will prevent any possible conflict "with outside business interests."

### Crawford finds voters uneasy

Even though she has the Republican nomination for District II commissioner already won, Diana Crawford's door-to-door campaign to meet the voters has not slackened.

However, she is glad not to have the run-ff pressures of run-off Democrats Ferrell and Taylor.

"It's going to be a tough run-off; to be geared up like that to almost a fever pitch is exhausting," she says. She and her husband Joe live near Coyle.

The office manager-accountant for Mesa Enterprises Construction Co. in Oklahoma City says that she has encountered a mix of enthusiasm and suspicion from Logan Co. residents on the campaign trail.

"The county commissioners have been the butt of jokes in the past year. Since I've been meeting people out here they seem to be really interested in county government," she says.

Recently, two Logan Co. commissioners and a retired county official pleaded guilty to charges of accepting kickbacks. They became part of a state-wide crackdown on abuses in the office.

"People are suspicious of county government. They say, 'what's the ulterior motive here,' when candidates show up.

The three candidates got quite a reception at a town gathering earlier this week in Woodward, she says.

"Woodward was the first time all three candidates had been together. The community thought it was fantastic," she says.

"I have been unemployed since after I filed for office. "I quit my job," he says. "If you were able to do it, you would be better able to serve the people."

County commissioners across the state have gotten considerable spotlight across the state in recent times. Several have received federal and state indictments for bid-rigging, accepting kickbacks and other illegal management activities.

Ferrell says that recent state legislation in the form of House Bill 1578 will bring a number of changes to county government.

Among these, it will establish a county purchasing agent and county road and bridge engineer positions. Ferrell says that smaller counties will hopefully be able to share an engineer rather than having to each pay their own.

"The act looks to me like it is geared more to the larger counties which can afford more what the act calls for," he says.

Ralph Taylor, also wary of previous commissioner pitfalls, has kept his campaign promises to a minimum. He says he is making just one.

"I'll do the best job I can if they want me for their commissioner. That's all I have to say," he notes.

Taylor, along with Ferrell, showed up at the Langston Co. Fair on Thursday night. Republican Diana Crawford was there also.

Taylor recounted his day's travels.

"I've been meeting with the people over in Langston-Coyle. I'm weak over there, I may be weaker now," he says with a smile.

He knows the campaign is tight, and refuses to make predictions. "We'll just wait until the votes are counted. I just don't know what to think about it," he says.

Taylor says he is not impressed with Ferrell's platform of being a "full-time" comissioner.

"A full-time commissioner is one who works at it for 24 hours a day, 365 days a yeer," says Taylor. He plans to keep his rental houses and his construction business.

"I've worked since I was six years old, and I don't plan to stop now. I've worked for what I've got," he says.

As a final push before the campaign, Taylor and supporters are sponsoring barbecue Monday night at the American Legion Hall. He is planning for around 700 people.

"I'd rather have too much rather

(See COMMISSIONER–Page 12)

## Today

**BALLOTS AVAILABLE**

Lorray Dyson, Secretary of the Logan County Election Board stated today the absentee ballots for the Mulhall-Orlando special school bond election are now available at the election board office, 311 East Harrison, Guthrie. Absentee application must be made no later than 5 p.m. September 22.

**AFS WELCOME SOCIAL**

A welcome ice cream social in honor of the two new foreign students at Guthrie Highschool sponsored by the American Field Service will be held Sunday at 4 p.m. at the home of Mr. and Mrs. Norman Jacobs, 810 East Cleveland. The event is open to members of the AFS and would-be members. The students to be welcomed are Susi Fabricius, West Germany, and Adrian Stutz, Switzerland.

**ROTARY SPEAKER**

Bill Wagoner, superintendent of Guthrie schools, will be the speaker at Rotary Club luncheon Monday noon at the American Legion Building. Marley Smith is program chairman.

**BEEKEEPERS TO MEET**

Logan County Beekeepers Assn. will meet at the Fairgrounds Tuesday, Sept. 21, from 7 to 9 p.m. Make Vandeventer, apiary specialist, will present the program.

**SATURDAY DECA CARWASH**

Guthrie's chapter of the Distributive Education Clubs of America will a carwash from 9 a.m. to 8 p.m. today at the school bus barn, 802 E. Oklahoma. Cost is $2 per car or pick-up, others negotiable.

## Ambulance system rides on EMS levy

If the Emergency Medical Service levy does not pass on Sept. 21, the Guthrie fire chief sees the City Council as having three main options for continuing ambulance service.

The council can raise water bills $2.50 a month, quadruple ambulance rates or discontinue ambulance service.

Guthrie's city ambulance service, which the fire department operates, did not receive state recertification in July. The ambulance service has until Dec. 31 to come up to standard or "go out of business."

Chief Bill Ward says that training and equipment status are two areas of deficiency. And as an added problem, the ambulance is projected by city estimates to lose over $100,000 this year.

Authority to establish EMS districts comes from a 1976 amendment to the oklahoma constitution. The amendment allows local government bodies to establish levies of up to three mills per thousand dollars of assessed valuation to fund the districts.

For a $40,000 home assessed at $4,000 with a $1,000 homestead exemption, the city estimates the levy would cost the taxpayer $9 a year.

Crescent is awaiting the results of the vote on the Guthrie School District EMS levy. The town has had a district, but is counting on Guthrie to provide training for the county, says Ward.

Presently Guthrie has four paramedics certified, who also serve as firemen. The city needs four more to meet state rules. None, however, are certified as EMS instructors.

Currently, the paramedics also serve as firemen. Ward would like to see them do either one or the other.

Presently, said Ward, no funds are budgeted for EMS training.

Also, none of the city's three ambulances are up to certification. The city's most serviceable vehicle is a rented one.

It costs about $30,000 to $38,000 to purchase a high-top van and outfit it an ambulance. And, the vehicles generally are retired after 60,000 miles.

Leonard Anderson, director of the Emergency Medical Services Division of the Oklahoma Department of Health, says that the district levy would create an entire EMS system for the area.

Many areas establish 911 emergency numbers answered by a central dispatcher. The dispatcher then sends either police, fire or emergency medical care personnel to the emergency site.

Victims are then taken to the nearest medical facility with the appropriate critical care team for their condition. Four state helicopters and the Military Assistance for Safety and Traffic (MAST) unit from Fort Sill augment the local districts.

So far, 16 counties and seven school districts have established EMS districts.

Anderson became a firm believer in quick, on-the-site medical care when his twin-engine Army Mohawk observation plane was forced down near the Cambodian border during the Vietnam war.

"I had the misfortune of ejecting in Vietnam, but I also had the fortune to be picked up by a copter. I only had a sprained ankle and a few other problems, but I sure was glad to see them show up," he said.

**Fig. 14-27a** *The* Guthrie Daily Leader *before redesign. It was in typical, but undistinguished, optimum format. Note the floating flag.*

# GUTHRIE DAILY LEADER

91st Volume -- Number 33 | Historic Capital of Oklahoma | TUESDAY, OCTOBER 26, 1982

## HOLMES AUTHORS SECTION

### *RECOUNTS DEVELOPMENT*

### CITES CITY PLANS

The author of the historical articles in this special souvenier edition of the Guthrie Daily Leader is Helen Freudenberger Holmes, Guthrie historian and journalist.

Mrs. Holmes is the editor and principal author of the recently published Logan County History, in two volumes, and the 1982 Souvenier 89er Celebration program, which detailed the history of that event commemorating the Run of April 22, 1889.

A native of Logan County, Mrs. Holmes holds a bachelor's degree from Oklahoma State University and a master's degree from the University of Wisconsin, and is a member of the Logan County Historical Society and the Oklahoma Historical Society.

She was the first member of the Women's Army Auxiliary Corps selected from Oklahoma in World War II, and is a retired major in the U. S. Army. She served as mayor of Guthrie, 1979-81.

Recently retired after a period as Women's Editor of the **Guthrie Daily Leader**, Mrs. Holmes is again devoting her time to historical research and writing.

## BISHOPS WANT NUCLEAR ARMS CUTBACKS

WASHINGTON (UPI) — A committee of Roman Catholic bishops is urging a freeze of nuclear weapons at a minimum deterrence level as a step toward progressive disarmament involving "negotiated bilateral deep cuts."

The committee Monday released a second draft of its controversial 110-page pastoral letter, "The Challenge of Peace: God's Promise and Our Response," which the nation's 300

**(See BISHOPS--Page 10)**

## SHOOTING INVESTIGATED

A Guthrie farmer died in a shooting accident near his home just before midnight Oct. 25.

Joe Musil, who lived with his wife Agnes north of Vet Corner, had gone out behind his barn to investigate a noise. He had taken a small-caliber rifle with him, and had evidently stumbled and discharged the weapon, said the sheriff's report.

The bullet struck him in the head, and he was pronounced dead at Logan Co. Health Center early this morning.

The body was taken to the state medical examiner's department in Oklahoma City for routine examination.

Musil farmed in the Crescent area, said friends of the family.

## SOUVENIR COPIES AVAILABLE

Copies of the Guthrie Daily Leader Souvenir edition may be mailed by the Leader office to relatives and families for $1.25 per issue. Orders may be placed at the Leader office weekdays 8:30 a.m. to 5 p.m.

**Brick worker Kirby Jantz scrapes mortar away from above the cornerstone after removing the time capsule.**
**(Leader Staff Photo by John Patrick Orr)**

## TIME CAPSULE FOUND AT MUSEUM

### *BEHIND CORNERSTONE*

Eighty years ago, workmen building the State Capital Printing Co. building at Second and Harrison left a time capsule behind the cornerstone.

The building now houses the State Capital Printing Museum, and museum personnel learned of the "tinder-box" capsule through research of early newspapers.

Guthrie brick worker Kirby Jantz removed the cornerstone Monday morning. He pulled out an old Social Smoke cigar box for the curators.

In the box were two yellowed copies of the building dedication program dated Aug. 7, 1902, and a three-inch rusted building nail.

Work crew members from the construction had signed the backs of the programs. Handwriting in pencil included the following:

August 8, 1902: This corner built by J.W. Perris, Bill Noris, El Blincal, superintendent and agent ..(ILLEGIBLE)...of Laisure new General Rauslerleaut. J.K. Hoffmur, mason; M.S. Heffurn, Alexander Hill, J.W. Brodie, N.S. Atwell, W.H. Shargf.

Robert Rhodes of Pulaski, Tenn., Frank C. Bell, Sidney Phillips, George T. Sartain.

Ezra Wright was water boy.

R.P. Pearson was mortarman.

The program contained a headline which said:

**Assemble at Masonic Temple at 2:15 p.m. and March to State Capital Building--List of Afternoon and Evening Speakers.**

At 7:30 p.m., 14 speakers plus a band at each end and interspersed choral performances, made the evening.

Featured among the speakers and topics were: President Barnes on "Guthrie Newspapers and Its Commercial Club;" Mayor C. G. Jones, Oklahoma City, on "Newspapers and Legislature;" Hon. H. E. Asp, "The Relation of the Press and the People;" Col. Roy V. Hoffman "The Two Greatest Professions, Law and the Press;" Hon. William Grimes, "Advantages of a Strong Newspaper to the State;" Mrs. N. M. Carter, "Woman's View of the Mission of the Newspaper;" Dr. D. R. Boyd of University of Oklahoma, "The Part of the Press in Educational Advancement;" Sen. C. Porter Johnson, "Young Men as Editors and Statesmen."

Assistant curator Cathie Zusy said that she and Curator Ludd Lentz were somewhat disappointed by the contents. Old records listed copies of the State Capital newspaper and a historic penny as contents of the box.

The penny had supposedly survived the fire which had burned the preceding State Capital building, which was located at 118 E. Oklahoma.

Frank Hilton Greer had come to Guthrie during the '89 land rush and set up shop in a tent. He busied himself with printing business cards and flyers before starting his newspaper.

He later moved to the Oklahoma Avenue location and developed physical plant worth, according to early newspaper accounts, $200,000. However, he only had it insured for $25,000 at the time of the Easter Sunday fire on March 30, 1900.

Zusy said that the town rallied to help Greer out of his predicament.

Leslie Niblack, editor of the Democratic rival **Leader**, opened his printing facility the next day to the **State Capital**. Greer, a Republican, never missed an edition.

Townfolk pitched in also, gathering $50,000 in a day to help Greer get started again. Greer refused the money as a gift, but offered to take it as a loan at 6 percent interest.

Turning down offers by Oklahoma City bigwigs to relocate his operation to the south, Greer bought the plant of the El Reno newspaper and brought the machinery to Guthrie.

[illegible] then commissioned Guthrie architect Joseph Foucart to construct the present building. Greer set up in temporary facilities until the new plant was completed.

## TAINTED TYLENOL FOUND

### *SUSPECT QUESTIONED*

### REFUSE COMMENT

CHICAGO (UPI) — An eighth bottle of cyanide-tainted Extra-Strength Tylenol has been found and police questioned a reported suspect who had a violent argument with one of the seven victims of the poisoned capsules.

A WMAQ-TV report Monday also said there was a chance one other bottle of the deadly capsules has yet to be found.

The station said there was a possibility the poisonings were an effort to cover up one slaying and that the other six deaths were randomly staged.

Investigators refused to comment on the case beyond confirming the new bottle was purchased at a supermarket in Wheaton, a western suburb.

In Denver, poison experts today identified a "deadly" mercury compound as the substance that critically injured William Sinkovic, 33, who took altered Excedrin capsules — the third case of product tampering in Colorado in 24 hours. Officials first thought the substance was arsenic.

Sinkovic was in "very critical" condition early today.

In Grand Junction, Colo., health officials said Monday they had found rat poison in a bottle of Maximum Strength Anacin, and local supermarkets removed frozen pies after finding one that contained a tranquilizer capsule.

The Chicago Sun-Times, in today's early editions, said the unidentified suspect in the Tylenol case had been questioned by authorities who have been working on the case for nearly a month. The seven deaths occurred between Sept. 29 and Oct. 1.

The man is a relative of one of the Tylenol victims and the two reportedly had a violent argument before the poisonings occurred, the

**(See TYLENOL--Page 10)**

## CHAMBER COFFEE SCHEDULED

The Chamber of Commerce Coffee will be at Pruitt Chrysler Dodge, 323 N. Division at 10 a.m. Wednesday.

## LEADER FORMAT CHANGEOVER EXPLAINED

### *LOOK WILL REFLECT TERRITORIAL ERA*

### MONTHS OF PLANNING COME TO FRUITION

If you've read your **Leader** recently, you know that the format is undergoing a drastic change. That change is before you now.

The change is not without reason. In light of the extensive renovation now taking place in Guthrie, our city's return to its historic past, it was decided to make the paper reflect the changes that are now taking place.

The basic idea for the format change to that of a Territorial-era paper was **Leader** General Manager Larry Adkisson's.

"It occurred to me", said Adkisson, "that with the restoration taking place and people coming into town to see that restoration, it would assist the town's image if, when people picked up the paper, the paper would reflect that image."

Adkisson discussed the idea with numerous people around town, and executive of the Donrey Media Group, of which the **Leader** is a member, and decided to try the change.

Donrey's three-person art staff, headquartered in Fort Smith, Ark., was given the problem of designing a paper that had the flavor of a Territorial-era paper, yet still retain modern production techniques, integrity and consistency.

The art department, along with the Donrey research and development director John Jopes, arrived at the basic format after intensive research and experimentation.

Newspapers at the turn of the century and earlier had a design that was basically vertical, while modern newspapers now have a make-up that is more horizontal. To train the **Leader** staff to design a paper that basically goes against all rules of "modern" newspaper design, John Jopes was called in from the west coast for a week of intensive training.

Jopes developed several rules of thumb for the staff to go by. One of the most obvious is the fact that most stories will now run down the page, as opposed to modern papers which run stories horizontally across the page. Another very obvious difference is the exclusive use of capital letters in all headlines. Neither of these practices are often seen and both are normally considered taboo in modern newspaper design.

One more apparent difference between today's paper and yesterday's is the size of the type you are now reading; it is quite a bit larger now.

Other changes are not so obvious, and would probably be of little interest to anyone not intimately involved with newspaper design and production. But the staff of the **Leader**, who have worried about the change and burned the midnight oil to bring you this souvenir edition, are excited about our new paper and hope that our readers find it as exciting as we do.

## TEEN NIGHT TONIGHT

"Teens Unlimited" will be presented Tuesday, from 6-9 p.m. at the Logan County Fairgrounds. There will be a program for teens and parents plus a panel discussion. The program is sponsored by the Logan County Extension Homemakers and the Logan County OSU Extension Center.

## TRANSPORTATION ANNOUNCED

Logan County Transportation for the Elderly will be in the Langston-Coyle-Meridian area Wednesday to take persons 60 and over for doctor's appointments, shopping, etc. Thursday the busette will be in the Crescent area, and Friday in the Marshall-Mulhall area. Call 282-1803 for appointments.

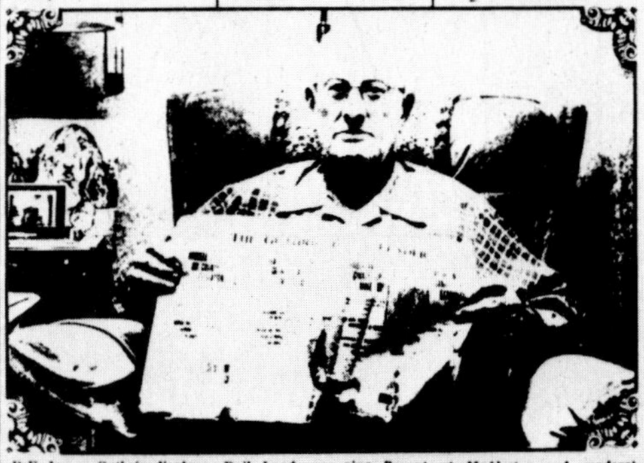

**R.E. James, Guthrie, displays a Daily Leader dated Nov. 17, 1908. Among others, the page carried stories about an address by then-governor Charles N. Haskell, Williams Jenning Bryant at McAlester and readers' reaction to the Leader anniversary issue which was printed the day before.**
**(Leader Staff Photo by J. Carmack)**

**Fig. 14-27b** *The* Guthrie Daily Leader *after redesign. A Territorial-era format was selected to reflect the personality of the community.*

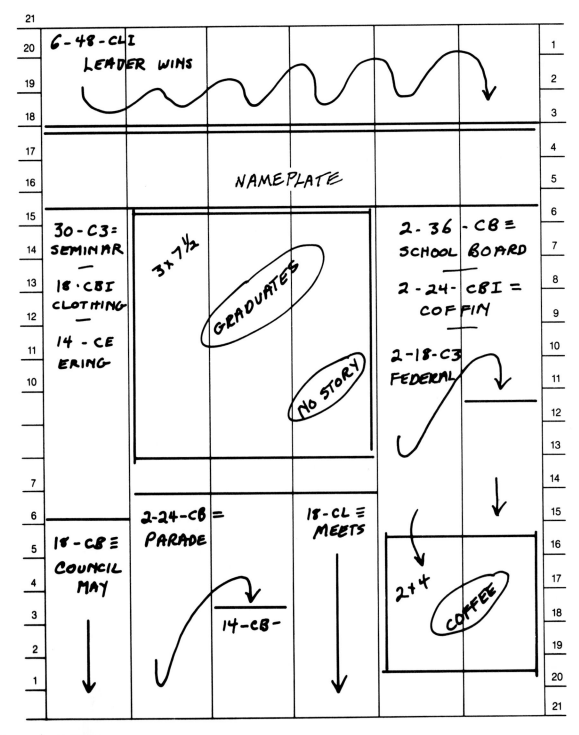

**Fig. 14-28a** *Dummy for prototype page of redesigned* Guthrie Daily Leader *as prepared by the staff. Several prototypes were dummied and composed during the project.*

*Sports Page*

1. All heads will be boldface, but slant may vary.
2. Top heads will be head and one deck; below the top will be headline only.
3. Banner heads will have no decks.

The newspaper page shown as the prototype:

# LEADER WINS PRAISE OF INDUSTRY

# GUTHRIE DAILY LEADER
### Historic Capital of Oklahoma

## SEMINAR PLANNED TUESDAY

### CLOTHING NEED GREAT

#### BRING MONEY

Interior furnishing has begun on two of the apartment buildings at East Towne.

Village on East Perkins Avenue. Mike Trovsie, 21, Route 1 unloads Wohler Co. cabinets for installation in the two buildings. Developers (Leader Staff Photo by J.

## PARADE TO DRAW STATE TALKING DUCK

## MEETS WITH NEED.GREAT FOR CLOTHING

## COUNCIL MAY TAKE ACTION ON SALARIES

## DETECTIVES HARD AT WORK

# SCHOOL BOARD HEARS PUBLIC BUS PROPOSAL

## COFFIN ADDRESSES PANEL ON PROJECT

### FEDERAL FINANCING WILL BE REQUESTED

The Yard of the Week this week, as selected by Spade & Trowel Garden Club, belongs Camerer, 15 Mockingbird are Gertie Carson, Ruth Camerer, Alice Crooks and

**Fig. 14-28b** *The completed prototype page for the* Guthrie Daily Leader *redesign project.*

*Inside Page*

1. Bold- and lightfaces will be mixed, as with slant.

2. Top heads will be head and one deck; headlines below that will be headline only.

3. Banner heads will not have decks, unless containing sidebar and related stories on the same page.

*Headline Mechanics*

**1.** Size designations will be noted on the dummy and on the copy to be set by the headliner. The following style will be used:

2-36-CB—two-column, 36-point Century bold, three lines.

A full headline with decks would be indicated thus:

2-36-CB—two-column, 36-point Century bold, three lines.

2-24-CBI—two-column, 24-point Century bold italic, two lines.

2-18-CB—two-column, 18-point Century bold, one line.

Before the redesign was put into production, various techniques were tested, and several prototypes were constructed before the final specifications were developed. Adkisson reports that the change has been well received by both readers and advertisers.

Although the changes made in the design of the Guthrie *Leader* might not be right for most communities, they carry out the basic principle of effective newspaper design—the appearance of a newspaper should reflect its editorial philosophy and the audience it seeks to serve.

## Effective Design Checklist

- Make sure that all essential elements are included in folio lines and masthead.

- Avoid setting type in unusually narrow measures. Studies show that 9.5 and 10 pica widths simply are not read.

- Keep basic headline types within the same family. If another family is used, it should be used sparingly and for contrast.

- Avoid jumping stories from one page to another. If stories are jumped from page 1, try to continue them all on a convenient page, such as the back page of the front section or page 2. Studies indicate that 80 percent of readership is lost on most jumped stories.

- Arrange advertisements so there is effective editorial display. Square off columns of advertising, and if the well or pyramid style is used, keep ads as low on the page as possible.

- Avoid pictures (usually mug shots, called "pork chops") that are less than one column wide. Try to use mug shots that show what a person is like, rather than what that person looks like.

- Don't run headlines too wide for the type size. A good rule is to keep headlines to thirty-two characters or less regardless of type size.

- Try to have a "stopper"—art or a dominant head—on each page. Never separate a picture from the story it accompanies.

- Eliminate barriers. But if long copy is broken with art or large subhead arrangements, make sure they do not confuse the reader.

- After a page is designed, try to judge it from the reader's point of view. Is it easy to follow, interesting, attractive?

## Graphics in Action

1. A major project in newspaper design could be redesigning your hometown newspaper. Examine current copies of the newspaper and then outline a complete plan for redesign. Make prototype pages by cutting heads, art, and body copy from newspapers that use the styles you would like to adopt. Write justifications for the changes you make.

2. If newspapers did not exist and you decided that a daily printed medium of news and advertisements was needed, how would you design it? What form would it take? What would be its page size? How would the contents be presented? Explain your answers.

3. Obtain a copy of a newspaper. Assume you have inherited the ownership of this newspaper. Since you are interested in graphics, you take a long, hard look at the paper. How would you change the front page? Don't forget that this is a profitable business and you do not want to take a chance on the new design adversely affecting reader acceptance and thus circulation and advertising revenue.

4. Redesign an inside page of a newspaper. Examine the pattern of advertisement placement. If the pyramid or well is used, redesign to magazine or modular. Redesign the editorial content to make its display more effective.

5. If possible, find a nearby community that does not now have a newspaper. Study the community and create a design plan for a newspaper that would reflect the character of the community and thus attract readership. Or choose a community and write to its chamber of commerce to obtain the community's characteristics and demographics to use in this activity.

## Notes

1. Don March, *Editor & Publisher*, October 16, 1980, p. 15.

SGMA is heard on the Hill before Congress recesses:   SGM
mpact of trademark counterfeiting and infringement on th
try before the House Energy and Commerce Subcommittee on
tigations.  Congressman John Dingell (D-MI), Chairman of
sked SGMA for a statistical assessment of international
erfeiting, trade dress and infringement on industry jobs
capital and expand markets.
Members are urged to give SGMA Washington Office individ
   The statistical assessment will be published in the Co
ng Record as an addendum to SGMA testimony.
SGMA members who have experienced international, commerc
f their trademark and products...submit written verifica
ems to the International Trade Commission by Monday, Sep
nfo on testimony guidelines, contact Maria Dennison, 202

Along the same lines, SGMA scheduled to testify later th
horization of the Generalized System of Preferences (GSF
y on the issue will be in the mail to you in the next co
will head coalition effort to condition duty-free treatm
ct to a country's protection of U.S. industrial property

An estimated $5 billion in increased trade and 200,000 j
f the U.S. Government's and SGMA's "Aluminum Bat" victor
rs announced to SGMA bat manufacturers.
Bat makers presented honorary, engraved aluminum bats to
, Secretary Malcolm Baldrige, Senators Heinz (R-PA), Dan
uddleston (D-KY) for their efforts.  SGMA's "Big Stick"
ws which permitted 32 U.S. industries access to Japanese

H.R. 2769, the Caribbean Basin Economic Recovery Act.pas
egislation is estimated to create $1 billion in addition
ts.  To enter duty-free, product must consist of at leas
e Caribbean except that a certain percentage (15% of tot
made components may be counted toward this 35% minimum.
all manufacturers.

Laser beams, word processors, editing terminals, cable television, videotext—these are all electronic miracles, and they are causing revolutionary changes in our communications systems. But no matter what the new technology may bring during the coming decades, one ancient form of communication is sure to survive—and prosper. The newsletter seems certain to keep its place in the communications mix.

Communicators agree that the success of an information program often rests on producing a medium for the information on a regular basis and supporting it with auxiliary tools to reinforce and repeat the message. For many organizations and businesses, the ideal tool for accomplishing this basic, regular communication is a *newsletter.*

The newsletter is not a new communications tool. It has been in existence for a long time. Researchers report that the Han dynasty in China published a daily newsletter in 200 B.C. The forerunners of the modern newspapers were leaflets and pamphlets—newsletters—which described an event or happenings from some other place. These were called diurnals, curantos, and mercuries, and they were printed and sold in the streets. And the first successful newspaper in America was called the *Boston News Letter.*

The modern American commercial newsletter can be traced back to 1923 when Willard Kiplinger brought out the first issue of the *Kiplinger Washington Letter.* Today the newsletter is one of the fastest growing segments of the printing industry in the country. There are more than 100,000 newsletters being produced and distributed on a regular basis. They range from the small mimeographed parish or club sheet to elaborately designed and printed publications that are more closely related to magapapers or in-house magazines.

It is estimated that 3,000 to 5,000 of the 100,000 published newsletters are sent to paid subscribers who pay from one dollar to several thousand dollars a year to receive them. The newsletter with the largest circulation is the *Kiplinger Letter.* It has more than 600,000 paid subscribers.

The newsletter is so popular that many magazines use its format for special interest and updated information pages. *U.S. News & World Report* includes five separate newsletter pages in each issue. Business and organizational publications have found that a page of upbeat information in newsletter style has high readership.

Why are newsletters so popular?

They are liked by communicators and readers. Communicators find the newsletter an ideal communications link with various audiences. A special audience can be targeted easily and reached on a continuing, regular basis. Since the newsletter is brief and to the point, it can be aligned easily with the interests of the target audience. Identification with the interests of an audience is one of the criteria for effective communication.

Messages in a newsletter can be tailor-made for the situation, the time, the location, and the audience. The newsletter can have

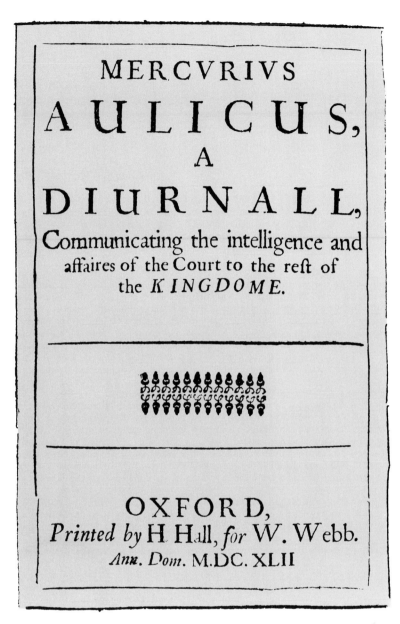

**Fig. 15-1** *Newsletters were popular before newspapers came into existence. Many "newsletters" or news pamphlets were sold in Europe in the 1500s and 1600s.*

a personality, and it can come closer to one-on-one personal communication than most other forms of mass communication. Its chatty style can resemble a personal letter.

In addition, the newsletter can accomplish its goals at a low cost because it can be produced very economically. It would be difficult to find a more cost-efficient method of effective printed communication.

Audiences like newsletters because they contain specialized information that cannot be found elsewhere. The newsletter usually condenses information from many sources. Often newsletter readers do not have access to all these sources or the time to pursue them. People like the resemblance to a letter, and they like to receive information in brief, to-the-point writing.

# THE KIPLINGER WASHINGTON LETTER

*Circulated weekly to business clients since 1923— Vol. 60, No. 52*

THE KIPLINGER WASHINGTON EDITORS

1729 H St., N.W., Washington, D.C. 20006 Tel: 202-887-6400

*Cable Address: Kiplinger Washington D C*

Dear Client:                                            Washington, Dec. 30, 1983.

<u>This is all about the rest of the century</u>...the next 16 years.
Shifts and trends in business, population, politics, technology.
What to expect, how to plan for it, how to make money out of it.
It's an upbeat story of progress and better standards of living.
Also new growing pains and new crises...never an end to them.

<u>Start with these assumptions</u>:
<u>No nuclear war</u>.  Each side has credible deterrents to an attack
and too much to lose by walloping the other.  But tensions will continue.
<u>No long-lasting oil shortage</u>.  We no longer depend on imports
as we did five years ago.  There'll be enough energy to meet our needs.
<u>We'll muddle through third world debt troubles</u>, but it will take
healthier economies around the world and concessions by the big lenders.
<u>And make some headway against gov't deficits</u> in next few years.
But it will be painful...higher taxes and tighter controls on spending.

<u>Business growing about 3% per year</u>...on average.
<u>That's quite good</u>...stronger the next 16 years than the past 16.
Sure, there will be recessions.  But they should be shorter and milder
than in the '70s and early '80s.  And the upturns will be more solid.
<u>Better productivity</u> is one reason.  It sagged from 1973 to 1982,
which worsened inflation.  Should grow at a good clip in the years ahead
due to a more seasoned labor force, increased capital investment and R&D
and more stable business conditions...less of a roller-coaster ride.

<u>"Moderate" inflation</u>...averaging 5% to 6% per year now to 2000.
(An item that you buy for $100 today will cost around $235 in 16 years.)
<u>Interest rates</u>, about 2% below present levels...on the average.
<u>Rising profits, higher incomes, higher standards of living</u>...
result of the greater productivity, milder inflation, stronger economy.

<u>Investment in new factories and equipment will climb 4% a year</u>,
slightly faster than the general economy.  More GNP going to investment.
<u>On saving, investing and managing</u>...back to basics will pay off.
Conventional strategies...less go-go speculation and fancy leveraging.
Stocks, bonds, CDs will probably beat gold, silver and futures trading.

<u>Among the hottest lines</u>: Computers.  Consumer electronic gear.
Telecommunications and satellite TV.  Health-care services and products.
Robotics.  Office automation.  Travel, restaurants, leisure industries.
Cellular radio and phone systems.  Financial services.  Autos.  Housing.
Defense & aerospace.  Genetic engineering.  Food processing & exporting.
<u>For career planning</u>, youngsters should look into math & science,
engineering, computer specialties and health.  LOADS of opportunities.
<u>Higher skills are a must</u> for the future...every line, every job.
Manual as well as mental or intellectual.  Hammer this home...SHOUT it.

**Fig. 15-2**   *The pioneer commercial newsletter, the* Kiplinger Washington Letter, *was founded in 1923. It set the design style that has been known as the "classic" newsletter format. The fourth page of the "classic" newsletter concludes with an ending similar to a personal letter. (Reproduced by special permission of the Kiplinger Washington Editors, Inc.)*

Financial services...a fast-changing industry.  Lines will blur
between banks, S&Ls, insurance firms and stockbrokers as they compete
across state lines for business.  There will be less gov't regulation,
more reliance on the market, more people using home computers to bank.
Computers will become more standardized and simpler to use...
able to "talk" with each other.  They'll run whole shops and warehouses.
Their capacity to gather, store and mold information will keep growing.

"High-definition" TV will be hot...sharp as a motion picture.
More satellites...worldwide voice, data and video transmission.
Fiber optics will deliver electronic signals, telephone service,
cable TV, etc., into homes and offices...cheaply and more efficiently.
Robots will boom, helping to make uniform parts with less waste.
You 20-year-olds, 30-ish, 40-ish, take note of what lies ahead.
Great changes are coming...for you, your children, your grandchildren.

No space-based defense system in place until well into the 2000s.
But the first steps will be taken...funding for chemical lasers,
nuclear-pumped lasers or particle beams for intercepting Soviet missiles.
Competition with Russia will continue in the years ahead, but...
An arms agreement will probably be reached sometime in the '80s.
And Russia has an economic mess that it must straighten out soon.
We think that it will gradually move toward a hybrid marketing system...
away from central planning...recognizing the present system is a flop.

Politically, we won't wander very far from middle of the road,
even though the long-term drift has been to the left...to bigger gov't.
The House will be more southern and western after 1990 Census
and reapportionment...more seats for Calif., Fla., Texas, Nevada, Ariz.
Taken away from N.Y. and other states that are going to be losing people.
Women on the national ticket by 2000.  VP...or even President.
And perhaps Blacks or Hispanics as they develop political clout.
Plus growing involvement of religious groups in public policy...
the Catholic bishops and Evangelicals are at the leading edge of this.

In the past 20 years, we've had to absorb some major jolts:
Kennedy's assassination.  Vietnam.  Watergate and Nixon's resignation.
The drug explosion and "counterculture."  A 10-fold rise in oil prices.
Runaway inflation.  And the hardest economic times since the Thirties.

Now things appear to be getting back on a more even keel,
a steadier, more normal footing.  There should be fewer shocks ahead.
The baby-boomers are on the verge of the most productive phase of life.
(We've already survived their teens.)  They'll be forming new families,
furnishing households...moving into their earningest, spendingest years.
We're beginning to pull together better as a nation, maturing.
Even the young people seem to be returning to more traditional values.

                              Yours very truly,

Dec. 30, 1983                 THE KIPLINGER WASHINGTON EDITORS

P.S.  Just for the fun of it, put down your age __.  Add 16, making __.
That's how old you will be when all of these things have taken place.

THE KIPLINGER WASHINGTON LETTER—(ISSN 0023-1770)
SUBSCRIPTION RATES: $48-ONE YEAR, $86-TWO YEARS, $118-THREE YEARS, $182-FIVE YEARS
SECOND-CLASS POSTAGE PAID AT WASHINGTON, D.C.

**Fig. 15-3** *Newsletters are so popular many magazines adopt the format for informational pages. For example, U.S. News & World Report publishes five "newsletters" in each issue of the magazine. (Copyright 1984, U.S. News & World Report, Inc.)*

## NEWS You Can Use.

### IN YOUR PERSONAL PLANNING

2300 N Street, N.W.
Washington, D.C. 20037

**HOW MUCH ARE YOU WORTH?**

Whether your goal is to buy a home, put the children through college or plan for retirement, it helps to know how much you're really worth.

FIGURING YOUR NET WORTH. Finding out how many assets you've been able to accumulate and then keeping track of them year after year will help you learn how close you are to your financial goals, advises Citibank.

Assets. Start by listing in one column the value of your assets. Figures should be fairly precise and for the same approximate date. Start with available cash; bank or money-market-account balances; cash value of life insurance; value of stocks and bonds, and equity from company fringe-benefit plans, such as vested pension plans, deferred profit sharing, stock-purchase plans or company savings plans.

Property. Follow with the value of your home, car, home furnishings, clothing and such personal possessions as antiques, silverware, collectibles and hobby equipment. Try to be reasonable, not sentimental, in setting values. Let them reflect what you could sell the possessions for--not their original or replacement costs.

Business. If you own all or part of a business, record your equity in it. Also, list any other special items, such as money owed you or the value of an estate or trust that's being held for you.

**LIST ALL DEBTS**

Liabilities. In a second column, write down all debts. List: The amount of outstanding bills, including unpaid utility and medical charges; outstanding balances still owed on mortgage, home-improvement and car loans, and credit-card and charge accounts. Also, insurance premiums, unpaid balances on any insurance-policy loans and college-tuition loans and any installments still due on estimated federal and state income taxes and school and property taxes.

The bottom line. Now add each of the two columns separately. The difference between the two is your net worth. If you own more than you owe, you have positive net worth. If the reverse is true, you have negative net worth. Once you have the final figure, it's fairly easy to update it each year. But don't forget to adjust for inflation, which is always nibbling away at the value of a dollar.

**IRS EYES ABUSIVE SHELTERS**

TAX CRACKDOWN. As part of its crackdown on abusive tax shelters, the Internal Revenue Service intends to notify investors--before they file tax returns--when a shelter's purported tax benefits aren't considered allowable. In deciding which shelters are abusive, IRS investigates whether promoters have (1) overvaluated assets, (2) made false or fraudulent statements or (3) abused technical formulas, such as methods of allocating excessive interest in time-sharing transactions.

CORDLESS PHONES. An owner of a cordless or portable telephone who forgets to place the phone in the "talk" position before lifting it to

## Designing the Newsletter

The newsletter is a rather uncomplicated printed communication. It doesn't seem to offer much challenge to the editor or designer. But therein lies the problem. It is such a basic form of printed communication that it can be put together too easily. As a result, too many lose effectiveness because they look inept and amateurish. But they don't have to. Application of basic typographic and design principles can change an unattractive, ineffective newsletter into one that is an asset to its publishers.

As always, before the designer or editor begins to make decisions concerning the format and graphics of a newsletter, it is necessary to consider its purpose. A thorough understanding of the reasons

The Community Relations

# REPORT

February 1983 Vol. 2 No. 3

*The Best in Corporate Community Relations*

## CR Videotapes

John Westfall, director of business issues action, business promotion, for Phillips Chemical Company, believes that community relations should be a part of each plant manager's responsibilities. So much so that he planned a training seminar for key people in all their 22 plant locations to attend—but that fell through when the economy fell through. Instead of giving up, he did a creative thing: he put the seminar on videotape and sent it to the plant managers and their internal community relations representatives.

"I made eight tapes and we're sending one a week to the plants along with a booklet," says Westfall. Each CR representative and his or her plant manager views the tape. Of all the tapes, only one is generic to Phillips. The others are about various community relation subjects, such as "the legal aspect of community relations;" "how Monsanto meets the media—and survives;" "why the chemical industry needs community relation programs;" and "an overview of community relations."

Westfall will make these tapes available to any *CR Report* subscriber on a loan-out basis. All eight tapes total three hours in length but can be viewed separately.

"One of our publics is our employee audience," says Westfall." If the employee thinks you have a problem, then you have a problem. The community relation representative must work together with those in employee relations." (please turn to page 2)

## INSIDE

**Phillips Chemicals**........1-4
**2% Club**..........5
**Volunteer Book**....6
**BG&E CR**........7
**Highlighting CR**...8
**IS Newsletter**.....9
**Contributions**.....10
**CR Notes**......11-15
**Ideas**...........16

**TIP:** Don't make a contribution to those who send you a form letter. If they don't go to the trouble of writing a personal letter, why should you go to the trouble of contributing to their organization?

**ANOTHER TIP:** Don't make contributions to telephone requests. These usually come in the form of a solicitation for money—and often it is not the organization itself calling, but a professional calling service and they may be questionable.

**HAVE YOU READ "MEGATRENDS"?** It's a good book that will give you a better understanding about the trends going on in society. The author is John Naisbitt. You can find it in your bookstore for $15.50.

## A New Look

This issue marks a different look to the *CR Report*—we start off the new year by redesigning the publication. Why? Because we want to make it look more attractive and conducive to the editorial material.

Good design is pleasing, gets people interested in what you have to say, and doesn't get in the way. We felt that the type was hard to read on the brown paper we were using—a point a number of you told us.

Some of you said it would be nice to have a table of contents on the front of the newsletter so it would be easier to go back at a later date and find things in the publication.

We also realize the short amount of time you have for reading.

If your in-box is anything like mine, it makes you wonder about how much paper is being used—and wasted today. We want the *CR Report* to be quick to scan and if there is a particular article that interests you there should be enough material about it for you to learn the basic details. That way you can decide whether or not it is worthwhile to contact the person for more information. The part most readers seem to like is the listing of the person's address and phone number at the end of each piece. We'll keep that up.

(continued on page 15)

**Fig. 15-4** *This newsletter was a gold award winner at the 1983 International Newsletter Conference. The* Report *nameplate is unusually bold and is printed in red ink, providing quick recognition. Note the use of rules and initial letters. Square Serif types are used throughout except for the contents box on page 1. (Courtesy of the* Community Relations Report.)

the newsletter is being produced will help make its appearance appropriate to the subject matter and the audience.

A description of the planned contents and a definition of the audience should be written as a basic policy guide for editing and designing. Potential readers should be described according to such characteristics as their professions, age category, education, sex, beliefs, attitudes, interests, hobbies, and family situation, or whatever else is relevant.

Out of this preliminary research should come some ideas on how to develop the newsletter's personality. Each newsletter should have its own personality, look, and style. This helps it establish its niche in the communications spectrum. The goal should be to design a newsletter that will be welcomed as a letter from a friend each time it appears.

A consistent style means each issue will look basically the same as all the others. Since the design elements of a newsletter are rather limited compared to many other printed communications, this may cause us to worry about producing a monotonous product. But the page that we spend one or several hours on will only be seen for a few minutes by the reader. And many newsletters have been produced in the same basic design for years with great success.

Nevertheless, this does not mean that the simple newsletter format cannot have sparkle and variety. Although a basic, consistent style is important in newsletter design, we should keep in mind that even the smallest change will become immediately apparent to the reader. A different size head type or a boxed item will stand out in a newsletter when it might be virtually unnoticed in a more complicated layout.

If an item is boxed or a few words underlined or set in italic type, the design change will be so apparent to the reader that it will grab attention and send the signal that something of considerable importance from the rest of the contents is being presented. Changes in design elements should thus be made very carefully. If change is made continually, nothing will stand out and the newsletter will become a confusing design hodgepodge.

Remember, the design of the newsletter sends out signals to the reader. The design tells the audience the attitude of the publication, its approach to the subject matter, and which items are especially important. A feature that is always boxed, for instance, or set in the same typeface every issue tells the reader something about the contents of the feature. Readers will get in the habit of seeking this element for certain information.

Since the design of a newsletter appears rather simplistic and unchallenging, some designers have been inclined to pay little attention to it. Designing a newsletter doesn't seem to deserve much time or thought except for a few decisions concerning the nameplate, width of columns, and a type for setting the contents.

However, Howard Penn Warren, publisher of the *Newsletter on Newsletters* and founder of the Newsletter Association of America, has reacted to the comments of some newsletter publishers that visual appearance and graphic quality are the least important characteristics of a successful newsletter by writing:

> . . . even as "least important," graphics are of some importance—and often neglected. Having reviewed thousands of newsletters which have filtered through this office, we come to these conclusions:
>
> **1.** Regardless of content, some NLs [newsletters] are more attractive, "more readable" than others.
> **2.** Some typefaces including typewriter are more pleasing than others.
> **3.** Some headings express better the subject and flavor of the letter than others.
> **4.** Some headlines and handling of body copy "grab" you more than others.
> **5.** Some color combinations are more inviting than others.
> **6.** Some printing is better than others.
>
> The simple 8½ by 11 format of most NLs is capable of infinite variations. When we speak of graphics for NLs, we are not thinking of coated stock and four-color illustrations. We are speaking of doing the most effective job within given limits.[1]

News and Notes on Sports Industry Matters

Vol. 7, No. 4                                   September/October 1983

Dear Member:

The stage is set and excitement is building. Not a single booth remains.
Buyer pre-registration is running 55% ahead of 1982. Buying groups from 30
nations have already pre-registered. New York hotel reservations are up
sharply.
SGMA's EXPO '83, America's Premier Sporting Goods Market, is the best
"open to buy" exhibit in years with the biggest buyer attendance ever.
The October 1-4 event will feature 1,100 sporting goods lines..."hosting
over 16,500 buyers and a few thousand tire kickers," says Show Chairman
George Stangel (Spalding).

A full slate of business seminars will enable retailers to sharpen their
professional skills. "Taking the Mystery out of Computer Selection" leads off
the Expo '83 seminar program. In the market for a computer, make sure you
attend...Saturday, October 1 at 10 a.m. and 2 p.m. and Sunday, October 2 at
2 p.m. Computer equipment demos held on the same days in the Canada Room where
retailers may personally consult with seminar leaders.
Other "must" seminars scheduled for Monday, October 3, include:
  9:30 a.m.  "Planning a New Store"
  11:30 a.m.  "Tennis Shop Management"
  2:00 p.m.  "Building a Line from the Manufacturers and Retailers
             Outlook" (footwear buyers)
These seminars will be held in the United Nations Room, 2nd floor south.

The SGMA Industry Breakfast, scheduled Sunday, October 3, from 8-10 a.m.
in the Imperial Ballroom of the Sheraton Centre Hotel is the social highlight
of Expo '83. Secretary of the Interior James G. Watt will keynote. Ticket sales
are well ahead of last year's for this event. For reservations, contact
Bobbie Hundley 305/842-4100.

High School Federation insurance policy said to shift liability to manufacturers. SGMA is studying the situation and will take action. Gymnastic
and helmet manufacturers very concerned. See NOCSAE story-page 4.

An SGMA trade show survey for both exhibitors and buyers has been distributed to the entire industry...results will provide a more factual basis from
which to guide trade show decisions. Survey includes personal interviews with
more than 2,000 retailers and the entire manufacturing community.
Of special interest is the "almagamation" of trade shows initiated by the
CSGA centered around a January-February time frame. Send comments on trade
shows to Tony Kucera, SGMA Vice President.

SPORTING GOODS MANUFACTURERS ASSN.
200 CASTLEWOOD DRIVE  •  NORTH PALM BEACH FLORIDA 33408  •  (305) 842-4100

**Fig. 15-5**  Action Update, *published by the Sporting Goods Manufacturers
Association, follows the "classic" newsletter format. It won a gold award for the best
in the "association" category in the 1983 International Newsletter Conference
competitions.*

Billiard and Bowling Institute of America (BBIA):  "It was good to see so many BBIAers at the SGMA New York Show," said BBIA President Dave Grau (Ace Mitchell House of Champions and Bowlers Mart).  At their Board meeting held at the 1984 Convention site in San Antonio, programs and socials were looked at first hand by Directors.  <u>Woody Woodruff (AMF) was chosen recipient of the 1984 Industry Service Award.</u>

Non-Powder Gun Products Association (NPGPA):  <u>Dr. Sherman Kearl, LAOOC Shooting Commissioner, and Dick Daniel (Daisy), NPGPA's President, were recognized at the SGMA Annual Industry Breakfast for their efforts on behalf of the air gun industry and the 1984 Olympics.</u>
Dr. Kearl stated that the LAOOC now has financing for a permanent facility for the '84 Olympic Air Gun Event and this new range, when built, will provide the U.S. with a permanent world class air gun facility.

<u>SGMA welcomes new members:</u>  Diamond Sports Company and Amoco Fabrics Company.

                              Sincerely,

                              SPORTING GOODS MANUFACTURERS ASSOCIATION

**SPORTING GOODS MANUFACTURERS ASSN.**
200 Castlewood Drive
North Palm Beach, Florida 33408

```
BULK RATE
U.S. Postage
PAID
West Palm Beach, FL
Permit No. 386
```

Please route to:
_____
_____
_____

**Fig. 15-6**  *The method of distribution will play a part in newsletter design.* Action
Update *devotes half of the back page to the mailing requirements. Note the closing*
*that resembles a letter to give that personal touch.*

## The First Step: Selecting a Size

The first step in designing a newsletter is to settle on a size. Just as certain sizes have developed into the standard for newspapers and magazines, so has the 8½ by 11 page become the standard for newsletters. There are a number of reasons for this. The 8½ by 11 page is the same size as the standard business letter. This size is easy to file or to punch and put into a binder. It folds easily to fit a number 10 (business size) envelope.

In addition, a four-page 8½ by 11 newsletter can be printed on an 11 by 17 sheet, two pages at a time, in most "quick print" or in-house printing facilities. The 11 by 17 (or 17 by 22) sheet is stocked by most shops and so is readily available. It is the standard sheet out of which business letterheads are cut.

However, there are alternatives. Sometimes the method of printing will determine, or at least affect, the page size. If a mimeograph is used, the page size will be limited to a "legal-size" sheet that is 8½ by 14 inches. The legal-size sheet can be folded in half to create a four-page 7 by 8½ inch newsletter. A small organization

**Fig. 15-7** *The page size of* In Touch *is only 6½ by 7¼, but a lot of graphics are packed in to attract the customers of the Minnegasco in Minneapolis.*

**with Minnegasco**

February/March, 1983

## How to Avoid Estimated Bills

During the winter, Minnegasco makes every effort to read your meter once a month. But from time to time, we must estimate your meter reading. As a result, your gas bill is based upon the estimated reading instead of the amount of gas you actually used.

There are several things you can do to obtain an actual reading. If your meter is outdoors, make sure the reader can get to it by removing any snow and ice on or around the meter. If your meter is indoors, make arrangements to allow the meter reader to gain access to your home on the scheduled meter reading date. Many customers provide us with a house key. You can send your key with your next bill requesting that it be kept on file for regular meter readings.

You can also read your own meter. Simply write or call the Minnegasco Office nearest you for a supply of meter reading cards. Follow the instructions on the card

*It's easy to read your gas meter. Just draw lines on the dials above exactly as they appear on your meter. Then mail in your reading by the next meter reading date listed on your gas bill. (Customers in Minneapolis may call in their reading — 340-0556.)*

and mail in your reading. (If you live in Minneapolis, you can phone in your reading by calling 340-0556.) The reading must be received by Minnegasco by the meter reading date which is listed on your gas bill.

## Heating Equipment Needs Fresh Air for Safe Operation

Keeping warm is part of our daily lives during the winter season. To keep comfortable indoors, we weatherize our homes and rely on our furnaces and fireplaces. For outdoor activities like camping and ice fishing, we depend on recreational heaters. And when we're traveling from place to place, we let our car engines idle longer to warm up.

*(Cont. on p. 3)*

or business might find this a workable size. It could also help the newsletter stand out from the more standard-size communications.

A newsletter produced on an office duplicator could be an 8½ by 11 sheet folded in half. This would make four 5½ by 8½ pages.

Another possibility would be to fold an 8½ by 11 sheet to make six 3⅔ by 8½ pages. An accordion or gate fold could be used (see pages 348-349). If such a format is selected, many of the design techniques used in producing brochures could be employed (see pages 346-352).

Probably the best solution if printing capabilities are limited to 8½ by 11 or 8½ by 14 is to stick to one 8½ by 11 sheet printed on both sides. If more than one sheet is used, a method of binding the sheets together will be needed. Sometimes sheets are held together with a single staple in the upper-left corner. This should, however, be avoided as it is a flimsy device and the pages come apart easily. A better solution is to leave a wider margin on the binding side of the page than on the outside and staple the newsletter in sidewire fashion, like a magazine.

Newsletters can be found in all shapes and sizes. Some, called *magaletters*, are actually more closely related to magazines or tabloid newspapers in format. Some, called *magapapers*, are a mix of newsletters, magazines, and tabloid newspapers. The designer of these hybrid publications can employ some of the design techniques of all three in planning such a publication.

### Designing the "Classic" Newsletter

Let's begin our discussion of newsletter design by considering the "classic" or "standard" newsletter format. This is an 11 by 17 sheet folded in half to produce four 8½ by 11 pages. More pages can be added, of course, but four 8½ by 11 pages seem ideal in size for the content and design of one issue of a newsletter. If there is so much material that it will not fit into a four-page issue, it may be time to consider more frequent publication.

The classic newsletter format has been developed for the 8½ by 11 page size. Its characteristics include:

- Typewriter composition (or the use of "typewriter"-style type if set on equipment other than a typewriter) with one column for each page.

- A short, punchy writing style in which obvious words are often left out and key sentences, phrases, and names are underlined.

- A limited number of graphic elements designed with care and used consistently. Simplicity is stressed.

- One style of type for the content; sometimes italic or boldface is used for limited emphasis.

- Preserving the feel of a personal communication as much as possible.

- Avoiding making the newsletter look like a magazine.

# Minnegasco News

**Volume 32
Feb. 15, 1983
No. 4**

## DEI reports increased earnings

*Minneapolis* — Diversified Energies, Inc. in unaudited figures, reported earlier this month net income for the year ended Dec. 31, 1982 of $20.1 million and earnings per common share of $4.18.

Net income was up $3.7 million, or 22 percent, from $16.4 million reported in 1981. Earnings per common share was up $.75 cents, or nearly 22 percent, from $3.43 a share in 1981.

The increase in net income was attributable primarily to increased sales of natural gas by Minnegasco, Inc., the natural gas distribution company of DEI.

While 1982 weather was slightly warmer than normal, it was 19 percent colder than weather in 1981 — which was an abnormally mild heating season.

## Utilizes company CPR training

## Metro meter reader saves resident's life

*Minneapolis* — An elderly Minneapolis man is alive today only because of the alertness and extra care exhibited by a Minnegasco employee.

The man, a south Minneapolis resident whose age is listed in the 60s, was saved

from certain death Jan. 27 by Metro Meter Reader Martin Torrez.

Torrez spotted the potentially lethal situation — a car motor running in an enclosed garage — and took it upon himself to open the

**LIFE-SAVER / *page 2***

Marty Torrez, with the assistance of fellow meter reader, Dick LeTourneau, (on floor), simulated the life-saving technique that he used to save the life of a customer. He received his CPR training through a company training session.

## Minnegasco to sell refrigerators, dishwashers

*Minneapolis* — Should one good merchandising offer lead to another?

In the case of Merchandising's successful introduction of microwave ovens in December, the answer is a decided YES!

And so, beginning Feb. 14 and continuing through March 12, Retail Sales will offer Whirlpool and Kelvinator refrigerators and dishwashers in a pilot program at its three Minneapolis-area locations.

"We will introduce the lines with very competitive prices," said Dave Osgood, product manager, Merchandising.

"We will also offer customers a large selection of models complete with the most asked for features in each appliance line," he said.

Kelvinator offers quality lines at competitive prices while Whirlpool has long been known as a leader in the appliance industry, he noted.

If the pilot program proves to be successful, plans call for the models to be offered at other key locations in the franchise area, said Osgood.

**Employees again have the opportunity to take advantage of special introductory sale prices. Details on page four.**

"The program is another in Merchandising's goals to improve its profitability and to establish Minnegasco as a full-line merchandiser in the eyes of the customers," he said.

## New study to aid future marketing efforts

*Minneapolis* — A recently-completed comprehensive study of Minnegasco customer attitudes will serve as a major guide to company marketing and communications in the year ahead.

The study — perhaps the most extensive done by Minnegasco in more than a decade — was prepared by Yankelovich, Skelly, and White, Inc. (YSW) of New York, a respected nation-

wide research firm. It reinforced some long-time beliefs Minnegasco management had about its customer base; supported some other existing views; and pointed up some new potential opportunities for working with customers.

YSW has done other studies for utilities across the country and has worked with the American Gas Association on research programs. Local market

research firms were also employed in the actual gathering of information for the Minnegasco customer study.

More than 600 Minnegasco Minnesota customers were interviewed to determine overall attitudes toward the company and to provide information to launch future marketing and communications strategies and programs. The study will also serve as a benchmark against which progress can

be measured in the future.

Subsequent articles in the *Minnegasco News* will cover the study findings in detail, YSW's study approach, and how the study will serve the company's marketing and communications plans. Findings on the customer's familiarity with attitudes toward the company will be covered Mar. 1.

**SURVEY / *page 5***

**Fig. 15-8** *Modular design using boxed rectangles and the same typeface throughout create both unity and harmony. At the same time, each graphic unit retains individuality in this well-designed newsletter.*

That is the classic newsletter format. It was developed by Kiplinger, and many newsletters follow it faithfully.

However, there are a number of alternatives to consider, and the first concerns the *widths of columns*.

One of the immediate criticisms of the single-column page is that the column width, usually about sixty characters for pica typewriter copy, is too wide for easy reading. However, since this is a standard for typewritten letters, people are used to it. If you prefer narrower line widths, an alternative is indenting the columns and placing the heads for items in the left-hand margin.

Even with one column, using wider margins and more space between paragraphs can help readability. If the margins are, say, 6 picas, the line width can be held to about forty-five characters.

There are two ways to handle a two-column page format. One is to vary the widths of the columns. The left-hand column can be 14 to 16 picas wide, for example, and the right-hand column

**Fig. 15-9**   *The single-column newsletter in 8½ by 11 format can have a narrower and more readable column width if heads are placed on the side of the reading matter.*

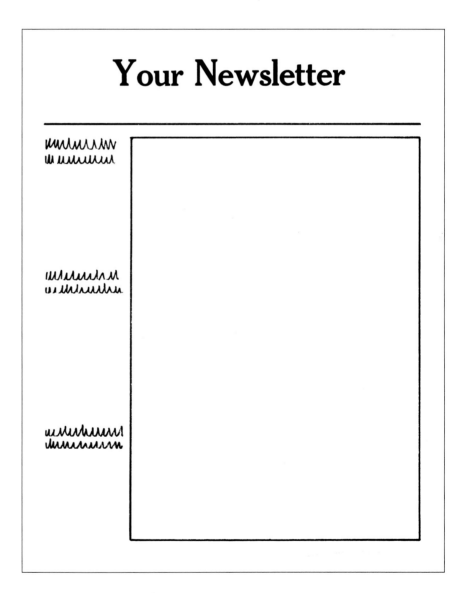

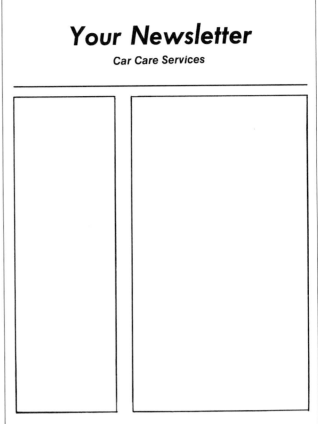

24 or 25 to 30 picas wide. The other, of course, is to plan two columns of equal size.

The two-column format has a number of advantages. It produces a more readable line width, and more words can be accommodated on a page compared to a single-column page. There is greater opportunity for creative design, and more variation and interest can be worked into the layouts. It is easier to use graphics such as charts and illustrations.

If a three-column format is adopted, the newsletter moves toward a magazine or miniature newspaper in appearance. It is necessary to have the body copy typeset for it to look attractive. Typewriter type will not work well on a narrow column unless it is reduced. If it is not reduced, the lines will be too short for good word spacing and the entire page will look amateurish. But, then, if it is reduced below 9 point, readability suffers.

Also, the three-column format tends to look like a magazine in the eyes of readers, and it might be judged as such. Since most newsletters are not produced with the extensive talent and mechanical resources of a large magazine, the newsletter will suffer by comparison.

However, the three-column page gives the designer an opportunity to blend the best qualities of magazine design with those of the newsletter.

**Fig. 15-10** *Two possibilities for a two-column newsletter format. Two equal-width columns or one narrow and one wide can be used. Often an identifying slogan can add impact and memorability to the logo.*

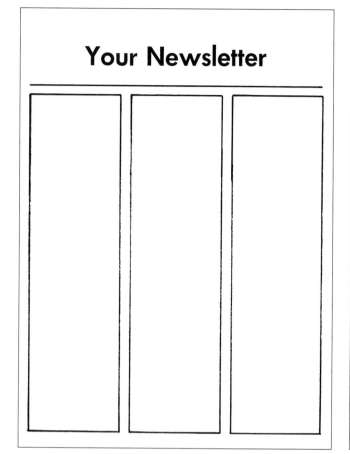

**Fig. 15-11** *The newsletter with a three-column page approaches the magazine format. Magazine design techniques can be used.*

**Fig. 15-12** *Some newsletters achieve orderly format and memorability plus quick identity with ruled borders around the pages and a symbol added to the logo.*

Along with deciding on the number of columns per page, we need to *determine margin size*. Page margins should be at least 3 picas all around. If the pages are to be punched for a binder, the margins should be wide enough to prevent the punch holes from obliterating some of the reading matter. As mentioned, if the newsletter is typewriter-set in a single column, margins of 6 picas all around are not too much.

White space between columns should not be more than 3 picas if copy is typewriter-set or 2 picas if typeset. Too much white space between columns can destroy unity by creating a wide white alley in the middle of the page. But white space should be at least 1½ picas wide for typewriter-set copy and 1 pica for typeset copy if it is to do a neat job of column separation.

Some newsletters are designed with *rules for framing* the type spaces and separating the columns. Rules can be effective design devices, but they should be added to a page only if they serve a useful purpose. A rule across the top and bottom of each page, bled to the edge, can help unify the whole newsletter and be an identifying device. Thin lines under headings can add individuality to the newsletter.

Reading matter that is typewriter-set can be ragged right. It is possible to justify typewriter-set copy, but it really doesn't seem worth the bother. It does not increase readability, and it can cause some awkward spacing between words. If the copy is set ragged right (either typed or typeset), the page will often look more organized if vertical hairline column rules are used. These rules should be centered between columns in at least 1 pica of white space. If hairlines are not used, care should be taken in selecting thicker rules between columns. If they are too thick they can create disunity and can give the page a "funereal" appearance.

Rules and borders that are too heavy and too complex should be avoided. Such ornamentation usually succeeds in attracting attention to itself rather than enhancing the whole layout. Wide borders, if used, can be toned down by screening.

## Newsletter Design Decisions

Along with the basic format for the newsletter, a number of graphic decisions must be made. These include the design of the nameplate or logo, headline treatment, constants such as masthead and folio lines, and heads for regular features, as well as the design of the body type.

## The Logo

The newsletter logo deserves serious consideration. In this discussion the term *nameplate* refers to the actual typeset name of the publication and *logo* to the whole treatment of the name plus any symbols or slogans. The logo creates the first impression, and it should identify the newsletter and its scope quickly but not overpower the other elements on the page. It should not occupy more than 20 percent of the page, in most situations.

The newsletter name should be imaginative—it should distinguish the newsletter from the thousands of others that are in circulation. Designers suggest avoiding using a name that can become dull and that cannot be expressed with some imaginative graphics. Such names as the initials of the organization with the word *newsletter* or *bulletin* tacked on the end can be dull.

The logo design should help translate the title, and the type style used should be appropriate for the purpose of the newsletter. It should provide contrast with the headline type, but it should not dominate the page to the point that it overshadows the content. It should be distinctive so it will not be confused with the headline types.

Often a symbol or design can be incorporated with the name to create a distinctive logo. This logo can be made in different sizes

PUBLISHED FOR OCHSNER EMPLOYEES                    VOLUME 7, NUMBER 4 • 1983

# INSIDE *Ochsner*

## Ochsner Makes All Out Effort Against German Measles

A program to immunize everyone who works at Ochsner — including employees and physicians in the clinic, hospital and foundation and the Brent House hotel — against rubella (German measles) is currently underway. It is designed to protect patients, particularly pregnant women and children, as much as possible from getting the disease.

The procedure requires that all employees and physicians must first be screened by blood test to determine if they need to be immunized against rubella. If it is found that they need the vaccine, then they are called in to receive it. The sweeping decision to guard everyone against rubella, a relatively mild form of measles which can cause deformity in the fetus when contracted by women in the early stages of pregnancy, was made by the board of management of the clinic and the board of trustees of the Alton Ochsner Medical Foundation. The foundation is funding the project.

Testing in the clinic, which has some 800 employees, is nearing completion — both with the screening test and the vaccinations, says Francis F. Manning, administrative director. At the foundation and hospital, which employs some 2700 people, screening and vaccination, if necessary, of all new employees began some two years ago, says assistant hospital director Otis L. Story, who is in charge of the project. Testing of all other employees will get underway shortly in order not to overburden

lab facilities, Mr. Story points out, adding that the hospital is presently involved in completing the series of three shots given to about 1000 of its high-risk employees against Hepatitis B.

The inoculation program against rubella, which has been in the planning stage for some time, was given added impetus recently by the Center for Disease Control in Atlanta, Ga.,

when it reported serious outbreaks of German measles in several hospitals throughout the country, particularly those in California. "The literature reveals that about 90% of all people are immune to the disease, either from having had rubella in childhood or from being immunized at some point in their lives. But, we are discovering that only 2% of Ochsner Clinic employees screened

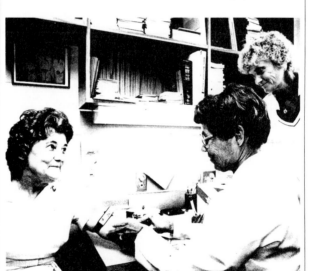

*Etta Lockbaum, R.N., left; Kitty Plemmons, R.N.; and Nita Betillier, L.P.N., standing.*

require immunization," Mr. Manning explains. "However, because we must offer our patients and employees the most complete protection we can, the Ochsner Clinic board of management believes it of sufficient importance to make immunization against rubella a condition of employment for future employees and physicians," he adds.

Screening in the clinic began during the summer when two nurses in each department were assigned to draw blood of a number of employees on a specified afternoon and subsequently inoculation is to take place in the section on infectious diseases. Dr. Shannon Cooper, head of the Ochsner Blood Bank, and Dr. Charles Genre, head of the pathology department, cooperated in planning the undertaking.

"In the hospital, immunization against rubella actually began in 1979 when the first efforts were made to immunize employees against rubella on a voluntary basis," Mr. Story states. Again in 1981, not only was rubella screening and immunization introduced in the preemployment physical, but all employees who had contact with children and pregnant women were immunized, including those in pediatrics, obstetrics and gynecology, and those working in all nursing units on the medical and surgical floors.

The foundation will shortly begin to screen those employees who haven't been previously tested and immunize those who need it.

**Fig. 15-13** *This award-winning newsletter uses a reverse for its folio line and a hairline rule to box pages plus 6-point cutoff rules. Although there is liberal use of rules, they do not interfere with readability. (Inside Ochsner, Ochsner Medical Institution, New Orleans. Editor: Luba B. Glade; designer: P. Douglas Manger)* to be used in the masthead, house ads, letterheads, envelopes, and so on. The more the logo is used, the better it can help create identity and recognition.

The logo should not be so large or strong that it interferes with the content of the newsletter. Designers say the logo plus the folio lines should not take up more than 2 inches at the top of page 1. However, as with most "rules," there might be situations where the exception is the most effective design device.

When Kiplinger created the name for the *Kiplinger Washington Letter* he deliberately left the word *news* out because his plan was to write about the news rather than report it. Many newsletter publishers have adopted this personalized style. There is the *Granville Report* on stocks, and the *Lundborg Letter* on oil, for instance.

A touch of distinction that can set a newsletter out of the ordinary is to print the logo in color. It is possible to do this inexpensively if arrangements are made with the printer to print a supply of blank paper for the newsletter when color is on the press. Then the body of the newsletter can be printed in black, or whatever, at a later date. Some newsletter producers have a year's supply of colored logos printed at one time at a considerable savings.

Other ways to add color and brighten the newsletter is to print a screened tint block across the top of the first page and surprint the logo over it. Or a rule that extends across the top or both the top and bottom of all pages can be printed in color. The logo can be printed from a reverse plate in color, too.

Some newsletter names are printed in all lowercase letters. But this design technique can cause problems. One newsletter is titled *communications briefings*. There is no problem when the title appears in the content of that newsletter because it is always set in italics. But if it were to appear in another publication, it could be confusing. Then there was the headline that appeared in a newspaper trade journal announcing "presstime staff changes." Readers had to know that "presstime" was the name of an association publication that elected to use a lowercase *p* for the first letter in its name. Readers should not have to stop and figure things out when it can be avoided.

**Fig. 15-14** *Two logo approaches to avoid. All-capital letters in Black Letter, Script, or Miscellaneous typefaces most likely will be unattractive and unreadable. A logo in all-lowercase letters can cause confusion when used within reading matter or if it appears in articles in other publications.*

**Fig. 15-15** *Note the design elements that were used to make this effective inside page of* Write Up. *The uneven column endings harmonize with the contour of the art, and a drop-in ruled quote is placed effectively to give added weight to the upper half of the page and break the gray of the reading matter. (Courtesy of Marie L. Lerch, Booz-Allen & Hamilton, Inc.)*

# Researchers study food poisoning causes

*Continued from p. 5*

The incidence of parasites in raw fish and shellfish found in Hawaiian waters is another task on the agenda. With the rising popularity of sushi and sashimi in this country, parasites that would normally be killed in the cooking process are kept alive in the raw fish. These may pose potential dangers. Research in this area is being conducted at the University of Hawaii.

The risk of botulism poisoning in improperly smoked fish is being studied at Virginia Tech. Following botulism outbreaks from contaminated smoked fish in 1960 and 1963, the FDA proposed Good Manufacturing Practice (GMP) regulations for smoked fish which, due to high processing temperatures, would insure destruction of the Clostridium botulinum organism. However, fish produced under this GMP were unacceptable to the consumer. As a result, a Federal court ruled against the FDA on enforcement of the GMP and smoked fish processors here ignored its recommendations. The purpose of the current research sponsored by FDA is to find procedures which ensure the safety of the product while providing a more palatable smoked fish.

> "...a deeper understanding of the molecular biology of bacteria and toxins will be gained..."

The findings from these and other tasks may be used by the Bureau of Foods to develop new Good Manufacturing Practice requirements to assist industry in processing safe, quality foods. The objective is to develop better food processing and packaging procedures while gaining understanding of diseases caused by contaminated foods.

Booz·Allen's involvement in the FDA-sponsored research program will continue at current levels for another two years. Some of the direct benefits will be the development of new methods for differentiating disease-producing from benign bacteria in foods, and finding new techniques for detecting contaminated or decomposed foods. In the area of food processing, study of bacteria and parasites will help identify food processing techniques (such as heat, freezing, preservatives) that provide the best protection. A deeper understanding of the molecular biology of bacteria and their toxins will also be gained.

After verifying the results and final reports from each task, the firm will assist the investigators and the FDA in disseminating the results. □

*Researchers are studying parasites in raw fish and shellfish*

---

Sometimes a slogan can be useful. It might be incorporated with the nameplate and, perhaps, a symbol to create an effective logo. Such phrases as "all about airplanes" or "your financial adviser" can help identify the newsletter and create memorability.

## The Folio Line

Newsletter design should make it easy for the reader to find out by whom, where, and when the newsletter is produced. A good practice is to include the volume number, issue number, and date in a folio line just below the logo. The name of the originator, address, telephone, and copyright information can be added in small type at the bottom of page 1. This information, plus staff members, subscription data, and so on, can be incorporated in a masthead at the bottom of page 4. This plan is standard practice for many four-page newsletters.

Repeating the name of the publication, page number, and date on every page is not necessary in a four-page newsletter. However, if the publication is filed or stored for future reference and a semi-annual or annual index is issued, it might be worthwhile to consider a page-numbering system.

One such system follows the style used by the printers of "mercuries" in England in the late 1500s and early 1600s. The mercuries were series of news pamphlets of continuing accounts of affairs. The first pamphlet of a series might contain pages 1 through 4. The second issue would have pages 5 through 8, and so on until the series was completed. *National Geographic* follows this page-numbering system today. sequential p. #'ing

In addition to their own system of filing, some newsletter publishers obtain an International Standard Serial Number (ISSN) and include it with the page 1 or masthead information. Anyone can obtain an International Serial Number at no cost. This number goes into a worldwide computer data bank, and libraries refer to it when subscribing to publications. Information concerning the number can be obtained from the National Serials Data Program (Library of Congress, Washington, DC 20540).

## Headlines

Headline type for newsletters should harmonize but stand out from the body type. Since newsletter design stresses simplicity, an uncomplicated Sans Serif or clean modern Roman type will work well for headlines. The headlines should be kept small, usually 12 to 18 points are adequate. If the newsletter is typewriter-set in typical typewriter Roman, a Sans Serif of the same size but in all capital letters can be effective.

Some newsletter designers simply set the heads in all capitals of the same type as the body or set the first few words in the first paragraph of an item in all capitals. Others do not use heads or capitals but simply underline the first few words of the first paragraph.

Regardless of the style selected for headline treatment, it should be consistent. If some headlines are set flush left, all should be flush left. If some are centered, all should be centered. The flush left is the simplest and quickest to use, and it can be given distinction by indenting it an en or em instead of lining it up with the body type. This will let more light into the page. But no matter what style is adopted, allow ample white space around the heads to help them stand out.

## Subheads

Since the newsletter thrives because it gives information quickly, most articles are short. When a long article is included, *subheads* should be used to break it up into short takes to enhance the punchy

---

### Creative Communication

Sometimes it all comes together. And sometimes nothing seems to work!

When the creative effort seems stymied these techniques may open the thought gates:

- Consider new combinations of old techniques or devices.
- Devise simple patterns out of what were complex patterns.
- Bring elements together that were considered unrelated.
- Search through, around, over, under, and beyond the obvious confines of the problem.

Creativity breaks from established patterns and rules and considers the whole picture beyond the problem as well as the problem itself.

**Fig. 15-16a**   Write Up *is an International Newsletter Conference gold award winner in the corporate external newsletters category. (Courtesy of Marie L. Lerch, Booz-Allen & Hamilton, Inc.)*

appearance of the newsletter. Subheads are not needed often in newsletters, but when used they look best when set in the same type style, though in a smaller size, as the main heads.

Some designers do use a different type style for subheads, but one that harmonizes well with the main head type.

For example, they say there is nothing wrong with using a Sans Serif subhead with a Roman main head. But they do suggest that an old style Roman of one family will not mix well with an old style Roman of another family. The same basic principles of good type selection apply to newsletters just as they do to all other printed communications.

Italics or lightface of the same family as used for the main head work well for subheads. One rule of thumb concerning subhead size is to make the subhead about half the size of the main head.

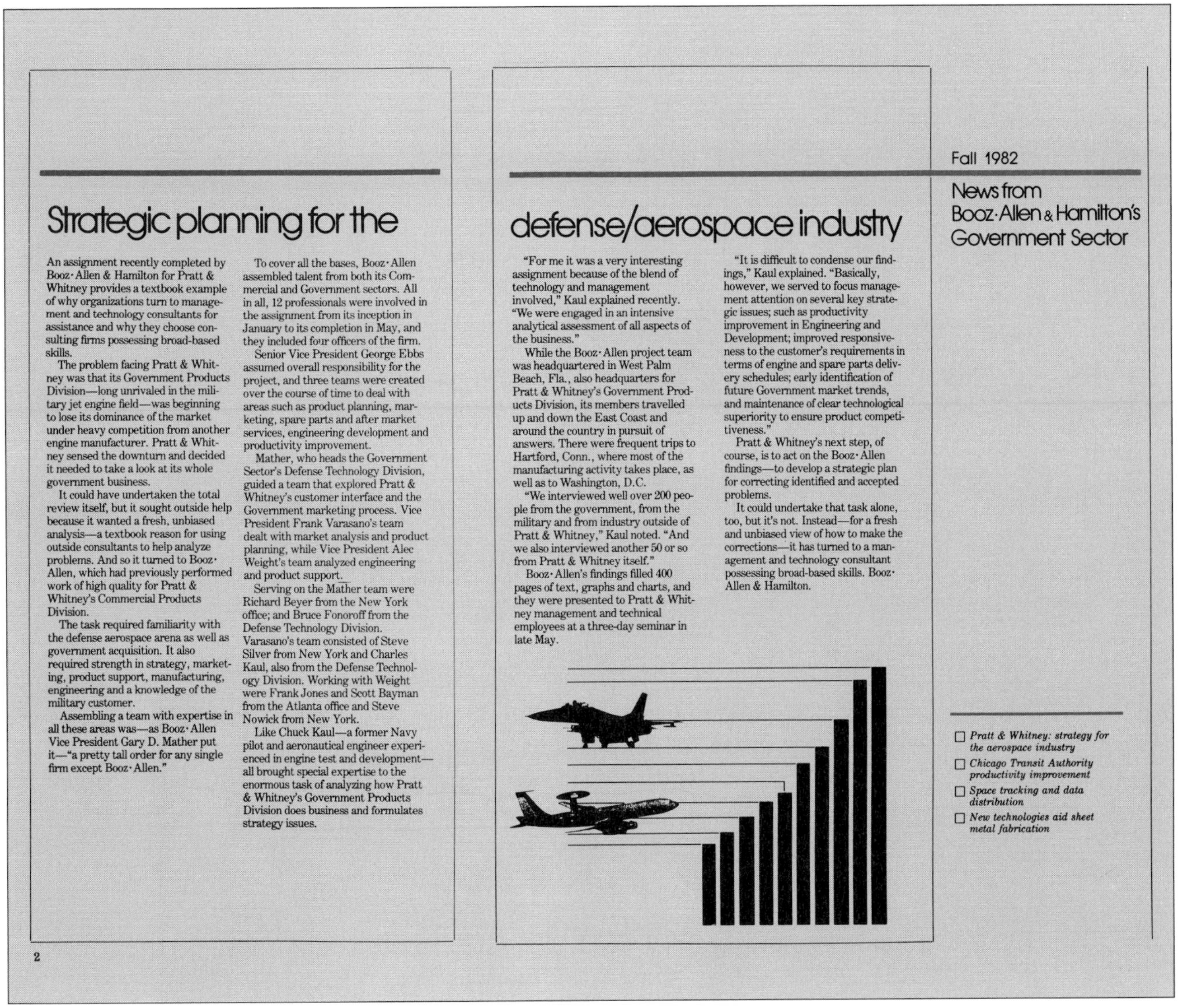

**Fig. 15-16b** *A unique feature of* Write Up *is the two-thirds size page that opens to present an arresting initial spread to the reader. (Courtesy of Marie L. Lerch, Booz-Allen & Hamilton, Inc.)*

If this practice is used, the subhead should be checked to ensure that it is at least the same size as the body type. Subheads should be placed so they do not interfere with the story line of the article. They should be in natural breaks. Also, they should not confuse the reader by appearing to signal the start of an entirely different article.

Punch can also be added by using typographic devices such as bullets or stars to emphasize points in the body copy.

## 5 Standing Heads

Newsletters often contain features that continue from one issue to the next. Many times these regular features are titled with heads such as "A Chat with the President" or "Front Office Notes" that never change. These standing heads can make a newsletter seem

**Fig. 15-17** *The* Getty Newsletter *is a six-page 8½ by 11 format with two parallel folds. This arrangement could be effective in smaller page sizes as well. Note how unity is achieved with a rule running across all pages.*

dull and static. We should plan a method of handling them so the material they identify comes alive.

A standing head can be supplemented with subheads, or, better yet, the identifying head can be used as a *kicker* (a head above the main head, usually underlined) so the subject head can be changed with each issue. An arrangement such as this can help:

**A Chat with the President** *standard*

## Things Are Looking Up; Membership Is Increasing

### Things to Avoid

One newsletter designer summed up the shortcomings of some newsletters: small, difficult-to-read typefaces for reading matter; crowded pages; dull and static layouts with little accent or variety; too much gingerbread in the designs. Other shortcomings included tiny photos that should have been enlarged for more impact, group shots in which faces were hardly recognizable, and inconsistency in design.

## Award-Winning Newsletters

A competition has been conducted since 1972 by the *Newsletter on Newsletters*, published by the Newsletter Clearinghouse. This competition is held in conjunction with the International Newsletter

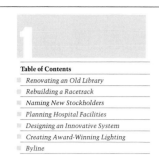

# DESIGNLINE

PUBLISHED BY EWING COLE CHERRY PARSKY, ARCHITECTS, ENGINEERS AND INTERIOR DESIGNERS, PHILADELPHIA, PENNSYLVANIA, AND MOUNT LAUREL, NEW JERSEY.

**SPRING 1983**

*Renovating an Old Library*

## RENOVATION: ITS PRICELESS VALUE

The high cost of building has made renovation a popular alternative to new construction. The $45 billion spent annually on renovations nationwide makes good economic sense. Its value, however, cannot be measured only in dollars.

Many of the most forward-looking institutions served by Ewing Cole have a rich tradition-filled past, and their buildings have great sentimental value. For these clients, renovation enriches the present by preserving the memory of the past.

Hamilton College in Clinton, New York, is one such client. Buildings on the campus of this private, liberal arts college are individually impressive. Together, they form a collection illustrative of the history of American collegiate architecture.

In the Fall of 1980, Hamilton College asked architects and engineers at Ewing Cole to study the James Library, built in 1913, and vacant since 1970. After comparing renovation with rebuilding, economics and tradition made renovation the preferred approach for converting the library into a multi-use facility.

To accommodate three art galleries, a television studio, photographic dark-rooms, language laboratories, conference rooms, faculty offices, classrooms and reading rooms, 10,000 square feet were added. To create the additional space, the original glass and steel library stack floors and a plaster vault were removed. An atrium, a mezzanine, and two new floors were built inside the building. A new addition containing a new entrance, fire stairs, and lavatories was also built.

On the interior, an eclectic approach provided a mix of old and new materials, finished and unfinished surfaces, and spatial experiences not found in the original building. In the new faculty offices, for instance, brick walls were sandblasted to reveal the natural brick surface. In the new art galleries, the walls were upholstered with Italian linen. The contrast between rough natural surfaces and highly finished surfaces is very dramatic. *(Continued)*

**Fig. 15-18** Designline *received a silver award for overall excellence, appropriate design, typography, photographic quality, and printing quality at the 1983 International Newsletter Conference. The logo on page 1 is embossed.*

Conference. Awards for overall excellence are made to newsletters that exhibit design, typographic, photographic, and printing quality. Judges for the competition are selected from the communications and graphics industries.

Comments made by judges in recent contests indicate that they do not like odd, unusual layouts. They pay particular attention to the designs of nameplates. (After all, the nameplate is the major design element of many newsletters.)

They applaud the use of color. They are impressed by newsletters that are printed on colored paper stock rather than white paper. And they point out that color can be an important element in creating identification for a newsletter.

On the other hand, the judges have had some negative things to say about some newsletter design. They criticize the use of nondescriptive names and initials for newsletter names. They note that such tags make it difficult to identify the newsletter quickly. If initials are used for a newsletter name, they should be followed quickly by a descriptive phrase.

The judges also criticized many newsletters for using small, difficult-to-read type. (We have recommended that a newsletter not be set in less than 10-point type.) They found that type packed into a newsletter without heads for items or breathing space caused reading difficulty. White space should be used to get air into a newsletter page just as it is used for all types of printed communication. Packed pages are unappealing and tend to turn readers away from newsletters.

An effective newsletter should be attractive and neat. Its design should be uncomplicated and consistent from issue to issue.

## Effective Design Checklist

■ Use a large initial letter at the start of each article. However, (don't use initial letters if subheads are being used) as too many elements in a newsletter can create a typographic mishmash.

■ Use a different type style for cutlines, or a different size or weight of the same type family as the body type, to brighten the page. The cutlines should all be in the same style and used in the same form, however.

■ Use a distinctive style for handling bylines to add a touch of contrast. But use one style for all the bylines.

■ Set off a list of specific points in an article by numbers or appropriate small ornaments. Or indent the points an em or so to bring in additional white space to brighten the page.

■ Since so much printed material is produced on white paper, consider using colored stock and/or ink to make your newsletter stand out from the rest.

■ Typewritten body copy will save space and look more like professional typesetting if reduced 10 percent.

■ Once the basic format is designed, stick with it and do not make format changes from issue to issue. Such changes can be costly and time consuming.

■ Study the effects of various screen percentages on the ink used. Often the effect of a second color can be obtained without the cost.

# 𝔜our 𝔑ewsletter

| Volume 00 | April 0, 1900 | Number 00 |

## Offerings of Sea and Shore

The other is called tomato wilt, which starts as a yellowing of the lower leaves. Leaves wilt and die as the disease progresses upward, resulting in stunted growth and low yields. The best control is buying disease-resistant plants. Look for the symbols "VF" on the tag as insurance against tomato wilt.

Now for the insects, those great purveyors of joy and sorrow. Let us not forget how many good things these creatures do for us; they till the soil, transform nutrients into useable forms for plants, provide evening serenades . . . but we will deal with the "pests."

In your excursions through the garden, you may happen upon a pale green, segmented larva feeding on leafy plants. This creature, the cabbage looper, can be controlled if you use a contact insecticide (spray or dust) registered for use on vegetables. An alternative biological control is Bacillus Thuringiensis (BT for short), a bacterial compound which is nontoxic to beneficial insects and humans. You can eat something sprayed with BT immediately after spraying. It is sold under several brand names, including Dipel and Thuricide.

Root maggots provide their share of headaches to the gardener. They are white larvae that feed on roots and underground stems, weakening root systems and girdling plants. A sign of root maggot infestation is stunted plant growth or wilting in hot weather. Control root maggots by using a contact insecticide, such as rotenone or diazinon. As a preventive measure, spread approximately three inches of sawdust around the base of the plant; this prevents the adult, a small gray fly, from laying its eggs at the base of the plant. A circle of tarpaper cut to size will also accomplish the task.

Small round holes in plant leaves probably indicate an infestation of flea beetles, which are shiny blue or bronze jumping beetles. They are relatively easy to control by dusting or spraying a contact insecticide on the plant.

One of the "bad guys" in the pest arena is the cutworm, of which there are several species. It usually appears as a fat, curled larvae in the top one to three inches of soil. Its nasty habit of cutting or girdling the plant near the base wreaks havoc on many gardens.

*Phil DeVito proudly displays the "Top 100" award for Salishan's 1982 wine list.*

### Diggers Face Razor Clam Shortage

Razor clam enthusiasts will find lean picking on Oregon's coastal beaches this summer, says Dale Snow, assistant supervisor of the Fish and Wildlife Department's Marine Region in Newport.

"In most years I would suggest digging any place from Tillamook Head near Seaside to the Columbia River," he says. "This year, however, I cannot recommend any place in Oregon as being good. Winter storms severely eroded our beaches and killed many clams," he said. "As a consequence, razor clam digging will be poor this year and until some time in the future."

Razor clams are extremely vulnerable to weather and environmental conditions that affect the beaches where they live. These changing conditions are beyond anyone's control, and the fluctuations in clam populations that result must simply be accepted. This cycle of abundance and depletion has always existed and always will.

### Now Open to Public

Perhaps the most important point is to repeat the spray or other treatment for insects and disease. Read the label carefully. Spraying simply kills adult insects, leaving the eggs to hatch out at a later date. Retreating eliminates this new generation of pests.

While improving your summer tan, be sure to communicate with your yard and garden. With a good feeding and watering program, along with careful inspection for pests and disease, you'll be steps ahead for blooms and bounty all summer long.

## RESTAURANT GUIDE

Last issue in this column we mentioned that we were mailing out 2,000 survey letters to a random selection of our subscribers, to get some input about what they did, or did not like about OCM. We have had a tremendous response from that mailing, and have received almost 1,000 completed surveys. That's a response rate of almost 50 percent, which is virtually unheard of in this business. We sincerely thank each and every subscriber that took the time to complete the survey, and especially thank those of you who went to the additional trouble of providing narrative information, beyond the questions asked. You can be sure that every single survey has been personal

In case you did not already notic the cover of this issue, this is our special "WHALE" issue, and we hav a 16-page feature section on the subject starting on page 21. We thinl that there is quite a bit of intriguing information in this special section, bu we realize that we have just scratche the surface of a very interesting topic Perhaps we will be able to do a second edition on the same subject a few months from now, if our readers are interested.

Ornamentals also play host to pe during warmer months. Root weevils attack a variety of plants and bulbs, plant mortality is usually caused by t weevil feeding on the roots. Noticeab signs of their presence are small.

**Fig. 15-19** *This prototype newsletter page was prepared by a student. Materials used were obtained by clipping headlines, body copy, illustration and caption from two pages of* Oregon Coast *magazine. What are the design and typography strengths and weaknesses of this prototype?*

## Graphics in Action

1. The prototype illustrated in Fig. 15-19 was created by a student in a graphics class. Evaluate it on the basis of good design, appropriate type styles, and balance, unity, harmony, proportion, contrast, rhythm. Make recommendations for revisions.

2. Plan the format for a four-page 8½ by 11 newsletter about your favorite hobby. Begin by outlining the research you would do, including evaluation of the target audience. Then design the logo, folio lines, number of columns per page, and all the other graphic and typographic elements. Explain what you did, and why.

3. Design and paste up a prototype for the front page of a newsletter. Select a size for the page after investigating production possibilities (for instance, if a 10 by 15 or 11 by 17 press is available in your shop, the prototype might be designed so it

could be printed with one or the other). Find headline types, body-type blocks, illustrations, and other design elements in magazines. Clip and use them in the project. Use elements that resemble as closely as possible what you would specify in reality—such as ragged-right body type in the size you would select, if the newsletter is to be set ragged right.

4. Find a four-page newsletter that has a one-column page and redesign it to a two-column format. Be creative and consider using such innovations as pages boxed with rules, tint blocks for surprinting the logo, screens of various designs for illustrations.

5. Select a section from a metropolitan Sunday newspaper (sports, business, travel, and so on) and plan a newsletter devoted to that area of interest. Write a prospectus for such a newsletter including the research that should be done and a description of the format and graphic elements the newsletter would contain.

6. Type page 1 of a newsletter on your own typewriter. First type it ragged right and then again justified. Type headlines and decide if you want to use bullets (which can be made by filling in the lowercase o), asterisks, or numbers to set off points or important information.*

## Notes

1. Howard Penn Hudson, *Publishing Newsletter* (New York: Scribner's, 1982), p. 48.

*J.F. Paschal, University of Oklahoma, uses this project to help students understand the mechanics of typewriter-set newsletters and realize the assets of electronic typesetting.

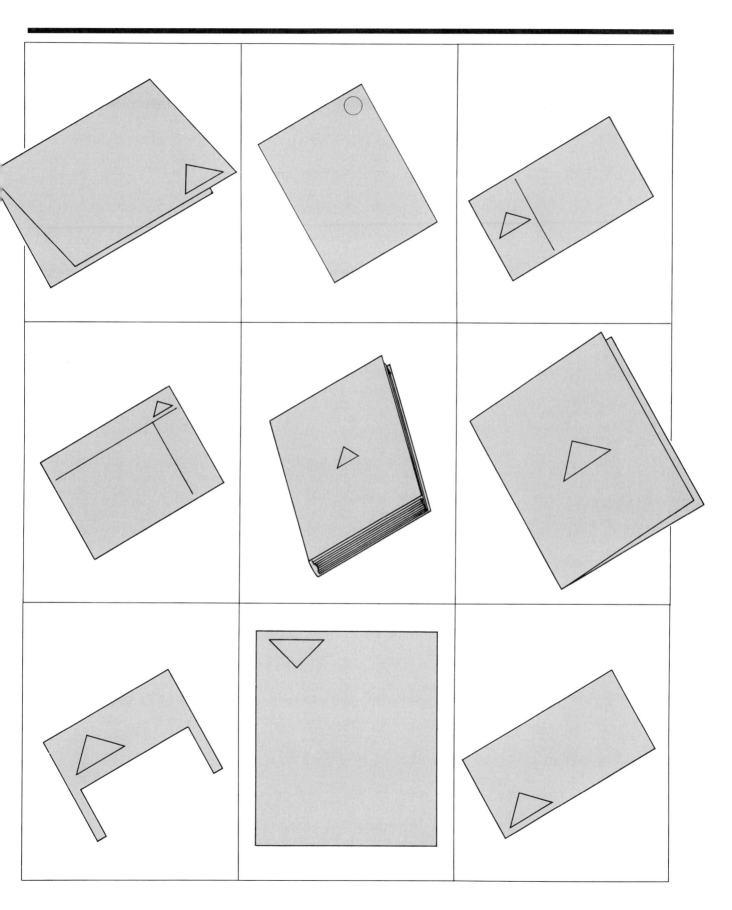

Every time an image is impressed on a piece of paper, communication should ultimately take place. No matter whether the production is an elaborate magazine, metropolitan newspaper, or a letterhead, the same care should be taken to ensure that it is doing all it can to perform its function to the fullest.

To get right down to it, *every* printed communication should exhibit the attributes of good design principles—and be legible and readable. In this chapter we will examine some of the printed communications that most of us in the profession will encounter and see how these principles can be applied.

Brochures will be considered first since they are "first cousins" of newspapers, magazines, and newsletters. Then we will examine stationery, programs, and pamphlets.

## Designing the Brochure

Let's say we are to design a brochure that will be part of an organization's communications mix. The brochure will serve as an informational piece, or an introduction to prospective members. Where should we begin? How do we move from inception to the completed project?

### Planning

While adjustments must be made to fit the particular situation at hand, there are some steps that can serve as a guide in handling any brochure or folder design execution from start to finish. *Planning* is the first step. The more details that can be worked out in the early stages of the project, the more effective and cost-efficient the end product will be. Planning should include (1) forming a statement of purpose, (2) determining the audience and its characteristics, (3) making a checklist of the essential information to be included, (4) listing the benefits to the audience of the information, and (5) making a timetable for execution and distribution.

The planning could be organized around the "three Fs" of communication—function, form, and format. Consider the brochure's *function*. What is its purpose? What are some possibilities? Usually these purposes will fall into one of three or four alternatives. It might announce a workshop or program of some sort. It might be used mainly to provide information. (In this case, we need to determine if the brochure is an end in itself or a supplement to other communications such as an advertising campaign or a lecture series.)

Perhaps the brochure is to serve several functions. It might be a mail-out announcement and at the same time a bulletin board notice. It might be part of a series of brochures that the audience will be encouraged to keep in a binder for future use or reference.

The distribution method and the life expectancy of the brochure should play a part in design planning. Will the brochure be mailed, distributed in an information rack, or handed out at a meeting? Will

**REFORMATION AND REVOLUTION:**
The 500th anniversary of the birth of Martin Luther

**Thursday, November 10, 1983**

| | |
|---|---|
| Lecture/Recital: | Dr. Deborah Teplow, Dr. Harry Bernstein, Patricia Halverson and Randy Wong Stanford University |
| THEME: | "German Musical Life in Luther's Time: a lecture/recital" |
| Time: | 7:00 p.m. Alumni Lounge, Jot Travis Student Union |

**Thursday, November 17, 1983**

| | |
|---|---|
| Lecture: | Dr. Carl Christensen, Professor of History University of Colorado, Boulder |
| THEME: | "Luther and Reformation Art" |
| Time: | 7:00 p.m. Alumni Lounge, Jot Travis Student Union |

**Friday, November 18, 1983**

| | |
|---|---|
| Panel Discussion: | Dr. John Christianson, Professor of History Luther College, Decorah, Iowa |
| | Dr. Jeannine E. Olson, Assistant Professor of Church History San Francisco Theological Seminary |
| | Dr. Susan Karant-Nunn, Associate Professor of History Portland State University |
| THEME: | "Reformation and Revolution in the Sixteenth Century" |
| Time: | 7:00 p.m. Alumni Lounge, Jot Travis Student Union |

**For more information, call 784-6855 or 882-9262.**

Sponsored by the University of Nevada Reno Medieval and Renaissance Studies Board, funded by the Nevada Humanities Committee.

**Fig. 16-1** *This pamphlet serves a dual purpose. It can be used as an announcement that can be mailed or posted on a bulletin board. Notice the choice of type and art to give the flavor of the medieval period. The tan paper with a ribbed finish further enhances the image of antiquity.*

it be used just to announce an event, or will it have more permanent use?

It will also, of course, be necessary to consider budget factors. How much money can be spent on the production? Money can be a limiting factor on the size, number of illustrations, use of color, quality of paper, and so on.

As this preliminary visualization of the situation progresses, a form may begin to evolve since form follows function. What should the physical size be? What shape should the brochure have? There are a number of possibilities. It could be simply a flat sheet; it could be folded in any number of arrangements.

Now might be a good time to start considering a rough dummy. Try this. Settle on a size and take a blank piece of paper and see what can be done with it. For example, suppose we decide our brochure will be printed on an 8½ by 11 standard typewriter-size sheet of paper. We have determined that the brochure will have a multi-informational purpose and that it should be easy to mail, place on information racks, and pass out at meetings.

What can we do with this piece of paper to make the most effective brochure?

There are a number of alternatives. The first is to make the brochure a flat sheet, printed both sides. This could be punched to be kept in a ring binder. Or it could be designed as a combination flyer and bulletin board notice. One side would be designed as a poster and the other could contain general information, or be left blank, or have an address box for mailing.

Other possibilities might involve folding the sheet of paper in certain ways. But before we can explore those possibilities, we should become acquainted with paper finishing and folding operations.

## Folding

If we are going to produce a brochure or pamphlet that requires folding, that operation should be a part of the planning. Michael Blum, a printing instructor, wrote in *In-Plant Printer* that "approximately 35 to 40 percent of the labor cost of the average printing job is in finishing."[1]

Modern equipment is capable of producing many different types of folds. But all folds are basically either parallel or right angle. *Parallel folds* are used for letters where two folds are required to fit the letter into the envelope. This same fold, when the sheet is held horizontally, becomes a six-page standard—also called *regular*—fold.

An *accordion fold* is another parallel fold. It, too, is popular for brochures and envelope stuffers. The most basic parallel fold is a simple fold to make a four-page folder. The two-fold accordion made from an 8½ by 11 sheet is popular for brochures as it creates a handy size that mails easily in a number 9 or 10 commercial envelope. It also has good design possibilities. Accordion folds can be made with additional folds to create eight, ten, or more pages.

A popular fold for invitations and greeting cards is the *French fold*. This is an example of a right-angle fold, which is made with two or more folds at right angles to each other. The French fold is also used to create an eight-page publication that can be saddle stitched if desired and trimmed off at the head, or top, of the folded sheet.

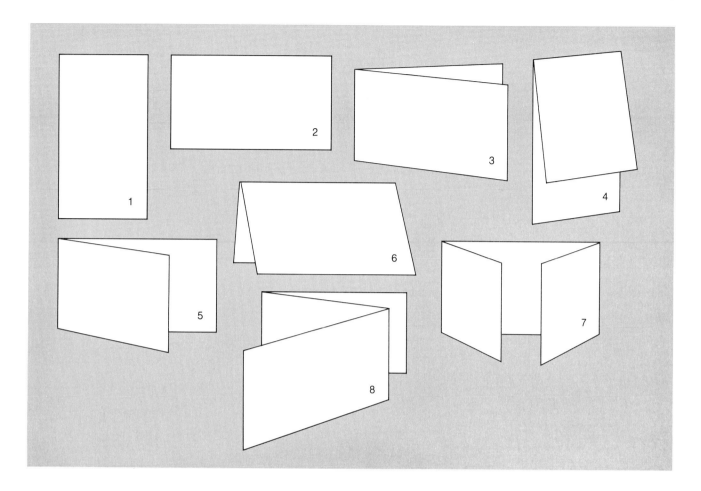

**Fig. 16-2** *The possibilities presented by various types of folds should be considered in brochure planning. Here are some alternatives: 1, vertical parallel fold; 2, horizontal; 3, book fold; 4, short fold vertical; 5, short fold horizontal; 6, tent fold; 7, gate fold; 8, z fold.*

Folders can handle signatures of many pages to create booklets and publications of twelve, sixteen, twenty, twenty-four, or more pages. Some machines are equipped with pasting attachments to produce paste-bind booklets (booklets with the pages pasted rather than stapled).

There are many other options for folding depending on the equipment available. These options should be considered when brochures and other printed communications are planned. Thus it can be quite worthwhile to discuss all possible options with the printer or binder operator. Sometimes the capability to make certain folds can spark ideas for a new and unique way to design the brochure.

Now take the blank sheet of paper and experiment with the fold possibilities for your particular brochure. How many alternatives can you devise considering all the factors that went into the planning so far?

## Planning the Format

Once a size is determined, the format can be planned. This should include (1) the size and form of the margins, (2) the placement of heads and copy blocks, (3) the use of borders, illustrations, and other typographic devices, (4) the selection of type styles—and the overall determination of how the principles of design will be applied.

*Offering three very special films...*

For more than a century, The American Dream has been fueled by abundant and reliable energy. In fact, in every corner of the world we see an undeniable relationship between progress and energy availability.

But with this quest for progress, man needs to concern himself with his impact on the environment. Fortunately, a heightened public awareness and a responsible commitment by government and the private sector have begun to exert a positive influence on our air, land, water and wildlife resources.

We have, in fact, arrived at that day when energy and the environment are not only compatible — they are complementary. The three films offered by Sierra Pacific Power examine this unique relationship and illustrate how an improved environment actually can be a by-product of modern technology.

Please use the handy tear-off panel to order any of these award-winning motion pictures. If possible, we would appreciate two weeks' advance notice.

**A SECOND CHANCE**

Across America, countless species of plants and animals share lands and waters used by electric utility companies to generate and transmit energy. This film demonstrates how careful research and the responsible development of power projects can satisfy our world's need for energy while contributing to the well-being of nature.
*Sound and color/16mm/27 minutes*

**SILVER WIRES, GOLDEN WINGS**

Seven years of research went into this artfully photographed film which earned a Certificate of Excellence at the World Wildlife Film Festival. It outlines the work of Morlan Nelson, internationally acclaimed authority on birds of prey, who sought to prevent their electrocution by utility power lines. Beautifully filmed footage of the golden eagle is featured. Mr. Nelson's research was sponsored by Sierra Pacific Power, Edison Electric Institute and four other western utilities.
*Sound and color/16mm/30 minutes*

**THE CHOSEN PLACE**

American wildlife has found a "chosen place," in the shadow of today's technology, where nature not only survives, but thrives. Thanks in part to electric utility planning, wildlife habitats are being enhanced. As a result, birds of prey benefit from improved hunting conditions . . . shrimp and other aquatic life flourish . . . and all manner of species discover year-round bountiful supplies of food. A portion of this film features Sierra Pacific's work with the golden eagle in northern Nevada.
*Sound and color/16mm/25 minutes*

**YES!** We want the following films:

☐ A SECOND CHANCE
☐ SILVER WIRES, GOLDEN WINGS
☐ THE CHOSEN PLACE

NAME _____
HOME ADDRESS _____

PHONE _____
BEST TIME TO CALL _____
DATE DESIRED _____
ORGANIZATION _____
MEETING ADDRESS _____

PHONE _____
MEETING TIME _____
ATTENDANCE _____
MY ORGANIZATION WILL PROVIDE A
SCREEN     YES ☐   NO ☐.

EXTENSION CORD     YES ☐   NO ☐.

**Fig. 16-3** *Some basic considerations in brochure design are illustrated here. The art helps communicate the theme and purpose. The return coupon is placed so the brochure message remains intact and usable after the coupon is detached. (Design by Mel Mathewson, Graphics Unlimited.)*

Now we can begin making rough layouts on paper. A good idea is to take several sheets of paper, fold them into the final brochure form, and sketch roughs of possible arrangements. Some designers like to make thumbnails in smaller but exact proportions to the final layout. Others prefer to work with full-size roughs. Whichever we choose, once we have selected a general arrangement, we would produce a full-size rough or comprehensive, following a procedure similar to designing an advertisement. Then we would mark the rough and submit it plus typed copy and illustrations to a printer. Or we might have the type set and then do the pasteups for comprehensives or completed mechanicals. These would be photographed and the negatives used to make plates for printing.

### Two Ways to Design Effective Brochures

Although the design for the brochure may evolve out of the preliminary planning, if we get stuck getting started, there are other

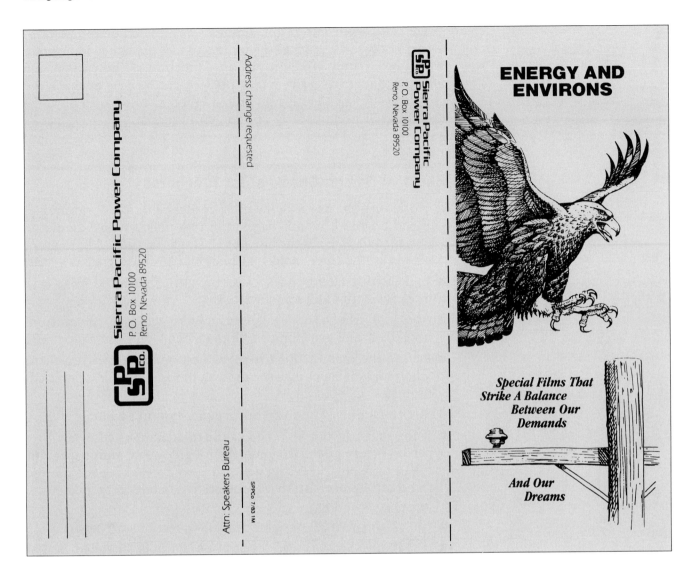

ways to approach the overall design. One might be called the "headline method," and the other the "attention to action" approach.

The *headline method* involves devising a brochure outline around the headlines to be used. First is the feature head, or the title for the brochure. This head stresses the most compelling reason for the target audience to read the brochure. It should set the theme for the brochure by answering the question, Why should I bother to read this brochure?

This feature head can become the title line for the brochure, and it can be amplified by *main support heads.* These can number two or three to six or more, and they become the heads for the copy blocks in the brochure. Often each copy block and head cover one topic or point to be made.

If the copy block under the main support head is long and involved, it can be broken down by "reinforce heads" or subheads, each with a brief copy block. This approach can be used as an outline for writing the brochure copy as well.

The *A-I-D-C-A (attention, interest, desire, conviction, action) formula* some advertising copywriters use, as explained in Chapter 9, can be a handy guide in planning brochures. The parts of the formula that are relevant to the situation can be used to check the copy and to plan the layout. This method also helps to organize the material in an orderly and forceful manner.

## Effective Design Checklist for Brochures

- Work with the pages as the units readers will see. For example, if the brochure is four pages, the two inside pages should be designed together. If the brochure has two parallel folds, to make six pages, the three inside pages should be considered as a unit.

- In designing facing pages, cross the gutter with the same care as if designing magazine spreads.

- Apply all the basic design principles—balance, proportion, unity, contrast, harmony, rhythm—when laying out a brochure.

- Define the margins for the pages first and work within them when making layouts. Use ample margins and avoid a jammed-up look.

- Stress simplicity and careful organization in layouts.

- If the rough layout is to be examined and approved by another person before production and the roughs are on thin paper, cut the spreads apart. Paste them on heavier backing for a more impressive presentation. A protective flap or cover taped at the top will help, too.

- Check to see if all possible readers' questions are answered.

- If a mail-in coupon or registration form is included in the design, place it where it can be detached easily and where it will not destroy pertinent information such as a program listing when it is removed.

- Use big, bold display when the brochure is to double as a bulletin board announcement.

- Have the purpose and content dictate the design: the announcement of an event calls for stronger display than an informational brochure does.

- Don't try to achieve too much in one brochure. Designers often need to limit the quantity of information to be included in a single brochure.

## Choosing the Right Paper

Choosing the right paper for a brochure or any other printed communication requires making two basic decisions. One is *selecting the proper finish and weight.* The other involves *planning the size* of the printed piece to obtain the most paper for the least amount of money.

Once the format of a job has been determined the next step is to select the best paper. This should be done after deciding the mood of the message, the type styles, and the kinds of art being used. All will play a part in determining which papers will work best.

In addition to antique finishes, machine finishes, bonds, and coated papers, there are papers of bold colors, pastel colors, iridescent colors. Nearly every color imaginable is available to call attention, set a mood, or add distinction. There are even "duplex" papers with a different color on each side.

The printing process and mailing costs will play a part in the paper choice. Offset and bond papers are closely related and are finished to take the water involved in offset printing and writing with ink. Screen printing can be accomplished on almost any kind of paper or other material.

In selecting papers, their reflectance or brightness and opacity should be considered. The more light the paper reflects, the brighter it will appear. This is its *reflective* quality. A glossy paper will appear bright, will show the contrasts in art to their maximum, and will bring out the tones. These papers will print colors vividly. However, glossy papers can be tiring to the eye if used for large amounts of reading matter.

The *opacity* is the ability of a paper to help prevent printing on one side from showing through to the other side. Opacity is an important quality to consider when selecting a paper that will be printed on both sides.

Since the paper has such an important effect on both the design and the quality of the printing, it is helpful to obtain samples of possible papers to use from the printer or paper company before starting a design project.

Another aspect in selecting paper is its size in relation to the size of the printed piece. As was noted in Chapter 7, unless papers are manufactured in rolls, they are produced in standard-size sheets.

This creates no problem where letterheads are concerned. Since the standard letterhead is 8½ by 11 or 5½ by 8½ inches, and the standard bond paper sheet is 17 by 22, four 8½ by 11 sheets or eight 5½ by 8½ sheets can be cut from each full sheet with no waste.

But it is worthwhile to understand how the printer prices and cuts paper stock. Sometimes a slight adjustment in the format of a project can create significant savings in paper costs.

Here is how it works. Say we are planning a brochure. It will be a simple, four-page folder with each page measuring 8 by 10 inches. The folder will be created by using a parallel fold on a 10 by 16 sheet. We have decided that the folder will look best if printed on machine-finish book paper. The standard size is 25 by 38. We require 5,000 brochures.

The printer will calculate the number of 25 by 38 sheets needed and cut them to make 5,000 10 by 16 sheets. This is the formula he or she will use:

## Creative Communication

It could be called a malleable finite cylindraceous cell wrought of parallel axes with azimuthal terminates. Or called a paper clip.

It remains one of humanity's best designs because it works all the time; it is cheap, fast, versatile, and above all else, *simple.*

As with paper clips, simplicity is also a great virtue in graphics. Keeping the graphics simple leads readers to a quicker and more comprehensive understanding of the information. Keeping the graphics simple leads to quicker production by the artist and generally easier production all through the publishing process.

A good rule of thumb is: if the graphic is easy to produce and easy to read, the information within will be easily understood.

—Adapted from *ASNE Today,* published by the graphics staff of *USA TODAY* for a conference of the American Society of Newspaper Editors, Denver, Colorado, 1983.

$$\frac{\text{Paper width}}{\text{Brochure width}} \times \frac{\text{Paper length}}{\text{Brochure length}} = \begin{array}{l}\text{Number of 10 by 16s}\\ \text{that can be cut}\\ \text{from a 25 by 38 sheet}\end{array}$$

That is, the printer will divide the widths and depths to get the most cuts out of a sheet. This may be affected by the grain of the sheets if the brochure is to be folded, especially if printed on heavy stock. However, in this case, we get

$$\frac{25}{10} \times \frac{38}{16} = 2 \times 2 = 4 \text{ 10 by 16 sheets from each 25 by 38 sheet}$$

If the 4 is then divided into 5,000, we find that 1,250 full-size sheets will be needed for the job. We will be billed for that number plus about 5 percent for spoilage in printing and processing.

However, if the brochure is designed for a 6 by 9 page rather than 8 by 10, it can be printed on a 9 by 12 sheet cut out of the 25 by 38 size.

$$\frac{25}{10} \times \frac{38}{16} = 2 \times 4 = 8 \text{ 9 by 12 sheets from each 25 by 38 sheet}$$

Now the job will require only 625 sheets, cutting the paper cost in half even though the brochure page size is only reduced by 1 inch in one direction and 2 inches in the other.

The economies of choosing sizes for the final printed products that correspond to standard paper sizes cannot be overemphasized. A designer can always choose any unique size, but that designer must be prepared to pay for higher levels of waste. Also remember that sizes that can be cut efficiently from bond papers will not cut efficiently from book papers because of the different standard sizes. One designer has pointed out that beginners often design a communication on standard office (8½ by 11) paper and then specify book papers for production. This causes confusion and increased costs.

**Fig. 16-4** *Careful planning that considers paper sizes can be cost efficient. On the left, six cuts, possibly eight if paper grain is not a factor, produce 7 by 10 inch sheets from a 25 by 38 sheet. By reducing the size just 1 inch for both width and depth to 6 by 9 inches, sixteen cuts can be obtained. The paper cost would be decreased by about 50 percent.*

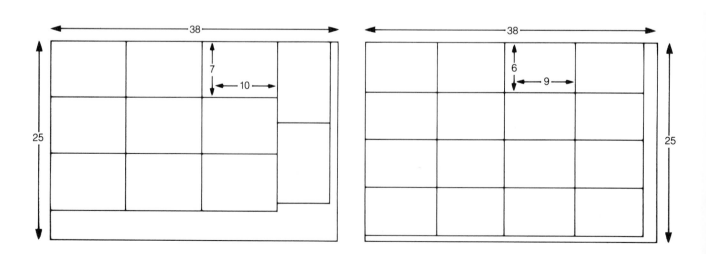

## Designing Effective Stationery

Letterheads, statements, invoices, envelopes, business cards, and other printed materials needed to make the wheels go round may not appear to offer much challenge. However, even something as deceivingly simple as a business card should receive thoughtful consideration. The principles of good design apply here just as they do for all printed communications.

The design of these items should be coordinated so they all work together to create the desired impression. Often it is effective to use the same layout but perhaps in a smaller size for statements and invoices, envelopes and cards, as is used for the letterhead. And

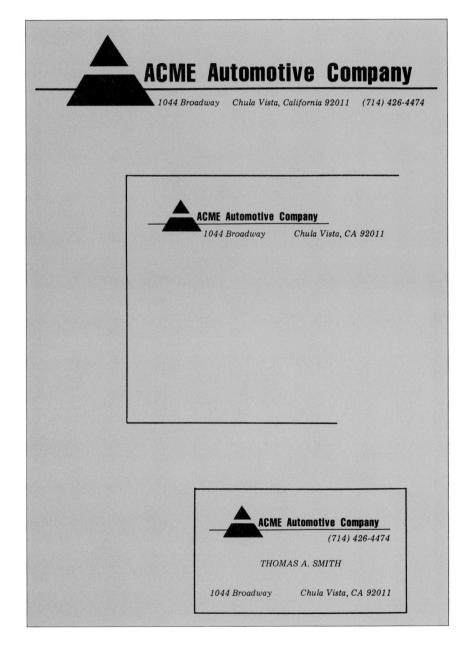

**Fig. 16-5** *Coordinating the design of letterhead, envelope, and business card can aid communication by adding recognition and continuity. (Printers Shopper.)*

even though a different design may be chosen for each, depending on its use, it is worthwhile to use the same logotype or typeface for the name of the organization on all printed pieces. This will help build recognition and memorability.

If a logo is designed it should be done with two basic considerations in mind. The first involves characteristics that will make it effective in printed communications. The second is its adaptability to all the identity requirements of the organization.

An effective logo should identify the organization when it stands alone. It should be simple enough to reproduce well on office copiers and more sophisticated printing equipment. It should reduce or enlarge without losing its design subtleties. It should reflect the tone of the organization, and it should not become outdated as times and styles change.

**Fig. 16-6**  *"Where to position the logo and the type, which typeface works best visually and best represents the client, and what size and shape the letterhead should take are some of the things that make every letterhead job an exciting challenge," according to "A Letterhead Production Guide" by the Gilbert Paper Company (1981). Here are some possibilities for locating the logo.*

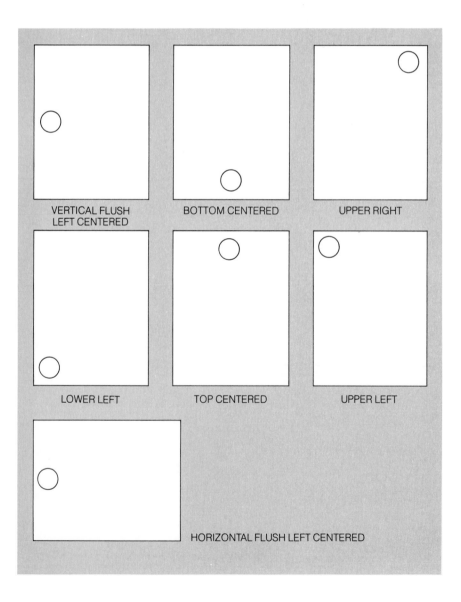

The logo should be executed with consideration of the possible expansion of the organization or company into new areas or activities. And the design should be suitable for use on vehicles, work clothes, uniforms, and so on.

## The Letterhead

Often the letterhead is the initial contact the receiver of a message has with the sender. Not only that, but many times the letter is the only contact made between an organization and its prospective clients. The letterhead, then, carries the weight of creating an impression as well as transmitting a message.

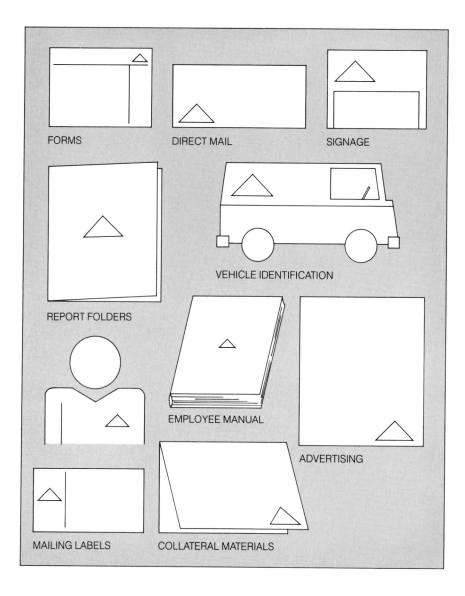

**Fig. 16-7** *The design can be incorporated into a total identity and marketing program for a business or organization.*

The letterhead should make a statement about its originator. The type styles selected and their arrangement help set the stage for the message. Effective letterhead design generally should be neat, dignified, and orderly. It should have character but not be obtrusive. It should be unique but restrained in terms of type sizes, tonal values, and utilization of space.

Letterhead designers suggest that the most effective results are obtained by skillfully accentuating the name of the firm, product, or logotype in relation to the other less important type elements while maintaining harmony, balance, and tone. In seeking this goal, designers usually consider two approaches: traditional or modern.

These are also referred to as formal and informal letterheads.

In the *traditional design*, type groups are usually arranged in either a square or inverted pyramid. If a trademark or symbol is used, it is centered. Sometimes rules are included but if they are, the formal symmetry is maintained. One feature of the inverted pyramid arrangement is that it forms a downward direction motion toward the message.

The *modern approach* involves creating a basically asymmetrical arrangement while maintaining the principles of good design. The type can be arranged on an imaginary vertical line or it can be

**Fig. 16-8** *Traditional layout in letterheads with symmetrical balance. (Woodbury and Company, Inc., Worcester, Mass.)*

CHAPS·RALPH·LAUREN

The spirited tradition.

CHAPS & COMPANY · THE WARNACO GROUP · 261 MADISON AVENUE · NEW YORK, N. Y. 10016 · 212 599-5770

Hathaway

Hathaway Women's Division · 1411 Broadway · New York, NY 10018 · Telephone 212 221-1290 counterbalanced. If larger type is used for the company name on the left of the page, a smaller two or three-line address may be placed on the right for balance.

Rules are sometimes used to add motion to the letterhead. Decorations can give a letterhead individuality, but they should be selected and used with discretion. Color should also be considered. Remember, though, that the typographic embellishments should not draw attention away from the type.

Papers are available in a variety of finishes—linen, wove, pebble—to add individuality and distinction to a letterhead.

*Margins* are important in letterhead design regardless of the arrangement selected. Side margins of type lines should approximate fairly closely the usual line width of the typed message. Sometimes elements, such as the name and position of the person sending the messages, are placed on the right of the page, to balance the typed name and address of the recipient of the letter.

Some organizations insist that long lists of officers be included on a letterhead. This can cause design problems, but they can be solved. If only a few names are involved, they can be listed across the bottom of the sheet. The other obvious alternatives are to list the names down the left or right margins. These lists should be

**Fig. 16-9** *(below left) Modern design in letterheads is neat, orderly, and appropriate, but the balance is informal. (Woodbury and Company, Inc., Worcester, Mass.)*

**Fig. 16-10** *(below right) Another informal, modern letterhead design. The handwritten script and push-pin art help create the proper atmosphere. The phone numbers at the bottom are perforated so they can be detached and saved. (Courtesy of Hammermill Papers Group.)*

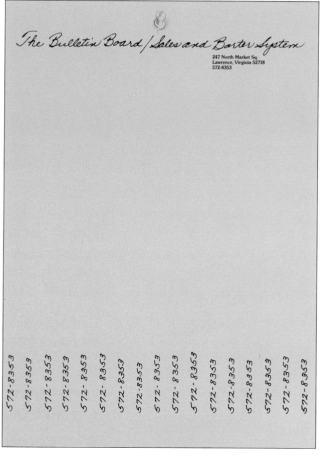

**Fig. 16-11** *The problem was to list eighteen names on the letterhead. It was solved creatively rather than following the outdated impulse to list them on the side and clutter the message. (Courtesy of Hammermill Papers Group.)*

kept as unobtrusive as possible. Sometimes printing them in a lighter color will help. Of course, placement of all elements should always be made with consideration of the format of the letter to be typed on the sheet.

A typographically effective letterhead printed on a carefully selected stock that reflects the character of the organization can create a favorable impression and help project the desired image.

## Effective Design Checklist for Letterheads

■ Letterhead design should never interfere with the utility of the letterhead, which is to convey a message.

- The *monarch size* (7¼ by 10½) can add dignity for professionals such as doctors, designers, architects, executives.
- When color stock is used the color should fit the character of the organization or the service it renders. It should not interfere with the typed letter.
- Half-sheets (5½ by 8½) can save money, and they can be folded twice to fit a 6¾ envelope.
- The logo should be original, stimulating, imaginative, and straightforward. It should be adaptable as well.
- Always keep in mind that a letterhead is a platform for words.

## Special Processes

There are several processes that can be used in producing letterheads and other printed communications. These can add effectiveness and distinction and should be considered. They include engraving, embossing, hot stamping, thermography, and die cutting.

*Engraving*   Engraving is an excellent method for projecting a high-quality, prestigious image. The sharp lines and crispness of an engraved announcement or letterhead project elegance, strength, and dignity. It reproduces fine lines and small type well. And it brings out the subtleties of shadings and patterns in a design.

A chromium-coated copper or steel plate with an etched-in design plus a smooth counterplate are used on a special engraving press. The plate is covered with ink, then wiped dry. The ink remains in the etched portions. Paper is fed into the press, and the impression transfers the ink to the paper.

Keep in mind that most engraving plates are limited to 4 by 8 inches. Also, paper selection is critical because of the stress exerted by the press. Paper lighter than 20 pounds should never be used.

*Embossing*   This technique is enjoying great popularity. It involves using heat and pressing paper between dies to produce a raised effect. It provides a distinctive element to a printed communication, and introduces a third dimension for added memorability.

The embossed effect seems to work best alone. The visual impact is impaired when printing or color are added to the embossed image. When embossing is used remember that the paper is formed, or molded, and this will use more of the paper than the layout might indicate. So, type and other elements should not be too close to the embossed area.

Often new life can be added to an old logo by using embossing.

*Debossing* is another technique. It is embossing in reverse—the image is depressed rather than raised.

*Hot stamping*   Hot stamping uses the same heat-pressure process as embossing, but it goes one step further by transferring an opaque foil material to the surface of the paper. A variety of foils and designs are available, but the most common hot-stamping techniques use gold or silver foils.

Hot stamping is used for greeting cards, ribbons, paper napkins, and so on. However, new hot-stamping presses are being marketed, and it is becoming a popular technique for business cards and letterheads.

In hot stamping a very thin ribbon of foil is fed into a press and releases its pigment onto the paper when pressed between a die and a hard, flat surface as heat is applied.

Hot stamping is expensive. It can cost as much as 10 to 15 percent more than engraving or embossing. Also, the process can discolor certain colors of paper stock, especially browns, yellows, and oranges.

*Thermography*   Thermography produces a raised printed surface. The image is permanent and chip-proof and crack-proof. It is considered by some to be similar in appearance to engraving, but it can be added anywhere on a sheet of paper and is not limited by a plate size, as is the case with engraving. It can also be used with any color ink.

*Die cutting*   Die cutting is rather like cookie cutting, except paper instead of dough is used. It can be an effective and dramatic attention-getting device. The cuts can be straight, circular, square, rectangular, or any number of special shapes.

Delicate or lacy patterns, which tear easily, should be avoided. Also, since it is difficult to maintain a tight register in the die press, elements should not be designed close to the cuts.

Die cutting is not expensive compared to some of the other special-effect processes, but care is needed in selecting paper with sufficient strength to take sharp, clear-cut lines.

## The Envelope—A Tale of Diversity

The part played by the envelope in printed communications is another tale of the vast size and diversity of materials available. Here again is another tool that if used properly can make communications effective. The communicator should be able to sort out the different styles of envelopes and select the best one for the job.

But there are so many to choose from! The Old Colony Envelope Company, which produces the most extensive line of envelopes in the United States, offers more than 1,700 different styles and sizes. Other converters (which is what the envelope people call themselves because they take flat sheets of paper and cut and fold and glue

**Fig. 16-12** *The top of the sheet for this letterhead was die cut to resemble trimming by pinking shears to provide identity, memorability, and distinction. (Courtesy of Hammermill Papers Group.)*

them to create envelopes) also offer envelopes in hundreds of sizes and styles for thousands of uses.

Fortunately, though, they have settled on some basic sizes and grades that are easy to sort out and that will take care of most of the designer's and communicator's needs. Selecting and using just the right envelope need not be difficult. There are four main points to consider: (1) sizes and styles, (2) paper weight and texture, (3) graphic design, and (4) Postal Service regulations.

The sizes of envelopes are given in inches with the shortest dimension first. A 6 by 9 envelope is 6 inches wide and 9 inches deep. Designations also include the location of the opening and the styles of the flap and seam. There are several devices for closing the envelope, and each should be considered.

**Fig. 16-13** *Standard envelope flap styles; left to right: commercial/official, square, square with pointed flap, square flap.*

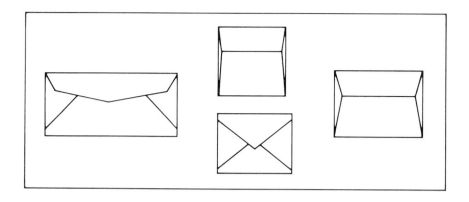

For example, most standard stationery envelopes are "open side" with the seal flap and opening on the long dimension. "Open end" envelopes have the seal flap and opening on the short dimension. Flap styles are called pointed, square, wallet, and mail-point. Seam styles are determined by the construction and location of the parts of the paper folded and glued to form the finished envelope. These styles include a diagonal seam that is used most commonly in business correspondence, a pointed flap used for announcements, and side seams used for mailing programs and booklets. A center seam is used in making envelopes that must be rugged to withstand heavy duty.

Envelopes can also be classified by the way they close. There are gummed flaps; flaps with metal clasps for added security; and "button-and-string" tied-down flaps, which were designed for envelopes to be used over and over again. Some converters have other patented closures such as self-sealing adhesives.

The envelope manufacturers and the graphic arts industry have settled on a variety of standard sizes and styles. Although a number of others are available, these are the most common (the first number is used to designate the size when ordering):

- *Commercial/official:* This is the standard business and personal correspondence envelope:

  | | |
  |---|---|
  | 6¼ commercial: | 3½ by 6 |
  | 6¾ commercial: | 3⅝ by 6½ |
  | Monarch: | 3⅞ by 7½ |
  | 9 official: | 3⅞ by 8⅞ |
  | 10 official: | 4⅛ by 9¼ |

  *(Note:* The 6¼ size fits into a 6¾ envelope and can be used as a return envelope.)

- *Booklet:* These are used for annual reports, brochures, sales literature, manuals, and so on (it is an open-side envelope):

  | | |
  |---|---|
  | 6: | 5¾ by 8⅞ |
  | 6½: | 6 by 9 |
  | 9: | 8¾ by 11½ |
  | 9½: | 9 by 12 |

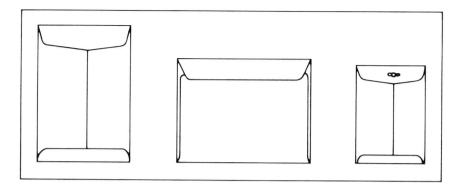

**Fig. 16-14** *Basic envelope styles for catalogs and pamphlets; left to right: catalog, booklet, clasp.*

- *Catalog:* These are used for catalogs, publications, and large booklets (it is an open-end envelope):

| | |
|---|---|
| 1 catalog: | 6 by 9 |
| 1¾ catalog: | 6½ by 9½ |
| 9¾ catalog: | 8¾ by 11¼ |
| 10½ catalog: | 9 by 12 |
| 13½ catalog: | 10 by 13 |

- *Clasp:* These are used for heavy publications or bulky contents:

| | |
|---|---|
| 75: | 7½ by 10½ |
| 90: | 9 by 12 |
| 97: | 10 by 13 |
| 110: | 12 by 15½ |

- *Square:* These are characterized by square flaps and are designed for announcements, booklets, and promotional material:

| | |
|---|---|
| 6½: | 6½ by 6½ |
| 8½: | 8½ by 8½ |

We can design the printed material and then seek the proper envelope. However, time and money can be saved and a much more effective communications package produced if a listing of styles and sizes of envelopes is consulted first.

When selecting an envelope, we need to consider the size and bulk of the material to be inserted and how it is to be stuffed. An envelope for inserting by hand should be from one-eighth to one-fourth of an inch wider and one-fourth to three-eighths of an inch longer than the material it contains. If a machine at the printing plant or at a mailing firm will be used, the inserter should be consulted. The whole package must be compatible with the mechanical system.

Once the size and style have been selected, thought should be given to the envelope paper stock. There are impressive envelopes, envelopes that attract attention, and envelopes that harmonize in texture and color with the messages they contain.

All envelopes, however, need to conform to Postal Service regulations. The Postal Service classifies envelopes as nonmailable, mailable with no surcharge, and mailable with possible surcharge.

Since the regulations are subject to change, they should be checked before printing is designed to be sent through the mails.

## Graphics for Envelopes

The envelope can introduce the contents. It can help create the stage setting for the message. Often this communications bonus is overlooked and little attention is paid to envelope graphics. However, good envelope graphics produced with some thought can aid in getting the container opened. Direct-mail advertisers know this, and they do all they can to design envelopes that will get the prospect to look inside.

Envelope graphics should be determined by the nature of the message and the sender. The types selected and their arrangements should harmonize with those used on the message.

There are three principal categories of envelope graphics: those designed for direct-mail advertising, those to accompany letterheads, and those for pamphlets or publications. Direct-mail envelopes are designed to use every device possible and proper to attract attention and get the prospect to open and read the contents. The envelope is an integral part of the whole sales plan, just as art or headlines are used to lure a reader to read a newspaper or magazine advertisement.

**Fig. 16-15** *Envelope graphics are important. The envelope is often the initial contact with a target audience. (Top courtesy of Dyna-Graphic Printing, Reno, Nev.; bottom courtesy of Printers Shopper, Chula Vista, Calif.)*

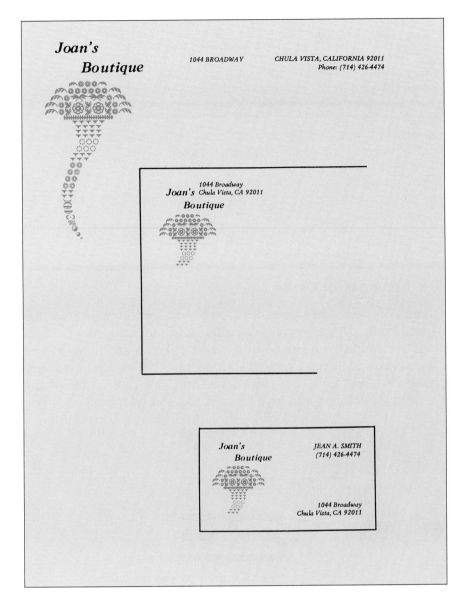

**Fig. 16-16** *Coordinating letterhead, envelope, and business card can create added memorability by repetition of the design and message. (Printers Shopper.)*

The graphics of envelopes that accompany letterheads should extend the basic letterhead design. The same types, logos, and symbols used on the letterhead but in suitable smaller sizes can help create the tone and recognition impact of the message.

The graphics of envelopes used for publications or pamphlets should reflect the contents and project the same type and tone harmony.

That is, whatever the purpose of the envelope, there should be a strong visual relationship between it and the contents. This includes the graphics as well as the color and texture of the paper.

Sometimes business reply cards or envelopes are included in a mailing. Here again, there are certain Postal Service regulations governing the graphics, sizes, and information that can be included. The designer should become familiar with these regulations.

**Fig. 16-17**  *Traditional layout for a formal business card.*

```
                              PHONE NUMBER



                     NAME OF BUSINESS
                   DESCRIPTION OR SLOGAN


                                       STREET AND NUMBER
         NAME OF PERSON                   CITY AND STATE
```

**Fig. 16-18**  *Modern design for business cards emphasizes symbolism and bold display for recognition and memorability.*

## The Business of Cards

Business cards are like letterheads—they can be formal or informal depending on the person or organization they identify. Most *formal cards* are carefully arranged to preserve balance and dignity. The copy should identify, explain, and locate. That is, it should emphasize the name of the person or firm, tell the nature of the business or service, and give the address and telephone number. In the formally balanced card all elements are balanced along a

PINE MOUNTAIN LUMBER CO.
P. O. BOX 535 · YREKA, CALIFORNIA 96097 · AREA CODE 916 842-4176

TYSON-CURTIS ADVERTISING, INC.

237 SOUTH SIERRA, RENO, NEVADA ■ FAIRVIEW 2-9411

Mark Curtis

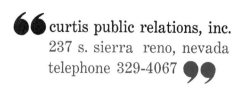

66 curtis public relations, inc.
237 s. sierra  reno, nevada
telephone 329-4067 99

mark curtis

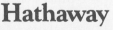

MAUREEN McMULLAN
SALES EXECUTIVE

**Hathaway**
C.F. Hathaway · THE ■WARNACO GROUP
90 Park Avenue · New York, N.Y. 10016 · Telephone 212 697-5566

visual vertical line down the center of the card with attention paid to the optical center.

*Informal cards* still retain the attributes of good design and typography, but are less rigid in arrangement. The designer has greater freedom in selecting type styles and arranging them on the card. Scripts, Romans, Sans Serifs, or Square Serifs can be used along with rules and small symbols or logos as long as they reflect the nature of the organization or service. Of course, all the essential information should be included in legible typefaces.

There are several standard sizes for cards. The generally accepted business card is identified as a number 88. It is 2 by 3½ inches. Resist the temptation to be different by using a different size. Odd-sized cards are often thrown away, and they will not fit the standard desktop file systems for business cards that serve as an excellent reference source for busy people.

In preparing business card layouts, don't place the type lines too close to the edge of the card. A margin of 12 to 18 points should be allowed on smaller cards and at least 18 points on larger cards. If a card is a number 88, 3½ inches wide, the type should be designed in an area 18 picas wide.

## Programs

Programs for plays, concerts, and other events do not necessarily follow a standard size or style. As a result they offer an interesting design challenge. However, the same basic criteria for good layout and typography used in all graphics work still apply.

The simplest plan for a program is a single sheet. The dimensions should follow the principle of good proportion while cutting most economically from the paper size chosen.

There is a rather agreed-upon format for programs. Most four-page programs with printing on two pages are designed with a title page on page 1 and the program itself on page 3. If three pages are printed, the program copy occupies the second and third pages. If a menu and a program are included, the usual format is the title page, the menu on page 2, and the program on page 3.

The typography should be consistent on all pages. A single family, with italic or oblique, if contrast is needed, is usually best for harmony and a pleasing appearance. If other type styles are used, they should be used sparingly, for heads, or for contrast, as long as they harmonize in design and tone.

Lines of dots or dashes are used to separate items on many programs. These devices are known as *leaders*. They are also used for setting what is called tabular material such as financial statements. Hyphens or periods can be used in place of leaders, with a standard separation between each period or hyphen. Most designers find that 1 or 2 ems is about right.

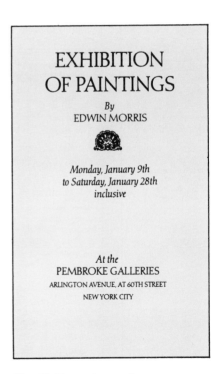

**Fig. 16-19** *Title page for a program, illustrating proper word grouping, proper type choice for the subject, and good balance and unity. (From U&lc, publication of the International Typeface Corporation.)*

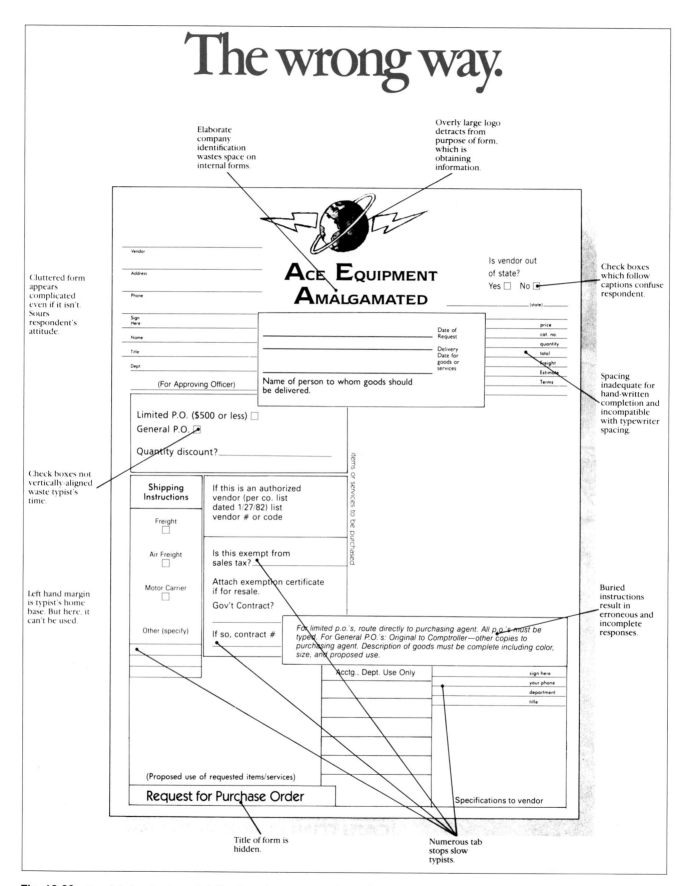

**Fig. 16-20**  *Careful planning is needed if business forms are to perform efficiently and provide all necessary informa-tion. The form on the left illustrates many common shortcomings of form design. The improved version is shown on the right. (Reprinted courtesy of Potlatch Corporation, Northwest Papers Division.)*

# The right way.

For internal forms, the company identification should be as simple as possible.

Logo is excluded or tastefully small.

Place form title top left for visual prominence. Describe purpose of form in the title.

Place Instructions ("Type or print", Press hard") below form title.

Printed screens help direct the eyes to important questions.

Align check boxes vertically for typing ease. Boxes *precede* captions.

Allow space for five characters per horizontal inch.

Fill-in space is adequate for the information being obtained.

With large margins, form can be handled without smearing information entered on the form.

## ACE Equipment Co.

40201 Anyroad Place/Somewhere, Minnesota   612-555-1212

### REQUEST FOR PURCHASE ORDER

• Type or print • If printing, press hard for 3 copies

### Vendor Identification

Name

Street address

City, state, ZIP

Acct. No. (see back for list)

### Purpose

☐ New acquisition

☒ Addition or modification of existing equipment

☐ Replace existing equipment

### Authority

☐ Existing contract # _____

☐ Officer approval required

**ROUTE:**

**Check only one**
☐ Limited purchase order (under $500)
    All copies to purchasing department

☐ General purchase order ($500 & over)
    Original to Comptroller
    All other copies to purchasing dept.

**SHIPPING:**

☐ Freight

☐ Air Freight

☐ Motor Carrier

☐ Other (specify)

_____

_____

**Leave this blank**

| Quantity | Catalog Number | Model Name and Number | Unit Price | Total Price |
|----------|----------------|------------------------|------------|-------------|
|          |                |                        |            |             |
|          |                |                        |            |             |
|          |                |                        |            |             |

Specify conditions to vendor

| Purchase Order Requested By: | | Delivery | |
|---|---|---|---|
| Name | Title | To Name | |
| Dept. | Phone | Dept. | |
| Division | TELEX | Phone | |
| Signature | Date | Delivery date | |

Form 107A—Revised 10-81

Routing stands out in upper right corner. List distribution instructions on the form.

A form that looks easy to complete usually is. The clean and tidy appearance not only pleases the respondent, it enhances efficiency.

Use box-design style with caption in upper left corner for efficiency.

Space lines compatibly with typewriters, 3 to the vertical inch.

Date form to prevent use of obsolete versions.

## Books and Pamphlets

Communicators often become involved in the writing and designing of books and pamphlets. It is thus helpful to know a few principles and practices concerning the format and design of these publications. They will be treated very briefly here as, once again, the basic tenets of good design and typography apply.

Let us begin by considering the standard arrangement used in the book industry and see how it can be helpful to us. This standard arrangement is followed for an average book and followed or modified depending on the size and nature of the book or pamphlet.

The order of arrangement of the contents of a typical book includes, from front to back, the following pages and sections:

Cover

Half-title

Title page

Copyright information

Dedication

Preface

Acknowledgments

Contents

List of illustrations

Introduction

Text

Appendix

Glossary

Bibliography

Index

All of the segments except the copyright information, which often includes the printer's imprint, begin on right-hand pages. The copyright information and printer's imprint usually appear on the back of the title page. This order of contents can be used as a guide for orderly arrangement. Of course, items can be eliminated. For instance, on booklets the cover can also serve as the title page. Even many full-sized books do not contain all of the sections.

The half-title is a page containing only the title of the book usually placed at the optical center. The title page gives greater prominence to the title and usually includes the author's name. The publisher's name and address and the date are often included on the title page. These are arranged and designed to harmonize with the content and to have proper balance on the page.

A colophon can be included, usually at the end of the book. It describes the technical aspects such as typefaces and paper used and printing techniques.

Harmony is an important design element, and the types used should work together throughout the book. The preface and

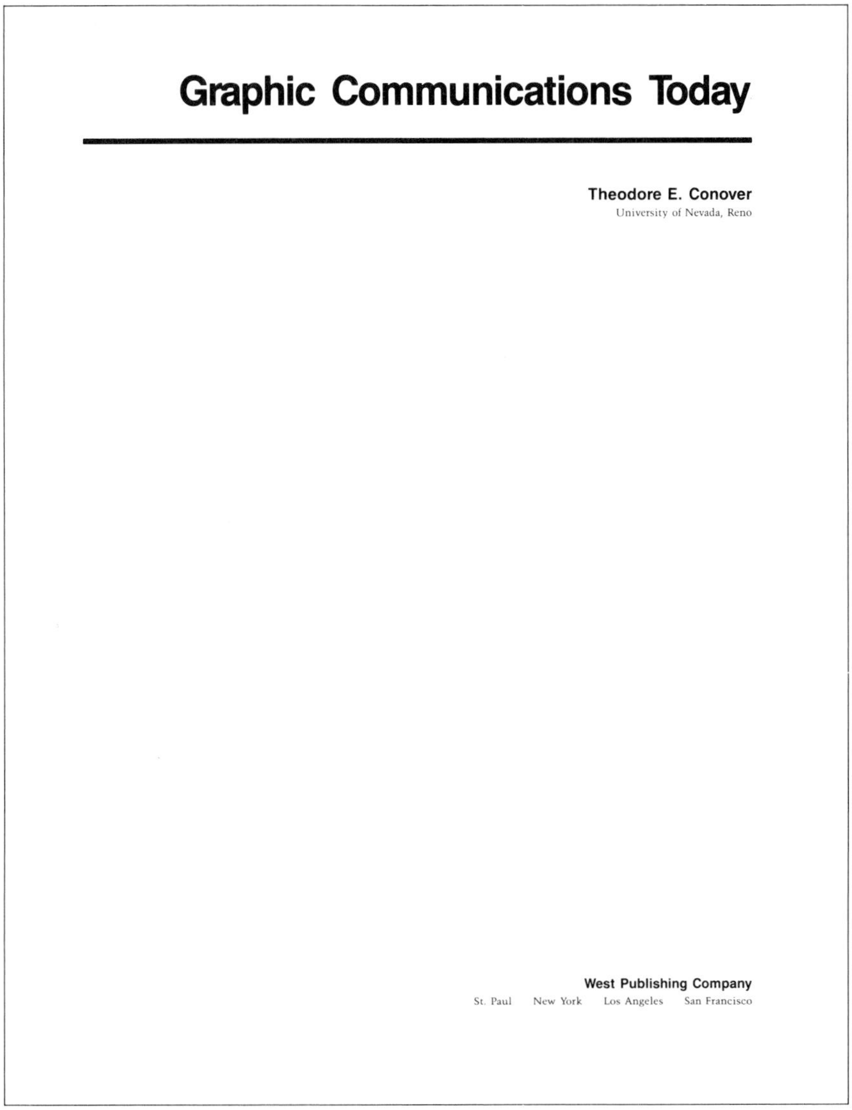

Fig. 16-21 *A typical title page layout.*

**Graphic Communications Today**

Theodore E. Conover
University of Nevada, Reno

**West Publishing Company**
St. Paul   New York   Los Angeles   San Francisco

ackowledgments are usually set in the same style and size of type as the text matter. Other material is often set in a smaller type size.

Some typographical features of book design that apply to booklet planning include folios, running heads, and margins. *Folios* are the page numbers of a book. The standard practice is to use Roman numbers (xii or XII) to number pages of the sections preceding the text, called the *preliminaries*, and Arabic numbers for the text and ending sections, called the *back pages*.

The numbering of the preliminary pages begins with the half-title. It is important that the numbers are placed consistently throughout the book.

*Running heads* are the lines at the top of pages that identify the book or chapter and often contain the page number. These heads usually consist of the title of the book on the left-hand page and the title of the chapter on the right. Running heads on preliminary pages ordinarily identify the contents of these pages.

Running heads offer the opportunity of adding a little variety and contrast to the page. But they still should harmonize with the title page and the body matter. Here are some examples of running heads:

GRAPHIC COMMUNICATIONS TODAY

*Graphic Communications Today*

**Graphic Communications Today**

*Margins* play an important role in book design. They frame the type much like a mat frames a work of art. They help the eye focus on the type area and create a pleasing appearance to the page.

Book designers recommend that there be more margin at the bottom of the page than the top. This will help prevent the

**Fig. 16-22** *Margins are important elements in book design. Progressive margins (top) and progressive margins with hanging shoulder notes (bottom) are shown.*

appearance of the type falling out of the page. The inner margin should be smaller than the outer margins. This will help make two facing pages appear as a single, unified whole. Careful attention to margins will not only enhance the appearance of a book but will help legibility as well.

Much care is taken in setting type and arranging elements for books. If some of the practices of page layout that are standard in book production were followed closely by others in the printed communications field, much of what we read would be improved.

## Effective Design Checklist for Books and Pamphlets

- Eliminate widows. *Widows* are the final words of a paragraph carried over from one column to the top of the next, or from one page to the next. They often contain only a word or two. This practice breaks the unity of a paragraph and creates an uneven contour to the column or page.

- Do not end a column or page with the first line of a paragraph.

- Do not divide a word from one column or page to the next.

- Avoid more than three consecutive lines ending with hyphenated words.

- Prevent "rivers of white" from flowing down columns. *Rivers of white* are obvious gaps between words that run down the columns. They are the result of poor and uneven spacing in the lines of type. To avoid rivers of white use a smaller typeface on the same measure; use the same typeface but in a longer measure; set the copy ragged right; use the same measure but a more condensed typeface.

**Fig. 16-23** *Two problems encountered in preparing reading (or text) matter for attractive design and pleasant reading. In the top example, the righthand column contains a widow, the last line of a paragraph carried to the top of the adjoining column. The lower example contains rivers of white, vertical gaps in successive lines caused by excessive spacing between words. Both situations should be eliminated.*

Further costs accrued if the person injured was transferred out of one county's hospital to a larger facility. If the bill became uncollectible from the patient, the county where the accident occurred was billed. The study defined what accidents occurred and what number of those resulted in uncollectible bills.

Harris said the long standing problem was partially addressed when the Nevada Legislature passed Assembly Bill No. 218. The bill created a fund provided through an ad valorem tax to help cover the cost of transient indigent care.

But the research showed that because of the volatile nature of the mining and agriculture industry of some communities, many more indigent accidents happen to in-state rather than transient patients. Harris thinks those financial burdens will have to addressed some day.

The economic impact of the agricultural school research is obvious in the case of the EMS study. It is harder to assess in such studies as the one being conducted in Lander County.

Another matter, closely connected with even spacing and complementary to it, is the question of close spacing. We have become accustomed to wide gaps between words, not so much because wide spacing makes for legibility as because the Procrustean Bed called the Compositor's Stick has made wide spacing

## Graphics in Action

1. Select the types to use to design a coordinated 8½ by 11 letterhead, number 10 commercial envelope, and number 88 business card for your own use. If you are associated with an existing business or service, use that. If not, devise a fictional name for a firm in your major field of interest. The types and arrangement should reflect the characteristics of the business or service.

2. Outline the procedures you would follow to create an informational brochure for an organization with which you are associated. This brochure would be printed on an 8½ by 11 sheet that would be mailed to prospective members. Its objective is to convince prospects that they should consider joining the organization.

3. Prepare a rough dummy for the brochure planned above.

4. Design one letterhead in the traditional format and one in modern design for a company, either existing or fictional. Use the same copy for each. Use an ornament or devise a symbol. Consider using a rule for the modern format. Analyze the two designs and decide which would be most appropriate for the company.

5. Plan and design the title page for your autobiography. Select types and ornaments or borders that you believe would best fit the subject and enhance the page. The use of ornaments or borders is up to you. The page size is 6 by 9 inches.

## Notes

1. Michael Blum, *In-Plant Printer*, April 1982, p. 48.

Throw away the paste pot, the scissors, the razor blades, and the T squares—the age of computer design is here. Well, not entirely here, but this is an era of transition in the world of printed communications. In many ways the profession is moving from a paper-based system for the transmission of words and graphics to a digital base.

What this means is that those who are working in printed communications during the next few decades will be using a mixture of the traditional and the computer-based tools. Some will be designing with pencil and paper for the foreseeable future. Others have already traded the drawing board for the display terminal.

Richard Hess, design director of the award-winning *Champion Magazine*, sees the technology as a challenge and a creative threat:

> I would not take interest in a direction of work that technology makes available to anyone with the appropriate code . . . I prefer to stay ahead of the machines rather than join . . . It may be an ever decreasing area that will be available to me, but that will be enough. I'll make it interesting and enough.[1]

**Fig. 17-1** *The tools of the pasteup era replaced those of the hot type era in most shops during the past three decades. (Courtesy of TEXET Corporation.)*

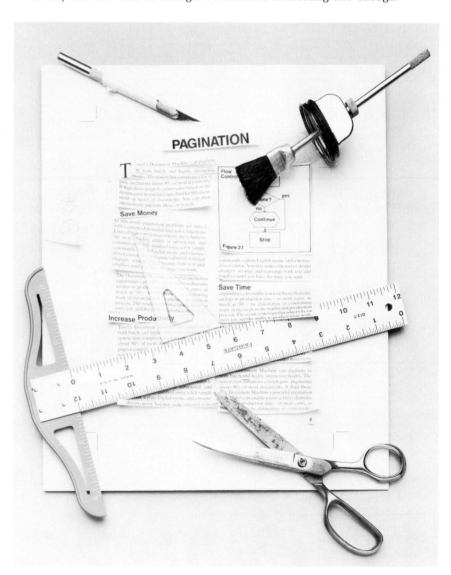

At the other end of the spectrum is the publishing operation where editor and art director perform their functions with a computer. They make copy and design decisions and arrange the material, which is not touched by human hands until a plate is clamped on a press.

The change that is occurring can be illustrated by what happened in Utica, New York, on a cold day in January 1983. There, for the first time, a daily newspaper used a computer-directed laser beam to etch a press plate on command from an editor.

Gone were the ten or more composing-room stations where humans, who were on the job when letterpress and hot type were used, could catch errors and back up the editor. Gone were the compositors who operated the photocomposition equipment, and gone were the pasteup, camera-room, and plate-making personnel of the cold type era. All that remained between the editor and the press were a computer and a laser beam. The computer directed the laser beam, which etched a press plate. The editor or graphic journalist directed the computer.

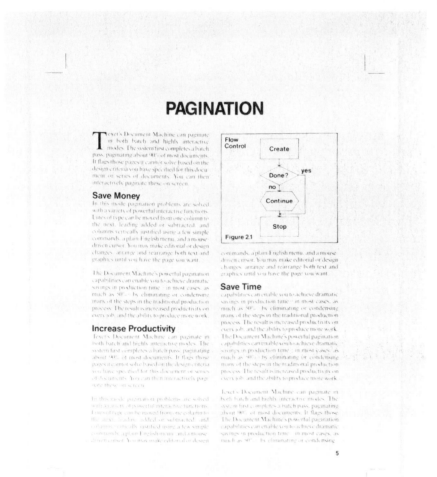

**Fig. 17-2** *This page was created simply by keyboarding. No tools were used. The video display terminal and the computer are replacing the tools of the pasteup era. (Courtesy of TEXET Corporation.)*

**Fig. 17-3**   *A video display pagination
system. This editing and design tool of
the future is moving into editorial and
production departments today.*

The newspaper was the *Observer-Dispatch*, the new process is
called *computer-to-plate pagination.* Staff members in the editorial
and advertising departments use pagination terminals to create full
newspaper pages complete with type, advertisements, and art—all
produced entirely by electronic composing machinery.

The *Observer-Dispatch* and its morning counterpart, the *Daily
Press*, were produced entirely by the system by January 1984.
Although the sophisticated computer-to-plate pagination system
employs advanced technology, the actual operation of the system
is not complex.

The reporters route their news copy to editors as has always been
the case. The editors edit the stories and write the headlines at their
computer terminals. Then the stories go to a designer at a special
design terminal. This designer-journalist adjusts and checks the
fit of the page and headlines. Photography and other art are scanned
and fed into the computer on a special machine.

At the same time, in the advertising department, copy is typed
into one terminal and forwarded to a design terminal where
headlines, art, and copy are designed and the layout completed.
When the arrangement is finished, the advertisement is given a
number and stored in the computer's memory.

Back in the newsroom, an editor calls up a page from the computer memory that contains the advertisements and completes the
page layout by arranging the editorial matter and the
advertisements.

The completed page is forwarded to a computer that breaks all the elements into computer bits. *Bits* (short for binary digits) are digits of a binary number. (Binary numbers are any numbers of the base 2. For example, the binary number 10 is composed of two bits.) Computers use binary numbers because they are easy to represent as on and off states in simple circuits. They are easy to process as well.

These bits transmit the information about the page to a laser platemaker that "reads" the bits and produces an aluminum plate from the instructions. The plate is placed on the press and is ready for printing about 5 minutes after the editor has sent it along its way.

This whole process means shorter deadlines and fewer people. In a rather simplified way, that sums up what designing in the electronic era is all about—more speed and fewer people involved in the production of printed communications.

## Many Changes on the Horizon

Change is taking place so fast, as Cliff Kolovson, media relations manager of Atex, Incorporated, pointed out in the fall of 1983, that "we have a problem here preventing our new manuals and advertising material from being obsolete by the time it is printed."[2] But some directions editing and designing will take in the electronic era are emerging. It is generally agreed that the new technology

**Fig. 17-4** *A designer uses a "mouse" (also called a "puck") to instruct the pagination device in laying out a newspaper page. The arrangement can be monitored on the video display screen.*

will make the communicator's job easier and open opportunities to expand creativity.

Here are some of the things prognosticators believe print communications will be able to do, and in some cases are doing now:

- Create colorful art on a keyboard.
- Take photographs with cameras that have no film and phase these photographs into a layout without using prints or paper.
- Make countless thumbnails and roughs without pencil or paper.
- Make revisions and corrections instantly.
- Press a button and send a layout to a machine that will make a hard copy or a printing plate.
- Transmit a page with type, line art, and screened halftones to another part of the world in minutes.
- Crop and size art automatically.
- Enlarge, reduce, condense, expand, oblique, inline and outline a typeface instantly.

Those who are working with word processors now know how easy it is to make changes and corrections in reading matter. The new technology will enable the communicator to make graphic changes and decisions as quickly and as easily.

The new tools will not, however, replace knowledge, good taste, and good judgment. They will aid the designer and editor, but they will not do the thinking. They will enable communicators to make full use of the principles of good design, legibility, and readability for maximum effectiveness.

In order to work effectively and advance in the years ahead, the communicator will not have to become an electronic genius. The frightening aspect of facing a world of complex circuits, blinking lights, and forbidding machines need not concern us today any more than the workings of the linotype and Elrod concerned the designer or journalist of two decades ago.

What will be expected of the communicator, however, is a knowledge of what the new technology can do and how it can be used to do things better or in new and more effective ways. It goes without saying, too, in this "bottom line"-oriented society, that the new equipment will enable the communicator to do the job faster and at lower cost.

## Editing and Design Equipment

Computers can create graphic designs in two ways. One method is for the designer to instruct the computer to produce a certain arrangement, and the computer will do it. In this case, the computer can create squares, circles, curves, ovals, and other designs. These can be enlarged, reduced, merged, or arranged in other ways to create the final layout.

**Fig. 17-5** *A page directory and layout appear simultaneously on the Atex Graphics Terminal, making it easy for graphics journalists to design magazine or newspaper pages. The designer uses a mouse with his right hand to move an arrow on the screen that indicates the positions for elements on the electronic layout dummy. The keyboard is used to select elements from the directory list, also on the screen, and to enter commands to the system.*

The other method, and it is being used for most graphics and editorial equipment now coming on line, employs the "mouse" technology. This eliminates the complicated keyboard procedures and instruction codes that were needed to command the computer.

The mouse is a hand-held device that controls a pointer on the video screen. Rather than enter keyboard commands, the operator directs the pointer to symbols that represent the functions to be performed. This system allows operators to create a wide variety of visuals such as charts, graphs, shading, and symbols. An almost limitless range of graphics can be drawn on the screen. Lines, rectangles, circles, and freehand shapes can be moved, reduced, expanded, and duplicated on the screen and then stored to be included with other elements. If needed, a hard copy printout can be produced for pasteup or other use.

Systems are being marketed for both large and small graphic and typographic operations. Compugraphic Corporation is an example. It now has a "personal composition system" that will link a computer to typographic output units. These systems are becoming practical for smaller operations, and in the winter of 1984 a plant could install a system for about what the most advanced models of new linotypes were costing 15 years earlier. The system is capable of producing high-quality typographic output and fast, easy creation of text and graphics.

## Pagination

Pagination is usually considered an editorial function, the process of dummying pages on a video screen rather than on a sheet of paper. But it is a lot more than that. It is a process that involves people

**Fig. 17-6** *The terminal illustrated here is used to plan and produce pages for a publication. It can be used for text editing as well as a graphic design work station. This is the Atex Graphics Terminal.*

throughout the newspaper. Writers, editors, graphic designers, and advertising and production personnel play a part. Design, layout, copy fitting, cropping and sizing of art, all are involved.

The design director, layout editor, or graphics journalist can perform the following functions with a pagination device:

- Give stories page and edition assignments.
- Determine the number of words needed for certain layout situations before the story is written.
- Order the size and style of headlines.
- Jump stories over any number of pages.
- Reserve space for graphics and cutlines.
- Change elements from one page to another automatically.
- Move items around on a page.
- Change headline sizes at will.
- Mix type sizes and styles on a page.
- Remake pages easily.
- Track progress of stories and pages through the production process.

The rate of installation of pagination systems in American publishing firms has been picking up speed. An example is the history of Atex, Incorporated, now the leading manufacturer of computer text-processing systems for the publishing industry. Atex was just 10 years old in 1983, and the company could claim that one out of every six copies of daily newspapers sold in the United States was produced on one of its systems.

Systems are being developed for magazines as well as graphic arts shops, in-plant and commercial printers, and newspapers. Publications such as *Forbes, Newsweek, Reader's Digest, Time, U.S. News & World Report,* and a number of corporate magazines are now being designed and composed on pagination equipment.

Magazine editors and designers can create full pages complete with text and graphics on a screen. In addition a magazine layout system has been developed that works in conjunction with the editorial system developed for newspaper pagination. The system reduces costs and speeds production. And it gives art directors and editors greater control of production and greater creative freedom.

Atex, for instance, has developed a graphic system that provides each work station in the editorial department with four main components: (1) a high-resolution video monitor on which the work of laying out a page is displayed; (2) an electronic mouse for positioning elements on a page; (3) a keyboard for transmitting instructions; and (4) a graphic controller located at the host computer. The controller eliminates noisy fans and excessive heat from the work area.

The designer sets up a grid on the video screen that corresponds to the page dummies. Stories, captions, headlines, quotation inserts, credit lines, graphics, advertisements, and other elements are positioned on, moved within, or removed from the page. When the page is ready, the machine creates all the necessary typesetting formats for each element on the page. The page as it will appear in print is displayed on the screen with all text in place. Even the small body type is readable in either black on white or white on black.

**Fig. 17-7** *Materials produced on a typewriter or word processor can be produced, complete with graphics, at a desk with this Compugraphic system linked to a small computer.*

**Fig. 17-8** *Example of a graphic produced on an electronic composition system.*

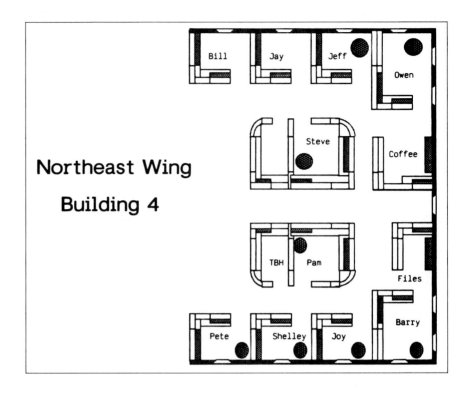

Northeast Wing

Building 4

**Fig. 17-9** *A writer at* Sunset *magazine makes final revisions on his text. The photographs and pencil layout on the work table indicate how the article will look in print.*

Another type of pagination device consists of three basic elements: a work station, a system control pedestal, and a graphics tablet. The Harris Corporation introduced such a system in late 1983. A full page is displayed on the terminal, or the screen can be split with the layout appearing on the right side and reading matter on the left. The reading matter can be edited on the screen.

The operator composes the page layout by moving a cursor on the graphic tablet that contains the commands, or instructions, for creating and placing elements on the layout on the screen. So it is possible to combine copyediting and design on one screen by one operator.

The editors of *Sunset* explained the new era of electronic publishing to their readers in a "Letter from *Sunset*" in January 1984. *Sunset* had been using electronic data processing for a number of years, but in 1982 computers were first used for processing copy, editing, and formatting pages.

"As we write this (on a computer terminal, of course)," *Sunset* told its readers, "the system has undergone its second diagnostic maintenance—akin to a 15,000-mile checkup—through a telephone link to Boston. After one memory circuit board was replaced, the system was given a clean bill of health."[3]

*Sunset* noted that writers and editors used the terminals daily to produce the sixteen issues of the magazine and the more than 1,800 articles that were processed since the equipment was installed.

It took us a while to jettison old ways and get used to the new. We had to learn new words, a seemingly endless number of abbreviations and acronym codes, and how to use the extra keys that buttress the VDT keyboard. But once the mysteries were unveiled, writers abandoned their once-loved typewriters so readily that more terminals had to be ordered, in a hurry . . .

A *Sunset* article usually goes through many drafts before the writer feels it's good enough to turn in. The words don't come any easier on a computer, but it does make revision simple and lightning fast. With just a couple of keystrokes, we can move a paragraph, copy it, or delete it. Another keystroke and the machine sets the text to the width of a magazine column and tells how long it is.

These instant results give writers more time to research, write, and polish their articles. Then they push a few more keys and their articles go to our copy department for editing and fine-tuning, again on VDTs.

Soon each article is ready for electronic formatting, positioning the text, photographs, and captions on the page. This step has given us a flexibility in page makeup that we never had before. With complex commands and minute adjustments, we strive for the best visual balance from headline and caption placement to the white space around each photograph. These changes, though not apparent to our readers, make for a more readable magazine . . .

The benefits of electronic publishing are evident to our staff. Just ask our writers how many would trade back their VDT for a typewriter.[4]

**Fig. 17-10**  *The article and page are formatted on a large-screen typesetter right in* Sunset*'s editorial offices. The operation replaces a traditional typesetting shop.*

## Other Electronic Era Trends

The electronic era has affected messages, typefaces, typesetting, and printing methods.

The volume of messages is expanding as we move into the information age. This will create increasing pressure to make messages shorter. This trend could affect the designer in at least three ways. One is the likelihood that messages will be shorter and more to the point. The "quick read" approach to covering the news is illustrated by the arrival of *USA TODAY* on the communications scene.

A second is the designer's ability to compress type—to employ minus letterspacing and minus leading to crowd more and more words into an area at no added composition expense but perhaps with the risk of reduced legibility.

The third and equally significant method of handling information is the increasing utilization of graphics to record, store, and transmit information. Often a chart, graph, cutaway sketch, or diagram can transmit information more concisely, clearly, and quickly than words that might occupy much more space. It is safe to assume that graphics will play a greater and greater role in printed communications. And graphics can also be used to store information in a compact manner.

### Trends in Type Design

At the same time communicators are faced with the task of handling more and more messages, there are some trends in type design that will affect the planning and execution of layouts. Readers consistently react favorably to larger type sizes that increase readability. Even though some designers are fascinated with the ease with which they can torture type with the electronic devices, it

**Fig. 17-11** *Graphic produced by In-House Business Graphics System. Such a system is simple to operate and can cut costs dramatically. The system produces slides, transparencies, full-color laser report sheets, and pen plots from 8½ by 11 inches to 3 by 5 feet.*

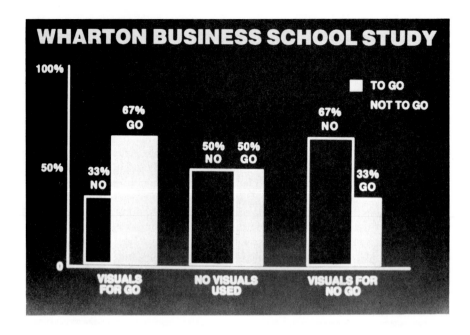

would seem that this destruction of readability will end and that the long-range movement will be toward larger size in body types and tighter editing.

Another change taking place in the use of types as a result of the electronic era is the adoption of the same type design for body matter and display. It has been the practice to make a fairly clear-cut distinction between most type families as being basically suitable for either text or display—reading matter or headlines. Now that types can be enlarged or reduced, expanded or condensed simply and that more full families are available at the tap of a key, the distinction between text and display types is disappearing. Of course, this does not apply to the Black Letters, Scripts and Cursives, and Novelty faces.

The communicator will have a greater variety of type styles to choose from in the electronic era because of the low cost of photo fonts as compared to the costs in the days of hot type.

### New Typesetting Equipment

Typesetting is changing, too. Now it is possible for a designer or editor to obtain automated text processing.

This equipment is so sophisticated it can be programmed to hyphenate properly according to definitive rules of logic and to a stored word dictionary. It can be instructed concerning the minimum number of characters permitted before hyphenation and the minimum number of characters that can be carried down to the next line. In addition, the maximum number of allowed consecutive hyphens can be controlled.

Some of the awkward word and letter spacing that was common in earlier phototypesetting equipment has also been eliminated.

*A B C D E F G H I J K L M N O P Q R S T U V W X Y Z & a b c d e f g h i j k l m n o p q r s t u v w x y z ., - ' : ; ? ! fi ff fl ffi ffl $ 1 2 3 4 5 6 7 8 9 0*

Typical font of characters available
in foundry (hot) type composition.

abcdefghijklmnopqrstuvwxyz
ABCDEFGHIJKLMNOPQRSTUVWXYZ&
1234567890$¢£ 1234567890$¢ 1/8 1/4 3/8 1/2 5/8 3/4 7/8
/ .,.:;----!?'*%#()[]†‡§'"@° +=×

A font of characters available on a diskette for
electronic typesetting.

Finer typesetting adjustments that increase readability have been incorporated in the new equipment. This equipment can be programmed to justify within precise minimum and maximum word spacing limits. The computer does the same thing over and over again with no deviations, and with, it is hoped, human frailties eliminated.

At Granite Graphics, a typography and typesetting firm in New Jersey, such typesetting systems are setting twelve 8½ by 11 pages a minute. Type also can be set at a 1,720-lines-per-minute speed. Hundreds of typefaces are available, and the cost of setting type is about 50 percent less than it was a few years ago.

**Fig. 17-12** *The number of characters available to the editor or designer has been expanded, and the font modifications that can be obtained at the press of a key have opened the door to creative opportunities in the electronic era. (Type samples courtesy of Varityper.)*

### Changes in Printing Methods

If projections of the experts in the field are correct, there will be some changes in printing methods in the coming years. (We have

**Fig. 17-13** *Although the new technology presents expanded creative possibilities, creativity is still the product of a human mind. (This impressive graphic was designed and executed by M.J. Baumwell of M.J. Baumwell Typography, New York.)*

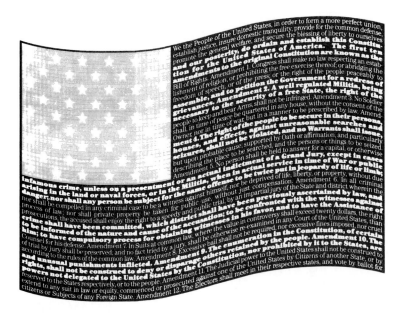

already discussed some of the new systems, such as ink jet and electrostatic printing.) But it appears that changes in the basic methods of printing will come gradually and will not affect the communicator to an alarming degree. For example, a small increase in the share of printing volume is expected by 1990 for ink jet, electronic, collotype, and screen printing. There will be a slight decline in the market share for lithography, especially offset lithography, and a noticeable increase in the use of gravure and flexography (see below), particularly in magazine and newspaper work.

The decline in offset may be caused by the increase in electronic printing for office and short-run business work plus the increase in gravure and flexography for publications. Many publishers are not happy with the waste involved in offset and the slow-drying qualities of the inks, especially in newspaper production.

There is considerable newspaper production presently being done with *flexographic* printing. This method employs relief images on rubber plates, rather like letterpress. It has been used for printing on foil, food cartons, cellophane bags, waxed paper, and such. Now newspapers such as the *Miami Herald, Atlanta Constitution, Providence Journal,* and *Washington Post* are making trial runs with flexographic presses, using photopolymer (plastic) plates.

Those interested in "flexo" cite its advantages. It uses a soft, shallow relief plate, printing directly on paper with water-base inks rather than the paste ink used in other methods today. It seems to be capable of exceptional quality at low cost, especially for color work. The ink dries hard, the density is more even than offset, and it has reduced show-through on lightweight newsprint.

Advances are also being made in letterpress printing, and they have led some in the profession to predict a return to letterpress by some of the plants that converted to offset a few years ago. These developments include thin relief plates that can be produced by computer and laser; water-based inks that do not rub off as readily as inks now being used; and finer screens for halftones that permit better definition and contrast for illustrations.

The laser will play an increasingly important role in the graphic arts, as well as in the mechanics of pre-press preparation. Rapid progress is being made in using the laser to reproduce art, and this will open new opportunities for the designer. The day may not be too far away when three-dimensional art will be an added tool for the communicator in both the print medium and television.

Although there were earlier experiments of printing three-dimensional art, in March 1984 *National Geographic* produced a three-dimensional illustration on its cover. This was the first *hologram* to be printed by a multi-million circulation magazine. (Holography is a relative of photography. Film is used but there is no lens, and the exposure is made by the light of a laser.)

William E. Garrett, *National Geographic* editor, explained the hologram to his readers and added some comments about

**Fig. 17-14** *Minutes after adjustments are made and an unprocessed plate is fed into the processor, a plate emerges from this NAPP system of automatic plate making for letterpresses. Within seconds after the plate emerges it is ready to be clamped on a press. This processor can produce 120 plates per hour.*

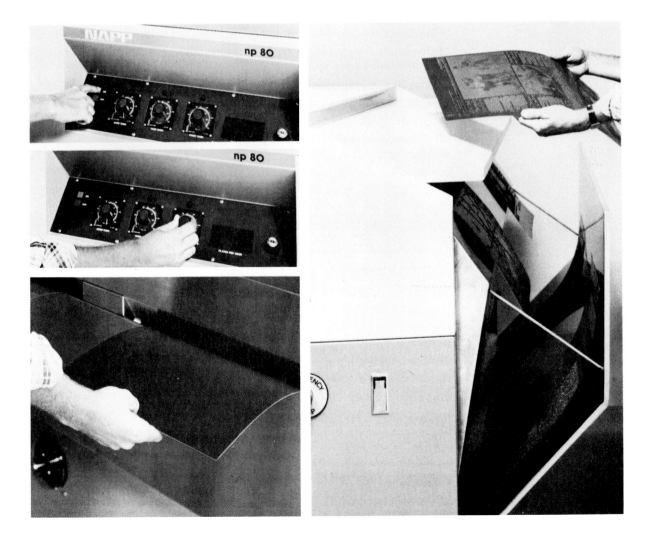

publishing in the electronic era: "At the *National Geographic* all the words and photographs for each issue's articles are electronically scanned and engraved onto printing cylinders with an accuracy of one-thousandth of an inch. . . . On the press, 13,500 miles of 6-foot-wide paper flies over these cylinders at 30 feet a second with near perfect register of the five to seven colors."[5]

## Television Graphics: A Growing Opportunity

The video display terminal is playing an increasingly important role in the work of editors and designers. But anyone who is investigating graphics in communications should consider it from another aspect—its function as a conveyor of information to an audience—its role in television.

Television graphics is a growing area of opportunity for designers. The medium offers challenges quite different from those of the print media. The more senses a message can stimulate, the more impact it can have. Television offers the opportunity to combine motion, sound, and color to create presentations that thus utilize several senses.

While the basic principles of design, type selection, and the use of illustrations still hold for television, there are unique differences in their application.

First of all, graphics for television are viewed in a rectangular area that is in the ratio of 4:3. All design elements and art must be prepared with this in mind. Television screen sizes are measured on a diagonal line from one corner to another. Thus the actual viewing area of a 22-inch television set is 17.6 by 13.2 inches. A 26-inch set has a viewing area of 20.8 by 15.6 inches.

The designer concerned with preparing visuals for television also needs to know how these visuals are transmitted. A television picture is made by a series of fine horizontal lines. The image is scanned much like a person's eyes scan a printed page while reading. An electronic beam traces the visual in a 525-line zigzag 30 times each second. As a result, it is difficult for television to transmit delicately drawn lines or fine shading. Typefaces with very thin strokes or serifs can be distorted or become virtually illegible when seen on the television screen. Spacing is also an important factor in type placement for television transmission. Lines and letters that are too close together can merge and become blurs.

The amount of the total picture that leaves the station to be seen on various receivers can vary depending on the types and sizes of the receivers used by the audience. The designer must be aware of this and allow for a "safety margin." This is a margin or frame around the visual to compensate for the loss of the full picture by some receivers. If a visual is made on a 12 by 9 card, for example, the actual design area should be only about 10 by 7 inches.

The designer must be aware of viewing conditions on the receiving end of the transmission, too. If the program is viewed in the home by a few people sitting 6 to 8 feet from the screen, the design elements should be quite different than if the program is educational and intended for viewing by a large audience in a classroom.

As a general guideline, designers believe that the minimum size for type in a graphic for television should be at least one-twenty-fifth of the total picture height. The type size used in a 12 by 9 layout should be at least 36 point if this guideline is followed.

The designer of graphics for television has to become skilled at working with a number of techniques that do not apply to design for the print media. Probably the most complex is the whole area of animation. Then there are such devices as inlay, overlay, back projection, color separation overlay, and split-screen effects, to mention a few.

Inlay is a technique by which part of a television picture is cut out electronically and replaced by visuals from another source. Overlay is accomplished in a similar way. Foreground material from one camera is projected on top of background originating from another source.

Back projection involves showing an image of a photographic transparency on a translucent screen. Then a person or object in front of the screen is recorded by the television camera along with the image. Color separation overlay is another method of projecting graphics and art from two sources at the same time. Split-screen effects also enable the producer to project material from more than one source simultaneously.

All of these techniques require close coordination between the designer and the other staff members involved in producing a television program. It is obviously helpful for the designer of graphics for the video screen to become familiar with all phases of television production.

## Preparation for Today's Graphics

Where does all this leave the communicator or someone planning a career in journalism or the graphic arts? How should a person prepare to work and advance in the world of graphic communications today?

One thing seems certain. Communicators will not be as restrained in their creativity and effectiveness as many have been by the equipment available. The new tools will give them greater flexibility and scope. Another fact seems equally certain. Production speed will increase, changes will have to be made faster, and design decisions, as a result, will have to be made quickly. Communicators thus will need a solid background in all aspects of graphic design, plus a broad knowledge of the world around them.

"There will be no careers in the publishing field that won't be touched by computers. More especially the design field in particular will rely more and more on computers," comments David B. Gray,

---

**Creative Communication**

"New wave" graphics is the buzzword in the world of communications design today.

The new wave graphics philosophy has been interpreted by some as an anything goes approach to design. Spacing between letters and lines follows no pattern proven by readership studies. Type is lined up vertically whether it is intended as decoration or as something to be read. Some lines produced by some designers resemble ransom notes in which the words were cut from various sources and pasted together on the layout.

"Type has always been the weakest aspect of American design and the situation has deteriorated of late. The reason, we believe, has to do with the New Wave vogue," wrote Martin Fox, editor of *Print*, in that publication's *Regional Design Annual, 1983* (July/August 1983, p.84).

New wave graphics, careful designers maintain, means knowing what rules are being destroyed and why. It means informed awareness of basic design principles and putting them aside to create something that is new, different, and commanding rather than a disunified chaotic presentation.

graphics editor of the *Providence Journal.*[6] Gray also teaches a course at the Rhode Island School of Design in electronic publication.

"My students at RISD are beginning to grasp the fact that change is inevitable and accelerating. As soon as we tell them something, it is already 'old hat,'" Gray notes.[7]

An example of the changes that are occurring is the Society of Newspaper Design. The organization was 5 years old in 1983 but it already had 1,000 members. And there is a shortage of qualified people to fill the "graphic editor" or "assistant managing editor—graphics" positions on newspapers. Gray notes that it is even difficult to find graphic journalists to fill entry-level artist or informational graphics jobs.

Gray also suggests that people planning careers in communications should have strong liberal arts backgrounds. He points out that some of the best writers and reporters on his newspaper were liberal arts majors. In addition, he believes design schools should spend more time on writing and journalism schools should spend more time on design:

> As we approach pagination, we are consolidating the makeup function into fewer people . . . centralizing the makeup function. The sheer cost of the terminals themselves will force this kind of organization on newspapers that do not already function in this way. The need for competent designer-editors will grow. On the really well-designed newspapers the designer is an editor . . . the say as to where stories go, and the play they get, is as much a designer's function as an editor's function. The real problem, as I see it, is to get designers with a sense of news, a feel for what is important, a feel for editing.[8]

Designers and editors have been consistent in recommending that students preparing for careers in print communications should learn all they can about design and computers. They suggest that there is far too much to learn, however, about technology and change to concentrate on the machinery.

The art director of a major New York publishing corporation suggests that students who wish to function effectively with design and graphics in the electronic era learn as much as possible about the principles and philosophies of the great movements or schools of design, such as Bauhaus, Swiss design, and international architectural style.

In addition, this art director believes the student should learn about the principles, philosophy, and richness of typographical design and be interested in all the graphic arts, especially drawing and photography. And, he adds, the student should study newspaper layout. The idea is to know the rudiments of design, but perhaps more important, to know what the artist and designer are trying to accomplish. It is also important, he believes, to learn the principles of statistical and informational graphics.

The art director urged students to learn to think of design and typography as absolutely integrated and interrelated with the journalistic processes of communication, not as a decorative optional appendage.

Some study of computers was recommended. The student should be knowledgeable in the use and possibilities of the computer for typesetting, pagination, and making charts and maps on the screen. However, Carl P. Palmer, writing in *Graphics Arts Monthly*, advises, "while the computer can be programmed to do all sort of things, only human creativity can produce usable, technically acceptable, and aesthetically pleasing results. This means there is a need for people having solid backgrounds that link design with computers."[9]

Palmer also notes that "spotting where illustrations and then captions go and the proper distribution of space on a page requires knowledge of design and typography."

Schools should concentrate on teaching students to think, the professionals tell us, to explore, to question, to wonder, and to approach old problems with new solutions.

And, we should all remember that even with the expanding technology for producing printed communications, these communications are still "consumed" with a device that has not changed in the nearly 550 years since Johann Gutenberg cast the first piece of movable type—the human eye. Design should always help, not hinder, the human eye when it encounters printed communications.

## Career Tips from Professionals

- Computers are here to stay. Learn as much as possible about them, but don't get bogged down in the bits and bytes.
- Broaden your horizons by reading, studying, learning—in the liberal arts.
- Start now and make a habit of reading the leading trade periodicals in the world of printed communications.
- Study publications and advertisements on a regular basis to monitor trends in graphics and typography.
- Read the popular books that are concerned with the directions society is taking as we move into the information age.
- Writers and editors should learn as much as they can about design, and designers should learn as much as they can about writing and editing.

## Graphics in Action

1. Collect samples of unusual type arrangements and see if you can determine if minus letterspacing or minus leading was used. Analyze the samples to determine if the arrangements helped or hindered readability.

2. Arrange a field trip to a newspaper, graphic arts firm, or printing plant that is using electronic editing and design equipment. Try to get some hands-on practice.

**3.** Prepare a research paper on electronic equipment, how it operates, and what it is capable of doing in your particular area of interest—advertising, newspapers, public relations, magazines, and so on.

**4.** Devise a model program of courses of study you believe would be suitable for someone planning a career in print or electronic graphics in the information age with emphasis on your area of special interest.

**5.** Devise a "printed communications IQ test" that a person could take to determine if he or she were acquiring the attributes that would lead to a successful career. Include a scoring system weighted according to the relative importance of the items you include.

## Notes

1. Richard Hess, personal communication, November 22, 1983.
2. Cliff Kolovson, personal communication, October 10, 1983.
3. *Sunset*, January 1984, p. 136.
4. Ibid.
5. William E. Garrett, *National Geographic*, March 1984, p. 281.
6. David G. Gray, personal communication, November 26, 1983.
7. Ibid.
8. Ibid.
9. Carl P. Palmer, *Graphic Arts Monthly*, November 1983, p. 148.

It would be impossible and most likely not even worthwhile to include an endless list of publications. Thus the books listed below were chosen to form a comprehensive basic library for the graphics communicator.

Adams, James L. *Conceptual Blockbusting.* Stanford, Calif.: Stanford Alumni Association, 1974.

*A concise, readable approach to creative problem solving with thought-provoking ideas of value to all who write or design.*

Arnold, Edmund C. *Designing the Total Newspaper.* New York: Harper & Row, 1981.

*A comprehensive examination of all aspects of newspaper design by America's leading newspaper designer for many years.*

Beach, Mark. *Editing Your Newsletter.* Portland, Ore.: Coast-to-Coast Books, 1982.

*A guide to the writing, design, and production of newsletters. Excellent for beginners in newsletter production.*

Birren, Faber. *Creative Color.* New York: Van Nostrand Reinhold, 1961.

*An introduction to color principles and the application of color to design; it includes simple to complex exercises to help one understand and use color.*

Craig, James. *Designing with Type.* New York: Watson-Guptill, 1983.

*A new edition of a basic introductory workbook/text on typography. It includes complete alphabets and simple how-to information.*

Garcia, Mario R. *Contemporary Newspaper Design.* Englewood Cliffs, N.J.: Prentice-Hall, 1984.

*An outline of the basics of newspaper design, very contemporary, with many illustrations plus examples of redesign projects completed by the author.*

Graham, Walter. *Complete Guide to Pasteup.* Philadelphia: North American, 1975.

*A comprehensive, fundamental guide aimed at the "quick print" and newsletter producer. It is an unsophisticated introductory book, ideal for the neophyte.*

Hudson, Howard Penn. *Publishing Newsletters.* New York: Scribner's, 1982.

*This is considered the most complete guide to all aspects of newsletters, including editing and design.*

Hurlburt, Allen F. *The Grid, A Modular System for the Design and Production of Newspapers, Magazines and Books.* New York: Van Nostrand Reinhold, 1978.

*An overview of the use of the grid in publication layout, helping one understand pagination and computer design techniques.*

International Paper Company. *Pocket Pal.* New York: International Paper, 1983.

*A must for all those working with graphic arts. Write International Paper Company, 220 East 42nd Street, New York, NY 10017.*

Kneller, George F. *The Art and Science of Creativity.* New York: Holt, Rinehart and Winston, 1965.

*Easy reading, concise, and a good introduction to creativity.*

Lem, Dean Phillip. *Graphics Master 3.* Los Angeles: Dean Lem Associates, 1983.

*A workbook of planning aids, guides, and graphic tools for the design and production of printing; it also contains a line gauge and ruler, copy-fitting charts, and a photo sizing proportion scale.*

Lindegren, Erik. *ABC of Lettering and Printing Typefaces.* New York: Greenwich House, 1982.

*A collection of representative typeface alphabets from the various races to use in selecting and tracing types.*

Moen, Daryl R. *Newspaper Layout and Design.* Ames, Iowa: Iowa State University Press, 1984.

*This paperback gives a well-balanced overview of newspaper design, with emphasis on how it is done.*

Munce, Howard. *Graphics Handbook.* Westport, Conn.: North Light, 1982.

*A guide for beginners; a good book to help neophytes design simple printed pieces.*

Nelson, Roy Paul. *Publication Design.* Dubuque, Iowa: Wm. C. Brown Company, 1983.

*Emphasizes magazine and periodical design, and touches on newspapers and typography. It was originally published in 1972. Many illustrations.*

Nesbitt, Alexander. *The History and Techniques of Lettering.* New York: Dover, 1957.

*A classic by one of the leading students of letter forms and typography; it traces the development of letter forms and the basic races of types as well as their uses in typography and graphic design.*

Rosen, Ben. *Type and Typography.* New York: Van Nostrand Reinhold, 1976.

*A workbook for students of graphic design and all those who work with type. It contains more than 1,500 specimens and alphabets of text and display types.*

Sanders, Norman. *Graphic Designer's Production Handbook.* New York: Hastings House, 1982.

*A valuable, very comprehensive reference work for anyone involved in the creation and production of printed communications. It explains with illustrations and diagrams such processes as overlays, keying, preparing for printing.*

Sausmarez, Maurice de. *Basic Design: The Dynamics of Visual Form.* New York: Van Nostrand Reinhold, 1983.

*A classic introduction to the basic elements and dynamics of design.*

Silver, Gerald A. *Graphic Layout and Design.* New York: Van Nostrand Reinhold, 1981.

*An overview of principles and practices of graphic arts in easy-to-understand language. A good self-teaching book for those desiring to sharpen layout skills.*

Stevenson, George A. *Graphic Arts Encyclopedia.* New York: McGraw-Hill, 1979.
   *The encyclopedia of printing and graphic arts; a valuable reference for any professional's library.*
V and M Typographical. *The Type Specimen Book.* New York: Van Nostrand Reinhold, 1974.
   *Complete alphabets of 544 different typefaces in more than 300 sizes.*
Van Uchelen, Rod. *Pasteup Production Techniques and New Applications.* New York: Van Nostrand Reinhold, 1976.
   *A profusely illustrated, easily understood introduction to pasteup; it contains simple projects that can be produced with a minimum of tools.*
Watkins, Don. *Newspaper Advertising Handbook.* Wheaton, Ill.: Dynamo, 1980.
   *Although devoted mainly to designing newspaper advertisements, it contains many valuable tips for all types of graphic design. Available from Dynamo, Inc., P.O. Box 175, Wheaton, IL 60187.*
White, Jan V. *Mastering Graphics.* New York: R.R. Bowker, 1983.
   *A handy reference tool for those who edit or produce internal or external publications for businesses or organizations.*

## Sources for New Publications

In the fast-paced world of the information age, new books are being produced constantly. The following are sources for books on graphics and typography. Lists of current offerings are available.

Dynamic Graphics, Inc.
6707 North Sheridan Road
P.O. Box 1901
Peoria, IL 61656-1901

Print Book Store
6400 Goldsboro Road
Bethesda, MD 20817

## Periodicals

*Communications Arts*—A bimonthly publication containing detailed reports on designers, illustrators, photographers, and art directors. *Communications Arts*, 410 Sherman Avenue, P.O. Box 10399, Palo Alto, CA 94303.

*Communicators, The—A monthly publication of the International Association of Business Communicators that contains many articles and regular features on magazine design. IABC, 879 Market Street, Suite 940, San Francisco, CA 94102.*

*DESIGN*—A quarterly journal of the professional society dedicated to improving newspapers through design; it provides information on newspapers undergoing design overhauls, computer graphics, trends. The Society of Newspaper Design, The Newspaper Center, Box 17290, Dulles International Airport, Washington, DC 20041.

*Fourth Edition*—An annual publication of the Society of Newspaper Design showing the winners in numerous categories of design. Issued yearly as First Edition, Second Edition, and so on. The Society of Newspaper Design, address above.

*Newsletter on Newsletters, The*—A twice-a-month newsletter for those who edit and produce newsletters; it contains a frequent "Graphics Clinic" section. The Newsletter Clearinghouse, 44 West Market Street, P.O. Box 311, Rhinebeck, NY 12572.

*Print*—A bimonthly, profusely illustrated design periodical; a source of new ideas and trends in design and typography. *Print*, 6400 Goldsboro Road NW, Washington, DC 20034.

*Typographic i*—A great little publication for ideas, information, and inspiration for anyone involved in producing printed communications. Typographers International Association, 2262 Hall Place NW, Washington, DC 20007.

*U&lc*—A quarterly tabloid-size free magazine about typography; an excellent source of ideas. U&lc, International Typeface Corporation, 2 Hammarskjold Plaza, New York, NY 10017.

| | | |
|:---:|:---:|:---:|
| T | T | T |
| ROMAN TYPES | SANS SERIF TYPES | SQUARE SERIF TYPES |
| T | T | T |
| SCRIPT AND CURSIVE TYPES | BLACK LETTER TYPES | MISCELLANEOUS AND NOVELTY TYPES |

# Roman Types

36 POINT BERNHARD MODERN BOLD

# ABCDEFGHIJKLMNOPQRSTU
# VWXYZ
abcdefghijklmnopqrstuvwxyz
1234567890

36 POINT BERNHARD MODERN BOLD ITALIC

*ABCDEFGHIJKLMNOPQRSTU*
*VWXYZ*
*abcdefghijklmnopqrstuvwxyz*
*1234567890$*

24 POINT BERNHARD MODERN BOLD

ABCDEFGHIJKLMNOPQRSTUVWXYZ
abcdefghijklmnopqrstuvwxyz
1234567890$&

24 POINT BERNHARD MODERN BOLD ITALIC

*ABCDEFGHIJKLMNOPQRSTUVWXYZ*
*abcdefghijklmnopqrstuvwxyz*
*1234567890$&*

72 POINT BERNHARD MODERN BOLD

# ABCDEFGHI
# JKLMNOPQR
# STUVWXYZ
# abcdefghijklm
# nopqrstuvwxyz
# 1234567890

36 POINT BODONI BOLD

# ABCDEFGHIJKLMNOPQRSTUV WXYZ
abcdefghijklmnopqrstuvwxyz
1234567890$&

36 POINT BODONI BOLD ITALIC

# *ABCDEFGHIJKLMNOPQRSTUV WXYZ*
*abcdefghijklmnopqrstuvwxyz*
*1234567890$&*

24 POINT BODONI BOLD

ABCDEFGHIJKLMNOPQRSTUVWXYZ
abcdefghijklmnopqrstuvwxyz
1234567890$&

24 POINT BODONI BOLD ITALIC

*ABCDEFGHIJKLMNOPQRSTUVWXYZ*
*abcdefghijklmnopqrstuvwxyz*
*1234567890$&*

72 POINT BODONI BOLD

# ABCDEFGHIJ

# KLMNOPQR

# STUVWXYZ

# abcdefghijklm

# nopqrstuvwxyz

# 1234567890$

**36 POINT CASLON OLD STYLE**

# ABCDEFGHIJKLMNOPQRSTUV WXYZ

abcdefghijklmnopqrstuvwxyz

1234567890&$

**36 POINT CASLON OLD STYLE ITALIC**

*ABCDEFGHIJKLMNOPQRS TUVWXYZ*

*abcdefghijklmnopqrstuvwxyz ABCD EGJKLMNPQRT 1234567890*

**24 POINT CASLON OLD STYLE**

ABCDEFGHIJKLMNOPQRSTUVWXYZ

abcdefghijklmnopqrstuvwxyz

1234567890

**24 POINT CASLON OLD STYLE ITALIC**

*ABCDEFGHIJKLMNOPQRSTUVWXYZ*

*abcdefghijklmnopqrstuvwxyz ABCDEGJK LMNP RTUY& 1234567890&$*

72 POINT CASLON OLD STYLE

# ABCDEFGHIJ
# KLMNOPQRS
# TUVWXYZ
# abcdefghijklmn
# opqrstuvwxyz
# 1234567890&$

36 POINT CENTURY EXPANDED BOLD

# ABCDEFGHIJKLMNOPQRST UVWXYZ
abcdefghijklmnopqrstuvwxyz
1234567890

36 POINT CENTURY EXPANDED BOLD ITALIC

# *ABCDEFGHIJKLMNOPQRST UVWXYZ*
*abcdefghijklmnopqrstuvwxyz*
*1234567890*

24 POINT CENTURY EXPANDED BOLD

ABCDEFGHIJKLMNOPQRSTUVWXYZ
abcdefghijklmnopqrstuvwxyz
1234567890

24 POINT CENTURY EXPANDED BOLD ITALIC

*ABCDEFGHIJKLMNOPQRSTUVWXYZ*
*abcdefghijklmnopqrstuvwxyz*
*1234567890*

72 POINT CENTURY EXPANDED BOLD

# ABCDEFGHIJ
# KLMNOPQRS
# TUVWXYZ
# abcdefghijklmn
# opqrstuvwxyz
# 1234567890

**36 POINT GARAMOND BOLD**

# ABCDEFGHIJKLMNOPQRSTUV WXYZ

abcdefghijklmnopqrstuvwxyz

1234567890$&

**36 POINT GARAMOND BOLD ITALIC**

# *ABCDEFGHIJKLMNOPQRSTUV WXYZ*

*abcdefghijklmnopqrstuvwxyz*

*1234567890$&*

**24 POINT GARAMOND BOLD**

ABCDEFGHIJKLMNOPQRSTUVWXYZ
abcdefghijklmnopqrstuvwxyz
1234567890$&

**24 POINT GARAMOND BOLD ITALIC**

*ABCDEFGHIJKL MNOPQRSTUVWXYZ*
*abcdefghijklmnopqrstuvwxyz*
*1234567890$&*

72 POINT GARAMOND BOLD

# ABCDEFGHIJ
# KLMNOPQ
# RSTUVWXYZ
# abcdefghijklm
# nopqrstuvwxyz
# 1234567890$&

36 POINT GOUDY BOLD

# ABCDEFGHIJKLMNOPQRST UVWXYZ
abcdefghijklmnopqrstuvwxyz
1234567890

36 POINT GOUDY BOLD ITALIC

# ABCDEFGHIJKLMNOPQRST UVWXYZ
abcdefghijklmnopqrstuvwxyz
1234567890

24 POINT GOUDY BOLD

ABCDEFGHIJKLMNOPQRSTUVWXYZ
abcdefghijklmnopqrstuvwxyz
1234567890

24 POINT GOUDY BOLD ITALIC

ABCDEFGHIJKLMNOPQRSTUVWXYZ
abcdefghijklmnopqrstuvwxyz
1234567890

72 POINT GOUDY BOLD

# ABCDEFGHIJK
# LMNOPQRSTU
# VWXYZ
# abcdefghijklmnop
# qrstuvwxyz
# 1234567890

36 POINT PALATINO SEMIBOLD

# ABCDEFGHIJKLMNOPQRSTU VWXYZ

## abcdefghijklmnopqrstuvwxyz
## 1234567890　1234567890

36 POINT PALATINO SEMIBOLD ITALIC

# *ABCDEFGHIJKLMNOPQRSTU VWXYZ*

## *abcdefghijklmnopqrstuvwxyz*
## *1234567890*

24 POINT PALATINO SEMIBOLD

### ABCDEFGHIJKLMNOPQRSTUVWXYZ
### abcdefghijklmnopqrstuvwxyz
### 1234567890 1234567890

24 POINT PALATINO SEMIBOLD ITALIC

### *ABCDEFGHIJKLMNOPQRSTUVWXYZ*
### *abcdefghijklmnopqrstuvwxyz*
### *1234567890*

72 POINT PALATINO SEMIBOLD

# ABCDEFGHIJK
# LMNOPQRST
# UVWXYZ
# abcdefghijklmn
# opqrstuvwxyz
# 1234567890
# 1234567890

# ABCDEFGHIJKLMNOPQRST UVWXYZ& abcdefghijklmnopqrstuvwxyz 1234567890$

# *ABCDEFGHIJKLMNOPQRST UVWXYZ& abcdefghijklmnopqrstuvwxyz 1234567890$*

## ABCDEFGHIJKLMNOPQRSTUVWXYZ& abcdefghijklmnopqrstuvwxyz 1234567890$

## *ABCDEFGHIJKLMNOPQRSTUVWXYZ& abcdefghijklmnopqrstuvwxyz 1234567890$*

72 POINT TIMES NEW ROMAN BOLD

# ABCDEFGHIJ
# KLMNOPQRS
# TUVWXYZ&
# abcdefghijklmno
# pqrstuvwxyz
# 1234567890$

60 POINT WEISS

ABCDEFGHIJKLM
NOPQRSTUV
WXYZ&
abcdefghijklmnopqr
stuvwxyz
1234567890$

36 POINT WEISS

ABCDEFGHIJKLMNOPQRST
UVWXYZ&
abcdefghijklmnopqrstuvwxyz
1234567890$

# Sans Serif Types

36 POINT FRANKLIN GOTHIC BOLD

# ABCDEFGHIJKLMNOPQRST UVWXYZ
# abcdefghijklmnopqrstuvwxyz
# 1234567890$&

36 POINT FRANKLIN GOTHIC BOLD ITALIC

# *ABCDEFGHIJKLMNOPQRST UVWXYZ*
# *abcdefghijklmnopqrstuvwx yz  1234567890$&*

24 POINT FRANKLIN GOTHIC BOLD

## ABCDEFGHIJKLMNOPQRSTUVWXYZ
## abcdefghijklmnopqrstuvwxyz
## 1234567890$&

24 POINT FRANKLIN GOTHIC BOLD ITALIC

## *ABCDEFGHIJKLMNOPQRSTUVWXYZ*
## *abcdefghijklmnopqrstuvwxyz*
## *1234567890$&*

72 POINT FRANKLIN GOTHIC BOLD

# ABCDEFGHIJK
# LMNOPQRSTU
# VWXYZ
# abcdefghijklmno
# pqrstuvwxyz
# 12345

# ABCDEFGHIJKLMNOP QRSTUVWXYZ

abcdefghijklmnopqrstuv wxyz& 1234567890

ABCDEFGHIJKLMNOPQRSTUVWXYZ abcdefghijklmnopqrstuvwxyz& 1234567890

*ABCDEFGHIJKLMNOPQRSTUVWXYZ abcdefghijklmnopqrstuvwxyz& 1234567890*

60 POINT FUTURA DEMIBOLD

# ABCDEFGHIJKLMNO
# PQRSTUTUVWXYZ
## abcdefghijklmnopqrst
## uvwxyz 1234567890

36 POINT FUTURA DEMIBOLD

## ABCDEFGHIJKLMNOPQRSTUVWXY
## Z abcdefghijklmnopqrstuvwxyz&
## 1234567890

36 POINT FUTURA DEMIBOLD ITALIC

## *ABCDEFGHIJKLMNOPQRSTUVWXY*
## *Z abcdefghijklmnopqrstuvwxyz&*
## *1234567890*

60 POINT HELVETICA LIGHT

# ABCDEFGHIJKLMN OPQRSTUVWXYZ abcdefghijklmnopqrst uvwxyz&1234567890

36 POINT HELVETICA LIGHT

## ABCDEFGHIJKLMNOPQRST UVWXYZ abcdefghijklmnopqrstuvwxyz& 1234567890

36 POINT HELVETICA LIGHT ITALIC

## *ABCDEFGHIJKLMNOPQRST UVWXYZ abcdefghijklmnopqrstuvwxyz& 1234567890*

60 POINT HELVETICA

# ABCDEFGHIJKLMN
# OPQRSTUVWXYZ
# abcdefghijklmnopqrst
# uvwxyz 1234567890

36 POINT HELVETICA

## ABCDEFGHIJKLMNOPQRS
## TUVWXYZ
## abcdefghijklmnopqrstuvwxyz&
## 1234567890

36 POINT HELVETICA ITALIC

## *ABCDEFGHIJKLMNOPQRS*
## *TUVWXYZ*
## *abcdefghijklmnopqrstuvwxyz&*
## *1234567890*

# ABCDEFGHIJKLMNOPQRSTUV WXYZ
## abcdefghijklmnopqrstuvwxyz& 1234567890

# *ABCDEFGHIJKLMNOPQRSTUV WXYZ*
## *abcdefghijklmnopqrstuvwxyz& 1234567890*

## ABCDEFGHIJKLMNOPQRSTUVWXYZ
abcdefghijklmnopqrstuvwxyz&
1234567890

## *ABCDEFGHIJKLMNOPQRSTUVWXYZ*
*abcdefghijklmnopqrstuvwxyz&
1234567890*

72 POINT HELVETICA BOLD

# ABCDEFGHIJKL
# MNOPQRSTUV
# WXYZ
# abcdefghijklmno
# pqrstuvwxyz&
# 1234567890

# ABCDEFGHIJ
# KLMNOPQRS
# TUVWXYZ
# abcdefghijklm
# nopqrstuvwx
# yz1234567890

# ABCDEFGHIJKLMNOPQ
# RSTUVWXYZ
# abcdefghijklmnopqrstuv
# wxyz&   1234567890

60 POINT OPTIMA

# ABCDEFGHIJKLMN
# OPQRSTUVWXYZ
# abcdefghijklmnopqrs
# tuvwxyz&1234567890

36 POINT OPTIMA

## ABCDEFGHIJKLMNOPQRST
## UVWXYZ
## abcdefghijklmnopqrstuvwxyz&
## 1234567890

36 POINT OPTIMA ITALIC

## *ABCDEFGHIJKLMNOPQRST*
## *VWXYZ*
## *abcdefghijklmnopqrstuvwxyz&*
## *1234567890*

60 POINT UNIVERS 45

# ABCDEFGHIJKLMN
# OPQRSTUVWXYZ
# abcdefghijklmnopqrst
# uvwxyz&
# 1234567890

36 POINT UNIVERS 45

## ABCDEFGHIJKLMNOPQRSTUV
## WXYZ
## abcdefghijklmnopqrstuvwxyz&
## 1234567890

36 POINT UNIVERS 46

## *ABCDEFGHIJKLMNOPQRSTUV*
## *WXYZ*
## *abcdefghijklmnopqrstuvwxyz&*
## *1234567890*

60 POINT UNIVERS 55

# ABCDEFGHIJKLMN
# OPQRSTUVWXYZ
# abcdefghijklmnopqrs
# tuvwxyz&
# 1234567890

36 POINT UNIVERS 55

## ABCDEFGHIJKLMNOPQRSTU
## VWXYZ
## abcdefghijklmnopqrstuvwxyz&
## 1234567890

36 POINT UNIVERS 56

## *ABCDEFGHIJKLMNOPQRSTU*
## *VWXYZ*
## *abcdefghijklmnopqrstuvwxyz&*
## *1234567890*

72 POINT UNIVERS 75

# ABCDEFGHIJK
# LMNOPQRS
# TUVWXYZ
# abcdefghijklmn
# opqrstuvwxyz
# 1234567890

36 POINT UNIVERS 75

## ABCDEFGHIJKLMNOPQR
## STUVWXYZ
## abcdefghijklmnopqrstuvwxyz&
## 1234567890

# Square Serif Types

24 POINT GOLD RUSH

# ABCDEFGHIJKLMNOPQ
# RSTUVWXYZ
# 1234567890$&

36 POINT HELLENIC WIDE

# ABCDEFGHIJ
# KLMNOPQRS
# TUVWXYZ
# abcdefghijklm
# nopqrstuvwxyz
# 1234567890

72 POINT P. T. BARNUM

# ABCDEFGHIJKLM
# NOPQRSTUVW
# XYZ abcdefghijk
# lmnopqrstuvwxyz
# 1234567890$&

48 POINT P. T. BARNUM

# ABCDEFGHIJKLMNOPQRST
# UVWXYZ
# abcdefghijklmnopqrstuvw
# xyz 1234567890$&

36 POINT LUBALIN GRAPH LIGHT

ABCDEFGHIJKLMNOPQRSTU
VWXYZ
abcdefghijklmnopqrstuvwxyz
1234567890

36 POINT LUBALIN GRAPH BOOK

ABCDEFGHIJKLMNOPQRSTU
VWXYZ
abcdefghijklmnopqrstuvwxyz
1234567890

36 POINT LUBALIN GRAPH BOLD

**ABCDEFGHIJKLMNOPQRS
TUVWXYZ
abcdefghijklmnopqrstuvw
vwxyz&
1234567890**

36 POINT STYMIE LIGHT

ABCDEFGHIJKLMNOPQRST
UVWXYZ
abcdefghijklmnopqrstuvwxyz&
1234567890

36 POINT STYMIE LIGHT ITALIC

*ABCDEFGHIJKLMNOPQRST*
*UVWXYZ*
*abcdefghijklmnopqrstuvwxyz&*
*1234567890*

24 POINT STYMIE MEDIUM

ABCDEFGHIJKLMNOPQRSTUVWXYZ
abcdefghijklmnopqrstuvwxyz&
1234567890

24 POINT STYMIE MEDIUM ITALIC

*ABCDEFGHIJKLMNOPQRSTUVWXYZ*
*abcdefghijklmnopqrstuvwxyz&*
*1234567890*

36 POINT STYMIE BOLD

# ABCDEFGHIJKLMNOPQRST UVWXYZ
## abcdefghijklmnopqrstuvwxyz
## 1234567890

36 POINT STYMIE BOLD ITALIC

# *ABCDEFGHIJKLMNOPQRST UVWXYZ*
## *abcdefghijklmnopqrstuvwxyz*
## *1234567890*

24 POINT STYMIE BOLD

## ABCDEFGHIJKLMNOPQRSTUVWXYZ
abcdefghijklmnopqrstuvwxyz&
1234567890

24 POINT STYMIE BOLD ITALIC

## *ABCDEFGHIJKLMNOPQRSTUVWXYZ*
*abcdefghijklmnopqrstuvwxyz&*
*1234567890*

# ABCDEFGHIJK
# LMNOPQRST
# UVWXYZ
## abcdefghijklm
## nopqrstuvwxyz
# 1234567890

48 POINT STYMIE EXTRA BOLD

# AABCDEFGHIJKL MNOPQRSTUVW XYZ
## aabcdefghijklmnop qrstuvwxyz
# 1234567890

36 POINT STYMIE EXTRA BOLD

## AABCDEFGHIJKLMNOP QRSTUVWXYZ
### aabcdefghijklmnopqrstu vwxyz
## 1234567890

48 POINT STYMIE OPEN

# ABCDEFGHIJKL
# MNOPQRSTUV
# WXYZ&
# 1234567890$

36 POINT STYMIE OPEN

## ABCDEFGHIJKLMNOP
## QRSTUVWXYZ&
## 1234567890$

24 POINT STYMIE OPEN

### ABCDEFGHIJKLMNOPQRSTUV
### WXYZ&
### 1234567890$

48 POINT TOWER

ABCDEFGHIJKLMNOPQRSTUV
WXYZ
abcdefghijklmnopqrstuvwxyz
1234567890

36 POINT TOWER

ABCDEFGHIJKLMNOPQRSTUVWXYZ
abcdefghijklmnopqrstuvwxyz
1234567890

36 POINT TRYLON

ABCDEFGHIJKLMNOPQRSTUVWXYZ&
abcdefghijklmnopqrstuvwxyz
1234567890$

# Script and Cursive Types

48 POINT BERNHARD TANGO

ABCDEFGHIJKLMNOPQ
RSTUUVWXYZ
abcdefghijklmnopqrstuvwxyz
1234567890

24 POINT BERNHARD TANGO

ABCDEFGHIJKLMNOPQRSTUUVWXYZ
abcdefghijklmnopqrstuvwxyz          1234567890

48 POINT CORONET BOLD

ABCDEFGHIJKLMNO
PQRSTUVWXYZ&
abcdefghijklmnopqrstuvwxyz
1234567890$

24 POINT CORONET BOLD

ABCDEFGHIJKLMNOPQRSTUVWXYZ&
abcdefghijklmnopqrstuvwxyz          1234567890$

72 POINT BRUSH

*ABCDEFGHIJ*
*KLMNOP2R*
*STUVWXYZ*
*abcdefghijklmnopqrst*
*uvwxyz1234567890*

36 POINT BRUSH

*ABCDEFGHIJKLMNOP2*
*RSTUVWXYZ*
*abcdefghijklmnopqrstuvwxyz*
*1234567890$&*

48 POINT LEGEND

ABCDEFGHIJKLMNOP

QRSTUVWXYZ

abcdefghijklmnopqrstuvwxyz

1234567890

36 POINT LIBERTY

ABCDEFGHIJKLMNOPQ

RSTUVWXYZ

abcdefghijklmnopqrstuvwxyz

1234567890

60 POINT LYDIAN CURSIVE

ABCDEFGHIJKLMN

OPQRSTUVWXYZ

abcdeefghijklmnopqrstuv

wxyz

1234567890

36 POINT LYDIAN CURSIVE

ABCDEFGHIJKLMNOPQRSTUVW

XYZ

abcdeefghijklmnopqrstuvwxyz

1234567890

48 POINT MISTRAL

# ABCDEFGHIJKLMNOPQRSTU
# VWXYZ&
*abcdefghijklmnopqrstuvwxyz*
# 1234567890$

48 POINT STRADIVARIUS

# Black Letter Types

72 POINT AMERICAN TEXT

# ABCDEFGHIJKLM
# NOPQRSTUVWXYZ
## abcdefghijklmnopqrstuvw
## xyz 1234567890

36 POINT AMERICAN TEXT

ABCDEFGHIJKLMNOPQRSTUVWXYZ
abcdefghijklmnopqrstuvwxyz.-:;,ˇ!?$&
1234567890

24 POINT AMERICAN TEXT

ABCDEFGHIJKLMNOPQRSTUVWXYZ
abcdefghijklmnopqrstuvwxyz
1234567890

60 POINT CLOISTER BLACK

ABCDEFGHIJK
LMNOPQ
RSTUVWXYZ&
abcdefghijklmnopqrstu
vwxyz 1234567890$

36 POINT CLOISTER BLACK

ABCDEFGHIJKLMNOPQ
RSTUVWXYZ&
abcdefghijklmnopqrstuvwxyz
1234567890$

72 POINT GOUDY TEXT

ABCDEFGHI
JKLMNOPQ
RSTUVWXYZ
abcdefghijklmnopqrstu
vwxyz 1234567890$

36 POINT GOUDY TEXT

ABCDEFGHIJKLMNOPQR
STUVWXYZ&
abcdefghijklmnopqrstuvwxyz
1234567890$

# Miscellaneous and Novelty Types

36 POINT AMELIA

ABCDEFGHIJKKLMNOPQRSTUVWXYZ
abcdefghijklmnopqrstuvwxyz
1234567890&!?$

36 POINT GALLIA

ABCDEFGHIJKLMN
OPQRSTUVWXYZ&
1234567890$
AERST

36 POINT JIM CROW

ABCDEFGHIJKLMNOPQRSTUV
WXYZ&    1234567890

36 POINT KISMET

ABCDEFGHIJKLMNOPQRSTUVW
XYZ
abcdefghijklmnopqrstuvluwxxyz
1234567890&$?

60 POINT POSTER ROMAN BOLD

# ABCDEFGHIJKL
# MNOPQRSTU
# VWXYZ&
# abcdefghijklmnopq
# rstuvwxyz
# 1234567890$

36 POINT POSTER ROMAN BOLD

## ABCDEFGHIJKLMNOPQRST
## UVWXYZ&
## abcdefghijklmnopqrstuvwxyz
## 1234567890$

36 POINT PRISMA

ABCDEFGHIJKLMNOPQR
STUVWXYZ&
1234567890$

36 POINT ROMANTIQUE

ABCDEFGHIJKLMN
OPQRSTUVWXYZ&
1234567890

36 POINT SMOKE

ABCDEFGHIJKLMNOPQRSTUVWXYZ

abcdefghijklmnopqrstuvwxyz

1234567890&!?$

36 POINT STENCIL

ABCDEFGHIJKLMN
OPQRSTUVWXYZ&
1234567890$

48 POINT STUDIO

ABCDEFGHIJKLMNOPQ
RSTUVWXYZ&
abcdefghijklmnopqrstu
vwxyz
1234567890$

36 POINT STUDIO

ABCDEFGHIJKLMNOPQRSTU
VWXYZ&
abcdefghijklmnopqrstuvwxyz
1234567890$

## A

**Access** To retrieve information from a storage device (internal memory, disk, tape). Access time is the time it takes to retrieve the stored data.

**Accordian fold** Two or more parallel folds with adjacent folds in opposite directions.

**Achromatic** The absence of color; black, gray, or white.

**Agate** This is 5½-point type. There are fourteen agate lines in 1 inch. The term is used to measure advertisements and can be used to designate tabular and classified matter in newspapers.

**Alignment** The positioning of letters so all have a common baseline; it also refers to the even placement of lines of type or art.

**Alphabet length** The width of lowercase (usually) characters when lined up *a* through *z*.

**Ampersand** The symbol used for *and* (&).

**Antique** A coarse and uneven paper finish.

**Ascender** The letter stroke that extends above the *x* height of a lowercase character.

## B

**Back shop** The mechanical departments of a printing plant.

**Bank** One line of a multiline headline.

**Banner** A large multicolumn headline, usually extending across the top of page 1 in a newspaper.

**Base alignment** The positioning of characters so the bottom of the *x* height lines up evenly on a horizontal line; in phototypesetting this alignment is used for the even positioning of different type styles on a common line.

**Ben Day** The regular pattern of dots or lines used to add tonal variation to line art.

**bf** The designation for setting type in boldface.

**Bidirectional printer** A printing device that speeds hard copy production by printing left to right and then right to left and so on until the printout is completed.

**Bit** BInary digiT. This is the single digit of a binary number; 10 is composed of two bits.

**Black Letter** A race or group of type characterized by its resemblance to medieval northern European manuscript characters.

**Bleed** To run a photograph to the edge of the page.

**Blind embossing** Embossing (see below) without printing.

**Block** A group of words, characters, or digits forming a single unit in a computerized system.

**Block letter** A letterform without serifs (the finishing stroke at the end of a letter), in the Sans Serif type group.

**Blueline** Copy composed of blue lines on a white background.

**Blurb** Copy written with a sales angle, usually in brief paragraphs.

**Body type** "Reading matter" type as differentiated from display or headline type.

**Boldface** Characters of normal form but heavier strokes.

**Bond paper** Paper with a hard, smooth finish for ruling, typing, and pen writing.

**Border** A frame around the type, art, or complete layout in either plane lines or an ornamental design.

**Bowl** The interior part of a letter in a circle form such as in a *b*, *c*, *d*, or *o*.

**Box** A border or rule that frames type.

**Bracketed serif** A serif (see below) connected to the character stem with a curved area at the connecting angle.

**Broadsheet** A standard-size newspaper page as contrasted to the small tabloid size.

**Brownline** A brown-line image on a white background.

**Bullet** A round, solid ornament resembling a large period: •.

**Byte** A number of binary digits, or bits, needed to encode one character such as a letter, punctuation mark, number, or symbol.

## C

**Calender** The process in papermaking that creates the amount of smoothness in the paper.

**C&lc** The symbols for setting type in which the first character of each word is in capitals.

**Camera ready** The completed pasteup from which the printing plate is made.

**Canned format** The specifications for composition and/or makeup of type kept on magnetic or paper tape for repeated use to command a typesetter.

**Capitals** Large characters, the original form of Latin characters.

**Caption** The term used in magazine layout for the explanatory matter accompanying art; usually called a *cutline* in newspaper editing and layout.

**Cast off** To determine the space a typewritten manuscript will occupy when set in type.

**Catchline** A line of display type between a picture and cutline.

**Cathode ray tube (CRT)** An electronic tube used to project images on a screen; it is also called a *visual* *display unit*; a television picture tube.

**Colophon** The data about design, type styles, and production of a book; usually found at the end of the book.

**Combination plate** Halftone and line art on a single printing plate.

**Composing room** The area of a printing plant where type is set and arranged for plate making or printing.

**Comprehensive** A completed, detailed layout ready for making a plate; also called a *comp.*

**Computer graphics** Any charts, diagrams, drawings, and/or art composed on a computer.

**Condensed type** A vertically compressed character.

**Constants** The typographic and graphic elements in a publication that don't change from issue to issue.

**Continuous tone** Any art, such as a photograph or painting, which contains black and white and the variations of grays between the two.

**Copy** Information to be printed or reproduced.

**Copy block** A segment of body type or reading matter in a layout.

**Copy fitting** Determining the area a certain amount of copy will occupy when set in type.

**Crop** To eliminate unwanted material or change the dimensions of art.

**Cropping L** The two right angles used to frame art to determine where it should be cropped.

**Cursive** A form of type that resembles handwriting.

**Cursor** A spot of light on a video screen that the user manipulates to indicate where changes in copy are to be made.

**Cut** A piece of art ready for printing; originally referred to as a mounted engraving used in letterpress printing.

**Cutline** The descriptive or identifying information printed with art—a caption.

**Cutoff rule** The dividing rule between elements, usually used in newspaper format.

**Cyan** A vivid blue color used in process (full color) color printing.

**Cylinder press** A printing press in which the form to be printed is flat and the impression is made on paper clamped on a cylinder that is rolled over the form.

## D

**Daisy wheel** A metal or plastic disk with typewriter characters on spokes radiating from its center. It is about 3 inches in diameter. Hard copy printers can be equipped with more than one daisy wheel to mix faces. On typewriters, the wheel can produce type with differential spacing.

**Dash** A small horizontal rule in layouts; also a punctuation mark.

**Debugging** Correcting errors in programs.

**Deck** One unit of a headline set in a single type size and style.

**Descender** A stroke of a lowercase letter that extends below the *x* height.

**Digital computer** A device used to manipulate data and perform calculations; most work on the binary number system (the number system based on powers of 2 rather than powers of 10).

**Digitized type** A form of type produced photographically by computer instructions created by patterns of black and white spots similar to the way television images are produced.

**Dingbat** A typographic ornament.

**Diskette** A flexible plastic recording medium, also called floppy disks or flexible disks.

**Double pyramid** The placement of advertisements on a page or facing pages to form a center "well" for editorial material.

**Double truck** A single advertisement that occupies two facing pages.

**Downstyle** A form of headline in which only the first word and proper nouns are capitalized.

**Dummy** A "blueprint" or pattern, usually half size for newspaper pages, used as a guide in making finished layout or pasteup.

**Duotone** A technique for color printing in which two plates are made from a black and white photo and printed in different colors to produce a single image.

## E

**Ear** The editorial matter alongside the nameplate (the name of the publication) on page 1.

**Em** A unit of space equal to the square of the type size being used.

**Embossing** The process of impressing an image in relief to achieve a raised surface over printing. Embossing on blank paper is called *blind embossing.*

**En** A unit of space that is the vertical half of an em.

**Extended** A form of type in which the normal character structure is widened.

## F

**Face** The style of a type, such as boldface.

**Family** A major division of typefaces.

**Flag** Synonymous with *nameplate*; the name of the publication in a distinctive design.

**Flexography** Printing from relief plates usually made of rubber as in letterpress but using a water-base ink rather than paste ink.

**Floating flag** A flag set in narrow width and displayed in a position other than the top of a page.

**Flush left** Type set even on the left margin and uneven on the right margin.

**Flush right** Type set with uneven lines on the left and even lines on the right margin.

**Folio lines** Originally the page numbers, but usually now the line giving date, volume, and number; or page number, name of publication, and date in small type on the inside pages.

**Font** All the characters and punctuation marks of one size and style of type.

**Form** All the typographic elements used in a particular printed piece arranged to be placed on a printing press.

**Format** The general appearance of a printed piece, including the page size and number of columns per page.

**Foundry type** Printing type made of individual characters cast from molten metal.

**Frame** A newspaper makeup pattern in which the left and right outside columns are each filled with a single story.

**Function code** A computer code that controls the machine's operations other than the output of typographic characters.

**Functional typography** A philosophy of design in which every element used does an efficient and necessary job.

## G

**Galley** A three-sided metal tray used to hold type; the term also refers to long strips of printed photographic or cold type ready to be proofread and used to make pasteups.

**Galley proof** The impression of type used for making corrections.

**Gothic** A group, or race, of monotonal types that have no serifs; also called *Sans Serif*.

**Gravure** An intaglio (see below) printing method that uses recessed plates.

**Grid** In graphic design, a pattern of horizontal and vertical guidelines for making layouts or dummies; in typesetting, an image carrier (a piece of film containing the characters) for a font of type for phototypesetting.

**Grotesk** The European name for Gothic type.

**Gutter** The margin between facing pages.

## H

**Hairline** The thinnest rule used in printing, or the thinnest stroke in a letter form.

**Halftone** A printing plate made by photographing an image through a screen so that the image is reproduced in dots.

**Hanging indent** A headline style in which the first line is full width and succeeding lines are indented

the same amount from the left margin.

**Hard copy** Printed or typed copy, usually the printout from a computer or word processor or similar device.

**Hardware** The actual equipment that makes up a computer system (see also *software*).

**Head** An abbreviation for headline.

**Headletter** The type used for headlines.

**Headline** The title of an article or news story.

**Headline schedule** A chart showing all the styles and sizes of headlines used by a publication.

**Highlight** The lightest portion of a halftone photograph; the area having the smallest dots or no dots at all.

**Horizontal makeup** An arrangement of story units across columns rather than vertically.

**Hot metal** Type, borders, and rules made of molten metal cast in molds.

**Hue** A color, or the quality that distinguishes colors in the visible spectrum.

## I

**Imposition** An arrangement of pages for printing so they will appear in proper order for folding.

**Impression cylinder** A printing press unit that presses paper on an inked form to make the print.

**Initial** The first letter in a word set in a larger or more decorative face, usually used at the beginning of an article, section, or paragraph.

**Ink-jet printing** A method of placing characters on paper by spraying a mist of ink through tiny holes in the patterns of the characters.

**Inline** A style of type in which a white line runs down the main stroke of the letter.

**Insert** Reference lines inserted in the body of an article; also called a *refer* or *sandwich*.

**Intaglio** A printing method in which the image is carved into, or recessed, in the plate; also called *gravure*.

**Inverted pyramid** A headline style in which each centered line is narrower than its predecessor; term is also used for a newswriting form.

**Italic** A form of Roman type design that slants to the right.

## J

**Jim dash** A small rule — usually used to separate decks in a headline or title.

**Jump head** A headline on the part of a story continued from another page.

**Justify** Setting type so the left and right margins are even.

## K

**Kerning** Placing two adjacent characters so that part of one is positioned within the space of the other; kerning may be controlled by the keyboard operator or programmed into the computer.

**Keylining** A process of using an overlay in a layout to indicate color separations, reverses, outlines, or other special effects.

**Kicker** A small headline, usually underlined, above a main headline.

## L

**Layout** A diagram or plan, drawing, or sketch used as a guide in arranging elements for printing.

**lc** The abbreviation for lowercase.

**lca** The abbreviation for lowercase alphabet.

**Lead** The space between lines of type, usually 2 points (pronounced "led").

**Leaders** The dots or dashes often used in tabular matter.

**Letterpress** A printing method that uses raised images.

**Letterspace** The space added to the normal spacing between the letters in a word.

**Ligature** Two or more characters joined to make a single unit.

**Lightface** Characters with strokes that have less weight than normal.

**Light pen** An electronic stylus used to position elements or indicate changes in copy on a CRT.

**Line art** A piece of art or a plate in black and white, not continuous tones.

**Line conversion** A line printing plate made from a continuous tone original by eliminating the halftone screen.

**Linen paper** A paper made from linen or having a finish resembling linen cloth.

**Lithography** A flat-surface printing method based on the principle that oil and water are mutually repellent.

**Logo** Abbreviation for logotype.

**Logotype** A distinctive type arrangement used for the name of a publication, business, or organization.

**Lowercase** The small letters of the alphabet.


**M**

**Magenta** Also called *process red*; it is a purplish red color and is used in process (or full) color printing.

**Magnetic ink** An ink that contains ferrous (iron) material that can be sensed magnetically.

**Makeup** The art of arranging elements on a page for printing.

**Markup** The process of writing instructions on a layout for the size and styles of types and the other elements desired by the designer.

**Masthead** The area in a publication that lists the staff, date of publication, and other pertinent information.

**Matrix (mat)** The brass mold from which type is cast (or molded) in the hot metal process.

**Measure** The width of the lines being set.

**Mechanical** A pasteup ready for plate making.

**Mechanical separation** Copy prepared by a designer with each individual color in a separate section.

**Mezzotint** A screen used for creating a crayon drawing effect on a printing plate.

**Minimum line length** The shortest width of lines of type of acceptable readability.

**Minuscules** Small characters.

**Minus leading** The elimination of space between lines, a technique possible with photographic or electronic typesetting.

**Minus letterspacing** Reducing the normal space between characters; a technique possible with photographic or electronic typesetting.

**Miter** To cut a rule or border at a 45-degree angle for making corners on a box.

**Mixing** Combining more than one style or size of type on the same line.

**Mnemonics** Ancient memory-aiding devices; also used to refer to abbreviations of complex terms used in encoding computer instructions.

**Mock-up** A full-size, experimental layout for study and evaluation.

**Modular makeup** The arrangement of elements in rectangular units on a page, also called *Mondrian*.

**Moiré** A distracting pattern that results when a previously screened halftone is screened again and printed.

**Mondrian makeup** The arrangement of elements into rectangles of various sizes and shapes, also called *modular*.

**Monotonal** Typefaces with strokes of equal thickness.

**Montage** A composite picture, usually made of two or more combined photographs.

**Mortise** An area cut out of a piece of art for the insertion of type or other art.


**N**

**Nameplate** The name of a publication set in a distinctive type form, also called *flag*.

**Newsprint** A low-quality paper mainly used for printing handbills and newspapers.

**Notch mortise** A rectangle cut from a corner of a rectangular illustration.

**Novelty** A category of type that is usually ornamental in design and does not display any strong characteristics of one of the basic races or species.


**O**

**Oblique** Letters that slant to the right, usually Sans Serif or Square Serif; Roman slanted letters are called *italics*.

**OCR (optical character recognition)** A device that electronically reads and encodes printed or typewritten material.

**Offset** A printing process in which the image is transferred from a printing plate to a rubber blanket to paper.

**Old style** A Roman typeface subdivision characterized by bracketed serifs and little difference between the thick and thin strokes.

**Opaque** Something that blocks light; in paper a lack of show-through.

**Optical center** A point about 10 percent above the mathematical center of a page or area.

**Optimum format** A format in which the width of the type columns is within the range of maximum readability.

**Optimum line length** The line width at which reading is easiest and fastest.

**Ornament** A decorative typographic device.

**Outline** A type design in which the letter is traced or outlined by lines on the outside of the strokes and the inside of the letter is blank.

**Overlay** A sheet of transparent plastic or paper placed over a piece of art or a layout on which instructions are written and areas to be printed in color are drawn.

**Overline** A display type heading placed above a picture.

**Overprint** To print over an area that has already been printed.

**Overset** Body matter that exceeds the allotted space.

**Oxford rule** Parallel heavy and light lines.


**P**

**Pagination** The process of arranging pages for printing; a computer-generated page layout; and/or the numbering of the pages of a book.

**Parallel fold** Two or more folds in the same direction.

**Pasteup** The process of fixing type and other elements on a grid for plate making; a *mechanical*.

**Pebbling** Embossing paper in its manufacture to create a ripple effect.

**Perfect binding** A method of binding that uses flexible glue rather than stitching.

**Photocomposition** Phototypesetting by film or paper.

**Photoengraving** A printing plate with a raised surface.

**Photolithography** An offset printing process that uses a plate made by a photographic process.

**Phototypesetter** A device that sets type by a photographic process; letter images are recorded on light-sensitive film or photographic paper that is then developed and printed.

**Pi** To mix type; individual metal characters that have been mixed up by accident.

**Pica** A 12-point unit of measurement.

**Planography** A printing process that uses a plate with a flat surface; offset lithography is a planographic process.

**Plate** A printing surface.

**Platen press** A machine in which paper is held on a flat surface and pressed against the form for printing.

**PMT (photo mechanical transfer)** A positive print that is ready for pasteup.

**Point** A unit of measurement approximately 1/72 of an inch.

**Pork chop** A small head shot of a person, usually half a column wide.

**Poster makeup** An arrangement of a newspaper's front page that usually consists of large art and a few headlines to attract attention.

**Prescreen** A halftone positive print that can be combined with line copy in pasteup, thus eliminating the need to strip in a screened negative with a line copy negative.

**Primary color** The colors red, yellow, and blue, which combine to make all other hues.

**Primary optical center** The spot where a reader's eye usually first lights on a page, the upper left quadrant.

**Process color** Printing the three primary colors in combination to produce all colors; full color.

**Proof** A preliminary print of set type or a comprehensive, used to detect errors before the final printing.

**Prototype** A mock-up; a model that is the pattern for the final product.

**Pyramid** An arrangement of advertisements on a page to form a stepped half pyramid.

**Q**

**Quad** A unit of space in setting type.

**Quad left, quad middle, quad right** Commands that instruct a typesetting machine to put space in lines.

**Quadrant makeup** A plan for a page in which each quarter is given a strong design element.

**R**

**Race** The basic division of type styles, sometimes called *species*; type groups.

**Ragged right** Type set unjustified (uneven) at the right margins.

**Ragged left** The opposite of ragged right.

**Readability** The characteristic of type and/or its arrangement that makes it easy to read.

**Readout** The headline or unit of a headline between a banner head and the story; also used to refer to devices for breaking up body matter such as quotes (called quote-outs or pulled quotes) set in display type and embellished with typographic devices.

**Recto** In book or pamphlet design, the odd-numbered, right-hand pages.

**Register** To line up color printing plates so the multiple impressions will create an accurate reproduction of the original.

**Relief printing** Printing from a raised surface; letterpress.

**Repro (reproduction proof)** The final image used for pasteup and plate making.

**Reverse** A printing area in which the background is black and the image is white.

**Reverse kicker** A headline form in which the kicker is larger than the primary headlines.

**Reverse leading** The technique of operating a phototypesetting device so superior figures or mixed display type can be added to the line.

**Rivers** Vertical strips of white space in areas of type created by excessive space between words; also called "rivers of white."

**Roman** A basic race or species of type in which the characters have

serifs and variations in the widths of their strokes.

**ROP (run of press)** Color or other matter that isn't given a specific special position in the publication.

**Rotary press** A press that uses a curved plate to print on a continuous roll of paper.

**Rotogravure** A recessed-image (intaglio) printing process on a continuous roll of paper.

**Rough** A sketchy dummy or layout to show the placement of elements.

**Rule** An element that prints a continuous line or lines usually used to frame type, art, or a layout.

**Run-in head** A headline that is part of the first line of the text.

**Running foot** A line at the bottom of a book page that indicates the book, chapter, or section title, and/or the page number.

**Running head** A line at the top of a book page that contains the same information as a running foot.

**S**

**Saddle stitch** A binding method for magazines or pamphlets that uses a wire stitch on the centerfold.

**Sandwich** A short notice placed within the body of an article.

**Sans Serif** A race or species of type without serifs (the finishing strokes on characters) usually containing monotonal letter strokes.

**Scale** To size art to certain enlarged or reduced dimensions.

**Scanner** A small moving light beam used for spotting images on an optical character reader, cathode ray tube, or laser typesetter.

**Score** To crease paper on a line to facilitate folding.

**Screen** A device, available in various densities used to reduce continuous tone art to a halftone plate.

**Script** A typeface that resembles handwriting.

**Scroll** To move a story up or down on a video display terminal screen, usually for editing purposes.

**Secondary color** A hue (color) produced by mixing two primary colors.

**Section logo** A typographic device used to identify a section of a publication.

**Series** A basic subdivision of a type family; it has family characteristics but an individual posture; all the sizes of that particular posture of a family.

**Serif** The finishing stroke at the end of a primary stroke of a character.

**Set solid** Type set with no leading between the lines.

**Shade** A darker hue obtained by adding black to a color.

**Shaded** Type that gives a gray instead of solid black imprint.

**Sideline** An arrangement with short display lines to the left of the cutlines.

**Sidestitch (sidewire stitching)** A binding in which the staple is placed on the side rather than on the spine as in saddle stitch.

**Signature** A group of pages printed on a single sheet.

**Silhouette** Art in which the background has been removed.

**Sinkage** A point below the top margin of a page where chapter openings or other material is set.

**Skyline** A headline or story at the top of the first page of a publication, above the nameplate.

**Slug** A unit of space, usually between lines of type and usually 6 or 12 points thick; a line of cast hot type; an identifying line on copy.

**Small cap** A capital letter for a font of type smaller than the regular capital letter.

**Software** The instructions or programs that cause a computer to operate and perform desired functions.

**Sorts** Characters that are obtainable but not ordinarily included in a font of type, such as mathematical signs and special punctuation and accent marks.

**Species** A basic division of type; a race of type.

**Spine** The midpoint area between the front and back covers of a book or magazine; the center point of the outside cover.

**Spot color** One hue (color) in addition to black, usually in a headline, display line, border, or ornament.

**Square Serif** A typeface characterized by monotonal strokes and heavy, squared serifs; also called *Egyptian*, *Slab Serif*.

**Standing head** A headline that remains the same from one issue of a publication to another.

**Stepped head** An arrangement of display type in which the top line is flush left, the middle line (if used) is centered, and the third line is flush right, and all the lines are less than full width to create a stair step effect.

**Stereotyping** The process of casting a printing form from molten metal by using a mold (called a *mat*) or paper, usually in a curved form, to create a curved printing plate for a rotary press.

**Stet** A term meaning "do not change," used in proofreading.

**Stick-on letters** Alphabet characters printed on paper, usually self-adhesive, for cold type composition.

**Straight matter** Reading matter; body type; the text material in a book.

**Streamer** A banner headline.

**Strike-on** Type produced by a typewriter or other percussion keyboard device that impacts character forms directly on paper.

**Stripping** Combining halftone and line negatives to create a comprehensive negative for printing plates that contain line and screened art.

**Subhead** A display line that is auxiliary to the main headline or used to break up masses of body type.

**Sunken initial** An initial inset in reading matter.

**Surprint** Something printed over art.

**Swash** A letter decorated with an elongated stroke, usually decorative.

**Symmetrical** An arrangement of elements in formal balance.

## T

**Tabloid** A newspaper format usually about half the size of a broadsheet or approximately 11 by 15 inches.

**Tabular matter** Statistics arranged in table or columnar form, such as stock market reports, financial statements, and so on.

**Terminal** A device in a communications network or system where information can be entered, removed, or displayed for viewing and arranging.

**Text** The Black Letter race or species of type.

**Text** Reading matter.

**Thumbnail** A small preliminary sketch of a possible arrangement of elements; also the term for a portrait that is less than a column wide and inset in reading matter.

**Tint** A value of a color created by adding white to a hue (color).

**Tint block** An area on a printed page produced in a tint, usually with type or art surprinted on it.

**Tombstone** Identical side-by-side headlines that compete for attention.

**Tone** Shading or tinting a printing element.

**Transfer letter** A letter for printing obtained by rubbing from a master sheet onto the layout sheet.

**Transitional** A subdivision of the Roman type race with characteristics of both old style and modern Romans.

**Type** The characters from which printing is done.

**Typeface** The distinctive design of an alphabet of letters and related characters.

**Typo** An error in set type.

**Typography** The use and arrangement of elements for printing.

## U

**U&lc** The designation for setting type in capital and lowercase letters where it is appropriate.

**Unit** A fraction of an em; in a 36-unit phototypesetting system, for instance, an em would have 36 units; more units allows more latitude in programming space between letters and words and in designating character widths.

**Unit count** A method of determining whether display type will fit a given area.

**Uppercase (uc)** Capital letters.

## V

**Value** Synonym for tone, or the relative tint or shade of a printing element.

**Velox** A black and white print of a halftone photograph.

**Video display terminal (VDT)** A device and screen for arranging elements.

**Verso** The even-numbered, left-hand pages.

**Vignette** An illustration in which the margins appear to fade into the background.

## W

**Watermark** A design, name, and/or logotype impressed on paper during manufacture.

**Waxer** A device for coating the back of layout parts with melted wax to attach them to a grid or layout sheet.

**Web** A wide strip or roll of paper that travels through a press for printing.

**Weight** The comparative thickness of strokes of letters.

**Well** The arrangement of advertisements on the right and left sides of a page so editorial matter can be placed between.

**Widow** A short line at the top of a column that completes a paragraph from the bottom of the preceding column; also used to refer to a very short final line of a paragraph.

**Wrong font (wf)** A type character set in a different family or series from the rest of the specified set matter.

## X

**x height** The distance between the baseline and meanline of type; the height of a lowercase letter excluding the ascender and descender.

## Z

**Zipatone** A transparent sheet containing dot or line patterns that provides a tonal effect similar to that provided by Ben Day.

# Index